Gustav Mahler's Symphonies

Recent Titles in Discographies

EJS: Discography of the Edward J. Smith Recordings: "The Golden Age of Opera," 1956–1971
William Shaman, William J. Collins, and Calvin M. Goodwin

His Master's Voice/Die Stimme Seines Herrn: The German Catalogue
Alan Kelly, compiler

The Johnny Cash Discography, 1984–1993
John L. Smith, compiler

Straighten Up and Fly Right: A Chronology and Discography of Nat "King" Cole
Klaus Teubig, compiler

Modern Harpsichord Music: A Discography
Martin Elste, compiler

Tantalizing Tingles: A Discography of Early Ragtime, Jazz, and Novelty Syncopated Piano Recordings, 1889–1934
Ross Laird

Berliner Gramophone Records: American Issues, 1892–1900
Paul Charosh, compiler

The Waylon Jennings Discography
John L. Smith, compiler

Ethnic and Vernacular Music, 1898–1960: A Resource and Guide to Recordings
Paul Vernon

Command Performance, USA!
Harry Mackenzie, compiler

The Fred Waring Discography
Peter T. Kiefer, compiler

The Decca Labels: A Discography (6 volumes)
Michel Ruppli, compiler

Gustav Mahler's Symphonies

Critical Commentary on Recordings Since 1986

Lewis M. Smoley

Discographies, Number 66

GREENWOOD PRESS
Westport, Connecticut • London

Library of Congress Cataloging-in-Publication Data

Smoley, Lewis M.
  Gustav Mahler's symphonies : critical commentary on
recordings since 1986 / Lewis M. Smoley.
       p.   cm.—(Discographies, ISSN 0192-334X ; no. 66)
  Includes bibliographical references (p.   ) and index.
  ISBN 0-313-29771-1 (alk. paper)
  1. Mahler, Gustav, 1860-1911—Discography. 2. Mahler, Gustav,
1860-1911. Symphonies. 3. Symphonies—Discography. I. Title.
II. Series.
ML156.5.M33S62   1996
784.2'184'092—dc20   96-18211

British Library Cataloguing in Publication Data is available.

Copyright © 1996 by Lewis M. Smoley

All rights reserved. No portion of this book may be
reproduced, by any process or technique, without the
express written consent of the publisher.

Library of Congress Catalog Card Number: 96-18211
ISBN: 0-313-29771-1
ISSN: 0192-334X

First published in 1996

Greenwood Press, 88 Post Road West, Westport, CT 06881
An imprint of Greenwood Publishing Group, Inc.

Printed in the United States of America

The paper used in this book complies with the
Permanent Paper Standard issued by the National
Information Standards Organization (Z39.48-1984).

10 9 8 7 6 5 4 3 2 1

I dedicate this volume with deepest gratitude to the many performers who have made Mahler's music a staple in the repertoire and to all those ardent admirers of his music whose unfailing support is largely responsible for the enormous increase in the number of recordings of Mahler's symphonies and, therefore, indirectly for this volume. I also dedicate this volume to my wife, Sally Yerkovich, without whose unflinching support, tireless assistance and remarkable patience this volume could never have been completed.

CONTENTS

Introduction	ix
Symphony No.1 in D Major ("Titan")	1
Symphony No.2 in C Minor ("Resurrection")	33
Symphony No.3 in D Minor	59
Symphony No.4 in G Major	81
Symphony No.5 in C-sharp Minor	107
Symphony No.6 in A Minor ("Tragic")	141
Symphony No.7 in E Minor ("Song of the Night")	167
Symphony No.8 in E-flat Major ("Symphony of a Thousand")	189
Das Lied von der Erde	205
Symphony No.9 in D Major	225
Symphony No.10 in F-sharp Major (Unfinished)	255
Bibliography	268
Index to Conductors	269
Index to Orchestras	284
Index to Soloists	298
Index to Choruses	322
Index to Record Labels	334

INTRODUCTION

The Mahler symphony boom continues. In the nine years that followed publication of my 1986 volume, **The Symphonies of Gustav Mahler: A Critical Discography**, 650 new recordings have been issued -- more than were made in all of the preceding years. This volume includes the completion or commencement of complete cycles by such noted Mahlerians as Abbado, Haitink (his second with the BPO), Bernstein (both on CD and video), Ozawa, and Vaclav Neumann (his second), as well as other conductors entering the field for the first time (e.g., Leif Segerstam, Gary Bertini, Hiroshi Wakasugi, Neeme Järvi, Giuseppe Sinopoli and Edo DeWaart).

It now seems incumbent upon virtually every prominent conductor as well as young hopeful to try his or her hand at at least one of Mahler's symphonies. Many have gone much further, recording several if not all of the symphonies. The latest crop of young maestros, while cognizant of past interpretive traditions, often approaches Mahler's music in a very personal manner, diverging considerably from both the score's many directions and the more conservative interpretive traditions of the past. The diversity of interpretive approaches to Mahler's symphonies has increased measurably during the past decade, now that Mahler's music has been widely accepted and frequently performed.

In earlier years a certain sense of authenticity attached itself to interpretations by such notable Mahlerians as Bruno Walter, Otto Klemperer and Jascha Horenstein, because they either knew and worked with Mahler or came into their profession in the wake of his heyday. Other conductors who championed Mahler when it was not fashionable to do so (e.g., Dimitri Mitropoulos, Sir John Barbirolli, Leopold Stokowski and Hermann Scherchen) built upon the traditions established by the "Germanic school" of conductors within the context of their individual stylistic orientations.

Leonard Bernstein offered a "modernistic" approach. He infused his readings with more energy and unnerving intensity than his predecessors and often heightened emotive or dramatic effects. While controversial, Bernstein's approach had merit and made a major impact, capturing the imagination of an audience coming to Mahler's music for the first time and dramatically increasing Mahler's popularity. In addition, his work inspired numerous divergent approaches to Mahler's symphonies which, in their enormous scope and remarkable diversity, are unique in the history of classical music interpretation.

In view of this deluge of heterogeneous interpretations, it is necessary that reviewers articulate the various criteria upon which their critical approach is based. Consideration should be given to a combination of factors, including the presence or absence of a conceptual overview for each piece, treatment of Mahler's detailed markings, evocation of contrasting moods, rendering of musical effects, and determination of tempi and their extraordinarily frequent modifications.

Mahler often said that he creates a "world" in each of his symphonies. This statement is key to any interpretive approach to Mahler's work, for without the conceptual overview it suggests, his symphonies can seem merely long-winded and confusing and will not communicate successfully with an audience. One might envision Mahler's symphonies as life-struggles between positive and negative forces. Many conceptual or philosophical reference points have been devised to orient the listener to extra-musical considerations. Although Mahler ultimately eschewed "program music," fearing that it would divert attention from the music itself to extra-musical imaginings, each of his symphonies clearly evokes a dramatic experience that demands some conceptualization, if not necessarily a narrative one. As "symphonic dramas," they create life-worlds of existential import that dramatize the human condition in a manner not unlike Greek tragedy.

Mahler's scores are filled with numerous details, markings, annotations and directions to the conductor and performer. Mahler expressed concern that conductors after him would wreck havoc upon his works, having not the slightest idea what he intended by his directions. While the numerous markings in Mahler's scores may reveal a slight paranoia about future generations of interpreters, they also provide instructions that are critical to the performance of each work. In my view, conductors must not ignore any of Mahler's detailed and unusual markings; they are not superfluous directions. The question is how to reproduce them effectively. Merely glossing over these markings without making an effort to utilize them in the service of the music will not lead to success in achieving Mahler's intentions. On the other hand, exaggerations in rendering effects often distort their value, thereby engendering a sense of mere artifice rather than musicality.

Only complete familiarity with Mahler's style can serve as a basis for determining how far to go in suitably executing his directions. Often interpreters reviewed here exaggerate the markings to produce extremes in tempo and dynamic levels as well as render lyrical material in a manner that distorts both the mood and the intended effect. The result can be untoward and disconcerting. An attempt to emphasize the highpoint of a melodic line or underline an especially evocative phrase by suddenly applying more pressure or holding up the pace markedly, if applied to excess, can disturb the musical flow by either losing hold too quickly of significant elements or causing a phrase or entire passage to linger on too long or out of context. On the other hand, the application of a slight degree of emphasis at the highpoint of a lyrical theme can enhance its beauty and a hair's breadth of hesitation in the midst of a climactic moment can heighten the feeling of anticipation and release that can create a thrilling climax. Just how much weight or prolongation will produce a satisfactory result is not a matter of concocting a definitive scientific formula but involves diverse considerations -- theoretical, intuitive and pragmatic.

A conductor should also consider how to handle the strong contrasts in mood that make Mahler's idiom so distinctive. Periodically, Mahler suddenly jolts the listener out of an established mood or pattern or shifts a set tempo radically, even in mid-measure. I suggest that these contrasts are vital to a Mahler performance and should not be de-emphasized. They are essential to the life-world which Mahler intended to create, exposing deep wounds and horrible torments and facing down painful vicissitudes. To what degree such contrasts need to be highlighted will depend on their significance within the context of the symphony.

Another important interpretive consideration is the rendering of Mahler's "grotesque" or "parodistic" elements. By these I mean his use of phrases, fragments or even single tones to either produce or heighten an horrific, even ugly effect or one of mocking irony. Mahler was not reticent to color these musical metaphors with strong, deep hues or intensify them with stinging thrusts. The feelings of dread, fear, and horror, as well as mocking caricature, cut deep. As a result, Mahler's works have been criticized as either vulgar or unmusical. His willingness to confront the most terrifying aspects of human existence by eliciting strange musical effects sometimes cuts to the core and can be difficult to bear. For Mahler is uncompromising in his representation of the positive and negative forces that struggle for the

INTRODUCTION

possession of the soul all of its earthly days. Yet in his symphonies Mahler seeks an antidote to the tragic side of life. For the most part, he sets up these negative forces only in hopes of finding a musical means to accomplish their ultimate defeat.

Tempo is always a major consideration in developing an interpretation of a symphonic work. As a conductor, Mahler knew that he needed to direct the flow of the music with special notations to achieve the effects he desired. More than any composer before or after him, he literally blanketed his scores with such directions, inserting them not just at the beginning of a section or movement to establish the tempo but within these contexts to moderate or enliven it. For example, Mahler knew that orchestral players often tend to speed up when rhythmic motion becomes more diminutive (say from quarter-notes to sixteen-notes). To mitigate against such a predilection, he would add *nicht eilen* ('don't rush') at such a point in the score as a warning to control this tendency. Unfortunately, many of these second-level directions are either ignored or exaggerated and performances suffer as a result.

Mahler sometimes caricatures aspects of the Austro-German musical tradition in his symphonies. March and dance rhythms abound, the former taking either an heroic or funereal guise, the latter presenting cosmopolitan and countrified folk music. These elements are often juxtaposed, and serve to contrast the dramatic with the caricaturesque, the sublime with the vulgar. They reflect Mahler's reaction to the decadence of *fin-de-siècle* Europe as well as his constant struggle to find meaning in life and death, and they give his works an existential import. Performances that speak to these considerations and engage the listener in the life-and-death struggle can be more successful for doing so.

A conductor's overall approach can be referred to as either "objective" or "personal" (presumably a euphemism for "subjective"). I use these terms here to orient the reader/listener to the way in which a conductor deals with the music's emotive content. An objective manner connotes an emphasis on technical precision over emotive expression; a personal approach may --but does not necessarily--connote the converse. Although admirable in its presumed concern with clarity, precision, consistency and cohesiveness in overall presentation, an objective approach can sap the music of its emotive impact and aesthetic essence, tempering the effectiveness of Mahler's dramatic vision. On the other hand, overemphasis on emotional outpourings can sound artificial. Obviously, a perfect combination of both frames of reference can be more successful than favoring one over the other.

One note about sonic reproduction. In this era of supersonic technology and hyperesthetic reaction to high volume, it is not surprising to find many record producers trying to compensate for a lack of interpretive insight or the inadequacies of the orchestra or chorus by supercharging dynamic levels. Climaxes are often distorted by such exaggerations and inner-voice parts overemphasized. While the sensitivity of modern recording equipment can enhance the audibility of inner voices, its usefulness in this respect can be overplayed, creating a one-dimensional perspective than flattens depth of field and results in inappropriate balances among various instruments or ensembles.

Now to the symphonies themselves. While each may be said to create a distinct music-world, they all seem to fit together, as Pierre Boulez aptly put it, as if they were parts of one gigantic musical piece. The so-called "Wunderhorn" symphonies (a term coined by Donald Mitchell referring to the first four symphonies by reason of their references to Mahler's *Des Knaben Wunderhorn* songs) have "nature" and/or "spirituality" as conceptual reference points. Mahler often evoked both images in the same symphony, relating to Nature as he might to God. It is imperative that these quintessential aspects of Mahler's aesthetic are brought out in a characterful and convincing manner. A fluid musical line with sufficient flexibility to be pliant but not so much as to sag or become distended can help achieve that end. References to folk or popular music should be idiomatic without sounding forced or unnatural.

The First Symphony presents numerous interpretive issues. How does one set the tempi for the first movement so as to make its shape as one long accelerando more obvious? How doggedly should the bass strings dig into the ländler rhythm in the second movement? How melismatically should the oboe sing the Yiddish theme in the following movement? Where is the ultimate climax of the finale to be found? The answers to these questions--and so many others--should not be considered as definitive, but most come from total immersion in Mahler's idiom. The storm scene that opens the symphony's expansive finale needs to capture the urgency and intensity that create the first crisis in the work; then, its heroic apotheosis needs a full measure of dramatic weight to achieve the effect of winning through to victory.

Mahler sought the meaning of life through an intensely personal communion with both Nature and God. In the Second Symphony, he seeks redemption, but it is more spiritual than worldly. Mahler intensifies the drama of the work by plumbing its emotional depths in the first movement in a manner that must have seemed terrifying, if not ugly, to early audiences. As in the First a funeral march appears, but it now has a profoundly spiritual character. Giving sufficient weight to the funeral march tread will set the tone for the entire work. Throughout his *oeuvre,* Mahler uses instrumental color to create atmosphere or add character to a particular musical line. Occasional thrusts, outbursts, or fragmentary material intrude upon the music with a terrifying, painful or even demonic character. Downplaying or smoothing over these elements will only detract from their effect and diminish the depth of emotion that should be conveyed. The minuet in the second movement should be paced comfortably so that it exudes charm and grace. In the Scherzo (third) movement, Mahler develops the art of parody to an even greater degree than in the funeral march movement of the First Symphony. A flowing rhythmic and melodic line infused with enough energy to keep its momentum going, but not too much to make it seem unduly nervous, should provide the right atmosphere within which to develop this caricature of his Wunderhorn song about Saint Anthony preaching to the fishes. *Urlicht,* with its prayer for redemption, provides a perfect prelude to the awesome opening of the finale. I have always felt that this magnificent movement, with its quasi-religious quest for redemption, comes off more convincingly if presented as a positive resolution of the tragedy of the first movement. Yet another reason to give full measure to that movement's tragic muse.

The Third Symphony is pantheistic in character, combining references to Nature and God in a progressive development from the former to the latter. Its string of six diverse movements has led some critics to conclude that it is not truly a symphony, but only an orchestral suite. However, presenting these movements merely as a set of unrelated divertissements neglects their subtle musical and dramatic interrelationships and also overlooks Mahler's deft fusion of the aesthetic and dramatic aspects (again Nature and Spirit) of his First and Second Symphonies in the Third. As in the Second, the funeral march with which the first movement of the Third opens (after the initial horn theme) should be given due weight. The Pan march that follows should be as contrastingly bright, joyous and filled with enthusiasm as the funeral march was terrifying. The unanticipated mood swings between these two sections should heighten their contrast. As indicated in the original titles for the following two movements, Mahler pays homage to the wonders of Nature, particularly "flowers" and "animals." Charm and delicacy, sprinkled with wit and playfulness, should cajole the listener at every turn. In contrast, the fourth movement, sung by a contralto to a text by Friedrich Nietzsche, is a dark, brooding song with deep philosophical meaning. Here Mahler finds his existential voice in a text for the first time, expressing life's longing for joy in the face of sorrow. Too many conductors who may not be in sympathy with this philosophy gloss over this movement and do not even attempt to fathom its depth. This symphony's concluding movement is a cornerstone of the entire work. For the first time, Mahler ends a symphony with a slow movement. In fact, some of the main considerations here relate to tempo. How slowly should the main themes be paced, and how consistently should the opening tempo be applied during the movement's progress and at its conclusion? It is my feeling that the tempo set at the

INTRODUCTION

beginning should correspond with the tempo of the conclusion. Recently, some conductors have defused the sense of release and overwhelming fulfillment of the closing measures by playing them briskly. I believe that this practice is contrary both to Mahler's directions and the symphony's basic aesthetic. Three times during the movement our attention is diverted from the gradual build up of its hauntingly beautiful themes by sudden references to the dark, funereal section of the first movement, a reminder of what is being overcome. All the dread evoked by these stark images should be laid bare.

After the heaven-storming spirituality of the Second Symphony and the Pantheistic world-view of the Third, the Fourth Symphony seems infinitely simpler, less emotionally troubled and spiritually transcendent. Lightness, simplicity, charm and grace seem (on the surface) to wipe away the memory of the earlier intense symphonic dramas. Yet the Fourth is even more contrapuntally complex than its predecessors. How inner musical lines are juxtaposed with principal material will be an important consideration in judging the merits of a performance. Just as significant is the way in which Mahler builds the entire symphony around the song finale. Thematic references to its principal tune are scattered throughout the work; these are especially apparent during the dynamic E-major flourish that precedes the coda of the *Adagio*. Nature, in the sense of the pastoral conjurings in the previous symphonies, seems strangely absent; the spiritual only appears in a curiously homespun song of the daily doings of "Heavenly Life" that replaces the more typically massive and dramatic finales found in the first three symphonies. Parody--an element only hinted at before--now comes to the fore. In the first two movements, Mahler parodies the decadence of modern life by presenting popular Viennese music (some of which recalls the strains of Haydn, Mozart and Schubert) in caricaturesque fashion. The sometimes mocking, sometimes grotesque way in which Mahler characterizes such well known and beloved musical styles did not go unnoticed in his day. Nor should it in performances today.

Mahler's fascinating compositional ingenuities become more highly developed here as well: for instance, the overlapping of sections by beginning a new section's theme at the same time as the previous one is concluding, what I call "telescoping." Such an intermeshing of themes in transition should be handled so that the audience is aware of what is happening musically. A second technique is the increasingly sophisticated manner in which Mahler uses motivic references. The pizzicato rhythm in bass strings that opens the third movement forms a motto (with a telling relationship to one of the two "heartbeat" mottos of the Ninth Symphony's first movement) that is significant throughout the movement. If this motto is not distinct when it first appears (though marked "*p*"), later, more forceful references to it will not have sufficient import.

I often refer to two other interesting sections of the Adagio movement. About two-thirds of the way into this movement, after Mahler returns to G major, he presents a series of tiered allegro segments in a lighter vein than the ethereal music of the principal thematic material. Each segment becomes progressively faster until the lighthearted mood is dispelled at its height by a sudden, unprepared return of the main theme in variation. The mood softens and soon becomes suspended in peaceful repose on hushed string harmonies over the opening rhythmic motto in the bass strings. Then the orchestra suddenly bursts out with a sky-opening *ff* flourish of Brucknerian grandeur in E major during which hints of the finale's main theme are presented. I often discuss how well these contrasting sections are handled. In the finale, the soprano should have a light vocal quality and an angelic manner of expression. The use of a boy soprano (in two recordings) is interesting but not necessarily successful in performance, depending largely upon the vocal timbre of the soloist.

The middle symphonies, Nos. 5 through 7, are often referred to as a group because they are considered more abstract, contain no sung text and no overt, readily discernible extra-musical references, and are more texturally complex than the earlier symphonies. Mahler's primary themes of Nature and God, so evident in his first four symphonies seem absent at first; however, Mahler refers symbolically to them with cowbells and bird song (Nature) and cataclysmic climaxes (God). Moreover, these middle symphonies are no less symphonic dramas than their predecessors. By means of musical allegory, they present different life-worlds, struggles against negative forces that threaten annihilation (Death). In all but No.6 the positive, life-enhancing elements are victorious. Parody and motivic symbolism also dominate these symphonies. As with the first two movements of No.4, Mahler builds upon his mocking commentary on modern decadence in dance movements with even more outrageous mimicry and burlesque. Each of the middle symphonies is filled with overtones of the *Rückert-lieder* and *Kindertotenlieder*, as well as references to the earlier symphonies, sometimes by theme or motive, at other times by general outline or conception.

In Part I of the Fifth Symphony, Mahler intensifies the tragedy and its tormented passions by strongly contrasting its many moods, often in such a sudden, unanticipated manner as to shock the listener. In Part II, negative emotions give way to a whimsical parody of contemporary cosmopolitan life, caricaturing popular Viennese dance forms in a mad whirl of carefree thoughtlessness that is interrupted periodically with unnerving doubts. One should feel caught up in this frivolous sense of complete abandon, yet also distressed by its moments of disturbing reflection. Recently, much controversy has arisen about the tempo and emotive evocation of the Adagietto movement. Whether or not Mahler intended it as a love-song to his bride-to-be Alma Schindler (as Wilhelm Mengelberg contends) or a morose reverie, possibly of lost love, filled with Mahlerian *angst*, the interpreter should apply the chosen approach consistently and with conviction. The current trend favors the former perspective over the latter for well-founded reasons. Whatever emotions are stirred up in this movement, the finale should be a celebration of joy. Yet the shapes of Mahler's main themes seem to work against this feeling, the first theme beginning with a downward motion that would normally have the opposite effect. The whole symphony connotes the transformation of tragedy and pain into joy and well-being. When the recollection of the Grand Chorale from the second movement appears, it should feel like the crowning glory of the symphony, conveying a sense of worldly redemption.

In the Sixth Symphony, Mahler takes up the life-struggle against tragedy and death once again. This time he fashions it as a Faustian music drama in which the hero of the first movement (characterized by the visceral strength of a muscular march theme) is confronted with his Mephistophelian shadow side (in the Scherzo) with such mocking irony that he loses faith in himself and is ultimately defeated. Tempo is a major factor here, particularly in establishing the temperament of the work at the very beginning. The first movement's march theme has caused much controversy in this regard: how fast should one set *allegro energico ma non troppo* (literally, an energetic allegro but not too much)? Since a heroic presentment should be evoked here, too much speed may produce a freneticism that detracts from the sense of boldness and robust resoluteness that this music should convey. (One might take a hint from the *allegro energico* of the Wunderhorn song, *Revelge*). Also controversial is the order of the inner movements, about which Mahler changed his mind at least once, if not twice.[1] Since I

---

[1]The first published edition of the Sixth, in 1906, had the Scherzo placed second, while the second edition reversed the order of movements. Some say that Mahler changed his mind, returning the Scherzo to its original position when last he performed the work. But several reviewers of this performance indicate that the slow movement was, in fact, still placed second. (Donald Mitchell suggests that Mahler may have tried out the original order at a rehearsal that may have been attended by only one reviewer who noticed, and criticized, the change of movement order.) Mahler also eliminated the third hammer blow in the finale, presumably for

view the Scherzo as a parody on the opening movement, in which Mephistopheles "frets and struts about the stage" mocking the hero's valorous pose, it fits best when placed after the heroic first movement. The main pulse for both movements should be essentially the same (notice the *wuchtig* (weighty) marking at the beginning of the Scherzo). A numbed reverie pervades the slow movement, as if seeking an unattainable peace (with poignant references to Nature symbolized by cowbells). The huge finale gives most conductors the greatest difficulty. How its extensive and complex, but remarkably cohesive, structure is contoured will have a major impact upon the quality of the performance. As with most of Mahler's dramatic symphonies, the finale, in every aspect, should be given time to unfold and weight to heighten its dramatic impact. Merely turning up the volume at strong climaxes or enhancing the hammer blows will not suffice.

Mahler's Seventh Symphony is probably his most controversial. Some commentators have denigrated its lack of cohesion and inspiration. I have always found such negative comments to be quite extraordinary, because Mahler develops some of his most brilliant compositional techniques in this work. The two *Nachtmusiken*, composed before the larger outer movements, are sources of Mahler's muse here. The first recalls Nature in a world reminiscent of the Wunderhorn songs; the second is a serenade of chamber-like simplicity, embellished with mandolin and guitar. A spectral vision of Night casts its spell in the opening of the Scherzo, using waltz and ländler themes in grotesque parody.

Although many explanations of this strange work have been offered, including those based upon Mahler's often cryptic remarks,[2] I suggest that Mahler is mocking himself here. If the Sixth speaks of the tragic irony of life's struggle, the Seventh carries the notion of self-mockery (appearing only in the Sixth's scherzo movement) to its ultimate extreme. Notice how he begins with yet another funeral march, now set to the strains of a grotesquely vulgarized theme on a tenor horn.[3] In the second movement, march and waltz themes are subject to caricaturesque treatment, as they are even more outrageously mimetic in the finale. There Mahler even caricatures his beloved Wagner by refashioning the festival march from *Die Meistersinger* and making it sound vulgarly pompous. Mahler even mocks his penchant for dramatic heaven-storming. In the Seventh, it might be said that he becomes the Mephistopheles to his own Faust! He dances with his own demon. One also senses this pervasive parodistic mode in the third movement that contrasts a sinister web of interweaving triplets with an absurd little waltz tune. Even the slow movement is not free of it, listen to how the moonlight serenade is decorated with little skipping rhythmic figures. The latter may very well have had their source in Beckmesser's impish character, as if to say that behind every lover there is a foolish little devil mocking him. The finale takes parody to previously unknown extremes, juxtaposing a foot-stomping march with a coy, Haydnesque minuet. As the movement proceeds, Mahler contrasts these divergent themes with ever increasing frequency, bringing one to its height only to collapse into the other. Few have succeeded in bringing off this movement as well as Leonard Bernstein, who refused to smooth over these contrasts or wander aimlessly through

---

reasons of superstition, and thinned out orchestral textures. The Critical Edition of the score places the Scherzo second and does not contain the third hammer blow, replacing it with celesta and percussion. There seems to be no reason to consider either version more authentic than the other.

[2] Mahler is reputed to have said that the opening material came to him while rowing on a lake. It seems doubtful that this statement was meant to indicate that the rhythm of rowing somehow relates to the opening funereal march tread.

[3] Mahler once remarked that this theme was "Nature's roar."

the thicket of their interweaving contraposition. Of course, the interpretive conception offered here is not Mahler's but my own. It is not intended to be definitive but only to serve as a reference point.

For some commentators the Eighth Symphony is somewhat of an enigma, for in this massive choral symphony one finds nothing of Mahler's tragic muse: all is confident and untroubled from beginning to end. No funeral marches or painful episodes here to be overcome in a triumphant finale. It is as if the work were structured as two finales surrounding music of hushed mysterium, romantic passion and cherubic playfulness. The parody and caricature that give the middle symphonies so much bite and wit are also absent here. As I see it, the Eighth is as much a cleansing of Mahler's passionate struggle with death and the meaning of life as the middle symphonies were attempts to objectify that struggle. Here aesthetic elements from the Wunderhorn years--such as Spirituality--reappear in a formidably complex textural construction using texts that juxtapose religious and worldly metaphysical principles and that recall a similar contrast in the Second and Third Symphonies.

Apart from considerations of tempi and phrasing, much is apparent interpretively. A recreation of the moods of the work can succeed by careful attention to Mahler's directions, providing one has adequate forces. The difficulty here is in controlling the enormous number of performers the work requires with enough precision that the contrapuntal lines, often containing important motivic elements and easily buried under the weight of textural complexity, are distinct. The work presents a few motives that develop continuously until they achieve fulfillment in the closing moments. A performance that allows the listener to hear the development of these motives while creating the diverse atmospheres in which they appear can touch both the heart and the mind.

The symphony *cum* song cycle, *Das Lied von der Erde*, presents such an extreme contrast to the Eighth that many who come to the former for the first time after experiencing the latter find it difficult to believe that both works were written about one year apart by the same composer. Here the heaven-storming redemptive spirit of the Eighth gives way to the worldly profundity of oriental mysticism. One senses that *Das Lied*'s tragic muse is itself a reaction to the confident spirituality of its predecessor. Sweet nostalgia is tinged with bitter self-reproach made more cutting by painful images reminiscent of the demons that were to have been defeated in the *Wunderhorn* symphonies. At life's conclusion a plain parody of decadence will not do; a deep sense of impending loss pervades the atmosphere--loss of the most cherished gift of all, life. One must take the bitter with the sweet, the sad with the joyful, and affirm all to eternity. One should not fail to notice how Nietzschean these concepts are, even at a time when Mahler, according to his wife, had rejected the ideas of the German philosopher.

In *Das Lied*, the recreation of disparate moods is of prime importance to a successful performance. None of the biting ferocity of the *Trinklied* song, the bemused loneliness of the *Absolung im Herbst*, the sweet, lilting charm of On Youth and On Beauty, the ebullient abandon to Nature's muse in *Trunkene* or the profound transcendental mysticism of *Der Abschied* should fail to captivate the most insensitive disposition. Here again, Mahler seeks an answer to his quest for a key to overcoming life's struggle against Death. As in most of his earlier symphonies, the combat between life-affirming and life-denying aspects is presented in the outer movements, and the middle movements provide diversions, here as various aspects of earthly life from the joys of its beauty to the pathos of its loneliness. Pacing is often a key factor in setting an appropriate mood. Expressivity in both vocal and orchestral phrasing is of equal importance, the conductor needing to coordinate the orchestral accompaniment with the vocal part to support the effect to be engendered. Basic motivic elements that occur throughout the work should come through within the context of the musical fabric. The extremely complex rhythmic construction of the finale (with its contrapuntally diffuse hemiolas) should flow easily and suggest both a sense of weightlessness and timelessness (even Mahler confessed that he

INTRODUCTION

wasn't sure how to conduct some of the closing passages!). It is very important, especially in the finale, that the vocalist pay careful attention to dynamic markings. Markings of *p* or softer in high registers can put a strain on the singer, as they often do on such words as *"lacht"* or *"Traum"* in the *Trunkene* lied. But if the soloist ignores them, the feeling of simple wonderment at the beauties of Nature to be conveyed here is lost. One particularly important place in the finale where such markings appear is at #58 when C major is firmly established on the words *"Die liebe Erde"* near the close. Mahler even adds an exclamation point to both the tempo (*Langsam*) and the dynamic markings (*ppp*). Too often the etheric beauty of this passage is diminished by excessive sound and speed. If the alto/baritone soloist can produce a liquid tone that floats through the closing measures, her or his performance will be unforgettable (witness the great contralto Kathleen Ferrier in her classic reading under Bruno Walter's direction).

Das Lied von der Erde and the Ninth and Tenth Symphonies form a trilogy the aesthetic core of which concentrates more fully upon Life and Death, and the struggle within the former to overcome the latter, and find meaning in the tragedy of its inevitability. The Ninth begins with two principal rhythmic mottos that can be considered as metaphors for a normal and abnormal heartbeat, the latter of which was supposedly a rhythmic representation of Mahler's arhythmic pulse. However this symphony is conceived, it presents a profound conflict for the human soul between positive and negative forces. To what degree the conductor is able to make this conflict impress itself upon the listener, however painful to the ear and heart it becomes, will determine the effectiveness of his or her interpretation. Just as significant is the need for an orchestra that can meet the demands made upon it in this work. Rich, full-bodied sonorities are necessary to adequately reproduce the thematic material and complex harmonies presented here, requiring warmth of tone in lyrical sections, dynamic thrust in soaring climaxes and marked articulation of certain inner voice parts. Tempi are again a major consideration. The second movement contains three principal subjects based upon dance music (ländler, waltz and minuet), whose tempi need to be adroitly juxtaposed. Effectiveness in coordinating contrasts in mood within movements is also an important consideration.

Mahler's penchant for parody and ironic caricature continues to play a significant role in each of these symphonies. The Scherzos of the Ninth and Tenth contrast music of raucous frenzy with that of lilting charm. Vitality and urgency should heighten the effect of brusque, even rude mockery that Mahler conjures up here as a commentary on modern times. Once again, the conductor should not shirk from presenting the contrasts between light and dark, positive and negative forces with all the ferocity that Mahler must have imagined in writing this music. In the Tenth, the shattering dissonant chords of piled-on thirds that appear in the outer movements in a horrific vision of annihilation should shock the audience. Some conductors try to play down their awesome character in a wayward effort at deconstruction. They miss the point. Enormous outbursts of this kind should make as strong an impression on the audience as possible. Here, timing, pacing, balancing and the way in which the climax fits within the context of the whole--and not mere volume--will determine their impact.

This brief introduction does not--and could not possibly--contain all that should be taken into account in reviewing a performance of a Mahler symphony. Moreover, no matter how objective the judgment is intended to be, subjective elements undoubtedly come into play. To avoid a merely personal approach, the reviews that follow try to balance an overall impression with a critique of specific passages considered significant. Whenever possible, I have included timings and score references for these passages.

Many recordings reviewed in the 1986 volume that have been reissued since its publication are included here with revised commentary and updated recording information. Sonic quality is only mentioned if it is a significant aspect of the reissue. It was difficult to decide whether to include all, some or none of the many private recordings that have appeared in the last nine years. After much deliberation, I decided not to include most of them, except for those recordings of special interest or significance. I have included reviews of all known commercially-issued videotape recordings.

The release of historical recordings, particularly those of Pierre Boulez and Bruno Maderna, has been most instructive and illuminating. However, one might question the willingness of certain record companies to release every single recorded performance by a famous Mahler conductor, regardless of quality. Even great conductors have off-days. If their interpretations of particular symphonies are already available on disc, it seems unproductive to release performances of the same work that do not show the conductor in the best light.

Listings are in alphabetical order by the last name of the conductor, and include the names of the orchestras, choruses and soloists where applicable, as well as recording data, dates of issue and total timings. One word of caution about timings. Higher numbers do not necessarily indicate slower tempi. Longer performances could result from a more spacious treatment of transitions, longer fermatas, etc. If one were to compare the timings of the first three movements of the Third in Leonard Bernstein's first recording (for Columbia) with the timings for the same movements in his later reading (for DG), one might get the impression that the later performance is slower than the earlier one. Not so! Tempi throughout the former are consistent with those in the latter. The performance in the DG release, however, has a greater urgency and intensity of the sort often generated in a live performance. Nevertheless, do not expect slower main tempi. Some sections (the posthorn passages of the third movement, for instance) are more broadly treated, as are some transitional passages in the first movement. So don't be misled.

As in the 1986 volume, I have marked each review with the following symbols to indicate my preferences. They appear at the end of each heading.

    ** excellent
    *+ very good
    * good
    + adequate

The absence of a marking indicates that the recording is not recommended.

These critiques should not be taken as definitive but as attempts to offer commentary on performance practice and interpretive concepts as they appear in the enormous number of recorded performances of Mahler's symphonies. I have tried to point out when and how I believe they succeed or fail, both at specific points and as a whole.

   I wish to express my boundless gratitude to some of my fellow Mahlerians for their kind assistance: Donald Mitchell for his extremely helpful critique of a portion of the book; Peter Fülöp for providing me with copies of several recordings I was otherwise unable to obtain; and Henry-Louis de la Grange for stimulating my thinking about performance practice and interpretation.

                         L.M.S.

Gustav Mahler's Symphonies

SYMPHONY NO. 1 IN D MAJOR ("TITAN")

Movements:

1. Langsam, schleppend/Im Anfang sehr gemächlich
[2."Blumine" - Andante] (omitted by Mahler from original version)
2. Kräftig bewegt, doch nicht zu schnell
3. Feierlich und gemessen, ohne zu schleppen
4. Sturmisch bewegt

ABBADO, CLAUDIO/Berlin Philharmonic - DG 431 769 (1991) [54:43]; DG video 440 072 273-2 (1991/1992) [55:05] "Abbado in Berlin: The First Year."*+   Nearly ten years after his recording with the Chicago Symphony (see Vol. 1, p.3), Abbado's approach seems less frenetic, exaggerated and self-conscious. His more stable and comfortable reading is enhanced by iridescent brass and radiant strings, especially compelling in the ethereal opening and heroic close. A warm, summery atmosphere is established immediately in soft, whispy high strings, a mere hint of distant fanfares and sparkling woodwinds. The main theme is mellower, even tender, and remains at *pp* until the rollicking close of the exposition. Characteristic of this more relaxed demeanor is the way the celli ease up ever so slightly at the end of the main theme's first statement during the repeat of the exposition. Playing generally flows more comfortably, with more liquid legato, lyricism and charm. This easy manner continues at the start of the development, yet with a gentle underlying momentum. How beautifully the BPO horns intone the bright fanfare theme at #15. One senses a slight tug-of-war thereafter, as Abbado tries to control the tempo yet moves it forward ever so gently. Pacing is more easy-going than unnervingly agitated. While the closing section is energetic enough to sound youthful, one comes away feeling less exhausted than one did in Abbado's CSO recording.

   A strict reading of markings sometimes can cause more problems than it resolves. For instance, Abbado takes the metronome marking at bar 5 of the second movement to mean that the previous four measures should be in a different, presumably slower tempo. Consequently, the opening whoops in strings are in one tempo and the theme in another. Aside from this quirk, the main theme has sufficient bounce, even if it seems slightly harried for a country dance. Abbado shows off the subtleties of the BPO in soft shadings (at #11). Some slight hesitations creep into an otherwise brisk Trio section, making it sound too sophistocated for its bucolic character. The ländler returns with a will, closing in racy and rough-hewn style.

A generally excellent third movement is particularly noteworthy for a characterful reading of the Yiddish music, despite an unmarked glissando between G and A at #7 on its return (3:05). The middle-section song theme is imbued with soft tones and touching simplicity. During the return of the opening march, in an attempt to highlight its parodistic character, the solo oboe takes some liberties with the minor-key version of the Yiddish theme before the close. Without overdoing it, Abbado gets up a good head of steam to open the finale, but he suddenly holds back to dig in more intently at #8 (1:45) and then just as abruptly pounces on the stormy opening once again. Very jagged, spasmotic spirts of energy exaggerate the fragments of the main theme that end the first subject (c.3:00). Like Bernstein, Abbado squeezes every drop of emotion from the introduction to the second subject, yet the lyrical theme itself is songful, and only slightly hesitant. (But what happened to those BPO horns at 5:24?) The concluding section of the second subject is rather slap-dash; it lacks any ritard and contains a very harsh swell at the closing cadence. When the heroic trumpet theme first appears (marked p), Abbado adds a momentary ritard, presumably to mirror the ritard Mahler writes for the start of the theme's later, full-blown appearance. This affectation may have the virtue of consistency, but disturbs the linear flow and detracts from the dramatic impact of the theme's later, more heroic guise. At 13:35, Abbado has the celli play glissandi, distorting its lyricism. The build up to the final heroic climax is magnificent, enhanced by superb brass sonics, even though Abbado gallops through the climactic segment marked *Triumphal - pesante* without hesitation. The closing section is strong, dynamic and quite exciting. Some of the troublesome mannerisms that appear on the CD, are omitted here (particularly those in the last two movements mentioned above).

ABRAVANEL, MAURICE/Utah Symphony - Vanguard S-320 (1975); OVC 4003 (1991); 11-08.4013.79 (1995) [48:50] Spotty playing in the middle movements and strange ineffective mannerisms severely detract from the value of this recording. Abravanel tends to be somewhat stiff, angular or abrupt at times; this results in roughly-handled transitions and a detached overall presentment. In the outer movements, he does generate some energy, particularly in the closing sections; however, the second movement is much too hurried and the third simply routine. Abravanel's objective approach lends itself better to the more dramatic moments, leaving the tender or sentimental lyricism or subsidiary melodic material sounding dry and ineffectual.

ANCERL, KAREL/Czech Philharmonic - Supraphon SUAST 50675 (1967); 151068; Classic 991003; Crossroads 22160011; Supraphon SU 1953-2011 (1995) [50:24]
The most interesting moment here appears right at the outset. An extraordinarily lifelike rendition of the chirping bird calls in woodwinds creates a delightfully evocative pastoral atmosphere. Thereafter, the performance soon devolves into the lackluster realms of the mediocre. Marred by sloppy and unstylish playing, a dull ländler, a stiffly read funeral march and an uneven and understated finale with some awkward affects, this performance does not live up to the promise of its opening measures.

ANDREESCU, HORIA/Moldavia Philharmonic Symphony - Electrecord ST-ECE03111 (1984) [55] This recording suffers mostly from a dry reading, technical imperfections and weak sonic range. After a mild, timid introduction colored with soft hues and in appropriately sluggish tempo, the main theme begins without a tempo change until #4 (four measures into the theme). From there, the tempo, as well as the general atmosphere, is free and airy. Without taking the repeat of the exposition, Andreescu lets the tempo sag as the development begins, recalling the labored introduction, now with a strangely mournful aspect. Then he picks up the tempo abruptly, destroying any continuity. The closing section is lively but diminished volume, imprecise articulation and a slight affectation at m.408 are disturbing. Andreescu routinely dashes off the ländler movement. But the third movement has more character, with its idiomatic treatment of the Yiddish dance music and lovely, expressive playing by violins in the songful middle section. The opening storm scene of the finale is much too tame, rigid and dynamically confined. However, a flexible treatment of the second subject is appealing. Like Abbado and others, Andreescu holds on to the first few notes of the heroic main theme when it first appears in trumpet solo, then suddenly speeds up into tempo. Following the transition to the recapitulation, the pace slackens before #49, thereby making the long gradual build-up to the full-blown statement of the heroic theme seem endless. The ultimate climax of the movement is strong and hefty but lacks sonic punch. Since Andreescu's tempo was already weighty long before the *Triumphal* section, he disregards its *pesante* marking and continues with the previous tempo to the very end, ignoring Mahler's direction at #60 to move forward more quickly to the close.

BERNSTEIN, LEONARD/New York Philharmonic - Columbia MS-7019 (1965); 7069; CBS M-31834; MK-42194; 2-Sony SM2K 47573 (1992) [52:36]* Agitation and impulsion are the norm here. Nervous energy and intensity propel the faster sections forward while extreme mannerisms exude a languorousness into the middle movements. The outer movements are more satisfying; Bernstein whoops up a whirlwind of excitement during their closing sections. His mannerisms in the finale's lyrical second theme are extremely self-indulgent. Yet his may be the best rendition of the *rubato* cadence that closes the exposition. His energetic approach makes the closing pages of the symphony thrilling.

BERNSTEIN, LEONARD/Vienna Philharmonic (perf. 1975) - DG video 072 223 (1990) [54:52]** The by-word for this splendid aural and visual experience is "natural," the very quintessence of the symphony itself. Every nuance is rendered stylishly; the self-indulgence of Bernstein's first effort is measurably tempered. From the hushed serenity of the nearly motionless opening, one immediately senses how naturally the music flows forth. Even the gradual increase in tempo is unaffected and unforced, yet overflows with youthful exuberance. The rustic stomping of the ländler has just enough heft, without compromising its spontaneity with excessive mannerisms; and the charming trio is the ländler's perfect counterfoil, nuanced with ease and grace. As one would expect, Bernstein treats the Yiddish music in the third movement idiomatically but without over-indulgence. Then he wafts gently into the songful middle section, in perfect contrast to the raucous Jewish wedding music that interrupts the funeral procession. After the procession dies down to a whisper, the finale bursts in without a moment's hesitation. Wild and furious is the raging storm, haunted by woodwinds' dissonant cries of dispair. This time Bernstein holds back on the first four notes of the heroic main theme in its first appearance (despite no marking to this effect), presumably in anticipation of the same effect that Mahler calls for at the theme's full-blown appearance in the final apotheosis. No Mahler conductor can render the romantic lyricism of the second subject as Bernstein can. After a fine transition to the closing section, he holds back intently into the section marked *höchster Kraft* (16:50) with an overwhelming accumulation of power. The climax that follows is thrilling. As in his earlier version, Bernstein shifts the moment of resolution of the symphony's dramatic course away from the *Triumphal* section, thereby weaking its impact (Mahler writes *pesante* here for emphasis). Although he also anticipates Mahler's direction to become less broad in tempo in the final pages by several measures (at #59 instead of #60), the closing section is very exciting.

BERNSTEIN, LEONARD/Royal Concertgebouw Orchestra of Amsterdam - DG 427 303 (1988); 13-DG 435 162 (1992) [57]** While generally consistent in approach with his first complete cycle, Bernstein's second series contains some interesting stylistic differences. Many critics have already noticed the slower pacing. Yet if this tendency is evidence of a change in Bernstein's interpretive style, it is not apparent here. From the onset of the first movement, the opposite is clear. In recent years, conductors have taken more seriously Mahler's opening direction to let the tempo drag (*schleppend*). Bernstein may have found these efforts excessive because his pace is generally quicker. Within the introduction's brisker main tempo, woodwind and trumpet tattoos are not rushed and the entire section seems less labored than in many other performances. The tempo of the main theme is sprightly, without being hurried or excessively agitated. A spirited but not overwrought sense of youthful exuberance is tempered by the ease with which the theme floats gently onward. While Bernstein is intent upon eliciting every special effect with which Mahler enhances this lilting, summery song, he does so now with less exaggeration than he did in earlier performances.

Mahler asks that the passage leading to the climax of the first movement's recapitulation be played more and more broadly until the moment the orchestra explodes (marked with an asterisk in the score). At the same time, the bass string figuration becomes increasingly diminutive (from #25). The intention is to let the rhythmic motion propel the music forward while holding back the tempo itself; a virtual contradiction, but one that, if accomplished, can make the climax utterly shattering. Mahler's directions are especially difficult to execute and, therefore, usually ignored. Bernstein makes a valiant, if imperfect, effort to execute this passage as written. In the second movement, the tempo should have sufficient heft and the opening rhythm enough accentuation to capture the spirit of a rustic peasant dance (ländler). Bernstein accomplishes this by digging into practically every note of the ländler, aptly but not laboriously evoking the dance's characteristic foot-stomping and knee-slapping. As is Bernstein's wont, the trio contains some expressive nuances bordering on self-indulgence, but he has toned down many of these eccentricities in this new cycle. His flexive style now follows the ebb and flow of the musical line more naturally. This more controlled manner of expression is most evident in the third movement funeral march. While he treats the Yiddish klesmer music stylishly, Bernstein now seems to downplay its caricaturesque aspect. Most peculiar is the brisk tempo he chooses for the march, completely ignoring the direction *feierlich* (solemn). This approach might be intended to highlight the parody in Mahler's inspiration for this movement: Moritz Von Schwind's woodcut of a funeral procession in which a number of small animals carry a hunter on his bier.

Tempi chosen for the finale are far from restrained. The stormy opening tempo increases with each successive appearance to the ripping pace set for the final bars of the exposition. Overall, it is a stirring performance, that evokes the fury of the opening storm, the lyric beauty of the second subject and the grandeur of the heroic brass themes that bring it to a triumphant close. In his first version, Bernstein handled the *rubato* closing of the second subject even more brilliantly than he does here, moving naturally and expressively through the ebb and flow of each phrase to the final cadence. Most conductors merely rush through this segment. The lyrical second theme itself is less self-indulgently mannered here than in Bernstein's first version. The finale's many tempo modulations present major interpretive problems. From the beginning Bernstein insists (as do some others) on slowing up out of tempo every time that the heroic theme is presented. In the recapitulation, where the heroic theme reaches stentorian proportions, its first four notes are marked *pesante* (heavy) to emphasize its grand bearing. However, this marking does not appear when the theme is first presented much earlier in a more subdued manner. Emphasizing these notes on their first appearance, when softly intoned, anticipates and thereby diminishes the impact of their triumphant presentment during the symphony's closing moments.

Bernstein frequently shifts tempi or momentarily holds back where no tempo markings exist. For instance, at #28 he suddenly returns to the main allegro tempo. At #52, before the main climax of the movement and of the entire symphony (which happens at #56, marked *Triumphal*), Bernstein suddenly pulls up the reins, shifting the climax away from its intended locus. Therefore, when the triumphant climax occurs (to be played *pesante*), the effect is severely diminished. After #56 no tempo change is marked for 55 measures (until at #60 where the direction calls for the tempo to become less and less broad until the end). Bernstein, however, picks up the tempo much earlier (at #59). Others have also interpolated this tempo shift, but to less positive effect (e.g., Järvi, see below). Whether Mahler would have considered such variations from the score as either conscionable or even laudable is something we will never know. One could, know doubt, revise many of Mahler's tempo markings to suit one's personal tastes; Mahler himself was constantly revising his symphony scores and was heard to say that he approved of other conductors doing so if the circumstances required (he may have merely intended such remarks to relate to the necessity of making adjustments tofit the acoustics of a particular hall). Notwithstanding his own adjustments to the score markings but not necessarily because of them, Bernstein delivers one of the truly great performances of the First ever recorded.

BERTINI, GARY/ Cologne Radio Symphony - EMI CDC 7 54907 (1993) [54:42]*+
Within the limitations of this ensemble, Bertini offers a perfect combination of masterful control, idiomatic phrasing and attention to detail, in splendidly clear and well-balanced sonic ranges. His approach is clearly objective, but his handling of nuances, shaping of lines and phrases and pacing of tempo gradations show him to be a true Mahlerian. No affectations or mannerisms here, only a faithful rendering of Mahler's musical directions. Such a reading could become imprisoned in its technical precision; however, Bertini's does not. The first two movements are energetic, yet the first occasionally evokes a sense of daydreaming that makes its summery atmosphere so captivating, and the second contains a lilting and easy-going trio. The funeral march movement has few of the affectations that appear in more stylized readings. Bertini lets the music alone, and if the result is not particularly warm in the songful middle section, it does convey the spirit of the piece. In the finale, Bertini keeps the tempo of the opening storm scene under control without diminishing its energy and intensity. His overall sense of proportion in pacing, particularly during transitions, as well as his proportionate balances in dynamic levels, are well-conceived. A slight rigidity becomes apparent during the storm's relentless rapid string figuration, but the mysterious atmosphere of the transition to the return of the opening deluge (7:20) and the heaving motion that continuously increases its force are marvelous effects. Only brass seem restrained, particularly during the symphony's grand conclusion.

BOULT, ADRIAN/London Philharmonic - Everest 3005; 3359/12 (1958); EVC 9022 (1995) [46:28] Little can be said in defence of this unmahlerian reading. Tempi are completely misconceived: disjointed in the first movement, incredibly fast in the ländler, quick in the funeral march and rushed in the finale. Moreover, playing is simply atrocious: imprecise, unstylish and routine. Boult seems to have neither a feeling for nor an understanding of this music.

BUTT, YONDANI/London Symphony - IMP Classics PCD 941 (1990) [51:59] Butt's approach is almost devoid of romantic spirit; it suffers from lifeless tempi and colorless, lackluster playing as well as thoughtless "objectivity." The young maestro (originally from Macao but U.S.-trained) saps much of this music of its natural vitality, youthfulness and beauty. The intricacy of Mahler's brief tempo fluctuations are glossed over (e.g., during the symphony's introduction), while bland and lackluster playing bleeds the performance of any semblance of emotion. Butt tries to control the volume at sections marked *pp* and *ppp*, but softness need not result in dullness. His failure to repeat the exposition of the first movement is no longer considered appropriate. Bloated horns distort the ländler movement by being too pronounced. A brisk, graceless trio with a matter-of-fact reading of its beautiful cello tune bury the performance even deeper into obscurity. In the fascinating third movement, with its folk melodies presented within the context of an ironic funeral cortege, Butt makes an effort to stylize the Yiddish dance music, but the lyric song theme of the middle section breezes along too quickly to be endearing. Only in the finale does Butt make an effort to instill life and intensity into this anemic performance, but what seems like a vital opening deteriorates quickly into controlled routine. In the warm and tender sentiments of the second theme (an oasis in the desert), Butt makes an attempt at being expressive. An interestingly mysterious, shadowy prelude to the return of the opening section (7:25) ushers in a storm as uneventful as before. The heroic theme in brass has little dramatic presence until the final climactic moments. Overbalanced, fatuous horns, weak percussion, high volume (as a substitute for genuine power) and a cautious, constricted tempo contribute to what can only be described as a deadly dull rendition.

CASADESUS, JEAN-CLAUDE/Orchestre National de Lille - Forlane UCD 16643 (1991) [54:12]+ A straight and generally unaffected reading such as Casadeses offers here makes a strong argument for letting the music speak for itself. While basically routine and unadventurous, this performance is well-conceived and manages to bring out the essential qualities of the music without mannerism or exaggeration. The Lille ensemble is a middling group, with occasional intonation problems and inarticulate playing. Tempi in the first movement work well, even if Casedesus tends to move too rapidly in the development section. The länder is tame, without the folkish characteristics that make it so engaging. In contrast, the trio section seems flighty, even hurried, if not without charm. Lacking even a hairsbreath pause, the third movement's funeral march begins on the heels of the ländler. Once again the approach is straightforward, the tempo of the songful middle section rather brisk, and playing somewhat stiff. Brass seem uncomfortably rigid and restrained in the opening storm scene of the finale. Casadesus keeps the tempo under strict control throughout the first subject, never letting either the tempo or the level of intensity get out of control, but the effect is too temperate. A lovely reading of the lyrical second subject argues favorably for an unaffected approach. Opting for what is rapidly becoming an acceptable mannerism, Casadesus slows up for the first four notes of the main theme in its first appearance (8:10) and then tries to catch up with the proper tempo which this interruption left behind. The later incarnation of the heroic theme is glorious; its strength of character enhanced by an emphatic treatment of the motivic counter-theme in brass. Unlike most conductors, Casadesus pays attention to the *pesante* marking at #56, adding dramatic weight to the tempo, and maintaining it even beyond #60, where Mahler calls for increasingly more motion to the end.

DAVIS, COLIN/Bavarian Radio Symphony - Novalis 150033-2 (1988) [67:29] Davis' approach to the first movement is restrained, evoking a mild summery haze in the introduction which then permeates much of the entire first movement. The main theme exudes warmth and charm, but the overall effect is somewhat subdued. Even as the music becomes more agitated through the closing section, it never really rises to the occasion, remaining as confined as the rest of the movement. Such mild-mannered temperament has a debilitating effect upon the ländler movement. While Davis deliberately adds weight to the opening dance rhythms, he smooths over what should be heavier accentuation in the bass strings that carry the ländler rhythm thereafter, smoothing out the theme's rough edges. Such a legato style has a more positive effect in the lovely trio section, even with uncharacteristic affectations in the lovely cello theme at #20. Sentimentality pervades over gaiety here. Even without an especially idiomatic treatment of the Yiddish klesmer music, the funeral march movement works quite well. The reading is basically straight-laced. Slight hesitations in oboe solos and at phrase-openings sound forced rather than idiomatic. Suddenly the music comes alive in the opening of the finale; however, weak, frayed brass temper the dramatic effect. Restrained dynamic levels in the more powerful moments of this movement also diffuse their overall impact. The tender sentiments of the second subject are beautifully rendered. Davis, like many others, slows up for the first four notes of the initial appearance of the heroic theme at #26. Later, at #34, he gallops along ignoring the tempo markings *pesante* and *im Tempo (aber etwas gemässtigter)* and causing the reappearance of the symphony's introductory material to seem unduly abrupt. Brass fudge the marcato articulation that should enhance the power of the final peroration (##54-55). The imposition of a ritard into #60 (when the tempo should quicken) is not without precedent, but an *alla breve* tempo in the final measures unhinges tempo continuity, hurtling the symphony forward to its end.

DE WAART, EDO/Minnesota Orchestra - Virgin Classics VC7 91096-2 (1990) [55:43]**
DeWaart's first recording of a Mahler symphony is one of the finest versions to come along in years. From the hushed atmosphere of the opening chords to the dramatic intensity of the close, this performance is so well-conceived and natural in expression that one would think DeWaart is an old-line Mahlerian. A perfect combination of superb playing, excellent sonics and a knowing interpretive manner, without the imposition of unnecessary mannerisms are some of the many merits of this engaging performance. A easy musical flow permeates the entire first movement. Tempo choices are well-considered in the ländler movement. Here DeWaart renders the bucolic dance music with sufficient heft, while stylizing the trio with a touch of lilting grace, giving only the slightest hint of fluctuation in tempo. He even makes a considerable pause between this movement and the next, as Mahler indicates. .One senses a veiled, almost dreamlike atmosphere in the opening of the third movement. The Yiddish dance music seems to have been conjured up from the faintest of memories. A free-floating atmosphere pervades the middle section's song theme, colored with soft pastel tones. The finale explodes with fire and energy, but never runs away with itself. DeWaart handles the gorgeous second subject perfectly, combining tender lyricism with lush string sonics. He proves once more that one need not resort to exaggerated mannerisms to bring out the romance in this music. Nor will extreme speed alone produce excitement: the finale's stormy first subject generates plenty of heat, without incinerating the music. The horns seem to hold back a desire to burst forth after #22, so that their appearance at the final apotheosis is even more dramatic. DeWaart also handles the final moments quite sensibly, taking note of the *pesante* marking at #56 and holding on to a weightier tempo until #59, where he ever so slightly begins to move forward to a fine close.

DE WAART, EDO/Netherlands Radio Philharmonic - RCA 74321 276022 (1995) [55:54]
*   After DeWaart's satisfying account of the First with the Minnesota orchestra (see above), his latest version now with the NRP is somewhat of a let-down. No interpretive adjustments occur, nor do any serious problems arise. The NRP plays extremely well for an orchestra without a world-class reputation. Its many merits are derived from a long, rich history of local performances. DeWaart's first movement is well-conceived, from the breezy main theme through the well-paced tempo increases to a spirited close. Only the opening is flawed by high volume which projects the woodwind chorale too strongly. Robust bass strings dig into the ländler of the second movement and contrast with a expressively lyrical trio. The funeral march's folk material is idiomatically treated, and the Mahler song quoted in the middle section,

soft and lovely. Only the finale seems too restrained. DeWaart approaches it as he did with the Minnesota orchestra, but the vitality he elicited from that fine ensemble seems moderated here.

DOHNANYI, CHRISTOPH VON/Cleveland Orchestra - London 425 718 (1990) [54:46]+ Those who favor a precision-oriented, highly polished and effortless performance, interpreted objectively and without much personal involvement, will be well satisfied by this performance. Restraint in both dynamic levels and romantic fervor are the order of the day for Dohnanyi. Except for a fine introduction and lilting main theme, the first movement seems too inflexible to convey the intended sense of *joie de vivre*. Too frequently the musical aesthetic is sterilized, the playing too stiff and the reading overly studied. For example, the opening of the development and the horn quartet from #15 sound deadly dull. Instead of a natural and gradual tempo increase, Dohnanyi suddenly shifts gears to a livelier tempo at #27 [14:50]. Some inner voices penetrate to good effect here (horns at c.15'). Much the same detached orientation affects the ländler movement. No attempt is made to be idiomatic, just a straight, brisk reading, which moves along without any nuance and lays bear every dynamic marking. Dohnanyi's distance from the musical aesthetic makes the lovely trio section seem routine, breezed through without interest. Only the soft lyricism of the middle section in the third movement provides an oasis of songful lyricism in the desert of inexpressivity that pervades the funeral march and its Yiddish music references.

The lackluster finale is most unsatisfying. From the surprisingly weak opening outburst, the stormy first subject is reduced to a mere drizzle! String figuration, intended to add greater intensity to the driving spirit of the music, is played like a formal exercise. Yet the lovely second theme is conveyed expressively, giving us a rare opportunity in this performance to basque in the glory of the Cleveland strings. After the tempestuous opening section returns, without any added intensity, Dohnanyi speeds up the tempo without direction (at #28/8:38) in an attempt to energize the musical impulse. He accomplishes this momentarily into the explosion that crashes through at #34 [9:56], but then retrenches into a lifeless and stiff reading of what follows. Dohnanyi seems more comfortable with the warm lyricism of the second theme, which has the enchanting aura of a nostalgic reverie. But the triumphal closing section is robbed of power and majesty by rigid and bloodless playing, underutilizing the many resources of this great orchestra.

EDELMANN, HANS/Stuttgart Conservatory Orchestra - Xenophone 88513 (1989) [55:08] + In spite of the inadequacies in both orchestral playing and sound quality, the merits of this budget recording are considerable. One senses an involvement here that is too often lacking in more polished performances. From the atmospheric opening, broadly paced and highlighting Mahler's naturalistic effects, Edelmann elicits a most engaging reading, full of life and yet refreshingly relaxed. A quick step ländler, rough-hewn enough in the strongly emphatic bass rhythm to be idiomatic, is in perfect contrast with a lovely trio section, engendering much *gemütlichkeit* by ever so slight hesitations in the melodic line. Edelmann renders an unaffected but characterful third movement. The opening bass solo is presented inappropriately as a tender lullaby rather than a craggy folk tune, and a quacky, poorly tuned oboe solo and some inappropriately loud passages are also disturbing (what dynamic level is employed on the first three notes of the violins at #7 is anybody's guess). The opening of the finale is intensely alive, despite a lack of neatness in the string figuration, and its second theme has a lovely, rubato quality. Most impressive are the distant "horn calls" in clarinets during the calm before the return of the opening storm (#21), marvelous horns swells at #30, and terrifying woodwind outcries after #32. Much of what follows until the final climax is well-conceived and aptly rendered. But the heroic theme of the great apotheosis seems slightly pressed and the closing section from #57 races along intently in the final measures, in which blurred horn triplets completely engulf the accompanying string figuration. Despite many technical problems, these little known performers generate much excitement.

FARBERMAN, HAROLD/London Symphony - 3MMG-106X (1982); 2-Vox Box CDX2 5123 (1995) [58:34]+ Some truly great moments, especially in the ländler movement, and a conscious effort at attention to details are not enough to warrant a higher rating for this otherwise colorless and lifeless performance. Although the CD format is an improvement, the sound is still veiled, stifling the music's richness and vitality. Balances need adjustment at times.

FEDOSEYEV, VLADIMIR/USSR Radio & TV Large Symphony - Melodyia A10 00719 002 (1990) [48:56] Little can be said in favor of this seriously flawed performance. Neither the orchestra nor the conductor seem comfortable with the piece or in tune with its idiom. Even though the introductory section works adequately (despite a hurried main tempo which diminishes the intended contrast with rapid trumpet calls), and the main material has an easy, relaxed quality, Fedoseyev makes the now unacceptable *faux pas* of not taking the repeat of the exposition and begins the development in much too hurriedly. What should be a bright and charming horn quartet at #15 becomes stilted by frequent hesitencies. While the conductor recovers from such awkward phrasing in what follows, trumpets are too weak at #23 to be effective, and the gradual build up to the orchestral outburst (marked in the score by an *) is stiff and unnaturally constricted. By the closing section, Fedoseyev generates enough energy to make the conclusion of the movement exciting.

The middle movements suffer from a complete lack of involvement. By smoothing over the marcato markings on the bass string rhythm in the opening of the ländler, Fedoseyev makes this rustic country dance sound ineffectual. The trio section has warmth and charm, especially apparent in a delightfully fresh counter-melody at #21 (frequently taken too fast by others). But Fedoseyev ruins the return of the ländler by anticipating its tempo in the preceeding solo horn calls. Woodwinds often seems faint and colorless. The extremely hurried pace of the funeral march movement is most disturbing. One is reminded here of Boult's rapid tempo, that hurtles the music forward mercilously, sounding more like a military than a funeral march. The middle section is handled adequately, seeming gay rather than parodistic. Trumpets blare mercilously from #14 (marked *p*). Forced to retain the initial brisk tempo, Fedoseyev cannot execute the *plötzlich viel schneller* (suddenly much faster) direction after #16, so the *volte-face* effect of this sudden change in tempo is lost. What remains of this massacred movement is rushed, bloated and completely out of character. Uneven brass playing and rigid string figuration hamper the effect of the finale's opening storm scene. After a satisfactory second subject, Fedoseyev reads the tempo marking at #21 *langsam* as if it meant *moderato*, again smoothing over the contrast in tempo with that of the return of the opening turbulence, deflating the shock of what should be its sudden, unexpected return. When the heroic main theme appears in all its glory, Fedoseyev ignores the ritard written for the first 3 notes and just dives right into it. Clarinet miscues also mar this section. Ritards and breath pauses are ignored. The general impression is one of a careless reading, where details are ridden over in a mindless attempt to whip up energy. Yet during the climactic section where the march is at its most resplendent, strong timpani reinforce the heroic character of the music. As in some other versions, a timpani stroke is added to the final snap.

FISCHER, IVAN/Hungarian State Orchestra - 2-Hungaroton SLPX 12267/8 (1982); HCD 12730 (1986) [58:30]; *Blumine* **movement included [6:40]*** This recording claims to be of the "original version" but is actually the 1906 edition with the Blumine movement added. In his first effort at recording a Mahler symphony, Ivan Fischer provides a detailed reading, idiomatic for the most part and containing some interesting nuances. Inner voices are more audible than usual. Playing is expressive and well-balanced. Although the first movement is somewhat restrained, even laborious at times, Fischer's overall conception is valid and he achieves some excitement during the closing section. A brisk ländler movement is enhanced by a mellifluous rubato treatment of the trio. A more songful approach with less speed would have been more effective in the Blumine movement. Sensitive and characterful, Fischer's reading of the funeral march movement is marked by a spirited rendition of the folk music segments. The finale is energetic and evenly paced, brought to a thrilling climax at the final apotheosis.

HAITINK, BERNARD/Concertgebouw Orchestra - Philips 6500 342; 7300397 (1968); 420 080 (1988); 434728 (1993); 10-Philips 434 053 (1992); 442 050 (1994) [56:13]
Haitink's second recording of the First is a measurable improvement over his earlier effort (see vol.1, p.6). Excellent sound quality and superb orchestral playing are in themselves justification for this new issue. Haitink still offers a controlled and restrained performance. The opening movement is relaxed yet sprightly enough to elicit a gay, carefree spirit, particularly evident in the delightful introduction. But the ländler movement could have been set at a livelier tempo, while an easier, less brisk tempo for the trio would have been more satisfying. A superb third movement highlights an idiomatic treatment of folk elements and a heavenly song theme in the middle section. Listen to how trippingly the oboe plays its dance-like phrase near the opening of the movement, tempering its brusque arrogance in keeping with the sobriety of the occasion. But the finale is too restrained to be thoroughly convincing.

HAITINK, BERNARD/Berlin Philharmonic - Philips 420 936-2 (1988) [56:38]*+
Haitink's third recording is undeniably his best. His interpretive manner, always moderated by a temperate sensibility, has become more attuned to Mahler's idiom over the years. The sonority of the BPO strings radiates brilliantly, with the added advantage of crystal clear sonics. Inner voices, usually fudged in less well produced recordings, come through clearly and in perfect balance with principal material. Particularly engaging is the opening movement. Here both warm sonorities and bright sonic dimension (especially in the brass) help create a summery hue. The *ppp* trumpet calls of the introduction sound like faint echoes from a distant mirage appearing hazily on the horizon. Haitink lets the music develop naturally and comfortably, without affectation or flexive distractions. He eases gently into the main theme, and then allows the pace to quicken smoothly and evenly. During this movement Mahler directs that the tempo increase unnoticeably or gradually, often accomplishing what seems like more speed by invigorating the rhythmic underpinning. Haitink renders this perfectly. The Ländler has a robust, yet sprightly quality. Uncharacteristically, Haitink gives full vent to some tantilizingly wicked brass phrases (after #2) and highlights the double-stopped string *col legnos* after #10, often difficult to hear in other recordings. The trio is played expressively, again without extreme inflection or self-indulgent mannerisms. The warm lyricism of BRO's strings gives much pleasure here. Opening with an appropriately craggy bass string solo, the third movement seems a bit stilted because of clipped dotted rhythms and an unstylish rendering of the Yiddish dance. But the *cantabile* middle-section, based upon the last song in Mahler's *Lieder eines Fahrenden Gesellen*, is soft and lovely.

Yet the finale is disappointing. Here Haitink plays up the technical abilities of his ensemble while downplaying the intensity of the music. One senses more purposeful control here than elsewhere in this performance. In contrast to such an approach, Haitink goes overboard in his treatment of the lyrical second subject. Here the main theme has a languid quality highlighted by frequent hesitencies until after #17, where Haitink takes the marking *a tempo* to require a stricter beat. Again restraint is imposed upon the stormy principal subject when it returns, affecting the progress of its gradual build up to the final heroic apotheosis. At

#26, the trumpet solo holds back into the first statement of the heroic theme (an affectation I have denigrated elsewhere). Percussion also sound constricted at the climax appearing at #34. But the trudging bass string rhythm that follows (at m.367 et seq.) produces the marvelous effect of an impending explosion. When the second theme reappears thereafter, all seems like a distant dream, a vision of nostalgic yearning. As the triumphal climax approaches, some kinks need loosening (e.g., at #46 a clipped third beat in 2d violins). Haitink tries to draw out the dramatic impact of the closing section without over-emphasis. While he generally succeeds, one gets the impression that he is less inspired here than during his captivating reading of the preceding movements.

HAYASHI, CHIHIRO/Polish Radio National Symphony (Katowice) - Fontec FOCD 3155 (1989) [55:13]+ This straightforward performance suffers from several flaws but manages to make a positive impression in the last two movements. Intonation problems in woodwinds, straggly or rigid playing and sometimes confined brass volume plague the opening movement (played without the repeat of the exposition). Within the context of a traditional reading, Chihiro Hayashi sometimes ignores details (e.g., brief accelerandi in brass fanfares) but usually follows the score dutifully. Figuration often seems too formalistic, detracting from the music's spirit in both the opening movement and succeeding ländler. Hayashi doesn't attempt to add too much *schmaltz* to the Yiddish music in the third movement, so that it comes off well without sounding affected. He tempers the finale's opening storm and lingers over the lyrical subsidiary theme, but his reading of the remainder of this movement is well-conceived. In the closing moments, he maintains a pesante tempo for the heroic theme (beginning before the *Triumphal* section marked *pesante*) until Mahler calls for more motion at #60, although he adds a slight ritard into it. Stronger brass and less stiff playing would have improved this performance measurably.

HORENSTEIN, JASCHA/Vienna Symphony - Vox PL 8050 (1956); 3-Vox VBX 116 (1960); Turnabout 34355E (ES) (1970); 2-Vox Box CDX2 5508 (1993) [56:55]**
Amongst knowledgeable Mahlerites this performance is still considered the definitive reading, notwithstanding a mediocre orchestral performance and dated sound quality. All tempi are perfectly paced. Every nuance is rendered with a thorough understanding of Mahler's style. Listen to the closing section of the finale at #56 marked *pesante*, a direction which is all too often ignored or observed only for a few measures. Horenstein holds the weightier tempo straight through to #60 as Mahler directs, and the effect is magnificent for its dramatic bearing. No untoward mannerisms mar this perfectly idiomatic reading. The performance is replete with unique insights into the way this youthful work can be best interpreted.

HORENSTEIN, JASCHA/Vienna Symphony - Preludio PHC 3143 (1988); Tuxedo Music TUCD 1048 (1990) [57:15]*+ Recorded at a concert in Vienna in 1958, this Horenstein recording has little more to offer than his 1953 version. Horenstein again offers an interpretation that ranks among the best ever recorded. His natural mode of expression and knowing way of handling Mahler's unexpected diversions in a seemless manner comes from his long association with this score. Horenstein's finale still serves as a benchmark for all competing versions, especially for his brilliant treatment of the final moments in accordance with Mahler's directions. Notwithstanding technical problems, his 1953 performance still has the edge over this one.

INBAL, ELIAHU/Frankfurt Radio Symphony - Denon C37-7537 (1987); 16-Denon CO 72589/604 (1989) [54:46] Concentration on technical precision and placement of musical details overshadow an interest in characterization or stylistic nuance in this neat and clean, if not especially evocative, performance. Inbal makes little effort to go beyond the surface interpretively. Until the supercharged finale, not much happens of interest. Notwithstanding such a conservative approach, the first three movements come off well, despite brushes with routine note-spinning. A delightfully expressive main theme and lingering celli on the 3-note motto that opens the development section are singularly notable aspects of the first movement. However, too much of this movement sounds homogenized, with the restrained tempi leaving an uncomfortably cool feeling until the closing section, when Inbal races to the finish line. After a matter-of-fact rendering of the ländler theme in the second movement, Inbal's mannered rendering of the trio seems out of place. When the ländler returns it now sounds extremely rough. Within the context of a routine funeral march, Inbal leans heavily on accents to stylize the folk material, but this only makes it seem overly caricaturish. Sonic range is amplified for the finale, which literally hits us in the face with its opening outburst. While the main tempo for the opening storm seems restrained, Inbal elicits forceful playing enhanced by full-blown dynamics. Wiry strings, sterile brass and only middling dramatic power do little to bring out the majestic aspect of the heroic conclusion.

JÄRVI, NEEME/Royal Scottish National Orchestra (includes *Blumine* movement) - Chandos CHAN 9308 (1995) [59:54]*+ The line between creative interpretation and solipsistic score tampering may be a thin one, but the benchmark for distinguishing between these two should be whether a particular nuance or deviation from the printed score serves the composer's intentions. Neeme Järvi's approach is certainly innovative. He makes numerous retouchings to tempo markings that sometimes enhance musical expression while at other times radically depart from the text with little justification. For the most part, Järvi's strong tempo contrasts work well in the opening movement, juxtaposing youthful exuberance with leisurely pacing. Slight hesitations elicit a comfortable, easy musical flow. For example, at #8 (4:40), Järvi ever so elegantly eases into the highpoint of the cello theme for a lovely effect (repeated later with even more emphasis). After a slightly attenuated treatment of the thematic fragment played by the celli at 9:20 of the development, Järvi holds back slightly for the D major horn quarter, giving it a gently wafting quality. Later, he adds dramatic weight to the dynamic horn theme at 14:17, making it ring out with stentorian tones, foreshadowing the triumphant conclusion of the symphony. From there to the movement's close one is caught up in Järvi's enthusiasm, infused with a light, airy quality that makes it thoroughly captivating. Rarely has anyone being so successful in treating each phrase with such delicacy, without appearing too self-indulgent. The *Blumine* movement (which would normally follow the first movement if placed where it belongs in the original version) is inserted as the last cut, presumably to allow for it to be treated as part of or separate from the symphony by reprogramming. Järvi's reading is expressive, producing a heavenly repose with lovely string sonorities. In the middle section, he presses forward intently but not excessively. The ländler movement has just the right heft, Järvi keeping its tempo steady and secure. In contrast, the romantic trio is very relaxed and furtively free-wheeling (N.B., this section is marked *zeit lassen*, the German phrase for rubato). Järvi eases into, speeds up for and slows down at the end of phrases here in a very flexible manner. Notice how he holds on tightly to the third eighth-note from the end of the cello figuration which closes the trio (7'), virtually adding a fermata above it. Then comes the funeral march. Here Järvi opts for a very quick tempo, hardly suitable for this purpose, unless by way of caricature. One is reminded of Adrian Boult's extremely fast tempo here (see above). Yiddish themes are rendered in a stylish manner, starting slowly and pressing forward into a lively tempo. Järvi treats the song theme of the middle section expressively, with slight hesitations which do not impede the musical flow.

A powerful opening outburst hurtles us into the furious storm of the finale. Unlike many conductors Järvi has enough confidence in his strings to let them make a mad dash through their rapid-fire figuration, producing unusually wild turbulence. He slows up on the fragment of the trumpet's heroic theme that suddenly cuts into this storm, thereby wrenching it out of context and causing the fury unleashed in the opening measures to abate momentarily. Otherwise, his pacing is well-conceived. Also impressive is his treatment of the lyrical second subject, phrased with just the right hesitation to be both provocative and captivating. When it returns later, one is caught up in a reverie that melts the heart. Generally, ritards into sections are lengthy, but the luftpause demonstratively written at #4 (9:25) in midst of the heroic main theme is completely ignored. Järvi makes every effort to heighten the dramatic impact of strong orchestral sections (e.g., by holding back mightily on the trumpet volleys that enliven the return of the main material leading to the final apotheosis). Tempo contrasts are markedly emphasized. Heavy underlining of the heroic theme further enhances its grandiose character. One is reminded of Horenstein's brilliant reading (see above) at the segment marked *Triumphal,* where Järvi takes the *pesante* (weighty) direction seriously and maintains this more robust tempo for the principal theme thereafter, as he should. But instead of holding on to it until #60, as Mahler directs, he suddenly speeds up over a dozen measures earlier, thus changing the entire effect of the closing. Such tampering with the score markings disengages the closing coda from its moorings. Momentary detractions aside, Järvi provides a very interesting, effective and-- depending on personal tastes--captivating reading. His Scottish forces perform beautifully and Chandos gives the performance a full sonic dimension.

JOÓ, ÁRPÁD/Amsterdam Philharmonic - Sefel SECD-5022(1984); Aurophon US 71822 CD (1992); ARTS CD 447239-2 (1995) [54:00]*+ Accolades should be given to all concerned for this superb recording. Remarkably clear and vibrant sonics are a definite advantage. The Amsterdam Philharmonic, a relatively new ensemble (organized in 1953), plays with immaculate precision and fine tonal quality. The players treat this music in such a thoroughly idiomatic manner that one might assume they had played it all their lives. Listen to the crisp brass tattoos in the outer movements, the perfectly intoned bass fiddle solo in the funeral march and the accuracy of the rapid string passages that open the finale, just to mention a few examples. Conductor Joó's brilliant interpretation speaks for itself. He also deserves high praise for the refined playing he elicits and his diligent attention to detail. As for the performance itself, almost every nuance works without a hitch. All the youthful exuberance of the opening movement comes through in a completely idiomatic manner without excessive speed or untoward mannerism. Tempi and tempo gradations (in the introduction and the end of the exposition) are perfectly wrought. Joó's approach to the tempo of the main theme here is more sprightly than easy-going but evokes a feeling of sparkling gaiety. Every detail is given its due (e.g., one rarely hears the ritard taken into #14). Again his characterful style captures the ländler movement in just the right ebullient spirit. Notice the impishly arrogant repeated eighth-note fragments played by muted horns. All inner voices are perfectly balanced without exception. Even the harp is audible on its rendering of the *Frère Jacques* tune during the opening section of the third movement. The funeral march tread is ideal but the middle section's song theme is paced too quickly to be completely satisfying. Joó is more restrained in the finale, possibly to maintain greater control over his players. Yet what the stormy opening lacks in furiosity, the heroic main theme makes up for in its dynamism. Joó observes the *pp* marking for the opening of the rapturous second theme, which is still given a passionate reading without indulging in mawkish mannerism. As the movement proceeds to its close, Joó builds up intensity masterfully but fails to put much weight on the *Triumphal* climax (marked *pesante*). Otherwise, the approach to the closing moments is strong and expansive. A marvelous first effort for all concerned.

JORDAN, ARMIN/l'Orchestre de la Suisse Romande - Erato 4509-919713 (1993) [52:17]
*+   Unlike his versions of the Third and Fourth, Jordan's reading of the First is exceptional. He shapes the opening section perfectly, pacing it leisurely and evoking a warm glow which distant military tattoos do not disturb. His easy manner with the main theme and natural shaping of phrases produces a lyrical flow that evokes the sounds of nature without sounding artificial. Just as natural is his pacing, which moves gradually from a comfortable allegro for the main theme to a lively close, without excessive agitation. In the second movement, a sprightly ländler closes with a strangely mournful horn call introducing a lively, song-like trio. Jordan reads the funeral march movement as written and in perfectly Mahlerian style, avoiding *kitsch* for the Yiddish dance music. Unlike many conductors he keeps down the volume level of the gypsy dance rhythms in the section marked *mit parodie*. Without a moment's hesitations, we are thrown into the storm music of the finale. Jordan captures its fury with urgency and intensity; one can almost feel the billowing waves rising and bursting upon the shore. Notice how he hesitates slightly on the augmented appoggiaturas at the close of the storm (3:15), as if providing a hint of lurking fatality. The second theme (3:30) is beautifully shaped, being paced flexible without maudlin exaggerations. Jordan creates an atmosphere of mystery in the sotto voce passage before the storm's return (c.7'). The approach is unaffected, sticking closely to the score for the most part. He omits the luftpause at #34 into the first full statement of the heroic theme and, unfortunately, ignores the *pesante* marking at *Triumphal* toward the close, missing an opportunity to create as near perfect a performance as we have heard in years. The Suisse Romande orchestra plays well and with enthusiasm (except for tempered brass and percussion in the finale).

JUDD, JAMES/Florida Philharmonic - Harmonia Mundi HMU 907118 (1994) [64:15]*+
     What a pleasant surprise! This young conductor and little-known regional ensemble provide a thoroughly marvelous performance. James Judd paces, shapes and phrases the entire work as if every note first germinated in his mind. That is not to say that he in any way takes liberties with the score. On the contrary, Judd seems to know just how to express this music without sounding forced or mannered. A warm pre-dawn glow suffuses the introduction with a hazy sheen, leading into a soft and easy main theme. Masterfully, Judd increases the main tempo of the exposition gradually, so that its spirited close sounds perfectly natural. Even the repeated exposition shows his creative mind: notice how his delicate nuances on the main theme make it sound even warmer and more lyrical than earlier. His stylish manner shows an intuitive identification with Mahler's idiom (e.g., a slight stretching of the three-note thematic fragment in the cello during the opening of the development). How delightfully comfortable he and his players seem throughout this movement. Judd does not ignore the placement of the tempo marking (dotted-half = 66) 5 measures into the second movement and brings the tempo up to speed there rather than beginning the movement in the main tempo. This tempo is on the weighty side and is not enhanced by over-emphasis on the supporting rhythm in bass strings. But as with the entire performance, all is clear and extremely well played. One drawback is the rather low volume level. The trio theme (3:32) is soft and lovely, with slight hesitations that make it ever so charming. In the third movement, an evenly-paced march tempo leads to a thoroughly idiomatic treatment of the Yiddish dance music played without excessive mannerisms. The counter-theme for trumpet duet in thirds at #16 sounds as if it were right out of a Jewish wedding. Also impressive is the lovely oboe solo on the Yiddish tune appearing thereafter. Only the finale seems to retreat from the promise of what preceded, because the FPO simply does not produce sufficiently full sonority needed to make a strong impact in the stormy opening. Yet Judd handles the lyrical second theme beautifully. How naturally and comfortably he wends through this romance with stytlistic flair. He even treats the rubato closing section skillfully; not merely rushing through it as many do, but, as Horenstein and

Bernstein have done, flexing the tempo in coordination with the musical line. Even without the forces he needs to achieve the ultimate in dramatic power, Judd manages to produce a thrilling conclusion. Blumine is included here, not within the symphony but as an extra cut that can be integrated into or played separately from the symphony.

KASPRZYK, JACEK/London Symphony - Collins Classics EC 1029-2 (1989) [54:42]; same as Collins Quest COL 3005 (1992) including *Blumine* movement [7:42]   The jacket notes refer to the 1992 issue, which includes the *Blumine* movement, as a recording of the "Berlin Version" -- whatever that may mean. In any event, the performance is just fair to middling. Its merits appear in the first movement that opens in the serene calm of a summer morning and gradually becomes more exuberant and joyful as it proceeds. *Blumine*, placed as the last cut, is bathed in warm colors with a gently flowing lyricism. Technical problems occur occasionally (e.g., where is the trumpet at 2 before #10 in the ländler movement?), and one senses a certain degree of self-consciousness and insecurity (e.g., in the opening of the development of the first movement). Although Kasprzyk is usually careful with details, several diversions from the score are troublesome, particularly in the complex finale. In that movement he slows up suddenly at m.603 and later at #58 after which he shifts into fast gear at #61, all without benefit of any markings in the score. Frequently, the brass playing is spotty and horns sound tired rather early in the finale (by #6). Lacking stylishness and character, the middle movements seem rather pallid and routine. Yet Kasprzyk generates much warmth and tenderness in the lyrical moments of the finale. But the final section has too many extreme tempo shifts to make its point consistently.

KEGEL, HERBERT/Dresden Philharmonic - Eterna 8 27 438 (1981); Berlin Classics 0090382BC (1995) [55:43]+   Herbert Kegel offers an interesting, even provocative reading that addresses itself to the symphony's many musical representations from that of youthful exuberance in the first movement to rustic merriment in the second. He has a tendency to ease up at the high point of thematic material, but this mannerism is not without its advocates. After a fairly straightforward introduction that is paced without unduly dragging its feet, the main theme has a certain bounce (made apparent by sharp string articulation). As the exposition progresses from an amiable demeanor to a more agitated one, Kegel presses forward intently, only easing up to hold on to a melodious phrase in full bloom. Unlike most conductors, Kegel brilliantly negotiates the difficult build-up beginning at 13:15 to an orchestral outburst, marked in the score with an asterisk, holding back as Mahler directed into the huge crash to give it more dramatic impact. However, mannerisms become the mainstay of Kegel's reading of the second movement. A longish hesitation after the 16th-note of the upbeat to the ländler theme is added, and becomes tiresome after many repeats. Kegel emphasizes the rustic quality of this countrified waltz with hefty strokes the first time around and then makes it sound snappy and fresh on its return. The trio section is extremely affected, with tempo so loose that no two measures occur in succession at the same pace. Such over-indulgent romanticizing is a matter of taste, but might very well be far beyond Mahler's own sensibilities. Kegel applies the same mannered treatment to finale's lyrical second subject. In the funeral march movement, he slows up measurably into the Yiddish dance music, maintaining a slowish tempo for its oboe tune in strong contrast to a brisk, perky pace for the gypsy band music that follows. The finale's storm has a fiery temperament, full of vigor and urgency. On its return after an extremely indulgent, even maudlin second theme, the furious storm is held up momentarily for the first half of the heroic trumpet theme on its initial appearance (marked *p*) at 8:36. Half way through it, Kegel shifts gears and lets the storm loose as before. When that heroic theme reappears at 16:25 (marked *Tempo I*), Kegel urges it onward aggressively. From there to the close, the performance is stirring, despite Kegel's overlooking the *pesante* marking at the *Triumphal* section and shifting the place where Mahler wanted the tempo to press forward thereafter from #60 to #59 (as do Sinopoli and a few others).

KOBAYASHI, KEN-ICHIRO/Hungarian State Symphony - Canyon Classics PCCL-00168 (1992) [58:34]+   Kobayashi projects the warm, summery atmosphere of the opening movement and the heroic quality of the finale with more assurance than he does the folk tunes in the inner movements. He lets the main theme of the first movement swing gently in soft breezes and coaxes it gradually into the energetic tempo it takes on at the close of the movement. Only a sudden, effusive slow-up at 12:20 (m.275) is not unnoticeable as Mahler directed. The ländler tempo is too rigid for the weight imposed upon it. A slight luftpause at the highpoint of the ländler theme (2:44) is inappropriate (and unmarked). Kobayashi's lack of familiarity with the Yiddish idiom of the third movement is obvious in his heavy-handed approach to the beginning of the swaying wedding dance music. During the reprise another awkward slow-up for the rocking violin phrase before the sudden mid-measure tempo shift requires a one-measure tempo increase into the unexpected return of the gypsy dance. Both inner movements seem overly studied. A strong outburst ushers in the finale. The storm music seems slightly controlled, with a measure of marcato on the thematic material which anticipates Kobayashi's demonstative manner with the heroic theme during the concluding section. After a lovely, expressive lyrical theme, handled without exaggerations, Kobayashi again touches up the score: he indulges in the unfortunately fashionable affect of slowing up for the first appearance of the heroic trumpet theme played *p* (at 9'); ignores the heavily-marked luftpause into the heroic theme at #34 (10:47); adds unmarked full-stops at m. 483 (15:55), where a reverie on the second theme begins to fade, and at #47 (18:10). A strong, weighty closing section anticipates the *pesante* marking at *Triumphal* (thus ignoring it when it does occur). In yet another concession to a popular quirk, Kobayashi shifts Mahler's direction to move forward in the final measures from #60 to #59, 16 measures before Mahler directs the tempo to change in this manner (21:22).

KOSLER, ZDENEK/Slovak Philharmonic - Enigma Classics CD 7 74649-2 (1988) [52:57]; Naxos 8.550120 (1992); Stradivari SCD 6011 [52:57]   Uneven playing and sonics, together with too many affectations and errors in detail, mar this otherwise adequate performance. The rather lightweight ensemble, particularly weak in brass, simply cannot deliver enough power to make the symphony's glorious conclusion hit home. Although Kosler establishes a relaxed atmosphere in the introduction and exposition of the first movement, it seems to affect the rest of the movement, stifling what should be increasing agitation as the movement proceeds to its end. Some intonation problems (in high violins) and awkward affectations (often at the high point of a melodic line) are also disturbing. The dance rhythms of the ländler movement lack sufficient heft and accentuation to capture the bucolic spirit of this music. Playing seems too stiff and constricted. While timpani overpower, brass are restrained. The performance lacks personality, nuance and *joie de vivre*. A crotchety old fiddler opens the third movement. Here tempo seems slightly pressed. The entire movement suffers from overly loud dynamic levels. The Yiddish dance music is played with little effort to sound idiomatic and the song theme of the middle section wants stylishness, even if played softly. Curiously, the movement closes with a bang rather than a whimper. Kosler can only energize his forces in moderation for the stormy opening of the finale. Uneven brass balances (underscoring the tuba), unpleasant sonic timbre (blaring trumpets) and generally mediocre playing temper the overall effect of this dramatic movement. Tempo shifts which Kosler imposes upon the score frequently interfere with the flow of the music (at #26, 28, 49, 50, etc.). A few segments work well: a *misterioso* atmosphere embellishes the interlude between the second subject; the sudden return of the first subject at #22 is well-handled; and the section that begins at #40 with the return of a rhythmic tread from the first movement is rendered expressively. After Kosler dives headlong into the piu mosso after #42, what follows is simply too unheroic in character, disjointed in tempo and overbearing in effect to be satisfying.

KUBELIK, RAFAEL/Bavarian Radio Symphony - DG SLPM 139331(1968); DG (Resonance) 429 157 (1990); 10-DG 429 042 (1990) [49:34]* Kubelik's reading is even more mannered than his earlier version with the VPO (see vol.1, p.10). But the orchestral performance is more impressive, even if details are frequently ignored or unduly modified. The finale and ländler movements are best. Curiously enough, the first movement's exposition repeat is observed this time, while the ländler repeat is omitted (a strange choice!). Typical of early DG, dynamic levels are extreme at both ends of the sonic spectrum.

LEINSDORF, ERICH/Boston Symphony - RCA LSC-2642 (1963); Victrola ALK1-4983; RCL-1014; RCA ALK1-4983 (1984) [49:33]*+ Leinsdorf's first version is still one of the best straightforward performances ever committed to disk. The middle movements are very effective; some especially enjoyable highlights being a lovely trio in the second and an unusually clean-sounding bass solo in the third (though the tempo here does tend to drag slightly). Leinsdorf's comfortable treatment of the main theme in the first movement and his moderately exciting rendition of the finale are further evidence of his sureness of approach.

LENARD, ONDREJ/Shinsei Japan Symphony (perf. 9 June 1990, Nuengewandhaus Leipzig) - Jod JOD-104 (1994) [52:02] These newcomers to the Mahler oeuvre produce a respectible, if not particularly interesting performance. The relatively young Japanese orchestra shows itself as a promising, still middle-level ensemble. Playing is generally stiff and confined in stronger sections but warm and charming in more lyrical passages (particularly in the trio of the second movement and the lyrical theme of the finale). Despite frequent horn cracks, momentary string pitch problems and underdone woodwinds (listen to the shy clarinet cuckoo at 7:04 of the first movement), the level of orchestral precision shows promise. But Mahler's music requires more dynamic thrust and power than this orchestra seems able to provide, especially in the finale. Also wanting is an idiomatic rendition of the folk material so essential to the third movement. Lenard gives the symphony a standard reading with only a few adjustments. For example, trumpet tattoos in the introduction to the first movement start slowly, in keeping with the hushed and serene atmosphere, and quickly become more rapid. Most conductors race through them as if the bugler had long been awake and fresh in the early hours of the summer morning. But a disturbingly awkward hesitation in the middle of the finale's second theme (5:36) and excessive stretching out of the passage preceding the first appearance of the heroic trumpet theme in the same movement (7:53) work against the grain. Contrary to the modern trend, Lenard does not take the exposition repeat in the first movement. Obeying the *pesante* marking at the climax marked *Triumphal*, he speeds up almost immediately thereafter, ignoring the absence of any direction to quicken the pace more than 40 measures (until #60).

LEVINE, JAMES/London Symphony - RCA ARL 1-0894 (1974); RCA RCD1-80894 (1987) [54:49]* Levine's first recording of a Mahler symphony suffers from too much of a good thing. The appearance of numerous stylistic nuances indicate a deep commitment to Mahler's idiom; but the exaggerated manner in which these affectations are rendered seems too forced to capture the spirit of this work. Uneven treatment of detail is also troublesome. A laborious introduction leads to an overblown exposition in which the playing and style are uncomfortably rigid. The ländler movement is generally pressed but ends with enthusiasm while the funeral march is slightly on the torpid side. Inconsistent tempi mar an otherwise exuberant finale. This performance has the advantage of precision playing, but an overtly conscious effort to be idiomatic results in a stylized, sometimes inflexible reading.

LITTON, ANDREW/Royal Philharmonic - Virgin Classics VC 790703-2 (1988) [53:03]*
Although his orchestra is British, Andrew Litton is a product of American shores, born and trained here. Only in his mid-twenties, his youth is a plus here, for this performance abounds in energy, vitality and romantic panache. While tempi are generally brisk--sometimes (as at the close of the first movement) nearly running amok--they rarely leave traces of inappropriate exaggeration or untidiness in their wake. Some still may find the tempi set for the main theme of the first movement and the funeral march of the third slightly hurried, but the exuberance Litton's energetic approach adds to the former and the sureness of measured step he applies to the latter are certainly enhancements. In comparison, one recalls the agitated impulse of Abbado's first version (now deleted), particularly in the outer movements. The first movement overflows with exuberance, gushing over from section to section with little self-control. One might have wished for a smoother transition into the first appearance of the main theme in the opening movement. Also disconcerting is the heavy underlining of the first four notes of the heroic trumpet theme when it first appears in the finale, an increasingly popular affectation. But the romantic spirit of the first movement and the dynamic power of the finale are certainly captured here. As for the middle movements, the second's most attractive quality is the strong *ff* accentuation given bass strings on the stomping rhythm of the ländler. Otherwise, the trio is extremely mannered, with frequent hesitations and heavy emphasis on the third beat. Litton's routine reading of the third movement lacks an idiomatic treatment of the folk elements as well as expression in the middle section's song theme. Too many passages seem to replicate stylistic nuances in vogue amongst those conductors who dispense with or revise Mahler's markings: for example, Litton slows up for the first appearance of the trumpet's heroic theme and ignores the *pesante* marking at the *Triumphal* climax (#56).

MAAZEL, LORIN/Vienna Philharmonic - CBS IM 42141 (1986); MDK 44907 (1992); 14-Sony SK14K48198 (1992) [57:44] Maazel's heavy-handed treatment of this symphony wastes the talents of a great Mahler orchestra. After setting a quick pace for the introduction, despite the *schleppend* (dragging) marking, Maazel broadens the tempo for the principal theme. With his usual reserve, he treats the theme without the slightest sense of youthful spirit, letting it drag on lifelessly. Even the VPO sounds uncomfortably stiff under his direction. Tempo shifts are abrupt and exaggerated, possibly applied to generate some semblance of energy, but the effect is often jolting and audacious (e.g., after * in the exposition). During the development Maazel maintains his tiresome pace, diminishing the music's spontaneity by heavily underlining musical fragments. Then another abrupt change of tempo occurs at #27, marked *etwas bewegter* (somewhat more agitated) and he speeds to the movement's close. Maazel's heavy-handed, extremely legato treatment of the ländler movement, devoid of all marcato accentuation, is similarly ineffectual. The lyrical trio is so deliberately affected that it borders on the outrageous. Notice how Maazel starts #22 very broadly, then moves the tempo forward from #23 only to get caught up in his own hesitations, which wrench the line from its moorings. Such exaggerated tempo adjustments sound merely contrived. The same problems spoil the funeral march. When the reading doesn't sound routine, it is because Maazel interjects an unnatural affectation at #7. Yet when Mahler asks for a sudden shift in tempo (such as after #16), Maazel ignores it! The opening outburst of the finale sounds like dishes being smashed! What follows has no more pleasing effect. Restraint in both spirit and dynamic levels is the order of the day. Mahler's furious storm is reduced to a tempest in a teapot. And where is the gorgeous tone one has come to expect from the VPO strings in the beautiful second subject? Only the celli offer a modicum of expression (at #19). At the first appearance of the heroic trumpet theme, Maazel not only hangs on to the first few notes, but slows up for the entire theme. At such a sluggish tempo, try as he might to press forward, Maazel simply cannot generate enough vitality and power to make a strong dramatic impact. Overbearing cymbals clutter up the closing measures.

MACKERRAS, CHARLES/Royal Liverpool Philharmonic - EMI 0777 7 64508-2 (1992) [54:20]* Mackerras, a relative newcomer to Mahler, offers much to savor in this performance. He lets the music breathe naturally, while eschewing extremes in tempo changes and lyrical expressivity. His pacing, as well as his overall approach, is assured and unaffected. While moderation is the order of the day, there is still enough energy and spirit to evoke enthusiasm. From the hushed glow of a summer sunrise in the introduction to the youthful exuberance of the close, the first movement is thoroughly captivating. No nonsense here, just a natural, uncomplicated reading of this nature music as it was intended to be presented. Notice how Mackerras impels the music forward from 13:00 to what is clearly the climax of the first movement at 14:18, where he holds back ever so slightly before the entire orchestra literally erupts with a volley of brass tattoos. Even the sound comes alive for his jubilent closing.

With strong emphasis on the third beat, the ländler opens with just the right rustic spirit. The trio section is marvelously phrased without excessive effusiveness. In an effort to avoid kitsch, the lovely cello theme (at #20) seems a bit too lively, requiring Mackerras to ease up at its cadence. But the overall effect is simply enchanting. More consciously emphatic is his reading of the third movement. Here his efforts to render the Yiddish folk material in an idiomatic manner sound artificial, and the gypsy dance music too boisterous in contrast with its surroundings. Then something goes awry during the rhythmic introduction to the song theme of the middle section. While Mackerras tries to elicit a nostaglic feeling here, the strings sound too dry to please and woodwinds have a fuzzy timbre. After a hushed fade-out at the close of the third movement, the finale starts off with a bang. What follows, unfortunately, fails to live up to the promise of its strong beginning. Although the energy level is adequate, volume rarely goes beyond *forte*. The lyrical second theme is fairly expressive, closing with a marvelous whoop up in the violins to high F (m.218) before the final cadence. Upon the return of the opening tempestuous music, the strings lose intensity. Mackerras opts to follow those who slow up upon the first entrance of the heroic theme at #26 [8:10], but only for the first four notes of it. Then he presses forward at #28. Mackerras' interpretation is excellent thereafter. Listen to the bittersweet longing evoked by brief reminiscences of the second theme at 13:45 et seq. (Yet why does he stop short after the 4-bar string phrase at m.483-6?) He is most most impressive in the final apotheosis, with an exciting build-up to the climax marked *höchste Kraft* (highest power). Unlike some of his colleagues, Mackerras takes seriously the *pesante* marking at the *Triumphal* section (18:50). Following the score, he holds on to this weightier tempo until #60 (over 40 measures later) until Mahler directs that the tempo moves forward to the end. Mackerras' may be the best treatment of the concluding section since Horenstein's definitive reading.

MARKEVITCH, IGOR/RAI Torino Orchestra - Stradivarius STR 10010 (1989); 2-Memories HR 4193/94 (1991) [44:22] This performance, given on March 10, 1967, predates Markevitch's performance with the French National Orchestra by only a few months. His reading is rapidly paced and electrifying in intensity but sloppy in precision (made more apparent by close miking). Frequent affectations (particularly at the height of melodic phrases) and mercilous cuts are also serious drawbacks. One senses a complete lack of self-restraint in Markevitch's approach. Frequently, Mahler's directions are completely ignored, e.g., during the closing section of the finale. Markevitch weaves in and out of tempo at will. While much of his subjective manner may go against the grain of a purist, he generates much energy and excitement in the outer movements. He rips through the ländler movement without any attempt to render the folk material stylishly, treating the dance music as if it were a citified waltz; even the trio is infected by Markevitch's unrelentingly brisk tempo. Similarly unimpressive is the third movement, with its sloppy entrances, the first oboe missing his cue into the Yiddish theme and the flute failing to appear at all before #9. Even an exaggerated ritard before the close of the song doesn't produce a positive effect. Although the finale's opening storm is spirited, awkward tempo shifts get in the way of its forward motion. After a nicely-handled second theme, the storm scene returns with all its unrestrained ferocity. Although Markevitch holds up for the first appearance of the heroic theme in the trumpet, he takes off from willfully (ignoring the later *pesante* marking in the process). Then he slices big chunks out of the movement (from m.400 to m.408 and from m.417 to m.424). Passing through a rather uninteresting return of the symphony's introduction (with disturbingly loud celli), the aggressive forward thrust of the storm returns and never lets up. The result is just a complete jumble: not one of Mahler's many markings from #45 are attended to; the percussion are absent before #47; the *pesante* marking at the *Triumphal* climax (#56) is ignored; a massive cut is made from m.667 to m.691; and the cymbals get confused after #60, adding a few extra crashes while missing a few. Markevitch creates as much confusion as he does excitement.

MARKEVITCH, IGOR/Orchestre National de France - Disques Montaigne WM 332 (1989); Originals CD SH 840 (1995) [44:56] This is another Markevitch aircheck, this time of a performance on June 21, 1967. It goes like the wind, making the musical excursion as brief as possible. To that end, he omits the important repeat of the exposition in the first movement and makes an unpardonable cut of twenty measures near the end of the finale. Otherwise, the entire performance is extremely hurried, generating much heat, but little warmth. Numerous *faux pas* distract (e.g., flaws in woodwind cuckoos and a wrong entrance into #26 in the first movement). Lack of clarity and proper balancing in the brass ensemble cause problems. Intent on stirring up as much intensity as possible, Markevitch sets a brisk pace for the main theme of the first movement. Consequently, the closing section is a mad dash for the finish line. Some of this propulsive energy spills over into the ländler movement. Even though Markevitch moves quickly in the trio section, the effect is offset by a few attempts to pull back. With a slight ritard on the solo horn passage that reintroduces the ländler, it returns with a vengeance. The French ensemble refuses to play softly during nearly all of the third movement. Instead, from the opening bass string solo, and throughout most of the movement, f or ff is the principal dynamic level. While there is an attempt at caricature here, there is little funereal character. After a rather long pause, the finale rushes in furiously. Markevitch tries to pull in the reins at #6 (not the best place to do so, since it is marked *energisch*). His flexible approach to tempi, particularly in the mannered treatment of the second subject, may seem excessive. Despite a rapid-fire return of the first subject, Markevitch holds up at the first appearance of the heroic main theme on solo trumpet, and then proceeds to pick and choose which tempo markings to apply and which to ignore. At #34 he drives forward intently even though the marking is pesante. After returning to a slightly faster main tempo, he holds back before #37 to try to get back in control. Though impassioned and fiery, the closing section loses many of the special effects Mahler built into it to heighten the dramatic effect. Instead of obeying the marking to hold back from #51, Markevitch gallops away into #52 (marked *höchste Kraft* -- with the greatest power). Completely ignoring Mahler's direction at #56 to give the tempo more weight (pesante), he drives blindly forward during what is left of the coda (after cuts from m.667 to m.687). Then in the last five measures, the tempo slackens slightly to make room for those whooping horns.

MASUR, KURT/New York Philharmonic - Teldec 9031-74868 (1992) [52:16]*+ Masur proves here that a conservative approach can be at least as satisfying as a more adventurous one. Throughout the performance it is evident that Masur has not only a sure command of his forces, but also a knowing way with Mahler's idiom. Rarely are untoward mannerisms imposed upon the musical line. Instead, an easy musical flow and stylish thematic treatment, reinforced by attention to detail, reign supreme. The first movement's main theme ambles comfortably along, as if caught in a daydream while on a morning stroll. And Masur moves the tempo forward gradually to the orchestral outburst (c.13:25) which ushers in the closing section, the upbeat to the main theme which follows, hanging momentarily in mid-air. Recorded at Avery Fischer Hall in New York (4/23-25/92), it is not surprising that brass and woodwinds are favored over strings and timpani. But sonic clarity is stunning. At first, Masur seems reserved in his treatment of the ländler, tempering accents in the bass strings that usually animate the spirit of this rustic dance. But as the movement progresses, through a charming trio section, Masur picks up the tempo slightly (c.5:30), enlivening the return of the dance music. A very faint opening tread in the funeral march movement builds naturally into the lilting Yiddish theme sung by the solo oboe. Masur handles the latter stylishly, easing into the oboe theme in a manner of a Hassidic wedding dance (2:25). The Mahler song that serves as the theme of the middle section has a slightly brisk pace. A monstrous bass drum stroke opens the finale with a bang, but dry sounding strings tone down the fiery brilliance of the storm scene. While Masur restrains the tempo and keeps a lid on dynamic levels, he still generates enough energy to achieve and sustain excitement. How captivating is his languid, but never over-indulgent, treatment of the romantic second theme. Like more and more conductors, Masur slows up for the first few notes of the heroic trumpet theme on its first appearance (8:05). Also the reappearance of the symphony's introduction is not in anywhere near its original tempo. In stronger sections one feels a lack of full sonic breadth, especially during the stormy first subject's return (10:40). Although some slightly abrupt tempo shifts occur (at #44), from 15:50 the tempo presses forward with natural impulse and urgency to a grand climax at 16:45. Masur's treatment of the closing section is an example of what frequently occurs: the *pesante* marking at *Triumphal* has no effect on the tempo, which merely moves along briskly to the end.

MEHTA, ZUBIN/Israel Philharmonic - London CS 7004 (1976); IMP 9005 (1990) [50:23] Mehta's reading is extremely mannered (especially in the finale), lacks overall cohesion and is marred by generally uncomfortable and uneven playing. A tendency to press forward is frequently disturbing in the outer movements. The final section is ruined by extreme speed and blaring trumpets.

MEHTA, ZUBIN/New York Philharmonic - Columbia IM-37273; CBS MK37273 (1982); Sony SBK 53259 (1993) [51:57]* Much improvement over Mehta's earlier version is evident, especially in the beautiful playing he elicits from the NYP. Sound quality is also much clearer and cleaner. In the opening movement, a basically conservative approach is distorted by abrupt tempo shifts and extreme speed at the close (the exposition is not repeated). An exceedingly mannered trio seems out of place in what is otherwise a traditional interpretation of the ländler movement. The middle section of the funeral march drags on unremittingly but the movement opens with a pleasant but uncharacterful reading of the string bass solo. A strong outburst ushers in the finale, but Mehta restrains the main material too markedly. Untoward mannerisms twist the lyrical second theme out of shape. In the closing section, Mehta ignores several markings that might have given the final moments a more heroic posture.

MEHTA, ZUBIN/Israel Philharmonic - EMI CDC 749044-2 (1988) (includes *Blumine* movement) [56:13/7:15]* Among the versions that include *Blumine* in its original position as the second movement, Mehta's collaboration with the IPO is one of the best. He handles both the opening movement and *Blumine* captivatingly, letting the music breathe naturally without unnecessarily disturbing the musical line. Even though the strings sound a bit wiry, are not always tonally secure, and sometimes untidy, they still manage to produce a pleasant sonority. The misty atmosphere Mehta creates to open the development of the first movement is particularly impressive. In comparison, only the closing section seems overly racy. A *misterioso* aura pervades the middle section of the *Blumine* movement, building gradually to a marvelous climax. During the course of the ländler movement, some problems occur. After a slightly pressed opening, the romantic trio is too self-consciously affectatious to be convincing. As the movement proceeds, a relaxed manner gives way to increased motion, so that by #22 the tempo has overrun itself and must be restrained (c. m.263) in order to bring it under control. Strings dig in more intently on the ländler rhythm upon its return. But the close seems unduly hurried for a countrified waltz (the final cymbal crash should also have been cut off more sharply).

Mehta handles the Yiddish folk elements of the funeral march movement in fine style, enhanced by expressive oboe solos. Sonorous strings enrich the *cantabile* middle section. But Mehta is least impressive where it counts most, in the finale. While he keeps the storm music under control, his reading of the lyrical second theme is exceedingly mannered. Mehta adds himself to the list of conductors who find it necessary to slow up at the first appearance of the heroic theme played softly by the first trumpet, without any such direction in the score. Attempts at eliciting a dramatic effect often seem contrived (e.g., the luftpause at m.411-412). Again one contrasts a hurried tempo for the return of the symphony's introduction with an overly effusive treatment of reminiscences of the second theme which follows. Long ritards replace *zurückhalten* (hold back) markings. Tempo shifts are sometimes jerky (from before #43 to after #44). Little underlying tension accompanies the progress of the principal themes to the climax at #52 (only extremely loud trumpets are audible). Then Mehta holds on with all of his might to the opening notes of the heroic theme, only to suddenly make a mad dash through what follows. Ignoring the *pesante* marking at the *Triumphal* climax (#56), he adds a big ritard into #58 and then rushes wildly through the heroic theme. Just for good measure, he slows up into #59 (also without benefit of a direction to that effect in the score) on his way to the final snap.

MITROPOULOS, DIMITRI/Minneapolis Symphony - Columbia 11609-14D(78s) (1940); ML 4251 (1949);SP-P14157; Theorema TH 121.152 (1994) [48:08]* For many years this recording was the only First available. A technically poor LP re-pressing was made, and now a new producer of historical recordings, Theorema, resurrected this important early performance, doing a remarkable job of editing and filtering. Finally, the merits of Mitropoulos' ground-breaking work can be fully appreciated. His rendition of the finale is outstanding. The opening storm scene bursts forth with tremendous power and ignites with flaming intensity. Just as engaging is the beautiful second theme, played charmingly without over indulging in its free-floating lyricism. While the Minneapolis ensemble has many problems, especially with string and brass precision and woodwind intonation, they play their hearts out here. During the development, Mitropoulos takes every opportunity to be expressive, particularly during its closing section. The symphony's triumphal conclusion is simply grand. Mitropoulos, like Horenstein, obeys the *pesante* marking at the section marked *Triumphal* and holds on to the weightier tempo he sets for it as Mahler required, ennobling the heroic final section (15:58). Fudged horn whoops hurl the final bars into an abrupt concluding snap.

In the first movement, a properly broad introduction, bestirred by very rapid wind tattoos, leads to a lively main theme. Mitropoulos shifts the pace both abruptly and often, causing some confusion in the orchestra. He evokes a light and airy atmopshere, energized by a spirited, sometimes darting approach to tempo. Much the same approach is taken in the ländler movement. After a few bars in heavier tempo, the dance theme rollicks along, Mitropoulos easing up or pressing forward by turns. As in the first movement, no repeats are taken. The trio section is extremely mannered, containing a very flexive cello theme. In the third movement, the funeral march tempo is rather quick, woodwind intonation slightly flat and the Yiddish dance not particularly idiomatic. For both historical reasons and for its marvelous finale, this re-issue is a worthy offering.

MUTI, RICCARDO/Philadelphia Orchestra - Angel DS-38078; CDC-47032 (1984); EMI Classics CDD 64287 (1992) [56:16]* Because this is one of the first recordings by Riccardo Muti as music director of The Philadelphia Orchestra and Muti's first effort at a Mahler symphony on disk, it is understandable that there would be some evidence of discomfort and lack of communication between orchestra and conductor. Consequently, the overall performance seems a bit too restrained and unsure of itself to merit high praise. Basically, Muti's reading has few technical faults; it merely sinks into the traditional style that the orchestra was accustomed to under Ormandy. Clearly, the strings have lost some of their brilliant sheen and brass sound rough-hewn and overbalanced. A straight and unaffected first movement with a quickish main theme is generally well done and contains some idyllic moments. Restrained dynamics and brisk tempi for both ländler and trio make the second movement less than satisfactory. Muti tries to get into the *gemütlichkeit* spirit of folk elements in the third movement with only moderate success. The opening funeral tread and bass solo are nearly inaudible. Again restrained dynamic levels and tempi weaken the finale which seems too controlled and understated despite some attempts at marcato treatment. Playing sounds uninvolved and some moments appear to be confounded (from No. 50 the tempo becomes disjointed). A firmer grasp of Mahler's style and more experience with this orchestra might have elicited a securer and more idiomatic performance.

NANUT, ANTON/Ljubljana Symphony - Stradivari Classics SCD 6011 (1987); 12-Digital Concerto CCT 999701 (1992) [53:31] {Incorrectly identified as Vladimir Petroschoff/Philharmonic Festival Orchestra - PILZ CD 160160 (1990); Pavel Urbanek/Prague Festival Orchestra - Laserlight CD 15529; 15828 (1988); and Alberto Vestri/London Festival Orchestra - Vivace 573 (1989) This budget recording is worthy of its price, if not much more. The performance is essentially routine, sometimes uneven, cautious and mild-mannered. Yet Nanut is usually careful with score markings, even if dynamic levels do not always come through as written. Numerous technical problems interfere, from occasional miscues to flattened wind and string intonation. Sonics are as expected: uneven, tinny and confined. An atmospheric opening is encouraging, set in an appropriately dragging tempo; trumpets calls are clear and crisp, horns soft and mellow (2:38). A lively main theme is charming, even though it begins to lose vitality toward the close of the exposition. The development section is played softly but with little expression. While Nanut increases the tempo naturally as the music builds to a fine climax (marked with an asterisk in the score), what follows seems too mild in contrast with the outburst that generated it. A stiff, edgy demeanor dominates the lively ländler that is also diffused by weak sonics, orchestral imprecision (sloppy *col legnos* after #10) and colorless sonorities. Pacing for the trio is much too rapid in contrast with the ländler. Exaggerated swells in celli at #20 add nothing to the lyrical beauty of this music. After speeding up to the close of the trio, Nanut suddenly shifts back to a slower pace for the horn solo that reintroduces the ländler. A timid, characterless bass solo opens the third movement. Most of what follows is similarly lacking in character or idiomatic gesture. The Yiddish song theme is too loud on its second appearance, after a noticeable splice. A clarinet miscue before #8 on the gypsy dance music should have been cleaned up. The middle section's song theme moves by quickly. A curiously comic trombone crescendo at #15 seems intent on producing some unimaginable effect. Nanut completely misses the mid-bar tempo shift after #16.

After an encouraging opening, the finale is soon mired in stiff playing and diminished sonic levels, leaving only heavily-accented, disintonated trumpets to catch the listener's ear. By #12 volume increases, but Nanut does not generate enough impulse to vitalize the storm music here. He elicits some expression in the lovely second theme, despite thin string sound. An unmarked ritard on the second part of the heroic trumpet theme after #26 is yet another distraction. Muted trumpets are too nasal, particularly in contrast with open trumpets' claring tone. Climaxes are underdone, due to weak brass and percussion; legato markings, particularly at phrase endings, are ignored; and dotted rhythms clipped (e.g., in violins at mm. 566 and 568). Nanut's admirable efforts to impel the music forward around #50 (16:22), add heft to the heroic theme at #54 and give some weight to the majestic climax from #56 (marked *Triumphal*) are worth mentioning. Unfortunately, the overall effect is still too mediocre to impress. Nanut adds a slight crescendo on the timpani roll into the final snap.

NEUMANN, VÁCLAV/Czech Philharmonic - Supraphon 1410 2963 (1981); 110 721 (1991); 111 970 (1993); [50:44]*   Generally, Neumann leads a fine performance through the second movement and then the level of involvement seems to wane. An excellent first movement with somewhat brisk tempi (except in the introduction) and good balances is deficient only in its failure to observe the exposition repeat. The ländler movement is not very strong nor is the trio comfortable but much attention is given to details. In the remaining movements, Neumann renders a cold and dispassionate reading that may be the cause for more uneven orchestral playing.

NEUMANN, VÁCLAV/Czech Philharmonic - Canyon Classics PCCL 00177 (1992) [50:23]   Familiarity may sometimes breed contempt, but here it seems to generate routine. Although the CPO performs proficiently, lack of enthusiasm and spontaneity result in an uninvolved and unimpressive performance. Neumann does not take this opportunity to re-think his earlier reading from his first complete cycle. Some strong playing in the finale might raise an eyebrow but fails to grab the listener's attention. This is also the only recording in recent history to eliminate the repeat of exposition in the first movement, a practice no longer acceptable.

OZAWA, SEIJI/Boston Symphony - Philips 422 329 (1987/88); 14-Philips 438 874 (1995) [53:54]   Ozawa does little here that is different from his earlier recording (see Vol. 1, p. 17). His reading is routine, lackluster and characterless. None of the introduction's impressionistic nuances come through Ozawa's colorless palette. Despite a *pp* marking, the horns suddenly burst forth before #4. The main theme is soft but sterile, and playing straight and stiff. When the tempo picks up toward the end of the first movement, one feels nothing of the youthful enthusiasm this music should convey. The ländler speeds along as if on wings rather than earthbound; its trio section has little expressive nuance. Ozawa strings sections together rather than organizing them within a cohesive and coordinated whole. After an absurd hesitation at m.247, the closing section is a race to the finish line. One senses complete disengagement from the musical aesthetic in the third movement. The march tempo presses along briskly and the folk-music elements are dashed off without any attempt to invoke their idiomatic characteristics. After a long pause between movements (Mahler directs that there be no break), the finale quickly takes on the character of the rest of this performance: routine. Brass are over-balanced and playing is rigid and sonically confined (particularly in the strings). Even the final moments fail to engender any dramatic impact, notwithstanding an added poco ritard into #60, where Mahler directs that the tempo pick up more and more to the end.

RATTLE, SIMON/City of Birmingham Symphony - EMI CDC 7 54647-2 (1992) [57:19] with *Blumine* movement [7:29]** Rattle is a conductor who delves deeply into the score, not just to be different from his colleagues but to reveal the work's essence. Yet his approach to this youthful symphony was criticized as too restrained or heavy-laden by some reviewers. What seems sluggish to some may sound creatively nuanced or characterful to others. Rattle's approach to the outer movements elicits such diversity of opinion. His manner with the principal theme of the first movement is very easy -- he lets it flow gently and languidly, as if floating on a cloud hovering over a hazy mid-summer morning mist. Out of the misty atmosphere of the opening bars comes a hint of distant volleys, tatoos and bird calls. A soft vaporous veil covers a whisper of horns (2:05), creating a suggestion of mystery. Rattle eases into the main theme, with a natural lilting quality gently prodded along by increasing momentum. As the tempo gradually increases, some sudden shifts intercede (c. m.128, after an effusive hesitation at m.125). Even during the rollicking close of the exposition, Rattle refuses to let the music run away with itself (as, for instance, Abbado did with the CSO). Unlike nearly all of his colleagues, Rattle sees no reason to repeat the exposition precisely as first rendered: notice how poignantly the celli play the main theme during its second go-round, and how urgently he presses ahead with the entrance of the same theme on the trumpet thereafter (6:54). Some lovely details in the development section are worth noting: a slight hesitation on the second note of the elongated cuckoo calls; a shimmering string accompaniment to the horn quartet; an evocative hesitation into the theme at 12:47. Even though some affectations are questionable (e.g., the big luftpause at 15:33), this reading is not really self-indulgent and rarely overly ecstatic or hard driven, and it never loses its momentum due to either sagging tempi or heavily underlined phrases. Energetic spirit is blended perfectly with a dreamy youthful romanticism. The ländler has fine heft and markéd articulation in bass strings. Its pacing is aggressive without being racy and returns more raucous than before in an energetic race to the close. Rattle's rubato style in the trio (4:27) is fitting, until celli appear in its second part (5:06) in a brisker tempo (unmarked), enabling Rattle to move gradually into the *frischer* (fresher) tempo Mahler asked for at #21.

Rattle gives a delightfully idiomatic reading of the folk elements in the third movement, easing into the Yiddish dance music as if he were accustomed to it. Notice the marvelous glissando into the fourth note of this same passage on its return at 3:30. After a lovely middle section song theme, the opening tread returns to usher in the Yiddish dance theme played by solo oboe (c.10') after an extended ritard. Focussing on dramatic weight rather than agitated excitement, the finale may seem temperate to some. However, those who see in this movement a musical representation of medieval Romance tales will find this approach thoroughly satisfying, if not thrilling. From the outset, one senses magic in this reading, evoked more by its muscularity and awesome power than sheer speed or agitation. To heighten the dramatic effect, Rattle articulates the thematic material demonstratively, adding breadth and depth to its bearing. Ritards are stretched out, marcato markings reinforced. The storm music surges forward in gigantic waves of sound. Rattle's effusive treatment of the second theme is reminiscent of Bernstein. Yet no over-emoting here, just lingering beauty that thoroughly captivates. After the storm's return, Rattle joins the many others who slow up for the first appearance of the heroic trumpet theme (8:22), then speeds up intently at #28 (8:58) to bring back the main tempo (all without benefit of Mahler's directions). After a huge orchestral outburst emblazoned by impetuous trumpet volleys (10:17), the main theme returns in all its full-blown glory. Some affectations seem contrived, such as the ritard placed before the return of the symphony's introduction (at 11:20). But other added touches in the introduction's reprise are captivating: have flute trills here ever sounded so much like birds? How movingly the languid references to the lyric second theme here stir the emotions. From the triumphant return of the heroic theme, Rattle's intuitive dramatic sense creates a magnificent impression. At the section marked *Triumphal*, he culminates this unique reading brilliantly, imposing just enough dramatic weight to give it added dimension. While he holds on to this weightier tempo thereafter-- as Mahler directs and most conductors do not--Rattle ever so gradually begins to move the tempo forward before #60 (where the first tempo change after the *Triumphal* marking appears), so that at #60 he has already reached an appropriate tempo from which to accelerate to the end. An excellent example of well-conceived restructuring that at least does not completely ignore Mahler's directions. Added as the last cut (reprogrammable for inclusion or exclusion from the symphony), the *Blumine* movement fits comfortably into Rattle's overall approach to the symphony. His pacing is easy and relaxed, enhancing the tender lyricism of the main theme without tugging too heavily on the musical line or letting it sag. The middle section is hushed and mysterious, with a plaint oboe solo followed by a lovely violin theme. Rattle shapes the melodic material beautifully (notice what a lovely effect the slight slow up makes at c.6:10). The closing moments take ones breath away.

ROSBAUD, HANS/Southwest German Radio Symphony - Stradivarius STR 10036 (1990) [52:34] This historical recording of a performance, given on September 13, 1961, is not the best evidence of Hans Rosbaud's usually intelligent and capable readings of Mahler's music. Too many technical problems are distracting, particularly weak sonics and uneven, imprecise playing. Moreover, Rosbaud makes little impression with his uninvolved reading. While the proper atmosphere is set for the opening, he moves the tempo forward too quickly into the main theme, so that he must make an early adjustment to ease up the tempo. After skipping the repeat of the exposition, Rosbaud takes the opening measures of the development hesitantly, creating a mood of hushed mystery, and invoking the sounds of a summer morning. But soon after rigor mortis begins to set in, and the music sounds constricted and inflexive. The feeling of spirited youthfulness that should be evoked here is lost in discomforting rigidity. The ländler movement is also disturbingly tight and forced, lacking a feeling of care-free abandon. Yet the trio section has a lilting quality, which provides a relaxing respite between straight-jacketed treatments of the ländler. A craggy, out-of-tune bass solo opens the third movement. The funeral march section moves along generally well, without leaving any special impression. Brass sometimes predominate (e.g., at #17). In the middle section, the atmosphere seems too extroverted to engender any touching sentiment. While agitated and intense, the finale's opening storm suffers from untidy string figuration and underdone dynamic levels. Rosbaud sets a hurried pace for the lovely second theme, yet tries to generate some feeling by slight hesitations. Later reminiscences of this theme move too rapidly, so that tempo adjustments are required (after #42). But as the movement proceeds to its heroic conclusion, Rosbaud shows his affinity for this music, particularly with his intelligent attention to Mahler's markings at the important *Triumphal* section. Miscues (where is the cymbal at the climax at #44?), blurry, inarticulate trumpets, and some awkward tempo shifts (an unmarked *subito a tempo* at #50, followed by holding back after #51, and a sudden return of the main tempo at #59), coupled with attentuated sound quality are some of the many flaws that makes this recording less than satisfying.

SCHERCHEN, HERMANN/London Philharmonic - Westminster XWN 18014 (1955); Heliodor 479032; 2-MCA MCAD2-99833 (1991); Palladio PD 4180 (1994) [49:18]*
Scherchen was a highly underrated, if eccentric Mahler interpreter. His First is one of the better of his many Mahler recordings for Westminster, and sonics are much improved in the latest CD issue. A superbly wrought first movement contains many usually understated details (despite omission of the exposition repeat). However, the entire second movement goes by in

a flash and the third movement is marred by uneven orchestral playing, even though the interpretation is well-conceived. The finale proceeds effectively until prior to the return of symphony's introduction where the tempo is rushed, and during the coda where tempo changes are too abrupt. The closing section is strong and dramatic.

SEGERSTAM, LEIF/Danish National Radio Symphony - Chandos CHAN 9242 (with Blumine) (1993) [60:14/6:33]+ Segerstam's reading exaggerates tempo contrasts and heavily underlines phrases within and at the close of various melodic lines to such an extent that it becomes disconcerting. He rarely overlooks an opportunity to stretch out a lyrical phrase. Conversely, accelerandos and piu mossos are very fast (witness the extremely rapid tattoos at the beginning set against the very slow opening tempo). What results seems extremely self-indulgent and without interpretive incite. Frequent slow-ups are imposed upon the musical flow. The marking *zurückhalten* is read as a ritard, so that Mahler's attempts to control the tempo are treated as tempo shifts. Segerstam lingers exaggeratedly on the first movement's main theme, yet the tempo increases with extreme rapidity toward the close. *Blumine*, placed as the final cut on this disc to enable the listener to place it where he or she will, seems slightly pressed. But the middle section has a nice lilt to it. An extremely fast pace is set for the ländler movement. A quirky treatment of fragmented material sounds forced (e.g., excessive underlining of the woodwind two-bar phrase into #18 (4:20) and treament of the two 16th notes that open each measure of the flute/violin counterpoint beginning at #22 as if they were grace-notes). Again frequent ritards both within and at the close of the Yiddish melodies exaggerate their folkish character. Listen to how each note of these tunes oozes out toward the close. Curiously enough, the opening storm of the finale seems mild, despite frantic increases in tempo. But again inordinate slow-ups tug at the line here and there (e.g., after #9; on the heroic trumpet theme at 9:10; and into #34 at 10:55). Add extremely agitated piu mossos, and the performance becomes a string of distortions and convolutions. Segerstam holds back at the *Triumphal* section (20:22), maintaining a *pesante* tempo straight through to #60 as written. This may be the most effective passage in an extremely fussy, self-indulgent reading.

SINOPOLI, GIUSEPPE/Philharmonia Orchestra - DG 429 228 (1990) [57:08]*+
Sinopoli offers a fascinating, personalized account, emphasizing contrasts in mood through considerable tempo fluctuations, belabored ritards that introduce or conclude sections or themes, and specialized effects, all as if to make a fresh argument for the work's wealth of musical invention. Such emphatic efforts on the symphony's behalf recall Bernstein's early attempts to educate audiences unfamiliar with Mahler's music by heavily underlining particular phrases or exaggerating nuances. So much of what Sinopoli accomplishes here is so significant that his version deserves a high rating. Few of his contemporaries have caught the symphony's opening atmosphere with such visionary beauty. A summery haze hovers over the dawning of a new day, that bestirs itself awake with a lazy yawn and becomes increasingly energetic, overcoming a desire to return to restful sleep. Having so deftly created this picturesque atmosphere, Sinopoli moves rapidly to the main theme [3:40+], only to shift gears awkwardly and pull back just before its initial statement. This slight disorientation has little impact on the theme itself, enchantingly rendered in a relaxed tempo. As elsewhere, tempi are flexible. Rather than replicating the main tempo in the exposition's repeat, Sinopoli varies the tempo with slight hesitations. The development section begins very slowly (more like mm. 76 than 96 as written), with emphasis on the recurring three-note thematic fragment in the cellos. At 10:28, horns are just barely audible (a true *ppp!*), seeming to peer ever so imperceptibly out from the misty ether, lingering hesitently before the main theme's reprise. Most of the remainder of the movement is handled with finesse and extraordinary sensitivity, capturing precisely the right mood. Only a exposed, slightly off-pitch first trumpet is a minor distraction. An unusual effect

appears around 14:00: unwritten trumpet swells on whole notes replace marcato markings. The closing section is hard-driven rather than breezy and gay.

Sinopoli takes even more liberties with the ländler movement. While the main material is crisp and sharp, laden with strong woodwinds and brass, the more lilting trio is expressively languid, subject to long ritards at high points or phrase endings (one is reminded of Kubelik here). An interesting diversion occurs at 6:19, marked *frischer* (fresher). Unlike most conductors who increase the tempo here, Sinopoli (to his credit) maintains the tempo but emboldens the music with added demarcation, certainly refreshing its spirit. When a horn solo ushers in the return of the ländler on a skipping rhythm in octaves, Sinopoli goes right into the ländler tempo rather than waiting for the return of the ländler theme itself, despite Mahler's direction to the contrary. But he adds a slight crescendo on the horn just before the ländler reappears, now sharper, rougher and more ribald than before. Again in the third movement, within the context of a generally well-rendered funeral march, Sinopoli exaggerates particular elements. The 3-note upbeat to the first Yiddish wedding dance is stretched to the breaking point, adding not a jot of authenticity to its ethnic character. The gypsy music that follows has its own faster tempo (again without Mahler's direction). The song theme of the middle section is exquisite, spun out with grace and ease, hesitantly but without mannerism. After the funeral march returns, notice how Sinopoli captures the strange mewings that appear toward the close of the Yiddish theme and just before the sudden intrusion of the faster gypsy music [9:52 et seq.]. This section seems uncoordinated, however, with its unmarked tempo shifts that sometimes anticipate what should be sudden tempo changes [10:10+]. In an effort to create a unique approach, too many twists and turns in tempo occur, further complicating a movement already convoluted with extreme and unexpected tempo changes. Notice even in the closing section how the tempo seems slower and faster by turns.

In the finale, Sinopoli's tendency to play up the big effect is given full reign. The opening section is stormy, generating much power and excitement, even if the main tempo seems to be held in check. Especially engrossing are the grotesque effects he elicits toward the end of the *wildheit* section [3:00]. But a nasal, underpitched trumpet becomes obtrusive. The lyrical second theme is beautifully handled (even if horns are sometimes too loud). Sinopoli is very effective in his long-lined treatment of the prelude to the return of the storm music [c.7'], again wild and raging. When the heroic trumpet theme first appears [8:30], he doesn't hold back as some do but waits for its later and more definitive appearance when Mahler so directs. From here to the close, ritards (even poco ritards) are stretched out in the extreme; brass overpower (particularly the first trumpet); big climaxes are wrenched from their context and elongated to be breaking point. Mannered thematic treatment is the order of the day. But the *höchster Kraft* climax is truly overwhelming [17:43], ushered in by a slight push at the end of the extensive rhythmic build up that precedes it. The last two or three minutes of the symphony present a perfect opportunity to pull out whatever stops remain untouched in this already indulgent reading. Sinopoli does just that. In fact, one could argue that he treats the main theme at 18:16 as the climax of the entire work. Each note of this heroic theme is not just played *pesante* (heavily) but as if written under fermatas. Having indulged in such over-dramatization, Sinopoli takes off at a gallop far beyond the previously set main tempo. He holds back at the *Triumphal* demarcation but gives it less emphasis then it deserves. From here Mahler makes no tempo change for about 40 measures. He wanted to retain the weight of the Triumphal climax until the cadence that occurs before #60 which ushers in the horn calls that close the symphony. Sinopoli finds it necessary to fill in these direction-free measures with his own markings, giving each segment its own special tempo. These tempo adjustments seem to be in keeping with his emphasis on contrast. Sinopoli is artful enough to render each phrase of this passage in a tempo arguably befitting the musical line. Even Bernstein at his most self-indulgent did not tamper as much with tempo markings in this symphony as Sinopoli does.

SYMPHONY NO. 1

SLATKIN, LEONARD/Saint Louis Symphony - Telarc DG 10066 (1981) ; 80066 (1987); 82004 (1993) [50:11]* Slatkin turns in a very fine performance for his first effort at a Mahler symphony. Spectacular sonics enhance clarity and ambience. Comfortable tempi, well-balanced dynamic levels and exuberant playing characterize a very effective first movement. The ländler is vitalized by a lively tempo but the trio lacks *gemütlichkeit*. The third movement also seems somewhat insensitive, primarily because of uncomfortably swift tempi. But the finale is strong and exciting, serving as the best evidence provided here of Slatkin's understanding of Mahler's idiom.

SOLTI, GEORG/London Symphony - London CS 6401 (1964); 417 701 (1987); 425005 (1991) [53:10]* Solti's first effort is still competitive. A quiet and somber, if slightly restless, introduction is enhanced by excellent wind playing. In what follows Solti indicates his complete mastery of this music and elicits much excitement and tender emotion. The ländler is portrayed as a rustic parody energized with typical Solti intensity, and its trio is infused with a soft, tender lyricism which never lingers but always sounds natural and comfortable. A scratchy yet quite intriguing bass solo opens the funeral march (conjuring up thoughts of **Fiddler on the Roof**). Solti takes no chances here, rendering this movement without affectations. He plunges into the violent storm which opens the finale with a will, easing up as the tempest subsides into a slightly less energetic main theme, counterbalanced by an expressive treatment of the lyrical second theme. However, the final apotheosis is slightly marred by unsettling trumpet intonation and abrupt tempo shifts.

SOLTI, GEORG/Chicago Symphony - London 411731-1; 2-LH (1984); 10-London 430 804 (1992) [55:41]*+ Solti's version with the CSO is recorded in sumptuous sonics. The performance reeks with confidence as if it literally poured out of the maestro with little conscious effort. All details are superbly rendered and very distinct. Playing is superb if sometimes on the cautious, squarish side. Solti seems more intent on clarity of line and highlighting the massive dramatic outbursts than emphasizing the subtleties of the romantic subsidiary material. Yet there is no denying that his manner is expressive in these softer moments. The main tempo set for each movement is right on the mark. One especially important detail in both the first and last movements is presented here as nowhere else: a lengthy crescendo that leads to the huge outburst marked *vorwärts* is played just as Mahler directed, continually more and more held back. The only sonic detraction is too much reverberation in the bass drum at climaxes. Otherwise, Solti turns in a magnificent performance. While some reviewers claim that Solti adds nothing to his previous effort here, more careful listening might change their perceptions.

TENNSTEDT, KLAUS/Chicago Symphony - EMI CDC 7 542172 (1991) [60:55]**
Tennstedt's second version is even better than his first with the London Philharmonic (see Volume 1, pp. 20-21). While tempi in the outer movements may seem too relaxed for some, they engender a warm, pastoral atmosphere in the first movement and strong dramatic weight in the finale. Having restrained his earlier tendency to over-emote in lyrical sections, Tennstedt more effectively balances the symphony's diverse moods than he did in his LPO performance. Imaginative coloristic effects create just the right shadings to evoke an atmosphere of pastoral repose (although trumpet calls are too pronounced), leading ever so gently into a tender treatment of the main theme. After an extremely affectatious slow-up at 5:50, the exposition closes in fine style without overrunning itself. Following a less indulgent repeat of the exposition, Tennstedt eases into the development, which is thoroughly captivating. One senses a reluctance to awaken from a summer night's dream with the coming of the dawn. Tennstedt's tendency toward effusiveness works well here. Easing into and out

of each thematic statement, he generates warmth and tenderness, coddling each phrase lovingly. Highpoints in the line are emphasized and trumpet swells (at 15:02) stretched to the limit. These tempo modulations fit well within the context of the languorous summer morning atmosphere he establishes early on.

Tennstedt's treatment of the ländler movement is also excellent. Strong bass strings generate heft in the bucolic dance, while the ease with which he handles the trio section recalls the mood of the first movement's main theme. An unwritten ritard on the closing cadence (6:16+) ushers in the ländler's return. Tennstedt's idiomatic reading of the third movement's folk material is also impressive, even if dynamic levels are relatively high where *pp* is called for. After the parodistic funeral march, Mahler tried to evoke tender sentiments of youthful innocence in a faint haze of recollection; he was not painting a trifling, rustic scene that might call for such boisterous treatment. An ineffective slow up into the mid-measure tempo change at 9:23 ruins what should be a sudden shift to a faster tempo that should knock the listener off balance.

A controlled pace tempers the ferocity of the storm scene that opens the finale. Even with an attentuated pulse, Tennstedt's reading makes a strong impact. Noticeably emphatic playing here helps to secure the main tempo against sagging or sounding long-winded. As expected, Tennstedt over-emotes in the romantic second theme with long hesitations and lingerings. One gets the feeling that he keeps trying for a big effect, yet he conveys both lyrical charm and drama with a less effusive approach. In his enthusiasm, he may have stepped over the line, but in most instances momentary excesses do little damage. His reading of the closing section is most impressive. The heroic apotheosis is gloriously majestic, with its resplendent brass flourishes. Tennstedt holds back slightly at the *Triumphal* section marked *pesante* (weighty), but not nearly as much as Horenstein does. The tempo Tennstedt establishes here is perfect for eliciting all of the grandeur of this magnificent conclusion, and he maintains it as Mahler directs until #60 (21:51), where the pacing presses forward to the end. Tennstedt's affectatious manner has tempered over the years, but it has not dulled his emotive instincts or his ability to build climaxes to dramatic heights.

TENNSTEDT, KLAUS/Chicago Symphony - EMI video ASVE 991244 3 (rec. May 31 and June 1, 1990; rel. 1991) [64:09]*+

This video version does not duplicate the CD issue made from these and other performances (see above). Tennstedt's mild, mature reading of the first movement still stands, but the introduction seems more earthy and direct. Slight hesitations (e.g., 1 m. before #7) add to the expressive character of his reading. If youthful ardor is slightly attenuated here, there is more of an aggressive pulse when the tempo increases than is apparent in the CD version. Notice how Tennstedt lingers yearningly on the cello phrase that opens the development, and how he stretches out the string syncopations before #20. One senses a desire to bring out all of the emotions inherent in every phrase and musical setting. The overall character seems more mature than youthful.

The remaining movements vary only slightly from the CD version. Although bass strings dig deep for marked emphasis on the ländler rhythm, Tennstedt keeps the mood in restraint and the pacing measured but not inflexible. His trio section is comfortable, yet lingers languidly. Caricature is at a minimum as he views Mahler's lighter whimsical touches from a mature vantage-point. In the funeral march movement, Tennstedt leaves the Yiddish dance music to its own devices, making no attempt to create any special effect, except for elongating the ritard that ushers in its return at #7. Dotted rhythms here seem too rigid, and slight hesitations bring back the mood of meditativeness which characterizes this reading. The awkward slow up at #16 compromises Mahler sudden shift into a faster tempo in mid-bar.

Tennstedt crashes into the finale with a big bang, but as on the CD, what follows is less propulsive than dramatic. Long ritards (e.g., after #9) add a gushing quality with to the romantic second subject. While intensity is almost entirely absent here, Tennstedt plays up the dramatic proportions of the final apotheosis magnificently, pouring forth in a profusion of brass the heroic music that forms the ultimate climax of the symphony. Horns virtually stand still (at #56) to further highlight this effect.

WAKASUGI, HIROSHI/Staatskapelle Dresden - Eterna 3 29 119 (1986) [53:15]+ This serviceable if not very impressive performance is aesthetically attenuated by an objective approach, that lacks nuance, inner impulse and dramatic impact. The first movement is best, conjuring up just the right summery atmosphere during the introduction and development sections to balance out a brisk main theme. The ländler feels stiff at times but has sufficient forward motion. During the charming trio, echoes of the muted horns interfere with the somewhat briskly paced musical flow. The third movement is merely routine, lacking Mahler's deliciously impish sense of irony. Dotted rhythms are played too strictly but the folk materials are well-handled, even if they are played too loudly upon their return. Strong percussion punctuate an agitated opening of the finale. From #4 playing becomes more cautious and even mechanical. Just a slight push might have enlivened the performance. Brass sound too constricted to give the symphony's magnificent conclusion sufficient sonic dimension. The second theme brings out more flexible, even sensual playing. Wakasugi opts for a slow-up at the first appearance of the heroic theme, an affectation that seems to have increased in popularity recently. Although he handles nicely the return of the symphony's introduction and subsequent transition to the main material, the brass are overpowered by percussion in the concluding section. A sudden increase in tempo at #50 (16:56) is uncalled for, as is the addition of a long unmarked rallentando into #60, at which point Mahler directs that the tempo should increase. While Wakasugi generates enough energy in the final moments to stir the emotions, his reserved approach throughout the performance limits its effectiveness.

WAKASUGI, HIROSHI/Tokyo Metropolitan Symphony (Budapest Version including *Blumine*) - Fontec FOCD 3274 (1989) [58:19]+ The only significance of this performance is its use of the score as it stood when the symphony was premiered in Budapest in 1889, at which time it included the *Blumine* movement. Mahler made many changes in the orchestration before the final version was published in 1898. Hearing these revisions may be of interest to some, but they reveal the wisdom of Mahler's final choices. Wakasugi's reading differs little from his earlier recording with the Dresden Staatskapelle (see above). A lovely *Blumine* movement is possibly the sole attraction. Wakasugi's objective manner and moderate temperament make for a mild-mannered, tame reading. The Tokyo Metropolitan Symphony sounds pale, sonically limited and sometimes insecure or imprecise.

WALTER, BRUNO/Columbia Symphony - Columbia MS-6394 (1963); Odyssey Y-30047 (1970); CBS MYK-37235 (1981); 2-Columbia M2K 45674 (1990); MYK 37235 [51:00]*
Many problems creep in to this generally fine performance. In the opening movement, smoother tempo changes, more even pacing and cleaner if not always idiomatic playing are improvements over his earlier NYP recording (see Vol. 1, p.21). A squarish treatment of the ländler and extremely reserved trio are disappointing. Repeats are not observed in the first two movements, a practice no longer countenanced. A lovely song theme does not redeem the slow movement from its uninteresting and unnecessarily mannered reading. The finale is too forced and deliberate to be sufficiently energetic. Themes are stated very slowly and the music tends to drag on lifelessly after an unfocussed opening. A disappointment for Walter fans.

WALTER, BRUNO/New York Philharmonic (perf. December 2, 1950) - AS Disc 402 (1991); Notes PGP 11006 (1992); Legend LGD 106 (1994) [49:07]* Not to be confused with Walter's commercial release with the NYP recording in 1954 (yet to be reissued on cd; see the 1986 volume, p.21), this first by the great Mahlerian maestro tends to press allegros forward hurriedly, particularly in the main material of the first movement and the trio of the second, and indulge in more mannerism than Walter's commercial recordings. Undeniably, his manner of expression is thoroughly Mahlerian. However, he abbreviates the first two movements by eliminating repeats and underplays the Yiddish folk material in the third. Imprecise playing also mars this performance, especially in the ländler movement. Dynamic levels are toned down in the finale. But Walter's reading of the opening section is intense and he never loses control over the slightly weighty tempo he begins with. Some unmarked *luftpausen* do appear, but never inappropriately (at #6; into #8; on the first appearance of the main theme at #26; and before #37). A flawed attack on the timpani's entrance at m.520 is unfortunately exposed. Before #51, the tempo seems to drag somewhat, forcing Walter to pick up the pace. He handles the final *Triumphal* section (at #56) impressively. In no other recorded performance does he give as much weight to this majestic climax.

SYMPHONY NO.2 IN C MINOR ("RESURRECTION")

Movements:

1. Allegro maestoso
2. Andante moderato
3. In ruhig fliessender Bewegung
4. "Urlicht" - Sehr feierlich, aber schlicht
5. Im Tempo des Scherzos.
   Wild herausfahrend. Allegro energico.

ABBADO, CLAUDIO/Chicago Symphony & Chorus; Carol Neblett, soprano; Marilyn Horne, contralto - 2-DG 2707094; 3370015 (1977); 2-DG 427 262 (1989)*+ While Abbado provides one of the better overall performances currently available, his extremely agitated fast tempi and abrupt tempo changes may not be to everyone's taste. He generates much excitement in the outer movements with an underlying energetic motion and vital intensity. He also creates some lovely lyrical moments (e.g., second theme of the first movement and in the cello countersubject in the second movement). A few phrase endings are treated affectatiously. Most distressing are the constricted, bassy sonics, weak percussion (where is the *ruthe* in the third movement?), unfocussed blend and uneven balances (particularly in the third movement), none of which are much improved in the CD reissue. Abbado makes a fine effort to attend to details and his interpretive style works well in stronger sections. Abbado takes the descending triplets that end the first movement at a rapid pace in keeping with the intense agitation he engenders throughout. The second and third movements are generally effective, if sometimes too tense. Percussion could be more prominent. In the Scherzo Abbado makes an unwarranted decision to speed up at #49. Marilyn Horne graces the brief *Urlicht* movement with her rich voice and expressive reading. Fuller and better focussed sound (particularly in the climaxes), a stronger, less distant chorus and more orchestral precision would have improved the finale. Abbado's ability to elicit excitement with energetic tempi and heightened intensity is his best asset here.

ABBADO, CLAUDIO/Vienna Philharmonic; Vienna State Opera Chorus; Stefan Woytowicz, soprano; Lucretia West, contralto (perf. 8 Aug. 1965, Salzburg) - 2-Hunt CD 542 (1988); 2-Arkadia 542 [79:01] This performance by Abbado and the VPO, given several years before his recording with the CSO (see above), while of some historical interest, is unsatisfactory. Technical problems with recorded sound and orchestral precision are serious drawbacks. Winds are frequently over-balanced and strings surprisingly messy in rapid tutti passages. Quacky oboe intonation in the outer movements is most annoying. The VPO must not have taken well to Abbado's way with Mahler's music. His approach is frenetic, with extreme contrasts in tempi that create a relentless underlying agitation. Abbado puts more weight on the march theme of the first movement than he does in his later version. He often darts forward nervously (at #12 and #18), wildly ripping through segments, as if fighting off the music. While he generates much excitement in this way, both precision and the movement's funereal aspect suffer. A curious combination of rigidity and affectation characterize the second movement. Beginning with timpani whacks that sound like cannon fire, the Scherzo's main tempo is consistently brisk. Strings, caught up in Abbado's nervous energy, keep pressing forward; yet trumpets have the completely opposite reaction and sound boorish and wallowy (at #40). Abbado makes an effort to produce a *cantabile* style for the lyrical material, but his quick pacing works against this. Some gradual tempo changes (to #44) are uncoordinated, and playing becomes extremely ragged at times. Abbado rips into and through the anticipation of the finale's opening and then calms down just as quickly and noticeably--Mahler marked the tempo change at the section's close *unmerklich* (unnoticeable). Dynamic levels are not in keeping with score markings: strings are bearly audible when they should be heard distinctly-- into #53--and the piccolo is too loud after #55.

Urlicht follows without a moment's pause. Lucretia West, an old hand at this music from the Mitropoulos era, has a robust vocal timbre but is too closely miked. The main tempo seems carelessly hurried and the music routinely played. Again excessive volume makes it difficult to elicit an appropriately hushed atmosphere. The opening of the finale is a mad rush, just as it was earlier when it was anticipated in the Scherzo. Blowing by so quickly, it fails to make much of an impression. What follows cannot help but be affected by such excessive speed. Hyped-up dynamics again take their toll (loud woodwinds in mushy timbre for the Dies Irae chorale marked *ppp*), yet the horn marked *in der Ferne* (in the distance) is all but inaudible (at m.84+). After a rather sluggish resumption of the main theme at #7, Abbado rushes the tempo into #10. Then he makes an unforgivable cut before the brass statement of the Dies Irae. Nervous energy and strong dynamic levels characterize much that follows, with straggly playing persisting throughout. Choral forces begin quite nicely, but an over-miked soprano and a blaring trumpet disturbs their longing for heavenly peace. Much of the remainder of the movement is either too fast or disregards Mahler's markings, such as holding back when the score says *nicht schleppen* (not dragging). In fact, Abbado presses so quickly into the choral climax that he has to stop literally in his tracks at #47 to take a breath. Notice also how the trumpets crescendo instead of decrescendo at the close of the choral section.

ABBADO, CLAUDIO/Vienna Philharmonic; Cheryl Studer, soprano; Waltraud Meier, contralto; Arnold Schoenberg Choir - 2-DG 439 953-2 (1994); 10-DG 447023 (1995) [87:12]+ In this performance Abbado has tempered the high-strung manner that made his CSO recording and earlier VPO performance so frenetic (see above). The first movement has more heft; tempi are broader, enhancing dramatic weight. Pacing is less agitated, producing a more majestic bearing. The result is often powerful and very expressive without being over-indulgent. In the middle movements, Abbado keeps things in their proper place without seeming to make a conscious effort at creative nuance, yet his reading lacks personality. In *Urlicht*, Waltraud Meier, despite her vocal merits, sounds uninspired at first but becomes more expressive as the music increases in intensity toward the close. Close miking of her voice is ill-advised for this ethereal intermezzo. The huge outburst that opens the final movement, punctuated by rock-hard timpani strokes, whizzes by in a flash. What follows seems to lack both mystery and inspiration; only overpowering sonics make a strong impression. Otherwise, Abbado's more temperate approach to both tempi and underlying impulse are memorable.

ABRAVANEL, MAURICE/Utah Symphony; Beverly Sills, soprano; Florence Kopleff, contralto; University of Utah Civic Chorale - 2-Vanguard VCS 10003/4 (1967); Vanguard Classics OVC 4004 (1991); 11-Vanguard 08.4013.79 (1995) [77:09]*
Considered one of the better early recordings on a budget label, this version should not be considered lightly. Abravanel's approach is restrained and temperate though generally well-conceived. Orchestral quality is only fair, lacking consistently refined playing and displaying woodwind intonation problems (listen to those quacky woodwinds at #7 in the finale). Choral forces are weak and Sills is not always comfortable; she sounds strained at times. A squarish treatment of dotted rhythms and slow tempi are somewhat compensated for by a generally sound if conservative reading. The first and second movements too often become sluggish. After setting a plodding pace for the main tempo of the first movement, Abravanel chooses to end it with rapid descending triplets. The choice of a proper and effective tempo for the closing notes has long been problemmatic. While the tempo is marked in most scores as "Tempo I," if the main tempo is labored the descending triplets that end the movement might sound ludicrous if played in that same tempo. Therefore, many conductors either play this passage at a moderate allegro tempo, while others (e.g., Klemperer) race through it hurriedly. (N.B., at least one version has "Presto" instead of "Tempo I" marked here) Abravanel sprinkles some sections with rather awkward affectations, usually at phrase-endings. But in spite of some shakey moments in the finale, the final choral climax is quite thrilling.

ASAHINA, TAKASHI/Osaka Philharmonic; Kiyomi Toyoda, soprano, Naoko Ihara, mezzo-soprano; Chorus of Mukogawa Women's University; Kansei Gakuin Glee Club - 2-Firebird K25C 475-6 (1987) [85:14]+   Takashi Asahina and his Japanese forces perform admirably despite various technical problems. The orchestra sometimes waffles between rigidity and unsteadiness, stiffening when rhythms are regular while shifting the tempo slightly from measure to measure. Woodwind timbres occasionally sour and brass have a raw tonal quality in forte passages. Notwithstanding these flaws, one can sense that the orchestra members are deeply committed to their task. Although the choruses sound weak at times, they sing the text correctly if not consistently in Germanic style. The alto soloist has a heavyish tonal quality and uses too many crutches, while the soprano sounds pale and reticent. Asahina approaches the score on its own terms, giving in a traditional reading faithful to Mahler's many markings. A suddenly slower tempo for the whiplashes that intensify the march theme at 14:57 of the first movement is an interesting touch. But a heavy-handed tempo for the opening of the finale (possibly taken to avoid precision problems that a faster tempo can sometimes cause) results in disruptions. Asahina brings out the martial character of the *Kräftig* march at 11' with demonstrative thrusts on each of the opening notes. Later, the trumpets are absent at #20 (c.14:07) after an orchestral outburst featuring a variant of the "anger" theme in the horns. Trombones tend to bury all competing brass when they play strongly. Close-miking causes softer choral sections to sound unduly loud (e.g., from 20:50). As the music moves toward the grand apotheosis of the *Auferstehen* chorus, Asahina adds to the tension by stretching out cadences and inserting a few unmarked ritards (at 31:45 into "*sterben werd' ich*" and into #51 in the final measures). The concluding climax is thrilling, even if the choruses recede slightly at its highpoint. Contrary to Mahler's directions to cut it short, the last stroke is emphatically prolonged.

BARBIROLLI, JOHN/Southwest German Radio Orchestra; Helen Donath, soprano; Birgit Finnila, mezzo-soprano; South German Radio Chorus; Stuttgart State School Choir; Stuttgart Darstallende Kunst Choir (perf. 19 June 1970) - Hunt CD 719 (1990); 3-Arkadia 719 (1995) [81:14]   Recorded at a performance given on June 19, 1970, at Stoccarda, Italy, this is the only version of the Second that we have thus far by Barbirolli.

Unfortunately, it suffers from numerous defects. Frequently sloppy playing, improper balances, and misjudged tempo changes mar what might have otherwise been an important statement by this noted Mahlerian conductor. If sonic distortion can be ignored, many moments in this recording are worthy of praise. Barbirolli's view of the opening movement can be compaired to Bruno Walter's: strong, weighty in the main material, tender and heart-felt in the lyrical subsidiary theme. While some moments seems distractingly objective (after #8; at the beginning of the reprise; and the closing section) and some strange tempo choices are made (at #16 where *sehr langsam* seems more like allegro), the overall results are positive. More impressive is Barbirolli's lovely reading of the second movement. Playing seems more under control here, even though several glitches appear (what is the harp playing before the beat into m.295, a glissando or an arpeggio?). Barbirolli plays up the gorgeous final variation and then breezes through the closing section. A brisk Scherzo movement finds the orchestra members in less than top form. Ticking off all of the miscues seems pointless. One also notices a curious tendency to over-sentimentalize one moment, e.g., at #40 (c.5'+) and then dash with little interest through what follows. Birgit Finnila has just the right timbre for the *Urlicht* movement, in spite of some pitch problems. Her reading is mostly secure and sometimes impassioned. Listen to the three rising notes in the viola come through at the close. The finale contains both the worst and the best of this performance. Although the opening is dashed off wildly and is embarrassingly sloppy, a fine choral finish makes up for it. While one might readily criticize what appears to be an approach that plays up the big moments and merely gets by the rest, the choral climax is so magnificent that it overshadows--if only momentarily--such reservations.

BERNSTEIN, LEONARD/London Symphony; Sheila Armstrong, soprano; Janet Baker, contralto; Edinburgh Festival Chorus - 2-Columbia M2 32681 (1974); 2-Sony SM2K 47573 (1992) [89:29]*+ While little has changed stylistically in Bernstein's second version (for his first, see the 1986 volume, p.24), better soloists and stronger sonics greatly enhance this performance. The first movement is still extremely mannered, luftpauses are sometimes inserted and the main tempo is treated so flexibly upon its several returns that it lacks overall cohesion. Much drive and robustness enhance the dramatic effect, if sometimes to a fault. One specific alteration here is the use of the more majestic Tempo I ending rather than *schnell* tempo for the final descending triplets. The second movement is too labored but the Scherzo flows evenly and gracefully, although disjointed tempo shifts and clipped phrases (after #54) occasionally put the music's forward motion out of kilter. Janet Baker sings beautifully in the *Urlicht* movement. In the finale, improved sonics have their most significant effect. Although tempi are still extreme, the resulting sense of urgency and dramatic intensity serve the music quite well, even if precision and details are sometimes lacking. Choral forces are still less than fully satisfying, sounding rather thin and lacking depth, but few would remain unmoved by the stupifying climax at the close.

BERNSTEIN, LEONARD/New York Philharmonic; Barbara Hendricks, soprano; Christa Ludwig, contralto; Westminster Choir - 2-DG 423 395-2 (1988); 13-DG 435162- 2 GX13 (1992) [93:15]*+ Bernstein's fourth and last recorded performance (including the video recording with the VPO) is both as marvelous and self-indulgent as most of his performances of this symphony. He takes a weightier approach to tempo in the opening movement. Although as in his earlier recordings (see above) many passages are supercharged with emotion, some moments lapse into unexpected sluggishness (particularly when Bernstein becomes mushy, as in the second movement). Bernstein often rearranges tempi to suit his sense of the moment. For example, Tempo I at #11 of the first movement is nearly twice as fast as in Bernstein's earlier recordings. But few can elicit such excitement in this music as Bernstein, particularly in the outer movements. Those who decry his mannerisms or his frenetic temperament must admit that they are not left unaffected by his reading. Yet he may overdo it at times, as in the final variation of the second movement. Christa Ludwig is superb in the *Urlicht* movement, while her soprano counterpart sounds heavy and unsteady in the finale. That movement is a Bernstein forte, and the NYP and Westminister Choir are in top form for him. Brass add raw power to the muscular main material. The *Auferstehen* chorus that closes the work is utterly magnificent, Bernstein stretching out the line (at #48) for all it is worth in an overpowering conclusion.

BERNSTEIN, LEONARD/London Symphony; Sheila Armstrong, soprano; Janet Baker, mezzo-soprano; Edinburgh Festival Chorus - DG video 072 200-3 (rec. in Ely Cathedral, 1973) (1988) [92]** Although this videotaped performance never appeared on CD, it may be Bernstein's most thoroughly successful account of the Second. He adds more dramatic weight to the outer movements here than in his other recorded performances and tempers his earlier tendency to over-indulge in tempo fluctuations in lyrical sections. Slight hesitations (for instance in the second theme of the first movement and the main theme of the second) never seem extreme but greatly enhance the beauty of Mahler's lyricism. Yet Bernstein still thunders across the stage with enormous power, particularly in the outer movements (e.g., at #12 and the closing of the exposition of the first movement; and from the brass Dies Irae in the finale). He utilizes the frenetic energy that invigorates his earlier versions to create an even greater impression of fury and cataclysm (e.g., at 14:55+ of the first movement). Listen to how beautifully he handles the second period of the first movement's main theme, without exaggeration yet with lovely portamenti, while obeying the marking to continuously hold back the tempo (18:50+). The second movement is perfection itself. A relaxed tempo gives this lovely music natural fluidity, while greater intensity stimulates the forward motion (from #6 to #8). Hanging ever so gently on each note, the final variation is simply gorgeous. Equally appealing are the Scherzo and *Urlicht* movements, the latter enhanced by that marvelously rich vocal timbre of Dame Janet Baker. In the finale Bernstein demonstrates his unequalled brilliance as a Mahler interpreter. The opening whirlwind overpowers, and what follows is dazzling in its immensity. At times the camera catches a brief glimpse of the structural marvels of the Ely Cathedral, providing a perfect visual ambience for this magnificent music. Other camera effects are equally marvelous: shining a light from above on the soprano when she is first heard. The choral forces are excellent as well. When Bernstein literally suspends the tempo on the final *pesante* which climaxes the entire symphony, the effect is overwhelming. If there is a more inspiring version of this symphony, I have not yet heard (or seen) it!

BERTINI, GARY/Cologne Radio Symphony; Krisztina Laki, soprano; Florence Quivar, mezzo-soprano; Cologne Radio Chorus; Sudfunk Choir, Stuttgart - 2-EMI CDS 7 54384-2 (1992) [82:33]* The promise created by a dramatic and impassioned first movement is ultimately unfulfilled, notwithstanding an expressive second movement and thrilling outburst opening the finale. Bertini's forces seem on edge, insecure and de-energized by the time the concluding apotheosis occurs. Many beautiful moments linger in memory: weepy string timbres in the first movement, particularly effective in adding a note of longing to the heavenly serenity of the second theme; Bertini's attention to detail; fine balances (except for weak bass strings and timpani at times); and a majestic brass chorale on the Dies Irae chant in the finale. A few tempo choices are questionable: a very brisk conclusion to the final variation in the second movement (despite Mahler's clear marking to hold back) and the hurried pace at #46 in the finale where the chorus begins its build up to the *Auferstehen* climax (marked *langsam*, slowly) which requires Bertini to hold back at #47 where the direction is *piu mosso*. The Scherzo is similarly pressed, causing some disjointed tempo adjustments (before the trio), and brass have difficulty keeping together on descending triplets. Florence Quivar's Erda-like timbre and sensitive expressivity enhances the *Urlicht* movement, yet its broad main tempo becomes sluggish during the middle section (#3/3:05). After a fine opening outburst, the finale works well for a time in spite of rather fuzzy and boxy sonics and some uneven playing. But from the demonstrative march after #14 (*kräftig*) the performance loses dynamic power and intensity and is further weakened by the excessive speed with which some passages are rushed through. Why is the solo trumpet in the foreground during the distant *der grosse Appell*? While fine choral forces might have redeemed the performance, the principal tempo used during half of the finale becomes pressed and detracts from the sense of spiritual grandeur which their music should convey. At first the soprano scoops into the high notes, but she later controls this annoying vocal crutch. Florence Quivar is darkly expressive in her solo, but when she teams up with the soprano they run away with the tempo. After the final climax, which is spoiled by a jittery cymbal player who anticipates his entrance, everyone runs out of steam. Church bells ring out (even when they don't appear in the score) and the conclusion is unbearably loud and obtrusive, leaving us with a disappointing end to what might and should have been a more appealing performance.

BLOMSTEDT, HERBERT/San Francisco Symphony; Ruth Ziesak, soprano; Charlotte Hellekant, mezzo-soprano; San Francisco Symphony Chorus - 2-London 443 350-2 (1994) [80:19]+ With the deluge of recordings of the Second bombarding the market of late, each trying to make its mark, some may find this consistently straight, unaffected but well-played version to their liking. None of the performers have appeared in a Mahler symphony recording before, so it should not be a surprise that they approach their various tasks intelligently and diligently, if without any especially Mahlerian flair. Blomstedt makes no attempt to super-impose himself upon the score, rendering it simply and directly, with every marking carefully produced and audible. Whether the impression it makes goes beyond that of mere correctness is another matter. No attempt is made to overwhelm or ingratiate; only to play what is written in a romantic style. Blomstedt makes both orchestral and choral forces sound powerful as well as hushed when appropriate. These admirable qualities unfortunately do not add up to a memorable dramatic event. Blomstedt keeps his tempi consistently on the move, where some inflexion might have made a more lasting impression. A "no frills" reading is certainly valid, and if neatness counts, add another plus. But concentration on precision without any personal involvement can result in stiff, constricted playing, lack of spontaneity, and little dramatic impact. The soloists sing admirably, with youthful timbre and expressivity. With a curious nod to Mahler's directions, five minutes of silence follows the end of the first movement, which fills an entire disc.

BOULEZ, PIERRE/BBC Symphony; Felicity Palmer, soprano; Tatiana Troyanos, alto; London Philharmonic Choir; BBC Choral Society (perf. 1973 London) - 2-Documents LV 915/16; 2-Enterprise LV-915/16 (1993) [83:23] Unlike his usually objectified reading, Boulez treats the lyrical material in an extremely mannered fashion. There is much dynamic force and majestic power in the outer movements, but so many tempo adjustments are required that many sections seem uncoordinated. He frequently slows up within and at the end of melodic phrases, thereby causing the lyric music to become overly gushy and effusive. Yet some great dramatic moments do occur, even where the tempo seems on the sluggish side (e.g., in first movement, before the reprise from #18 at 14', and in the menacing passage for horns before the final descent). A light, steady flow creates a pleasant mood in the second movement. Some slow-ups and hesitations occur (e.g., m.30 at about 1'), but the overall effect is lovely. Affectations are almost completely absent from the third movement. An appropriate balance of forward motion and natural fluidity result in a fine reading, which captures the semitic character of this music without mannerisms. Although Troyanos seems a bit insecure in the lower register at first, she becomes stronger and more focussed as the *Urlicht* movement proceeds. Boulez sets a weighty pace for the middle section. The closing section works well, even though Troyanos has to break the line on her high E-flat on the final appoggiatura. At this inappropriate place, a change of CD is required.

A huge outburst gets the finale off effectively. Then Boulez ignores the caesura marking and runs straight into the off-stage horn calls (which are pitiously flat). The woodwind choir produces a strange tonal quality for its Dies Irae chorale, and the brass version that follows is over-blown. A mournfully sluggish tempo follows, during which high woodwinds replicates the "cry of a wounded soul" of the First Symphony's finale. Thereafter, Boulez may be the only conductor in memory to take the *sehr zurückhalten* (very held back) marking seriously, giving more prominence to the pressure Mahler directs be applied to the tempo that follows. After #11, too many unmarked tempo shifts throw the music off kilter. Boulez tries to empower the drama by turning up the volume on brass, as into #25 at c.15', during the cataclysmic "grave-opening" section, played rapidly here. A blaring, messy trumpet solo mars *der grosse Appell*. Boulez sets a very broad tempo for the choral closing. Horns mercilessly clip notes after #33 (m.499) and woodwinds are frequently too loud. Boulez stretches out the music to its breaking point for the final apotheosis, so that it is no wonder that the chorus peters out in the closing moments. He tries to make yet another adjustment by speeding up to #32, completely ignoring Mahler's directions to the contrary. Bells are inaudible at the close.

CASADESUS, JEAN-CLAUDE/Orchestre National de Lille; Teresa Zylis-Gara, soprano; Ewa Podles, alto; Stuttgart Oratorio Chorus - 2-Forlane UCD 16654/55 (1991) [83:14] This performance just scratches the surface of Mahler's glorious choral symphony. Playing is unimpressive, lacking in both idiomatic expression and coloristic sonority. From the onset of the first movement's main theme one is aware of a tonal brightness inappropriate for a funeral rite. Casadesus' approach is objective to the point of lacking depth and tragic pathos. Pacing is hurried in the first movement, where it should be broad and weighty. Strings and brass sound dry and pale, often clipping dotted rhythms. Dramatic tension is missing, caused by quick motion from one section to another, players rarely holding on to full note values and frequently swallowing phrase endings. Routine, squarish playing dulls the finish of the lovely second movement. Without tonal beauty the strings cannot make this movement as captivating as it should be. Constant agitation requires frequent adjustments (at #9 and before #11). Only the charming perfumery of the final variation seems to relax the performers enough to play with more ease. Similarly, the Scherzo has little to offer. While fluid motion is established at the outset, the trio section seems hurried and characterless. Celli "whoops" at 1:50 are not as elongated when repeated at 7:53. Inner parts are over-exposed at times (e.g., trombones at mm. 201-4). The big climax from #40 (8:39) starts stiffly but tries to get up a head of steam into the preview of the finale's opening outburst. After dashing through this orchestral explosion in strict rhythmic motion, a laggard bass string upbeat at #53 indicates exhaustion (at #53). A wobbly alto, who scoops into high notes constantly, and hollow, tarnished brass, who play without the slightest hint of solemnity, do little to enhance the *Urlicht* movement. In the finale, as in the first movement, one detects little dramatic quality. The temperament is extroverted and the timbre bright. Brass seem too restrained until the final climax, where they overpower the choral forces. Sometimes Casadesus relies on speed alone to add a measure of intensity to stronger sections (e.g., in the "grave-opening" sequence). Soloists try to sing over each other in an impassioned duet through which they fly so rapidly that a noticeable slow-up is necessary to bring the tempo back down to earth. The final *Auferstehen* chorus begins with impetuous vitality that soon dissipates. Casadesus holds up its progress when more speed is called for at *etwas schneller* (somewhat faster). A big bass drum roll swallows much of the ensemble during final choral climax. Certainly not a competitor, this performance leaves much of the symphony's drama in the lurch.

DE WAART, EDO/Netherlands Radio Philharmonic; Charlotte Margiono, soprano; Birgit Remmert, contralto; Netherlands Radio Choir - 2-RCA 74321 276032 (1995) [86:12]* RCA provides excellent sonic quality for most of this performance, especially notable for clarity and strong bass response. What a pity that the final climax is so unfocussed. DeWaart's reading is traditional, akin in temperament to Bruno Walter's. The outer movements are weighty and majestic, with strong dramatic impact. The three inner movements are stylishly handled and naturally paced. DeWaart has developed his Dutch forces into a fine Mahlerian ensemble and chosen soloists who perform admirably. In the opening movement a hefty pace never wears down the listener. DeWaart heeds Mahler's many markings, sometimes to a fault: why start the third 16th-note run in bass strings that begins the opening section slowly just to obey the accelerando marking, and then fail to do it later at #15 (11:20)? After a lovely slow movement, the ebb and flow of the Scherzo's triplet rhythms create the feeling of gently swaying breezes. How lovely the trumpets sing in thirds at #40. After a hushed, devotional *Urlicht*, the finale opens with a strong salvo despite covered brass sound. The Call in the Desert at 5:40 sounds like the faint cry of a little child. DeWaart keeps his forces under control, sometimes to a fault, as the music progresses to the choral section. He tries to heighten the drama by maintaining a broad tempo for the *Auferstehen* chorus, rather than urging it forward as the directions indicate. Consequently, the pace sometimes slackens (c. 31:20). The vocal soloists are accompanied rather mildly until their duet builds to a passionate climax. After hurrying through the approach to the closing of the choral section (marked *Langsam*), the ultimate climax is well done despite unfocussed sonics.

FRIED, OSKAR/Berlin State Opera Orchestra; Gertrud Bindenagel, soprano; Emmi Leisner, contralto; Cathedral Choir - Polydor 66290-300 (78s) (1924); Bruno Walter Society BWS 719; 2-Opal 821/22 (1984); 2-Pearl PEAS 9929 (1992) [83:48]*+
This important historical issue is the first recorded performance of a Mahler symphony (made from several sessions taken during the 1923-24 season). It is a monumental performance as well. In fact, Mahler is said to have attended and apparently approved of Fried's earlier performances of this work. Although tempi are very flexible, they are rarely exaggerated and usually thoroughly Mahlerian. Most impressive is Fried's careful attention to detail, clarity and precision which becomes more and more apparent with each listening. A majestic and dramatic reading of the first movement unrelentingly builds to a flaming conclusion. Luscious string portamenti grace the lilting Andante movement, which is perfectly juxtaposed to a relaxed reading of the Scherzo. Tempi here are restrained but contribute to a steady musical flow. An abrupt entrance to the segment of the Scherzo which anticipates the opening of the finale jerks the proceedings somewhat off course, so that what remains of the third movement thereafter seems uncomfortably slow, even epileptic. A quasi-religious atmosphere pervades the *Urlicht*. After a brisk opening, the finale gradually becomes more and more expansive, building in intensity as well as grandeur to a thrilling climax. Although vintage sound quality is undoubtedly harsh to the ear, the producers have done everything conceivable to make this historical issue as listenable as possible.

HAITINK, BERNARD/Concertgebouw Orchestra; Aafje Heynes, soprano; Elly Ameling, contralto; Netherland Radio Chorus - 2-Philips 802884/85 LY (1969); 2-Philips 420234 (1988); 10-Philips 434 053 (1992); 442 050 (1994) [81:25]* In a conservative, unaffected reading, Haitink fails to generate enough vitality and intensity to satisfy thoroughly. His restraint does not enhance this overtly romantic and highly dramatic score. Details are carefully rendered and orchestral playing is solid. Weighty tempi in the first movement add a measure of dramatic weight but sap life from the inner movements. The finale promises more than it delivers.

A strong beginning degenerates into an uneven mixture of well-conceived yet generally spiritless sections that at least have the virtue of noticeable details. Veiled, distant sonics are often at fault even if the sound is clean and clear. Some marvelous moments occur (e.g., the climax after #26). Ameling sings with much assurance and better vocal quality than her soprano counterpart. Choral forces are sometimes too distant and unfocussed. Brass overpower almost all the remaining forces in the final climax.

HAITINK, BERNARD/Berlin Philharmonic; Sylvia McNair, soprano; Jard Van Nes, contralto; Ernst-Senff-Chor - 2-Philips 438 935-2 (1994) [86:05]+ Haitink's approach has changed little from his earlier recording with the Concertgebouw, his conservatism remaining unaltered. The result is as disappointing as it is uninspired. Even one of the world's great orchestras, two of the best female vocalists available and remarkably clear and vibrant sonics, the performance only makes a strong impression in its closing moments. For the most part, one senses that the performance has been well homogenized. Much of the work's dramatic intensity is toned down; in its place we are offered precise, highly polished playing. Brass give the impression of having performed this work so often that it would take much more than the likes of Bernard Haitink to inspire them. While inner details come through because of close miking, this sometimes causes softer sections, where an atmosphere of heavenly serenity would be preferred, to sound too strong and bright (particularly in the finale). In the opening movement, Haitink emphasizes fluidity of line, foregoing a sense of dramatic urgency which might have impelled the music forward and heightened the dramatic effect. The three middle movements are pleasant enough, if lacking in stylistic nuance. Jard Van Nes graces the **Urlicht** movement with her splendid vocalism, despite an otherwise uninvolved performance from the orchestra, complete with an unduly sloppy glissando in solo violin at around 3:35. Taking full advantage of sonic techniques, the finale's opening promises much with an enormous orchestral outburst, which Haitink does not race through as others do. But even well-conceived tempi will not heighten either the intensity or dramatic impact of Haitink's reserved reading. Only at the electrifying march, marked *wit Mut* (with fury) (CD 2, Index 4 at 3:05) and the glorious final chorus does the performance come to life. Such magnificent moments are not enough to erase the memory of the lackluster character of much of the rest of this performance.

HORVATH, MILAN/Slovene Philharmonic; Olga Gracelj, soprano; Eva Novzak-Houzka, contralto; Academic Choir Ljubljana "Iwan Gorgan Kovacic" - 2-Digital Concerto CCD 669-79 (1992); 12-CCT 999701 (1992); ZYX Classics CLS 4193 (1993) [83:51]+ This obscure recording offers more than might be expected from its budget-label and little known performers. Horvat approaches the symphony in a traditional manner, emphasizing its noble grandeur with broad tempi in the outer movements. He keeps a tight rein on his forces, but seldom does his strong control cause the music to sag lifelessly. In fact, Horvat knows how to propel the music forward without abruptly changing tempo. How deftly he rounds out sections and integrates them with the structural framework of each movement, and how brilliantly he infuses climaxes with dramatic weight (e.g., the perfectly paced progression to the reprise of the first movement at Index 8). While sonics are far less than first rate, they do not seriously interfere with the performance. Even with a mediocre orchestra, Horvat can make a strong impression. Listen to the accents in strings toward the close of the first section of the second movement (Index 2 at 1:12+). He generates much energy in the third movement, pressing the main tempo foward urgently and intently. But it is in the massive finale that Horvat shows himself to be a thorough-going Mahlerian. His reading is consistently true to the spirit of the music. When the magnificent *Auferstehen* choral climax occurs, he holds on to a weighty tempo for dear life, producing an overwhelming effect with little help from weak choral forces. If he is able to generate so much intensity and excitement from these performers, one wonders what he could produce from a highly-polished orchestra, a stronger chorus and more secure soloists.

INBAL, ELIAHU/Frankfurt Radio Symphony; Helen Donath, contralto; Doris Soffel, soprano; Chorus of Norddeutsche Rundfunk; Dale Warland Singers - 2-Denon 60C37 7603-4 (1986); 16-Denon CO 72589/604 (1989) [85:02]+ Brilliant sound quality and clear, well-balanced inner voice are the most significant aspects of this recording. Given Inbal's brisk tempi, powerful climaxes appear as quickly as they disappear. One misses a sense of dramatic weight and depth in the first movement. Orchestral playing is deliberate and precise in the main march section and lovely and expressive in the lyrical second theme. But Inbal's tendency to hurry forward fast tempi, coupled with an annoying proclivity for clipping dotted rhythms, produces an underlying agitation that undermines the symphony's religious or philosophical character. A rigid manner of playing the principal thematic material works against establishing a funereal atmosphere in the opening movement. Consequently, the entire reading fails to respond to the movement's depth of feeling and dramatic import. While the second movement opens in a refreshingly warm and gentle manner, the main tempo presses forward nervously at times, creating an inappropriate uneasiness. Celli become over-emotive in the "Midnight Clear" counter-subject, overlooking their *p* marking. Inbal takes the *vorwärts* (forward) marking at #11 at such a clip that it seems almost violent, out of character with the lilting charm of this movement. Fast pacing mars what should be an easy-going musical flow in the third movement. Another *vorwärts* direction (at #37) is taken in double time. Later frequent tempo adjustments are required to bring the music anywhere near an appropriate pace. Exaggerated swells in strings after m.522 detract from otherwise fine progress into #53. Tempo control seems to be a problem here. In the *Urlicht* movement, notwithstanding an appropriately solemn mood, the severe, school-marmish tone of the contralto sounds more critical than prophetic. Donath is in harsh voice at first but becomes more expressive toward the close. Her pronounciation also leaves something to be desired ("je" is sung as "ge" with a hard "g").

After a fine opening outburst, Inbal intensifies the principal theme of the finale with nervous energy. Although inner voices are clearly audible, they sometimes become too pronounced (e.g., trombones at #5). Some moments contrast with Inbal's generally agitated manner, such as his weighty *kräftig* march. The ultimate apotheosis begins briskly at #, 46, despite the *langsam* marking. But extremely long ritards into #47 and at the highpoint of this section are insufficient to counteract the generally hurried pace. Choral forces are excellent here. However, the soloists are closely-miked, causing a dreadful mismatch between them and the chorus at the climax appearing at #48. Even bells are out of pitch. Trumpets dominate the final page in what seems like a never-ending final chord.

JANSONS, MARISS/Oslo Philharmonic Orchestra; Felicity Lott, soprano; Julia Hamari, contralto; Oslo Philharmonic Chorus; Latvian State Academic Choir - 2-Chandos CHAN 8838/9 (1990); 6595/6 [83:28]*+ For his first Mahler recording, Jansons offers an electrifying performance. Orchestral playing is articulate and sonics clear and bold. One senses youthful ardor that creates an underlying feeling of nervous energy. Jansons does not labor over the "funeral rites" opening movement, setting a pace that has internal motion without excessive speed. He takes care in rendering the welter of dynamic markings judiciously. Excellent sonics enhance the performance immeasurably, especially in brass-dominated climaxes. When a soft touch is required, Jansons imbues it with either romantic ardor or a hint of mystery (e.g., the coda of the first movement at 19:15). Although paced briskly, the second movement proceeds steadily and never gets overly agitated. Violins cover celli in the "Midnight

Clear" counter-subject and a slight hesitency ushers in the final variation. The Scherzo is also set at a breezy pace. Climaxes are never overbearing but set in perspective. At #37 [3:40] Jansons lets his forces loose suddenly at *vorwärts*, as if by magic. His treatment of the lyrical material beginning at 4:50 is warm and charming. Notice how subtly and deftly Jansons gradually moves the tempo forward from 5:58 to 6:20. The *Urlicht* movement begins as if from afar; both the contralto and the brass chorale are reduced to a bare whisper. A long-lined and hesitant tempo conveys a feeling of reverence here. What at first seems rather mild becomes more intense as the movement progresses, closing in heavenly serenity.

The massive finale opens with a powerful outburst, toward the close of which the harps are extremely pronounced. Some pianissimos become only faintly audible, as in the echos of the horn calls that follow. Woodwinds have a strangely nasal timbre in the Dies Irae chorale, and brass seem uncomfortably stiff in their later rendition of it. But the full-blown appearance of the Auferstehen theme at #11 is overpowering. Also impressive is the *kräftig* march segment [10:48], enhanced by pronounced martellato in strings and immense power (with bells *ad libitum*). Each of the orchestral climaxes is perfectly coordinated and makes an enormous impact. Choral forces are generally adequate, even if fortissimi are shouted rather than sung. The contralto, while expressive, has a pale, colorless timbre and atrocious pronunciation ("*glaube*" becomes "guloubu"). In the vocal duet, both soloists fail to generate enough passion to sound convincing. From there to the final choral climax, the performers seem to run out of steam. In spite of all this, one cannot deny that Jansons shows himself an intelligent Mahler interpreter.

KAPLAN, GILBERT/London Symphony; Benita Valente, soprano; Maureen Forrester, contralto; The Ardwyn Singers; BBC Welsh Chorus; Cardiff Polyphonic Choir - 2-MCA 2-11011/MCAD 11011 (1988) [82:37]*+ Gilbert Kaplan, millionaire publisher and Mahler lover, fulfilled a life-long dream: to conduct his favorite symphony. Without benefit of musical training, he put all of his resources into studying both the music and the art of conducting it. The result is quite remarkable given his amateur status. Having purchased an original manuscript, he made it his goal to follow Mahler's numerous directions to the letter as had none before. For the most part he has fulfilled this laudable mission. Rarely has so much care been taken with Mahler's many score markings. The often misread opening movement fairs best in this regard. Kaplan renders each and every special effect in good form, producing a strong and majestic reading of the funereal first subject and an expressively lyrical reading of the second. He balances inner voices extremely well, revealing elements often lost in other performances. Only occasional inaccuracies in string ensemble work are drawbacks here.

The next two movements are also striking. Kaplan's main tempo for the second movement is amiably relaxed, but strings sometimes sound rather removed from its charming lyricism. His pacing of the Scherzo is also well considered, even if a similar sense of business-like detachment impedes the fluency of the music. Once again, markings are rendered as written (few obey the marking *zurückkehren Tempo I*--move back into Tempo I--into #54), with the exception of rather strong violins for *pp* at #41.

Maureen Forrester, much honored Mahler vocalist, seems rather worn here. Her usually liquid vocal production and secure linear flow now requires frequent crutches and is infected with a slight wooble. But she still sings the *Urlicht* with a depth of emotion that few can match. Kaplan sets a fairly slow tempo and takes a back seat to his soloist. The magnificent finale, again correctly performed in its details, seems to lack atmosphere. Playing often sounds colorless, even bland. One also senses that the brass are kept under wraps. Yet most of the purely orchestral sections are well-conceived. While the distant band sounds boxy, the beautiful string melody that accompanies it is sung more lyrically than any other string passage in this performance. Power, weight and intensity figure much in the final moments of the orchestral section that precedes the entry of the chorus, but trumpets in poor intonation and messy articulation protrude at #30. The soloists seem too uninvolved to sing with conviction. Choral forces, on the other hand, perform impressively. The ultimate climax is thrilling, enhanced with *ad libitum* church bells (real ones, not tubular substitutes) and a strong organ pedal. Conductors who are only moderately acquainted with this work might turn to this recording for an example of what can be accomplished by careful attention to detail and total immersion in the score and Mahler's idiom.

KLEMPERER, OTTO/Concertgebouw Orchestra; Jo Vincent, soprano; Kathleen Ferrier, contralto; Holland Festival Chorus (1951) - 2-IGI-374; Decca D264D2; K264K22 2-Verona 27062/63 (1990) [70:51]*+ Recorded at The Holland Festival on July 6, 1951, this performance is characterized by Klemperer's tendency to rush through climaxes in an aggressive manner and make abrupt transitions. Orchestral playing is woefully inadequate, at its worst at the beginning of the finale and in the Scherzo. The level of dynamic intensity that Klemperer elicits in the outer movements is very impressive. Also well-wrought is the lovely Andante movement, enhanced by gorgeous string portamenti. This recording is worth its price if only for the appearance of that unequalled Mahler singer, Kathleen Ferrier, who graces the *Urlicht* and the finale with her superbly rich and expressive voice.

KLEMPERER, OTTO/Philharmonia Orchestra; Elizabeth Schwarzkopf, soprano; Hilde Rossl-Majden, contralto; Philharmonia Chorus - 2-Angel 3634 (1963); EAC-50033/34; 2-Angel CDM 69662 (1990) [79:13]*+ Despite better orchestral forces and the appearance of the incomparable Schwarzkopf, Klemperer's last studio recording is certainly an improvement over his VSO performance but falls short of what he was able to achieve at the 1951 Holland Festival. A forceful and dynamic first movement is characterized by a sense of urgency, even if sometimes unduly pressed. The *Andante* movement seems extremely cold and lacks concentration, while balance problems (especially in percussion), a restrained principal tempo and disjointed rhythmic treatment result in a stodgy Scherzo. Though Rossl-Majden is heavyish at top-range, she is still quite expressive in the *Urlicht*. But for fine singing, the finale also seems stuffy with sluggish tempi and little intensity. Much of Klemperer's earlier dynamic impulse seems to have decreased with age.

KLEMPERER, OTTO/Vienna Philharmonic; Galina Vishnevskaya, soprano; Hilde Rössl-Majden, mezzo-soprano; Vienna Singverein (perf. 13 June 1963, Vienna) - 2-Disques Refrain DR 910007 (1991); Music & Arts CD 881 (1995) [77:57]*
Klemperer's approach is much the same as in his recording of the same year with the Philharmonia Orchestra (see above): fiery and intense, tending to become extremely agitated in fast passages. His mastery of this score, evidenced in so many recorded performances, is never in doubt. Unfortunately, the radio transcription tapes from which this recording was taken severely distort orchestral timbres, causing woodwinds to sound mousy, brass and strings raw and ragged. Also troublesome are occasional lapses in control (e.g., in the opening of the finale). Yet the entire performance breathes life into the work with much fire and passion. A seemlessness in execution integrates Mahler's divergent material. And Klemperer creates an electricity in the outer movements that is unsurpassed, especially when he builds momentum and intensity as he drives a passage forcefully to its climax (e.g., first movement from 7:45). Yet all is not conveyed with agitation: witness the muscularity of the *kräftig* march of the finale (10:44) or the martial bearing of *mit einem Male etwas wuchtiger* (suddenly somewhat weightier) at 12:59 in the same movement. Klemperer moves quickly through the final moments with an urgency that achieves ultimate resolution at the cost of diminishing the impact of the soloists' passages and the grandeur of the choral apotheosis. Sonic troubles abound: an

inaudible distant band in the finale, poorly balanced choral forces and considerably confined dynamic levels, especially at climaxes.

KLEMPERER, OTTO/Bavarian Radio Symphony Orchestra; Heather Harper, soprano; Janet Baker, contralto; Bavarian Radio Symphony Chorus (perf. 1965) - 2-Nuova Era 6714-DM (1988); Hunt CD 703 (1990); Enterprise (Documents) LV 937 (1994) [78:56] ** Of the many recorded performances of the Second by Klemperer, this one may be his best. Balancing dramatic power with underlying intensity, he produces a thrilling performance. All of the players and singers associated with this marvelous performance are to be congratulated. Klemperer imposes more dramatic weight upon the first movement's main tempo than in his earlier versions. The tension implicit in Klemperer's approach adds a dynamic undercurrent which impels the music forward without making it too hard-pressed. Although this same quality affects the second movement, tensing up what should be a more relaxed linear flow, the tempo is steady and fluid. Overall, this movement works well without a hint of mannerism or unduly high dynamic levels. Beginning at a leisurely pace, the third movement's opening tempo picks up rather quickly, as does the volume. One senses a klesmer-like quality in Klemperer's treatment of movement's proto-Semitic material, but tempi sometimes lack pliancy. In the trio section, more flexibility results in greater warmth. After the scherzo theme returns, Klemperer takes a strangely weighty approach to the section preceding the enormous outburst that foreshadows the finale's opening, and, as a result, it takes him some time before he sets a comfortable tempo.

Baker sings beautifully in *Urlicht*, despite close miking. The finale is a veritable masterpiece. Klemperer again achieves underlying urgency without excessive speed. Most of the purely orchestral sections preceding the chorus' first entrance are simply magnificent: strong, weighty and thrilling, particularly at *kräftig* (powerful) and *mit einem Male etwas wuchtiger* (suddenly somewhat weightier). At #25, the music surges forward with driving intensity, nearly bursting its seams. The opening horn calls of *der grosse Appell* are not treated as call-and-echo but are played at nearly the same dynamic level. An audible miscue in trumpet on concert F# appears at m.455. Choral forces are superb for the most part, although close miking makes pianissimos nearly impossible. The vocal soloists rise to the occasion in their exciting duet, after which follows a thrilling final apotheosis. Thereafter, Klemperer moves swiftly through the final measures to a satisfying close.

KLEMPERER, OTTO/New Philharmonia Orchestra; Anne Finley, soprano; Alfreda Hodgson, contralto; New Philharmonia Chorus (perf. 16 May 1971, London) - 2-Hunt CDHP 590 (1991) [98:52]* Klemperer's last recorded performance is both his longest and, in some ways, his most disappointing. The orchestra has difficulty following him from the very beginning, resulting in numerous imperfections. As in his 1965 performances, and unlike his earlier readings, he gives more dramatic weight to the outer movements. Much of his earlier fire has peetered out, but he still can elicit the wonder and mystery that make the work so appealing and create enough tension to produce a stirring effect (e.g., in the first movement at c.11:25 into *vorwärts*). Despite failing health, Klemperer maintains control over these forces, especially at critical moments (e.g., his perfectly paced tempo increase to the return of the opening at #15 (c.12:50+). In the coda slight hesitencies underline the music's funereal character, and the build up to the final climax is thrilling. The second movement becomes stiff and tightly controlled at times, possibly caused in part by the first violin's wrong entry after #3. Following the cello variation, Klemperer relaxes the pacing and playing becomes more legato. In contrast, brass seem very stark, even frightening, at #6 in their version of the triplets of the second subject. At times the main tempo plods along heavily. The violins shine beautifully in the gorgeous final variation, intoxicating the atmosphere with exquisite musical perfumery. The third movement opens on the heavy side but picks up soon thereafter. A legato treatment of the main material replaces urgent impulse with grace and charm. One has the feeling of being caught in a nostalgic daydream (e.g., at 7:10+ to the return of the opening section). Yet when a precursor of the finale's opening outburst approaches, Klemperer sounds a call to arms (10:25) that culminates in an enormous explosion. The last violin segment contains a piercing upsurge after which all the musical material dissembles, to disappear with a strong final tam-tam whack.

Urlicht starts without a moment's hesitation and in a fairly brisk tempo that eases up for the brass chorale. Hodgson's lustrous voice is fitting for this song, but her reading would have been more satisfying had she been accompanied by better-tuned trumpets. Generally, volume needs to be toned down. The opening section should be heard as a soft whisper. At #3, the tempo becomes sluggish. A momentary lapse in coordination between singer and oboes before #5 is also disconcerting. Yet Hodgson gives a bravura performance of the passionate final section. A marvelous orchestral outburst opens the finale. Klemperer impresses just enough weight upon the main theme to bring out its majestic character. From around #11 the musicians have already exhausted themselves from Klemperer's controlled tempo. Moments of insecurity develop, partly because the tempo becomes sluggish and players probably find it more difficult to stay together. Brass seems to fade after *mit einem Male etwas wuchtiger* (suddenly somewhat weightier) and the funeral march appearing thereafter sounds like a pomp-and-circumstance procession. As the movement proceeds to a climax (c.#20), things begin to come apart. One is grateful for the CD break at #21. Slowish offstage trumpet calls follow, accompanied by a lovely lyric string line. With terrifying furiosity, the graves burst open and a soft cello intones the hope of resurrection. Unfortunately, the trumpets are hopelessly lost by now (after #27); loud timpani cover the trumpet calls during *der grosse Appell*. Choral forces sing softly, even if Ms. Finney does not. From #33 too much volume works against the intended effect of soft passages. While Ms. Hodgson sings well, her vocal counterpart has a weak, insecure top and needs crutches to reach it. As the music builds to the grand climax, timpani fail to appear (at #47) and cymbals seem to be reading from a different score, adding cymbal crashes to those Mahler provided. The result is a terrible mess, ruining what might have been a fine conclusion. As all settles down for the final chord, Klemperer begins it piano (instead of fortissimo) and crescendos to the final stroke.

KUBELIK, RAFAEL/Bavarian Radio Symphony; Edith Mathis, soprano; Norma Procter, contralto; Bavarian Radio Symphony Chorus - 2-DG 139 332/33; 13149-4GW (1968); 2-DG 413 524 (1988); 10-DG 429042 (1990) [76:18]** A magnificent performance! The approach is strong and weighty rather than agitated and intense. All of the majesty and drama of the first movement is revealed in one of the best-recorded versions ever produced. Few conductors handle the martial dotted rhythms as well as Kubelik. Only the second movement seems distractedly objective and less expressive. But the Scherzo moves along at just the right pace with a steady rhythmic flow, audible inner details and fine tempo modulations. Although Norma Procter sounds somewhat heavy and scoops into high notes at times, she is still very expressive. The finale is nothing short of thrilling, from the awesome power of the opening outburst to the overwhelming choral climax. While setting a slightly brisk main tempo, Kubelik keeps his forces under control without becoming rigid or constricted. Except for some brass intonation problems in the finale, orchestral playing is consistently excellent, choral singing vibrant and full-bodied. All these superb forces are reproduced to marvelous effect in clear, clean and reverberant sonics. This sleeper of a performance deserves more attention than it has generally received.

MAAZEL, LORIN/Vienna Philharmonic;Eva Marton, soprano; Jessye Norman, contralto; Konzertvereinigung; Vienna State Opera Chorus - 2-CBS I2M 38667; M2K-38667 (1984); 14-Sony SK14K 48198 (1992) [88:36]*+   Maazel turns in a most impressive reading, particularly for one of the most dramatic first movements ever recorded. All the weight and depth of this mini-music drama is emerges without the piece ever becoming dull or tiresome. Lyrical material is treated with great expressivity but without over-indulgence. Details are carefully and stylistically observed. Playing is consistently excellent even if the strings sound somewhat wiry. The *Andante* movement has a gorgeous linear flow (listen to those string swells and glissandi!) which exudes much warmth and charm. An easily paced Scherzo emphasizes the parodistic aspect of this music. Rarely have details been so carefully attended to and well recorded, but a loud hissing noise and buzzy bass response, especially annoying during strong climaxes, are disturbing. Tempi flow evenly and comfortably; tempo changes are never abrupt or unseemly.

Jessye Norman is deep-throated and profoundly expressive in the *Urlicht*, although the orchestral accompaniment is merely straightforward. Close-miking creates imbalances in the finale. Maazel's reading is so strong and well-conceived and choral forces so superb that such a minor detraction has little negative impact. Dramatic intensity is gradually increased to a magnificent climax, paced with perfect control and timing. Though Eva Marton is slightly harsh she sings with authority and Jessye Norman is simply exquisite. Unfortunately, Maazel rushes through the closing pages after the choral climax (a practice that has become more popular in recent years). One would think he was embarassed by this closing section and wished to move it quickly to its end. Yet in this recording, Maazel offers his most insightful and effective recorded performance a Mahler symphony.

MATA, EDUARDO/Dallas Symphony; Sylvia McNair, soprano; Jard Van Nes, alto; Dallas Symphony Chorus - 2-Audio Plus CDD 479 (1989); 2-Pro Arte CDD 479 [82:26]
Primarily a showpiece for Dallas' newly refurbished concert hall, this performance offers little beyond the routine. Playing is neither articulate nor stylish and Mata's rendition has no flair or interpretive nuance. Pale strings sonorities (hampered further by intonation problems in lower strings) and weak brass undermine any attempt to show off the new hall's acoustics. Mata races through the first movement without eliciting much dramatic impact. He maintains his straight-and-narrow interpretive approach where more flexibility is needed (in the Scherzo) and over-emotes where less would have been more welcome (in the main theme of the second movement). Tempo coordination lacks consistency at times (particularly in the main tempi of the first and third movements). Jard Van Nes sings expressively in a broadly paced *Urlicht* movement. The finale suffers from stilted playing and lack of cohesion. Brass seem underdone when strength is required (e.g., during the "grave-opening" sequence). With fierce intensity the orchestra builds to the climax marked *mit einem Male etwas wuchtiger* (suddenly weightier) after a brisk march tempo at *kräftig* (powerful), yet dramatic weight and breadth of vision are still lacking. Special aural effects during *der grosse Appell* provide a singular instance in which the new hall's acoustics enhance this performance. Choral forces maintain a proper *ppp* hush when they first appear. Mata takes his time, letting the music progress naturally from here, but the glorious apotheosis that crowns both this movement and the entire symphony is still too restrained.

MEHTA, ZUBIN/Israel Philharmonic; Florence Quivar, mezzo-soprano; Sylvia Greenberg, soprano; The National Choir "RINAT"; The Tel Aviv Philharmonic Choir; The 'Ihud' Choir - CDI 28901 (1989); Pickwick (PWK Classics PWK 1136 [77:48]; Kultura video 1229 (1989)   Recorded atop Mount Masada in Israel for a special Independence Day celebration, this performance is more significant as a national event than a musical one. The performance seems on edge, as if dangling from the mountainside. Tempi are pressed, playing is often ragged. Mehta stretches out the climaxes and hurries through intervals between them to heighten the tension, but with little success. Brass are surprisingly weak in the finale, and both high strings and celli sound rough-hewn. Probably under-rehearsed, the IPO's performance lacks coordination and concentration. Quivar is disconcertingly gutteral and wobbly, beginning *Urlicht* on the wrong note (C instead of D). Here tempi are brisk or heavy by turns. Percussion go all out during the opening and closing of the finale, but what happens in between has little effect. Frequent unmarked tempo adjustments are needed to corral generally hurried tempi. Trumpets and percussion often overpower at climaxes, resulting in little more than an orchestral blur. Mehta is not in full control of his forces. Dynamic levels are often too high (e.g., the choral section after #33) and playing often imprecise. Quivar is more expressive here than earlier, but the soprano seems lightweight and rather uninvolved. What this performance lacks is essentially what this music is all about: majesty, mystery and the joy of redemption. A curious failing for such a celebratory occasion.

MEHTA, ZUBIN/Israel Philharmonic; Nancy Gustafson, soprano; Florence Quivar, alto; Prague Philharmonic Choir - Teldec 4509-94545-2 (1994) [78:24]   Zubin Mehta here presents what seems more like a contrived theater work than a grandoise symphony with religious overtones. Rarely, if ever, does he plumb the depths or soar to the heights of emotion that the work demands, preferring to concentrate on orchestral precision. Consequently, this performance has that homogenized quality that sometimes results from such an orientation. Unlike his earlier Masada performance, all is now neat and tidy, but lacks spontaneity, adventursomeness and vision. Mehta glosses over the symphony's climactic passages, especially in the finale. This performance has all the earmarks of modern commercialism: no risks, all the notes set in place, and sonics brilliant and swept clean of any distractions (even those appearing in the score). Florence Quivar, with her special manner of vocal production, is closely miked in the *Urlicht* movement, and sings adequately against a standardized accompaniment. Nancy Gustafson sounds too imposingly operatic to convey the feeling of deep longing for redemption which the text connotes. Mehta handles the finale, as he does the entire symphony, in such an ordinary, disinterested manner as to compromise any of the theatricality his treatment of the opening movement promised. The last movement just happens: strong passages are loud but not powerful, calmer ones soft but not either endearing or serene, and climaxes unimpressive.

NEUMANN, VÁCLAV/Czech Philharmonic; Gabriela Beňačková-Čápová, soprano; Eva Randová, contralto; Prague Philharmonic Chorus - 2-Supraphon Pro Arte 2PAL 2011; 2CDD-2011 (1981); Supraphon SUP 0020 (1988); 111 971 (1993); 11-SUP 111860 (1994) [75:06]   Neumann's approach is objective, cold and impersonal. Sharply clipped rhythms and a tendency to press tempi are also pervasive characteristics of this performance. Recorded at a high volume level, the stronger sections are merely loud rather than powerful or dramatic. String playing sounds jagged, not always in sinc, and brass are sometimes over-balanced. Soloists are harsh and guteral, while the chorus is sometimes messy and lacks sufficient tonal breadth. The choral climax of the finale fails to generate excitement despite high volume. Erratic and uneven, this performance also lacks cohesiveness.

NEUMANN, VÁCLAV/Czech Philharmonic; Livia Aghová, soprano; Marta Benacková, contralto; Prague Philharmonic Choir - Canyon Classics EC 3692 (1994) [76:38]
    While the CPO seems to handle Mahler's idiom more convincingly than in Neumann's earlier recording (see above), with less tendency to clip phrases and more marcato in brass, Neumann's reading is no less detached and ineffectual. Only the opening movement, despite

somewhat pressed tempi, has a moderate degree of dramatic strength and vigorous playing. Neumann leaves little room for the music to breathe, debilitating what should be visceral strength, cooling any warmth of expression and avoiding emotive outpouring. Inflexible tempi sometimes cause stagnation to set in, yet pacing is often on edge. Neumann rarely underlines a highpoint or makes much of the symphony's dramatic effects, remaining indifferent to its aesthetic and spiritual essence. At the height of a moderately paced *molto pesante* build-up into the reprise, he takes the final snap not in Tempo I as written but as if part of the long ritard. The result sounds like two emphatically demonstrative quarter-notes instead of two eighths. The main tempo of the second movement is more moderato than andante, and certainly not *sehr gemächlich* (very relaxed). Little of the charm and grace of this movement survives Neumann's straight-laced treatment. Conversely, the Scherzo seems on the lumpy side, its slackened pace causing stiffness at times, despite steady motion. Following an unexpressive *Urlicht*, the finale opens not with a bang but a whimper. When the main theme first appears, Neumann turns the tempo marking around, moving forward instead of holding back as Mahler directs. Yet more speed does not necessarily generate more excitement or urgency. Nor does the weak chorus (though closely-miked) or the uninvolved vocal soloists provide any enhancement. The best moment here occurs before the "*O Glaube*" solos, where Neumann generates a warmth of expression felt before only in the first movement. A totally uneventful *Auferstehen* chorus closes this lackluster performance.

OZAWA, SEIJI/Boston Symphony; Kiri TeKanawa, soprano; Marilyn Horne, contralto; Tanglewood Festival Choir - 2-Philips 420 824-2 (1986); 14-Philips 438 874 (1995) [79:49]
With the superstars and high-level technology that this recording offers, it should have been more successful. Ozawa's reading is uninvolved and uninteresting. The first movement passes routinely, requiring more blood and sinew. Moments of enormous dramatic power seem underdone, while softer ethereal passages lack atmosphere. Bland brass playing, heavy treatment of dotted rhythms and a sluggish main tempo are primarily at fault. Much the same can be said for the two movements that follow: colorless playing, characterless treatment, brisk tempi and lack of nuance. While Marilyn Horne is a superb choice for the *Urlicht* (even if she sounds a bit unsteady), Kiri TeKanawa could only have been chosen for her popularity. She puts very little into her part, even shouting at the end of her duet with Horne in the finale. Little if anything happens in that magnificent movement. After beginning with a huge blast and hurtling past what remains of the cataclysmic opening, Ozawa returns to his routine manner. Orchestral lapses (mostly in the brass, with an additional flute miscue during *der grosse Appell*) may result from lack of concentration in this uninvolved performance. The massive orchestral climaxes before the entrance of the chorus are very rapid (particularly at *mit einem Male etwas wuchtiger*, suddenly somewhat weightier), yet such dizzying speed fails to produce much excitement. Beginning in very broad tempo, the chorus makes a good impression at first, singing their opening music softly and clearly, but an air of mystery is missing. The male chorus races through their part in an agitated manner, as if impatient for the redemption to come. Even the final apotheosis seems rushed and the bells that chime in the glorious conclusion are completely inaudible.

RATTLE, SIMON/City of Birmingham Symphony and Chorus; Arleen Auger, soprano; Janet Baker, contralto - 2-EMI CDCB 47962 (1987) [85:44]** Simon Rattle has become one of the most highly acclaimed Mahler conductors since Bernstein. His reputation is mostly due to his unique reading of this symphony. He rethinks many aspects of the symphony and relates his sometimes unusual but always interesting interpretive nuances with conviction. Even though there are differences of opinion regarding details, the overall effect is highly engaging and impressive for its stimulating ideas. A sense of urgency pervades the entire performance, only moderated by orchestral and choral limitations. The opening contains some troublesome quirks: starting the third set of 16th-note runs in string bass slowly so as to adhere to accel. marking; heavy emphasis on sforzandi in woodwinds on the first theme; clipped dotted rhythms detracting from the intended majestic character of the music. But Rattle is consistently successful in delivering an abundance of dynamic power, forcefulness and intensity. He clearly views this movement as based upon extreme contrasts. Wild furiosity resolves into a maddeningly slow molto ritard on flatted-ninth chords into the reprise. Rattle paces the second movement briskly, creating an undercurrent of agitation that undermines the lilting quality of its principal theme. Even if he eases up for the cello variation and hesitates after #11 without benefit of a marking, pacing remains generally on edge. There is even sudden unexplainable agitation in the middle of pizzicato section (at #13). Setting a fine tempo for the Scherzo, Rattle holds his forces to the written pianissimo for the main subject, a marking so often ignored. Dotted rhythms are slightly stiff and ensemble work not always precise. Listen to that audacious bassoon after #34, recalling the haughty clarinet "*keck*" from the First Symphony's funeral march movement; and the usually buried flute trills before #42 that come through and decorate the musical fabric. Some minor technical problems get in the way, however: timpani are too distant; trumpets are slightly off pitch; and strings and *ruthe* are not in sync.

With nary a moment's hesitation, Rattle jumps into the *Urlicht* movement. Baker is in fine voice, singing clearly and securely. Only an overly loud oboe detracts from this otherwise entrancing interlude. Some restraint imposed on the opening orchestral outburst of the finale (despite loud tam-tams) makes it less than an ultimate experience. Even though Rattle sets a weighty pace for the Dies Irae, certain segments are noticeably untidy (#6-7). The general effect is strong and dramatic, but some moments get lost in an effort to overwhelm (e.g., the percussion swell to #14). Extreme tempo contrasts appear between the section marked *mit einem Male etwas wuchtiger* (suddenly somewhat weightier) and the rapid *piu mosso* at #20 (where the complex texture becomes muddled). Much excitement is generated into #26. Notice how deftly Rattle slows up for the Dies Irae fragment before #27. Balances seem more engineered than natural in the segment that contrasts the distant band with a lyrical string line. Choral forces are youthful and enthusiastic. Baker sounds uninvolved at first but seems to plead for redemption into #44. Even if dynamic levels still are confined, the final *Auferstehen* chorus and magnificent closing scene are imposing. Rattle seems to consider the section beginning at #51 (which follows upon the final choral statement) to be the movement's ultimate climax, placing more emphasis upon it than is usually given. An emphatic, rather than sharp cut-off closes one of the most interesting readings to come along in years.

SCHERCHEN, HERMANN/Vienna State Opera Orchestra; Mimi Coertse, soprano; Lucretia West, contralto; Vienna Academy Chorus - 2-Westminister XWN 2229; WST-206 (1958); MG S6204; 2-MCA Classics MCAD2-99833 (1991); 2-Theorema TH 121 203-4 (1993); Palladio PD 4180 (1994)*+   Tempi are on the slow side: lugubrious in the first movement and replete with affectations; stodgy but generally effective in the middle movements with exaggerated tempo changes in the Scherzo. A lovely last variation in the Andante is worth noting. The *Urlicht* movement is extremely broad, sometimes so much so that it seems to virtually stand still. While the orchestral section of the finale is quickly but unevenly paced, tempi become extremely heavy in the chorale section. A very personal approach is taken to each section, and the overall effect seems disjointed due to extreme variations of fast and slow tempi. Choral forces are effective but soloists have some difficulties (particularly the scooping soprano). The final climax is stretched to the breaking point and bell sounds are distorted at the close. Careless playing is a major detraction. Yet the several interesting interpretive nuances are worthy of high praise. Scherchen displays his unique ability to effectively balance flexible tempi with control and cohesiveness of approach. The CD reissue eliminates much of the sonic distortion that tarnished the original LP issue.

SCHURICHT, CARL/Orchestra & Chorus of National de Paris; Edith Selig, soprano; Eugenia Zareska, contralto (perf. 1958) - 2-Melodram CD 27504 (1990) [81:51]+
Schuricht's reading differs little from his 1960 performance (see below), but he seems to have more difficulty with this Parisien ensemble than he had with the Hessian forces. Sonic quality is below par: by turns distorted, tinny, harsh and veiled. The first movement seems on edge in the first subject but calms nicely from the lyrical second theme. Tempi are generally brisk, intensifying the electricity that Schuricht's reading engenders. The last note seems to overlap with the opening of the next movement. Here expressive playing with much portamento is pleasing, even if the celli sound wooden and dry in the Midnight Clear variation. Except for a few miscues (e.g., the horn's early entrance into #37) and excessively high volume levels, the Scherzo breezes along effectively. Schuricht adds a slight rallentando into the huge outburst that anticipates the finale. In the *Urlicht* movement, after some early pitch problems, the contralto settles in nicely, gracing her lines with a mellow and dark timbre. Would that she were not so closely miked. A distorted, tinny cymbal crash ushers in the finale, the opening whizzing by without much impact. A flat glockenspiel sticks out like a sore thumb, and close-miking detracts from what should be a sombre mood thereafter. Schuricht produces moments of great dramatic power (at #7 and *mit einem Male etwas wuchtiger*), although he hurries past sections which might have developed more effectively had they had a chance to unfold without being under such pressure (at #11). The distant band section is taken extremely slow but the build-up to the "grave-opening" section is monumental. As one might expect, probably the most effective aspect of the entire performance comes at the choral ending. The chorus and soloists sing with passion and depth. Schuricht keeps the tempo under control (even if at #46 he ignores the *langsam* marking for a quicker pace), and, after a long pause before #47, he broadens the tempo, giving immense dramatic weight to the glorious *Auferstehen* climax.

SCHURICHT, CARL/Hessian Radio Symphony; Ruth Margret Puetz, soprano; Marga Hoffgen, alto; Frankfurt Singakademie Chorus; Hessian Radio Symphony Chorus (perf. 1960) - 2-Originals SH 819/20 (1994) [83:25]+ Given the many orchestral imperfections and weaknesses in the choral ensemble, Schuricht renders an interesting and generally well-conceived performance. He treats the opening movement as a traditional allegro, set in a quicker main tempo than is customary. Within that context, modulations are seemless and well-turned. Fierce intensity develops, giving the movement an almost horrific aspect at times. That characteristic is felt occasionally even in the succeeding movements. The Hessian orchestra manages as best it can, but imprecision, general overplaying of wind parts and intonation problems occur. After the opening outburst, the finale settles in at a broad, majestic pace. Only at #6 (4:22) where the woodwinds intone a fanfare (repeated at #11) might one question Schuricht's tempo choice. He moves quickly through this section, ignoring Mahler's notation to hold up on the triplets in winds. Restraining his forces early on to heighten the impact of the final chorus, Schuricht then has some difficult controlling them. After the disc change (at #21), the trombone becomes confused during the "Call in the Desert" segment, because of the sudden shift by Schuricht to an extremely slow tempo. The alto soloist gets through "*O Glaube*" well enough, notwithstanding her being accompanied by a flat English horn. The vocal duet is not pressed, obeying Mahler's direction *aber nicht eilen* (but not fast). The choral climax is moderately effective. But where are the cymbals at mm.721 and 724? Even with its flaws, this performance shows that Schuricht understood the basic aesthetic perspective of Mahler's idiom.

SEGERSTAM, LEIF/Danish National Radio Symphony; Tina Kiberg, soprano; Kirsten Dolberg, alto; Danish National Radio Choir - 2-Chandos CHAN 9266/67 (1995) [91:24]
Segerstam's self-indulgent style, with its highly conscious, but rarely successful attempts to overwhelm, produces a heavy-handed, affectatious performance of the Second. He lumbers through the first movement sluggishly, except in a few passages (*vorwärts* at #12) where he whizzes by in an almost maniacal rage. Most of the movement plods along in dirge-like fashion, never approaching the *maestoso* marking Mahler placed at its head. A long hesitation on the upbeat that begins the second movement provides a hint of what is to come: a tiresomely sluggish movement laden with mannerisms. Lacking any sense of motion and replete with awkward luftpausen (the cello counter-theme after the pizzicato trio is overplayed), the movement projects an odd combination of characteristics: both lack of inspiration and self-indulgence. For the Scherzo movement, Segerstam sets a lively pace and maintains it relentlessly throughout; however, except for an explosive outburst at 8:05, little offered here is especially evocative. After a relatively uninteresting *Urlicht* (sung nicely by the alto soloist), Segerstam offers one of the most uninspired renditions of the finale in recent memory. He tries to stretch out every phrase, climactic section and lyrical passage to such a degree that this sprawling movement often threatens to collapse of its own weight. With few exceptions (e.g., the "grave-opening" section at 15:37) his efforts result in increasing the feeling of tedium an elongated reading of an already extensive movement can cause. So many misguided mannerisms occur here that they might fill a monograph (*nicht schleppen* is read as *piu mosso*; awkward hesitations are made on the quarter-note/eighth note triplets at #6 and #11; ritards are stretched to the breaking point, etc.). One senses that the funereal character of the opening movement hangs like a dark cloud over the entire performance. Choral forces perform admirably but are ill-used. The DNRSO remains slightly below the level of sonic dimension required by Mahler's music, despite Chandos' efforts to make compensating technical adjustments. The closing section is drawn out for all it is worth, with trumpets blaring and percussion thundering out. If this be resurrection, is it worth the effort?

SINOPOLI, GIUSEPPE/Philharmonia Orchestra & Chorus; Brigitte Fassbaender, mezzo-soprano; Rosalind Plowright, soprano - 2-DG 415-959-2 (1985/86) [85:47] *
The performers do not seem to give their utmost in this performance. Generally hurried tempi combined with temperate dynamic levels in major climactic sections reinforce this impression. A general sense of agitation is noticeable from the very beginning with rapid 16th-note runs and a clipped, snappy first theme. Thus the *maestoso* character of the first movement is sacrificed to underlying tension, and dramatic power succumbs to restrained dynamic levels. Expressivity abounds in the heavenly second subject, with a few affectatious touches added for good measure. The same feeling of undue haste characterizes the second movement, counteracting the lilting quality of its thematic material. As if to emphasize the romantic quality of this music, Sinopoli consistently employs manneristic luftpauses at thematic highpoints. While the Scherzo seems more naturally fluid, the result is merely listless and bland. Brass seems uninvolved (e.gs., at #39 and #49). In *Urlicht* despite a *mosso* tempo, the brass chorale sounds majestic and solemn. Fassbaender sings admirably for the most part, even if she sounds slightly gutteral and rushes too abruptly into the high E-flat appoggiatura at the close. An enormous deluge of sound follows the opening cymbal crash of the finale, pressed urgently forward in high-powered dynamics. The orchestra appears to be more involved here, yet too often brass lack the nobility of tone and bearing that this work demands. One misses the sense of might and majesty that should come through in the *kräftig* (powerful) and *mit einem Male etwas wuchtiger* (suddenly somewhat weightier) segments. Balances are sometimes troublesome, both when welters of sound flood over important inner voices and when too much distance separates the listener from the internal band. Notwithstanding these detractions, some

powerful moments do occur (e.g., the outburst at #20 with very strong percussion and trombone). But a sense of spaciousness is missing from *der grosse Appell* (the Last Trump) section. The choir (probably chosen due to the location of the recording, Tokyo) is ill-suited to this work. The singers have difficulty with the language as well as the idiom and are often untidy at entrances. Sinopoli tries to elicit some emotion from the vocal solos, but his tempo choices--presumably employed for this purpose--are at odds with Mahler's directions (at #37, marked *a tempo*, he slows down and becomes more hesitant). A broad-lined legato treatment of the ultimate climactic section fails to impress. At the closing bars of the *Auferstehen* chorus, a fine reverse swell is ruined by being punctuated as it diminishes by a frightfully exposed timpani stroke. And where are the *fff* horns before #49? Sinopoli adds an unbearably long crescendo to the final chord, as if to make one last attempt to convince the listener that he or shes has in fact witnessed a great music drama.

SLATKIN, LEONARD/Saint Louis Symphony Orchestra & Chorus; Kathleen Battle, soprano; Maureen Forrester, contralto - 2-Telarc DG 10081/82; CD-80081/2 (1983); 2-Telarc CD-80081/2 (1985) [81:19]* Although Slatkin provides a basically fine performance, Telarc's usually high standards of sound quality are missing here. Muffled, constricted sonics and buzzy bass at high levels have an extremely negative impact. Slatkin's overall approach is somewhat cool and controlled; the effect being rather stiff, lacking vitality and intensity at times (particularly in the second movement). More impressive is the excellent balance of orchestral and vocal forces and careful attention to details, highlighting important inner voices too often buried under the weight of the full orchestra. Despite Slatkin's general detachment, some impressive moments occur in the first movement. An understated Scherzo moves to a rapid close. The *Urlicht* movement finds Maureen Forrester in slightly worn condition (she sang much better earlier under Walter). After a gigantic if rather quick opening, the finale goes fairly well despite muddy sound in the climactic sections. Battle sounds young and fresh and Forrester is impressive as usual. Choral forces are on the thin side but sing adequately. Slatkin manages to elicit a powerful if not very dramatic choral climax enhanced by an audible organ.

SOLTI, GEORG/London Symphony & Chorus; Heather Harper, soprano; Helen Watts, contralto - 2-London CSA 7217 (1966); 2-London 425005 (1991) [80:44]* This is still a great performance, even if sonically surpassed by Solti's later version (see below). A strong and energetic first movement is embellished by sharp, clear sound quality and a thoroughly idiomatic reading. Solti's intense, aggressive style adds forward thrust yet still achieves weight and breadth. The *Andante* movement is light and charming even if sometimes slightly pressed. A smooth linear flow underlies the Scherzo; but the trio is too quick and affects the return of the scherzo material by forcing it into a faster pace than previously applied. Helen Watts is full-bodied and expressive in a *mosso* treatment of *Urlicht*. The finale is stark and intense, ending in a magnificent climax with a fine chorus and generally solid soloists (Harper has some difficulty at extreme ranges but Helen Watts is very impressive).

SOLTI, GEORG/Chicago Symphony & Chorus;Isobel Buchanan, soprano; Miri Zakai, contralto - 2-London LDR 72006; 41020-2 H2 (1981); 10-London 430 804 (1992) [80:48] *+ A high-powered version of Solti's earlier effort, this recording has the "virtue" of extremely loud sonic levels and digital technology (except for some strange sounds in strings at times). This is the version for those who like their Mahler to explode in sonic cataclysm. A very strong, taut if sometimes disjointed first movement is followed by a more relaxed and comfortable *Andante*. The superb sound quality greatly enhances the details of the Scherzo, rendered basically as in the earlier version. The only disadvantage in the last two movements is the less than adequate soloists (imprecise and insecure as well as closely-miked). The finale is very exciting, filled with depth and power, making the best possible use of sonic dimension and the intenity generated by Solti's nervous energy. The closing section is unforgettable.

STOKOWSKI, LEOPOLD/Philadelphia Orchestra; Veronica Tyler, soprano; Maria Lucia Godoy, mezzo-soprano; The Singing City Choir (perf. 9 Nov. 1967) - Leopold Stokowski Society of America LSCD-26 (1989) [77:16]+   This issue is more important for its historical value than for the performance, given during Maestro Stokowski's waning years when he was not always physically able to control the forces at his command. As an experienced Mahlerian, he can give a coherent and conceptually sound reading that has much dynamic force, yet here, within the context of generally brisk tempi, he makes many quirky tempo adjustments. He creates a few memorable moments in the opening movement: a gorgeous second theme at 6:32 (listen to the celli at 7:35+ for their purity of tone) and a magnificent approach to #11 from 10:10. Some sections come in like a lion (with rapid urgency) and go out like a lamb (with unmarked ritards). Too often speed serves in place of underlying tension, even if it does generate some excitement (e.g., after #18). Stokowski's frequent shifting between rapid propulsion and demonstrative underlining make lengthy passages feel awkward --as if the musical material was pushing and pulling against itself. He skips through the *molto pesante* cadence into the reprise, taking no notice of the tempo marking. But his treatment of the build up to the final climax of the coda is magnificent (21:49). The descending triplets on the final page are played rapidly. A charming reading of the second movement follows, highlighted by a soft and warm "Midnight Clear" counter-subject in celli. For some reason, Stokowski dampens the second snap in timpani that opens the Scherzo movement. An energetic tempo works better here, even if it becomes almost breathless at times. Our sympathies are with the clarinet soloist, whose miscue on the main theme is part of the toll taken by the excessive speed. In fact, many of the movement's highlights are glossed over in the haste of the moment. Stokowski also sets a quick pace for the *Urlicht* movement. Godoy has a soft and pleasing voice but has difficulty with the language as well as her entrances.

Stokowski's cuts in the finale (#7-10; 21-22, before #51) are simply unpardonable. Again tempi are generally rapid. While an energetic pulse stirs up some excitement, problems with control over these large forces are exacerbated by the maddening pace set here. The orchestra runs out of energy long before the chorus' first appearance, leaving little strength in reserve for the magnificent closing moments. From #37, a broader pace finally asserts itself (easing up further on the violins' high A-flat before #38) leading into one of the best renderings of the section preceding the alto solo in recent memory (to #39). The alto sings with little expression in contrast to the lovely soprano solo. Shouting much of their declamation, the male voices sing unmusically. Stokowski has the chorus accompany the duet using Mahler's ad lib choral line. After adding a ritard at the end of this section (against Mahler's instructions not to let the tempo drag), Stokowski loses his choral forces to total fatigue. They do more shouting than singing as Stokowski keeps them moving. The ultimate climax is marred by blaring, cracking trumpets. Church bells are wonderful in the final pages, but they cannot erase the memory of the many deficiencies of this performance. A long, loud crescendo that begins measures before it is marked finally puts this performance to rest.

SUITNER, OTMAR/Staatskapelle Berlin; Magdalena Hajossyova, soprano; Uta Priew, alto; Chorus of the German State Opera, Berlin -2-Eterna 827875 (1985); 2-Tokuma 32TC-104/105 (1986) [78:14]   This merely passable performance from what was once East Germany is most notable for the energy and intensity which heighten the impact of the outer movements. Tempi are generally pressed and agitated, sometimes requiring disconcerting adjustments. Suitner elicits demonstrative playing from his orchestra when called for. He keeps his eye on the score generally but not consistently. Strings lack the warmth and polish which might have enhanced such segments as the lyrical second theme of the first movement and the string variations of the second. One senses a lack of consistency in tempo choices in the outer movements, so that in the opening movement the passage at #16, marked *sehr langsam*, is paced more like the main tempo (*allegro maestoso*). Yet segments requiring a more muscular treatment are sometimes given due weight (e.g., in the finale at #11). Inner movements are presented in a routine manner. The second movement lacks warmth and expressivity, and even slight affectations (into #14 and at the end of the phrase at m.274) fail to inject a sense of charm or delicacy. The middle section (at #6) has a racy, hard edge, more harsh than energetic. At first, the Scherzo seems to have caught the fever pitch that made the first movement sound so anxious and agitated, but it calms down slightly after #33. The main tempo seems pressed, causing some imprecision in string figuration. Again unmarked tempo adjustments indicate lack of control. In *Urlicht*, a light, soft and youthful alto soloist sings with little expressivity and too much vibrato in the higher register. After a fierce and strong opening, the finale proceeds mildly, offering little to savor. Sometimes Suitner rises to the occasion such as in his demonstrative treatment of the strong and majestic music at #11. Brass and volume levels are generally too restrained. As a result such powerful sections as *mit einem Male etwas wuchtiger* (suddenly somwhat weightier) seem underdone, in spite of rapid tempi. Suitner races through much of the orchestral music preceding the choral section. But when the choral forces appear the previous *mosso* temperament that lay beneath the surface of this reading gradually eases up, so that by the return of the main theme at #34 Suitner settles into a broad tempo that is well-considered. Choral work from there is well done, clear and soft. After cursory readings of the vocal solos, the vocal duet enlivens the proceedings. Suitner presses forward as the music builds to the ultimate climax (from #42). Thereafter, he readjusts the tempo once again following a full stop at #47. Despite such an uneven performance, the symphony's culminating *Auferstehen* chorus comes off in fine fettle.

TEMIRKANOV, YURI/Symphony Orchestra and Chorus of the Kirov Opera & Ballet Theater, Leningrad; Yevgenia Gorokhovskaya, mezzo-soprano; Galina Kovaleva, soprano - 2-Melodyia C10-154485-8 (1982) (LP) [80:35] Both a routine reading and too many technical problems keep this version from becoming a serious competitor. With only minor exceptions, mostly in the finale, Temirkanov handles the work in a straightforward manner, sometimes inflexibly and often impersonally. Little subtlety of line or refinement of nuance occurs. The Kirov ensemble is unsuited to Mahler's idiom, sounding lightweight and playing stiffly in apparent discomfort. A sense of detachment pervades that is most disconcerting in the lyrical sections. An occasionally heavy emphasis on brass (e.g., #17 of the first movement) is also unattractive. Following the upbeat which opens the second movement, Temirkanov adds an awkward hesitation, as if to spice up his generally lackluster reading. Otherwise, his reserved demeanor is probably responsible for the rigid, inflexible manner of orchestral playing and the lack of shadings in dynamic levels, too often resulting in unvaringly high volume. Much the same can be said of the scherzo. After quickly deadening the timpani snaps that open the movement, Temirkanov sets a strict tempo in a reading that tightens phrasing and causes the musical flow to stiffen.

Even an expressive mezzo-soprano with a fine voice cannot save *Urlicht* from being below par. Dynamic levels are generally too high. Although the main tempo works well, Temirkanov chooses to speed up at #4 and #6, causing too much agitation in the closing section. The finale opens with a strange bass string run (what notes are being played here?) that comes to a complete hault before the orchestral outburst. Then the tempo becomes extremely rapid until another sudden, lengthy pause is taken for the comma at #2. From there dynamic levels are rarely below *mf* despite frequent *ppp* markings (at #6). The main segments of the orchestral section have enough weight and power to pass muster (if one can ignore imprecise and piercing brass playing). Sometimes too much agitation detracts from the dramatic effect (e.g., in the build up to the huge outburst at #26). The side break, mislabelled on the jacket as occurring before the chorus' first appearance, actually happens before #29 during *der grosse Appell* (the Last Trump) segment. Choral forces are passable but recorded too strongly to sound appropriately hushed for their initial appearance. Thereafter, too many flaws make the concluding section as unattractive as the rest of the performance: closely-miked soloists, an overmiked male chorus, a screaming soprano heard over the final chorus, poor choral balances (emphasizing the tenors' A-flat over the sopranos D-natural at #49) and a routine climax.

TENNSTEDT, KLAUS/London Philharmonic & Choir; Edith Mathis, soprano; Doris Soffel, contralto - 2-EMI/Angel DS-3916; 4X2S-916; EAC 90081/82; CDC-47040 (1979); 10-EMI CMS7 64471-81 (1993) [87:49]* Frequently self-indulgent in the extreme, Tennstedt's over-romanticized approach can appeal only to those who see Mahler's early symphonies as gushing with excessive sentimentality. In an effort to extract every ounce of emotion and drama, laboriously slow tempi with frequent mannerisms in lyrical sections are combined with abrupt tempo shifts in the first movement. Since tempi are neither consistent nor well-coordinated, one must raise a question about Tennstedt's powers of control. Though akin to Bernstein's rubato approach, Tennstedt's reading seems more self-conscious and forced rather than effortlessly idiomatic. A slightly tired opening of the Andante gives way to a more comfortable tempo that sometimes seems too deliberate but is beautifully played (except for some awful glissandi toward the end). The Scherzo is too agitated and disjointed in tempo changes, resulting in spotty playing. An interminably slow and tiresome *Urlicht* suffers from harsh singing (it is a wonder the alto can hold out at such a slow tempo!). Disjointed tempo shifts mar the finale. Harsh choral sound and a poor vocal duet are further detractions. But the reading is strong, if slightly pressed. The bells are inaudible at the conclusion.

VONK, HANS/Hague Philharmonic; Maria Oran, soprano; Jard Van Nes, contralto; Dutch Theater Choir - 2-HPO 6818.663/4 (1986); Vivace E 337 (1991) [79:12]*
Originally released privately by the Hague Philharmonic and then reissued on CD, this performance offers much to admire even with occasional orchestral problems in cohesion and precision. Hans Vonk clearly knows how to handle the symphony. For the most part, his tempo choices are well-conceived. The opening *allegro maestoso* has impressive dramatic strength even if some sections scurry by with much agitation (e.g., *Tempo I* at #11 and *vorwärt* at #12). Vonk's approach is essentially conservative with an intelligent juxtaposition of vigor and muscularity. Brass sometimes sound blaring and nasal. In keeping with Vonk's level of intensity, the final descending triplets are rapidly paced rather than in Tempo I as marked. The frequency with which this quick tempo is taken by conductors at this point--often to avoid what may sound lackluster at the main tempo--makes one suspect the existence of an underground version of the score (N.B., Jack Diether claimed to have a score which marked these measures *Presto*; in its previous incarnation as *Totenfeier*, the passage is marked *Allegro*). A lilting *grazioso* quality makes the lovely second movement quite endearing. Vonk follows markings carefully and balances ensembles and inner voices generally well. He elicits much expression from the strings in the final variation. After an elongated second timpani snap, the Scherzo movement steadies into gracefully flowing motion. Playing is idiomatic and precise, engendering some lovely songful moments in the middle section. Sometimes Vonk pushes the tempo aggressively (e.g., from #38, at #44 and toward the close). In the *Urlicht* movement, a broad main tempo serves well as accompaniment to the contralto's expressive reading. Van Nes is in full command of her lovely voice and sings softly when she should, even

accomplishing a marvelous diminuendo on high E as the movement ends. After a fine opening outburst, Vonk delivers a broad-lined, demonstrative reading of the finale, emphasizing its majestic and dramatic qualities. Pacing is generally well-conceived. Some offstage effects are lost in the distance (horn echoes), while the external band seems less distant than merely quiet. Choral forces perform admirably throughout, even if they do not have the requisite strength to do the final climax justice. As with much that precedes it, the ultimate climax is thrilling, perfectly timed and well played. After the sounds of the chorus fade, the final pages seem anticlimactic: bells and organ are hardly audible and the final chord produced with less than full strength. Only inconsistent orchestral playing diminishes this otherwise meritorious performance.

WAKASUGI, HIROSHI/Tokyo Metropolitan Symphony; Shinobu Satoh, soprano; Naoko Ihara, alto; Shin-yukai Chorus - 2-Fontec FOCD 2705/6 (1990) [84:27]+
Maestro Wakasugi has replaced the opening movement with *Totenfeier*, a symphonic poem which Mahler composed before the symphony and later used as its first movement in revised form. Wakasugi's decision to replace the final version of this movement with the original symphonic poem is highly questionable, particularly because Mahler made major changes in both the scoring and content of this movement to better coordinate it with the whole work. Otherwise, Wakasugi's reading is conservative and his approach objective. He delivers a respectable performance given the fact that his Japanese forces are not completely at home in the Mahlerian milieu. Both orchestra and chorus perform in a formal manner that stiffens linear flow, clips phrases and, when combined with Wakasugi's objective approach, significantly limits expression and dramatic impact. Credit should still be given to both orchestra and chorus for dedication and commitment, which often results in success notwithstanding technical drawbacks. The soloists, who do not have especially attractive voices, sing expressively.

WALTER, BRUNO/New York Philharmonic; Emilia Cundari, soprano; Maureen Forrester, contralto; Westminster Choir - 2-Columbia M2S 601 (1957); 2-Odyssey Y2-30848; 2-Columbia M2K 42032 (1986); MB2K 45674 (1990); M2K 45674 (1990) [79:18]*+ This performance is now a classic, having established a tradition which seems conservative in light of more adventuresome later readings. Reissues on compact disc bring out inner voices splendidly, revealing much more detail than the original shellac recordings. Despite technical flaws, Walter's reading remains one of the most popular ever committed to disc. Although choral forces are not always perfectly focussed and some miscues occur in the orchestra, no other conductor has achieved a more insightful, more satisfying reading of this score. The music speaks as it was written, with sufficient weight, depth and dramatic effect but without the neurotic agitation of Bernstein and Solti or the mawkish emotionalism of Tennstedt. Walter elicits a performance of monumental dimensions which, despite what some may consider too moderate tempi, generates much power and intensity. Tempi are perfectly appropriate and playing very expressive (listen to those rich strings in the *Andante* movement, infused with warmth and tenderness). The slightly agitated tempo of the Scherzo spills over into the *Urlicht* which could be more broadly treated. Maureen Forrester sings with dramatic depth and vocal assurance. The finale is simply magnificent. Walter illuminates this powerful music with a glowing ethereal quality, yet with equal brilliance he intensifies the music's dramatic impact to awesome proportions. His pacing is always appropriate and each section is given its requisite weight, infused with power and emotive depth. While later versions provide more electricity, few if any have attained the profundity of Walter's dramatic sense or his warm lyricism. Vocal soloists sing well but choral forces need better focus and more sonic strength. The final apotheosis is still one of the great moments in the history of this symphony on disk.

WIT, ANTONI/Polish National Symphony; Hanna Lisowska, soprano; Jadwiga Rappé, alto; Cracow Radio & TV Choir - 2-Naxos 8.550523/4 (1993) [85:21]*+   Antoni Wit's straightforward, detailed and thoroughly idiomatic reading of this score is quite striking. Given his middling choral and orchestral forces, Wit delivers a performance rich in dramatic impact, graced with tender lyricism and interpretive nuance. Evidently not looking to overwhelm or overindulge himself, Wit pays careful attention to the score and delivers often overlooked details in a well-balanced, intelligent manner, without sounding studied or perfunctory. His tempo choices are rooted firmly in the Germanic tradition; his sensibly steady way of handling gradual tempo changes deserves praise. What is missing is sufficient volume, reverberation, full-bodied sonority and orchestral/choral precision without which any performance of this dramatic symphony would probably fail to the heights of emotion it is capable of. But why not revel in the details before measuring the inadequacies?

Listen to the marvelous glissandi into #6 of the first movement and the beginning of the second (4:28); the sure-fire Tempo I at #11 of the same movement (so often rushed); the perfectly graduated tempo increase marked *unmerklich* (unnoticeably). Some points may seem minor (e.g., the opening of the pizzicato section of the second movement, where the *mf-diminuendo* marking is actually audible!). But what a wonderful impression they make. Witt even eases up for the final variation of the second movement, taking note of the marking *Breit* (broadly). What follows to the close of this movement is a study in careful reading of tempo variations. It appears that Wit is more willing to give Mahler's markings their due than many more renowned conductors. No exaggerations or mannerisms distract. Some unattractive stiffness occurs during the middle section of the third movement, but the *Urlicht* is a pure blessing. Jadwiga Rappé has the perfect vocal timbre for this music: warm, full, completely secure and yet dark and expressive. She adds a crescendo on the final appoggiatura on "*Leben.*" Then comes a magnificent outburst to open the finale, neither rushed nor blurred, but powerful and dramatic. From there each section is well-conceived and ably rendered. Wit proves that exaggerations are not needed to bring out the glories of this thrilling symphony. Notice how deftly he handles the sudden hush that follows the cataclysmic outburst of the Grave-opening segment. But the horn calls of *der grosse Appell* (The Last Trump) are nearly buried. Choral forces are broadly paced and sing well, despite their apparently meager numbers. The alto impresses in her *O Glaube* solo, but the soprano needs crutches to reach the top of her range. What ultimately disappoints is the grand apotheosis. Fatigue saps both energy and strength from the performers, undermining the power of the final climax. Possibly without intention, the final chord stresses the fifth in horns rather than the root. Overall, this is a fine performance, worthy of attention.

SYMPHONY NO.3 IN D MINOR

Movements:

1. Kräftig. Entschieden.
   ("Pan Awakes; Summer Marches In")
2. Tempo di menuetto. Sehr massig.
   ("What the Flowers of the Meadow Tell Me")
3. Comodo. Scherzando. Ohne Hast.
   ("What the Animals of the Forest Tell Me")
4. Sehr Langsam. Misterioso. (Text by Nietzsche)
   ("What Man Tells Me")
5. Lustig im Tempo und keck im Ausdruck.
   ("What the Angels Tell Me")
6. Langsam. Ruhevoll. Empfunden.
   ("What Love/God Tells Me")

ABBADO, CLAUDIO/Vienna Philharmonic; Jessye Norman, contralto; Vienna State Opera Chorus; Vienna Boys Choir - 2-DG 2741 010 (1982); 3382010; 410715-2 (1982); 10-DG 447 023 (1995) [103:33]*+ One of the better versions on disk, this recording combines excellent sound quality with an engrossing and well-conceived reading. Tempi are quite appropriate though at times slightly extreme (e.g., the end of the first movement moves by like a stampede). In the first movement, Abbado sharply defines the contrast between the abysmal images of the first section and the ebullient Pan march in a well-considered rendition. Though balances are sometimes uneven (e.g., weak percussion and bass strings), inner voice placement is generally adequate. A straightforward, squarish treatment of the second movement elicits some lovely moments, and the third movement generates a delightful sense of frolic, perfectly counterpoised with the pastoral atmosphere engendered by a beautiful posthorn solo. In the closing moments, energy seems to wane just when it should gain momentum. Jessye Norman is in excellent voice, providing a rich and profound reading of the Nietzsche movement. Vocal ensembles are marvelously clear and brilliant. A genuinely sensitive finale is broadly paced but loses steam toward the end.

ABRAVANEL, MAURICE/Utah Symphony; Christina Krooskos, contralto; University of Utah Civic Chorale - 2-Vanguard VCS 10072/3; VSQ 30008-9(quad)(1969);

2-Vanguard OVC 4005/6; 08 400672 (1991); 11-Vanguard 08.4013.79 (1995) [97:21]
Possibly the least attractive effort in the Abravanel complete series, this performance lacks intensity, sensitivity and idiomatic phrasing. The result is a dull, uninvolved reading. Laborious tempi, unclear playing and square rhythmic treatment hamper the darker moments of the first movement, though the Pan march tempo is generally well-conceived, if somewhat constricted. A mild, mellow temperament defuses energy in the inner movements, particularly the second and third which seem uninspired and lack grace and delicacy. An expressive, dark-hewn alto adds depth to the Nietzsche movement, which otherwise suffers from frequently clipped playing. Though choral forces sound thin and confined, the Angels movement has the virtue of consistent forward motion and better clarity. Abravanel and his Utah Symphony offer their best work in the finale: it opens restfully and is paced broadly. Some awkward tempo changes occur but the primary problem here is the sloppy and sometimes poorly tuned playing.

ADLER, F. CHARLES/Vienna Symphony; Hildegard Rossl-Majden, contralto; Les Petits Chanteurs de Vienne - 2-SPA 20/22 (1952); 70/71 (1955); Harmonia Mundi HM2469; Revolution RCB 14/15 ; 2-Harmonia Mundi 43501/2 (1990) [104:03]* This recording has the distinction of being the first Third to be released, although on an obscure label with limited distribution. As one of the early champions of Mahler's music, Adler had the traditional background that also distinguished his colleagues Bruno Walter and Otto Klemperer as devoted and knowledgeable Mahlerians. For many years Adler's version seemed to satisfy, possibly because of the lack of alternative recorded versions. But the over the years, strong competition has placed his reading in perspective and it seems to have tarnished with age as a result. Adler's trudgingly slow pace sometimes impedes forward progress, even as it adds character to the opening section of the first movement and lingers a bit too long on the lilting themes of the third. Uneven playing and spotty sonics are less troublesome in the compact disc reissue. A mighty, forceful introduction seems inconsistent with the generally lyrical approach to the first movement. Adler's tempi tends to become so weighed down at times that he loses the thread of the movement's progress, causing distention that robs the music of the very force it generated in the opening measures. A light and brisk tempo for the second movement, although engendering a few endearing moments, often seems hurried and causes precision problems. Adler imposes a weighty approach to tempo upon the third movement, until approximately its mid-point, where the tempo picks up slightly, although unevenly. But it fails to generate enough impulse to vitalize the closing coda. Then the Nietzsche movement follows with virtually no pause. This time Adler moves the pace along smartly, thereby missing an opportunity to create an appropriately transcendental atmosphere to serve as musical support for Nietzsche's profound text. Yet the alto soloist sings with conviction, intensifying the closing section with a passionate reading. The "angels"seem uninvolved though they sing well. Hauntingly beautiful strings open the finale. Adler moves the main themes forward cautiously; brilliantly shapes their gradual progress, interrupting them with terrifying references to the dark music of the opening movement; and brings the performance to a dramatic and powerful conclusion.

ASHKENAZY, VLADIMIR/European Community Youth Orchestra; Christine Cairns, mezzo-soprano; Stockholm's Boy Choir; Ladies' Choir of Royal Academy of Music, Sweden (perf. 15 Aug. 1991, Stockholm Konserthus) - 2-Digital Classics (1992) [98:40]
*   Vladimir Ashkenazy's only Mahler recording demonstrates that he fully comprehends Mahler's idiom and can effectively communicate it to a relatively new and young orchestra. In his basically traditional reading, Ashkenazy renders Mahler's many directions stylishly, choosing tempi to fit the work's diverse moods and aptly handling transitions, both sudden and gradual. But the finale is the highlight of this performance. In the third movement's touching allusion to

the serenity of the finale (13:25), Ashkenazy gives us a glimpse of what is to come. From the outset of the closing movement, he shapes the long-lined themes beautifully, building gradually and naturally to each climax. His main tempo is fairly broad, and one wonders whether he will be able to maintain it to the end. Ashkenazy's success in doing so is a tribute to his conducting skill, and a welcome antidote to the several other conductors who undermine the apotheosis of the final measures by speeding through them.

BARBIROLLI, JOHN/Berlin Philharmonic; Lucretia West, mezzo-soprano; Women & Children's Chorus of St. Hedwig's Cathedral (perf. 8 March 1969, Berlin) - 3-Hunt CD 719 (1990); 3-Arkadia 719 [99:18] Barbirolli clearly had difficulty with the Third. He treats the sprawling outer movements sectionally, failing to provide a cohesive overview. He has a hard time keeping the BPO under control; his frequent tempo adjustments strain ensemble coordination. Tempi are generally brisk, even though some of the lyrical material in the opening movement seems sluggish. After a quick opening horn theme, the first subject is given a heavy, demonstrative reading that conjures up a dark and foreboding, if sonically confined, atmosphere. The Pan march is energetic, but Mahler's devilish grotesqueries are toned down. Frequently untidiness also mars the performance. Attempts to infuse lyrical material with effusive hesitations and slow-ups do more to disrupt than enhance the emotive effect (e.g., at #39/20'; after #55/26:15, etc.). The first trumpet appears either too far in the distance or too affected to please (before #70/33:35). A huge luftpause into #75 after yet another big rallentando at the final climax (35:30) are further examples of intolerable self-indulgence. Again in the second movement, the main tempo seems hurried. Even with fewer mannerisms than in the previous movement, Barbirolli's reading still lacks the spirit of carefree playfulness which the music should evoke. In the Animals movement constriction and rigidity prevail, particularly in the merely time-beaten rendition of the posthorn solos. Too often volume levels are excessively high, particularly toward the final section, and lack of concentration produces noticeable imprecision. Even the clarinet soloist loses his way at m.475. After adding an unwritten harp arpeggio at the opening of the Nietzsche movement, Barbirolli sets yet another inflexible tempo that further stiffens the musical flow. Lucretia West, however, is perfect for this music, with her dark, Erda-like tonal quality. After a lively and sometimes uneven Angels movement, the finale offers little hope of being the Phoenix that will raise this performance from the ashes. By now Barbirolli has lost control of the strings, who fail to keep together in the long-lined opening section. As the movement proceeds, he quickens the pace, emphasizing the passionate second theme. Too much of this movement sounds disjointed and spasmotic, however, as if Barbirolli thought he needed to make his points with a heavy hand. By the climax at #20 high volume is all that is offered to make an impact. Trumpets mess up high notes roaring over the orchestra (after #26). Consistent with the many flaws of this performance, the timpani tread in the closing measures enters at a quickened paced, completely ruining what should be an inspiring conclusion.

BERNSTEIN, LEONARD/New York Philharmonic; Martha Lipton, mezzo-soprano; Boys' Choir of Church of the Transfiguration; Women's Chorus of the Schola Cantorum - 2-Columbia M2S-675 (1965); 2-Sony SM2K 47576 (1992) [99:11]** Although it later became undeservedly controvertial for allegedly being long-winded, Bernstein's first version still serves as a benchmark against which each new recording should be measured. Challenged by a few excellent versions (including his own later version for DG), this performance may still be the most dramatic and profound to have ever been recorded. Bernstein completely captures the spirit of the music with all its variety and complexity. (There are some, however, who do not cotton to his generally affectatious style.) While some moments in the first movement and the opening of the finale are extremely slow, they work convincingly. In the first movement, a strong and weighty opening is perfectly balanced against the delightful abandon of the Pan march, decorated with pronounced grotesqueries and permeated with extroverted energy, rhythmic spirit and full-bodied, panoramic orchestral sound. Though some important details are de-emphasized, the overall effect is stunning. A delightfully graceful and delicate Flowers movement seems effortless, breathing the fresh air of a summery pastoral scene. Here Bernstein exhibits sureness of tempo control in his perfect handling of the "telescoping" of one section into another. A relaxed, yet dance-like quality pervades the Scherzo, enhanced by Mahlerian parodistic effects. John Ware deserves special mention for his spellbinding reading of the posthorn solos (played beautifully on an F-trumpet). The Nietzsche movement is the least impressive for its brisk underlying motion and less than adequate vocalist. Some over-balancing and fudged dotted rhythms hamper an otherwise splendid Angels movement. An extremely slow string opening in the finale may not be to everyone's taste, but it is remarkable for its evenly paced legato line and beautiful playing. While the climaxes seem to pass by too quickly, the closing section moves with stately majesty -- a thrilling conclusion to a monumental performance.

BERNSTEIN, LEONARD/ New York Philharmonic; Christa Ludwig, alto/contralto; New York Choral Artists; Brooklyn Boys Choir - 2-DG 427 328 (1988); 13-DG 435162-2 GX13 (1992) [102:29]** While Bernstein makes few stylistic changes here from his ground-breaking first recording, this performance is in many respects even more thrilling than its magnificent predecessor. The clarity and precision of the orchestra, as well as the intensity of their concentration and involvement are most impressive. That Maestro Bernstein can still elicit such qualities from this orchestra in a live performance after the passage of so many years since he was its music director is a tribute to his music-making and total command as well as evidence of the affection the orchestra has for him.

Listen to the precise execution of trumpet calls and rapid triplet rhythms in the first movement (the brass deserve special praise here); the bright woodwind sonics blend in with other ensembles perfectly in strong tutti passages; and rich, full-bodied string sound, especially advantageous in the finale. Close miking makes the performance somewhat larger than life and robs it of greater sonic dimension, yet one can hear as many of the inner details as one is likely to hear in any recording of this complex work. Bernstein lets his brass players (particularly the trombone soloist in the first movement) play true and often overpowering fortissimos.

The first movement's opening section and its frequent reprises convey a stark, icy atmosphere, filled with nihilistic dread. In contrast, the joyous spirit of the Pan March is no less captivating than in Bernstein's thoroughly satisfying earlier version, with its sense of Dionysian abandon. Bernstein does hesitate frequently in rendering the charming themes of the Flowers movement. His earlier recording was quite successful without such mannerisms, although some thought its pacing too slow. The delightful Animals movement has the advantage of a more distant sounding posthorn (although John Ware on an F-trumpet conveyed a more pastoral mood than does the soloist in this recording). In the Nietzsche movement, Christa Ludwig is, as ever, a marvelous Mahlerian singer. Sounding somewhat less weighty and dark than Maureen Forrester did in the earlier recording, she renders a less doleful reading, capturing with greater intensity the uplifting last lines of this profound passage from **Thus Spake Zarathustra**. Yet here as in the previous recording, the opening section lacks sufficient spaciousness to conjure up a cavernous atmosphere infused with primeval stirrings. After a slightly brisker fifth movement, sung well by all (choral balances being especially well proportioned), the great finale arrives. Since Bernstein's first version was released, several conductors have chosen a more moderate tempo than his for this long-lined slow movement. Bernstein, if anything, slightly broadens the pacing in the beginning. The gradual build-up to the three climaxes that temporarily interrupt the basically serene, sometimes impassioned main material with terrifying visions of the first movement's demonic side are incomparably rendered. Thereafter, when the great climax that caps the entire work is at hand one cannot fail to grasp how deftly Bernstein has steered us through the long, progressive build-up to its final destination. On first hearing it seems that Bernstein might have been somewhat more weighty in his pacing of the final measures (when the timpani tread enters), as he was in his earlier reading. But repeated hearings dispell reservations in this regard. In the face of what appears to be a recent unfortunate trend to downplay this magnificent conclusion by picking up the tempo of the final timpani tread, minimizing Mahler's clear intention to bring the huge symphony to a noble close, one is greatful that Bernstein gives these final measures their due weight.

BERNSTEIN, LEONARD/Vienna Philharmonic; Christa Ludwig, mezzo-soprano; Konzertvereinigung Weiner Staatsopernchor; Wiener Sangerknaben - DG video 072 515-3 (rec. Vienna Musikverein Grosser Saal, April 1972) (1991) [105:35]** Filmed intelligently with an eye on the score, this video documents Bernstein's unparalleled manner of eliciting every nuance of this complex work. Interpretively, Bernstein stays within the context of his earlier reading with the NYP (see above). But he seems to have more difficulty engendering particular effects from the VPO than he did with his own NYP. Minor flaws aside, could one imagine a more perfect unison of 8 horns than occurs at the reprise of the first movement? Or more magnificent climactic passages in the outer movements (at #73 in the first movement and #19 in the finale)? Slight hesitations at highpoints of phrases are turned with such aplomb (notice how a momentary luftpause at the climax of the first movement at #73 makes its impact more impressive). Bernstein sets a somewhat brisker tempo for the second movement than in his earlier recording. This underlying propulsion hurtles the middle section forward like a whirlwind and causes the telescoped return of the main theme to miss the mark. A soft, heavenly posthorn (visually super-imposed over the orchestra) graces the Animals movement. Christa Ludwig could not be a better choice for the Nietzsche movement, with her dark, richly colored vocal timbre, profound expressivity and angelic demeanor. A delightfully up-beat Angels movement rarely quiets down. But the finale is Bernstein's own. From the beautifully rendered opening string theme to the magnificent closing section, Bernstein once again captures the spirit of this music in a moving, personal statement of grand nobility and deeply-felt spirituality.

BERTINI, GARY/Cologne Radio Symphony; Gwendolyn Killebrew, alto; Boys' Choir of Collegium Josephinum, Bonn; Women's Chorus of Bavarian and West German Radio - 2-EMI CDS 747568 8 (1986) [104:58]* This issue in the Bertini cycle reinforces Bertini's status as a true Mahlerian. While the CRS strings may not have the sheen and thrust necessary to do the outer movements justice, such deficiencies are amply compensated for by Bertini's thoroughly captivating reading and clear, strong sonics. Notwithstanding a rather mild opening horn theme, some underdone climaxes, a few overly hurried segments (from #39) and temperate percussion, the opening movement comes off satisfactorily. Just listen to those 4 piccolos saunter down the Prater on the Pan march at #49! Given a slightly brisk pace for this most extroverted of Mahler's rare excursions into the Dionysian realm of joyous abandon, Bertini's pacing projects a Germanic martial bearing that makes the march theme so majestic. Again a *mosso* tempo is set for the Flowers movement, but here a quacky oboe tarnishes the beauty of the opening theme. In much that follows, one misses the warm glow that can make this music so captivating, at least until the lovely final variation on strings. Bertini emphasizes the raucous and playful qualities of the Animals movement, set at a frisky pace. The posthorn solo, properly distanced from the orchestra, is played nicely, superbly balanced with the horns in its final appearance. Gwendolyn Killebrew has a deep, rich, if heavyish, timbre that suits the profound, other-worldly atmosphere of Nietzsche's poetry. One would only wish that she had attended more carefully to the softer dynamic markings. In spite of constricted string tone and Bertini's tendency to rush into climaxes, the finale works well. Overall, this is a fine addition to Bertini's complete cycle.

BOULEZ, PIERRE/BBC Symphony; Yvonne Minton, mezzo-soprano; BBC Choral Society (Women's Voices); BBC Singers; Hartfordshire County Youth Choir; West London Youth Choir (perf. 1974, London) - 2-Artists FED 024.25 (1993) [95:42]+
Boulez offers an exacting, concise if sometimes inflexible reading. Brass frequently sound larger than life but clarity of line and concern for inner voice placement overcome most balance problems. Tempi are frequently pressed but in most instances not ungainly. A strong opening horn theme ushers in a contrastingly dark-hued atmosphere for the heavy-laden first subject, intensified by monstrously obtrusive brass. The Pan march seems to lack energy at first, but by 6:20 when the clarinets decorate the proceedings with trills, the tempo becomes more spirited. Boulez treats the return of the dark first section, with its stentorian yet doleful trombone solos accompanied by a Verdian "death" motif (6:52), in a rather routine manner. Even the reappearance of the Pan March is constrained at first but soon becomes more energetic. Generally, the movement proceeds in a straight, unwavering manner. The sudden return of the first subject in horns, carreening off a massive orchestral onslaught (into #29 at 14:20) is most impressive. Boulez captures the rowdy spirit of the close effectively. A charming, delicate Flowers movement follows. Lyrical phrases are nicely shaped in this generally straight, unmannered reading. Debilitating inflexibility sometimes stifles the otherwise congenial surroundings and some dynamic levels overstep their boundaries (at the start of the final variation in violins, also taken rather hurriedly), but the overall effect is delightful. A perky tempo is set for the "animals" to romp around in, but again it soon becomes too stiff and inflexible rather than natural and free-wheeling. A too distant posthorn is not balanced well against horns in their haunting trio. But the passing hint of the finale's heavenly calm between posthorn solos is beautiful rendered, and the sudden reappearance of the threatening trombone from the opening movement magnificent. The Nietzsche movement has a mysterious aura and more spacious pacing. Brass are recorded too closely and play stiffly, but the soloist is adequate, despite an indistinct first entrance. After a generally fine Angels movement (but for close miking of the children's chorus), the finale provides an apt conclusion for Boulez's generally pressed and inflexible reading. Although the climaxes are strong and impassioned, the string themes lack nuance and breathing room. The entire movement should proceed in such a manner as to make the final bars seem inevitable, serving as the crowning glory of the entire work. Unfortunately that does not happen here.

DANIEL, JOSIP/Zagreb Radio & TV Symphony; Eva Novzack-Houzka, contralto; Women's Choir of Zagreb Radio & TV; Children's Choir Rade Koncar - 2-Digital Concerto CCT 731-2 (1991); 12-CCT 999701 (1992) [91:38] This performance from Yugoslavia, buried in a boxed set of the complete cycle issued on a budget label, offers little reason to unearth it. Conductor Daniel, a virtual unknown, provides an unintelligible reading, characterized at best as routine, mild and lacking in style and nuance of phrasing. The Zagreb orchestral and choral forces are not up to the symphony's mighty challenge. Strings are colorless, thin and imprecise, woodwinds quacky, percussion weak and brass prone to clipping phrases (particularly disturbing are the trombone solos of the first movement). Tempi tend to wander off course frequently, mostly on the side of greater speed. Mahler's markings are frequently ignored (listen to the trombone solo at 26' of the first movement, where none of the accelerando and rubato markings are followed). Most egregious is the unforgivable cut in the second movement, ripping out all but the beautiful violin thematic variation at #16 before the close! All inner movements but the fifth suffer from rigidity, overly high volume levels and unstylish phrasing. So too the finale, with the added detraction of a pressed main tempo that increases in speed throughout. Lacking sensitivity, nuance and orchestral color, the players go through the motions without the slightest effort to communicate the music's emotive qualities. Although Daniel broadens the tempo for the final pages, blaring brass overwhelm the closing moments.

DEWAART, EDO/Netherlands Radio Philharmonic; Larissa Diadkova, contralto; Ladies of the Netherlands Radio Choir; City Boys Choir Elburg - 2-RCA 74321 276042 (1995) [101:10]* Edo DeWaart offers a respectible if not always inspired reading. Tending to confine its dramatic dimensions, he makes no attempt to overwhelm or indulge in interpretive fancies. His approach is straightforward and generally in keeping with Mahler's directions. The NRPO performs admirably, as do both the contralto soloist and women's chorus. Beginning with a strong horn theme, dark, sometimes demonic brass make the first section of the opening movement sound gruesome. Pacing throughout the movement is well-conceived. What it lacks is both dramatic presence and a strong personality. A breezy second movement and sprightly third are well turned but fail to enchant. The Nietzsche movement is sung clearly and with expression, though some lines are delivered out of character with the text (e.g., *"tief noch als Herzenleid"* is merely run through) while others add their own special characterization (e.g., the last line projects a sense of joyful discovery). After a gay and spirited Angels movement, the finale is treated spaciously, its soft and tender melodies beautifully played but its terrifying reminiscences of the dark section of the first movement less than threatening. Throughout the final moments, DeWaart maintains the broad tempo he set at the opening of the movement. Too many conductors speed up the closing measures from the entrance of the timpani tread and lose the feeling of nobility and dignity that should characterize the final bars. DeWaart deserves praise for having his timpanists pound out the stalwart march rhythm at the close, so as not to diminish the grandeur of this magnificent ending with a brisk tempo.

HAITINK, BERNARD/Concertgebouw Orchestra; Maureen Forrester, contralto; Women's Chorus of Amsterdam; Boys' Chorus of St. Willibrord Church - 2-Philips PHS2-996; 802711/2 (1969); 2-Philips 420 113 (1988); 10-434 053 (1992); 442 050 (1994)
This performance may be the least successful in Haitink's complete traversal of the symphonies. Essentially unidiomatic and uninteresting, his reading lacks intensity, is replete with inconsistencies and uninspired playing, and is further hampered by constricted sound and squarish rhythmic treatment. In short, little happens here that might evoke a favorable response. Shakey trombone portamenti distort the opening movement's first section, while a rather quick and unadventurous march, stiffened by clipped rhythms and confused by poor brass balances, mars the remainder of the movement. Although maintaining an appropriate tempo for the Flowers movement, Haitink produces a stitled reading, lacking the grace and effortlessness needed to make this music sing. A nasal oboe tone putrefies the sweet smell of these "flowers" with an irritating pungent odor. Tempo changes rarely mesh well, creating confusion. A swift tempo for the third movement results in a rigid and lifeless performance, further disturbed by poorly tuned horns. A C-trumpet replaces the posthorn and is played without nuance or color. The closing section is strong, heavy-laden with percussion. A characterful if somewhat brisk reading of the Nietzsche movement is enhanced by the Erda-like tones of Maureen Forrester, but a strained choral group and a routine reading tarnishes the "angels'" halo. In the finale, Haitink provides a valid alternative to Bernstein's more languid approach, with more moderate pacing that deflects sentimentality. Little intensity is generated into the final climax, that is further impaired by poorly tuned brass.

HAITINK, BERNARD/Berlin Philharmonic; Jard Van Nes, contralto; Women of the Ernst-Senff Chor; Tölzer Knabenchor - 2-Philips 432 162 (1991) [103:10]* Although Haitink here seems more comfortable with this sprawling work than in his earlier recording, he still seems to distance himself from the work until the finale. While the dark atmosphere of the opening movement's funereal subject has a terrifying aspect (primarily elicited by huge brass sound), playing seems too precision-oriented, sometimes even perfunctory. The BPO renders the dotted rhythms of the Pan march in a more Germanic style than the Concergebouw in Haitink's earlier recording (see above), and much of its *joie de vivre* comes through. One is more impressed with the well-polished performance and the clear and full-bodied sonics than with the reading itself, however. Haitink evokes little of the charm and grace that the second movement has to offer, despite a few nuances of phrasing (4:21). The "animals" seem rather tame and the posthorn somewhat pale and merely precise. The appearance of the orchestral outburst riding on a freshet of orchestral sound toward the close is more evocative than anything else offered here. Close miking detracts from Jard Van Nes' excellent rendition of Nietzsche's poetics. Given the rich quality of her voice and the vitality of her expression, she would have been more effective placed at a distance, thereby evoking a more transcendent aspect. Haitink's sober reading is neither atmospheric nor uplifting. Only the *fp* swell in the first violins before the close of the middle section (m.110/c.7:10) raises an eyebrow. After a relatively fine Angels movement (except for weak woodwinds), Haitink offers a superbly wrought finale. Here he seems more attuned to the music's lyrical expression, gracing it with lustrous string sound, heavenly atmosphere and fluidity of line. The three unnerving climaxes which call to mind the dark side of the first movement, are most impressive--unlike many other conductors, Haitink does not race through them without giving full effect to the contrast between their terrifying aspect and the serenity of the movement's main material. He infuses these unsettling moments with a deeply tragic quality by not resorting to rapid accelerandi. For example, during the denouement of the second climax, the strongly articulated c-sharps in strings, appearing in staggered entrances, fiercely thrust out from the gradually diminishing chords that close the segment (14:50). While no match for the best of his competitors in the preceding movements, Haitink's reading of the magnificent conclusion is certainly one of the most successful.

HORENSTEIN, JASCHA/London Symphony; Norma Procter, contralto; Ambrosian Singers; Wandsworth School Boys Choir - 2-Unicorn PHS 302/3; 2-Nonesuch HB 73023 (1970); 2-Unicorn Kanchana UKCD 2006/7 (1988) [97:58]** Horenstein's Third is still considered one of the best of the more traditional interpretations. Although hampered by some uneven playing (particularly in the first movement), Horenstein's is as close as we may ever come to a definitive reading. His approach is more sober and less self-indulgent than Bernstein's and frequently brings out more of the inner parts to better advantage. A strong introduction gives way to a robust funeral march that treats the demonic passages as they were conceived. Tempi in the second movement tend to be on the quick side but bring more lightness and delicacy to the music than Bernstein's more languid treatment, although it offers less contrast in the progressively-faster middle section. Crisp, clean playing, a perfect main tempo and great ensemble balances, together with a beautifully-intoned posthorn solo (played on a flugel horn) add to the charm of the Animals movement. Norma Procter sings effectively but with little stylistic nuance in a straight reading of the Nietzsche movement. Good strong choral work and a marvelously threatening climax in the Angels movement provide a fitting contrast for the finale that follows. Horenstein avoids extremes of tempo in the finale. Climaxes are weighty and the final tread is noble and magnificently performed.

INBAL, ELIAHU/Frankfurt Radio Symphony; Doris Soffel, mezzo-soprano; Limburger Domsingknaben; Women's Chorus of Frankfurter Kantorei - 2-Denon 60C37-7829/30 (1986); 16-Denon CO 72589/604 (1989) [98:11]*+   This performance may well be the best in Inbal's entire cycle. While pacing in all but the finale tends to be brisk and playing is sometimes slightly stiff and clipped, his approach to the outer movements is consistently well-conceived. In a broadly paced and full-throated treatment of the funereal section of the opening movement, enhanced by lurid brass swells and dives, Inbal emphasizes Mahler's penchant for the grotesque. He urges the Pan march forward with much spirit, although thereby causing some imprecise entrances and ensemble incohesiveness. Balances vary (e.g., the woodwinds are lost as the Pan march progresses before #70). While dynamic markings are generally followed, some exceptions are inevitable (e.g., from #63-65 all is much too loud for *pp/ppp*). Generally unaffected, Inbal's reading is sprinkled with occasional slow-ups (e.g., at the highpoint of the Pan march toward the close before #73) and hesitations (e.g., before the final coda, despite the *wieder vorwärts* marking). The "flowers" seem slightly agitated, as if disturbed by a slight breeze. Inbal tries to smooth over the telescoped returns of the main theme with slight ritards, thereby downplaying Mahler's ingenious technique of overlapping themes and telescoping the transition of one into another. The more raucous middle section, if too strong for *ppp*, is spiced with delightful spiccati in violins. Inbal's tendency toward inflexibility detracts from the effusive beauty of the final variation. Though more relaxed, the third movement is still slightly pressed, with emphasis placed on its playful quality. Again balance problems cause the melody to be suppressed (e.g., in the clarinet at m.199). Quiet and restful posthorn segments could have been improved by avoiding clipping of dotted rhythms. A rather bland treatment of the Nietzsche movement fails to evoke its profound atmosphere, even if dark sonorities provide an appropriately somber background. More comfortable in the upper reaches of her voice, Doris Soffel doesn't make much of an effort to evoke the existential nature of the text. Choral "angels" sound thin and sing in speachified fashion in faster passages. Inbal is most at home in the finale. Inbal establishes a main tempo in perfect compromise between Bernstein's very broad pace and the more quick tempo of Mitropoulos. Inbal elicits marvelous legato playing from the FRSO strings. Unlike much of what preceded it, the finale does not seem pressed. When agitation is called for, Inbal knows just where the boundaries are located. The three climaxes referring back to the first movement are handled with intensity but without excessive speed. Steady progression during the long build up to the glorious conclusion increases dramatic intensity, which adds to the feeling of release in the final bars.

JÄRVI, NEEME/Royal Scottish Orchestra; Linda Finnie, contralto; Women's Chorus and Junior Chorus of Royal Scottish Orchestra - 2-Chandos CHAN 9117/8 (1992) [99:08]*   Perhaps Järvi and Chandos hope that hyped-up dynamic range and sonic boom will be sufficient to attract a wide audience, in spite of the weaknesses of the orchestral and choral forces used here. Simply put, the RSO is not a Mahlerian orchestra. Järvi doesn't help much with his tendency to aggressiveness and unrestrained impulse. These problems aside, his reading of the sprawling first movement is spirited and contains deeply etched characterizations. Some segments seem to be on automatic pilot, but overall the performance makes a strong impression, particularly the lively Pan march and brass grotesqueries that intensify the funereal march sequences. In the following movement, the "flowers" seems to have lost their luster and sweet perfume. Järvi seems uninvolved here, and the orchestra catches his disaffection and plays with little stylish nuance. The marvelous overlapping of themes at 2:50 and 6:18 are merely strung together. Järvi seems more at home in the Animals movement. Emphasizing its impish playfulness and gruffness, he keeps the tempo brisk. The off-stage posthorn is well-positioned and beautifully played. Some moments still lack conviction here, however. In the Nietzsche movement, the slightly gutteral quality at the top of Finnie's voice can be disconcerting. She waits until "*aus tiefen Traum*" before showing any sense of involvement. Women's voices smother the boys' chorus in the "Angels" movement, which is wrought in a mild, inconsequential manner. Had Järvi not closed the finale with an anticlimactic fast-paced march (more appropriate for the Pan March), the finale would have been thoroughly satisfying. But the unremitting undercurrent of motion he generates draws the wrong conclusion. Järvi adds a crescendo at the end of the finale chord.

JORDAN, ARMIN/l'Orchestre de la Suisse Romande; Jadwiga Rappé, contralto; Ensemble feminin de Musique vocale de Lausanne; Maitrise du Conservatoire populaire de Musique de Geneve (perf. 20,22 April 1994) - 2-fnac 592329 WM 351 (1994) [92:43]
+   Armin Jordan offers a standard, restrained reading that is inconsistent in the attention paid to Mahler's directions and often concentrates on precision to the detriment of characterization and dramatic quality. Either he is overly fussy with details (such as at 10:40 of the first movement where he highlights the *mf*-to-*f* sequence in the first few measures of the march theme) or completely ignores them (for example, during the approach to closing moments of the symphony, where all directions to broaden the tempo or press forward are overlooked). The Suisse Romande orchestra is obviously unfamiliar with Mahler's idiom, and sometimes sounds uncomfortably four-square, pale and unstylish. For the most part, the result makes little impact. In the first movement, an energetic Pan march is pitted against a straight reading of the opening dark demonic section, except for the sluggish horn call at 2:55, which ignores the marking *bewegter* (agitated). While Jordan generally avoids mannerism, he adds an unnecessary luftpause before the interlude that precedes the return of the march theme at 18:40. Brass are kept in check, while the march tempo presses forward intently. Isolated attempts to add character occur (e.g., nasty horns on the opening theme as it appears in march tempo at 29:20) but too infrequently. Jordan fails to capture the lilt and charm of the Flowers movement, only offering a stiff, routine reading. While his "animals" are sprightly, playing is still too rigid to evoke the *gemächlich* (leisurely) quality Mahler sought here. The closeted posthorn solos are dampened rather than distant and give off a pale tonal effect. Even the dramatic orchestral outburst that ushers in the scampering close is just wimpy. Not even the beautiful tone quality of Jadwiga Rappe's splendid voice can awaken the Nietzsche movement from its slumber. After an undistinguished Angels movement with a rag-tag children's chorus, the finale begins in a moderately slow tempo. Jordan keeps moving along, giving phrases little breathing space. When each climax approaches, he ignores Mahler's directions to press forward intently and trudgingly lopes through them. His restraint robs the music of its passion and drama. Sforzandi are smoothed over and Mahler's tempo changes during the long approach to the symphony's conclusion are ignored, thus Jordan fails to produce that the overwhelming sense of release which the final measures should bring.

KNESS, WALTER/Festival Philharmonic and Choruses; unidentified soloist - 2-Quadrifoglio VDS 2/15 (1978) [83:29]   This recording, released only on LP, provides no information regarding the "festival" during which the performance was given or the names of the vocal soloist and choruses. But no matter. The performance has little merit and would interest only a Mahler historian. Although the record jacket refers to the symphony as "*La Programmatica*" (a curious invention), the performance itself fails to characterize the music in any descriptive fashion, not to mention one that evokes images that might be drawn from Mahler's original program notes. Sonic reproduction is very spotty, frequently fading in and out of focus. Conductor Kness provides a mild, uninteresting reading, offering nothing appealing. Orchestral forces are not up to the demands of this difficult work, playing sloppily and without the slightest sense of Mahlerian style. A quick-step tempo for the second movement and an unpardonable cut of the beautiful last variation in high strings in the same movement are serious flaws. The finale suffers from too much underlying momentum. One can only guess at the language being sung in the two vocal movements. Certainly it is not the original German; it may be Russian or Slavic.

KUBELIK, RAFAEL/Bavarian Radio Symphony Orchestra & Chorus; Marjorie Thomas, contralto - 2-DG 139337/8 (1969); 2-DG 413 525 (1988); 10-429042 (1990) [91:33] This rather disjointed and inconsistent performance suffers from troublesome brass intonation and articulation, an eccentric reading of the first movement, a quick and insensitive rendition of both the second and third movements and an extremely fast and characterless finale. The opening of the finale contains some of the loveliest and best-played moments in this rarely satisfying performance. Less acceptable is the Pan march from the first movement, unevenly and unidiomatically played. Choral forces seem small and the vocal soloist has difficulty in the upper register in the Angels movement.

MAAZEL, LORIN/Vienna Philharmonic; Agnes Baltsa, mezzo-soprano; Vienna Boys Choir; Women's Chorus of Vienna State Opera Chorus - 2-CBS 12M 42178 (1986); 2-CBS M2K 42403; 14-Sony SK14K 48198 (1992) [100:23] As is his wont, Maazel indulges in sluggish tempi in the first movement, setting the tone for a long, drawn out performance. When nuance is desired, he is inflexible; when flexibility is employed he is merely affectatious. Balances favor brass over strings, causing a piercing sound at climaxes. Temperament seems restrained when it should be aggressive. More than a casual sense of involvement is missing throughout. Maazel proves that even Mahler's own orchestra can sound stiff and uninvolved when performing his music under an uninvolved technician. One senses that the vocal soloist is affected by such distancing from the music's aesthetic core. In the Nietzsche movement, her cautiousness and restraint may stem from Maazel's broad main tempo as well as his tempo "revisions" (on *"Lust tiefer noch als Herzleid"* he rushes despite the ritard and pushes the tempo at #9, ignoring the *Langsam* tempo marking). The children's chorus in the Angels movement heavily accents the final consonant of their "bimm bamms," often out-singing the women's chorus. While the main tempo of the finale is appropriate, it rarely varies, even when tempo markings call for more motion. So for half an hour we hear this deeply felt homage to Love and God treated so stiffly that it becomes an unendurably endless procession.

MADERNA, BRUNO/Orchestra & Chorus of RAI, Milan; Ursula Boese, contralto (perf. 12 Jan. 1973, Milan) - 4-Arkadia CDMAD 028.4 (1993) [86:16] One of the few Mahler advocates in Italy who gave numerous performances of his symphonies there during the third quarter of this century, Bruno Maderna took a very personal approach to Mahler's music. His reading suffers from both overly fast tempi and unnatural attempts at emotive inflexion. Maderna bathes the entire score in Mediterreanean sunlight, a quality that underplays the dark side of this music, but no amount of solar-generated illumination can cover the orchestral imprecision and unidiomatic phrasing that permeate this performance. Lack of familiarity with the music and insufficient rehearsal time are the most likely causes for these problems. Fast pacing sets the tone. Even the Pan procession in the first movement hurries along more at a trot than a march. Maderna's reading can sometimes be compelling for its vigorousness and thrilling climaxes in the outer movements (e.g., the electrifying intensity of the return of the funereal subject in the midst of a climax of the Pan march at around 6:30, and the three climactic passages in the finale that evoke nightmares of the first movement). But too often Maderna seems merely impulsive and self-indulgent--awkwardly surging forward and then holding up only to dash off once again. The middle movements also suffer from this gushing, over-emotive quality alternating with breakneck speed. Consequently, the "flowers" cool in the breezy pacing, and none of the affectations imposed upon lyrical phrases here work well. Although the

Animals movement is headed with the tempo marking "without haste," Maderna races through it unimaginatively. So too with the Nietzsche and Angels movements. Only in the finale does he calm down. But after he spins out a long-lined opening, Maderna presses onward, interrupting his forward motion with distracting hesitations and long ritards. High volume at sections marked *pp* or *ppp* is also annoying. By the close, there can be little doubt that this work and Maderna are either not simpatico or that he compromised his interest in it so as not to tax his audience with such a long symphony.

MEHTA, ZUBIN/Israel Philharmonic; Florence Quivar, mezzo-soprano; Israel Kibbutz Choir; The Israel National Choir "Rinat"; The "Ankor" Children's Choir - 2-Sony S2K 52579 (1993) [95:02]*+ Much of what is commendable about this recording has more to do with the superb sonics and superior orchestral performance than the quality of Mehta's reading. The IPO sounds remarkably well when bathed in such bright, clear sonic ambience. Clearly, their precision and polish have improved measurably over the years. Zubin Mehta's handling of the symphony has as well. Now much more comfortable with its many diversions than in his earlier version, Mehta lets the music pour forth more naturally, without either unnecessary affectations or inflexible pacing. His reading of the opening movement is energetic but sometimes lacks breathing room (especially between segments). The dark first subject is embellished with sneering trumpets and ghoulish trombones plumbing the depths of the abyss into which the music often sinks. As a perfect counterfoil, the Pan march is perky and good-spirited. Horns ride the crest of an enormous orchestral wave that ushers in the return of the dark side at #29 (13:35). Most impressive here is the thoroughly captivating wildness of the Pan march before the reprise (c.21-22:34). A tendency to overplay this music creates unduly loud dynamic levels (e.g., at the beginning of the coda), but this is only a minor flaw and does not detract from Mehta's accomplishment. He handles the Flowers movement nicely (but for a rather abrupt transition to the main theme at #6), gently gliding through its sweet, pleasantries with an air of gentility. While the "animals" seem rather agitated throughout their movement, they prance in and out of sections with aplomb. Only the posthorn segments seem to lack personality. One also senses a reserve in the Nietzsche movement. It would not be unlikely that the IPO members do not cotton to a philosopher so blatantly (if wrongfully) appropriated by the Nazis. Florence Quivar has a lovely mellow quality to her voice, that might have overcome Mehta's impersonal reading had she not been placed so close to the mike. To create an mystical aura, dynamic levels should be not sound above a hush until the vocal part becomes more impassioned toward the middle of the movement. High volume levels make the appropriate atmosphere impossible. The "angels" whizz by playfully, but are too strong in quieter passages. Mehta's pacing for most of the finale is superb. Climaxes are thrilling and phrasing beautifully shaped. But toward the close he begins to press forward, ignoring the warning signs against exertion of more energy (e.g., *immer breiter*, always broader). Unfortunately, Mehta trashes the magnificent conclusion by setting a jaunty march tempo from the entrance of the timpani tread, as if he were on a casual stroll down the boulevard, instead of in a majestic procression. Some have criticized the ending as an allegedly over-romanticized embarassment. Is this part of a subtle conspiracy to deconstruct Mahler's spiritualism? What a pity that Mehta, who offers a fine version of all that leads up to the magnificent ending, choses to present its grand apotheosis in such a unfulfilling manner, perhaps to be trendy.

MITROPOULOS, DIMITRI/New York Philharmonic; Beatrice Krebs, contralto; Westminster Choir - 8-Fonit Cetra DOC 43; 3-Cetra LO514 (1979); Hunt/Arkadia CD 557 (1989) [77:37] This pitiful performance took place on April 14, 1956, and should be relegated to oblivion of the archival shelves. Tempi are fast in the extreme: Mitropoulos practically gallops through the Pan march in the first movement, romps through the Flowers movement and maintains a fast pace for all but the opening of the finale. Orchestral playing is far from up to par. Stylistically harsh, insensitive and emotively frigid, the performance generates no feeling for stylistic nuance or insightful understanding. What seems always apparent is a rush to close. The most unforgivable commissions here are numerous cuts in the outer movements and instrumental embellishment in the brass (in the fourth movement at #8 and the fifth after #9). One unusual aspect is the use of an English translation for the texts. Krebs sounds a bit heavy yet sings fairly well, but the choral forces are distant and blurred. Although the finale begins smoothly, an uncomfortable feeling of agitation takes over early on and only eases up at the conclusion. Mitropoulos' Cologne performance is much to be preferred (see below).

MITROPOULOS, DIMITRI/WDR Cologne Symphony; Lucretia West, contralto; WDR Cologne Symphony Women's Chorus; Boys' Chorus of Schola di Cologne - 2-Fonit Cetra DOC 4 (1981); 2-Enterprise LV 10001 (1995) This live performance dates from October 24, 1960. Best here is the first movement, solidly wrought and quite idiomatic with a fine Pan march section and strong, though often sloppy brass. The second movement lacks charm and aesthetic quality, breezing along at a rapid pace often indelicately adjusted and not well coordinated in the terraced allegros of the middle section. A playful, frolicking Animals movement has some captivating moments, but is spoiled by a rather perfunctory posthorn solo. Although this movement catches fire at the close, the remaining movements completely douse the flames! A straight, uninteresting Nietzsche movement, replete with too many horn miscues to ignore, is only redeemed by a fine soloist. Yet the alto labors through the Angels movement and childrens' chorus is too weak to be effective. Uneven tempi are disjunctive here. But the women's chorus sings admirably and bells are audible. A very objective reading of the finale contains some agitated and impassioned passages (particularly in the climactic sections); however, the performance overall is too uneven to satisfy.

NEUMANN, VÁCLAV/Czech Philharmonic Chorus & Orchestra;Christa Ludwig, contralto; Kuhn Boys' Choir - 2-Pro Arte 2PAD 206; 2-CDD-206 (1983); 3-Supraphon 111 972 (1993) [90:34]*+ A very impressive recording from all aspects, this may be Neumann's finest performance in his entire cycle. In the first movement, clarity of line, a jaunty rhythmic treatment of the Pan march section and well-conceived tempi are pluses. All goes without a hitch despite restrained, mellowish sonics and weak brass and percussion. A quick second movement (which holds back the tempo in the middle section when it should become more pressed) provides little contrast with the succeeding movement. But the "animals" are delightfully cute and playful. The posthorn solo is beautifully played if closely miked. More interesting is the Nietzsche movement. Christa Ludwig is a perfect choice, imbuing the text with a profound sense of human pathos, enhanced by Neumann's spacious tempi. The "angels" are clear and tightly phrased, lacking only in excessive dynamics. Neumann strikes a perfect compromise for the main tempo of the finale, setting it at a moderately slow pace. He becomes more demonstrative with each climax. Pouring out all of the passion which his other interpretations of Mahler's symphonies often lack, Neumann seems to have found the spark necessary to ignite his Mahler performances. But as the movement progresses many directions are ignored, and some of the denser segments are muddled. Particularly disturbing is a highly pronounced trumpet. As he nears the closing section, Neumann thwarts the growing sense of anticipation by his brisk tempo for the final apotheosis. This tempo, completely unwarranted for so noble and majestic a conclusion, is clearly contrary to Mahler's own directions. It is a pity that such an excellent performance should be brought to so ineffective a conclusion.

OZAWA, SEIJI/Boston Symphony; Jessye Norman, contralto; Tanglewood Festival Chorus; American Boychoir - 3-Philips 434 909-2 (1994); 14-Philips 438 874 (1995) [97:11]* Ozawa nearly replicates Bernstein's reading, diverging from it only in the closing measures. There, after the timpani enter in march tread, he speeds through the final bars in what appears to be another concession to a radical fringe of Mahler deconstructionists. Some claim that after such a long-lined movement, these final bars sound pompous and overbearing. Maestro Bernstein (the symphony's greatest interpreter) disagrees. In fact to my ears, adopting a brisk march tempo not only spoils the movement's majestic grandeur and nobility but also undermines the entire work. Otherwise, Ozawa's reading is not inappropriate but also not illuminating or inspiring. The BSO is in superb form, although throughout the first three movements one senses a casualness that borders on the routine. While neat and clean, clear and sonorous, their playing lacks spontaneity and involvement. Sonics are excellent (except for unfocussed choral forces). Tempi are well-conceived and tempo modifications handled stylishly, but no especially interesting personality emerges. Ozawa smooths over the rough spots and emphasizes the lyrical line with languid inflexion. Brass are kept under wraps and climaxes somewhat confined. The Pan march of the first movement seems matter-of-fact rather than ebullient, and the delicate, graceful lyricism of the Flowers movement seems more artful than natural. But the "animals" of the next movement are in high spirits. The pastoral quality of the posthorn solos here are reminiscent of John Ware's captivating reading in Bernstein's first version. In the often glossed-over Nietzsche movement, Ozawa adopts a broader tempo than usual, evoking a mystical quality appropriate to Nietzsche's profound declamations. Jessye Norman's smooth, lush vocality beautifully captures the soulful character of this poignant midnight song. The Angels movement follows trippingly, though not sonically focussed. Despite his nod to radical revisionism at the symphony's close, here Ozawa slows up for the soprano's chorale (that reappears in the finale of the Fourth), an unmarked nuance which was once but is no longer in fashion. The finale begins in a spacious, legatissimo style and one wonders whether Ozawa can sustain the broad pace consistently throughout. It is to his credit that he does so almost to the very end, while eliciting a beautiful tone from the BSO strings. Unfortunately, he rejects this tempo at the close and weakens the impact of the three climaxes that harken back to the dark, foreboding elements of the first movement.

RÖGNER, HEINZ/Berlin Radio Symphony; Judwiga Rappé, alto; Boys' Chorus of Berlin Radio Children's Chorus; Women's Chorus of Berlin Radio Chorus - 2-Eterna 827877 (1983); 3-Tokuma 32TC-85-87 (1986) [95:38] This rather routine performance has few distinguishing features. Rögner views the work from a distance, giving an impersonal reading that works best in its more energetic moments. The orchestral performance is flawed by frequent inaccuracies and improper ensemble balancing, only made more audible by overamplified dynamic levels. Sonics in the CD pressing are hissy and muffled, strings sounding harsh and brass blaring. Tempi are generally pressed and playing often stiff and expressionless. Rögner is most impressive in the opening section of the first movement. But he often ignores details, particularly in dynamics. The Pan march saunters along nicely if still sounding controlled at times. Greater personal involvement here might have resulted in a more spirited performance. The second movement suffers from stiffness, lack of expression and unstylish playing. Rögner sets a lively, bouncing pace for the third movement, but it soon becomes inflexible and later hard-driven. It is doubtful that the posthorn part is taken by the usual flugelhorn, for its timbre sounds too pinched. In Rögner's detached reading, ritards are ignored so that transitions or cadences are not smoothly rendered. Rappe has a robust, heavyish vocal quality that gives her reading of the Nietzsche song more depth, but she is closely miked, and any sonic perspective that might have made her voice sound like a call from the abyss is thus eliminated. The best position for the contralto would be behind the orchestra (or in Erda-like fashion, below it). The solo oboe tries with varying success to lip slur its rising-thirds motif. As the song becomes more impassioned, the tempo increases and the soloist finds herself either ahead of or behind the orchestra. Strong bells, marked *nicht zu stark* (not too strong), ring out harshly to open the Angels movement, sounding harsh and hurried rather than joyous. Rögner establishes a fine tempo for the finale that contains some of the best string playing in the performance. As the music becomes more passionate, he presses forward intently, and brings the climaxes off well in spite of imprecision. But the closing section is a quick step march which sounds too earth-born for a heavenly apotheosis.

SCHERCHEN, HERMANN/Leipzig Radio Symphony; Sona Cervena, alto; Women's Chorus of Leipzig Radio; Greater Children's Chorus of Leipzig Radio (perf. 1 Oct. 1960) - 2-Tahra TAH101 (1992) [94:15]*   Scherchen's erratic approach to tempo gives his reading a nervous quality. The orchestra is merely passable: strings have a raw timbre and brass sound harsh and often seem distracted. Sonics are clear but closely miked and boosted in volume. Scherchen energizes the opening horn theme, in strong contrast with his heavy-handed reading of the funereal section. The Pan march has just the right lift and parade-like stridency to sweep one along. Scherchen takes some liberties here (as is his wont), but for the most part he sticks to the score and gets impressive results. Only the closing coda seems out of step, extremely flabby in the context of an energetic reading. For the second movement, Scherchen sets a brisk pace, that seems too much in a hurry at times. Although the closing moments have an easy, rubato-like inflection, their *grazioso* quality comes through. Miscues are too frequent to catalogue. Scherchen's usual penchant for affectation is absent from his agitated reading of the Animals movement, yet he indulges in revising tempo markings (e.g., c.8:10 is not in Tempo I). The posthorn segments are most effective, particularly when accompanied by two horns. During the second half of the movement, the main tempo hurries along as if to cover technical problems. An atmospheric bass string opening sets the stage for the Nietzsche movement. The alto soloist has a clear and clean voice that tends to waiver off pitch at the top of her range. In her impassioned reading of the closing section (at 7'), she rushes ahead of the orchestra. A sprightly chorus contrasts with a now morose, less secure soloist in the Angels movement.

Contrasts are the order of the day in the finale. The main tempo seems to float lazily in mid-air. But when the mood becomes more passionate, Scherchen races ahead, rushing headlong into climaxes. The result can be very intense, if one can filter out the miscues and balance problems (especially in over-miked trumpet solos at 18:14). Toward the close Scherchen completely ignores Mahler's tempo markings, gradually increasing the pace rather than broadening it (from c.21') so that the final bars accompanied by the timpani tread are in quick-step. This seems counter to Mahler's intention. The close should reaffirm the broad tempo set at the beginning of the movement, giving due weight and meaning to the message of redemption through love which this magnificent ending should convey. Curiously enough, the accompanying booklet contains an extensive and impressive quotation from Scherchen on "philosophy in music." If this performance was supposed to present Mahler's "philosophy," its success is questionable.

SCHURICHT, CARL/Stuttgart Radio Symphony; Ruth Siewert, contralto; Knabenchor des Eberhard Ludwig Gymnasium; Mitglieder des Sudfunk Chor (perf. April 1960) - 2-Stradivarius STR 10051 (1992); 2-Archiphon 02.6/7 (1993) [87:04]   For the most part, this performance seems to have been given under severe time constraints. Tempi are generally hurried, musical lines, phrases and paragraphs nearly run into each other, ritards virtually ignored. But for a CD change between the first two movements, the movements are played without pause. With such an unrelenting forward impulse, it is not surprising that the orchestra has difficulties in keeping up. Yet such unremittingly brisk pacing does not result in a spirited performance. In fact, when Schuricht keeps a fast tempo under control, as in the Pan march of the first movement, the pace feels just right. However, the rapid tempo set for the lyrical second movement diminishes the effect of its charming lyricism, only apparent in the final measures. Schuricht's haste in the Animals and Nietzsche movements detracts from the relaxed atmosphere that should permeate the main material in the former (despite Schuricht's gruff and frolicsome treatment) and the profound sensibilities of the latter. The high volume level is yet another problem. Written pianissimi rarely sound below mezzo forte; this becomes most annoying in the quiet moments of the Flowers and Nietzsche movements. The strong presence of the contralto soloist in the latter (who swallows word-endings and has difficulty following the tempo) is yet another distraction, despite her otherwise secure vocalism. Without the pause of a single breath, the finale begins in an *andante* rather than *langsam* tempo. Again high volume dispels the desired feeling of tender repose. Schuricht seems to sense this fact as the movement proceeds, and by the final coda he has set a much broader pace, enabling the closing moments to express the sense of grandeur and nobility Mahler intended.

SEGERSTAM, LEIF/Danish National Radio Symphony and Choir; Anne Gjevang, contralto; Copenhagen Boys' Choir - 2-Chandos CHAN 8970/1 (1991) [104:20]+

Put simply, this performance fails in certain areas most essential to success: idiomatic playing and a sense of commitment and involvement. Segerstam just seems to run through much of the work casually, except when he overreacts to the beauties of a lyrical phrase. Despite marvelous sonics, strings sound weak, brass overdone in climactic sections and balances not properly adjusted. The first movement opens in a quick tempo on the dynamic horn theme, played with only moderate fullness of tone. The succeeding funereal music has some character, but Segerstam's straight, tight and detached rendition of the Pan march makes little impression. Long stretches of uninvolved note-spinning suddenly give way to an occasional injection of over-emotive inflection. Segerstam's gushingly emotive mannerisms may not be to everyone's taste (e.g., a huge ritard on the horn theme before the closing coda, m.842). And when these affectations occur in the context of a generally standoffish treatment of the whole, they sound artificial and contrived. The middle movements suffer from the same lack of involvement until a particular note or phrase strikes Segerstam as worthy of strong emphasis. He reels off the charming music of the succeeding movement in a mechanical, colorless and plodding manner, the "flowers" seeming faded and wilted in his hands. Much the same sense of routine pervades the Animals movement, their playfulness lacking impulse. Even the distant posthorn, although well played, is devoid of warmth and tenderness. It should sound almost like a lullaby. Only when overpowering volume accompanies the orchestral outburst that leads to the final accelerating coda does something happen to attract one's attention. In the Nietzsche movement, stilted pacing, routine playing and a closely-miked soloist detract from the transcendental atmosphere that should be evoked here. Following a routine Angels movement, Segerstam opens the finale promisingly with a long-lined first theme. But his apparent lack of sympathy for the music's soulful quality becomes evident early on. His tendency to lunge forward in spurts during the more intense moments, then hurry into and out of climaxes, generates energy but not depth of feeling. This movement should build purposefully in successive waves, aborted by climaxes that conjure up the dark regions of the first movement, to the final majestic procession. Only then can the finale serve as the spiritual antidote to those dreadful visions evoked in the symphony's opening movement. Segerstam's pacing does not achieve such a gradual progression or that feeling of inevitability so necessary to a full realization of the overall conception of the work.

SINOPOLI, GIUSEPPE/Philharmonia Orchestra; Hanna Schwarz, contralto; Women's Voices of Philharmonia Chorus; New London Children's Choir - 2-DG 447 051 (1995) [99:23]** This excellent performance of the Third is a fitting conclusion to one of the best of the more recent complete cycles. Over the years under Sinopoli's direction the Philharmonia Orchestra has come a long way to becoming one of the premiere Mahler orchestras. How stunningly the horns intone their opening call-to-arms in full-throated, brilliant sound. Throughout the entire performance the brass perform superbly and Sinopoli lets them show off their strong, pure tone without restraint. In doing so, he adds depth to the darker music of the first movement and strength to its Pan march. Not that the rest of the orchestra does any less: strings have full-bodied sound in all ranges (especially in the bass) and play articulately (listen to those perfectly executed yet rapid 16th-note runs in the first section of the opening movement); while the woodwinds are expressive and well-coordinated. Rarely have the contrapuntally complex segments of the first and third movements been played so clearly and crisply. Only the Flowers movement is their a sense of tightness and rigidity, caused by the combination of sharp staccato at a relaxed pace. But when raucousness or rough-house play is to be conveyed, it is much in evidence (e.g., in the "march of the rabble" at 21:33+ in the first movement and throughout much of the stronger music in the Animals movement).

Although the second movement wants for more lyric charm, elsewhere Sinopoli turns a melodious phrase gently and warmly, particularly in the marvelous finale and the hint of it at 14:36 of the Animals movement, where an unusually slow, yet dreamy violin theme engages the ear without sounding maudlin. Nietzsche's profound text could have been more movingly wrought in the fourth movement but is sung well, if not in an especially mystical atmosphere. What sound like real church bells grace the Angels movement. Sinopoli handles the last movement superbly. Tender lyricism combine with surges of passion and terrifying visions of the first movement's funereal music intervening periodically. His broad pacing of the final bars conveys the nobility that Mahler sought to express here.

What is most fascinating about Sinopoli's reading is the care with which he attends to Mahler's many markings. Gone are the disturbances in musical flow, the exaggerated contrasts and the inflexive mannerisms that characterized his earlier Mahler symphony recordings, wrongly presumed to be Mahlerian stylistic touches. Now Sinopoli functions totally in the service of Mahler's directions; and he renders them so deftly that they come through without sounding too studious and exaggerated. This last issue in his cycle may very well be his best Mahler performance on disc.

SOLTI, GEORG/Chicago Symphony Orchestra & Women's Chorus; Helga Dernesch, mezzo-soprano; Glen Ellen Children's Choir - 2-London LDR 72014; 414268-2 LH2 (1983); 10-London 430 804 (1992) [92:06]*+ Not only a vast improvement upon his earlier reading, Solti's performance is excellent in its own right. Stunning sonic clarity and immense volume are literally awesome! The massive power of the opening is magnificent. Full and strong brass, sharp, dynamic playing (listen to the horns at #29) and vibrant string sound combine with a sauntering Pan march tempo to create a very impressive and idiomatic first movement--all on one side. Although the Flowers movement seems to lack sufficient warmth and grace, it is still effective, particularly in the well-balanced treatment of the terraced allegro segments in the middle section. An agitated but well-wrought Animals movement is embellished by an excellent posthorn solo, even if treated on the cool side. Helga Dernesch sings strongly as a converted Wagnerian soprano, even if her voice is slightly raw on top. The Nietzsche movement seems to evoke a frozen wasteland. In the succeeding movement, the "angels" are closely miked and seem to strain in the upper register. Solti is one of the few conductors who refuses to add a *ritenuto* before the famous chorale in this movement which later appears in the finale of the Fourth. Stylistically, the greatest improvement is in the finale. Warmer and more emotive than in the earlier version, the music takes on a rhapsodic quality as it gradually presses forward to the ultimate climax. Unfortunately, Solti has not rethought the closing measures, which he plays in moderate tempo, far faster than the original tempo of Mahler's directions.

SVETLANOV, YEVGENY/Russian State Symphony; Olga Alexandrova, mezzosoprano; Russian Academic Choir of TV "Ostankino"; Moscow Boys' Capella - 2-Saison Russe RUS 288111.12 (1995) [96:54] After a stalwart presentation of the opening horn theme, a dark veil hovers over the brass that begin to develop a satanic character that seems to effect the entire performance. Brass play here with terrifying ferocity, unafraid to evoke the demonic character of the first section with monstrous power, creating images that could only be conjured up in the worst of nightmares. Otherwise, the orchestral performance is seriously flawed: woodwind timbres are tinged with intonation problems; string sonority is lusterless; brass lack polish; and a disquieting sense of insecurity, sometimes resulting in miscues, is pervasive. One senses a lack of familiarity with Mahler's idiom. Svetlanov, probably well aware of the weaknesses of his players, takes a strict, inflexible approach to tempi, which causes nervous energy to propel the tempo forward aggressively (particularly in the Pan march of the first movement) and elsewhere results in stiff, plodding motion (e.g., in the second theme of the "Flowers" movement). The second movement opens at a leisurely pace, but the manner in which its lilting melodies are presented fails to do justice to their lyric beauty, both because the strings lack sufficient tonal luxuriousness and the pace begins to slacken early. Lacking a sense of spontaneity, the third movement suffers from inflexible, leaden tempi and stiff playing, making the "animals" appear heavy-footed when their rhythmic figures indicate that they should prance about light-heartedly. Only when the peaceful strains of the finale are anticipated in strings (at 14') does the orchestra relax momentarily. The Nietzsche movement lacks weight and soulful expression. A tendency to waiver in pitch on the part of the vocal soloist is yet another problem here. Yet Svetlanov manages to provide a fine reading of the finale. His steady pacing works well enough in the opening section, but hinders the intensity and drive that should heighten the shock of the sudden intrusions of the opening movement's demonic side. Svetlanov even tries to make the last of these climaxes sound grandiose rather than horrific by slowing up the tempo. One senses that the negative forces that take command in the opening section of the first movement hover over the entire performance, hampering any effort to lighten the mood in the second and third movements and causing the reappearance of these dark elements in the finale to temper rather than heighten the effect of ultimate redemption at the close.

TENNSTEDT, KLAUS/London Philharmonic Orchestra and Ladies Choir; Ortrun Wenkel, contralto; Southerd Boys' Choir - 2-EMI/Angel 835/36; S3912; Z2S-3902; EAC-80600-1 (1980); 10-EMI CMS7 64471-81 (1993) [96:41] Tennstedt offers an extremely uneven and mostly unimpressive performance which has little to recommend it. Careless playing, disconcerting brass intonation (particularly in the trombone), an overall perfunctory reading plagued by quick tempi, especially in the middle movements, and a cold, objective approach are serious detractions. Brass are overbalanced (most noticeable in the third movement) and the orchestral performance is simply out-classed by several others. While the first movement contains some fine moments, Tennstedt plays down its more demonic aspects, tending toward an Apollonian approach. Controlled, legato playing sometimes seems forced and gives way to unwanted affectations (e.g., several times in the second movement). Wenkel has a wide vibrato and sings with a heavy, throaty tone. Details are sometimes glossed over. The volume level in the Nietzsche movement is disturbingly high, obliterating all sense of subtlety and dread. A very straight and uneventful reading of the finale is marked by quickened pacing in the more passionate effusions of the main themes. The final moments are deficient in dramatic weight necessary to bring this monumental symphony to a satisfying conclusion.

THOMAS, MICHAEL TILSON/London Symphony Orchestra & Chorus; Janet Baker, contralto; Southend Boys' Choir - 2-CBS M2K 44553 (1988) [102:42]*+ Given his affinity for Mahler's music evident in various performances over the years, it is unfortunate that Michael Tilson Thomas has only recorded one Mahler symphony. His training with Bernstein--possibly the best interpreter of the Third (Horenstein excepted)--bears much fruit in this superb reading. Thomas displays both a thorough understanding of the work and an ability to render its myriad nuances and provocative characterizations with aplomb. From the opening horn theme, one senses a vibrant energy and dramatic strength that is sustained throughout the movement. Some technical problems in orchestral precision, ensemble balances and over-engineered dynamic levels occur, but the brilliance of Thomas' reading, particularly in the outer movements, consistently impresses. He knows just when and how much to slacken the pace to add a sense of profundity (in the funereal sections of the first movement and in much of the finale) and when and how to energize the tempo to generate intensity or passion without excess. His Pan march is marvelous for its vitality; a big slow-up two measures before #73 at the highpoint of the march theme being the sole exception to an unaffected reading. Thomas also sets an energetic pace for the second movement that belies its leisurely lyricism. While careful with details here, he fails to captivate. Dynamic levels are overdone in the quicker segments. For some inexplicable reason, Thomas pauses before the final variation, which moves along so briskly as to seem more virtuosic than beauteous. Why does he slow up for the violin passage five measures before the close (when Mahler indicates "a tempo subito")?

The "animals" are lively and sound more vigorous than delicate or gentle. Placed at a proper distance from the orchestra, the soft, gentle posthorn contrasts nicely with the frolicsome main theme that precedes it. Now the intermittent orchestral segments seem to lumber along more sleepily, as if cradled by the posthorn's lilting lullaby. All their initial vigor spent, the animals take their time to waken from langourous daydreams after a rather tame orchestral outburst before the close (coming out of the depths of the opening movement). Subterranean murmurings in bass strings create just the right mystical atmosphere to serve as background for the Nietzschean text. Janet Baker, as always, is in fine voice and aptly expressive. But she swallows the "sch" on Mensch on her first appearance and creates broad swells on whole notes (swells are written only on the upbeats to these notes). The female "angels" sound rather dry and the boys lack sufficient resonance in their "bim bams." But clarity of line and fine balancing are pluses here.

In the finale Thomas shows himself a thoroughly knowledgable Mahlerian. His pacing is superb throughout. The opening string theme is not as long-lined as Bernstein's. Thomas sets a tempo that works perfectly without either undue weight or propulsion. When the music becomes more impassioned, he doesn't sacrifice depth of feeling for intensity by hurtling forward to climaxes; he gives them their due without appearing overly neurotic. The result is Mahlerian drama as it was meant to be: strong, demonstrative and awesome. *Luftpausen* are intelligently placed. Notice how Thomas holds up ever so slightly on the upbeat to the brass entrance at m.213. Few of his colleagues have created such a sense of underlying inevitability as the movement moves toward its magnificent conclusion.

VONK, HANS/The Hague Philharmonic; Jard Van Nes, contralto; Residente Kamerkoor and Rotterdam Kamerkoor; Boys' Choir of the Koorschool St. Bavo, Haarlem - 2-HPO 6818.547/8 (1986) [94:19] Released only on LP by The Hague Philharmonic, this obscure performance presents a subdued and controlled reading of the the Third, eschewing characterization for structural cohesion. Volume is restricted so that powerful orchestral climaxes sound muted. Precision is occasionally flawed. Yet within the context of these limitations, Vonk offers a straightforward, unaffected reading that has its moments. The massive first movement seems too toned down, unadventurous and routinely rendered to have much of an impact. Accentuation is often smoothed over and grotesqueries downplayed. The "flowers" seem rather pale, more pastel than brilliant in coloration. In contrast, Vonk evokes a more appropriate characterization of the "animals", highlighting their delicacy and playfulness within moderation. His subdued approach works best in the Nietzsche movement. Here just the right subtle sense of mystery accompanies a splendid reading by Jard Van Nes, who has deservedly achieved high acclaim as a Mahler singer. While passions remain restrained as the music becomes more agitated, Van Nes' expressivity takes the lead over the mellow orchestral treatment. The "angels" sing well throughout a fine rendition of their movement. Vonk holds back for the chorale cadences (which appear in the finale of the Fourth) and seems to press forward intently from #10. A fine, flowing line is established at the outset of the finale. But Vonk gradually increases the tempo long before Mahler directs. Certainly the strings need much more fullness of tone for this music, and ensemble cohesion could stand improvement. Vonk lunges forward abruptly during the intense build up to each of the terrifying climaxes that interrupt the flow of the heart-warming main themes. Brass often clip notes, reducing their dramatic impact. Overall, this is an adequate performance that does not remain long in memory.

WAKASUGI, HIROSHI/Tokyo Metropolitan Symphony; Naoko Ihara, alto; Tokyo College of Music, female chorus; Tokyo Broadcasting Children's Chorus Group - 2-Fontec FOCD 9018/9 (1990) [96:23]* Hiroshi Wakasugi deserves much credit for eliciting such an admirable performance from his Japanese forces. His approach is conservative and straightforward. He is careful with details, intent on making his musicians and singers perform in as close to a Germanic style as possible. That he succeeds in this ambition for the most part, despite occasional stiffness, is a remarkable tribute to his dedication to and intelligent direction of Mahler's music. The true test of idiomatic playing is the finale (not the stricter tempi of the contrasting marches in the first movement), where the manner of expression, nuance and general style, particularly in the strings, is indistinguishable from many fine European orchestras. One senses the influence of Bernstein (possibly through Bernstein's student and Wakasugi's fellow countryman Seiji Ozawa). But Wakasugi is more objective in temperament than the great American Mahlerian, controlling the Dionysian effusions that abound in this score and keeping dynamic levels within pre-determined limits. Wakasugi doesn't try to overpower (Fontec engineers react accordingly) or over-emote, but his reading is undeniably Mahlerian and often impressive. Inner voices could have been better blended into the musical fabric at times. Naoko Ihara's Erda-like vocal quality works extremely well in both the Nietzsche and Angels movements, and the choruses sing securely in the latter. Wakasugi's finale is strikingly expressive. Opening in a steady *adagio*, he abjures the long-lined approach to the thematic material for which Bernstein is noted. Yet Wakasugi offers an intelligent, well-conceived reading that may be on the cool side but is well-phrased and capably wrought. Unfortunately, he chooses a brisk tempo for the closing timpani tread.

WIT, ANTONI/Polish National Radio Symphony; Ewa Podles, contralto; Cracow Philharmonic Choir; Cracow Boys' Choir - 2-Naxos 8.550525-6 (1995) [101:06] +
Antoni Wit stays close to the score and delivers a reading that seems content to engender precise playing if not much spirit, that is until the finale. There broad and even pacing combine with well-turned phrasing to draw the movement gradually to its magnificent conclusion. While the preceding movements sometimes suffer from rigidity, restricted temperament, and confined sonic dimension, the last movement is notable for the absence of these limitations. Wit handles its themes more flexibly, gently caressing them, yet never over-indulging himself in unnecessary affectation. He lets the three internal climaxes assert themselves strongly without speeding through them as others do. One wonders at how so much routine, docile and disinterested note-spinning in the other movements could have generated

this marvelous finale. What the opening lacks in Mahlerian *angst*, the Flowers movement in beauteous tone and nuanced phrasing, the Animals movement in spirit and the Nietzsche movement in depth of perception, the finale makes up for in sensitivity and dramatic power. The PNRS plays quite adequately if not with much Mahlerian flair. Close-miking sometimes over-emphasizes inner parts and brass are frequently too restrained.

SYMPHONY NO. 4 IN G MAJOR

Movements:

1. Bedächtig. Nicht eilen.
2. In gemächlicher Bewegung. Ohne Hast.
3. Poco Adagio. Ruhevoll.
4. Sehr behäglich ("The Heavenly Life")

ABBADO, CLAUDIO/Vienna Philharmonic; Frederica von Stade, soprano - DG 2530 966; 413354-2 GH(1979); 10-DG 447 023 (1995) [57:43] Abbado's reading is very uneven, replete with annoying mannerisms, inappropriate tempi and untoward dynamic shifts. Generally agitated motion produces a forced, hard-driven effect. Only in the finale does all go quite smoothly, especially graced by the beautiful voice and expressive reading of Frederica Von Stade. The preceding movements simply do not hang together. While the first movement begins in an appropriately relaxed mood, Abbado's usual sense of urgency pushes the music beyond the limits characteristic of the Viennese *comodo* style being evoked here. In the second movement, the same process occurs, interrupted only by disturbing mannerisms (Abbado constantly slows up for the clarinet *keck* phrase), resulting in a disjointed reading. The Poco Adagio movement drags on mercilessly but an underlying tension disturbs what should be a restful, somber atmosphere. Again, strange and uncomfortable shifts in tempo and dynamic levels play havoc with transitions. Yet the closing section is beautifully played. Balances and sonics are generally good and the playing excellent despite self-conscious brass.

ABRAVANEL, MAURICE/Utah Symphony; Netania Davrath, soprano - Vanguard C-10042 (1968); Vanguard OVC 4007 (1991); 11-Vanguard 08.7013.79 (1995) [51:55]
In keeping with the general stylistic approach apparent throughout his symphony cycle, Abravanel offers a temperate, detached reading the only virtue of which is that it tends to stick closely to the letter of the score. Playing is generally fine but for some lapses in precision in the middle section of the third movement. Sonics are adequate but close-miking sometimes distorts balances, especially in the third movement. The best work occurs in the finale, played with a delightfully light touch and sung in a youthfully coquettish manner. The other three movements fail to satisfy with their uneven tempi and phrasing in a generally agitated and objective approach. Essentially, the performance rarely rises above the routine.

BARBIROLLI, JOHN/BBC Symphony; Heather Harper, soprano (perf. 16 Jan. 1967, Prague) - Intaglio INCD 7291 (1992) [60:40] This lifeless, colorless and uneven performance offers little that pleases. Close-miking, distorted balances and unpleasant woodwind timbre make the listening experience even more of a chore. Unfortunately, it is the only Fourth we have from the first maestro who championed Mahler's music in England, John Barbirolli. Beginning with a sluggish tempo and dark-hewn atmosphere, the opening movement plods along aimlessly. Longish ritards, disjointed tempo changes and forced expression further detract from this ice-cold reading. Barbirolli distances himself from the Viennese charms of the first movement. His detached approach works better in the Scherzo movement, where the altered tuning of the solo violin captures its devilish spirit effectively. But the veil of darkness that hovers over the first movement still cloaks the second. Barbirolli tries too hard to evoke the heavenly magic of the latter's trio section, with harsh playing at high volume. Tempi seem to be patched together and do not flow naturally. The third movement opens with a nearly inaudible bass string rhythmic motto played pizzicato, ushering in a long-lined reading of the beautiful string themes, but harsh, close sonics undermine what should be the tender sentiments of a soft, lovingly gentle lullaby. Too much volume is a major problem throughout the quieter moments of this extensive *Adagio*. What results has little warmth, color or sensitivity. Barbirolli presses into climaxes intently, gushing over with passion which seems out of place in an otherwise unemotional reading. The tiered *allegro* segments, which serve as the movement's lighter centerpiece, begin in more of a *largo* than *andante* tempo, sounding almost like a pulseless recitative. A strangely awkward ritard is inserted into the following *allegretto* (against Mahler's explicit directions). The movement's closing section evokes a sense of heavenly peace, despite stimulation from underlying forward pressure. The dark hues of the symphony's opening reappear in its closing movement. A heavy tempo and an unevocative, dry manner of expression keep it from evoking the lightness of spirit that can make this music so captivating. Heather Harper's tonal quality and characterization is perfectly in tune with Barbirolli's leaden, sombrous reading. She tries to pick up the tempo at times but without much success. Interminably slow and long, the end finally brings relief.

BERNSTEIN, LEONARD/New York Philharmonic; Reri Grist, soprano - Columbia MS 6152 (1966); Sony SMK 47579 (1992) [54:57]* A typical early Bernstein reading, replete with affectations, disjointed tempo shifts, neurotically agitated fast tempi and over-sentimentalized lyricism. Such a personal approach works well only in the *Adagio* movement, where delicately sensitive lyricism is juxtaposed with intense passion. One particular effect worth noting is the exquisite string glissandi before the closing section. Excessively rapid tempi and awkward mannerisms wreak havoc in the first movement. The Scherzo is briskly paced and its trio section contains excessive affectations bordering on the vulgar. Bernstein saunters through the finale in a more straightforward manner. Reri Grist is charming and radiant, especially in the heavenly chorale cadences. Overall, this performance does not rank among Bernstein's best Mahler offerings.

BERNSTEIN, LEONARD/Vienna Philharmonic; Edith Mathis, soprano (perf. 1975 Musikverein, Grosser Saal, Vienna) - DG video 072 223 (1990) [57:48]* This performance communicates a strange sense of discomfort, perhaps due to the fact that it was recorded live. Bernstein is as captivating as ever, in spite of underlying tension. While contrasting youthful vigor and impulse with expressive lyricism, he presses into and out of sections in the first movement in an agitated manner, making it seems hurried and edgy. In the second movement, such agitation works to better advantage. Here a few affectations add a lilting touch to the melodious quality of the trio. Opening with a faint pizzicato motif in bass strings, the *Adagio* movement also seems on edge. The main tempo is on the brisk side, detracting from what should be a restive feeling, that is tinged with bittersweet sentiment. This restlessness is most disquieting in the heartbreaking climaxes at 6:20 and 11:15. Following a speedy reading of the tiered allegro segments, the VPO strings imbue the heavenly main theme with gorgeous sonority, and, after a magnificent E major orchestral outburst, the movement concludes in sublime tranquility. To counter the feeling that the finale's opening is anticlimactic after the heavenly beauty of the preceding movement's close, Bernstein begins in a relaxed tempo, relating the opening theme to the tender sentiment of the Adagio's closing section, and then gradually becomes more agitated as the movement progresses. Edith Mathis has a hard edge to her voice but sings intelligently and pleasantly, if sometimes too loudly (e.g., on "*Saint Ursula selbst da zu lacht*" in the closing section).

BERNSTEIN, LEONARD/Concertgebouw Orchestra; Helmut Wittek, boy soprano - DG 423607-1 (1988); 13-DG 435162-2 GX13 (1992) [56:59]*+   The most significant aspect of this performance is the use of a boy soprano for the finale rather than a more mature female singer. Whether this innovation works well or not, it influences Bernstein's interpretive approach to the entire work. Each of the earlier movements projects elements of childlike innocence, youthful bravado and adolescent agitation in a manner that is truly unique amongst all recorded versions of the Fourth. The opening tempo, marked *bedächtig* (cautious, prudent), is not rendered with the assertive assurance characteristic of maturity but is more evocative of the mindless daydreaming of youth. Moreover, moments that break the mood with fits and starts are exaggerated, calling to mind adolescent nervous energy and sudden, extreme shifts of attention (e.g., into #3 and #5). Lyricism is infused with the languid ease of carefree youth (into #4) or the hesitant uncertainty of awkward teenage (#18 to #19). Elsewhere, a brusque, youthful assertiveness (at #19) contrasts with lyrical romantic musings (after #20, *schwungvoll*). Listen carefully to the opening of the development section. This passage takes on a curiously spooky character, as if evoking aspects of a child's nightmare, replete with numerous sforzandi that pierce like daggers the already frightening atmosphere. Yet throughout the first movement one senses that the music is not projected in full bloom. Dynamics are restrained and tempi are very relaxed (with the exception of those moments of utter madness which set in greater contrast the wistful main material). Viennese *schmaltz* is held in check; yet few recordings contain a more idiomatic treatment of the lead-in to the final statement of the waltz theme that ushers in the closing section. Although Bernstein does take liberties--as one has come to expect--he is extremely careful to bring out each and every nuance, sometimes requiring several tempo shifts within a single bar. Examples of such attention to details are replete (from #9, particularly in the violins). Equally painstaking is the care and stylistic assurance with which he observes all commas (often ignored by others). But most impressive--whether one accepts them or not--are the variety and unusual character of the moods Bernstein evokes and the new interpretive slant that he presents on this movement.

The Scherzo movement carries many of the characteristics of the the first movement to extremes. The opening tempo scurries along smartly, Bernstein making the most of movement's many parodistic elements. After #3, a strident clarinet rudely parades across the scene, holding back the proceedings momentarily with its bold intrusion. At times the main tempo seems to wander or linger hesitantly, as if unsure of itself, possibly a reflection of adolescent insecurity. Daydreams (from #10) and spooky nightmares (closing section) again recall youthful fantasies. Swells are often exaggerated; changes of tempi sometimes occur a few measures from where Mahler placed them (at M.109 and after #9). But an argument for their re-location can be made in the futherance of Bernstein's evocation of youthful sentiments and sensibilities. Yet sometimes he goes too far. The section marked "sich noch mehr ausbreitend" (here even more broadly) seems too cool and detached. After #12 and into #13, Bernstein reverses Mahler's direction to hold back and simply moves faster and faster.

Bernstein's reading of the slow movement is most surprising. Rather than opt for a lingering pace which one might have expected from him here, he moves the tempo forward in a slightly hurried manner, emphasizing the songfulness of the main material without gushing sentimentality. Emotions are held in check for the most part; even if a few moments of wrenching heartbreak pierce through in soaring violins (at m.86). Consequently, the more wistful, dream-like segments recall their counterpart in the first movement; but the more controlled passages could imply the insecurities of youth rather than merely connoting an objectivity which would be out of character in any Bernstein interpretation. While details are carefully attended to, dynamics are controlled, rarely if ever mounting to a *fff* or even *ff* where called for. String glissandi are deftly played and glowingly grace the music's lyrical beauty. Yet woodwind timbre in tutti passages and an over-miked lead trumpet (into #8) are disturbing.

In an otherwise temperate reading, Bernstein brilliantly infuses each section with a special character yet maintains overall cohesiveness. Notice how he evokes the awesome feeling of hovering over an abyss in the surging violins after #8 in the slow movement, imbuing this intense moment with a tragic presentment that looks forward to the sobering drama of the Sixth. As the music gradually modulates back into G major after #9, Bernstein's hesitant approach takes on a presentment of fear in the face of change. Progressively faster and more joyful segments that follow literally overflow with unrestrained excitement, only to be suddenly broken off at their climax with the unexpected return of the main theme's serene reverie. Even with a moderate approach to tempo, Bernstein captures much of the romance as well as the awkwardness of youth without being excessively self-indulgent. After the heavenly music of the Adagio, a childlike, angelic voice would be most welcome. Thus, the choice of a boy soprano has wonderful possibilities. It is ironic that the boy soprano used in this recording sounds more like a scruffy youth than a little angel. Although the liner notes provide us with no information about Master Wittek, other than that he has soloed with the Tolzer Knabenchors, his vocal quality places him in early teenage. His voice has nothing of the smoothness of tone that a more mature female soprano could project. Possibly, Bernstein considers the playful text more characteristically rendered when sung in this manner, but this version will probably not satisfy those who desire a more angelic quality in the soloist.

BERTINI, GARY/Cologne Radio Symphony; Lucia Popp, soprano - EMI CDC 7 54178 (1990/1991) [58:55] Bertini's cool, objective approach, overladen with excessively strong dynamic levels, lacks warmth, charm and tenderness. Treating the music's lyric sentiments in a brisk, aggressive manner, he concentrates more on the lighter sections of the first movement. An underlying energy imposes itself not only upon this movement, but upon the entire symphony, generating an aggressive demeanor which works best in the Scherzo movement, where its temperament has just the right impish quality. Notice how deftly Bertini makes the transition to the second theme of the Scherzo at #3. But little variety in dynamic levels undermines the playful devilry of Mahler's intrusive grotequeries. Woodwinds sometimes stiffen up (at 5:15) or recede into the background when they should come through strongly (c.6:00). Replacing *pianissimo* with *mezzo-forte* causes strings to seem harsh when they should project a warm glow. Lack of tonal and dynamic shading is a serious drawback. These problems take their greatest toll in the *Adagio* movement. Its tender sentiments are only occasionally apparent in this rigid, unreflective reading, such as before the layered *allegro* sections around 14:00. There is no sense of proportion in these progressively faster segments so that almost no distinction is made in progressing from *allegro* to the closing *allegro molto*. These playful segments simply collapse into the unanticipated return of the andante theme, falling to the floor like split milk!

The sonic quality of the finale is fuzzy and unfocussed. Paced rather sluggishly and with little dynamic variety. The accompaniment provides less than an accomodating backdrop for the soloist's charming soliloquy. Lucia Popp treats the song like an opera aria, sounding too strong to capture the song's heavenly, lilting charms. Only in the final verse does she lighten up enough to evoke the feeling of heavenly serenity with which the symphony comes to a quiet close.

CASADESUS, JEAN-CLAUDE/Orchestre National de Lille; Margaret Marshall, soprano - Forlane UCD 16563 (1987) [54:28] Tempi are the main problem in this performance. All but the *Adagio* movement is paced briskly and unevenly. From the woodwinds' entrance at the 7th bar of the first movement, one already senses a tendency to press forward hurriedly; ritards are barely noticeable and tempo markings often contradicted (e.g., at #4 the tempo is quick even though the marking calls for less motion). Whenever Mahler asks for more speed, Casadesus gives him more than may be desirable. Casadesus also interjects ritards into and at the end of phrases, perhaps making an attempt at stylishness (e.g., into #9 on the main theme and before #15). The contrast between these slow-ups and frequently rapid tempi undermine the aesthetic quality of this work. Orchestral playing is at best mediocre (what is the timpani doing after #11?) and balances favor brass over strings. Although a little agitation is appropriate for the Scherzo movement, Casadesus goes beyond acceptable limits. Untidy playing and awkward contrasts result. By way of relief, the Adagio is paced more comfortably, but the tempo becomes uneven and inconsistent, and icy cold playing and objective detachment deflate the music's emotions. At strong climaxes, high volume levels do not achieve a sense of power by themselves. In the finale, Margaret Marshall displays a youthful voice, although she is slightly unsteady and weak at the bottom of her range. She tries to be characterful, but her sometimes unwieldly efforts get in the way of her vocality (e.g., the protrusive high E in "*Himmel*"). Casadesus gives her a fine tempo to work with. Mannerisms spoil the return of the sleigh bells from the opening movement (at #3). Marshall tries to keep the volume down and sounds perky and sprite, but the lovely final verse is blandly served up, and the closing measures are hurried, detracting from the serene beauty that should linger long after the final low harp note punctuates the close.

CONLON, JAMES/Gurzenich Orchestra; Cologne Philharmonic; Soile Isoloski, soprano - EMI CDC 4 78235-2 (1993) [58:06]*+ For those who know James Conlon to be a fine Mahler interpreter, this recording should come as no surprise. Conlon handles the Fourth superbly from beginning to end, rendering every nuance stylishly and without over-emphasis. Tempi are perfectly conceived within a traditional, no-nonsense approach. Conlon captures the Viennese *gemütlichkeit* of the first movement as is he were a native. He adds just the right degree of agitation to the pacing of the Scherzo and imbues the *Adagio* movement with tender warmth without succumbing to over-emoting. The strings of his combined orchestral forces play beautifully and with deep expression (e.g., at 17' into the third movement). Soile Isoloski has a pleasant voice and sings softly throughout the captivating finale. EMI has provided brilliant sonics, with an unusually resilient bass line. Bravo to all concerned with this excellent recording!

DEWAART, EDO/Netherlands Radio Philharmonic; Charlotte Margiono, soprano - RCA 74321 276052 (1995) [59:44]* DeWaart adopts a traditional, objective approach. He handles each of the movements in fine style. His spirited reading of the first movement captures its Viennese charm without resorting to affectation. The Scherzo movement has just enough underlying agitation to keep it on edge without excessive speed, and tempo gradations are paced naturally and sometimes even unnoticeably. The woodwinds sparkle in the first subject. A warm and gentle lyricism pervades the *Poco Adagio* movement. While one senses a slight distance from the emotional essence of this music, the reading still captures enough of its tender sentiments to please. A relaxed opening tempo for the finale provides a fine accompaniment to the soft, if somewhat matronly charms of the soprano soloist. While some may prefer a more personal approach, DeWaart's conservative, straightforward reading will bear repeated listening.

DOHNANYI, CHRISTOPH VON/Cleveland Orchestra; Dawn Upshaw, soprano - London 440 315 (1994) [57:03]* With an orchestra as polished as Cleveland's one can revel in the gorgeous string sonorities, even without feeling immersed in the hyped-up dynamic levels with which London's engineers tried to empower the performance. Heightening sonic levels seem out of keeping with the delicacies of Mahler's lightest symphony. Instead of achieving a heightened impact they result in inverted balances and over-studious exaggerations of minor details that work against the lightness of texture, and an unnatural aesthetic that underplays the work's emotions.

Dohnanyi has an acute eye for detail and he brings many often-buried inner parts to the surface. But these are only the fragments of music, the conglomeration of which do not constitute the whole. Dohnanyi can be credited with a lovely reading of the first movement; he unaffectedly presents its Viennese gracefulness without smoothing over the contrasting grotesqueries. Such a combination of detail, excellent playing and characterful reading is rare. Most impressive is his deft handling of tempo modifications and transitions, such as into #7 at the end of the exposition (4:12). In a no-nonsense reading, Dohnanyi never indulges in extremes or overly-inflexive tempos. The result is a completely satisfying first movement (*pace* a minor tempo adjustment before #21 which runs over the marking *a tempo*, driving hurriedly into the third theme in woodwinds). Although the Scherzo has many positive qualities (splendid playing and vital characterizations), the trio seems rather detached. Dohnanyi's fussy attention to each and every detail is most disconcerting in the slow movement. Of course, the lush and expressive Cleveland strings are enchanting, but as the music becomes more agitated one senses a lack of spontaneity, as if emotions need be forced from the musical fabric (notice at 11:10 how much is made of the celli before the climax of this section). Dohnanyi handles the tempo changes intelligently, and the result is virtually seamless. Notice how he tries to make a strong impact by hyping up dynamic levels in percussion during the huge E- major outburst before the final coda. Now one finally hears the skipped-beat motto, nearly inaudible at the outset. Of course, the closing pages are gorgeously played, but the effect is tempered by Dohnanyi's cerebral manner. Dawn Upshaw brings much intelligence and youthful spirit to the finale. Despite a somewhat sluggish main tempo and darkened woodwind timbre accompanying her, she lightens up the mood immensely with her pert, tomboyish style. Again concentration on detail abounds (at 3' listen to the low horns on a fragment of the main theme). Achieving an optimal balance between technical precision and emotive expression is always difficult; it often comes down to a matter of taste in the measuring of technique against feeling.

FARBERMAN, HAROLD/London Symphony; Corinne Curry, soprano - 3-MMG 106X (1979); 2-Vox Box CDX2 5123 (1995) [60:49]+ Farberman provides a generally sound if uneven performance. While the sun shines through on a few isolated occasions, too frequently an objectivite sensibility dims its brilliance. Drab and lifeless are the only adjectives adequate to describe the impressions elicited in the first movement. Some tempi are inappropriate to Mahler's idiom, and little sense of identification with his style comes through. A sentimental approach to the Scherzo seems to contradict the approach taken in the first movement and tempi seem to get out of control. Yet the movement has a delightfully piquant quality. The *Poco Adagio* opens quietly, building to very powerful, yet desolate climax. Moments of stirring beauty occur despite occasional lack of control and intonation problems, particularly noticeable in the celli. Corinne Curry sings well, displaying a fine lower range even if her top register is slightly harsh. But the overall performance lacks a sufficiently appropriate stylistic sense to be completely satisfying.

GIELEN, MICHAEL/Southwest German Radio Symphony, Baden-Baden; Christine Whittlesey, soprano - Saphir INT 830.856 (1988) [56:27]*+   Although Michael Gielen is noted more for his work in the expressionistic vein, he has become one of the few conductors associated with modern music whose Mahler interpretations are usually quite idiomatic. Each nuance of phrasing is stylishly handled, each tempo change masterfully wrought. He also offers superb clarity of line and proper balance of inner voices. His swaggering way with the main theme of the first movement is as delightful as his refusal to compromise Mahler's ghastly sputterings and jabbings in the development section. A heavenly reverie pervades the lovely *ruhig* (restful) section before the final coda. The same relaxed feeling pervades the Scherzo, eliciting more charm and romance from the waltz segments than is usual. Allowing enough breathing space for the main material to unfold naturally adds to the music's gracefulness, belying its more agitated qualities. For the most part, the Adagio movement is played gently and expressively; Gielen is not above an occasional hesitation to enhance lyrical sentiment. How nostalgically he lingers over the brief reference to the first *Kintertotenlieder* song during the cadence before #3. Moments of stronger passion seem to lack cohesion and appear abruptly aggressive. At c.7' a dramatic climax conjures up dark shadows that hover over what follows. Gielen handles the tiered *allegro* sections in fine proportion and without undue speed, leading deftly into the *subito andante* return of the main theme. He achieves a gorgeous *pppp* on sustained strings at the close. After an easy-going opening tempo, the finale suddenly takes on more motion at #1. The vocal soloist has a youthful, child-like voice. Even if she is not perfectly steady throughout (having some difficulty in the upper register), her reading is clear and characterful. Gielen keeps her in balance with the orchestra, enhancing her charming music with delightful nuances (e.g., low notes in horn after #6 give the music a wonderfully playful character). As a Mahler interpreter, Michael Gielen should not be underestimated.

HAENCHEN, HARTMUT/Netherlands Philharmonic; Alexandra Coku, soprano - Laserlight 14 139 (1994) [55:11]+   This performance has all that one could reasonably expect from a budget-label issue: fine, generally accurate and idiomatic playing (despite compressed sonics and a relatively narrow dynamic range), clear lines and proper balances, and an interpretative approach that stays close to the text, producing a reading that is well-shaped, nicely phrased and aptly paced. Haenchen follows tradition without innovation or self-indulgence. What results is simply fine music-making from forces giving all they have to give. Of course, one might wish for more fullness of sound and more polished playing; but this ensemble turns in a generally well-rendered performance by any standard. In the opening, Haenchen moves into the main theme without the slightest hesitation. One notices a tendency toward briskness (he speeds up for the woodwind entrance at m.63, three bars before Mahler directed), but tempi never get out of hand. Haenchen's approach is both stylish and nuanced but never either overbearing or disturbed by heavy underlining. His reading makes the point that Mahler's music (at least in the Fourth) can work without over-emphasis on contrasts, as long as the emotive quality is there. And it is. Just listen to the *Adagio*: even with the limitations of this orchestral, the beauteous quality of this etheric music is evident throughout. The finale is equally pleasing: a light soprano sings softly, accompanied by a respectfully light touch in the orchestral treatment. This performance could be aptly categorized under the ancient Greek rubric "nothing to excess."

HAITINK, BERNARD/Concertgebouw Orchestra; Roberta Alexander, soprano - Philips 412 119-1; 2 PH (1984); 10-Philips 434 053 (1992); 442 050 (1994) [55:01]*+
 Little interpretive changes are made in this second version by Haitink (see the 1986 volume, p. 53). But the advent of digital sonics and revamped orchestral forces certainly enhance the performance. Again the reading is essentially straightforward and unaffected. A slight underlying agitation gives a detached, coolness to the first two movements, but orchestral playing is superb as are sonics and balances. The slow movement has more of an objective quality than appears in the earlier version, although in neither case does this approach detract from a satisfying overall reading. Roberta Alexander has a lovely, youthful voice that sounds especially delightful in a flawless finale. But the magic of Viennese warmth engendered by Horenstein and Kletzki is still missing here.

HAITINK, BERNARD/Berlin Philharmonic; Sylvia McNair, soprano - Philips 434 123-2 (1993) [58:27]** In his third recording of the Fourth, Haitink has found the perfect balance between relaxed lyricism and idiomatic characterization. Given the benefits of working with the magnificent BPO and gorgeous Sylvia McNair, one of the best soprano voices available for the finale, Haitink captures this charming work brilliantly. He sets a comfortable tempo for the opening movement, letting its lyricism float naturally and with sufficient breathing room to enable him to shape phrases beautifully. Some might find his pacing too languid, but he never exaggerates to make a point or indulges in untoward mannerisms. In fact, his attention to detail is both remarkably acute and perfectly integrated into the whole so as not to seem studied or overdone. Despite the easy-going tempo, the music's demeanor never seems lumpy or unnatural. When more agitation is needed, Haitink adds just the right amount, again without becoming over-wrought. Climaxes have dramatic impact, particularly because Haitink builds into them gradually. Nor is his reading without character: listen to the dark, unearthly sound produced by the trombone that accompanies the trumpet call after the climax before the reprise (10:12). Haitink's vision is not weighty or stolid; he can be as swaggering and joyful as he can be dramatic. (Yet the pause on a fermata in mid-theme before the reprise is somewhat long). In the Scherzo Haitink begins rather objectively, without attempting to embellish the devilish aspect of the opening. As the music progresses, one becomes aware of the fact that a straight, unexaggerated reading can still create the appropriate effect by nuanced phrasing and proper gradation of dynamic levels and well-defined details. While inflexibility sometimes stiffens the musical flow, or an edginess increases the pulse, these distractions are minor when compared to the many merits of this performance. Haitink's pacing of the beautiful Adagio movement is also impressive. He shapes each phrase seamlessly without unnecessary affectation. The music breathes with warmth and tenderness. Only the opening pizzicato notes, which form an important motto throughout the movement, are too inconspicuous to make an impact. When the music becomes more impassioned, Haitink does not merely rely on increased speed to create more intensity. The result is a deeply emotive reading, achieved without excess or over-indulgence. Listen to the final four minutes, sit back and let your spirits soar heavenward.
 Sylvia McNair's voice perfectly combines youthfulness, clarity, luscious tonal quality, warmth, security and expressivity. Haitink introduces her with a comfortable tempo, played *ppp* as written. At times McNair expresses herself as if in an aside, gossiping about the goings-on of the heavenly Host. Notice how gradually Haitink increases the intensity of the music at #8 (3:55), as Mahler directed, and how delicately McNair shapes the beautiful phrases of the closing section, which dies out to a mere hush. In all, a superlative performance worthy of high praise for all concerned.

SYMPHONY NO. 4

HORENSTEIN, JASCHA/London Philharmonic; Margaret Price, soprano - Monitor S-2141 (1974); Classics for Pleasure CFP 159 (1970); Angel 34415 (1985)**   A splendid reading from one of the greatest Mahler interpreters; his knowing way with Mahler here readily servicable as a guide to performance. Tempi are comfortable; nuances evocative and expressive; climaxes thrilling. In the opening movement, Horenstein never hurries yet excitement rarely flags. A charmingly "naughty" Scherzo is perfectly juxtaposed against the coyish, yet easy-going treatment of the trios, where playful exuberance runs high. Rarely has any conductor captured the soft, tender sentiments of the *Poco Adagio* with such airy lightness and ease of manner, or the more passionate music of the middle section with more pathos and intensity. A comfortably paced finale could have been much improved by a less heavy-sounding soprano who might have provided a smoother tone and more delicacy of line that this heavenly music calls for.

HORVATH, MILAN/Zagreb Radio and TV Symphony; Eva Andor, soprano - 2-Digital Concerto CCT 731-2 (1991); 12-CCT 999701 (1992) [53:54]   Little need be said about this routine performance included in a budget cycle from the former Yugoslavia. Recorded at high volume, the first movement sounds gruff and harsh when it should be soft and mellow. The Zagreb orchestra plays adequately but with little Mahlerian coloration or stylistic flair. Conductor Horvath goes through the motions competently but with little nuance of phrasing, so necessary to elicit the Viennese style parodied here. Lacking such qualities, much of this music moves along stiffly and perfunctorily. The same can be said for the Scherzo movement. The strings lack sufficient warmth and tonal beauty to captivate in the slow movement, especially when paced so inflexibly throughout the principal theme. Emotions are in short supply for such deeply moving music. While the tempi in the finale are generally well set, the orchestra sounds pale and thin (especially in woodwinds during the opening). The soprano has an operatic quality that she tries to keep within the bounds of this light song. She sings softly but, as with most of this performance, never rises about the mediocre.

INBAL, ELIAHU/Frankfurt Radio Symphony; Helen Donath, soprano - Denon 33C37-7952 (1986); 16-Denon CO 72589/604 (1989) [56:17]   Inbal's tendency to agitate his pacing with tension gives a nervous edge to this performance. Such an undercurrent of pressure is not well-suited to this light-hearted, easy-going and rarely troubled music. Inbal's handling of glissandi, oozing them from the strings in mercilessly long stretches, only succeeds in distorting lyrical passages. Clipping of dotted rhythms results in rigid, constricted playing that detracts from what should be a comfortable, relaxed manner. Given Inbal's emotive detachment, little of the Viennese charm of the opening movement or the heavenly repose of the *Adagio* come through. Tempi are often uncoordinated, set in fits and starts in the larger movements, causing sectional fragmentation. Notice how rapid the 16th-note passages sound during the opening of the symphony compared with the rest of the music and the push-pull of extreme tempo changes in the same movement (e.g., from m.289). At least Inbal keeps the volume level down when he should. The second movement is well-paced at the start, but by the close tempi become uneven and exaggerated, as do some special effects (e.g., clarinet fragments marked *keck* (audacious) and staccato strings from #9). The pizzicato motif in bass strings that opens the Adagio is nearly inaudible, despite the high volume at which the movement is recorded. Playing is harsh and cool, yet glissandi are overdone. Some imprecision and fragmentation (at the huge E major outburst before the final coda) do occur. None of the many beautiful moments are given their due. The finale fares no better. Helen Donath's vocal timbre has a harsh edge, that sounds far from angelic or child-like. Moreover, she seems unsteady, even shaky, at times, sings too loudly throughout, and gives the impression of being harried or distressed rather than playful or charming.

INOUE, MICHIYOSHI/Royal Philharmonic; Yvonne Kenny, soprano - ASV CD RPO 8017 (1989/1990); 5007 [58:49]*+   Inoue offers a splendid reading of this briefest of Mahler symphonies. He pays close attention to tempo markings and dynamic levels and creates a mild, pleasant mood without ignoring Mahler's many caricaturesque details. In the first movement, his approach works perfectly. Keeping dynamic levels at bay and exaggerations to a minimum, Inoue captures the Viennese lyricism of this movement stylishly. Tempi are both well-conceived and flexible enough to let the music breathe naturally. The Scherzo has a similarly mild ambience, with many of its devilish grotesqueries toned down. Rarely has the solo violin's errant tuning sounded so eerie or the clarinet's bold fragment marked *keck* so outrageous, especially when set against gorgeous string harmonies. The *Adagio* is beautiful, sensitive and warm in the lyrical sections, strong and dramatic at powerful climaxes. But its opening pizzicato notes, which form an important motto in the movement, need more definition. The finale opens in a true *ppp*, something rarely encountered here, but the soprano soloist is less than ideal. Her voice suffers from thinness and insecurity. The main tempo seems rather slow, as if weighed down by the preceding Adagio. To overcome this sluggishness, Inoue suddenly presses forward at #2, sacrificing tempo consistency in order to bring the tempo to a more natural pace. Nevertheless, the performance as a whole succeeds for its lyrical beauty.

JÄRVI, NEEME /Royal Scottish Orchestra; Linda Finnie, soprano - Chandos CHAN 8951 (1991) [57:08]+   Järvi's manner with Mahler's music is aggressive, extroverted and often brusque. He wields a magic baton when caricature and parody are required, but lets moments of tenderness and serenity pass by without effect. Järvi often plays with tempi but his purpose in doing so in unclear. From the somewhat disjointed opening theme, one is immediately conscious of a lack of Viennese style. In the first movement, Järvi seems more concerned with emphasizing the contrast between cosmopolitan charm and countrified gruffness (with noticeable stress on the latter) than balancing these characterizations. Tempi often press on agitatedly, requiring distracting adjustments between sections. The reading is as spirited as it is simply blunt (particularly during the development), evoking a roughness and awkward distention that plays indulgently with the musical flow. Järvi makes much of the grotesqueries that permeate the Scherzo: the mistuned solo violin slinks about with oily devilishness; horn swells and brass sforzanti add to the ghostly aura; and the woodwinds are impressive in the broad range of their musical characterizations, from coy to impudent. Again Järvi makes adjustments in Mahler's tempo markings and adds a few of his own: sometimes they work well to emphasize a parodistic effect (7:00), elsewhere they are in defiance of the intended impression (2:58). In the Adagio, Järvi fails to convey a feeling of heavenly serenity, and as a result this movement seems endless. Covering the opening pizzicato motive in bass strings completely, he sets a moderate tempo for the principal theme, robbing it of any tenderness or sensitivity. As the movement progresses, an impulsive restlessness becomes apparent, causing tempi to jockey back and forth unnaturally. Järvi intensifies the more passionate moments, but his cool, detached approach leaves one unmoved. After well-positioned tempo changes in the tiered allegro section and a fine E-major burst of sunlight, the closing moments are bathed in a glaringly white hue rather than a golden glow. Linda Finnie is miscast in the finale. Her voice is too strong, weighty and shrill for this angelic song. A warmer tone with youthful lightness would have served the music better. Järvi hastens through much of this movement without taking time to underline its playful qualities. But the closing moments are soft and lovely at last.

JORDAN, ARMIN/l'Orchestre de la Suisse Romande; Edith Wiens, soprano - Erato 2292-45628 (1991) [56:00]   While making every effort to adhere to Mahler's numerous dynamic markings, Jordan fails to elicit any Mahlerian spirit. His detachment from the tender sensibilities of the *Adagio* is particularly unattractive. All forces seem rather uncomfortable with Mahler's idiom, toning down climaxes and distancing themselves from the aesthetic core of the work. The perky opening bars of the first movement give way to an awkwardly long 3-note upbeat to the main theme, weighing heavily on the last of these notes for good measure in a too-conscious effort at stylishness. When brisker tempi are called for, Jordan becomes agitated rather than enlivened. Even if one cannot become accustomed to his affected manner of rendering the main theme, its permutations during the development build nicely to a climax (c.9'+). After having been ushered in with such urgency, the climax seems underdone. Jordan smoothes over the grotesqueries of the Scherzo, to the extent of prettifying the mistuned violin solo. Characterization is lacking here, a prime factor in the success of any performance of this movement. An easy, bouncing tempo opens the finale. Edith Wiens has a fine voice, if somewhat strained on top and with a slight edge to it. But she sings characterfully, in a reading more spirited than *bedächt*. How delightfully she scolds the residence of Heaven, whose domestic doings she relates so impertinently. Unfortunately, the finale alone cannot make this performance worthy of a higher rating.

KEGEL, HERBERT/Leipzig Radio Symphony; Serestyna Kasapietora, soprano - Tokuma 32TC-101 (1986) [55:45]*+ With this release Herbert Kegel proves himself a major Mahler interpreter. His flexibility with Mahler's fluid lyricism and his characterization of both parody and pathos are inspiring. Setting an easy pace, somewhat on the slow side, for the main theme of the first movement, Kegel enhances every nuance with either graceful expressivity or exciting bruskness, making their contrasting ethos most telling. Not reticent to add slight hesitations to the linear flow, Kegel has the know-how to use them wisely. Some passages get out of hand and require adjustment (after #18, on the sudden reprise of the main theme, Kegel senses that it seems too sluggish and presses forward into #19), but the result is enchanting, especially in the closing coda. Equally delightfully is the Scherzo. Applying his flexible approach to tempo, Kegel captures every mood marvelously. Notice the pompous clarinet phrase (marked *keck*), made more audacious by a slight hesitation. Kegel's sense of linear phrasing works perfectly to establish a fluid musical line (c.m.212; #10). Even more marvelous is the *Adagio*, rarely so beautifully played and movingly interpreted. When more passion is called for, Kegel provides excessive speed which can be counter-productive. The woodwinds sound too forward and produce a bright timbre out of keeping with the warm glow of Mahler's lyricism. The tiered *allegro* segments that end in overlapping anticipation of the reprise are perfectly co-ordinated. For the closing coda, Kegel sets a spacious tempo that enables his players to linger on the beautiful strains that end the movement. Notice how at this tempo the final bars look forward to the *Adagietto* of the Fifth. The finale is just as enchanting. In an easy, relaxed pace, Kegel captures each of its varied moods. The youthful, clear and light soprano compliments Kegel's unobtrusive accompaniment, even if she clips dotted rhythms and is suprisingly unexpressive in the charming final stanza. Notwithstanding, Kegel's thoroughly stylish reading does not fail to please.

KLEMPERER, OTTO/Cologne Radio Symphony; Elfriede Troetschel, soprano (perf. 21 Feb. 1954) - Memoria 991-005 (1988) [49:49]* Klemperer dashes off this performance as if it were second-nature. Tempi are not too fast but often agitated. Klemperer tends to round off the closing cadence of a theme by easing up slightly. The first movement rarely exudes any warmth or charm. In spite of a few technical problems (an early entrance of the timpani at #20; a wah-wah quality to the trumpet at mm.276-7), the Cologne Radio Symphony performs impressively. The Scherzo begins routinely, but after #3 Klemperer concentrates more on bringing to light its diverse characterizations. Again a hasty tempo chills his reading from the return of opening theme, despite slow-ups at cadences. Klemperer shows that the *Adagio*'s dreamy song theme can captivate when set at a moderate pace. Even if he makes little of the music's sentiment, and breezes through its more powerful moments, his comprehensive treatment of the movement is intelligently conceived. A harried pace causes problems, however: the abrupt tempo adjustment to andante at the height of the tiered *allegro* segments is botched because of the high speed of the *molto allegro* that is cut off in mid-stream by the sudden appearance of the andante main theme. Elfriede Trotschel graces the finale with a light, lilting, if not always focussed voice. Sonics are clear and distinct.

KLEMPERER, OTTO/Bavarian Radio Symphony; Elisabeth Lindermeier, soprano (perf. 19 July 1956) - 2-Arkadia CDHP 590 (1991) [54:29]*+ Tempi are light and bouncy but always under perfect control. Playing is generally superb, even with some brass problems. Klemperer deftly handles the graceful nuances of the first movement like a true Viennese. Notice how ever so slightly he lingers on the horn passage at m.10 and how he makes the clarinet play its *keck* phrase (13:30) more sprightly without actually increasing the tempo. Klemperer's flexible phrasing moves in sync with Mahler's directions. His timing of climaxes (c.10:18) is perfection itself. A brisk tempo is set for the Scherzo, which has just the right *lustig* (playful) quality. Again his approach to tempo is flexible (e.g., he speeds up on the 3rd horn during a statement of the main theme before #5). Some momentary problems in brass (an overbearing high F after #6 and spotty *gestopfs*) are distracting, but the strings shine luminously throughout. Klemperer eases so gracefully into #11 (6:34), even if on overly loud strings. He ignores the *gehalten* warning at #12 and urges his players on intently. The close seems somewhat hurried. The *Adagio* is thoroughly captivating, being paced broadly, played gracefully, with sensitve delicacy. A haunting *klagend* second theme is played superbly by the oboe solo. Klemperer's energetic intensity drives the more passionate music forward with urgency, sometimes becoming overly hasty. A change of mood at #4 (7:44) to a more sunny atmosphere seems forced. Climactic sections thereafter are run through hastily, as if spent before they happen. As a result, the main theme in its final appearance seems to have acquired nervous energy along the way. Yet the closing measures are heavenly. Without a moment's pause, the finale begins with much animation on its sprightly little tune. Lindermeier sings well, even though her vocal quality is slightly viceral. Some words are misplaced (e.g., is it Saint Martha or Saint Peter to whom she refers on the chorale-like cadence that precedes the return of the sleigh-bell motif from the first movement?). Klemperer doesn't dash through the reappearance of the opening movement's sleigh bells as others do, and he evokes a wonderfully calm feeling in the final bars. (What is that whistling sound at 5:39? Did a bird try to join the proceedings?).

KLEMPERER, OTTO/Philharmonia Orchestra; Elizabeth Schwarzkopf, soprano - Angel S35829 (1962); Seraphim S-60359; EAC 50035; EMI Classics CDM 69667 (1990) [54:10]* Surprisingly less effective in spots than his recorded live performances, this version is still one of the better versions available. A very Germanic reading of the opening movement begins easily and becomes more aggressive and demonstrative as the music proceeds. Good tempo control restrains unnecessary agitation but high volume sometimes spoils quieter passages, particularly in the coda. The closing section is also a bit too stiff. A rough-hewn Scherzo could stand reduced volume, lacking finesse and subtlety in the treatment of dynamic levels. In the *Poco Adagio*, a quick main tempo creates a slightly pressed undercurrent, ignoring Mahler's directions to establish a restful tempo. The principal melodies have a songlike quality, but lack warmth and sentiment. The middle section is very agitated, hard-driven and indelicate at times. Klemperer manages to elicit a few lovely if fleeting moments during the closing section. Only a moderate feeling of innocent cheerfulness pervades the finale. Schwarzkopf sounds too sophisticated and outspoken for this light and delicate music; but her voice is secure and lovely.

KONOYE, VISCOUNT HILDEMARO /New Symphony Orchestra of Tokyo; Sakaye Kitasaya, soprano - Japanese Parlophone E 10009/14 (1930); Denon 30CO-2111 (1988) [53:54]+   The first electric recording of a Mahler symphony, this rare issue dates from May of 1930. The reading has some merit, particularly for its careful attention to details. Taking into account an expected lack of familiarity with this music, the performers make a concerted effort to provide an idiomatic rendition. Tempi are basically well-conceived, even if the Scherzo is on the brisk side. Lyrical material (particularly in the first movement) has a lovely *cantabile* quality. In contrast, the violin solo in the Scherzo has a truly eerie character, rarely captured in later versions. Orchestral playing has a noticeably European sound, especially evident in the sinewy string portamenti in the slow movement. On the negative side, some passages sound stiff and uncomfortable (in the development of the first movement and the return of the opening movement in the finale). In the slow movement, the climax after #8 and the coda are treated harshly and a lengthy cut appears before the huge E-major outburst in the slow movement. A fluttering quality in the soprano helps her flit delicately through the finale. But Konoye's approach stifles her charming reading by enforced restraint of tempo. Notwithstanding the few miscues and moments of unsettling intonation problems, the orchestra performs admirably and the then new recording technique assists in making contrapuntal lines clearly audible.

KUBELIK, RAFAEL/Bavarian Radio Symphony; Elsie Morison, soprano - DG 139339 (1968); 10-DG 429 042 (1990) [51:41]   This entire performance is much too fast, harsh and insensitive. Both playing and interpretation are cold and objective. A few added nuances sound awkward. Depth of feeling, especially in the *Poco Adagio*, is completely lacking and climaxes are rushed. Percussion and brass often sound underplayed, especially when they should be more audible. Although the soprano has a shrill and heavy tone at first, her voice seems to lighten as the finale proceeds. Overall a cold, insensitive and generally uninteresting performance.

LEVINE, JAMES/Chicago Symphony; Judith Blegen, soprano - RCA ARL1-0895 (1974); RCD1-0895; RCA RCD1 0895 (1986) [57:39]+   While the orchestra plays sharply and precisely for Levine, too much control causes tightness and discomfort. Tempi are generally on the quick side and the music is played with little warmth or *gemüt*. Details are audible but some nuances seem awkward (e.g., string articulation in the *Poco Adagio*) and balances often inappropriate (e.g., celli at the opening of the finale are too loud, as is the harp and strings in the trio of the Scherzo movement). Levine's sensitive reading of the finale disrupted by some strange string playing. Judith Blegen lends her light, pretty voice to this enchanting movement, but she tends to treat the music too operatically and becomes unsteady in the coda.

LUDWIG, LEOPOLD/Saxon State Orchestra; Anny Schlemm, soprano - Decca DL 9944 (1957); Berlin Classics BC 2119-2 (1993) [49:46]*   A reissue of this fine performance is most welcome. Ludwig shows his complete mastery of the Mahler idiom in the first movement by the stylish manner in which he shapes phrases, handles transitions and sets perfect tempi without ever becoming stiff or awkward. Stunning clarity of line is a pleasant surprise for such an early recording. The middle movements seem slightly pressed (especially the brisk trio of the second movement) but never unduly mannered. The coda of the third movement is simply gorgeous, graced with lush string glissandi. Anny Schlemm has a lovely lyric voice with a fine high register and sings in a sprightly, easy-going manner in the finale. The close section does seem somewhat on the quick side.

MAAZEL, LORIN /Berlin Radio Symphony Orchestra; Heather Harper, soprano - Nonesuch 71259 (1967); Pearl SHE 552; Nonesuch XD 13205 (1988); Via Classics 642 314 (1994) [58:39] Even in his first Mahler recording, Maazel evidences the basic interpretive tendencies which will characterize his later VPO performances: a cool temperament, very detailed but not always idiomatic approach and a disturbing quirk of slowing up at phrase endings. If you accept Maazel's extremely relaxed, almost lazy tempo for the first movement, all works quite well. Some affectations do distort linear flow. The middle movements' main tempi are on the aggressive side, especially in the Scherzo. The *Poco Adagio* is restrained, even in the tiered allegro sections, but the climactic outburst at #12 is very heavy and affected. Maazel sets so lugubrious a pace for the finale that even the soloist has difficulties following him. In fact, the coda almost falls apart for being so limpid.

MAAZEL, LORIN/Vienna Philharmonic; Kathleen Battle, soprano - CBS IM 39072; MK-39072 (1984); CBS MK 39072 (1986); 44908 (1989); 14-Sony SK14K 48198 (1992) [60:45]*+ Maazel's interpretive manner has not changed since his earlier recording (see above), although the orchestral performance and sound quality are in another league by far. In Maazel's intellectualized conception, he emphasizes details rather than nuances and handles the latter without engendering an especially Mahlerian stylishness. The opening tempo might be interpreted as a strict reading the direction *bedächtig* (cautious, prudent) but sounds too labored. The result is a structurally well-conceived movement that lacks finesse and spontaneity and seems too controlled and antiseptic. Maazel's tendency to slow up at the end of phrases can become disturbing. While the Scherzo is pressed at times, everything is in its proper place and played superbly. A moderately cool, reserved treatment of the *Poco Adagio* lacks warmth of expression. Even an attempt to produce a strong climax at #12 is too heavy-handed. Similiarly, Maazel weighs down the finale with sluggish tempi. Kathleen Battle, who has a lovely voice, is better able to withstand the strain than Heather Harper in the earlier recording. After #7, Maazel shifts to a more appropriate tempo but then eases up again into #13 awkwardly. The close may be "heavenly" but it is treated in too matter-of-fact a manner to provide an effective conclusion to this light-hearted symphony.

MACKERRAS, CHARLES/ BBC Symphony; Sheila Armstrong, soprano (perf. 4 May 1977, Royal Festival Hall, London) - BBC Radio Classics BBCRD 9101 (1995) [56:51] + This BBC radio transcription starts promisingly with a felicitous reading of the opening movement, pleasantly at ease and charmingly graceful. Mood swings here are moderated, and inner voice details and sforzando intrusions come through the musical fabric in nicely balanced equilibrium with principal thematic material. The BBC is far from an ideal Mahler orchestra, with its raw-sounding horns and thinnish strings, yet Mackerras tries to put them at ease, and his efforts work well. In the Scherzo, the mistuned solo violin makes the main theme sound like a vulgar sneer (by emphasizing the *p-crescendo* that appears on the first complete measure after the three-note upbeat). Mackerras highlights other grotesqueries throughout the movement, adding a ghoulish touch to its agitated demeanor. When a glimpse of heaven appears in lush strings against a backdrop of perky woodwinds, Mackerras presses forward inflexibly, detracting from the sense of calm that should conjure up a prophetic vision of the serenity to come with the next movement. The Scherzo lacks flexibility in tempo and phrasing. Much the same may be said for the celestial *Poco Adagio* that follows. Given the lack of full string sonority and the sense that neither this ensemble nor its conductor cotton to the tender sentiments expressed here, even fine broad pacing of the main themes and inner-voice clarity are not enough to fully satisfy. Mackerras' reading is respectible but not captivating; he seems to go through the motions without becoming involved in the music. Sometimes inner voices are over-balanced: ff chords on low horns and trumpets at 12:28 distract from the principal subject in the first horn; heavy accentuation on legato inner strings at 17' and overstated swells thereafter distort the heavenly vision evoked here. High volume and close miking can never replace rich sonorities and proper balances. After an outburst of coughing from the audience, the finale begins in fine style. Sheila Armstrong does not seem at her best here; she is unable to reach low notes, shaky on high ones and lacks expression and stylishness. Mackerras' disinterest matches hers.

MARRINER, NEVILLE /Radio Symphony Orchestra of Stuttgart; Mitsuko Shirai, soprano - Capriccio 10358 (1991) [53:28]+ As one might expect, Marriner interprets the Fourth as a neo-classical symphony. He smoothes over the intended rough spots and straightens out tempo inflections so that everything sounds highly polished and refined but not especially Mahlerian. In taking a decidedly objective approach, he plays down the music's emotional content. Given such an orientation, Marriner provides a generally well-handled, unaffected reading, played clearly by the Stuttgart Radio Symphony. Much gaiety comes through in the perky, energetic treatment of the first movement, even if it is not especially Viennese in character. Brass have a harsh demeanor at times. In the Scherzo, Marriner smooths over Mahler's many grotesque instrumental nuances; yet why such a huge swell in the horns during the introduction to the second theme? Even if sprinkled with a few well-intended affectations, the movement lacks character, seeming more well-constructed than stylistic. The slow movement is beautifully played but is short on personal involvement. One exception is the heavenly serenity that precedes the E-major orchestral outburst before the final coda, where strings have a delicate and lustrous sheen. Set in an easy, comfortable tempo, the finale works well. Mitsuko Shirai has a clear, clean and vibrant tone that can become shrill on top, but generally suits the music's temperament. A compelling calm pervades the final stanza.

MENGELBERG, WILHELM/Concertgebouw Orchestra; Jo Vincent, soprano - Philips PHM 500-040(1939); Turnabout 4425; Philips 416 211 (1986); 426 108 (1990) [55:41]* Possibly the most controversial Fourth ever recorded! Could Mahler really have approved of such a performance? This version is a classic of a free-style, manneristic reading. Affectations are sometimes nothing short of outrageous! But at times the reading is straightforward (especially in the Scherzo) and the vintage style of orchestral performance is marvelous (listen to those string portamenti). Mengelberg subjects the opening movement to his wayward manner with frequent swelling of phrases and violently abrupt tempo changes. The *Poco Adagio* is less affectational (more like rubato) and reveals a few lovely moments, especially during the coda. Jo Vincent displays a more tart than delicately vocal quality but she does catch the spirit of the music as it proceeds. While the tempo set for the finale is easy and comfortable, the return of the jingle music from the opening movement seems too restrained. But whether the interpretive style is pleasing or not, the importance of this recording cannot be underplayed, not only for Mahlerians but as a rare document which exemplifies a romantic and effusive style of conducting that has been out of fashion for at least half a century and was in vogue during Mahler's own time. Those modern conductors who make clumsy efforts at imitation generally fail to capture such a flexible style without becoming jerky and disjointed. Surely, we can count Mengelberg among the greatest exponents of this romanticized style.

MORRIS, WYN/London Symphony; Patricia Rozario, soprano - Collins Classics 10442 (1989) [65:15]+ After an easy-going first movement and a generally well-rendered Scherzo, this performance falls apart with an excessively sluggish treatment of the slow movement. At first, Morris's handling of tempi and phrasing in the opening movement is extremely lumpy (with the possible exception of the end of the exposition before #6). Yet notice how deftly he moves the tempo forward after #22. As one might expect, Morris smooths over strong contrasts but carefully attends to score markings (even the string accents are audible after #11). Clarity of line and well-balanced ensemble work add to the merits of the first movement (one can even distinguish the celesta from the glockenspiel!). Expressivity is not lacking (e.g., at #7). Nor is shading: listen to those ominous low horns at m.226 et seq. A characterful treatment of its parodistic elements enhances Morris's reading of the Scherzo. Curiously, Morris ignores a contrast in mood at #8 (despite the marking *nicht eilen*), handling the same marking for the trumpet solo into the trio section in like manner. The coda has an eerie, grotesque quality which aptly characterizes the entire movement. But the *Poco Adagio* movement is a disaster. More *molto* than *poco adagio*, the tempo plods along so sluggishly that it soon becomes unbearable, especially when ritards further impede forward progress. Climaxes misfire (m.89) and brisker tempi in the middle section seem overly fast in contrast with the main tempo. Yet the more melancholy moments (c.#7), being treated weightily, overflow with tragic pathos. The heroic outburst at #12 is too leaden to evoke a sense of grandeur. What remains of the movement is so interminably long-winded that one wonders whether the end will ever come! While an easy pace works better in the finale, the soprano's robust vocal quality is too much for these lilting strains. Her voice is strong and hefty but inappropriate, particularly in the final stanza.

NEUMANN, VÁCLAV/Czech Philharmonic; Magdalena Hajossyova, soprano - Supraphon Pro Arte PAL 1068 (1981); Supraphon SUP 0035 (1988); 111 975 (1993); 11-Supraphon SUP 111860 (1994) [55:33]   As with most of Neumann's Mahler performances, we have a cool, detached reading. Distant and constricted sonics do little to embellish a fine orchestral performance. The opening movement moves along at a somewhat strident pace without ever feeling really comfortable. Neumann's interpretive manner is generally straightforward, but also includes a few minor affectations. A Slavic rusticity pervades the first movement, sometimes becoming fierce, even harsh and rarely warm or charming. Toning down the demonic aspects of the Scherzo makes this movement appear too tame. Some problems of tempo control and balancing occur here as well. While Neumann tries to evoke a restful mood in the *Poco Adagio* movement, the result is only tiresome. Some lovely string playing is not enough to overcome his extremely temperate, uninvolved reading. Only in the coda, after a heavy-handed climatic section at #12, does a ray of warm sunshine appear. But a harsh and heavy-sounding soprano pulls us down from the heavenly heights in the finale. Neumann returns to his cool reserved manner and ponderously walks us through the jingling music that returns from the symphony's opening.

OZAWA, SEIJI/Boston Symphony; Kiri Te Kanawa, soprano - Philips 422 072-2 (1988); 14-Philips 438 874 (1995) [54:03]+   Ozawa's Mahler performances with the BSO are rarely either revealing or adventuresome, being apparently more concerned with getting the most from this highly polished orchestra. His Fourth is no different. If one can be satisfied solely by brilliant sonics and clear, precise and gorgeous playing, this recording will please, notwithstanding its restrained emotional sensibilities. Each ensemble, from winds to strings, produces a lustrous glow which might have warmed the heart if used as a means of enhancing each mood with just the right degree of tonal ambience. But Ozawa does not guide the players beyond occasionally easing-up at cadences or section endings. Tempi are steady and even, if slightly restless. One misses the Viennese *gemütlichkeit* of the first movement, which is replaced by mere note-spinning. The impishness of the Scherzo is toned down; and depth of feeling is expurgated from the slow movement. The overall effect is staid, pristine and uncharacteristic of Mahler's aesthetic. Kiri Te Kanawa's expressive reading of the finale is probably the most impressive aspect of this otherwise unimpressive performance.

PREVIN, ANDRÉ/Pittsburgh Symphony; Elly Ameling, soprano - Angel SZ-37576 (1979); EMI Classics CDM 65179 (1994) [56:53] This performance has little to speak for it. Previn misconceives almost the entire work! Tempi and balances are generally inappropriate; attempts at stylistic nuances are untoward and stodgy; and the soprano is too harsh and heavyish. The first movement plods along at such a slow tempo that the music fails to flow evenly. Affectations and lack of tempo coordination are appauling. In contrast, Previn sets a quick pace for the second movement, which tends to be sectionalized, disjointed and simply dull. The *Poco Adagio* movement drags on endlessly. A squarish treatment of dotted rhythms stiffens the finale. Ameling is not at her best here. Fine sound quality is just about the only positive aspect of this recording.

REINER, FRITZ/Chicago Symphony; Lisa Della Casa, soprano - RCA LSC 2364 (1960); VICS 1048; AGL 1-5256; RCA 5722 (1987) [53:03]* Reiner seems completely detached from the symphony's aesthetic, although he elicits superb playing and his reading evokes some interesting effects, particularly in the first movement. He makes a valid argument for a perky tempo, for there is no lack of Viennese character despite such a brisk pace. The brilliant clarity and vibrancy of the old "Living Stereo" sound from RCA has not diminished in this CD transfer. After a lively Scherzo, Reiner's languid approach to the *Poco Adagio* movement catches one off guard. What turns out to be an objective reading does not engender much warmth or *gemüt*. Reiner handles the terraced *allegro* sections abruptly and some inner voices obtrude unnecessarily. A slightly lazy opening tempo for the finale moves forward without eliciting much interest, even at the return of the opening movement's jingling music. Lisa Della Casa has a demonstrative vocal quality that is not very sensitive to the delicate lyricism of her part and she sometimes has pitch problems in the lower range. Yet her stytlistic approach is generally sound, even if she changes some words at #13. The orchestral accompaniment is not always as light and delicate as desirable. Most impressive is the first movement and much of the first half of the third.

SALONEN, ESA-PEKKA /Los Angeles Philharmonic; Barbara Hendricks, soprano - Sony SK 48380 (1992) [58:10]*+ This young conductor shows great promise in his first Mahler recording. Salonen's combination of idiomatic treatment, youthful vigor, and creative nuance is most unusual in a premiere Mahler recording. In the first movement, a light, perky opening tempo still has enough *gemächlich* (relaxed) quality to elicit Viennese charm. In contrast, the second theme (3') is appropriately more fleeting. Before the return of the main theme at #6 (3:41), Salonen speeds up as if to imitate the initial treatment of the sleigh bells and then eases back into tempo for the main theme. Tempo inflections are generally well-wrought and affectations either absent or unobtrusive. The development conjures up the errant wanderings of Strauss's imagined mountain-climber in **The Alpine Symphony**. At first, one senses that an unknown force threatens to dispel the joyous mood. The characterization becomes more pointed and the tempo more agitated, as if anticipating danger. And when it comes, it comes quickly (before #10), on haphazard plunges into the abyss. As if running from some unknown spectre, the music presses forward, building to an inevitable confrontation with the pursuer. What follows is a vision both wonderful and horrifying (from 9:30). The sudden interruption that takes us back to the main theme in mid-stream provides welcome relief from these tense moments. Almost sheepishly at first, as if not yet willing to believe that the danger is past, the theme gathers up enough courage to return to its previous undaunted *joie de vivre*. Salonen shifts the tempo into forward gear each time the bold clarinet fragment, marked *keck*, and the sleigh-bell rhythms' return. While this quirk at first seems awkward, it adds vivacity to Salonen's characterful treatment. The restful close of the reprise (14:45) is beautifully played. Notice how Salonen suspends the elongated upbeat notes into the final coda evoking nostaglia for *fin de siecle* Viennese highlife then in decline.

In the Scherzo, Salonen uses more emphatic mannerisms, some of which seem perfectly appropriate, others overdone. The solo violin sneers provocatively on his "wrong note" E; while the clarinet overtly parades its little *keck* phrase with outlandish arrogance. Brisk pacing detracts from the movement's grazioso quality. Some conductors assume that a "scherzo" must always be agitated. This one starts off that way, but Mahler rarely keeps to any rigidified traditional format ("Tradition is laziness," or something to that effect, he is known to have said). The second theme seems more relaxed, if with affected hesitations and poco ritards at the end of cadences (before #10). Through many twists and turns of the movement, Salonen's approach is both intelligent and creative. The slow movement, while played accurately, sounds pallid, thereby tarnishing the full bloom of its gorgeous lyricism. When the music becomes more passionate, Salonen becomes more involved and presses forward hurriedly. Consequently, the climax after 12:40 seems forced, at its height literally hitting the listener over the head with an outburst of sound. No poignant pathos is evoked here. The tiered *allegro* segments work well, abruptly ending on a dreamy variant of the main theme in horns, giving the rest of the orchestra a chance to catch its breath. The heroic Brucknerian outburst that soon follows gives way to a very pronounced treatment of the anticipation of the finale's main theme in horns, accented rather than played staccato as marked. Salonen seems more interested in impressing at the big climaxes than eliciting a soulful reading of the lyrical themes. During the final pages, a flute chord gets in the way of an upward glissando (m.332), momentarily spoiling what is otherwise a beautifully played closing section. Barbara Hendricks' pretty voice sounds rather thin in the finale; it is particularly weak in the low range. She doesn't seem particularly interested in coloring her voice or creating any characterization with her words, except in the final stanza, where her luscious voice evokes a dream-like atmosphere. The chorale-like segments that recall the "angels" of the Third Symphony sound half-hearted. Salonen establishes a comfortable tempo for his vocalist at first but begins to hurry around #8. Strong, stark contrasts characterize the orchestral treatment, counteracting the soloist's lack of personal involvement. Sonics are marvelous throughout.

SINOPOLI, GIUSEPPE/Philharmonia Orchestra; Edita Gruberova, soprano - DG 437 527 (1993) [58:03]+ This performance exemplifies Sinopoli's "intellectualized" approach to Mahler. One senses that Sinopoli does not take naturally to the aesthetic character of this music. As a result, his way with Mahler's phraseology seems overtly self-consciously, with frequent gear-shifts and heavy underlining of what he takes to be interesting modular elements. Consequently, his reading sounds forced, over-indulgent and too fussy for comfort, or as Mahler himself put it at the head of the symphony's first page, *gemächlich* (comfortable). Sinopoli downplays the Viennese *gemütlichkeit* quality of the main theme by making it seem lighter and more frisky (and also by clipping dotted rhythms). One immediate result is lack of contrast with the brisker woodwind music at #2 (1:17). Then celli appear to over-emote on their lyrical line in an obvious effort to seem expressive. The tempo suddenly increases for the sparkling woodwind music after #4 (2:38), presumably because of the marking *etwas fliessender*, one of many tempo markings much abused in modern readings. The main theme seems to have several tempi, depending upon whether it is introduced by sleigh bells or not (at 3:35). But the orchestra plays superbly and, at the end of the exposition, Sinopoli creates a lovely summer-like atmosphere. He also injects a note of mystery during the first few minutes of the development, then presses the main tempo forward intently, rather than gradually to the section's climax. When the reprise occurs, a light-spirited gaiety prevails, contrasted *in extremis* with an overly effusive *schwungvoll* segment. Again fragments are picked on for emphasis, some appropriately, such as the clarinet's audacious rhythmic phrase at 12:27). Abrupt tempo changes, often invented by Sinopoli, and strong contrasts characterize Sinopoli's approach. The final allegro seems more harsh than enthusiastic.

Even more exaggerated tempo inflections appear in the Scherzo movement. Ritards are added to phrase endings and dynamic markings (especially in strings) are over-emphasized. The general character seems gruff rather than devilish. In contrast, the *gemächlicher* section at #9 (5:11) is torn apart by over-indulgent rubato. If the intent of these inflections is to elicit a feeling of spontaneity, one may question their success. Many of the same characteristics pervade the *Poco Adagio* movement. Sinopoli pulls apart the opening theme by lingering and hesitating awkwardly. Such flexibility does not produce the sensitive emotions this music should engender: warmth, dreaminess and repose. The main theme simply does not breathe in the right places (notice how the second violins snap off the end of the theme before #1). The important quiet statement of the rhythmic motto in pizzicato bass strings at the opening is completely lost, so that its triumphant appearance during the grandiose outburst before the final section cannot possibly have the significance it should. Sinopoli captures the dramatic aspect of more powerful sections, emphasizing the long plunges into the abyss at 5:45+, the tragic aspect of the climax at 6:35+, and the dramatic depth of the climax at 11:10 (by extra weight on the celli's longing theme accompanied by thunderous timpani rolls -- also notice how broadly he plays the string phrases that follow). A tragic presentment rather than dreamy reverie hovers over this movement. Long ritards (e.g., at 13:35+ into the *andante* before the tiered *allegro* sections), broad, languid tempi and a general mushiness weigh down the main theme's reappearance before the E-major orchestral outburst at 18:05+. Then comes the finale. Sinopoli foregoes affectations, if not always unmarked tempo changes, such as at #8 (c.3:45). The main tempo is comfortable and provides a perfect setting for the youthfully light and pleasant soprano. But the sudden return of the jingling sleigh bell motive from the opening of the symphony is loud and brash. After a lovely, languid treatment of the main theme on its sudden return after the soloist's quick chatty stanzas, the final section drags on. It all seems unnatural and unconvincing.

SKROWACZEWSKI, STANISLAW /Halle Orchestra; Alison Hargan, soprano - IMP Classics PCD 972 (1991) [61:01]+ Skrowaczewski shows himself to be a master Mahlerian in the first two movements, and then tempi prove to be his undoing. The first movement is light and airy, set in a comfortably relaxed pace perfectly adapted to both the delicacy and ebullience of its Viennese flavor. Only Skrowaczewski's insistence upon slowing up for the upbeat notes of the main theme whenever they appear (except in the development) is a temporary distraction. Otherwise, both the *grazioso* character of the music and its contrasting vigor come through in fine style. Also in the Scherzo, a natural sense of expressivity prevails, enhanced by coyish treatment of the second subject. Notice at #12 (7:50+) that Skrowaczewski, unlike all too many of his colleagues, takes the *gehalten* marking at its word, keeping the tempo at bay. Even the darkish, murky fade-out creates a shadowy atmosphere that are most appropriate here. Then comes the adagio. Skrowaczewski begins the movement in extremely broad tempo, but the Halle group, lacking sufficient fullness of tone, simply cannot sustain such long-lined pacing. Toward the end of the first subject, one senses the strain. Given such a slow pace, no contrast is possible with the slower *klagend* second subject (6:30). Emerging from such a long-winded beginning, the reading conveys much emotion in a painfully tragic climax (8:50). When the tempo increases, it provides some relief from the excruciatingly overdrawn exposition. Skrowaczewski elicits passion (e.g., to 15'), languid beauty (during the closing section), and power (at 20:26). What defuses the finale, by contrast, is not the easy, lyric opening but how much Skrowaczewski has to slow up for the soloists' entrance. Alison Hargan's vocal timbre is too robust for this light and delicate song. She wanders off pitch at times and often goes to extremes in trying to appear characterful. Skrowaczewski creates a feeling of heavenly peace during the final measures.

SOLTI, GEORG/Concertgebouw Orchestra; Sylvia Stahlman, soprano - London CS 6217; 6781 (1966); London 417 745 (1988) [51:45] Solti's hard-driving impulse envigorates this performance. Although he opens the symphony in an easy, comfortable manner, soon his tendency to press forward takes over, increasing the excitement if diminishing the restful quality of the lyrical music. Playing and balances are not always on target, but Solti's reading is generally well-conceived. The Scherzo movement is on the quick side but things calm down somewhat during the trio. Although generally agitated, Solti's style is idiomatic and he creates a jocular, yet sardonic character for the principal subject with the help of clipped staccati.Tempi become unsteady at times. Solti fails to establish a restful atmosphere in the opening of the slow movement until the entrance of the second violins. Here the celli are overly pronounced and the pizzicati bass almost inaudible. Throughout much of this movement, Solti drives the tempo forward to excess, and, consequently, fails to elicit a feeling of profound longing. The terraced tempi of the middle section are well handled, but Solti dives too quickly into the E-major outburst. Delicately clipped dotted rhythms in the finale lighten the atmosphere, but the return of the symphony's opening is too aggressive and the coda not very sensitive. On the positive side, the soprano has a charming voice and sings with spirit.

SOLTI, GEORG/Chicago Symphony; Kiri TeKanawa, soprano - London LDR 410 188; 2-LH (1984); London 436 618; 436 600 (1992); 10-London 430 804 (1992) [54:21]*+
A vast improvement in every sense over his earlier recording (see above), this performance can easily be considered in the top class. The sound quality is magnificent and playing excellent. Solti is more in control of his agitated temperament here than previously, although a tendency to press forward is apparent throughout. Tempi are mostly appropriate, balances excellent and the overall reading comfortably idiomatic. Nuances are beautifully phrased in a lively opening movement. The Scherzo is much more relaxed than in the earlier reading but the pace moves along smartly. Beautiful playing illuminates an emotion-charged *Poco Adagio* movement. As the music intensifies, underlying agitation increases and when combined with high powered sonics produces a strong effect. The climax at #12 could be more laid back, but from there to the close all works quite well. Solti's way with the finale is uncharacteristically light and sprightly. Kiri TeKanawa is a fine choice for the finale, singing expressively and with a delicate touch. Solti leads the performance with such complete assurance that it seems second nature.

SWAROWSKY, HANS /Czech Philharmonic; Gerlinde Lorenz, soprano - Supraphon 1101346 (1973); Supraphon 110625 (1988); Supraphon 110625 (1988) [57:15] This even-tempered, conservative reading is nicely-handled and well-played. Balances and inner voice placement are generally acceptable. Since Swarowsky never projects himself into or upon the music by inserting untoward mannerisms, little can be said to go wrong here. While some moments sound slightly stiff in the development section, the first movement is spirited and well-conceived. From #22, the tempo eases up into a more comfortable pace. Brisk motion pervades the Scherzo, its wry humor coming through without unnecessary affectations. A restful atmosphere pervades the *Poco Adagio* movement in which Swarowsky's level of sensitivity stays within the bounds of self-restraint. He never hangs on to phrases unduly but lets the music flow naturally. The *grazioso* section of this movement seems more peaceful than joyous; but a more poignant emotive quality is evoked in the *ruhig* section before #2. A calm contentment pervades the finale. Ms. Lorenz is in fine voice with a very smooth delivery, despite a slight waiver in the high register. Sharp articulation from bass strings is another positive aspect. Tempo modulations are well handled. Essentially, this is a satisfying performance in a straightforward mold.

SZELL, GEORGE/Cleveland Orchestra; Judith Raskin, soprano - Columbia MS-6833 (1966); CBS MY-37225; Columbia MYK 37225 (1988); MK 42416 (1987); Sony SBK 46535 (1991) [56:49]** Frequent reissues indicate the durability of this superb performance, possibly the best of the earlier versions. Szell's mastery of Mahler's style and excellent orchestral playing are mainly responsible for the high rating. The work is presented in a clear and concise manner but without the sense of detachment that afflicted Reiner's reading. The opening has a perky quality and the main theme of the first movement is handled with ease. The climax at #16 is simply thrilling. In the coda more passion than tranquility is evoked and some passages lack sufficient warmth. A strange miscue occurs after #4 when the bells enter too early. The Scherzo movement is on the quick side, but evokes a spirit of playfulness. Clear, bright sound quality helps the listener follow the intricate contrapuntal lines. Szell elicits some very beautiful and expressive playing in the slow movement, which is perfectly paced but never overbroad or mannered. He keeps the tempo moving rather than lingering on lyrical phrases. Climaxes are strong and dramatic, the flood of E-major at #12 being simply marvelous. After a gorgeous coda, the tempo Szell sets for the finale seems to drag slightly. Yet he treats the return of the "jingle bells" from the first movement in a playful spirit. Judith Raskin takes a narrative approach to the text while singing with moderate expressiveness. A lilting quality permeates the final coda of this superlative version.

TENNSTEDT, KLAUS/London Philharmonic; Lucia Popp, soprano - EMI/Angel DS-37954; EAC 90137; CDC-47024 (1983); 10-EMI CMS7 64471-81 (1993) [54:50]*
This very fine recording is most notable for superb sound quality and an excellent orchestral performance. Tennstedt's tendency to thickly overlay the music with numerous manneristic affects and exaggerated, unsteady tempi are serious detractions. The first movement opens pleasantly, but then distracting affectations creep in and tempi become generally pressed. However, balances are excellent and uncover some significant details. Tennstedt generates some excitement in the middle section but he is sometimes careless in reading Mahler's directions. The Scherzo is quick and perky yet when it returns after the first trio the tempo becomes restless. At the return of the trio, extremely flexible tempi result in disjointed phrasing. After lingering on each note of the opening, the *Poco Adagio* movement progresses at a lugubrious pace, holding dearly on to phrase endings. Yet Tennstedt elicits some thrilling climaxes here, probing the depths of this moving music with a deep sense of human pathos. Added *ritardandi* further stretch out an already extremely slow main tempo. The coda is heart-rending. While the opening tempo of the finale has a nice-and-easy quality, a feeling of discomfort still remains. If this reading is less than inspiring, the soloist adds little to enhance the mood. Although she sings well enough, her vocal production is on the heavy side and she seems too aloof to render a thoroughly pleasing account of the text. Tennstedt's overall approach can only satisfy those who enjoy Mahler's music when it oozes from every pore.

TSUTSUMI, SHUNSAKU/Tokyo City Philharmonic; Ruri Usami, soprano - Ray FHCR-1001 (1991) [57:58] This Japanese issue adds a subtitle to the symphony: "Ode to Heavenly Joy." As with most of the Japanese recordings, performers make a respectable effort to play the work stylishly, but they occasionally succumb to a strict, formalistic manner which lacks both nuance and flexibility. The finale is sung in Japanese by a full-voiced soprano. Sonics sometimes overplay inner harmonic voices, and woodwinds, too closely miked, have intonation problems. Yet the performance has some fine moments (particularly in the slow movement) and provides further evidence of the strong interest in Mahler's music in Japan.

WAKASUGI, HIROSHI /Tokyo Metropolitan Symphony; Kiyomi Toyoda, soprano - Fontec FOCD 9020 (1990) [56:16]*+   Once again Hiroshi Wakasugi proves that he is a well-versed and intelligent Mahler conductor in this recording, subtitled "Ode to Heavenly Joy." While he employs an objective approach, his reading is thoroughly stylish, eschewing mannerism and exaggerated dynamic contrasts. Excellent inner voice balancing and well-defined sonics also enhance the performance. The TMSO has developed into a fine Mahlerian ensemble. The first movement moves along at a frisky pace. A similarly brisk tempo is set for the Scherzo, sounding more agitated than relaxed. Wakasugi's reading captivates with its lilting strings, perky rhythmic treatment and seamless musical flow. From the opening notes of the slow movement, he immediately puts us in just the right mood for this tender, sometimes passionate, expression of love. Wakasugi elicits these emotions without becoming excessively sentimental. The finale contrasts perfectly the soft strains of the folk-like opening melody with its pert rhythmic accompaniment which recalls the first movement's sleigh bells. Tempo choices are well-conceived and sudden shifts well-handled. Soprano Toyoda has a fine, clear voice and sings softly and charmingly. Overall, this recording has much to offer.

WALTER, BRUNO/New York Philharmonic; Desi Halban, soprano - Columbia 11213-8D; ML 4032 (1948); Odyssey 32160026; CBS/SONY 20AC; Sony MPK 46450 (1990) [66:54]+   This recording does not present Walter at his best. Although his reading is mostly idiomatic, it is also surprisingly uninspired and on the cool side. Tempi are frequently handled in a flexible manner and details are not always carefully rendered. A perky tempo for the first movement does not prevent Walter from infusing the music with an appropriately Viennese quality. And he does conjure up some strong climaxes here; only the coda seems no more than routine. A mournful horn solo opens a rather brisk Scherzo, which while expressive still lacks sufficient sensitivity. The *Poco Adagio* also moves along smartly rather than lovingly, and Walter's powerful climaxes go by too quickly. One has come to expect more warmth and tenderness from Walter in interpreting Mahler's music. Worse yet is the finale, suffering from much too agitattion, uneven playing and a mediocre soloist.

WALTER, BRUNO/Vienna Philharmonic; Irmgard Seefried, soprano (perf. 24 Aug. 1950, Salzburg) - Varese Sarabande VCD 47228 (1985); Originals SH 836 (1994) [53:34]
     Compared to his commercial recording of the Fourth, this rag-tag, dashed-off performance comes as an unwelcome surprise, especially from one of Mahler's greatest champions! To suggest that tempi are treated flexibly is to vastly understate the case. Walter proceeds as if many of Mahler's frequent tempo shifts were deleted from the score. Rushing and slowing up at will, he wrenches any semblance of tempo consistency from its moorings. The result is often a case of conductor vs. orchestra. The VPO's performance is simply atrocious, disaffected by wiry string sound, raw, brash and inarticulate brass, intonation problems in woodwinds, brass and timpani, and serious miscues (what is that percussion doing before #17?). To make matters even worse, the sound quality leaves much to be desired. Walter's strange mannerisms in the slow movement are most disarming. Ignoring Mahler's markings, he holds back into #1, hesitates on violins after #2, where Mahler says *nicht schleppen* (don't drag), and suddenly speeds up at m.72, where Mahler writes *ruhig* (restful). Clearly, this performance caught Walter on an off-night. Other live performances (see below) are more representative of Walter's Mahlerian manner. Even Seefried does not give her best here. She sings loudly, coldly and with a harsh, school-marmish vocal quality. When Tempo I returns after #7, she begins *alla breve* while Walter insists on common time. He soon gives way to her

to dispel the confusion. Better to omit the numerous details of technical problems here than to make more of this performance than it deserves.

WALTER, BRUNO/New York Philharmonic; Irmgard Seefried, soprano (perf. 4 Jan. 1953) - Music & Arts CD 656 (1990) [52:52]+   Walter is much more at home with the New York Philharmonic than with the Vienna Philharmonic in this 1950 performance with the same soloist (see above). While still flexive and slightly *mosso*, tempi are much more comfortable and under control. High volume levels distort balances in quiet passages; audience noise becomes annoying. Playing is also much cleaner and truer than in the VPO performance. Strong accents and *sforzandi* in brass during the development section of the first movement help to bring out the devilish *in medias res* (at 8:50) only to push forward intently thereafter. How urgently he builds to the grandoise climax at 10:00+. By #19 (11:17), he again rushes forward only to hold back at *schungwoll* after #20. Brass timbres seem harsh at times. Underlying edginess detracts from the warmth and charm Mahlerites have come to expect from Walter. Such nervous energy works better in the Scherzo, where it enhances the caricaturish nature of the music. But one is reminded of Klemperer in the unhesitating coupling of section with section. Again Walter seems removed from the music he knows so well and usually renders with such complete assurance and stylistic charm. In the *Poco Adagio*, he seems more like himself. He mellifluously floats the long-lined opening theme, gracing it with slight hesitations that enhance its lyric beauty. As the music gathers strength and intensity, strings give the impression of being forced to move forward. By 2:20, the violins are far too loud for *pp*. The more agitated material following at #4 (c.8') seems hurried, but Walter works up to a strong climax at #11 without pressing into it too intently. Of course, Walter's handling of the *subito andante* that suddenly appears at the end of the tiered allegro segments is, as always, masterful. The finale opens in a comfortable tempo, with woodwinds in jaunty style. Seefried is more herself here too, singing clearly and securely. But she picks up the tempo on her entrance and sings more demonstratively than with innocent charm. By the final stanza things seem slightly off course: Seefried moving the tempo forward stridently, Walter trying to hold a more moderate course. The voice sounds too overbearing to convey either the light-hearted or peaceful visions of heavenly life that should be expressed here.

WALTER, BRUNO/Vienna Philharmonic; Hilde Gueden, soprano (perf. 6 Nov. 1955) - DG 435 334 (1991) [54:30]+   Walter and the VPO jell much better here than in their earlier recorded performances (see above). He presses forward agitatedly at times but more often than not in a natural and easy manner. This tendency to add impulse to the pace is evident early on: after establishing a relaxed main tempo, Walter thrusts for *frisch* second theme with much bravura. The cello melody which follows seems more forceful than lyrical. After a somewhat subdued beginning, the development moves urgently into its climax (7:15+), where dark clouds cover the otherwise untroubled atmosphere. While Walter hurries the tempo forward at times, his approach to the climax before the reprise is masterful--it culminates in a terrifying vision of the underside of heavenly beatitude. Conversely, the reprise is joyful and exuberant. Notice how gently Walter calms down the orchestra before the final coda (14:50) (tainted only by a miscue on solo horn). In the Scherzo, he sets an agitated tempo for a reading that lacks the usual Walterian charm. Nor do the clarinet's folk-like parodies get the usually idiomatic Walter treatment. Tempo eases up a bit for the trio, where true Mahlerian strings captivate at #11(6'). Toward the closing section, coordination becomes unstrung; the horns rush while solo violin holds back. As early performances indicate, Walter's reading of the *Poco Adagio* movement never lacks warmth, passion and intensity. His handling of the tiered *allegro* sections is most impressive, especially in how deftly they give way at the height of their agitation to the calming main theme. Hilde Gueden sounds charmingly youthful. Her pianissimos are lovely and her phrasing expressive. But she has difficulty with "*Sanct Peter im Himmel seht zu*," stopping abruptly on the last note; her top range sounds somewhat shrill; and she has a tendency to push the tempo forward. At subito tempo I after #7 (3:07), Gueden seems confused by Walter's tempo and starts in double time. Walter has to adjust to her as he did with Seefried in the earlier VPO version.

WALTER, BRUNO/Orchestre National de France; Maria Stader, soprano (perf. 5 Dec. 1955) - Nuova Era 2233 (1989) [51:34] This is another recorded performance by Walter that should not have been issued. Except for the slow movement, Walter just dashes off the music with little interest or involvement. Sonics are often too loud and frequent volume adjustments are noticeable, sometimes diminishing the effect of climaxes (at #7 and #8 in the *Poco Adagio* movement). The first movement whizzes by without any of Walter's usual stylishness. The Scherzo is given a brash, indelicate and routine reading. While the slow movement is expressive, high level sonics ravage the intended mood of restful contemplation. Even Walter's usually assured handling of the tiered *allegro* sections, which end so abruptly with an andante transition to the main theme, suffers from dislocation and dissociation of tempi: the opening *andante* drags sluggishly; the *allegretto* that follows is suddenly much faster; and the *molto allegro* ending zooms forward as if shot from a gun! Brass miscues clutter the closing section. In the finale, the soprano seems to have her own ideas about tempo, often at odds with Walter's. Close miking detracts from her otherwise pleasing voice. She tries to be perky and cute in the quicker sections, but generally conveys little delicacy or fluid lyricism elsewhere. Her tendency to hurry the tempo along is yet another distraction. This release truly serves little purpose, except to undermine the deserved reputation of a great conductor.

WALTER, BRUNO/Vienna Philharmonic; Elizabeth Schwarzkopf, soprano (perf. 29 May 1960) - 2-Bruno Walter Society 705 (1976); 2-Music & Arts CD 705; 2-Arkadia CD 767 (1993) [59:22]+ While this recorded performance shows Walter in a slightly different light from his studio recording, the sonics are very disturbing at times. Again the first movement is best, with its easy-going tempo and Viennese *gemütlichkeit*. Here more details are audible but tempi lack consistency. The Scherzo is again on the brisk side in a straight, detailed reading. But the performance seems somewhat on the dry side. A much more lush, sometimes even milked treatment of the slow movement provides some beautiful moments of yearning passion. Yet at times a cool breeze seems to waft over the music producing a rather harsh effect. The E-major outburst at #12 could have been more effective but the following pesante is appropriately dolorous. Schwarzkopf sounds lighter and softer here than in her recording under Klemperer. While she does sing with much expression, her vocal tone simply doesn't have that quality of childlike innocence which would better serve this music. Although Walter's treatment of the finale is much more acceptable here than in his studio recording, the overall impression still can only be described as adequate.

WELSER-MÖST, FRANZ/London Philharmonic; Felicity Lott, soprano - EMI Eminence CD-EMX 2139 (1988) [62:59]** With his first recording of a Mahler work, Franz Welser-Möst became an overnight sensation. His handling of the Fourth matches in stylistic nuance, attention to detail, characterization and emotive quality the best of existing versions. His approach, while personal, is not affected or overly mannered. He knows how to give a lyrical phrase just the right inflection to be stylish without going overboard. Notice how touchingly he renders the close of the first movement's exposition; how he achieves urgency in building to the climax of the development without undue speed; and how delicately he leads his forces into the final coda, gently stroking each of the first few notes of the main theme until he coaxes them forward to an exuberant close. The Scherzo has spirit as well as an appropriately devilish character, enhanced by perky woodwinds and highlighted sforzandi. By contrast, lyrical material melt with exquisite string portamenti (at #4). Few more experienced conductors realize the meaning of the direction *hervortretend* (expressive) as impressively as Welser-Möst. While he takes a weighty tempo to open the *Poco Adagio*, he makes an extremely persuasive case for it. His pacing here is strict but at least never sags. Mahler's nostalgic sentiments are conjured up with delicacy and sensitivity. The important bass ostinato rhythm at the beginning of the movement has rarely been given as much prominence. Had the strings been richer and warmer, the superlatives would be unending. This young conductor knows how to produce a tragic climax as well (e.g., after #3). He can fire the music with passion (after #7) and let it breathe with gentle fluency (such as during the entire coda). The finale is no less impressive. Setting a comfortable tempo, he balances the vocal soloist with the orchestra by placing her within it. Even with a slight edge to her voice, she sings the final "*Kein Musik ist ja nicht auf Erde*" beautifully, ending with a portamento at #14 that would melt the hardest heart. Notice how Welser-Möst picks up the half-measure dotted-rhythmic figure appearing at the close of this section as a reference to the impish Scherzo. This is a brilliant reading from a very talented young conductor.

WIT, ANTONI/Polish National Radio Symphony; Lynda Russell, soprano - Naxos 8.550527 (1992) [56:54]+ The most obvious characteristic of this performance is its moderation. Working within the limitations of this ensemble, Wit maintains order and control, careful attention to dynamic markings and generally well-conceived tempo gradations. But the overall effect leaves one unmoved. From the sluggish opening jingles, blandness permeates this performance. Strings sound scrawny and brass attentuated. Sonic quality is clear but lacks depth of field and underbalances woodwinds and bass strings. Wit knows how to handle this music proficiently and maintains a firm hand throughout, possibly at the expense of needed flexibility. The main thematic material of the first movement is spirited if somewhat constricted. During the development Wit generates a sense of urgency that impels the music forward to a fine climax (9:40+). But at the sudden return of the main theme in mid-stream at the beginning of the reprise, we are a long way from what should be the main tempo (10:30), requiring a later unmarked tempo adjustment to enliven what otherwise would be a stultifyingly slow tempo. The Scherzo has a sprightly, impish character, as well as a strong impulse that is achieved without undue speed. Tempo changes (into #9 at 5:10) work well without affectation. Again Wit carefully renders dynamic markings that highlight the movement's devilish character. Lovely high strings at #11 (6:38) would have been more captivating if played more softly. Unlike others, Wit takes care to hold back at #12 (7:30), marked *gehalten* (halting), and then presses forward as Mahler directs, so that the return of Tempo I at #13 is perfectly timed. A gushing, darting quality pervades this entire movement. The *Poco Adagio* is most disappointing, for it fails to project much emotion or sensitivity. Although Wit can arouse his players to some measure of feeling when called for (6:35+), the somber main theme needs more flexibility. Wit downplays the important rhythmic motto first presented in bass strings at the outset. Some sore spots are all-too-audible: overdone horn swells at c.7:30 and fatuous horns following the climax after #7 (11:25+). While the return of the main theme at 15:37 is handled beautifully, the movement as a whole has little impact. After a relaxed opening tempo is set for the finale, the clarinet intones the main theme in a strangely dark and cool manner. Placed properly within the orchestra, the soloist sings well enough, despite some insecurity at the extremes of her range. But again the reading merely scratches the surface of the movement's many diverse qualities, strongly contrasting a nearly ferocious rendering of the jingles motive (5') with the heavenly calm of the final stanza (6:22).

SYMPHONY NO.5 IN C-SHARP MINOR

Movements:

Part I:
1. Trauermarsch. In gemessenem Schritt. Streng. Wie ein Konduct.
2. Sturmisch bewegt. Mit grosster Vehemenz.

Part II:
3. Scherzo. Kräftig, nicht zu schnell.

Part III:
4. Adagietto. Sehr langsam.
5. Rondo-Finale. Allegro.

ABBADO, CLAUDIO/Chicago Symphony - 2-DG 1707 128 (1981); DG 419 835 (1988); 427 254 (1989) [72:13] In an effort to be stylish, Abbado engages in exaggerated mannerisms and extremes of tempo. An over-emotive funeral march sometimes played by weeping woodwinds infuses the music with an extremely morose quality. Yet a more restrained, even studious approach is taken in second movement. Much too tame for this violently angry music, Abbado's reading seems sapped of vitality before it gets started. Although Abbado does achieve a strong climax before the coda, phrases are clipped and the return of the scherzo subject is not well-coordinated. Part II (Scherzo) begins nicely but soon loses energy, plodding along spiritlessly. Balances could be improved and the faster sections before the coda could have been more cleanly played. The final section is rushed abominably and recorded too loudly. Although the *Adagietto* is expansive, it lacks stylish nuance of phrasing and depleting its emotive effect, it drags on without direction. The finale opens well (even the sound and balances improve) and playing is more energetic although lacking sensitivity and warmth. Some vulgar mannerisms occur and contrast strangely with rushed climaxes. The performance breaks loose in the final moments coming to a rapid, rollicking close.

ABBADO, CLAUDIO/Berlin Philharmonic - DG 437 789-2 (1993); 10-DG 447 023 (1995) [69:29]+ If excellent playing and superb sound quality were all that was necessary to make a performance succeed, this would be one of the best available, but the music's dramatic force and joyful spirit are so tempered that it fails to impress. The first movement makes a promising beginning; the funeral march theme has just the right hesitency, accentuation makes a promising beginning; the funeral march theme has just the right hesitency, accentuation and weightiness to make it doleful without seeming gushy. In shocking constrast, the trio abruptly interrupts the plaintive lamentation of the march with an impassioned dramatic thrust, surging forth mightily without excessive speed. But from the opening of the second movement, one senses a weakening of purposefulness. While the funeral march theme's return is deeply felt and the rising violin motif at #7 (2:45) willfully draws the rest of the music with it, the violent anger on which the movement concentrates seems too temperate. Abbado makes a few interesting points, such as at 4:35 in the cello interlude, where he plays the first two measures *mf* and the remainder of the passage *pp* as marked. Later, the broadly-paced march theme becomes menacing when hints of the opening violence bestir themselves in bass strings (6:15+). Yet emotive force seems restrained, confining the intensity of this outpouring of rage. Abbado manages a powerful Grand Chorale (11:50) and a thrilling climax of the scherzo material before the coda. But restraint and control sedate the wild spirit that should permeate the middle movement. A lack of personal involvement becomes evident. In the *Adagietto*, Abbado follows the current trend of pacing the main tempo more briskly than was once accepted by some noted Mahlerians, particularly Leonard Bernstein and Hermann Scherchen. The rationale for this approach is to avoid creating a dolorous mood that would contradict Mahler's alleged intent to write a love song for Alma Mahler and not a lugubrious dirge. While the main theme has a *cantabile* quality, its overall impact is lessened by lack of personality. Abbado also imposes an unusual effect upon the main theme by fussing with the first beat of the measure that follows the rising three-note upbeat with which the theme begins. The finale also suffers from halfheartedness. From the section marked *frisch* (fresh) near the beginning of the movement, one senses a mildness of spirit which becomes more animated only momentarily (c.6:30+; 9:25+). From #27 (11:38), the performance takes on a segmented quality, becoming a patchwork of dissociated moods. After only a moderately intense build-up, the Grand Chorale's enormous power seems to be self-generating.

ABRAVANEL, MAURICE/Utah Symphony - 2-Vanguard SUR 321/2 SD (1975); 11-Vanguard 08.4013.79 (1995) [61:25] This very tame and basically uninteresting performance is typical of Abravanel's stylistic approach. Square rhythmic treatment and an overcautious manner result in a fussy, lifeless and sometimes awkward reading. Although Abravanel rarely takes liberties with the score, his approach lacks direction, coordination and cohesion. He tends to smooth over the rough spots, defusing the music's grotesqueries. Some fine moments do occur, such as in the funeral march of the first movement which has just the right mournful quality. Frequent intonation problems and other technical difficulties are disturbing. A feeling of ferocity is completely lacking in the second movement, which seems simply hard-driven, especially during the climaxes. Much the same can be said for the Scherzo. While it opens with a gaily tripping principal subject, the music soon becomes stiff and stilted. Phrases are either pressed, very agitated or routinely read. Brass are confined and woodwinds have a tendency to go off pitch. The tempo for the *Adagietto* movement is moderately slow, but playing lacks sufficient sonic dimension and expressiveness, contributing to a lack of warmth and sensitivity. A spirited tempo in the finale is not enough to inject life into this sterile, directionless and often stilted reading in which playing lacks polish and idiomatic treatment. The *pesante* climax is taken at too fast a clip but the closing section has a gingerly snap to it. Overall, this performance is mediocre at its best.

BARBIROLLI, JOHN/New Philharmonia Orchestra - 2-Angel SB-3760 (1969); 2-EMI CDM 64749 (1994) [74:17]* Barbirolli's reading is generally labored, heavy-handed and stiff; only in the fervent moments of the opening movement and the passionate segments of the *Adagietto* does Barbirolli provide enough spirit to satisfy. Yet his compatriots at Gramophone magazine find this approach completely appropriate. Slower tempi tend to drag mercilously, especially in the opening funeral march, yet Barbirolli rips into more energetic sections with a will. Consequently, some moments in the opening movement are profoundly moving and intensely exciting but contrast with the overcautious approach found elsewhere. The second movement is rather tame: weak percussion and squarish playing rob the music of intensity and forward motion. A lyrical rather than coquettish treatment of the Scherzo is also plagued by stiff playing, lack of vigor and unidiomatic effects. After a songful *Adagietto*, Barbirolli presents an uninvolved, tired and aimless reading of the finale, robbing it of its *giocoso* character.

BERNSTEIN , LEONARD/New York Philharmonic - 2-Columbia M2S 698 (1965); Sony SMK 47580 (1992) [69:22]*+ Bernstein draws much power and intensity from this work in one of the most exciting versions ever recorded. While his proclivity for affectation is evident, it rarely disturbs, and often enhances, the music's emotive exuberance. Without stretching the opening funeral march to excess (as Barbirolli does), Bernstein evokes a deeply mournful feeling as well as rock-solid strength and dramatic furvor. Although he hesitates on the march theme, it never seems to drag or lose intensity. Clear details and taut playing are further pluses. While the second movement could be more vehement and is frequently marred by forcefully abrupt tempo changes, it is still well played and builds to an energetic if not very grandiose climax. The Scherzo movement is a delight. The music whirls and swirls as if in a whirlwind, without becoming affected or disjointed. Bernstein's extremely slow and inflexive reading of the *Adagietto* may not be in vogue at present, but it does not want for tenderness and sensitivity, as do other versions which take a quicker pace and are less supple in phrasing. Bernstein captures the essence of the finale perfectly. All its good-natured joyfulness is elicited with spirit and verve. One is especially taken with Bernstein's way of gradually, even unnoticeably, increasing the forward motion until the final glorious return of the brass chorale of the second movement. Although this grand climax could be taken more broadly and infused with a more noble aspect, Bernstein whips up the tempo in the closing section to a frenzy which is nothing short of thrilling.

BERNSTEIN, LEONARD/Vienna Philharmonic (perf. May-June 1972, Vienna Musikverein Grosser Saal) - DG video 072 225-3 (1991) [71]*+ One of the first recorded performances of Mahler by Bernstein and the VPO finds them not always as much in sync as in later performances. Consequently, inaccuracies in precision occur and restraint in temperament constricts expressivity, especially during Part II. Sonic levels sound remote, particularly in the brass. Memory of these detractions seems to vanish in the outpouring of deeply felt emotion and exuberance in Part III. In the first movement, Bernstein's march theme is solemn yet touching and his trio section is fired with passion. Later, he speeds up intently to the massive *klagend* outburst before the final coda. While taking a marked ritard in the opening measures of the Scherzo, Bernstein ravages the principal subject with fierce, seething energy. Yet he moderates the extreme tempo and dynamic levels of his earlier NYP recording. Even so, the level of intensity and dramatic impact is still high. With marvelous urgency, Bernstein builds to an anticipation of the Grand Chorale, only to be dashed to pieces by the violence of the main theme. From there, the music seethes with passion, racing forward to that wonderful moment when the sky opens, foretelling of ultimate redemption. After such a thrilling climax, the scherzo's return seems sluggish, as if overwhelmed by the grand vision that preceded it. Set against such heaven-storming vision, Part II lacks Bernstein's usual ebullience. There is much gracefulness and idiomatic nuance in the dance themes, but some moments seem forced, tempered or uncomfortable (e.g., the returns of the opening). From *kräftig* to the end, this uneasiness abates, and the movement relentlessly presses forward to the close. Bernstein reads the *Adagietto* as a moving statement of heart-felt passion mixed with profound melancholy. While his approach might seem out of vogue today (especially when taking 12:14), the depth of emotion he evokes should not be overlooked. Moments that hang suspended in mid-air contrast with those of surging intensity. This performance need not elicit sadness but a passionate longing for both the tenderness and intensity of love. The finale is a perfect counterfoil to these emotions, overflowing with *joie de vivre*. Not only is the *Adagietto* theme presented here in a more joyful guise, but even the hint of the violence of the second movement (after #23) has a mocking presentment. Torrents of sound build with great intensity to the reappearance of the Grand Chorale, resplendent in its heroic grandeur. The finale coda leaves one breathless.

BERNSTEIN, LEONARD/ Vienna Philharmonic - DG 423 608-1 (1986); 13-DG 435 162 (1992) [75:00]** Those familiar with Bernstein's earlier recordings of the Fifth will immediately notice how age has tempered his approach to dynamic levels and tempi. Frenetic intensity is less pervasive here. One senses a greater degree of control that was missing from earlier versions. Rather than having a negative effect on the performance, his broader tempi work well here. Bernstein seems more deliberate in his treatment of the score's numerous dynamic markings, yet he does not over-emphasize them. Using sectional miking, he creates near perfect balances of inner voices, revealing more of the complex textural interweaving of thematic fragments in this highly contrapuntal score. In fact, Bernstein achieves greater linear transparency than most of his colleagues in this work. Bernstein offers a sensitive and profound reading, with few of the exaggerations. His flexible but unaffectatious approach to the march theme provides a well-deserved lesson to those who have stretched this theme out to its breaking point. A *cantabile* treatment of this doleful yet yearning melody can create the desired effect without either setting an extremely slow pace or over-indulging in mawkish luftpausen. (A curious lesson to come from Bernstein!) A fluid, legato line for this theme with just the slightest hesitation on its two-note upbeat sets he mood for the entire performance. Listen to the final statement of the theme before the trio section (beginning at bar 307): how utterly devastating! Notice also how deftly Bernstein handles fluctuations in tempo and transition passages (e.g., into #11). Whether overwrought with intense passion (at #7) or overwhelmed with tragic pathos (c. mm. 253-6 and #17-18), the effect is devastating.

Even if age may have slightly tempered Bernstein's energies, he renders the stormy second movement with aggressive intensity and dynamic thrust. Inner workings come through more clearly and dynamic levels are more carefully balanced and coordinated. For example, he highlights the usually inaudibile countertheme played by the clarinets and bassoons at #13. Accents are also more pointed, sharpening the edge of the *scherzando* material with rapier-like precision (e.g., into the return of the *scherzo* section at #9). Even minor elements leave a strong impression, such as the echo effect produced in the strings at *piu mosso* after #16. Although Bernstein elicits much passion as the music builds to the Grand Chorale, when it is reached it seems to lack sonic power sufficient to fully convey its grandeur and nobility. More forceful is the huge outburst of dispair marked *klagend* toward the close. A weightier tempo for the third movement may sound sluggish to some listeners familiar with Bernstein's more energetic approach in his earlier version. But Mahler added the phrase *nicht zu schnell* (not too fast) to the tempo marking for this movement. Bernstein's treatment evokes a nostalgia for lost youth rather than the mindless whirl of cosmopolitan life. (Could this music have had personal meaning for the Maestro?) Again linear details and dynamic markings are clearly rendered. Waltz material is handled with knowing grace and charm (e.g., notice how the waltz theme enters ever so slowly at the beginning of the trio at #6 and then gradually moves forward in truly Viennese fashion). But there are a few distractions. The strong hesitation into bar 614 is uncalled for in light of Mahler's direction to render the hesitation *unmerklich* (unnoticably).

Bernstein's manner elicits a feeling of weariness (at #26) until he wisely choses to pick up the tempo. Also troublesome is the inaudibility of the bass drum rhythm at the opening of the coda. In the Adagietto movement, Bernstein seems more concerned with clarity than self-indulgent emotionalism. He treats the main theme songfully, with warmth and tenderness; yet one might wish for a more subdued harp here. In the finale, Bernstein holds back the tempo of the main theme at first, becoming more aggressive as the movement proceeds. By the time we reach the section marked *grazioso*, he is clearly into it, so that the closing moments overflow with *joie de vivre*. One still feels that more volume is called for, but it is nearly impossible not to be caught up in the sheer joy of it all.

BERTINI, GARY/Cologne Radio Symphony - EMI CDC 7 54179-2 (1990/91) [67:52]+
Bertini seems less motivated here than in most of his other Mahler symphony recordings. Consequently, he provides a straight, unaffected but often inflexible reading that rarely gets to the dramatic core of the music. Within such an objective frame of reference, there is still much to admire in his conception, particularly in the relentless impulse with which he drives Part II and the high spirits he generates in the finale. But the high volume levels engineered here do not make up for the overall lack of emotion and dramatic impact (e.g., in the funeral march theme of the first movement and the section leading to the climax at 4:15 of the second movement). Nor can high speed into climaxes (occurring frequently in Part I) replace more natural progression (e.g., #10 at *klagend* in the first movement). A tendency to highlight solos, particularly in the trumpet in Part I, recalling Leinsdorf's version (see below), becomes distracting. Bertini seems more involved in the maddening whirl of Part II, where unflagging spirit drives the music forward and deliciously provocative tidbits offer fascinating characterizations. Notice the wickedly nasty trumpet snarls on a fragment of the main theme at 4:25 and the uncharacteristically moody horn solo interrupted by musing on snatches of the waltz theme (5'). Otherwise, all passes by like the wind, with little contrast or significance. Bertini plays up the movement's ups and downs, fits and starts. How tellingly he pauses ever so slightly at #26, then gets up another head of steam only to be interrupted again by that bemused horn solo, going on as if it hadn't noticed that the wild dance had come to an abrupt halt. Yet with all of the movement's strength and mad frivolity, one senses a lack of underlying tension and urgency that should drive the musical protagonist to an untimely end. A surface reading of the *Adagietto* follows, detached from its emotive essence. If this music was intended as a love song (as some claim), it is more declaimed here than sung. The finale is lively, joyful and exuberant, if somewhat lacking in inflexion. As with Ozawa, one senses that the music here is sometimes put on automatic pilot. With the anticipation of the Grand Chorale's return at #21 (c.9'), the reading becomes forced and runs out of energy. A feeling of inevitability which should drive the music to its majesterial climax never comes through. Even the whirlwind coda feels too stiff and constricted.

BOULEZ, PIERRE/BBC Symphony (perf. 1968, London) - Nuova Era 2326 (1989); 2-Arkadia CDGI 754 (1992); Enterprise CDEN 901 (1993) [64:28]* Boulez's Mahler performances are too frequently given short shrift as unidiomatic and too intellectual. Despite the occasional awkward turn of phrase and questionable tempi, his reading of the Fifth has many merits, particularly a clarity of line and balancing of inner voices, most apparent in the finale. From the stentorian trumpet calls of the opening, one expects a strong, demonstrative first movement . . . and gets it. The march theme is properly hesitant and mournful, touchingly phrased without undue inflection, even if it seems sluggish at times. In contrast, Boulez whips up a virulent storm of passion in the trio section. Dotted rhythms seem heavy-laden occasionally (at #12), but his reading is often impressively perceptive (e.g., how telling is the slight swell in lower woodwinds before #14). Ponderous moments thereafter give way to an entrancing stillness in the return of the trio section. The deeply tragic "cry of lament" (marked *klagend*) before the close seems temperate in comparison with the surging emotions aroused earlier. Boulez emphasizes the mournful quality of the succeeding Scherzo movement in a reading that combines fierce anger and touching expressivity. His handling of the many mood swings here is well-conceived for the most part. But some of his adjustments seem incomprehensible: after taking the long view into the return of the scherzo theme at #14, he does not begin it in tempo but continues the *poco ritard*; then he shifts the unexpected return of Tempo I in mid-measure to the beginning of the measure. Boulez nearly stops for the return of the theme here, then trudges through the subsequent section marked *piu mosso subito*. His approach to the following *pesante* is also misguided: no ritard into it, but a sudden quick burst of speed at *drangend* (pressed), hardly unnoticeable as directed. The return of Tempo I thereafter makes a marvelously wild contrast, aggressive yet rambling. But its vigorous intensity spills over into the march theme that follows, making it seem strangely passionate. After #23 Boulez ignores the marking *nicht eilen* (not fast), keeping the tempo brisk, so that the climax at *wuchtig* (weighty) is given less heft and has less impact than it should. Too often here Boulez hurries the tempo where Mahler calls for a more restraint (before the return of the scherzo at #26). Following a generally fine Grand Chorale, Tempo I is hard-driven until it comes up against a big ritard to #33. For Part II Boulez sets a lively pace, also driving the music forward relentlessy at times. But since this movement bespeaks wild abandon and unremitting bustle, such pressed tempi are not out of order. Some awkward moments occur: slowing up for two measures of the theme at m.67 and again at m.114. Curiously, he does not repeat this mannerism in the trio, where all is charming and gracious. Some slight hesitations seem superimposed (at #20), but they rarely interfere with the chaotic whirl which hastens on incessantly to the close. Boulez comes close to the timing for the *Adagietto* that Mahler is alleged to have pencilled in at the beginning of the movement in the score after a performance (clocking in at 7:37) but the moderate tempo he sets does not detract from the music's expressivity. Boulez gives a passionate reading of this popular movement, making a strong argument against a heavy-laden approach to tempo. Just as convincing is his rendition of the finale, full of joyous *elan* and refined charm. Inner voices are well delineated and balanced. Now the tempo set for the *Adagietto* theme makes infinite sense in its reappearance in this movement. Listen to how effectively Boulez builds up the excitement into #15. Unlike his free interpretation of markings in the second and third movements, he shows how deftly Mahler's directions can be handled to enhance the effect. But for some awkward maladjustments appearing in the earlier movements, this performance merits a higher regard than it has been given by some thoughtless critics.

BOULEZ, PIERRE/BBC Symphony - Hunt CD 718 (1990) [64:03] Less impressive than their 1968 performance, this 1970 performance finds both conductor and orchestra more detached from the symphony's dramatic character. Boulez avoids the experiments in phrasing which clutter the earlier reading but his previous spontaneity and sense of adventure have vanished. Little has changed in the straight, surface reading of the first movement, but the second movement lacks intensity, drive and thrust. While structurally well-conceived, it has minimal dramatic impact. Frequently, the main scherzo material is weighed down and from 5:45 and becomes plodding from 7:25, sounding like a pomp-and-circumstance march. Contrariwise, the funeral march of the first movement is sometimes hurried, and in a dash for the *wuchtig* climax, the orchestra trips over itself. Similarly, they fall haphazardly into the climax of the Grand Chorale. Part II is restrained, its light-hearted gaiety seeming more like tongue-in-cheek whimsy. The orchestra sounds discomforted and insecure. As one has come to expect from Boulez, there is much clarity of line and inner voice balance. But the music keeps stiffly grinding itself out without purpose or direction and with little temperament. Notice how pitifully Boulez tries to ease in to the waltz in Viennese style at the return of pizzicato trio (8:36), only stumbling into it clumsily while being whacked by heavy timpani strokes. Unlike the 1968 version, constant motion fails to produce seamlessness, instead causing fragmentation. Strings are frequently imprecise, and the solo trombone misses his entrance before #30 (14:22). Rather than unremitting abandon we feel nervous energy. Emotions are closeted in Boulez' reading of the *Adagietto* movement. While taking about 30 seconds longer than in his 1968 performance, his pacing has a breathless quality which it did not have earlier. By the finale, there is little hope of revivifying this performance. Tempi are sluggish, playing faulty and the spirit restrained. The *Adagietto* theme now sounds reflective, even moody. Boulez tries to energize the ensemble in the section that follows the wild *fff* tutti at #21 (9') and in the section that follows, but he plays down the trumpets' anticipation of the Grand Chorale to mere whisper (9:20). Shaky brass inhibit the next wave to 10:38. Some signs of life appear on the build-up to the Grand Chorale, but when it comes, Boulez hastens through it as if embarrassed by its grandeur. Tempo increases in the coda are staggered rather than smooth. Long before the close, the orchestra seems too exhausted to capture the music's joyous spirit.

CASADESUS, JEAN-CLAUDE/Orchestre National De Lille - Forlane UCD 16609 (1989) [67:38] One senses that neither conductor nor orchestra are atuned to this music. Casadesus tries to provide a characterful reading without being especially provocative, but too often his choices for emphasis and de-emphasis are questionable. Frequently, tempi press forward hurriedly, move in an unremitting straight path, or wander aimlessly. Many tempo changes are uncoordinated. In the second movement, the cello interlude at 4' limps along, ignoring Mahler's directions to press forward, while the funeral march theme of the first movement is set at a brisk pace. Casadesus seems most secure in Part III, where he takes a cantabile rather than languorous approach to the *Adagietto*, becoming more sensitive and tender as it proceeds, and vitalizes the finale with much energy. Least successful is his conscious and uncomfortable effort to inject both liveliness and character into the middle movement (Part II). His efforts to create a Viennese style for the waltz music are too studious to sound natural. At 12:30 he misreads *nicht eilen* as a direction to slow up in the midst of a lively, lighthearted section, thus causing its energy level to diffuse. The Lille ensemble is not particularly Mahlerian, sounding stiff and rigid, bright and glaring in wind coloration, weak in string sonority, and clipped in dotted-rhythms. Brass (particularly the solo trumpet) blare out mercilessly, sometimes smothering strings, and often playing without that Germanic martial quality that is quintessential to Mahler's symphonies.

CONLON, JAMES/Gurzenich Orchestra; Cologne Philharmonic - EMI 5 55320-2 (1994) [71:04] On the heels of Conlon's excellent recording of the Fourth issued only a year earlier, this performance of the Fifth is a big disappointment. While Conlon maintains his conservative, straight-laced approach, he treats this more intense work so tamely that he fails to make much of an impression. His moderation in temperament detracts both from the dramatic depth of Part I and the joyous conclusion of Part III. Only in the devil-may-care antics of Part II does he seem more attuned to the music's whimsy. Unlike the brilliant sonics EMI provided for Conlon's Fourth, sound levels are severly confined, adding to the limitations of this surprisingly uninspired performance.

DEWAART, EDO/Netherlands Radio Philharmonic - RCA 74321 276062 (1995) [74:11]
+   The key word that describes DeWaart's approach here is "moderation", for he keeps all elements of this performance under tight control and restricts expression of its diverse moods. While he renders Mahler's markings with care, he does not use them to enhance the symphony's dramatic character. A steady, sometimes squarish march in the first movement drags along

casually, and the trio section seems too tame. DeWaart tones down the vehemence of the second movement, merely concentrating on technical precision. A spirited Part II becomes too rigid for lack of spirit. The result sounds more studied than spontaneous. Part III is no less moderate in temperament. The *Adagietto* moves along smartly but without much nuance or passion, and the closing Rondo movement is only moderately jocose, lacking drive and personality.

DOHNANYI, CHRISTOPH VON/Cleveland Orchestra - London 425 438-2 (1989) [65:07]*+   Rarely have clarity and precision been so deftly combined with an intelligent interpretive sense as in this recording. Without indulging in manufactured effects or excessive mannerisms, Dohnanyi conveys the dramatic import of this symphony in a most capable manner. Tempi tend to be pressed, but *allegros* are energeretic and slower tempi have a nice lift. Sonic production is superb as are inner voice placement and balances. Within a moderate temperament and a straightforward reading, Dohnanyi manages to capture the spirit of the opening movement: it has dynamic force, even if the funeral march theme seems too evenly paced in its first appearance. After an aptly torrid trio, one detects a dispassionateness, which replaces dramatic weight with agitated intensity, crisp playing and softened accentuation. But how marvelously the horns give out on the ascending motive of yearning at m.225, and how forthrightly the antiphonal trombones play out after #17. Although increased motion intensifies the second movement, its dark, satanic side is hidden from view. Mahler's almost unbearable inner struggle rarely comes to the surface in this reading. Even the return of the funeral march theme feels hurried, like an objectified recollection of past sorrows rather of than an anguished contrast to the furosity that ushered it in. Dohnanyi handles the transitions back to the scherzo material with cunning and subtlety. His approach doesn't overwhelm but it does impress. He gives Part II an unpretentious reading, enlivened with hyper-tension. Notice how clearly he delineates counter-melodies (between upper and lower strings at m.47). But any excitement here seems generated more by calculation than instinct. The *Adagietto* movement is, as one might expect, also given only a moderately emotive reading. In *cantabile* style the main theme has a pleasant character, never wallowing in grief. Again clarity is a strong point: rarely does one hear the climax at mm.30-31 so clearly (particularly the 16-note figurations in inner strings). No strong sentiment, but no lack of emotion either. In perfect contrast, the finale spills over with gaiety, enthusiasm and vitality. A brisk main tempo works well, played to perfection by this jewel of an ensemble. Even the return of the *Adagietto* theme has rarely sounded as gracious. A thrilling close brings this exemplary performance to a thoroughly delightful conclusion.

FROMENT, LOUIS DE/Radio Luxembourg Symphony - Blackpearl BPCD 201 (1988) [63:13]   This budget-label recording adds the anachronistic subtitle "Death in Venice" to the name of symphony. Notwithstanding such nonsense and the middling level of orchestral playing and sonic reproduction, the performance has much in its favor. Froment gives the work a straight, unaffected reading, that is generally lively and sometimes fairly strong. While he rarely gets below the surface of the music's emotions, he handles the symphony's many twists and turns aptly. Unfortunately, what he is able to create cannot possibly overcome the technical inadequacies: weak, thin string sound; over-balanced brass; woodwind intonation problems; and dynamic levels either too high (in the *Adagietto*) or too low (in the finale).

HAITINK, BERNARD/Concertgebouw Orchestra - 2-Philips 6700 048; 7505069 (1969); Philips 416 469 (1987); 10-434 053 (1992); 10-442 050 (1994) [70:42]   Haitink's restrained, cautious approach works no better in this performance than elsewhere. Despite a strong opening and a good march tempo, playing is too stiff and square, dynamic levels restricted and intense moments toned down. After a strong, dramatic opening, the second movement loses steam and becomes ineffectual and boring. Haitink emphasizes the lyrical elements of the Scherzo movement, smoothing over the hard edge of its rough-hewn gaiety. Tempi here sometimes plod along but balances work well. A conservative approach to the *Adagietto* produces some lovely moments, but the finale is too mellow and inflexive to engender much excitement.

HAITINK, BERNARD/Berlin Philharmonic - Philips 422 355-2 (1989) [78:47]+
Haitink's reading suffers from a brooding character laced with sluggish tempi that defuse striking contrasts and detract from what should be a natural progression from melancholy to joy. As a result, much of this performance lacks both character and spirit. Even slight affectations fail to elicit the right expression. Haitink infuses the tragic character of Part I with such an overwhelmingly morose feeling that it hampers his ability to rise above its dark moods in Parts II and III. He weighs in heavily on climaxes (e.g., in the first movement at m.247; and in the second movement at *wuchtig* after #24) and clouds over the joys that should resolve the painful effusions of Part I in a restrained, precision-oriented reading. Notwithstanding such reservations, the BPO plays superbly. One cannot fault Haitink for careful attention to details or clarity of line, but his conception is so mired in darkness and negativity that energy levels are held down and emotive contrasts tempered. Part II fails to convey a spirit of devil-may-care abandon, yielding only momentarily to a contrastingly sober mood on horn solos. Waltz rhythms are given a squarish treatment, strong effects smoothed over and playing often stiffly precise. A mournful quality inhibits some of the waltz tunes. Rarely has the *Adagietto* been stretched out so mercilessly as here, yet Haitink's lugubrious tempo does not infuse the movement with any special emotive quality. Though one might expect a mournful demeanor from such a long-lined reading, it merely sounds sterile and expressionless. The finale is neither joyful nor energetic. Haitink settles for high volume and technical precision. Playing is very legato, smoothing over the rough-and-ready side of this music. Even the Grand Chorale merely sounds loud and deliberate rather than grandiose, and the final coda lacks impulse. Consequently, the performance negates Mahler's vision of overcoming despair through the joys of love.

HERBIG, GÜNTHER/Berlin Symphony - 2-Eterna 8 27 548-9 (1983); Curb Classic Collection D2-78005 (1995) [67:04]+ In true Kappelmeister fashion, Gunther Hertig turns in a traditional reading, uncluttered with affectation or mannerism and well within the mainstream of Mahler's idiom. In full command of his forces, Herbig sets appropriate tempi throughout and conveys the symphony's diverse emotions in a moderate manner. They are neither devoid of passion nor self-indulgently laden with *angst* or mawkish sentiment. His faster tempi are spirited in moderation, and he rarely lingers over a lyrical expression. Sonics are clear and reverberant, if slightly unfocussed in bass strings and recorded at high volume (this has a negative effect only upon the *Adagietto*). The BSO wind group produces quacky timbres at times, and horns and trombones often overpower trumpets and strings, yet Herbig gets them to play articulately for the most part. His sense of balances and inner voice placement is well-considered. With so many conductors making a conscious effort to be "creative" (meaning especially different), Herbig's straightforward, uncomplicated but thoroughly idiomatic rendition is a welcome relief from the more adventurous readings that wallow in self-impose mannerisms.

INBAL, ELIAHU/Frankfurt Radio Symphony - Denon 33CO-1088 (1986); 16-Denon CO-72589/604 (1989) [72:22]* As with much of Inbal's cycle, an energetic approach enlivens allegros and strong dramatic power heightens the emotive effect. Rarely does Inbal engage in affectation or mannerism, leaning more toward the objective, yet he elicits much depth of feeling in all but Part II. Inbal conveys the tragic desolation of the first movement, establishing a strong opening tempo with occasional slight hesitations. The entrance to the coda section is extraordinarily profound. After an intensely energetic opening of the second movement, the funeral march returns in brisk tempo as if the aggressive nature of what preceded it was only slightly abated by its reappearance. Playing here is generally fine if not always on the mark. The scherzo material is full-blooded, if not always rapier sharp, and some moments seem underdone, notwithstanding high volume (e.g., prior to the closing section). Inbal fails to capture the spirit of devil-may-care frivolity that should pervade Part II. His treatment of the waltz music is squarish, and he falls into a ponderous, lumbering tempi at times, lacking stylistic nuance (particularly disturbing the second trio). Sudden relapses into the opening horn call seem stiff while the main thematic material speeds along hurriedly, resulting in imprecision. Inbal offers a soulful reading of the *Adagietto*. While he never digs deeply into the emotions conveyed here, he does capture its romantic lyricism. He closes the symphony with a delightful rendition of the finale, full of spirit and vivacity.

INOUE, MICHIYOSHI/Royal Philharmonic - RPO CDRPO 7011 (1990) [75:23]

The only redeeming feature of this mild-mannered, perfunctory and generally unimpressive performance is its consistency. Inoue leads his forces straight through the music, merely grazing its heights and depths without much dramatic effect. Only in the *Adagietto* (paced in the now passé manner of a dirge) does he permit his otherwise objective temperament to go beneath the surface of this heart-rending music. For the most part, Inoue is more intent on eliciting a languid turn of phrase for lyrical themes (such as the first movement's march theme) than in heightening the intensity of more dramatic passages or enlivening more energetic material. The RPO, not being an especially Mahlerian orchestra, plays cautiously, with restraint and very little color. Most of the stronger, more intense sections are played through unadventurously, with little dramatic power and sonic dimension. Such a pallid rendition has no place beside the many satisfying versions of the Fifth currently available.

JÄRVI, NEEME/Scottish National Orchestra - Chandos CHAN 8829 (1990) [70:29]*

Järvi's first Mahler recording is a worthy effort, offering a reading much in keeping with his usual stylistic approach to the late romantic symphony. He emphasizes huge climactic effects while often just playing through passages that require more subtlety, sensitivity and structural coordination. His opening movement has enormous dramatic weight and muscularity, amplified by strong brass and high-level volume. The march theme is ever so slightly held back, affecting a sense of melancholy that never becomes burdensome. The impassioned trio section [5:30] is devastatingly tragic, particularly at its close [7:40], and especially in contrast to its soft and languid return [10:10]. The *klagend* (sorrowful) outburst just before the final coda is simply overwhelming. Although some unmarked rallentandos do occur, Järvi is generally careful in attending to Mahler's numerous directions and avoiding unwarranted innovations. The full dramatic thrust of this movement comes through with intensity and power.

The success of the first movement carries over into the second. Paced at a fairly brisk clip, the opening section grips the listener with its seething rage. When the first movement's march theme reappears, it no longer seems so hesitant but straightforward, even slightly livelier, impelled by the initial surge of negative energy. But from here Järvi encounters some difficulties, particularly in mastering the many tempo changes and sudden transitions. After a fine return to the scherzo material of the opening [6:15 et seq.], he sluffs off into the *subito langsam* (suddenly slow) return of the march theme [6:30], defusing the jarring effect of this unprepared reversion to the calmer march theme by nearly anticipating it. Later, he slithers too cautiously into the *subito piu mosso* (suddenly more motion) tempo change at 7:10, again ruining the immediacy of its impact. The sudden return of Tempo I after a preview of the Grand Chorale [8:55] is handled more deftly. An occasional nuance impresses, such as added emphasis on the cello rhythm supporting the viola/trumpet line, that is completely lost in most recordings. At the section marked *wuchtig* (heavy), Järvi produces a climax of awesome dread, as if all of the negative emotions previously exuded were amassed anew for a final annihilating assault. Yet at its lowest ebb--the music virtually spent from such debilitating exertion--comes the glorious Grand Chorale. Despite Järvi's effort to make its high point by slowing up into it, this magnificent heaven-storming passage seems to lack sufficient dramatic weight to overcome the furious anger of the main material previously unleashed. These negative musical forces that terrorized the opening of the movement are not far away. When they reappear, the Grand Chorale's glimpse of heavenly glory is shattered with even greater ferocity than before. A long ritard ushers in the coda's hushed mysterium.

Seeming to stagger from the preceding onslaught, the third movement proceeds rather debilitatedly, showing a weakened spirit with its lack of momentum. Järvi tries to propel the music forward periodically (not always when called for), but his reading lacks the feeling of abandon that this music should convey. Frequent hesitations and tempo shifts cause forward motion to become disjointed. Järvi changes tempo so often, without direction in the score, that sections seem disconnected from the whole. After generating some excitement in the second trio, everything falls flat with the return of the lumbering opening theme [11:34]. Järvi tries desperately to press the tempo forward to fit the mood, but overdoes it [13:20] and must pull back slightly at the sudden *pp* [13:48]. Thereafter, he works into sections by gradually increasing the tempo from a slowish start [14:50+]. When the coda is reached, calling for a return to Tempo I, Järvi, having already exceeded that tempo, simply ignores it and races for the final bar at break-neck speed.

Tempo flexibility is used more effectively in the *Adagietto*. A lovely main theme, somewhat on the weighty side but never sluggish, has a pleasant lyrical quality. But high volume detracts from what should be an all-too-fleeting moment of calm and tenderness. Jarvi rarely instills a sense of repose or serenity here; his reading, though lyrical, is also rarely subtle or tender. The climactic section is overly strong when balanced against what preceded it and the closing section too drawn out for the intensity that generates it. The Rondo movement has all of the spirit of a Dvorak finale. But where Mahler sought to create an atmosphere of joyous celebration, Järvi creates an underlying tension and urgency, continuously press toward the big climax of the Grand Chorale. As a result the music seems more on edge than light-hearted. Once again brass dominate, carrying the entire orchestra to the Grand Chorale with increasing energy. After that thrilling moment (and thrilling it certainly is here) has subsided, the closing section begins as if exhausted from the huge outburst that preceded it, so that Jarvi must stir his forces from momentary lethargy to finish with a rousing presto. He does so admirably, despite some slipshod entrances.

KOBAYASHI, KEN-ICHIRO/Japan Philharmonic - Canyon Classics PCCL-00152 (1992) [72:05]** This performance establishes Ken-ichiro Kobayashi as a major Mahler conductor. Not only does he elicit strong, vibrant and thoroughly idiomatic playing from the JPO, but his brilliant blend of attention to details and generally well-conceived nuances provide ample evidence of a conductor who is mindful of tradition but not a slave to it. Kobayashi's tempi are very flexible, with occasional slow-ups and speed-ups not written in the score. More often than not they enhance the emotions conveyed without seriously disturbing the musical flow. Obviously, both conductor and orchestra are deeply involved in this performance; they generate much passion, intensity, drive and excitement throughout. Kobayashi makes a strong impression from the very beginning, weighing into the chords that follow the opening trumpet tattoo with enormous power. No passive observer, Kobayashi clearly feels the depth of this tragedy to the fullest measure. He unleashes tremendous fury in the trio section, rising to the height of passion, then holds up on the huge *klagend* chords at 7:25 with almost threatening presentment. And that threat is upon us with unrelenting ferocity in the movement that follows. Kobayashi insists upon strong accents and sharp sforzandi that add to the thrust and parry of this violent music. He adds a full ritard into the sudden return of Tempo I (c.3:20) and, thereafter, has the celli begin very slowly but movingly on their lengthy intermezzo (4:18), gradually progressing to the main tempo. What impresses the most is how expressively he has the TPO play here and throughout the performance. Around 9' into this movement (at #20) he slows up suddenly before the return of the march theme. What power is unleashed at the appearance of the *wuchtig* climax (10:45) and what majestic vision is conjured up in the Grand Chorale (11:51)!

Kobayashi also does a fine job with the waltz music of Part II, even if his players need to get off the eighth note of the broken dotted rhythms more quickly. A languid trio might seem overdone at first, but it works its way nicely into a more comfortable tempo. Playing occasionally creaks with stiffness, but for the most part, the movement has character and is shaped brilliantly and creatively. Kobayashi strikes a perfect compromise on the main tempo of the *Adagietto*, beginning in a moderately slow pace but moving through the movement flexively. His is a passionate reading, wrapped in the music's strong emotions, expressing each phrase with a personal feeling that forces the listener to take notice. Minor deviations from the score usually work in the service of these emotions and show his intelligence and strong intuitive sensibilitiy. In the finale, Kobayashi's personal approach again enhances the music's impact. Each fragment of thematic material presented in the opening has its own character. Kobayashi takes the first measure of the main theme in horns as part of the preceding ritard, beginning the main tempo on the second measure; this makes enough musical sense to question just where the *allegro giocoso* marking should actually appear. That *allegro* tempo is light and frisky, giving an upbeat quality to the main theme. Both pacing and mode of expression are true and evocative. The strings have a highly polished, brilliant sound, dig into accents intently, and can even survive a powerful brass onslaught. How deftly Kobayashi lingers over the return of the *Adagietto* theme (at 12') and then aggressively urges his forces forward as fragments of the main theme reappear, all without really having left the principal tempo. Rarely has this movement come alive with such urgency and impulse.

KONDRASHIN, KIRIL/USSR Radio & TV Large Symphony - 3-Eurodisc 27398KGX (1974); 2-Musical Heritage Society MHS 3951/52 (1979); Audiophile APL 101.501 (1995) [63:50] Kondrashin provides a serviceable if not very involved performance. Playing tends to be on the hard-edged, jagged side. Lyrical sections are treated with little sensitivity, emphasis being placed on the more powerful moments. The opening funeral march has more of a mournful than defiant character; yet the second movement is filled with biting harsh intensity. Details and balances are well-conceived but ensemble work could be better coordinated. While the middle movement seems too restrained at times, Kondrashin does generate some excitement with his hard-driven tempi.

KUBELIK, RAFAEL/Bavarian Radio Symphony (perf. early 1970s) - Meteor MCD 024 (1993) [68:03]*+ Kubelik's rapid tempi virtually sweep one off one's feet! The drive, intensity and agitation that permeate this performance are nothing less than overwhelming. Part I is not treated as a doleful dirge followed by raging anger at the tragic inevitability of death. Instead, Kubelik almost never allows the mournful aspects of these first two movements to deplete the strength and resolve in the face of death. His approach to the first movement's funeral march is not morose but forceful and dynamic, so that when the passionate trio first appears it does not provide a marked contrast in mood from the march that preceded it. Brass are strong and vibrant, woodwinds bright and shining. Swells, accents and sforzandi are exaggerated. One senses that the first movement's hero is memorialized as he was in life not in death. This feeling becomes more evident from Kubelik's reading of the second movement. The opening violence seethes with intensity. Baying horns blare out their anger at the injustice of inescapable human tragedy. Again the funeral march moves along quickly, as if in defiance of its mournful nature. Only a few technical mishaps in percussion temper this white-hot performance (e.g., a weak cymbal at the Grand Chorale's climax). Most shocking is the speed with which Kubelik dashes madly through Part II. In record time he races through the opening section despite Mahler's warnings not to rush. But the music comes alive with energy. Even the waltz music of the trio moves quickly at first; and its pizzicato reprise is more like an *allegro* than a *molto moderato*. Articulation is sharp-edged to fit the mood of agitation, and the atmosphere is tinged more with nervous energy than carefree spirit. Yet it sweeps one along with it to the wild conclusion. An *andante* tempo sets the pace for a cantabile reading of the *Adagietto*, sounding more bright and extroverted than warm and soft. The Rondo finale is alive with spirit. Inner parts are exposed and well-balanced and the canonic figuration sharply articulated. What tension Kubelik builds with each wave of the music's ebb and flow! He keeps pressing on to the Grand Chorale with unremitting urgency. But where is the cymbal at its climax? This is a thrilling performance, even if tempi are unusually fast and Part I may not contrast in mood enough with the remainder of the symphony.

KUBELIK, RAFAEL/Bavarian Radio Symphony - 2-DG 2707 056 (1971); Privilege 2726064 (1977); 2543535 (1984); DG 429 519 (1990); 10-DG 429 042 (1990) [68:03]*

One of the finest performances in Kubelik's symphony cycle, enhanced by superb sonics and balances and audible inner details. Granite-like strength characterizes the opening fanfare, which eases off into a strongly accented funeral march and builds intently to a climax of thrilling proportions. Although the succeeding movement seems somewhat restrained, Kubelik still manages to evoke a moderate level of dramatic intensity. Very expressive playing, interesting nuances and crystalline clarity are positive characteristics, as well as a glorious Grand Chorale. After a somewhat sluggish opening, the Scherzo picks up to a more sprightly tempo which adds sparkle to the waltz segment. Kubelik generates much excitement from forceful and expressive playing. Flexible tempi add vitality and never seem excessive. The closing section is a maddening whirl. While an unaffected reading of the *Adagietto* does not rise to the occasion of its furtive emotions, it evokes a positive response. But the finale suffers from stiff, squarish playing and frequent affectations do not produce an appropriate effect. Orchestral performance is brilliant, pacing generally fine, details well-rendered and balances well-proportioned.

LEINSDORF, ERICH/Boston Symphony - RCA 60482 (1990); 09026-68365 (1995) [64:06]+ The extremely pronounced trumpet protrudes noisely throughout Part I; otherwise, this version has its moments. Clarity of inner details and fine sound are pluses. A strong and unaffected opening movement generates some excitement with agitated pacing. Vibrant intensity energizes the second movement but playing sometimes sounds harsh, jagged and rough-hewn. A flabby horn spoils the Scherzo's opening. From here even a lilting waltz section cannot generate enough spirit to enliven Leinsdorf's mild-mannered reading. Leinsdorf is not very endearing in his brisk reading of the *Adagietto*, but in the finale spirited tempi and expressive phrasing hold interest. Here Leinsdorf is at his most exhilarating, especially as he approaches the great chorale climax. But at this most important moment he lets us down by breezing through the section as if it lacks significance.

LENARD, ONDREJ/Shinsei Japan Symphony - Club la Boheme B-3012 (1994) [67:46] + Much improved since its recording of the First two years earlier and now enhanced by strong sonics, the Shinsei Symphony gives an admirable performance, no longer shrinking from the challenge of rapid figuration, complex contrapuntal interweaving and idiomatic expressivity. Lenard's reading is straight and non-idiosynchratic. The result is most impressive given the short history of this orchestra. Undoubtedly, much of the credit must go to its able conductor, Czech-born Ondrej Lenard. For the most part his approach is not unique but his superlative handling of the many convolutions in this score shows his understanding of Mahler's style. Only one major fault should be mentioned: a measured, straight and inflexible reading of the march theme in Part I. Otherwise, Lenard and his Japanese orchestra generate much excitement. They do not lack the capacity to be expressive; their fine rendition of the *Adagietto* is adequate proof of this. The strong, intense music gets their most committed attention. Evidence of their talents is most noticeable in Part II, a difficult movement for players not schooled in *fin-de-siecle* Viennese style. They do well in eliciting its free-and-easy manner, despite some awkward hesitations in the waltz material. What impresses most is the energy, spirit and excitement generated throughout this performance, particularly in the second and third movements. Only the finale seems untoward at first, the main theme beginning mildly and the *Adagietto* theme sounding overly sweet and languid. But as the movement progresses, Lenard energizes his players until they generate enough impulse to hurl the listener through the closing pages. Lenard weighs in mightily on the second part of the principal theme after the change of key to C major before #12 (at 5:43), then resets the tempo to allegro, scampering along even more quickly than before. Pressing urgently into the Grand Chorale, Lenard heightens the intensity generated during the build-up to its monumental climax. Given the relative obscurity of this ensemble, their recording leaves a strong and satisfying impression.

LEVI, YOEL/Atlanta Symphony - Telarc CD-80394 (1995) [72:38]+ In his first Mahler recording, Yoel Levi offers an accurate, if moderately temperate account of this increasingly popular symphony. One senses early on a reticence to evoke without restraint the diverse emotions expressed here, from tragic passion to exuberant joy, resulting in a performance that lacks an emotive dimension. More moody than tragic, the first movement frequently succumbs to a mildness of temperament and colorlessness of sonic quality that severely hamper its dramatic impact. One cannot fault Levi's careful and intelligent rendering of score markings, but his tempi seem restrained and dynamic levels confined. The funeral march theme is appropriately hesitant but sounds too pale and mushy. Some passions are stirred at the onset of the first trio but kept within bounds. But how expressionless the strings appear in the second trio (10') and how characterless the woodwinds on the march theme (8'). What finally emerges lacks personality.

Much the same criticism applies to the second movement. The enraged anger of the opening subject is so diminished as to become a mere rhythmic exercize; the return of the funeral march from the preceding movement sounds pale and feckless. So enfeebled, the music never comes alive. Levi elicits stylish playing from the ASO in the Scherzo (Part II), but a mild-mannered temperament again fails to evoke the feeling of carefree abandon that should be expressed here. Yet the waltz music of the trio has a delightfully dreamy quality and the segments for horn obbligato have a contemplative character. For the *Adagietto*, Levi chooses a tempo akin to that of Bernstein and Levine, slower than has become the fashion with those who see the movement as an expression of profound love rather than bittersweet longing. Although the ASO strings are not as lustrous as those of other ensembles, they play eloquently and with a simplicity and sensitivity of expression that is admirable. One curiosity should be mentioned: the addition of a glissando into the high D-natural in first violins into the cadence at #3.

After such a fine reading of the *Adagietto*, Levi's restrained manner returns to attenuate the joys of the finale, which never seems to fully awaken from the dreamy atmosphere of the preceding movement. Emotions are held in check and never break their confines. Even the *Adagietto* theme's appearance here sounds meek and shy, as a bashful lover hesitant to express his overflowing emotions. The gradual build-up to the Grand Chorale lacks force, thrust and energy sufficient to make the appearance of this grandiose climax to the symphony a significant event; even the cymbal crash at its height is quickly dampened despite Mahler's direction to let it ring out fully. Too much restraint makes this otherwise straightforward and generally well-played performance too lackluster to satisfy.

LEVINE, JAMES/Philadelphia Orchestra - 2-RCA ARL2 2905 (1978); RCD1-5453 (1995) [72:10]*+   Levine's perception of this complex work is stylistically insightful and conceptually sound. Orchestral performance is assured and Levine makes certain that percussion is audible throughout. He captures all the drama of the opening movement with stirring intensity and touching sensitivity. Although tamer than one would hope for, the vehement second movement is still spirited and builds to a fine chorale climax. Levine's treatment of the Scherzo's hustle-bustle is thoroughly captivating, with spirited though controlled pacing and careful treatment of details. The *Adagietto* is paced very broadly, but played with soulful expression embellished by those luscious Philadelphian strings. Few conductors on disk have been able to elicit such a fresh, joyous spirit as Levine does in the finale. The return of the *Adagietto* theme has just the right uplifting quality to evoke the joyful spirit of this music and the closing section reels with unrestrained elation.

LITTON, ANDREW/Dallas Symphony - Dorian DOR 90193 (1993) [71:00]   Severely restrained sonic levels and improper balances weaken the impact of this performance. Litton's mild-mannered reading simply does not do justice to the symphony's dramatic power. Occasional nuances and inflections do little to generate intensity or stimulate emotions. Although strong climaxes are sonically enhanced, Mahler's hard-edged ferocity is smoothed over. As a result, the performance seems forced when trying to produce a strong impression and unimpressive when not. The DSO does not produce an effective Mahlerian sound: neither dark and nor fearsome enough in Part I, nor bright and vibrant in Part II, nor rich in string sonority or brilliant in brass sonics in Part III. Tempi are confined as well, sometimes requiring unmarked adjustments to liven things up--even if Mahler directs otherwise, such as before the final coda of the first movement at 11:40. The second movement is too tame and lacks both richness and depth of feeling. Listen to how meekly the main material returns at 6:42. Yet in mid-movement, Litton drives forward to the anticipation of the Grand Chorale (8:10) and thereafter adds a splendid hesitation on the reappearance of the funeral march theme. His drawn-out manner in the Grand Chorale comes across as loud rather than powerful. Part II lacks the spirit of wild abandon that should characterize this extensive movement. Either playing is too restrained, cautious and stiff, or pulled apart by awkward luftpauses (e.g., at the horn entrance to the trio at 2:35). Beginning on the weighty side at first, the trio succumbs to *kitsch* upon its return (10:30). An awkward extended ritard into the return of the scherzo theme (11:35) detracts from the suddenness of its reappearance. At the close, speed and volume fail to elicit excitement. Yet Litton's approach to the *Adagietto* has more merit. Despite pale string tone, he produces some tender moments, especially in the middle section and return of the opening theme. One wonders why so many conductors pick up the tempo into the climax in the final measures, rather than press forward thereafter as Mahler directed. The finale's main material is set in a lively tempo, but suffers from inertia. Litton even slows up at the key change marked *l'istesso tempo* (the same tempo) at 5:43, requiring yet another injection of speed thereafter. Again he tries to energize the movement as it moves to a climax at #20 (8:45), but loudness and matter-of-fact playing in the brass are counter-productive to his efforts. Much of the movement seems superficial, colorless and smoothed over.

LOMBARD, ALAIN/Orchestre National Bordeaux Aquitaine - Forlane FF 059 (1991) [65:47]*+ Although Alain Lombard is not known as a Mahlerian, if his reading here is any indication, he should be. He not only produces details with extreme care and achieves remarkable clarity of inner voices, but also captures each of the symphony's contrasting moods. Clearly, he took great pains with this local ensemble, which probably has little experience with Mahler's music. That they play with remarkable concentration, precision and enthusiasm is yet another credit to Maestro Lombard. In Part I, he weighs strongly into the fortissimo chords that follow the opening trumpet call and highlights dynamic contrasts. How incredible is the raw power he generates at the *wuchtig* outburst in the second movement [10']. The *joie de vivre* of Part II comes through in sparkling, gilt-edged profusion. Keeping the main tempo breezy yet steady, the movement never flags for lack of a joyous spirit. How deftly Lombard works into the waltz theme of the trio at 9:16. The closing coda is a veritable romp. After a perfectly gauged opening, the *Adagietto* is paced on the brisk side at first, but when the celli offer the main theme, the tempo relaxes to a comfortable pace. More intense moments are passionate and softer sections both warm and expressive. Lombard presses forward long before the climactic chord that ushers in the final bars, but the effect of that final upsurge is riveting. He goes into the Rondo finale without a moment's hesitation. And what a movement it is: bright, spirited and overflowing with joy. As each wave carries the music forward, Lombard ever so slightly increases the tempo, so that when the Grand Chorale appears, he must pull up noticeably. But it is well worth the effort, for a Grand Chorale it is. From here to the close, a whirlwind of excitement is let loose. Only the slapstick sounds strange--like a large wood block. Forlane is to be congratulated for providing such crystal clarity and full-blown dynamics levels.

MAAZEL, LORIN/Vienna Philharmonic - 3-CBS D3 37875 (1983); CBS MK 42310 (1987); MDK 44782 (1989); 14-Sony Classics SK14K 48198 (1992) [71:15]* Unlike his usually detached approach, Maazel gives a very strong performance here, sumptuously recorded and superbly played. An enormously powerful opening ushers in a mournful funeral march, somewhat heavy-laden and on the squarish side. Dramatic moments are highlighted in an expansive and impassioned reading. Maazel's noted interest in clarity of line and attention to detail is evident here. A muscular approach to the second movement sometimes seems too hesitant, but power rarely abates and some interesting nuances are applied (e.g., an awesome woodwind outcry at #25). A magnificent chorale climax crowns this irascible movement with a glorious touch. Maazel emphasizes the parodistic aspects of the Scherzo in a coquettishly coy manner. Each nuance is carefully rendered to enhance the playfully devilish side of this movement. Sometimes Maazel holds back momentarily, but only to spill over with enthusiasm. Elsewhere, he exaggerates restraint in order to caricature the waltz theme. While Maazel seems to be caught up in underlining every special effect, he still makes them work to enhance the music's character. Toward the close, Maazel virtually sets the music on fire. But thereafter the performance goes awry. Maazel seems to lose interest with the advent of the *Adagietto*, giving a cold, forced reading. He manages to elicit the *grazioso* quality of the dance music in the finale, even if a sense of restraint and caution hinder forward motion until the very end. Troublesome affectations and stiff phrasing detract from what should be a jovial atmosphere.

MACKERRAS, CHARLES/Royal Liverpool Philharmonic - EMI Eminence CD-EMX 2164 (1990) [69:45]+ Mackerras' first Mahler recording is a serviceable, if not thoroughly idiomatic or especially impressive, performance. Its stylistic character is more truly Edwardian than Mahlerian, toning down extremes in temperament, except in the *Adagietto*. High volume sometimes takes the place of dramatic power or distorts calmer sections. A cautious manner is revealed in exposed solo passages. Mackerras tends to be overly self-conscious in his treatment of details and dynamic markings. Close-miking causes extreme highlighting of inner parts and imbalances or heightens the volume unduly in softer passages (such as for the funeral march theme in the opening movement). Brass and cymbals dominate the first movement. While Mackerras' reading here is generally conservative, playing is slightly stiff and too deliberate. The vitriolic second movement is becalmed, with underplayed and colorless strings dominated by brass and percussion. Inner voices either penetrate too obtrusively or are buried in an orchestral onslaught. The sudden shift to a slower tempo at 7:11 is poorly handled, while the *subito piu mosso* (7:50) that follows needs more pep. Mackerras treats the Grand Chorale as an English ceremonial march, adding an over-stretched slow-up to its climax for good measure. (What kind of mute is the trumpet using just before the coda?)

In Part II more vitality fails to overcome a self-conscious manner. Clipped dotted rhythms stiffen the rhythmic flow, and slight affectations in the trio sections do little to loosen things up. Swells are often over-emphasized. However, Mackerras handles the waltz segments nicely (c.5' and 9:12). While lacking subtlety, there is enough drive and impulse to hold the attention, particularly from 12:38 to 13:10. Mackerras clearly tries to engender more passion in the *Adagietto*, but dynamic levels are consistently too high. A gentle, tender main theme is quite attractive. Notice the false articulation in violins at mm.31-32 (3:18). Kept within bounds, the finale has spirit, even if playing is sometimes lackluster. In the opening measures, Mackerras has both the bassoon and oboe hesitate on fragments of the main theme (Mahler indicated such treatment only for the latter) Before the Grand Chorale's reappearance, the energy level seems to subside, causing Mackerras to try to enliven the proceedings (before #23). After a moderately effective climax, the final section begins in fast tempo and remains so, with the marked increases in speed ignored to the very end.

MADERNA, BRUNO/Milan RAI Symphony (perf. 23 Feb. 1973, Milan) - 4-Arkadia CDMAD 028.4 (1993) [69:44]*+ Maderna was probably the most important champion of Mahler's music in Italy during this century. His is an extremely personal approach, but not necessarily an unidiomatic one. He frequently ignores Mahler's directions, content to indulge himself in a plethora of stylistic nuances and mannerisms. Yet Maderna is clearly in sympathy with the work's emotive aspects, making every effort to elicit them in such a manner as to leave a marked impression. His orchestra has difficulty both with the music and his exaggerated inflections. After opening on a raspy trumpet, the horns suddenly hold back, weighing strongly on the first note of each martial figure in the cadence before the march theme and causing the introduction to die out sluggishly. Then the funeral march takes up this heavy-handed manner, underlining its mournful quality. At the beginning of the theme, Maderna sits on its upbeat dotted rhythm (3:00), and he repeats this mannerism throughout the movement. In contrast, the trio (5:30) whizzes by breathlessly, causing technical problems in the string figuration. Driving to a strong climax (c.6:50), Maderna infuses it with extraordinary power, slightly depleted by a shaky trumpet and quacky woodwinds. The return of the trio section (10:20) is quicker than in its earlier appearance, despite Mahler's direction to play it at the same tempo as before. Maderna again drives his forces forward to the *klagend* orchestral outburst, which seems sonically underdone for the urgency with which it was wrought. Again contradicting Mahler's directions, Maderna sets a slow pace for the closing coda (even the final flute tattoo is held back). Throughout the movement, Maderna either stretches out the thematic material or hurtles through more agitated sections with fiery passion. Ferocity and intensity characterize the opening of the second movement, but again Maderna counters its willful fury by slowing up for the main theme at #2, causing some dislocation. He also holds on to the upbeat into the funeral march theme in its reappearance here. The woodwind motive of repeated notes which punctuate it has an icy foreboding. At 2:12 Maderna slows up in mid-stream and then races forward; a tactic he uses frequently in this movement (e.g., at 5:50 and 6:30). Contrasts in tempo and mood are thereby highlighted and deepened. Some will find Maderna's long hesitations on appoggiaturas difficult to take (7:15). After a rivetting sudden return of the scherzo material following hints of the Grand Chorale, the tempo set for the funeral march theme is nearly the same as that of the scherzo (8:35)! Maderna suddenly reverses gears on the second period of the theme at 9:00 and then presses forward to a climax, holding aloft its highpoint (at #22) to make the equally sudden return of the scherzo more disquieting. He darts in and out of phrases agitatedly before the Grand Chorale. When it appears, Maderna continues to press through it to its climax, where he slows up not at its height but even before the trumpet tattoos that introduce it. A long ritard closes this section with a poorly tuned horn solo (12:10). The unanticipated return of the scherzo is simply frightening.

In Part II Maderna makes every effort to affect the carefree swagger of a true cosmopolitan. He treats the dance music very flexively, underscoring each individual nuance for good measure. Again he frequently propels the tempo forward only to rein it in at a denouement, thereby emphasizing the chaotic mood swings presented here. A bit sluggish to start, the trio section (6:05) evokes a dreamy atmosphere with its nuanced waltz theme (notice how bashfully the oboe soloist plays here). Some strange quirks occur in Maderna's incessant bobbing and weaving (11:20), but his approach captures the wild spirit of this movement. The result is so thrilling that temporary distractions caused by technical problems (e.g., clarinet at 15:04) can easily be overlooked. Just before the coda, notice how deftly Maderna eases up at the end of the cello passages (15:20) to evoke yet again a feeling that all is not well with this incessant madness. On paper Maderna's pacing of the *Adagietto* would not please those who think it should not be extremely slow and over-sentimentalized with anguished passion. Clocked at 12:40 one might expect a ponderously slow dirge. In fact, the main tempo is very broad for modern ears, but I fail to hear this approach as funereal or morose. Instead, what comes across is a reverie for lost love which is extremely moving. Hesitancies abound but enhance the emotive effect. The middle section is passionate but temperately paced. How gently Maderna comes off the climax before the key change at 5:50; how delicately he treats the slight comma (written only for second violins and violas) at 6:10; and how naturally he picks up the tempo to become more impassioned and then lets it recede to close the section, caressing each note ever so tenderly. The fluency of motion into the main theme's return is simply breathtaking. Maderna may have hit upon just the right treatment of the layered C-naturals that introduce the final section, delicately covering each other in a silky smooth texture. At this languorous pace, Maderna doesn't have to rush into the final climax as others mistakenly do. The finale is perky and spirited, except for an unfortunately heavy treatment of the *Adagietto* theme that impedes the musical flow and requires unsteadying tempo adjustments. At times, Maderna slows up for certain passages better left unaffected (the bass string figuration at 3:07). Upon the appearance of the *ff* violin thematic variant in C (5:24), he ignores the marking not to change tempo and holds back until the woodwind entrance on a counter-theme at #12. But from 6:12 to the anticipation of the Grand Chorale's return at 8:15, the performance virtually sings with an untroubled gaiety until it collapses from sheer exhaustion. Maderna usually handles sudden tempo changes deftly, except when he anticipates them (e.g., at 10:00). However, the orchestra has difficulty following him. The Grand Chorale is briskly paced but serves as a glorious climax to the symphony, and the performance closes with an uproarious coda.

MEHTA, ZUBIN/Los Angeles Philharmonic - 2-London CSA 2248 (1977); London 417 730 (1989); 433877 (1992) [63:22]   Mehta's approach lacks cohesion if not consistency. Where certain passages could speak better if played as written, he mangles them with numerous awkward mannerisms. When a flexible or sensitive treatment would enhance lyrical passages, Mehta seems out of touch. Orchestral performance also sounds uncomfortable and lacks polish. Restraint is the order of the day in the more intense moments of the opening movement. A slightly affected funeral march plods along intrepidly. This theme is too often treated as if it were intended to conjure up the scene of Christ bearing the Cross, but the yearning aspect of this theme is completely ignored. While Mehta seems to make an effort at projecting more temperament into the second movement, he simply fails to produce enough intensity to drive home its angry presentment convincingly. Consequently, his reading borders on the routine. Although the Scherzo opens in fine spirits, details are often fudged and playing lacks Viennese stylishness. Mehta's idiosyncratic manner of treating the waltz section may be part of the cause for the failure of his stylized reading to captivate. Nervous energy presses the music to a brisk close. The *Adagietto* is weak, only mildly expressive and lacking in warmth and soulfulness. Continuously hurried and imprecise, playing in much of the finale seems distracted until the performers get caught up in the thrill of the final climax and closing section.

MEHTA, ZUBIN/New York Philharmonic - Teldec 2292-46152 (1990) [69:48]*+

With this performance, Mehta has produced his finest Mahler recording to date. He has this work well in hand, and although some of his personal touches may seem out of place, they are only minor diversions from an otherwise marvelous reading. Clarity and precision are not considered among Mehta's strengths; yet, he ably demonstrates them here. Beginning somewhat moderately, with little hesitation on the funeral march theme, as if numbed by the awesomeness of the occasion, Mehta dives into the wild trio (#7), unleashing all its passion and intensity. Ritards are somewhat lengthy (e.g., into the second part of the trio at #9) but the dramatic closure before the return of the march theme is devastating. The trio's reprise is characterized by a combination of long-lined lyricism and strong rhythmic underpinning. A curious acceleration of tempo at m.377 (marked *poco meno mosso*) follows the huge depressing chords that precede the final coda. The second movement's vehemence is made more visceral by broad pacing. Mehta treats the return of the march theme flexibly and expressively, adeptly handling the many abrupt tempo and mood shifts. A brooding quality permeates the cello recitative interlude. Violins seem to search for meaning out of the violence on their rising scalar motive. One senses a slight retrenchment from the relentless tensions during the anticipation of the Grand Chorale, yet Mehta dives back into the scherzo's return willfully. Some unnecessary affectations creep in (into m.407 in the march theme), but the sense of overwhelming tragedy is conveyed masterfully: witness the awesome *wuchtig* climax. Mehta slows up into and holds on to highpoint of the Grand Chorale effectively. Before the final coda, the orchestral explosion is overpowering. Mehta aptly elicits the spirit of carefree abandon in Part II. The waltz trios have a slightly coy character. Alternating horn solos and orchestral fragments of the waltz are treated as melancholy reflections of a lost innocence. An underlying agitation propels the music forward, if sometimes against Mahler's directions (*nicht eilen*). At #14 Mehta ignores the *a tempo* marking, choosing to treat the cello passage broadly and expressively. The horn drags itself to the return of the trio, that moves briskly into the waltz theme long before Tempo I is marked. These details are only momentary distractions from the impulsiveness that characterizes this reading. In the *Adagietto*, Mehta takes the opening measures as written, holding back on each of the three notes that lead into its main theme. His reading is one of the most captivating on disc. A few details are worth mentioning: the clarity of the sixteenth-note figures in the first climax and the perfect placement of the harp within the orchestra. Mehta connects this movement with the finale (as Mahler intended) by opening it dreamily, still lost in reverie. He takes some time to shake off this wistful mood with the unrestrained joy of the Rondo. During at least half of this movement, the mood seems rather sober. Notice how Mehta eases into #21 where more *schwung* is call for; or how often he slows up into sections, smoothing their way clear of any rough edges. But when the Grand Chorale finally appears, any recollection of the *Adagietto*'s bittersweet melancholy is gone and general merriment is in full bloom to the end. Mehta's extensive experience with this work has borne fruit on disc at last.

MITROPOULOS, DIMITRI/New York Philharmonic - 4-Replica ARPL 32463 (1981); Hunt/Arkadia 523 (1989) [68:59]   Although this performance takes place on New Year's Eve, 1959, more than four and one-half years after the previous issue (see vol. 1, p.76), and some improvements can be cited, Mitropoulos' reading still tends to be uneven and affected. The opening movement moves along at a better pace, the march being treated spaciously but not laboriously. Mitropoulos dives into the *furioso* sections with a will and minimizes the intrusion of overdone mannerisms in the funeral march so as to evoke a more profound sense of tragic pathos. A steadier tempo works well here. In the second movement, his flexible style combines abrupt tempo shifts with sudden *ritardandi*. He does manage to generate some excitement despite a few affected intrusions. The remaining movements are read essentially in the same manner as in the earlier performance, although the waltz sections of the Scherzo are slightly less affected. While Mitropoulos' reading is still frequently at odds with both Mahler's idiom and his specific directions, some interesting moments occur.

MORRIS, WYN/Symphonia of London - Victor Independent SYM 3-4 (1973); Peters PLE 100/1; Collins 10372 (1990); IMP PCD 1033 (1993) [75:57]   Here we have Mahler as seen through the eyes of the English nobility! By means of this categorically unidiomatic reading, Mahler's music becomes stodgy and stuffy, even pompous and pretentious. The funeral march trudges along lugubriously. A blaring trumpet is too pronounced and infects the entire movement with a fatuous quality. Little happens in what should be a violently tempestuous second movement. Tempi are too slow and ponderous to invoke any intensity and, consequently, the movement drags on unmercifully. Though not very comfortable, the tempo Morris finally locates is fairly sensible for the third movement, even if the waltz sections still sound stuffy. Gradual tempo changes would have worked better in the coda in order to shift gears more deftly. The *Adagietto* is completely off the mark, totally devoid of sentiment, and given a light and tripping character. While the overall reading of the finale is satisfactory, too many sections still have a stodginess stifles the feeling of exuberant joy this music should convey. Orchestral forces are neither highly polished nor particularly stylish.

NANUT, ANTON/Radio Symphony Orchestra of Ljubljana - Pilz 160 182 (1990); ZYX CLS 4109 (1991); Fidelio 5003 (1991); Digital Concerto CCT 656 (1990) [63:18] {Incorrectly referred to as Alberto Vestri/London Festival Orchestra - Vivace 566 (1990)}
   This mild, ineffectual version is marred by weak and imprecise playing. A routine reading of the first movement manages to create some intensity in the wild, if jumbled, trio and a modicum of passion at #12. The last return of the funeral march theme has more nuance than in its earlier appearance. After a fine start, the Scherzo becomes rather mild, dry and under-energized, making little impact. Nanut presses into climaxes rapidly, substituting high volume for dramatic power. Part II suffers from a similar lack of tension. Rough edges are smoothed over and strong tutti passages are replete with technical imperfections. A tender, dreamy *Adagietto* has its moments, despite pitch problems in the strings. Too closely-miked, the harp entrance to #3 is over-exposed. Nanut elicits a feeling of joy in the Rondo, with dynamic levels that are more appropriate than in earlier movements. Now the *Adagietto* theme is more expressive, but Nanut rips through section-ending ritards and is unable to avoid clutter in forte orchestral passages. The finale is just another slapdash affair, neither joyful nor even interesting. Nanut rushes headlong into the Grand Chorale, although he presents it fairly well; however, one solitary moment of grandeur is not enough to redeem this otherwise ineffectual performance.

SYMPHONY NO. 5

NEUMANN, VÁCLAV/Czech Philharmonic - 2-Supraphon 1402511/2 (1978); Supraphon SUP 0021 (1988); 110 722 (1991); 111 976 (1993); 11-Supraphon SUP 111860 (1994) [69:30]   As is characteristic of Neumann's Mahler recordings, here we have another lifeless and uninteresting performance which fails almost at every turn to capture Mahler's spirit. Tempi in the opening movement are on the quick, snappy side and move along with little expressive nuance. The march theme is hardly treated as funereal but the more passionate trio (#7) is uncharacteristically mournful. An extremely objective treatment of the second movement finds Neumann more concerned about clarity of line than temperament or style. Consequently, his interpretation is too restrained and tempi too burdensome to elicit any intensity from this angry music. The Scherzo also sounds dull and uninspired, containing an extremely heavy-footed waltz theme. Neumann's reading is stiff and lifeless but the CPO play with Mahlerian flair. In moderate tempo, the *Adagietto* fails to captivate even if it is played beautifully. After establishing a fine tempo for the finale, things seem to finally catch fire. . .at least momentarily, but a mannered return of the *Adagietto* theme puts a damper on the proceedings and the remainder of the movement has an over-cautious quality which robs it of spirit. A grandiose climax is like an oasis in the desert of this lifeless performance.

NEUMANN, VÁCLAV/Leipzig Gewandhaus Orchestra - Philips 6703.016; Vanguard Cardinal C 10011/2 (1967); Berlin Classics BC2074 (1993) [65:41]   It is unfortunate that Neumann's performances with the Gewandhaus Orchestra of Leipzig are not more readily available. Even if this version has more to offer than his Czech Philharmonic performance, many problems still surface. The overall approach is straight and unaffected but again frequently lacks spirit and commitment. Playing tends to be constricted as are dynamic levels. While tempi are less brisk and tempo changes less abrupt than with the CPO, the first movement is still hampered by stiffness. But the succeeding movement completely misses the mark, jockeying between a very restrained treatment of melodic material and a tendency to jump into and rush through more intense passages. The Scherzo is quick and lively but does not captivate. More attention to details and better balances are helpful but most of the movement is simply tired and dull. The *Adagietto* is plagued by a brisk tempo, careless treatment of details and dynamic markings and complete lack of stylistic nuance. Although Neumann enlivens the tempo in the finale, he still fails to generate enough spirit to be completely satisfying, even though the great chorale climax works well.

NEUMANN, VÁCLAV/Czech Philharmonic - Canyon Classics 00205 (1993); Emergo EC 3972-2 (1994) [70:26]+   Unlike their earlier recording, Václav Neumann and the CPO now seem deeply involved in the music. Still, Neumann doesn't generate enough energy to propel the fast sections forward with urgency, and he often leaves an impression of weakness or exhaustion. While the CPO is a premiere orchestra, its string players tend to clip dotted rhythms and the brass often sound raw and piercing. In the opening tattoos, the trumpet rushes triplets and then slows up for dotted rhythms. But muscular strength predominates. The funeral march theme is well-treated, expressive without being maudlin, even if it drags slightly in the closing measures. Seering intensity heightens the drama of the trio, which builds to a thrilling climax at 6:00. At the height of the final climax, Neumann places dramatic weight on the huge chords marked *klagend*; but then moves rather briskly through the coda. His treatment of the Scherzo reminds one of Barbirolli's weighty approach. Bass strings dig in heavily on the opening figure. The main tempo is moderate for its stormy nature; anger being elicited more from sheer power than agitation. Played in strict tempo now, the funeral march seems stilted in contrast to the impulsive scherzo material. Neumann doesn't press into its return at 6:17, playing down the sudden shock of its reappearance. Notice how woodwinds sound stiff on the march theme at 6:50, controlling what should be a feeling of urgency that impels the music forward. While Neumann generates strength and emotional intensity, he does not sustain them over the long stretches Mahler requires. He treats the Grand Chorale (10:33) with a deliberateness that sounds self-conscious; after the scherzo's final return weakened by a feeling of exhaustion, he blurs the misty coda.

Neumann reads Part II as a recollection of youth from the vantage point of old age. A heavy main tempo lacks vitality and a feeling of devil-may-care abandon. Neumann handles the waltz trios with nuance and grace, giving them a dreamy nostalgic air. Stiff playing of canonic string passages works against the wildness of the music, and clipped playing in brass constricts forward motion. Full-bodied sonority and high volume can carry this movement just so far. A slight hold up for the last two bars, mirroring the opening measures, is an intelligent nuance. Neumann's reading of the *Adagietto* is emotive but recorded at a volume too high for such tender and meditative music. Weeping strings and weighty chordal support lend a touching quality to the middle section, but at the close too much restraint stifles the emotions generated earlier. Like so many other conductors, Neumann ignores the fact that the *molto ritard* into the return of the theme on a long downward glissando at #3 is to continue for five measures into the theme itself before Tempo I appears. A slight luftpause into the high A at the final climax adds depth as does the robust treatment of the final chords. The finale lacks spirit, both interpreted and played too temperately to be joyful. In contrast, the Adagietto theme seems more effusive here, when it should be played in tempo and with less hesitation so as to fit within the context of the movement's general feeling of joyous redemption. Tight reins hold back the driving quality of much of this music, and precision is achieved at the cost of high spirits. Notice at 12:47, where the *Adagietto* theme and the finale's main theme are combined, how the spirit of cheerfulness is restrained; it is as if the latter got bogged down in a recollection of the former. After a strong Grand Chorale (14:34), the closing coda tries to build up a head of steam, but sounds merely louder rather than wilder.

OTAKA, TADAAKI/Tokyo Philharmonic - Camerata 32CM-227 (1984) [70:39]*

If you listen to this performance after hearing Otaka's recording of the Fifth with the BBC Welsh Symphony made 10 years later (see below), you will see how early this young conductor became a thorough-going Mahlerian and how consistently he has maintained his interpretive approach to this symphony. Otaka has the advantage of leading Japan's premiere orchestra, one that plays more idiomatically than many other Japanese orchestras, despite occasional rhythmic rigidity and off-color wind timbre. Strings and horns need more sonic dimension, for they sound weak when they should be rich and full. As in his later version, Otaka takes a traditional approach, sticking close to the score's many details while avoiding affectation. Dynamic levels are restrained, never giving a full measure to the work's powerful climaxes and tempering the cutting edge of sforzandi and strong accentuation. Yet Otaka handles the music stylishly, turning each corner of this often disconcertingly unpredictable work with aplomb. A few moments are worthy of special mention: a touching cello intermezzo before the return of the march theme in the second movement (from 4:12); a jaunty march thereafter (at c.8') replete with growling and biting brass effects; and a surprisingly stylish Part II, that demonstrates just the right degree of control over its high spirits until they are let loose in the final coda. In the finale, occasional rawness in brass only adds to its rough-hewn rustic character. Higher volume levels would have enhanced this recording.

OTAKA, TADAAKI/BBC Welsh Symphony - BBC Music Magazine BBCMM 109 (1994) [68:12]*   Few experienced Mahlerians would expect such a strong and well-conceived performance from these relatively unknown performers. This release, issued privately by the BBC but available by subscription, provides a serviceable rendition of the Fifth. Even if the BBC Welsh ensemble lacks sufficient sonic dimension to be thoroughly Mahlerian, it plays well and makes a fine impression. Opening with a strong trumpet solo, broadly treated with dramatic weight, the first movement is handled in a straight, unaffected manner, with careful attention to details, without sacrificing spirit or temperament. An appropriately funereal quality enhances the main theme, and the furious trio section has much vitality. Otaka knows how to engender the symphony's diverse moods, whether of touching sensitivity (e.g., the trio's return at 9:25) or awesome dread (the *klagend* outburst at 10:34).

Despite low-powered strings, the Scherzo has much spirit. Otaka again attends to details and adjusts balances intelligently. Yet the sudden return to Tempo I at 6:08 could have been tuned more finely. Little dramatic weight underlies the anticipation of the Grand Chorale (7:30), but the combination of march theme and scherzo is well presented (8:00). Strong contrasts in somber and tempestuous elements lead to a shattering *wuchtig* climax (9:50). Aggresively pressing to the Grand Chorale, Otaka lifts its high point with a big ritard. The scherzo's return is fearsome and the closing section shadowy. A nice swagger enhances Part II, that is given a straight, unmannered reading; but as it progresses, weak strings and sluggishness diminish the feeling of unrestrained giddiness. The solo horn at 7:50 wanders in and out of tune. Before the trio's return (9:55), one senses a world-weary feeling rather than the contemplative reminiscence of past carefree days. Otaka handles the Viennese waltz segments stylishly and generates more energy and excitement to the close.

For the *Adagietto*, he sets a moderate pace and creates a mood of touching sensitivity without over-indulgent emotionalism. Taking his time, Otaka lets the music flow naturally, highlighting its *cantabile* quality. Notice how beautifully he brings back the main theme at 4:55 and how captivatingly he handles the closing moments from 8:25, where he holds back the final climax ever so gently. In the Rondo, Otaka makes more of the fragmentary opening than most, underlining each phrase. But strange instrumental timbres present a problem that becomes more acute in horns later. Thereafter, he succeeds in capturing both the rough peasant quality of the main theme and the overall spirit of joyous regeneration. Messy entrances and imprecise string figuration do not seriously impair this generally fine performance.

OZAWA, SEIJI/Boston Symphony - Philips 432 141 (1990/1991); 14-Philips 438 874 (1995) [71:32]*+ Ozawa's Mahler recordings often receive faint praise at best or downright rejection at worst. In this case neither are justified, for he delivers a very fine reading, as idiomatic as it is powerful. From the strong opening tattoos, set in steady march tempo, to the weighty, pliant march theme that follows, Ozawa shows that his many years of involvement with this music have borne fruit. With sensitivity and depth of feeling, impelled to powerful climaxes from the sudden outburst of the trio, the first movement teems with intensity. Only a continuously over-exposed solo trumpet is troublesome. Muscularity rather than agitation dominates the Scherzo. The return of the march theme from the first movement has a heavy-laden quality, as it had in its previous incarnation. Some balance problems occur (at 3:30 where the repeated-note motif is smothered by heavy timpani), but Ozawa is generally careful in attending to the multiplicity of dynamic markings and other details. During the section marked *piu mosso subito* (7:50), where both the principal and march themes combine, a hint of the Grand Chorale should have stirred up more anticipation. Instead, it it is hardly noticeable before the passage dissolves in the fury of the opening material. Ozawa generates more excitement on the way to the full-blown appearance of the Grand Chorale than he does when it actually occurs: trumpets clip their heroic theme and low brass drown out woods and timpani. Before the final coda, however, Ozawa draws a powerful climax that befits its tragic character.

In Part II, Ozawa emphasizes the contrast between the vitality of the main subject and the enchanting lightness of the trios. Spacial instrumental placement brings out the stereophony of certain segments (e.g., the horn's "call" and "answer" at c.2:18 before #6 and the whirling

F-naturals in horns at c.10). Strings play the languid waltz themes beautifully. In the latter half of the movement, Ozawa's unflagging approach to the main tempo underlines the sudden collapse from exhaustion which momentarily halts its progress, only to roust itself for yet another dizzying whirl (14:45+). Although brass seem restrained before it, the final coda is undauntedly wild. Ozawa takes a more traditional approach to the main tempo of the *Adagietto* than is taken now-a-days, playing it in the tempo Mahler provided (*sehr langsam*) rather than more fashionable *andante*. The reading is deeply moving without seeming either gloomy or over-emotive. The main theme is treated with much hesitancy (sometimes against Mahler's directions), but it captivates completely as it moves to the climax of the opening section, without pressing too rapidly into it or smudging the filigree that graces its highpoint. The closing of the middle section into #3 (at 7:48+) is heavenly, and the extended Cs that usher in the closing section seem to float on air. The Rondo begins tamely, but from the string figuration at #2, Ozawa picks up the tempo, even if the energy level remains only moderate. At a steady, controlled pace, he manages to be lively in what is one of the rare movements in Mahler untroubled by negative emotions. The BSO strings seem to hold their capacity for full-bodied sonority in reserve, but balances and sonic levels are excellent. Both the build up to and the appearance of the Grand Chorale before the close is glorious; and the coda generates much excitement without excessive speed. This performance deserves more sympathetic press than it received when first released.

RATH, GYÖRGY GYÖRIVANYI/Giovanile Italiana Orchestra - Caroman CRM 011 (1993) [69:39] This rare issue presents a performance as close to a chamber version of the Fifth as can be imagined. The young Italian ensemble plays extraordinarily well in this challenging work, but produces a diminutive sound that often lacks sufficient breadth to be effective. Close miking of soloists surrounded by a small-sounding ensemble adds to the chamber-like effect. The solo trumpet is too prominent throughout Part I. Conductor Rath, when he is attentive to markings, handles the score competently. He adds character to his reading of the funeral march theme of Part I by applying slight hesitencies, and creates a coyness in the way the violins play the first theme of Part II. But his deviations from the score, scattered throughout Part II and the Rondo of Part III only confuse. For example, in Part II he goes into one-beat to a bar after the ritard at m.152, slows up into the *langsamer* (slower) change of tempo at m.241, and maintains a brisk tempo in the finale, despite many *nicht eilen* markings, sometimes requiring uncalled for adjustments (e.g., at m.307 on the *ff* violin theme marked *l'istesso tempo*). Rath makes up in stylish nuance for what the orchestra lacks in precision and sonic dimension. Notwithstanding the meager sound they sometimes produce, the young players can muster enough energy to jolt one out of one's seat at the sudden appearance of the trio of the first movement. A few miscues are excusable in light of the high level of performance they achieve.

SARASTE, YUKKA-PEKKA/Finnish Radio Symphony - Virgin Classics VC 7 91445 (1991); 561130 (1994) [68:16]+ For his first Mahler recording, the young Finnish conductor Saraste handles the score intelligently, without any brash attempts at revisionism. While his orchestral forces do not exhibit a particularly Mahlerian style, they present themselves well. Saraste generates excitement as well as depth of feeling in the impassioned allegro sections of Part I, but calmer passages are sometimes stultified or bloated. In the chordal outbursts concluding the opening march, he rears back and hurls forth mightily into the wildly passionate trio section of the first movement (at 5'). But in the succeeding movement, playing tends to become stiff or doughy by turns. Much the same may be said for the Scherzo. While it contains a well-turned waltz tune (at 2:34), embellished with affected nuances, again rigidity sets in thereafter. Sometimes one gets the impression that high volume is employed to make

SYMPHONY NO. 5

up for lack of impulse (to 13:35), a strategy that rarely accomplishes its presumed goal. Saraste seems too remote from the emotions of the *Adagietto*, as if making a report of sentiment rather than expressing it; but in the finale, he has Mahler's ebullient mood well in hand. His energetic spirit enlivens the joyous mood, although sometimes it is better held in check, as during Saraste's hasty treatment of the Grand Chorale. But from 13' to the end, the performance catches fire, generating a flurry of excitement. Minor flaws aside, this is an impressive first venture into the Mahlerian world for both conductor and orchestra.

SCHERCHEN, HERMANN/Vienna State Opera Orchestra - 2-Westminster WAL 207; XWN 2220; WST 220 (1952); Palladio ENTPD 4121 (1993); Andromeda ANR 2516 (1994) [66:16]   Scherchen's reading is replete with harsh contrasts, flexible tempi and some quite interesting nuances. A serious drawback is the antiquated sonics and frequently sloppy playing. The opening is very dramatic even if the march is on the calm, legato side. Yet Scherchen generates an incredible level of excitement by activating wildly aggressive tempi that press forward unrelentingly. A maddening second movement riveted with biting intensity and extremely fast tempi would have worked better with cleaner playing and less affectations. After a rather down-played opening, the Scherzo becomes more buoyant in spirit as it moves into the trio section. Here the waltz theme is presented in an awkwardly square manner that sounds almost like a caricature and is marred by poorly tuned and jumbled strings. All hell breaks loose at *sehr wild*, but the level of playing cannot sustain Scherchen's rapid tempo and the passage gradually begins to fall apart. A moderately quick *Adagietto* is generally uninteresting and at times even harsh until about the midway point where Scherchen suddenly takes the music to heart. The finale begins neither *giocoso* nor *frisch* as directed but simply slowly and tiresomely until #2 where it swings into a livelier tempo. Balances are poor and playing uneven. A fast chorale climax has little grandeur and is hampered by atrocious brass sound. Yet Scherchen musters up enough energy to make the closing section appropriately animated.

SCHERCHEN, HERMANN/Orchestra della RAI di Milano (perf. 8 April 1962) - Stradivarius STR 13600 (1988) [57:47]   For a devotee of Mahler's music, listening to this performance might be the ultimate challenge of one's loyalty, if not of one's endurance. Scherchen, noted for his eccentricities, delivers what can only be described as an abusive reading of this symphony. With little respect for Mahler's score, he makes numerous lengthy cuts, massacring Part II, of which only 5 1/2 minutes survive, and ripping long stretches out of the finale, of which he retains less than 9 1/2 minutes. For those interested in particulars, #7 through #17 and #22 to the coda after #30 are omitted in Part II, and m. 329 through #24 (209 measures!) and mm. 749 to 759 are dropped from the finale. The eccentricities of Scherchen's reading are primarily found in extreme tempo choices, from carelessly rushed passages in the fast movements to lugubriously sluggish tempi in movements 1 and 4. These extremes have some validity in the first movement, where the contrast between the funeral march theme and the violent trio are heightened by exaggerated tempo contrasts. But too often Scherchen ignores Mahler's directions so unreservedly that he appears more than careless. Either he gallops through quick sections (#15) ignoring their dramatic import or stretches out the lyrical line mercilessly in slower sections (#19). To add to the problem, orchestral playing is generally sloppy and exposed errors abound (most notably the horn's sorry miscue at the opening of the finale). In the second movement, rushing into climaxes and slowing up endlessly before and during the final coda are serious abuses. Scherchen dashes carelessly through the dance music of Part II and then burdens the trios with extraordinary weight. The *Adagietto* gets milked for all of the emotionality it is worth (clocked at 13:12). Time seems to stand still before the final reprise at #3. The glissando that concludes this section is stretched out for what seems an eternity. After the opening horn miscue, the finale's main theme sounds bright and buoyant, but mucky playing and a dashed-off reading (with a characterless *Adagietto* theme, sectional treatment, uneven tempi and a mere run-through of the Grand Chorale) make the end of this experience most welcome.

SCHERCHEN, HERMANN/ORTF National Orchestra (perf. 1965) - Harmonia Mundi HMA 1905179 (1987) [53:05]   Little has changed from the earlier Milan performance (see above). Essentially the same cuts are made in Part II and the finale. Contrasting tempi and moods are highlighted, sometimes to such extremes that the musical structure is threatened. Like the orchestra in the previous performance, this ensemble has difficulty following Scherchen's impulsive bursts of energy; many miscues and general sloppiness result. This time the first movement takes less time than the second, more in keeping with their relative lengths. As before, the first movement, though by no means perfect, boasts an inflexible march theme, if well-coordinated with a furious trio section (N.B., the tuba plays certain notes an octave higher than written at m.259-260). Scherchen tends to push the music forward in faster sections, driving it to the brink of collapse. The same is true of the main material of the second movement that again contrasts strongly with a more hesitant and sluggish funeral march theme. But Scherchen makes more points in this movement than he did with the Milan orchestra. Despite hurried pacing, some transitions in tempo work better here (e.gs., before #9 and into #15). The climactic *wuchtig* outburst is awesome; but a weak trumpet solo and an awkward climax debilitates the Grand Chorale. Once again the concluding section is extremely slow and tiring. Very rapid tempi mar orchestral precision, and an extremely languid, indulgently caricaturesque treatment of the trio section are the only characteristics worth making about what survives of Part II, apparently not one of Scherchen's favorite movements. Again the focus is on the Adagietto, set in a *molto adagio* tempo and given the same soulful reading as before. Strings literally weep from m.56 and the close is heart-rending. This time it is the clarinet that messes up the introduction to the finale. But as before the main material is highly energetic and spirited. After a trumpet miscue at #11 (probably caused by Scherchen's wildly fast tempo), all the shreds of this movement emerge as if shot from a cannon.

SCHWARZ, GERARD/Tokyo Philharmonic - Fun House FHCB-2022 (1994) [66:37]+
    In his first recording of a Mahler symphony, Gerard Schwarz evidences a kinship with the work that communicates clearly to the Tokyo Philharmonic: the orchestra follows every twist and turn in the score with ease. After he tries to make a big impression in the powerful opening of the symphony, Schwarz settles into a traditional approach, one that takes the work at face value. His reading of Part I is well-conceived, but Part II lacks sufficient vigor and carefree abandon to captivate. His unmarked speed-up for the string figuration first appearing at #2 is his only divergence from the score. The waltz music in the third movement's trio section seems too languid and sugary when juxtaposed with the main theme's mild swing. After a song-like *Adagietto*, tender but not maudlin, the finale comes along like a wake-up call. Perky and smart with plenty of drive, the movement's lively spirit comes through with unrestrained enthusiasm. Schwarz hurries the main material forward to heighten the effect of its collapse at 9:55. The Grand Chorale is marvelous and the presto coda a whirlwind.

SCHWARZ, RUDOLF/London Symphony - Everest 3014-5 (1958); 3359/12; Murray Hill S4565; Everest EVC 9032 (1995) [69:44]*+   This version is the closest we will ever come to a Horenstein reading since Schwarz assisted him with the LSO. Sound and balances are superb for this vintage recording and playing is generally clear and precise as well as idiomatic. The opening of the first movement has a magnificent martial quality with a superb march tread. Details are rendered with care, percussion is strong and the solo trumpet crystal clear. The *klagend* outburst near the close is shattering. A mild-tempered second movement fails to incite much violence but playing, details, balances and sound quality are consistently excellent. Climaxes here are robust even though the *wuchtig* climax could be weightier. The long, gradual return to the intense opening material has a mean and menacing character. In Part II Schwarz elicits characterful playing that makes the scherzo and waltz-trio effervescent and charming, but the closing section is hampered by a sluggish tempo. Set in a fairly moderate tempo, the *Adagietto* is treated more songfully than soulfully and has the advantage of beautiful string playing. While the finale is replete with details, its restrained principal tempo puts a slight damper on what should be a joyous mood. Yet strong playing enlivens the movement until the coda where Schwarz fails to generate enough energy make this happy resolution of the conflicts of Part I convincing.

SEGERSTAM, LEIF/Danish National Radio Symphony - Chandos CHAN 9403 (1995) [75:16]* Segerstam's penchant for exaggerating both emotive expression and tempo contrast is no less evident here than throughout his nearly complete cycle. Lyrical lines are stretched out with many hesitations, ritards are sometimes unindurably long and special effects (such as biting sforzandi, swells or stopped notes in brass) are magnified. For example, his treatment of the funeral march in the first movement is extremely inflexive, to the point of virtually holding on to some notes for all the emotion that can be wrought from them. Yet his reading is deeply tragic and expresses a profound sense of human pathos giving way to impassioned fury in the trio. When Segerstam tries to make a strong impression here, he often succeeds. He is ably assisted by powerful, resplendent brass playing and full-blown sonics. How impressively the brass bray out their doleful descending phrases at the *wuchtig* climax of the second movement (10:20); and how gloriously they resound in the finale's Grand Chorale (14:30). Moreover, Segerstam's attention to details and inner-voice balancing is unqualifiedly brilliant. While high strings are often buried by brass during strong tutti passages, bass strings frequently penetrate the musical fabric with an important rhythmic pulse (e.g., at 7:35 of the finale). Segerstam's reading has much character but his excessive mode of expression can be wearing at times.

Wild fury rages forth in the second movement, only to give way to deeply mournful emotions. The Scherzo movement presents a few problems that Segerstam has more difficulty overcoming. What is missing here is the feeling of carefree frivolity. Forced disruptions and some plodding tempi detract from such a mood, producing either an artificality in the manner of expression or overly-bemused moodiness. Segerstam makes a critical interpretive error here and throughout this performance that impedes the musical flow. Whenever he encounters the marking *nicht eilen*, he suddenly engages a much slower tempo; and, conversely, when the direction *nicht schleppen* appears, he immediately speeds up. Making such exaggerated changes in the course of the music was not Mahler's intention, nor does it help to maintain a natural fluency of line. (See Introduction). Such radical tempo changes severely disturb the musical flow detract from linear consistency and structural cohesion.

Segerstam also takes a defiantly unpopular stance in the *Adagietto*. Instead of treating it as a love song of tenderness and affection, he reads it as a long-winded and over-wrought expression of deep sorrow. Taking nearly twelve minutes, he stretches the main theme to the breaking point in his efforts to project a profound sense of melancholy. He certainly accomplishes that, if against the grain of those who presume that Mahler would not have offered such music as an expression of his love for his wife-to-be. The finale also seems on the weighty side. There is much ebulliency to the main theme, which adds a skipping quality to its rustic characater. But sometimes a feeling of reserve tempers the joyousness to be evoked here. What mostly impresses is Segerstam's brilliant handling of contrapuntal lines, each one clearly audible but well-placed within the musical texture. His is a strong, characterful reading that consciously seeks to overwhelm, yet it produces its most successful moments when artfulness gives way to spontaneous and unaffected music-making.

SINOPOLI, GIUSEPPE/Philharmonia Orchestra - 2-DG 415 476 (1986)* For the first offering in his complete cycle, Sinopoli submits a taut and muscular rendering of the Fifth which can easily take its place among the best performances. His approach combines dynamic force with a keen sense of polyphonic clarity in an effort to drive home as many of Mahler's intricate details as can be audible in this jam-packed score. Rarely in recent memory has The Philharmonia Orchestra played with such assurance or sounded as robust. While string balances are superb throughout, one would have liked to tone down the piercing quality of the trumpets at times. Sinopoli handles the mournful opening movement in such a way as to capture its funereal spirit without sluggish tempi or overdone ferocity in the trio. His tempo control here, as throughout, is admirably assured. All the drama of this awesome music is conveyed without morbidity. There are moments of revelation: a feeling of terrifying dread is superbly captured at #11 as the music calms down from a passionate outburst; a touching sensitivity comes through in the closing section into #15 with its momentary reference to *Kindertotenlieder*. It may seem like a minor loss, but those intermittent drum rolls between tattoos at the close are inaudible. While the second movement has all the violence and fiery temperament it should have, Sinopoli seems to gloss over the triumphant climax (*pesante*, #27). Sometimes high volume gobbles up much of what is happening (e.g., into *wuchtig* after #24) and a few affectations at the return of the funeral march seem awkward. Least satisfying is the middle movement. Articulation is smoothed over where it should be sharp and much of the music just seems to happen ineffectually. Sinopoli's effort to drive home the subtleties of Mahler's dynamic markings (particularly the swells) borders on the excessive. The frantic, senseless whirl of modern life Mahler sought to satirize here could have been aptly engendered without the use of a sledge hammer to drive it home! Sometimes the waltz sections are treated manneristically, making them appear clumsy rather than lilting. A feeling of wild abandon is evident, but overdrawn.

Sinopoli takes a cool, rather uninvolved approach to the *Adagietto*. The main tempo (a subject of much controversy among Mahlerians) is on the moderate side, flowing quite evenly throughout. Emotions are restrained. At the change of key (to G-flat) and in the closing section (#4) Sinopoli's reading is more sensitive but such moments are too few make up for his general detachment. Once again exaggerated dynamic markings (particularly swells) interfere with the sense of deep longing that this music should convey. Sinopoli confuses the bridge passage into the reprise by misreading or ignoring the marking *zurückhalten*, thus creating a brief moment of disorientation. The closing bars could have been given more weight and thrust. In the finale, one senses cautiousness that keeps the main tempo restrainted and sometimes requires sudden or gradual tempo shifts to keep within the proper frame of reference. The feeling generated here is one of subdued joy, as if to imply that the musical content is unable to provide a curative for the tragedy of Part I. Notice how it becomes necessary to speed up the main tempo at times (e.g., to m.357) in order keep the forward momentum. At #23, Sinopoli needs to thrust the tempo forward suddenly in order to avoid falling behind. The return of the *Adagietto* theme still has a melancholy tinge, as if evoking a memory of past sorrow. Sinopoli does better with this theme toward the close (from #28). He may conceive of the movement as a gradual uplifting of the spirit rather than an a sudden shift of emotional gears. Again the majestic *pesante* climax from the second movement seems all too brief to be the crowning glory of this movement or of the symphony itself. A rapid-fire final section brings the work to an extremely impulsive close.

SOLTI, GEORG/Chicago Symphony - 2-London 2228 (1970); 414321; London 430 437-48; 430 635 (1991); 430 443 (1991); 436 619; 436 600 (1992); 10-London 430 804 (1992)

SYMPHONY NO. 5

[65:53]** This is still one of the best Fifths ever recorded, especially in its successful compact disc transfer. In his first Mahler recording with the CSO, Solti achieves a thrilling performance enhanced by strong, brilliant sound and superb playing. The overall approach is intense and dramatic but never fails to be idiomatic. A magnificent opening trumpet call is followed by a well-paced funeral march. *Furioso* passages are played passionately, climaxes are extremely powerful and details are audible and carefully rendered. All the violence and anger of the second movement comes through with burning passion. The return of the opening march theme has an appropriately doleful aspect and climaxes are tremendous. Solti elicits just the right Viennese touch in the middle movement. Fugal passages are artfully played and whip up much excitement, Solti driving undauntedly to a spirited close. Tempo for the *Adagietto* is on the moderately brisk side, the main theme being treated songfully rather than overly sentimentalized. Solti presses with much passion to the movement's heart-rending climax. Few conductors achieve Mahler's intentions in the finale so thoroughly as Solti. A joyful exuberance resounds from the outset and is enhanced by razor-sharp playing. The music literally bubbles over with enthusiasm as it drives forward to a riotously wild conclusion.

SOLTI, GEORG/Chicago Symphony (perf. 26 March 1986, Bunkakaikan, Tokyo) - Sony video SHV 46377 (1990) [70:07]*+ Solti's readings of the Fifth usually generate much intensity and dramatic power. This is no exception. Most notable is the spectacular brass playing, strong and forceful. From the opening, Solti's nervous impulse energizes the performance. As in his first recording of the Fifth with the CSO (see above), the dramatic impact throughout the opening movement is very strong. If anything has changed over time, it is Solti's ever more deft manner of shaping the march theme. How threatening are those stopped horns at mm. 139-141! And the trio literally smacks us in the face with a jolt. Just as unnerving is the shivering feeling that suddenly appears before #11. Always very expressive, Solti never over-indulges. Seething with anger and burning passion, the second movement is just as compelling. The CSO responds marvelously to every nuance of phrasing and abrupt tempo change. It is a sheer delight to listen to such a splendid orchestra play with such fire and commitment difficult music that they know so well. Energy is at a fever pitch, especially as the movement progresses to the Grand Chorale. At this magnificent apotheosis, Solti holds back enough to let its heroic character ring out in majestic splendor. A sense of devil-may-care cosmopolitanism pervades Part II, enhanced with a delightfully suave treatment of the trio's waltz segments. Some imprecision creeps in here (the viola miscues at m.316), but brass (particularly horns and the trombone solo) perform admirably. Even if a slight restraint seems to impede the progress of this movement momentarily, most of its many impetuous turns are handled superbly. Solti paces the *Adagietto* between the extremes that have caused much controversy. While hardly read as a love song, it is not as weepy as a more dolorous reading might have been. The ardent passion of the middle section evokes a impression of one in middle age recalling wistfully the memory of a past love. How dreamily Solti lingers on the layered C-naturals that introduce the final version of the main theme. Tenderness here never becomes maudlin. As expected, the finale is a delightfully spirited affair, full of verve and joyousness, and climaxed by a breathtaking Grand Chorale.

SOLTI, GEORG/Chicago Symphony - London 433 329 (1991) [69:29]+ Since Solti does not take this opportunity to rethink his interpretation, one wonders whether non-musical considerations may have prompted this issue. Musically speaking, however, he might have been better advised to let well enough alone, for this version neither supercedes his previous efforts nor reproduces them. What we have instead is a professional performance that never digs very deeply into the music's dramatic core, nor generates the spontaneity and intensity that made his first recording so splendid. Even the playing is adversely affected by this superficial reading.

The marvelous sense of spontaneity that characterized the video release (see above) is nowhere in evidence. Brass still play strongly but in a matter-of-fact manner. The rushed triplets of the opening trumpet tattoos signify less a sense of urgency than a desire to move things quickly to the finish. All the bite, thrust and underlying tension of the prior version has tempered. Sonics are improved as one might expect, but they do not, and cannot, take the place of personal involvement.

SUITNER, OTMAR/Staatskapelle Berlin - 2-Eterna 8 27 616-617 (1986); Tokuma 32TC-79 (1986) [63:54] This routine performance suffers from sloppy string playing as well as thin and fuzzy sonics. Suitner generates excitement by increasing underlying agitation, and sometimes drives the tempo beyond the capabilities of the orchestra. For the most part, one might characterize the reading as objective. Part I rages with violent passions, but they are primarily stirred up by wildly fast tempi. In the softer sections playing is expressionless, sound veiled and the atmosphere dry and static. There is also a tendency to clip dotted rhythms. Despite wild bursts of fury, Suitner underplays both the ferocious *wuchtig* outburst (at #24) that climaxes the movement's principal theme and the visionary Grand Chorale. For Part II, he maintains a lively main tempo, slightly on edge throughout. Strings sound brighter and more exuberant here, as well as better balanced, but untidiness occurs when Suitner turns up the heat. Some minor inflections in the funeral march theme interfere with its natural flow. The trio sections are ineffectual, played with little nuance; Suitner seeming more intent on racing madly through the wilder music to the close. String sonorities are too thin for the *Adagietto*. Played with some emotion, this movement still lacks soulfulness. The finale is moderately lively and gay, although colorless strings, a quick pace for the *Adagietto* theme's return, heavy brass that drown strings in strong tutti passages, and a pervasive raciness that desynchronizes the ensemble combine to undermine the effectiveness of this movement.

TENNSTEDT, KLAUS/London Philharmonic -2-Angel SZ-3883 (1979); CDC-47103; 10-EMI CMS7 64471-81 (1993) [75:10] Tennstedt misses the mark here, serving up an uneven reading further marred by veiled, indistinct sonics and poor balances. Frequent exaggerated affectations produce a forced, overly dramatic performance. The funeral march tends to plod along while the more *appassionato* trio is very intense. Brass and percussion generally overshadow strings and woodwinds, the overall quality of performance being too often imprecise and poorly tuned. The final coda to the first movement is dull in the extreme. Energy levels continue to be too low in the fiery second movement. The return of the march theme is dull and expressionless and playing often lacks clarity. Tennstedt frequently exaggerates ritards in an affectatious manner. Some moments (e.g., the *wuchtig* and *pesante* sections) are robust and demonstrative. Unsteady tempi, uneven playing, distorted sonics and an unimaginative reading severely hamper the Scherzo, at least until after #21, when the performance catches fire and builds to a strong and raucous close. A slow and soulful treatment of the *Adagietto* produces some very expressive and impassioned moments that might have been more effective without the addition of a few annoying affectations. Tennstedt misses the point of the transfiguring finale completely, giving it an almost mournful rather than joyous character. Restrained and inconsistent tempi often result in a uneven, sometimes strained and generally uninteresting performance. Tennstedt's affected approach rarely enhances the emotive quality and frequently disturbs the linear flow.

TENNSTEDT, KLAUS/London Philharmonic - Angel EMI CDC 7 49888 (1990) [73:24]
   Tennstedt's interpretation of the Fifth has changed measurably since his earlier recording. Now dark clouds hang heavily over much of the work, threatening to explode and sometimes actually exploding in torrents of power and emotion. Tempi are generally heavy,

SYMPHONY NO. 5

sodden with frequent luftpausen and extremely long ritards. Brass overplay their hand at the expense of strings. The extreme contrast between melismatic lyricism and abruptly hurled invective is sometimes oppressive. The opening trumpet tattoos are played in free, almost recitativo style (Mahler's direction requires a strict funeral march tempo). A properly hesitant march theme elicits a brooding melancholy that gives way to a racy torrent of violence at the trio (#7). Here Tennstedt follows his usual tendency to slow up in mid-stream to heighten emotions. He emphasizes the music's tragic aspect with weighty brass chords at climaxes. The same effect permeates the second movement. Violent enough when it opens, this mood is soon confounded by frequent slow-ups and stretched ritards. Brass often have a menacing aspect (before #9) and strings sound tearful in the return of the funeral march theme. Ensemble precision is sometimes adversely affected by Tennstedt's sudden tempo shifts. Loud percussion and brass overwhelm at the *wuchtig* climax and the Grand Chorale, sounding harsh and rough-hewn rather round, firm and full-bodied. Little *joie de vivre* comes through in Part II, again set in a sluggish main tempo. Uncharacteristically, emotional detachment and restraint reign supreme. Tennstedt seems unable to overcome the negative emotions generated earlier in this movement. With the *Adagietto* everything quiets down, giving us a rest from the high volume levels imposed upon the previous movements. In extremely slow tempo, Tennstedt takes the long-lined approach less favored these days. Playing seems disconcertingly harsh in the climaxes and rarely tender or sensitive elsewhere. The finale is hard-driven, eliciting more agitation than joy. Playing again seems befuddled at times. Occasional affectations do little to lighten the mood (#5 on theme; #21; m.581, etc.). After galloping to the Grand Chorale, Tennstedt holds up momentarily and then plunges into the closing section. His approach throughout seems overladen with tragedy.

VIS, LUCAS/Netherlands Youth Orchestra - NSO 0191LV (1992) [74:58]+   Most impressive here is the accomplished level of precision and stylish playing that this young orchestra displays. That they cope so well with conductor Vis's many attempts to infuse the score with added inflection and his frequent interpolations of Mahler's tempo changes is to their credit. When Vis holds back the tempo, the likelihood of technical problems increases. But rapid passages are played proficiently. The first movement's funeral march is morose, plodding and yet interestingly nuanced. A very rapid trio makes a striking contrast to the march theme, as does the sinewy opening of the second trio. But thereafter Vis rushes into the *klagend* orchestral outburst and moves rapidly through the following trumpet calls. He races like the wind through the next movement, horns ripping like blazing demons through the main subject. A strong contrast is created between the melancholy march theme and torrents of fierce anger. Unfortunately, Vis speeds through the *wuchtig* climax. Unusually strong emphasis is placed on the opening horn call of Part II. But Vis fails to engender much spirit from the main theme, until he quickens the pace for the string figuration at #3. The waltz segments have a coquettish quality that is most attractive. Vis moves in and out of tempo so often that it is remarkable that his orchestra stays with him so consistently. The profusion of tempo shifts adds to the wild character of the movement. A sensitive reading of the *Adagietto* seems to affect the opening of the finale, for it takes much time before the unrestrained joy of this movement takes hold. Vis generates some energy at times (by #24), but again his many unmarked tempo adjustments create confusion. By the rapid Grand Chorale and wild final coda we are certain that untroubled happiness has finally triumphed over the gloom of the opening movement.

WAKASUGI, HIROSHI/Tokyo Metropolitan Symphony - Fontec FOCD 9021 (1988) [71:11]+   Two serious problems hinder this recording's success: Wakasugi's reserved manner and Fontec's confined sonic levels. In a generally objective, straightforward reading, Wakasugi is prone more to be expressive in lyrical passages than overwhelming in powerful climaxes or urgent and intense in energetic allegros. Wakasugi lingers over the main theme of the *Adagietto*, giving a sensitive reading. The TMSO performs idiomatically throughout, in spite of the lack of full sonic dimension in strings and restrained brass. What is lacking further is the temperament that can make convincing the fury of the second movement, the gaiety of the third and the joyousness of the finale. The last movement is a big let-down, with its lumpishness and mildness. The most impressive moment in this performance is the extraordinarily powerful *wuchtig* climax in the second movement (10:50+). Wakasugi should be complimented on some fine tuning of details (e.g., the noticeable ritard at m.2 of the second movement) and intelligent handling of tempo gradations.

WALTER, BRUNO/New York Philharmonic - Columbia 12656-73D (1947); SL 171; Odyssey 32260016; Sony Classics MPK 47683 (1992) [61:52]*+ While later versions by other conductors have put the relative merits of Walter's ground-breaking reading in better perspective, the importance of this performance should not be underrated, for Walter's profound understanding of and identification with this music are qualities that many contemporary Mahler interpreters lack. It is also true, however, that Walter's tempi are sometimes on the quick side and he lets some sections go by without eliciting any special effect. A fairly brisk underlying motion in the first movement never causes Walter to gloss over the music's dramatic aspects, even if a few details are underplayed. Walter still generates much depth of feeling and intensity here. Weak sonics in repressings have toned down the vibrancy of the second movement. Although Walter's reading is rhythmically vital and energetic, one still feels that a measure of intensity is left in reserve. Moreover, the chorale climax could be handled with more weight, depending upon whether one sees this section as an anticipation of a later fulfillment or the achievement of it, later recalled in the finale. In a spirited Scherzo, Walter tends to press forward (especially in the trio) but he engenders much excitement. He sets a moderately brisk pace for the *Adagietto*, seeking to elicit its beauty without too much *schmaltz*. Many interpreters find this approach much sounder than a slower, more emotional reading, such as is offered by Levine and Tennstedt. The finale is bright and lively, moving forward purposefully to a strong chorale climax.

WIT, ANTONI/Polish National Radio Symphony (perf. 16-18 June 1990, Concert Hall of Polish Radio, Katowice) (1992) - Naxos 8.550528 [74:43]+ Structurally, this performance inverts the arch form in which the Fifth is organized. Its strong points appear at both ends, while it sags in the middle. Wit generates much intensity and depth of feeling in his reading of Part I, even if sonics sometimes blur strong tuttis. His pacing of the funeral march in both movements is hesitant and heavily-accented. In the first movement, notice how gently he holds back when the theme returns (2:53), as Mahler directs. All of this theme's heart-rending melancholy is forgotten when the trio section begins suddenly with wild furiosity. Throughout this movement and the next, one senses a deep personal involvement often absent from more glamorous performances. In Part II, however, this impulse loses hold. To make its point, this movement needs to evoke a feeling of carefree abandon, momentarily interrupted by second thoughts about the madness of cosmopolitan life. Instead, stiff playing and mild treatment rob the music of its energy, and temper the effect of contrasting bewilderment. Everything seems tired, especially the awkwardly flexible waltz theme. More sobering moments evoke a nostalgic mood, but do not contrast sufficiently with what should be lively dance music suggesting the decadent life of *fin-de-siecle* Vienna. Instead, Wit seems more involved in eliciting the emotions of the *Adagietto*. In a broad, long-lined tempo, he tries to convey its soulfulness without excessive gushiness, but he stretches the line almost to the breaking point, especially in transition passages. The return of D minor at 8:10 is simply gorgeous and the final high D-natural opens out of the harp arpeggio like a flower blossoming. Bathed in sunshine, the finale is light and gay, if sometimes moderated by self-conscious restraint. Milder moments are played with suppleness but stronger sections seem lackluster. A hesitant *Adagietto* theme (c.12') lingers in the mood of its earlier incarnation and does not glide by amiably. But Wit lets us enjoy the gradually growing elation that culminates in the return of the Grand Chorale. When it occurs, overladen with brass, it seems more strident than grandiose and one never senses that the darker mood of the earlier movements has been completely dispelled.

SYMPHONY NO.6 IN A MINOR ("TRAGIC")

Movements:

1. Allegro energico, ma non troppo.
   Heftig, aber märkig
2. Scherzo, Wüchtig.
3. Andante moderato.
4. Finale. Sostenuto - Allegro moderato.

(N.B.: In the listings, "Revised Version" refers to that in which the middle movements listed above are reversed.)

ABBADO, CLAUDIO/Chicago Symphony - 2-DG 2707117 (1980); DG 423928-2 GGA2 (1989); 10-DG 447 023 (1995) [83:06]* Abbado offers a generally fine, if somewhat uneven reading that has the added advantage of polished playing and excellent sound quality. Best is the first movement with a strong, vibrant march and a soaring second theme. Chorale-like transition passages are hauntingly beautiful and abrupt mood shifts are rife with passion. Abbado has complete command of Mahler's idiom. Now that it has finally become apparent to most conductors how important the first movement exposition repeat is to the overall structure, this repeat (rare in Mahler's works) is taken more often than not, as it is here. Abbado would have enhanced the devilish humor of the Scherzo if he had not insisted upon pushing the tempo rather than giving it more weight. Suddenly, his care in rendering details wanes and too many interesting nuances are overlooked. The *grazioso* sections are too cautious and are paced in a tiresome manner, while other sections are restlessly driven. Despite many affectations little of the irony of this caricature of Viennese style comes across. On the other hand, Abbado captures the dreamy lyricism of the slow movement with much sensitivity and expressiveness. Balances are not always appropriate (e.g., weak pizzicati in bass strings). A reflective mood pervades the softer passages, giving way to moments of poignant intensity that culminate in a heart-rending climax. Abbado elicits some strong playing in the finale, despite weak percussion. The absence of a thoroughly convincing overall conception is particularly hampered by Abbado's tendency to drag or press forward unduly at times.

ABBADO, CLAUDIO/Vienna Symphony (perf. 24 May 1967) [REVISED VERSION] - Hunt CD-553 (1988); Hunt/Arkadia CMHP 553.1 (1993) [79:07]+ This live performance is only of historic value. With close-miking, awkward woodwind intonation, almost no breaks between movements and merely passable sonics, it could not possibly be competitive. The VSO is clearly uncomfortable with this work, and Abbado's frequently driven tempi cause precision problems, particularly for the strings. Nevertheless, Abbado elicits much of the work's emotive qualities. Strong, dynamic thrust energizes the first movement (though sometimes to excess) and fiery vigor drives home powerhouse climaxes in the finale. Abbado dashes off the mocking Scherzo too quickly to catch its parody of the first movement's heroic bearing; and he brings out little of the bittersweet tenderness that can make the slow movement a moving experience.

ABRAVANEL, MAURICE/Utah Symphony - 2-Vanguard S-323/4 (1975); 11-Vanguard 08.4013.79 (1995) [70:33] Abravanel's perfunctory reading lacks overall conception, produces excessively fast tempi and slipshod playing. Balances are often uneven, particularly weak in the bass and timpani. Sonics are veiled and dullish and dynamic levels tend to be too weak and mellow. Little sense of drama is conveyed in the outer movements, none of the caricaturish humor of the Scherzo emerges, and little emotive pathos is evoked in the slow movement. Playing is often stiff and squarish. Hammer blows are weak in the finale, where several sections seem to be dashed off with little insight. Most disturbing is Abravanel's consistent use of rapid tempi. The music has little chance to breathe, resulting in a performance with little dramatic depth.

BARBIROLLI, JOHN/Berlin Philharmonic (perf. 13 Jan. 1966) [REVISED VERSION] - Hunt CD 702 (1989); Arkadia CDGI 702.1 (1993) [74:55]+ The dramatic weight with which Barbirolli burdens the opening march tempo contrasts markedly with his generally impulsive and agitated reading. The BPO, particularly the brass, sound less than up to par here. Balances are also problemmatic. During the first movement, Barbirolli gradually adjusts the pace of the main theme from its initial extremely broad tempo to a much quicker pulse. His tendency to rush in and out of sections is somewhat mitigated by a weighty brass chorale interlude and a restful return of the second theme (#23). A few big slow-ups do occur (e.g., 2 before #33 and before #35) but the music impells forward urgently throughout the movement. Barbirolli does not repeat the exposition. Taking the *Andante* movement next, Barbirolli establishes a comfortable tempo, in broad strokes with legato phrasing. He then picks up the tempo gradually, so that by #53 he is cruising along at a brisk pace. But with the return of the main theme, he calms things down nicely. Some confusion in inner voices occurs and attacks are not as precise as one would expect from this great orchestra. From around #57, Barbirolli again picks up the tempo to a rapid pace which he retains throughout much of what remains of the movement. As a result, his long ritard at #62 seems overly pronounced. Under-refined playing and a general sense of detachment defuse the mood of demonic parody in the Scherzo. Imitating the opening of the first movement, Barbirolli starts off in a weighty tempo and gradually increases the tempo to fit the musical character. On the other hand, the Haydnesque *altväterisch* (old-fashioned) segments are played without any stylistic nuance. Frequent weavings in and out of tempo cause many passages to seem disjointed.

Brass miscues mar the opening of the finale. A very sluggish woodwind chorale (#106) leads to a strong, heavy treatment of the fate motif (#107). Some slight affectations intrude before the appearance of the main theme. The Berlin horns shine for the second theme, which is treated briskly, but they often overplay their hand, drowning out their colleagues in *forte* passages. Barbirolli races through the return of the introductory theme (#119-120), but settles down during the calmer orchestral bridge passages, accompanied by cowbells that sound too close to produce the intended effect. Thereafter, the third theme presses forward relentlessly, inner voices again smothered by brass and strings. The hammer blows sound metallic, contrary to Mahler's specific direction that they sound like strokes of an axe. After the first blow, screechy strings on clipped dotted-rhythms threatened to tear apart the musical fabric. General agitation increases to the point of ferocity. When the introductory theme reappears, now in very broad tempo, a moment of relief from the tensions generated earlier is welcome. By m.566 Barbirolli is on the attack again, playing the next appearance of the motto-like theme now in double time. He even races through the fate motif before #163. Barbirolli eases up in time to make his inclusion of the rarely heard third hammer blow effective (even though again sounding metallic). He holds on tenaciously to the *sotto voce* chords that precede the devastating final outburst, putting all the weight of the opening march on the fate motive's final declamation.

BARBIROLLI, JOHN/New Philharmonia Orchestra (perf. 22 Jan. 1969) [REVISED VERSION] - Hunt/Arkadia CDGI 726 (1991) [73:35]* Barbirolli makes a few adjustments to what is essentially the same reading he gave the Sixth with the BPO a few years earlier. But now he has the added advantage of working with an orchestra more familiar with his manner and more willing to give him their level best. The overall result is greater cohesion, providing better evidence of Barbirolli's skills as a major Mahler interpreter. Unfortunately, poor sonic quality is a major problem: loud tape hiss, muffled dynamics, muddy bass, and harsh blurried *fortes*. One can discern enough to make the effort worthwhile, however. As in both other recordings, Barbirolli starts off with a heavy-laden, markedly accented march. Naturally, he is bound to move such a weighty march tempo forward as the movement progresses. But he does so with such deftness as to make this adjustment virtually unnoticeable. By the reprise, the march moves along with much energy and spirit. How demonstratively the timpani pound out the fate motto in the outer movements! An ever so slight hesitation into the reprise makes it an important event (11:40), and a ripping close ends the movement.

No longer as broadly paced as his earlier NPO reading, the *Andante*'s main tempo is comfortable and the fluid lyricism of the principal theme enchanting. Barbirolli's brilliant shaping of the movement's contours, giving just the right impulse to the passionate climactic section beginning at 10:26, makes for a satisfying experience. In the Scherzo, he tries to relax more in dealing with the trio's Haydnesque material. But by 7' he reverts to the hurried manner in which he paced this section earlier. Monstrous growlings in low brass are marvelous, though (6'). More secure playing and a more cohesive approach make the sprawling finale work better here than in either of Barbirolli's other recorded performances. A demonstrative main theme with strong emphasis on the Fate motto and agitated build-ups to the climaxes work extremely well. One is caught up in the urgency with which Barbirolli heightens the drama. However, sonic problems severely detract from the overall effect. After the added third stroke, Barbirolli provides just the right degree of somber repose in the quiet interlude for low brass that precedes the horrific orchestral outburst that ushers in awesome timpani strokes of Fate which close this extraordinary performance.

BERNSTEIN, LEONARD/New York Philharmonic - 2-Columbia M3S-776; GMS 765; MS 7021 (1968); 3-CBS M3K 42199 (1986); 3-Sony SM3K 47581 (1992) [77:35]*

Bernstein's approach is evident from the outset in the rapid tempo he sets for the opening march (Can anyone really march to this tempo?). Nervous energy pervades this reading, sometimes at the expense of more lyrical moments. The first movement literally attacks the listener with its violent raging. Yet certain passages fall all over themselves at break-neck speed. The second theme soars to the heights of passion, enhanced by beautiful string sound. Bernstein emphasizes the demonic aspects of the development section. In accordance with his overall conception, the Scherzo is very rapidly paced (not at all *wuchtig* as marked) but Bernstein captures all its devilish grotesqueries and handles its abrupt tempo shifts with playfull impishness. Superb sonics, perfect balances and excellent playing add to the movement's impact. In the *Andante* movement, Bernstein lapses into his typically mannered approach at times and tends to press forward during more intense moments, yet little of the movement's heart-rending poignancy penetrates a slightly detached veneer. In the finale, Bernstein's energetic approach works quite well. Again emphasis is placed on the more grotesque elements and both tempi and volume are set at excessive levels. Bernstein attends carefully to details but dynamic levels do not always measure up to the dramatic content. He sometimes rushes through one section in order to reach another, causing some unevenness. The tempo used for the return of the first movement march theme is less agitated than it was originally (possibly an indication of a loss of energy in life's ceaseless struggle). While the finale reeks with impassioned intensity, a sense of profound meaning is not obvious. One has an uncomfortable feeling that we have not heard all of what this great Mahlerian interpreter could have given to the symphony. One can readily verify this by listening to Bernstein's thrilling performance with The Vienna Philharmonic on videotape (see below).

BERNSTEIN, LEONARD/Vienna Philharmonic (perf. Nov. 1977, Vienna Musikverein, Grosser Saal) - DG video 072-2263-3 (1991) [84]** Yet another magnificent performance of the Sixth by a perfect team: Mahler's own orchestra and one of his greatest interpreters. Bernstein offers nothing radically different from his readings recorded both earlier and later. Still wildly frenetic and yet superimposed with immense dramatic strength, the first movement is rapidly paced and hard-driven. Given the brisk march tempo, the drama unfolds with riveting impact. Here is a depiction of the hero at the height of his powers, full of energy and passion. Beginning with a slightly weighty tread, the Scherzo gradually moves up to speed. This movement might be characterized as a Mephistophelian mockery of the hero depicted in the first movement, the dynamic march from that movement now caricatured in offbeat-accented triple-meter that smacks of twittering impudence. This quirky march alternates with coquetish classical dance music that is yet another caricature, this time of Mephistopheles flitting about in mocking distain of the hero's romantic presentment characterized in the opening movement. Bernstein makes as much of these depictions as he can. Yet he is as touching and sensitive in handling the slow movement as he is devilish in the Scherzo. The entire *Andante* is deeply moving and masterfully wrought. But it is in the finale where a conductor's mettle is truly tested, and Bernstein's finale has always been and still is a benchmark against which other performances are compared. One is conscious throughout of the inevitability of a tragic end, as the hero races madly to his doom. As he has done elsewhere, Bernstein includes the third hammer blow before the final coda. Watching these terrifying hammer strokes adds a thrilling dimension to yet another superlative Bernstein reading of this dramatic masterpiece.

BERNSTEIN, LEONARD/Vienna Philharmonic - 2-DG 427 697 (1986); 13-DG 435 162 (1992) [94:28]** Although many particulars are different from Bernstein's 1967 recording, his overall approach remains unchanged. The hero of this musical saga is still the intense, frenetic and somewhat schizophrenic paladin of Bernstein's earlier vision. His undaunted and unrelenting pace seems just as hard-driven, his romantic flair just as passionate (in the "Alma" theme) and disquieting (in the brass chorale bridge passages). The entire first movement seethes with tension, that sometimes gives way to wild abandon (at *piu mosso*, #37), and elsewhere is further strained by tempi that hold back and then press forward (from #40). One is confronted with essentially the same post-modern, nihilistic view of heroism, overflowing with power and overwhelming everything in his path with little concern for the consequences of his unrestrained exertions of superior strength. The Scherzo is a perfect foil to the hero's egoism. Now Mephistopheles appears, the barterer of souls, and shows our Faustian hero just what all his strutting and posing is really worth. The march rhythm of the first movement reappears as a distorted, constricted shadow of its former self. To make this caricature more effective, the main tempo of both movements should coincide, as they do to some extent here. But most impressive is Bernstein's pointed exaggerations of the numerous grotesque effects and mannered mockeries with which the devil's surrogate confronts his heroic prey. Awesome brass growlings open up like the jaws of a fearsome dragon, and low brass plunge to the depths of the abyss with horrific aspect. The minuet-like prancing of the trio sections, parodying the hero's self-satisfied swagger, is superbly handled with a touch of ironic mockery. The brief, scurrying interruptions of the dance seem to carry mimicry to the point of insult. Near the close, with a terrifyingly shrill orchestral outburst (at #100), the satanic spectre vanishes. We are treated to nothing less than a Mahlerian *Walpurgisnacht*. The impact on the hero is undeniable, if not yet discernable.

In the *Andante* movement, that impact is subtly manifest. Although the atmosphere is calm and restful, a sense of numbing detachment prevails. Soon this objectified calm is shattered by the hero's realization that he can no longer attain the peace he so passionately seeks. This feeling of existential doubt is conveyed with passion, but seems less poignant than in readings offered by others (e.g., Karajan). The finale has always been the most troublesome for conductors. Bernstein's first version of this massive and uniquely structured movement was hailed as a revelation when it first appeared. To this reviewer it seemed to lack structural unity, frequently pressing toward abortive climaxes as if in a mad rush toward ultimate annihilation rather than in a struggle against it. In this reading, these characteristics have disappeared. Bernstein takes a full 4 minutes longer with this movement, and to good effect. The opening section is more broadly treated, the soaring string theme magnificently played by the luxurious VPO violins. The grotesque swoopings in brass are literally hair-raising. No longer does Bernstein race to each climax. A notable example can be found is his perceptive treatment of the hushed brass section from the return of the finale's introduction before the last horrific outburst of the fate motif that closes the symphony. Shadowy fragments of the march theme now appear bereft of their previous vitality as a result of the preceding conflict. Bernstein creates an atmosphere of foreboding, holding back the tempo more and more, until the orchestra explodes with the Fate motto in a pronouncement of ultimate doom. Stirring pizzicati in bass strings demonstratively punctuate the end of this heroic struggle. Although this performance is certainly more effective than its predecessor, certain concerns remain. Several sonic effects are jumbled or too overladen with ragged brass. But aside from the breathless pace of the opening movement and the somewhat glacial slow movement, the performance is undeniably masterful.

BERTINI, GARY/Cologne Radio Symphony Orchestra - 2-Harmonia Mundi 153 1695353 (1985); EMI CDC 475 928 (1990) [83:05]* This performance is extremely impressive, particularly considering the fact that this is the first effort at a Mahler symphony on records both conductor and orchestra have given us. Bertini is not only to be congratulated not only for his insightful and inspired reading but also for the highly articulate and carefully balanced performance he elicits from The Cologne Radio Symphony. These musicians play with evident commitment and dedication to every detail. Most impressive is Bertini's overall conception of the work both philosophically and musically. According to his notes on the record jacket, he views the work not merely as an implicitly autobiographical statement of its composer's foreshadowed end, but as "the annihilation of everything human by an overwhelming fate." Seeing such a prophetic vision as the symphony's ultimate meaning, he treats it with more weight and depth than many have done previously. One of the most difficult determinations to make in this regard is the tempo of the opening movement. Those who read *allegro energico* literally and in isolation from its musical context (a dark, sinister march) have taken a brisk main tempo here (Bernstein, Kubelik, Karajan and others). The older generation of conductors intimately familiar with Mahler's music (and in some cases Mahler himself) see this movement as spiritually akin to Mahler's Wunderhorn song *Revelge* (also a military march) and take the tempo more deliberately and with greater weight and accentuation on each beat (particularly Horenstein and Adler). Bertini clearly (and I believe correctly) falls into the latter camp. While not very energetic, his first movement is full of stength and a dramatic presence which makes an excellent case for interpreting the word "energetic" unrelated to speed. Each effect is produced with care and attention to Mahler's numerous details without becoming fussy or excessive. Bridge passages have a sinister character, as if already foreboding a tragic ending (e.g., from #21 when the tingly cow bells first appear). Bertini is clearly an advocate of this music as is evident by his sensitive treatment of lyrical passages and dynamic rendering of more forceful sections. Some special moments worth mentioning are the huge build up to the reprise, the weighty *sostenuto* passage in the reprise and the thrilling final climax. In the second movement (Scherzo), Bertini recognizes the obvious rhythmic parody of the first movement march and so coordinates his tempo with the previous movement perfectly. Taking the marking *wuchtig* (weighty) literally (thereby paralleling his weighty approach to the first movement march tempo), his characterization of this musical parody emphasizes a demonstrative aggressiveness over rhythymic tension. Tempi are always in perfect control. He manages to conjure up the "dance of death," which he calls this movement, with perfectly devilish aplomb but without exaggerations of either dynamic markings or tempi. At this weighty main tempo, a spooky aspect hovers over many passages. In the *grazioso* material (a Viennese parody of its own), a light, lilting treatment is splendidly characterful in its childlike naiveté. The coda is infused with a brief but touching moment of regret (again foreshadowing doom).

Bertini handles the beautifully serene slow movement tenderly, as if evoking a distant vision of the peace and beauty of earlier days. Phrases are well shaped and played with loving care. A warm glow pervades the main thematic material. Some moments seem too restrained (at #53 in horns), as if repressing feelings of joy. Later, a subtle magic haunts the theme at #56, ending with a marvelous octave portamento on violins (at #58). Bertini elicits deep human pathos from the orchestra in the climactic moments. The extremely difficult finale, with its numerous sections which require careful deployment, is handled with a knowing structural sense. Tempi are generally well conceived and sections are well-placed so as never to appear disjointed or segmented. Again the main allegro is coordinated with its sister allegro of the first movement and is alive with dramatic intensity and vitality (without being unduly rushed). The conception of a hero weakened and finally destroyed by blows of fate does not temper the dynamic thrust of this music. Passages which build to and conclude with the two hammer blows are absolutely awesome. The only serious detractions are rapidly played cowbells and low bells (few conductors have tried the more atmospheric and sensible approach of isolated tones) and a rather brisk treatment of the fate motif in timpani (particularly disturbing in the final measures). Regardless of these flaws, this performance deserves high praise.

BOULEZ, PIERRE/BBC Symphony (perf. 1973, London) - Artists FED 032 (1993); Enterprise LV 995 (1995) [75:38] From the forceful and demonstrative opening march, one expects a muscular, weighty reading. But Boulez is unable to maintain this or any other main tempo for any of the movements. In each instance the main tempo keeps getting faster and faster, increasing in energy but leaving both consistency and precision by the wayside. The first movement seems more terrifying than heroic. Already much emphasis on grotesqueries in screeming woodwind cries, blaring trumpets and harsh brass sonics foreshadow inevitable doom. One senses early on that this hero is rapidly hurrying toward his end. While inner voice clarity is a quality we have come to expect from Boulez, hard-edged and blaring brass overpower in strong tutti passages, particularly when the tempo increases to a gallop at the close. Similar problems occur in the Scherzo movement. The parodistic character of the *altväterisch* sections is downplayed against the more devilish grotesqueries of the primary material. Again the main tempo set for the Scherzo keeps increasing throughout the movement

SYMPHONY NO. 6

until it veritably romps through its final appearance. Woodwinds have a curiously clucky timbre which adds to their satanic character.

The *Andante* movement starts off in fine style, with an expressive treatment of the bittersweet main theme, but again Boulez cannot hold on to the initial tempo, which keeps increases at each return of the main theme. From 6:24, after a basically straight reading, Boulez tries his hand at some mid-theme tempo inflections which sound too self-conscious to be effective. The brass seem rather uninvolved throughout this performance, only piercing trumpets making a noticeable, if negative impression. Boulez drives by the movement's climax (9:35) into yet an even faster reprise of the main theme. The sudden dark cloud that appears on the horizen during the closing measures on a minor chord in horns has no time to make an impact, and the movement comes to a rather mindless close. Weak strings on the opening violin theme and very rapid 32nds in woodwinds do not bode well for the opening of the finale. The layered build-up to the main theme is well handled, despite harsh, blaring trumpets which stick out like a sore thumb. Again the BBC orchestra cannot hold on to the initial tempo established for the main theme. Such unremitting forward motion projects an edginess which goes well with the general sense that the hero seems impatient in his progress toward what is to be his ultimate demise. As the allegro tempo increases, orchestral precision diminishes, especially in the brass. Mahler's directions are ignored if they detract from this general forward thrust. Despite an intense build into it, the first stroke seems somewhat of a let down. But a briefer prelude to the second stroke ends in a shattering climax. One is well aware that the battle will soon be lost. Frequent tempo adjustments in opposition to Mahler's directions follow, such as a slowing up at #145 (18'), where Mahler writes *fliessender* (more fleeting). The movements' dramatic character is sacrificed to speed and propulsiveness, Boulez apparently intent upon reaching the close as quickly as possible. One has to shift position to avoid the aural onslaught of the trumpets, who themselves cannot cope with such a rapid tempo. Just listen to how fast the fate motif is rushed through at 23:50. Absent the third hammer blow, the coda is merely a cut-time run-through. Even though the dramatic impact of this remarkable movement is sacrificed, Boulez finishes in well under a half-an-hour, perhaps the motivation for setting such rapid tempi.

BOULEZ, PIERRE/Vienna Philharmonic - DG 445 835 (1994) [79:22]*+   Boulez's conception of the Sixth has changed measurably from his more erratic approach in performances with the BBC Symphony more than twenty years earlier. Now he concentrates on revealing the score's inner depth in a traditional reading that eschews the re-touchings that were so prevalent in his earlier version. Tempo choices are well-conceived, beginning with a forceful and demonstrative march that coordinates well with the following Scherzo and the main tempo of the finale. The VPO is in top form, enhanced by brilliant sonics. Boulez never attempts to overpower or over-emote, but the symphonic drama comes through in all of its diverse manifestations, from the visceral strength of the first movement, through the impish parody of the second and warm sentiments of the third, to the conflict with Fate played out in the finale. Inner voice clarity is a major asset and sonorities are generally full and brilliant. After a strong, emphatic march, the "Alma" theme has a semi-sweet quality yet also much verve. How restful is the woodwind theme at #22 (12:45), evoking nostalgic sentiments. Only the Scherzo seems to lack sufficient contrast in shading and characterization between the mocking off-beat march of the opening and the *altväterisch* (old-fashioned) Haydnesque dance music. Boulez holds the emotions of the slow movement in check, but purity of string tone and his natural pacing make it attractive.

In the finale, Boulez no longer drives the music forward relentlessly, pacing it now to achieve maximum dramatic impact. Rich and vibrant violins intone the yearning theme that opens the movement. Horns growl like menacing monsters rising from depth of the earth (at around 2:10). Terrific timpani strokes of Fate pound out a warning of ultimate doom. Mystery is evoked in quieter wind chorales. Each wave of rising intensity in the introduction increases to an almost unbearable level into the exposition. The main theme bursts on the scene with powerful force and urgency. Bass strings dig deep into a fragment of the main theme at #122 (10:12). The sunlight of D major thereafter brings only momentary relief from the movement's unremitting drive, soon to culminate in a fight for prominence between the first and third themes. With such dramatic presence apparent throughout, the two hammer blows employed are relatively underplayed. Otherwise, Boulez and the VPO deliver a vibrant and powerful performance.

CHAILLY, RICCARDO/Royal Concertgebouw Orchestra - 2-London 430 165-2 (1990)
[84:31]+ Perhaps Chailly intended to give a straightforward, uncomplicated reading of this music drama; however, the result is so detached and restrained that it leaves the listener unmoved. Chailly's mild-mannered approach is evident throughout the first movement, not merely because of the moderate march tempo (which can be very effective if played demonstratively and with heft) but the temperate character of the performance. In the development, grotesqueries are smoothed over and lack sharp bite. Dynamic levels are restrained. In contrast, Chailly treats the Scherzo in typically romantic fashion by setting a brisk pace for its principal thematic material and underplaying the movement's harsh qualities and acrimonious mockery. From the opening of the *Andante* movement one senses the absense of warmth, expressivity and genuine feeling. Chailly has woodwinds add slight affectations to their solos, thus disturbing linear flow. Later, he hangs on to the last few notes in certain bars (e.gs., #47+ and #58+), again creating an awkward display of forced emotions. At #61 he makes a few interesting points, which unfortunately are insignificant and come too late. Otherwise, the movement proceeds aimlessly, without much tragic pathos. The last movement is presented as a typical (if overlong) romantic finale. Tempo gradations are smoothed over in an attempt to attain continuity, but the dramatic essence of this movement escapes the conductor. Either too much appears in broad daylight, particularly from #109 of the introduction, which should be shadowy, or is covered, such as the first appearance of the fate motif in timpani at #107. Woodwinds are overbalanced but not compelling into the first theme. Chailly simply moves through the intricate and challenging byways of this movement without communicating a sense of its dramatic significance. Although the hammer blows are well done, what precedes and follows them fails to measure up to their enormous power (despite Chailly's imposing what amounts to a fermata over the leading note into the second stroke). A weak introductory violin theme at m.524 after the close of the section that includes the second stroke is debilitating. Dynamic levels are sometimes toned down (*fff* on the Fate motif at m.622 becomes *f*). All seems like much ado about nothing. Yet the final bars provide a touching close to what was otherwise a non-event.

DEWAART, EDO/Netherlands Radio Philharmonic - 2-RCA 74321 276072 (1995)
[85:16] As with much of DeWaart's complete cycle, the Sixth gets a moderate, controlled and unadventurous reading, devoid of personality. Sonic levels are tempered, failing to make up for orchestral weakness, particularly in the strings. The outer movements suffer most from these flaws. Moderation is the order of the day in the first movement. Notice that the very first strokes of Fate on the timpani end with a diminuendo (but are written to be played *sempre f*). DeWaart even smoothes over the dynamic passion of the "Alma" theme. He paces the movement well, even if a few moments seem tiresome (e.g., the brass chorale of the development and the coda at 20:17). His tendency to slide into climaxes rather than hit them on the head is also distracting. The off-beat march rhythm of the Scherzo movement has a heftier feel than did its counterpart in the first movement, but DeWaart slavishly drags the pace

of the *altväterisch* subject, which quickly grows tiresome. (What sense would the exhaustion one should feel at 11' make if the music that produced it is already on its last legs?) Much of his reading here sounds like mere note-spinning. Consistently mid-range dynamic levels hamper the feeling of serenity which should pervade the first subject of the slow movement. Within the context of a fairly well-conceived reading, the finale fails to make much of an impression. It suffers from the same symptoms as the rest of the performance: too much moderation and not enough personality.

DOHNANYI, CHRISTOPH VON/Cleveland Orchestra - 2-London 436 240 (1992) [79:52]+ This performance might be characterized aptly as "politically correct," focussing on clarity and precision rather than communicating a sense of the Mahlerian drama. Dohnanyi offers a well-played, clean and emotively moderate performance which neither scales the heights nor plumbs the depths of this profound work. Taking the shock out of its dynamic contrasts, taking the sting out of its painful jabs and thrusts and tempering its fiery spirit, Dohnanyi concentrates in their place on precise articulation and properly balancing inner parts. He seems to treat this work as if it were nothing more than a Brahmsian symphony, wiping the score clean of any distractions that might mitigate against such an approach, aesthetically as well as structurally. There is little to savor of the work's dramatic character or profound emotions in this objectified reading. Perhaps the lovely variant on the second theme of the first movement at 12:35 in woodwinds and the strong climax before the final coda of the Scherzo will momentarily raise an eyebrow, but the tragic aspect of Mahler's most personal symphony is gutted in this performance. Beginning in moderately quick tempo, there is even a hint of mildness at the second entrance of the bass strings on the march tread. Moderation is the order of the day, and it serves neither to increase precision nor to clarify complexity. Notice how weak the pounding fate motive is in the outer movements; how timidly the two hammer blows fall upon awaiting ears; how caricatureless the *altväterisch* subject of the Scherzo; and how devoid of gripping intensity the awesome finale. Dohnanyi refuses to let the music flow naturally: he either presses it forward hurriedly or lets it wander aimlessly. One can frequently tell a true Mahler conductor from the way he or she handles the bridge passages. Notice how matter-of-factly Dohnanyi glides through the quiet somber coda before the final outburst that ends the symphony, as if this brilliantly-conceived passage, quiet yet darkly ominous, were mere padding.

HAENCHEN, HARTMUT/Philharmonia Slavonica - Digital Concerto CCT 676 (1989); 12-CCT 999701 (1992) [79:02] Although a budget recording, this performance should not be rejected out-of-hand. Sonic levels are considerably strong and playing surprisingly effective, even if the strings leave much to be desired. Haenchen hurries the pace of the opening march, giving the entire movement a sense of urgency and vital intensity. His approach is akin to Solti's, if lacking interpretive nuance. Strangely, the fate motive is consistently underplayed by timpani in the outer movements. Coordinating with the first movement's march tempo, the second movement is also set in a brisk pace, which often gallops through the many parodistic elements without special effect. Yet the Haydnesque *altväterisch* segments are light and delicate, if not adequately contrasted with the brief rapid figurative interjections which parody it. Haenchen sets a moderate pace for the *Andante* movement, emphasizing the song-like, rather than the bittersweet, quality of its main theme. Cowbells jingle too rapidly to convey a faint recollection of peacefulness that Mahler sought. After rushing through the finale's opening string theme, Haenchen settles into the movement with a well-paced introduction, played without any particularly engaging stylistic quality. The movement proceeds generally well, notwithstanding weak strings. But the first hammer blow and frequent appearances of the fate motif in timpani are too mild to produce even a twinge. For some inexplicable reason, high bells at #145 replace deep bells, producing an ineffectual tingle when a more robust sound quality is called for.

HAENCHEN, HARTMUT/Netherlands Philharmonic - 2-Laserlight 14140; 3-Capriccio 10 643 (1994) [82:49]   Haenchen takes a little more time with the first movement than he in his earlier version (see above), and to good effect. His is primarily a straight and unmannered reading, characterized by long stretches of measured, inflexible pacing, and producing only a moderate impact. Loud and rapid cow bells and a piercing trumpet sometimes cut too strongly through orchestral passages. Most problemmatic is the rapid tempo Haenchen sets for the Scherzo. He attempts to overplay the contrast between the main material and the *altväterisch* sections by substantially slowing down the tempo for the latter. Yet this *grazioso* music has little stylishness even in parody, being played in too much of a four-square manner. One interesting moment comes around 6:15 where growling low brass create a terrifying spectre. Haenchen's frequent meandering in and out of tempo does not enhance the musical flow or provide a substitute for lack of stylishness. Taken at a somewhat more relaxed pace than in his previous recording, the slow movement tries to be expressive but problems in woodwind intonation, little dynamic inflection and monochromatic timbre detract significantly. Only during its climax (c.13:12) does the movement come to life. A welter of brass smothers the first appearance of the Fate motto in timpani during the finale's introduction. This important motto is presented too weakly throughout the movement. Haenchen seems to be unwilling to come to grips with the work's tragic aspect. Long stretches of music are routinely played, with some sense of underlying propulsion and , except for some balance problems (brass vs. strings) and an overblown trumpet, the orchestra is moderately effective. The celli imitation of the violin's introductory theme on its return at 8:38 comes through noticeably. Again rapid cow bells do not produce a nostalgic yearning for the simple pleasures of Nature. At #122 (marked *poco piu mosso*), Haenchen holds on to the woodwind chords as if placed under fermatas, while playing the celli's dotted rhythmic figures which follow in tempo (9:40). Yet the two hammer blows are absolutely awesome, sounding axe-like as Mahler intended. Given such strong strokes, one wonders why the Fate motto is so severely underplayed at 21:42 where it is marked *fff*. Haenchen quickly runs through the closing coda, rattling off the final ouburst on Fate without a moment's hesitation, his performance demonstrates that one cannot render this symphony effectively by trying to make its tragic aspect disappear.

HAITINK, BERNARD/Concertgebouw Orchestra - 2-Philips 839797/8 (1970); 2-Philips 420 138 (1988); 10-442 050 (1994) [80:77]   Haitink's mild approach generally tempers the harshness so pervasive in this symphony and fails to generate much warmth in its few tender passages. Sonics are clear and vibrant but percussion is weak and veiled. The opening march set in moderate tempo projects little impulse. Some sections are pressed while others are rigidly measured. Although the Scherzo tempo is appropriately weighty, Haitink makes little of the music's Mephistophelian character. The trio sounds like an tiresome waltz rather than a mocking caricature of the Viennese rococo style. In the slow movement, Haitink manages to produce some moments of tender lyricism and a poignant climax, but much of his reading is dry and superficial. Lack of intensity and vitality are serious detractions in the finale. Orchestral playing is clear and precise if not full-blown and luxurious. The work demands a sense of drama that this version lacks.

HAITINK, BERNARD/Berlin Philharmonic - 2-Philips 426 257 (1990) [81:21] +
    Haitink focuses his vision of the Sixth on the finale. Unlike his rather detached reading of the preceeding movements, the massive, complex last movement receives his most ardent and responsive attention. The BPO gives him stronger brass (sometimes overbearing) with

which to make as much of an impact as his rather objective orientation will bear. Haitink rarely digs deeply into the soul of this music, chosing to smooth over the excesses and exaggerations which are so important to this work. Set in moderately swift tempo, the first movement makes only a moderate impression. Dynamic levels are diminished (despite blaring trumpets), in character with the general sense of mildness that works against the nature of such demonstrative music. Even the "Alma" theme sounds sweet and endearing rather than ardent and impassioned. While essentially understated, if clear and distinct, a few interesting effects catch the ear: the seering violins on the main theme at 9:40 and the hint of mystery following the entrance of cow bells in the development. While Haitink coordinates the main tempo of the Scherzo with that of the first movement (the former being a caricature of the latter), he minimizes the many grotesqueries that should heighten its mocking character; only the overgrown growling of low brass (4:50 and 6:35) contribute to this end. After a soft and serene, though rather pointless, slow movement, the finale bursts open forcefully. It is here that the tragic essence of Mahler's vision is prominent, and, consequently, here that Haitink takes his stand. Evocative instrumental coloration intensifies the atmosphere generated by the sprawling introduction (e.g., the eerie bass clarinet and whooping brass). The mystery evoked by these weird sounds becomes a shroud in which the entire movement is enveloped. Dynamic thrust propels the music forward, orchestral involvement increases, driving home the three threatening crises, each concluding with a stroke of Fate (the last omitted here). Yet between blows one senses a lack of urgency, with the tempo only picking up as the music builds to each devastating climax. Even the Fate motto in timpani is sometimes unduly restrained (23:34). If one overlooks some of these contradictions, the finale sounds quite imposing. Unfortunately, the aesthetic link with the preceding movements not apparent and the tragic character of the work is underdeveloped.

HORENSTEIN, JASCHA/Stockholm Philharmonic - 2-Nonesuch 73029 (1975); 2-Unicorn-Kanchana UKCD 2024/25 (1989); 4-Music & Arts CD-785 (1993) [86:39]*+

Despite some technical problems, Horenstein delivers yet another insightful and intelligent, as well as moving, performance of one of Mahler's most powerful symphonies. While any Mahlerian would be grateful for having a performance of the Sixth by this great Mahler conductor, the orchestra, clearly unfamiliar with this music, makes it more difficult for Horenstein to realize fully his vision of the work. Too often one senses a cautiousness in the orchestra which may have caused the square rhythmic treatment and stilted, unidiomatic playing. Horenstein intelligently avoids the quick tempo for the opening march that is chosen by all-too-many conductors, but he has difficulty maintaining his weighty pace consistently; more accentuation and flexibility would have been helpful. If others may jog too briskly through this movement, Horenstein seems only to lumber through it. The Scherzo is set in an appropriately weighty tempo but little is made of the grotesqueries that make this music so delightfully devilish. Instead, the movement sounds slightly forced and playing is often cold, stiff and imprecise. Most disturbing is the brisk pace set for the trio that consequently lacks grace and charm, remaining in a scherzo-like mode. Least problemmatic is the *Andante* movement in which Horenstein elicits a restful and serene atmosphere as well as some of the finest playing of the performance. Cow bells are excellently presented, creating an atmosphere tinged with distant memories of a long-lost peace. Horenstein makes every effort to produce a strong and insightful finale and his success in rendering subtle nuances and thrilling climaxes at each hammer blow is unquestionable, but elsewhere the performance is hampered by a lack of energy (particularly in the development) and some insecure and weak playing (e.g., at the end of the exposition and after the second hammer blow). Although this recording may have more to offer interpretively than most, its many problems are difficult to overlook.

INBAL, ELIAHU /Frankfurt Radio Symphony - 2-Denon 60C-1327 (1987); 16-Denon CO 72589-604 (1989) [83:49]* Inbal offers a competitive performance, heavy on brass in strong climaxes and laced with quick pacing and electric intensity. His tendency to press forward pulls tempi out of gear at times and overpowering brass sometimes bury the rest of the orchestra. Inbal's agitated pacing works best in the outer movements, but it fails to capture the bittersweet reverie that the slow movement should evoke. Inbal handles the parodistic grotesqueries of the second movement impressly. Here the *grazioso* segments mimic the eighteenth-century *galante* style peppered with interjecting bits of rapid figuration in self-mocking irony. The finale is excellently rendered: all the drama is there, punctuated by magnificent hammer blows. However, string sonorities do not penetrate the musical fabric sufficiently to do justice to this music.

INOUE, MICHIYOSHI /Royal Philharmonic - 2-RPO CD RPZ 001 (1989) [82:57]
Characterized by confined sonics, restrained playing and an uneven and undistinguished reading, this performance makes only a moderate impact. Most troublesome are the orchestral weaknesses: anemic strings, diminutive brass and a general lack of involvement. Although the first movement opens in a fairly well-conceived tempo, slightly heavy-laden with forced marcato, the march theme fails to make much of an impression. Even more disconcerting is the sluggish and mild treatment of the "Alma" theme. With such a consistently moderate temperament, the performance simply never rises to the occasion. Transitions are sometimes hurried; grotesqueries too tame; and tempi too heavy-laden (e.g., the brass choral at 12:20). For the Scherzo, Inoue sets an even more ponderous tempo than for the first movement's march theme, ignoring an opportunity to establish a tempo relationship between these movements. At such a weighted pace, he fails to make much of the movement's mocking parody. The contrast between the demonic main theme and the graceful *altväterisch* subject on classical dance rhythms is reduced to a mere semblance of itself. With lifeless, lackluster strings, the *Andante* movement is equally ineffective, lacking warmth, passion and poignancy. Much the same may be said for the finale, which is weakened by diminished sonics and restrained playing. The music trudges along without any underlying tension or dramatic impact. Even the first hammer blow sounds like a mere puff of smoke. Inoue too frequently smooths over dynamic contrasts. Although he occasionally brings some life to the final third of the movement (e.g., from 22:20 to the return of the *allegro* and at 23:28 into the main theme), he fails to pull this performance out of the doldrums.

JÄRVI, NEEME/Royal Scottish National Orchestra - Chandos CHAN 9207 (1993) [72:32] Here is a perfect example of how *not* to conduct this symphony! In his mad rush to record a Mahler cycle, Järvi hurtles through this profound masterpiece, using high-powered sonics and loud brass in place of a well-conceived interpretion. The inordinately fast march tempo he sets at the very beginning establishes his general approach to the entire work. Dashing unabatedly through each section, while overwhelming with a welter of sound, he ignores important motifs (at #7). Halfway through the first movement, he eases up a bit (at #21), giving the chorale interlude with cow bells and celeste a chance to breathe, but otherwise he drives through the movement without let-up. So too in the Scherzo. Even the *altväterisch* parody is briskly treated, thereby diminishing its coy character and mocking irony. At #81 (4:32), Järvi suddenly backs off the pace without apparent reason, necessitating the imposition of several tempo adjustments to bring him back to the main tempo. Brass are coarse rather than characterful.

A similarly hurried tempo is set for the slow movement, more *moderato* than *andante*. Järvi keeps his brisk tempo going with little relief, deflating the lyrical beauty of the thematic material. Only a few special touches are applied: emphasis on certain notes of the violin theme at 6:45 in mid-phrase; awkward tempo shifts in the main climactic section from 9:46; crude weight on accents in the theme played by the violins after #61; and added violin glissandi toward the close. In the finale nothing especially interesting happens either. A weak opening violin theme leads to some variably fine effects (e.g., brass whoops and rapid 32nd note woodwind phrases). The main theme has vitality and strength, but soon Järvi's tendency to press forward overwhelms, and the result is bombastic and devoid of any semblance of the tragic.

KARAJAN, HERBERT VON/Berlin Philharmonic - 2-DG 2707206 (1978); 415 099-2 (1986) [82:55]*+ DG gives us a sonic spectacular that captures the magnificent playing of the BPO in sumptuous and crystal clear sound and excellently proportioned balances. Tempi are generally fast (except in the *Andante* movement) but much excitement is generated. Overall, the performance is well-conceived and rendered without unnecessary affectations. Driving speed frequently results in less dramatic weight and little emotive depth or sensitivity, particularly at the close of the first movement and throughout the Scherzo. In the second movement, scherzo and trio sections are almost indistinguishable in temperament, the latter failing to elicit a *grazioso* feeling. On the other hand, Karajan's *Andante* movement is one of the best on disk. Gorgeously played, very poignant and thoughtfully rendered without exaggerations or disconcerting mannerisms, this movement alone is adequate evidence of Karajan's profound understanding of Mahler's deeply personal perspective. The finale is quite thrilling. Magnificent sonics, superb playing and vibrant intensity add to the dramatic impact made by this awesome movement. Although the main tempo is hard-driven, Karajan gives the music's profound emotions their due. Strangely enough, the second hammer blow is stronger than the first (the reverse in intended), but the urgent impulse that follows each of these musical catastrophes is overwhelming. Even if tempi might have been slightly more moderate, Karajan's is still an exciting, brilliantly conceived and excellently played reading.

KUBELIK, RAFAEL/Bavarian Radio Symphony - 2-DG 139341/2 (1969); 413 528 (1988); 10-DG 429 042 (1990) [70:54]* One of Kubelik's best efforts in the Mahler cycle, this too frequently overlooked performance is strong and vital, and has the advantage of crystal clear sound and superb playing. One must, however, accept the rapid pace that dominates his approach. The first movement march tempo may be the swiftest on disk, yet Kubelik generates much excitement from his energetic pace. Details are carefully rendered and audible. In coordination with the first movement main tempo, the Scherzo is set at a very quick pace, the music scampering about impishly (thus making a strong argument for downplaying the *wuchtig* tempo marking). The trio section is deliciously wicked. Despite a furiously-paced tempo for the Scherzo, Kubelik very skillfully slows down the proceedings for the final coda. Antiphonal violins add an interesting stereophonous effect to the tender lyricism of the *Andante* movement. Although some moments seems rather cold and uninvolved, Kubelik's treatment of stylistic nuances and his marvelous approach to the climactic section (#59) is every bit the equal of Karajan's thrilling performance (see above). A quick main tempo in the finale elicits much excitement. While very abrupt tempo fluctuations mar the introduction and the development is much too hard-driven, Kubelik's energetic reading vibrates with intensity. Timpani pound out the "Fate" motif with ferocity and the two hammer blows are very strong even if approached somewhat too quickly. Kubelik presses intently to the closing, but poor brass sound distorts the final coda.

LEVINE, JAMES/London Symphony - 2-RCA ARL-2 3212; RVC 2275/6 (1979); RCD2-3213 (1986) [80:56]*+ This fine performance continues to be competitive despite the increased number excellent recordings that have emerged since it was first issued. Dynamic levels are high and rich, full-bodied orchestral sound is superb, with Levine emphasizing strong timpani and sharp attacks. While generally intense, the approach is not as excessively agitated as others, such as Kubelik, Karajan and Bernstein, who take the opening march tempo at racing speed. Sonics are clear, balances well-adjusted and details aptly rendered. Levine treats the cow bells better here then in most versions, having them rung in isolated strokes rather than in rapid unrealistic and pointless trills. Although the march tempo used for the first movement is on the quick side, it works quite well, never allowing the tempo to lag during transitions, as in Horenstein's version (see above). The development section is marvelously devilish and played with panache (notice the fascinating affect at #26 on *nicht eilen*). Levine highlights more powerful moments with explosive strength and vibrancy. Before the final close, the music almost stands still as if challenging the might of the opposing negative forces. Equally superb is the Scherzo in which Levine enhances its biting humor and satanic grotesqueries with razor sharp playing and wickedly impish woodwinds trills. Nuances are never exaggerated but simply given due importance within the overall structure. Expecting a sensitive and emotion-charged *Andante* (especially after his *Adagietto* in the Fifth), Levine serves up a surprisingly cool reading that simply doesn't capture the poignancy and pensive melancholy of this too-often misunderstood movement. Frequently, dynamic levels are overbearing despite a tempered and straightforward approach. Levine must have been saving his energy for the finale. Unlike most other conductors, in the massive closing movement he provides a structural framework within which sections have just the right proportion and follow each other naturally and inevitably. He charges the music with dynamic force, assisted by expressive and highly-polished playing (even if strings are more vibrant in the first movement). Levine presses resolutely from climax to climax, each bursting forth with overpowering strength. Hammer blows are gigantic and the excitement generated keeps one literally at the edge of one's seat. Around #150 the orchestra explodes with terrifying power. One might imagine a scene in which the hero frantically runs off into the night screaming with the torment of his oppressors, until he meets the ghost of his youth (first movement march) taunting him with the spectre of how much he has lost!

LOMBARD, ALAIN/The Hague Philharmonic - 2-Hague Philharmonic 6818.677/8 (1986) [79:45]   This LP release by The Hague Philharmonic is a rarity, but the quick tempi in the first two movements and moderate sonic level make hunting for it a low priority. After an energetic treatment of the first movement's march theme, the "Alma" theme seems rather tame. Lombard plays up the many grotesque effects appearing in the development, but his treatment lacks the sense of tragic doom that should haunt the entire movement. His curious slow-up into #42 (marked *etwas drängend*, somewhat pressed) is one of the few affectations Lombard imposes upon the music. Coordinated with the first movement's march tempo, the Scherzo opens briskly, sharply accented and stylistically nuanced. Generally well rendered with some interesting effects, this movement still suffers from intermittent flaws (e.gs., a slow-up to the return of Tempo I at #82 and quick, harsh treatment of the music beginning after #91). Lombard's best work is done in the slow movement. In contrast with the first two movements, the *Andante Moderato* is broadly paced, the main theme hesitently languid. While Lombard's finale has much dramatic impact, particularly in the sections surrounding the two hammer blows, confined string sound and some momentary excesses in tempo fluctuations mar what is otherwise a moderately compelling performance.

MAAZEL, LORIN/Vienna Philharmonic - 3-CBS 13M-37875 (1983); M3K 42495 (1987); 14-Sony Classics SK 14K 48198 (1992) [83:00]*+   Maazel's approach is strong and weighty with much attention to detail and clear, precise playing. He brings out all of the power and depth of the opening movement by combining forcefulness with an expansive and muscular march tempo maintained with perfect control. The "Alma" theme sounds more tender-hearted than passionate. Maazel elicits more emotion than one expects from him without his usual erratic exaggerations of phrasing. Equally well executed is the Scherzo but for a few uninspired moments in the trio which fail to elicit the intended *grazioso* effect. The Scherzo tempo is well-coordinated with the first movement march (as it should be) and numerous hidden details come to the surface. While beautifully played, the *Andante* movement lacks warmth and sensitivity, thus failing to capture the underlying spirit of pensive lyricism that this music should convey. The finale opens strongly, highlighted by terrifying horn leaps after #105 and a very heavy *schwer* section. Maazel builds agitatedly into the allegro exposition. Here a spirited main theme lacks dynamic force and sufficient sonic fullness. One feels the life force being sapped out of the hero as the first hammer blow approaches. And then, with an horrific thud, all hell breaks loose. Maazel treats the second hammer stroke in much the same manner, but now the furious reaction evoked quickly wanes and the reading begins to suffer from fatigue. From here somber moments seem too fleeting in comparison with the breadth given more powerful sections. The coda would have been greatly enhanced by richer sound and a greater sense of anticipation.

MITROPOULOS, DIMITRI/Orchestra Sinfonica della WDR di Colonia - 2-Fonit Cetra DOC 5 (1981); Hunt/Arkadia 522 (1994) [74:06] This performance took place on August 31, 1959, more than four and one-half years after the NYP performances (see the 1986 volume, p.92). Orchestral playing is sloppier and less stylistically adept, while Mitropoulos' interpretive approach is more mannered and less effective. The pressing is defective (a few measures of the *Andante* are lost!) and volume levels are weak. As in the NYP performances, a flexible conducting style is evident throughout. Frequent affectations distort the musical line and interrupt rather than enhance the overall effect. The first movement suffers most from this approach (the repeat is not taken). A snappy tempo for the Scherzo is again used and the trio is just as brisk and dull as in the NYP performances, if far below their level of precision. Unfortunately, this more sensitive and better paced reading of the *Andante* movement is marred by tape distortions, and an exciting finale would have been better served by fewer affectations and awkward tempi, stronger sonics, better balances (horns and percussion are weak and cow bells blurred) and cleaner playing.

NANUT, ANTON /Radio Symphony Orchestra of Ljubljana - ZYX CLS 4110 (1990); Digital Concerto CCT 676 (1990) [79:03]+ Nanut and his Croatian orchestra offer a serviceable performance. Its primary impact is made by high-powered brass and percussion and Nanut's tendency to hurl headlong into climaxes, centering on the powerful highs, and letting much of what remains between them merely happen. Orchestral playing is adequate except for blaring trumpets, perfunctory horns, and numerous balance problems which blur important motivic inner voices. Nanut tends to hasten from climax to climax in all but the slow movement, creating an edginess that mitigates against the tragic aspect of the symphony. He sets a brisk pace throughout much of the opening movement. Yet quieter interludes elicit a soft, shimmering atmosphere and the final climax follows an energetic build-up. Coordinated with the first movement's march tempo, the Scherzo's main tempo is also very animated, but too rapid to give the parodistic elements their due. Contrasts in tempo which caricature the old-fashioned dance music in the trios are smoothed over, as are biting witticisms in brass and woodwinds. Lacking nuance and style, the Scherzo just happens. After a mild, restful main theme, the slow movement goes its way routinely until it becomes more impassioned in the final climactic section. Screaming horns bellow major-to-minor chords over a dampened pronouncement of fate in the timpani to open the finale. Nanut approaches the movement's lengthy introduction cautiously. But from the first appearance of the main theme, his reading is quite effective, even if his orchestral forces do not have the sonic dimension needed for a fully satisfying performance. An extremely strong tam-tam stroke at the second hammer blow makes it seem stronger than the first, which reverses Mahler's intention. But in isolation, the climax is impressive. Only the brass seem too restrained throughout, weakening the grotesque character of their distorted thematic material. Nanut often presses ardently through the music to get from one highpoint to another, requiring only high volume rather than a well-conceived approach to structural proportions in order to carry the climaxes.

NEUMANN, VÁCLAV/Leipzig Gewandhaus Orchestra - 2-Philips 6703.016; C71AX 306; AY 802807/09 (1966); 2-Berlin Classics 0090452 (1995) [80:33]*+ This performance is rendered with much more conviction and dynamic verve than Neumann's later effort with the CPO (see below). Neumann lets the music breath more fully, thereby eliciting greater dramatic impact, enhanced by sharp playing, better balances and fuller, clearer sound quality. The opening march is much stronger even if it is in basically the same tempo while the second theme is more passionate and robust. Dynamic markings are carefully rendered. A strong marcato tread adds to the force of the opening movement. Neumann creates more atmosphere by his intelligent use of cow bells. Even the Scherzo's main tempo has more weight but never drags; yet the trio section is on the quick side. Attention to details and articulate playing produce a positive effective. Listen to the marvelous yawn in the horns at #95. Greater sensitivity adds significantly to Neumann's reading of the *Andante* movement. He brings out the music's light-hearted sensibilities at #53, recalling long-lost joys. The climax is both powerful and heartrending. Stronger and cleaner playing invigorates the finale. Only timpani seems too muffled. The *allegro* exposition is pressed but generates much excitement. Individual effects are well-handled, particularly cow bells and deep bells. The sole defect is the metallic sound of the hammer which flies in the face of Mahler's specific instructions. But climaxes are spectacular. After #143 some things begin to go awry: the flute disappears before #144; a ritard replaces the direction *nicht schleppen* before #150; and the B-trumpet is missing at #162. Neumann's intense reading engenders much excitement as the work proceeds to its whirlwind conclusion.

NEUMANN, VÁCLAV/Czech Philharmonic - 2-Pro-Arte 2PAL 2019 (1982); Supraphon 11 1977 (1993); 11-Supraphon SUP 111860 (1994) [78:35] Too many problems mitigate against a high rating for this performance: uneven playing and balance problems, constricted sound and an approach which skims the surface of the music and frequently misreads important directions. A moderately quick march tempo opens the symphony, but weak strings, blaring trumpets and distant timpani sap much of the music's strength. Even the effusive "Alma" theme is smoothed over, making it more tender than effusive. Raw brass sound and a curiously indeterminate cow bell timbre are further detractions. Contrasts are generally watered down in a lyrical approach de-emphasizing the more powerful aspects of the work. In the Scherzo movement, a speedy tempo hurries past significant details and fudged accents smooth over rough edges. Neumann enhances the trio with lilting grace even if at its return the music becomes somewhat stilted. The *Andante* movement is comfortably paced, allowing the tender emotions expressed to come through naturally without being forced. However, at m.182 Neumann suddenly stops short, abruptly interrupting the musical flow. Stronger and played with more involvement that the preceding movements, the finale lacks sufficient dynamic force. Cow bells are too loud while deep bells are inaudible. Some strange sounds come from the timpani around #127-128 and the first hammer has a slightly metallic ring to it. From there the music acquires a sharper edge in too prominent brass. Although Neumann generates some excitement in the reprise, several misread directions and playing problems diminish the overall effect.

SYMPHONY NO. 6

OZAWA, SEIJI/Boston Symphony - 3-Philips 434 909-2 (1994); 14-Philips 438 874(1995) [83:41]+ As with the rest of his cycle, Ozawa presents the Sixth as if it were merely a typical romantic symphony in manner and form. He treats the second movement as a traditional Scherzo, setting a fast pace for the main theme, and ignoring the headnote marking *wuchtig* (weighty) as well as the parodistic relationship of this off-beat march in triple time with the four-square march of the first movement. The trio section, which caricatures classical dance-styles, is devoid of any attempt at parody. Instead, Ozawa presents it in a formalistic, straight-laced and unstylish manner. The outer movements lack sufficient dramatic impact. Ozawa restrains his forces so much that the performance seems almost nonchalant. For the most part his tempo choices are appropriate (with the possible exception of a rapid tempo for the principal subject of the Scherzo and a sluggish one for the trio). However, he rarely gets beyond the surface of the work. That is not to say that Ozawa has no ideas of his own, yet when he employs them, his choices seem ill considered. Sometimes he wears the music down with long, drawn out ritards, even interpreting the marking *etwas zurückhalten* (somewhat held back) at 6:20 in the second movement as a *molto ritard*. Elsewhere he ignores markings which he would have been better advised to heed, (such as *nicht eilen* at #26 before the reprise in the first movement). Only the warm lyricism of the *Andante* movement seems to attract Ozawa's sensibilities. Even here, however, a mildness permeates the movement, that becomes listless at times. Ozawa's total lack of conception in the finale is most disturbing. After a disjointed introduction, one wonders what the music is getting at. Where menacing anticipation should pervade the musical approach into the initial statement of the main theme, instead we hear mere note spinning. Ozawa's second stroke has a fearful presentment. Thereafter (c.18') he puts on the breaks when Mahler directs that the music press forward, producing a stilted effect, and then races through the Fate motto as if it had little significance. Even its terrifying return at 22:50 (marked *fff*) is surprisingly weak. Only in the quiet, weighty bass line that proceeds the final outburst is one aware of any dramagtic depth. Despite demonstrative and articulate string playing, the brass are either too overbearing (particularly the trumpets) or merely pedestrian, further diminishing the overall impact of this performance.

RATTLE, SIMON/City of Birmingham Symphony [REVISED VERSION] - 2-EMI CDS 754047 (1990) [85:36]* Simon Rattle choses the Revised Version of the Sixth for this recording, and, true to his bent, provides some diverting interpretive nuances throughout. What is missing is both a consistancy of approach and dramatic intensity. From the very outset, there is a mildness in both his reading and the orchestra's treatment of the main material. Rattle's tendency to suddenly rush headlong into, or stretch out approaches to, climaxes seems inconsistent with this temperateness. While a lyrical legato style softens the general impact of the first movement, it is occasionally contradicted by fits of frenzy (at 12:50 and 23:00). Major climaxes do not have the force needed to drive them home securely (e.g., at 20:30). Softer segments, such as the chorale intermezzi, provide a contrasting sense of peace, as do the opening moments of the coda. Rattle closes this movement with great ferocity that seems to come from nowhere, given his mild-mannered reading of the rest of the movement. He imbues the *Andante Moderato* with a tenderly pensive quality, attempting to lift the lighter rhythmic fragments that serve as a counterpoise to the tender sentiments of the principal theme out of the overall pacing by giving them slightly more motion. Some interesting effects are noteworthy: a gradual increase into the main tempo at 8:00 and a long glissando at 11:38. But taken together they offer little that is relevant to the drama presented here. Rattle marvelously conveys the unexpected appearance of a dark cloud upon the horizon toward the close. Yet it, too, seems inconsequential. Had the finale commenced immediately thereafter, this sudden shadow at the close of the slow movement would have provided an interesting prophetic touch. Instead, a brisk reading of the Scherzo follows, in which exaggerations in tempo contrasts are the main feature. While more grotesque images conjured up by lower brass (at 5:00 and 6:00 et seq.) are diverting, brass playing generally seems bland for this devilish music. Again an inconsistency in the treatment of grotesqueries is apparent. Rattle seems to pick and choose which effects he wishes to highlight and either gives them a hard edge or drives them on forcefully. As with the first movement, the finale stops far short of being a complete success. Confined dynamic levels, tempered impulse and a curious combination of threadbare meandering spiced with abrupt moments of violent fury (Rattle's reaction to the markings *drängend* and *nicht schleppend* respectively) simply leave his reading far short of what many had hoped would be a major statement. Rattle concentrates on the big climaxes, trying to overwhelm by increasing their sonic level. But all goes for naught, as neither the work's tragic aspect nor its dramatic power comes through with sufficient force (not just sound) or intensity (not just speed) to provide a thoroughly satisfying performance.

RÖGNER, HEINZ /Berlin Radio Symphony [REVISED VERSION] - 2-Eterna 817612-3; 3-Tokuma 32TC-85-87 (1986) [82:11]* Despite some spotty playing and excessively high volume, this relatively routine performance has some merit. Rögner opens with a weighty, emphatic march tempo that soon begins to drag for lack of flexibility. To sustain such a broad tempo requires both a muscular marcato on each pulse and an urgency that intensifies the steady march tempo. Rögner appropriately emphasizes the woodwind and brass grotesqueries in the development. Yet the level of intensity often flags and the strings sometimes sound uninvolved or too restrained. In lyrical sections, Rögner evokes warm and heartfelt sentiments, and produces a rivetting effect upon the march's return at #28 and after #40. His style has two quirks which become all too apparent: he hurries through ritards without letting up on the tempo and has strings play long glissandi. While the former detracts from the terrifying impact that should be made by the huge dissonant climax toward the end of the first movement (no ritard appears into it), the latter, occurring throughout the symphony, may offend some tastes.

Taking the *Andante Moderato* second in order, Rögner sets a brisk pace for the main theme. Expressively played by strings, the movement suffers from some stiff, detached brass playing. Intensity is replaced by high volume in climaxes (particularly from #59). The Scherzo movement has a spirited character, with wonderful effects in winds, but it is spoiled by lack of tempo contrast with the trio subject (even if the rapid figuration that intermittently interrupts the *grazioso* music is in proper contrast to it) and stiff, inflexible playing. An uneven finale has as many impressive moments as it has problems, however. Unduly brisk treatment of the Fate motto during the introduction contrasts with Rögner's well-coordinated tempo modulations into the exposition. As with the first movement's march theme, the principal theme has much heft. But tension falters as it proceeds, despite high volume, and trumpets bury strings. The orchestra blasts its way to the first hammer blow, yet it seems slightly underdone for what preceded it. The rapid string figuration that follows seems to over-react to this moderate blow with furious agitation. Unlike many conductors, Rögner takes seriously the marking *etwas wuchtiger* (somewhat more weighty), which appears at the Shostakovichian gallop (after #133), and he digs into the *kräftig* (powerful) march that follows with impressive strength. While his approach to the second hammer stroke seems too hurried, the effect of the blow is cataclyismic, heightened by terrifying trumpet screams. He then disinterestedly races through the next appearance of the "Fate" motto (after #143). Tempo contrasts thereafter run the gamut, from extremely deliberate to very racy. Upon its return (at #153), the main theme staunchly and emphatically clears the way for the reprise. Had what follows not been merely blasted out at excruciatingly high volume and had been paced more deliberately and flexibly, the overall effect would have been measurably enhanced.

SYMPHONY NO. 6

ROSBAUD, HANS /Southwest German Radio Symphony (perf. 1960) - 2-Datum DAT 12303 (1993) [81:11]* The main tempi in the first half of this performance might serve as a model for Mahler conductors. Rosbaud's demonstrative, visceral tempo for the opening march highlights its heroic quality and is remarkably consistent throughout the entire movement. He is able to keep his robust march tempo going with urgency and intensity, never becoming sodden or tiresome. With the exception of the exposition's repeat, Rosbaud follows Mahler's directions to the letter, and to excellent effect. Close miking sometimes distorts brass sonics at high pitch, giving trumpets a disturbingly piercing quality. Perfectly coordinated in tempo with the opening movement, the Scherzo maintains the weighty, marked character of the first movement's march, now evoked as its mocking counterfoil. Rosbaud eases into the trio, establishing a tempo not much slower than for the scherzo material (as Mahler directs) but still stylish, sounding gruffly Haydnesque. Rosbaud conveys the classical mannerisms parodied here with perfect aplomb. Low growling and yawning in brass add a grotesque aspect to Mahler's parody. Again Rosbaud maintains perfect control over tempi. A dishy tamtam mars the final climax, however (at 12:15), and the closing coda is treated too inflexibly to conjure up a mysterious aura. From here things begin to wear thin. The slow movement is taken more *moderato* than *andante*, seeming cool and detached. Again close miking distorts proper volume levels. Rosbaud hurries along here without much involvement. As a result, the passionate climax at #59 (11:02) sounds out of place.

By the finale, the orchestra seems nearly spent. What a pity! Opening the movement quickly, Rosbaud adds weight to the first pronouncement of the Fate motto in timpani, giving it a terrifying aspect, and he paces gradually to the major-to-minor chord at 4:20, yet it seems surprisingly unimpressive. He then sets the main theme in essentially the same tempo as the opening march, but he is not successful in recapturing its demonstrative strength. A legato style permeates orchestral playing, weakening dramatic power and depth. Only high volume (from close miking) heightens the overall effect. But urgency and impulse fail. The percussion are frequently absent, and even the first hammer blow merely brushes by. Only around 23' does Rosbaud slacken the pace somewhat to give the *grazioso* section (at #147) a chance to be expressive. After the final statement of the introduction's soaring violin theme, Fate is finally given its due, pounded out forcefully in timpani. Although generally well-conceived, the finale does not live up to the promise of Rosbaud's brilliant performance of the first two movements.

SCHERCHEN, HERMANN/Leipzig Radio Symphony (perf. 4 Oct. 1961, Kongresshalle, Leipzig) [REVISED VERSION] - 2-Tahra TAH 110/111 (1994) [53:43] Most Mahlerians would be shocked by this performance! Scherchen rips through the entire symphony at record-breaking speed, ignoring the repeat of the first movement and hacking away huge chunks from the Scherzo and finale. Billed as Scherchen's "abridged version," akin to his surgery on the Fifth, the recording contains notes *in apologia* which try to muster an argument in favor of his extraordinarily rapid tempi and massive cuts. We are told that Scherchen is an "expressionistic" conductor and that his vision of this masterpiece is best projected by these unorthodox devices. But even considering the extreme energy and maddening tension produced by consistently fast tempi (especially in the opening and Scherzo movements), too many subtleties of expression, contrapuntal nuances, important internal motifs and major tempo modulations are lost in a such relentlessly rapid pace. What is the aesthetic conveyed by such fury? Is the hero a savage beast raging through life uncontrollably? Could this approach have been conceived as an anti-heroic statement or a reaction to the bestial savagery of modern "heroes"? But then why is the *Andante Moderato* movement placed second in order? Possibly because Scherchen's reading of the first movement is itself a parody of heroism which the scherzo is supposed to represent.

The main brisk tempo of the slow movement comports well with its cool demeanor.

Scherchen most interestingly ushers in the section at #58 (9') by a long ascending superoctave glissando on A in violins. Yet when the main theme returns, welling up with intense passion, he breezes through it so rapidly that passion turns into near mania. Is this joyous exuberance or wild lustfulness? Despite a statement to the contrary in the accompanying notes, Scherchen makes no cuts in this movement. In the following Scherzo, he excises no less than 173 measures from #84 tp #99 (mm.222 to 395). Together with his extremely fast main tempo--completely devoid of any *wuchtig* quality--comparable to the earlier march movement, Scherchen runs through this movement in about 6 1/2 minutes. At least his approach is consistent in its unremitting mania. The caricaturesque nature of the trio is lost in a strict, measured reading. Scherchen's treatment of the finale is also remarkable, speed and intensity again its mainstay. Although the main material is not excessively driven, every time the Fate motto appears, Scherchen suddenly rushes by it as if he were unwilling to look destiny in the face. He also rushes through transitional passages with undaunted speed, and then cuts the entire next section including the second hammer blow! (from #129, m.336 to #140, m.479). Scherchen closes this wild (but not really tragic) excursion with a well-conceived final coda: a broadly stated chorale for low brass, followed by an enormous orchestral outburst which weighs heavily upon the Fate motto. Scherchen's only recorded performance of the Sixth may be more worthy of discussion for its controversial approach than of repeated listening.

SEGERSTAM, LEIF/Danish National Radio Symphony - 2-Chandos CHAN 895617 (1991) [87:41]* Segerstam relishes the many brilliant compositional nuances found here with the ardent enthusiasm of a composer/interpreter. But his orchestral forces lack the sonic breadth and richness that the Sixth requires to make it the overwhelming experience it should be. Strings are the worst offenders in this regard. The horns often lack enough reserve for powerful entrances. By contrast, the solo trumpet is sometimes overexposed, rattling the ear with its piercing tone. Chandos provides excellent sonics, making every effort to compensate for orchestral weaknesses. In the opening movement, taken at a moderately brisk clip, Segerstam minimizes the important contrast between the two main subjects, in a relatively strong if still tempered reading. His best work occurs in the quieter transition passages (the brass chorale at 12:40 and the sentimental second subject at c.14') and with woodwind and brass grotesqueries, which emerge from the musical fabric yet make only a moderate impression. Toward the closing minutes, Segerstam presses forward into ritards, stretching them out extensively into climaxes. Generally, the reading waivers between highlighting interesting effects and maintaining control over the intensity of dramatic thrust. Using the same brisk tempo of the opening march, the Scherzo movement might be characterized in much the same way. Well-rendered grotesqueries in devilish caricature are played off against a very adamant, slightly pressed main tempo, contrasted (only slightly at first, but later markedly) with the trio's *altväterisch* dance music. Again individual moments seem more engaging in isolation than as part of a well-integrated whole (e.g., the return of the scherzo at 12' and the climactic outburst at 12:44).

Segerstam's reading of the *Andante Moderato* allows the music to proceed naturally, capturing both its tender sentiments and passionate ethos. His composer's eye focusses attention on compositonal nuances, such as the long glissando at 11:25 followed by a hesitency in the solo oboe which adds a touchingly human quality before more fervent music suddenly sweeps aside all serenity. Violins give all they have on the soaring theme of the finale's opening measures. From there the remainder of the lengthy introduction contains some well-conceived effects, particularly in low brass. Most of the main thematic material is well-rendered. Segerstam holds back into each of the hammer blows (employing all three) and gives strong characterization to the chaotic fury that is unleashed by the first two. Yet the Fate motto is understated throughout. The finale is effective in some dramatic moments, but it is hampered by confined string sound and a perspective that seems more concerned with the particular than the general.

SINOPOLI, GIUSEPPE/Philharmonia Orchestra - 2-DG 423 082-2 (1987) [93:11]+

Sinopoli's stylistic proclivities are no more apparent than in this performance. His attention to detail is undeniably admirable as is his knack for bringing out Mahler's special effects that underlines their demonic quality without over-emphasis. He is also noted for infusing his interpretations with philosophical inflection. But as a whole, his Sixth somehow misses the mark. In this tragic symphony, Mahler presents us with yet another symphonic drama in which his hero struggles with life's negative forces--but, in this instance, he does not conquer them but ultimately succumbs. If the urgency of this drama is impressed upon the listener early on, attention will be less likely to dissipate as the lengthy work proceeds. A demonstrative, viceral march beat that has enough dramatic weight and muscularity yet also urgency and intensity can help to accomplish this end. Strong accentuation helps to mitigate against sluggishness and, if sustained over the long haul, should heighten the dramatic impact. Alternative versions of this tempo are extreme, from the rapid pace set by Kubelik, Bernstein and Karajan, to the weighty tread of Horenstein and Rosbaud. Sinopoli's approach fits comfortably between these two poles; he chooses a moderate tempo that still emphasizes visceral strength over energetic impulse.

The problem with his general approach becomes evident as soon as the main theme appears. From here and throughout much of what follows, the drama dissipates and dynamic levels become restrained. What is missing from Sinpoli's vision is the profundity of this heroic life-struggle that comes to a tragic end. Rather than portraying the hero in his prime of life, powerful and secure in his strength, he appears rather debilitated even before the battle has begun. The strokes of Fate, hammered out by the timpani periodically as a reminder of human fallibility, are distant and underplayed. Alma's impassioned theme is well played but sounds remote and dispassionate. In a work that could be described as a tragic *Ein Heldenleben*, Sinopoli's hero seems a mere shadow of a legendary champion, who is willing to face life's vicissitudes bravely and eagerly. What actually comes across is less than heroic, a life lived cautiously and with little bravura.

Musical material representing the hero's antagonist sometimes has the requisite demonic character (e.g., at the opening of the development section in strong brass sforzati) but brass playing is so often flatulent and matter-of-fact as to whitewash the hero's dark side. Moreover, much of this music lacks sufficient energy and articulation to make it truly wicked. Too often Sinopoli tries for an effect (many times without, or contrary to, Mahler's directions) and fails. At #21, what is marked *allmahlich etwas gehaltener* (gradually somewhat held back) is played as if it were marked *subito langsamer* (suddenly slower). From here the music lopes along without much involvement. The *grazioso* section at #22 is very restful but never graceful. By #25 where Tempo I returns, Sinopoli begins to liven up the proceedings. But by now is anyone still listening? A very slow start for the coda contrasts well with the later *piu mosso subito* section at #37, but an unmarked *rallentando* into #41 is nothing less than a tawdry affectation. Weak timpani keep the fateful undertone of this movement in check. Also notice how the main tempo has become rippingly fast by #45.

In the devilish second movement, intended as a grotesque mockery of the heroism of the first movement, *a la* Liszt's *A Faust Symphony*, Sinopoli also seems to downplay the demonic elements. While some grotesqueries come through (e.g., near the opening and at #84 in the brass plunges to ghostly depths), such moments are conspicuous for their rarity. One example of this problem is particularly disturbing. During the minuet-like prancing, which serves as a mocking commentary upon the already caricaturesque march of the opening, brief flurries interrupt. These short bits of figuration should sound like inane mimicry of Faust's heroic pose. None of this is evident in Sinopoli's casual approach to these contrasting measures. Has Mephisto grown tired and ineffectual, or does he (or Sinopoli) no longer find the joke stimulating? Sinopoli also tends to slow up at phrase-endings. This mannerism can work well when it is applied with finesse and need not impede the musical flow. Here it sounds awkward. The problem is not so much one of tempo consistency as it is lack of vitality. At #95, where a feeling of exhaustion from all of life's absurd trials and tribulations seems apparent, Sinopoli sets so slow a pace as to almost stand still!

In the third movement Sinopoli makes what might be an attempt at providing an explanation for the lack of intensity and dramatic impact of what preceded it. He conjures up an idyllic, blissful world free of the hero's painful self-doubts or the taunting mockery of his antagonist. All is lyrical, lingering, and longing for eternity; a dream-like atmosphere, unaffected by any foreboding of the tragedy to come. Nowhere does Sinopoli's reading capture the profound sense of human pathos which makes this movement so poignant. Again some affectations appear (into #50), but they serve more as unnecessary hindrances than embellishments of mood. After the strains of disquietude wane, a state of unabated joy prevails. Even expressions of peaceful serenity seem too sterile, however. If the hero has come through a brief crisis, he should bear the marks of a struggle, but no such signs are apparent. Sinopoli even downplays the sudden dark cloud appearing as a minor key intrusion at measure 190. All is merely untroubled peace--or is it?

And so we come to the crux of the matter--the massive finale with its terrifying hammer blows of fate that finally fell the hero. Has Sinopoli been leading us on by his rather objective, temperate approach? Are we at last to squarely face the awesomeness of Mahler's conception without blinders? I'm afraid not. Sinopoli evokes no greater intensity or dramatic power throughout most of this movement than he had earlier. Where is the unsettling undercurrent of the introduction, with its references to the demonic second movement? Where the mystery? Where the drama? Again the pronouncement of Fate in the timpani is restrained (almost inaudible at #107). The music seems encumbered and unemotive, while playing is cautious and sometimes stifled. Affectations are simply overbearing (e.g., slowing up into #117). Momentary sunshine from the third theme at #117 is ineffectually dim. Dynamic levels rarely if ever reach beyond *forte*. Idyllic moments, so well-portrayed in the third movement, seem merely quiet here. The music appearing before the first hammer blow is not filled with an ebullient spirit but seems dispassionate and uncommitted. Is this the hero whose demise Mahler saw as so tragic? Straight through into the recapitulation we are confronted with nothing evocative, nothing to stir the blood. When the impact of the second hammer blow fades, the lyrical section that follows is left unaffected by it. At #150 Sinopoli suddenly races through the music so that it literally falls over itself in an effort to get nowhere, for the subsequent return of the main tempo seems to hold back the proceedings rather than impell them forward. Moreover, weakness in violins after #164 (marked *fff*) exemplifies the main problem with this approach. One wonders what Sinopoli intends by all of this. Is it all much ado about nothing? Since Sinopoli sometimes takes a philosophical approach, could we conclude that he is engaged in interpretive deconstruction? Unfortunately, Sinopoli does not enlighten us with commentary.

SOLTI, GEORG/Chicago Symphony - 2-London 2227 (1971); 425 040 (1992); 10-London 430 804 (1992) [76:44]* As to be expected from Solti, a hard-driven impulse pervades this performance, highlighted by rich and full-bodied sonics as well as superb orchestral playing. Solti's treatment of the opening march is nervous and intense. Sometimes the music has the riveting effect of a jack hammer. Conversely, a tendency to gloss over more somber moments and emphasize the gigantic climaxes becomes apparent. Although Solti generates much excitement, a weightier pace might have been more dramatic. After a slowish start, the Scherzo also becomes racy as if driven in blistering heat. In contrast, the trio section is on the slow side and lacks a natural ease of pacing which would have been more conducive to achieving the intended *grazioso* effect. Frequently rushed tempi (e.g., to #87) and awkward adjustments (e.g., at #90) sometimes throw the musical progress out of kilter. Some lovely moments occur in the slow movement but one senses a lack of personal involvement until the passionate climax. Although much of the finale also seems pressed, Solti's expansive treatment of the introductory section is one of the most satisfying ever recorded. Brass sound brilliant and robust throughout. Solti rushes headlong into each hammer blow and generates electrifying intensity in the furious string passages that follow. While some inner details are ignored, the big moments are stupendous. In fact, it almost seems as if the deadly third hammer blow sounds at that point in the score where Mahler originally inserted it. No mention is made of this in the liner notes.

SVETLANOV, YEVGENY/USSR Academic Symphony - 2-MCA Arts & Electronics AED2-10207 (1991) [79:33] Svetlanov reads the Sixth strictly within the confines of nineteenth-century romanticism. Consequently, the Scherzo must be briskly paced and the finale's main tempo a standard *allegro*, while grotesqueries are tempered and sudden shifts smoothed over. Such an approach simply does not bring to the fore either the nature of Mahler's aesthetic or the many musical nuances he employed to enhance its variety of moods. Svetlanov begins in fine fettle. The opening march tempo has a strong if moderate tread. Only flatulent, piercing brass, booming timpani and some periodic clumsiness mar an otherwise no-frills reading. While there is much dynamic thrust in the main material (at 9:40+ in the development and at 15:43 opening the reprise), tendency to clip dotted rhythms in brass can be disconcerting. Generally, Svetlanov follows Mahler's directions, making some of his own adjustments in a few places (slowing up into the *alla breve* at 21:20 instead of pressing forward as marked). But the Scherzo virtually slaps one in the face from its inception. Ignoring the marking *wuchtig*, Svetlanov gallops through the principal subject faster than most of his colleagues. One positive result is that his rapid tempo is in strong contrast to the *grazioso* trios which caricature classical dance rhythms. While grotesqueries are moderately rendered, the ghostly music at 4:40+ elicits an appropriately eerie atmosphere. A generally straight reading of the *Andante Moderato* movement follows, seasoned with a few slight hesitations, but lacking in tender sentiment. Only during the passionate section that contains the movement's principal argument (from 11:05) does the music come alive with a curiously joyous aspect. Least satisfactory is the finale. After a rather ineffectual, disjointed reading of the long introduction, a raucous, rollicking treatment of the principal theme characterizes much of this movement. Pacing is hectic and nervous, punctuated by piercing trumpets which often clip dotted rhythms. Jumbled tutti passages and other orchestral imperfections may be attributed to the speedy main tempo. If the intent is to use such a fast pace to make this sprawling movement more cohesive, in the style of a traditional romantic symphony, it simply does not work.

SZELL, GEORGE/Cleveland Orchestra - 2-Columbia M2-31313 (1972); Sony Classics SBK 47654 (1992) [73:52]*+ Szell strikes an appropriate balance between the very intense approach of Bernstein and Kubelik and the milder and more lyrical style of Horenstein and Haitink. A strong and vital march theme in moderate tempo opens the first movement. Szell dives into the "Alma" theme with a will, driving it home with much verve and great exuberance. The exposition is not repeated and the remainder of the movement is rendered conservatively but in fine style. However, weak brass and percussion tone down the dramatic effect. One could not ask for a better choice of tempo for the Scherzo, giving it sufficient weight. But the trio is paced too quickly and lacks stylish treatment. Little warmth or sensitivity comes through in the slow movement, set at a moderate pace. Szell saves most of his dynamic thrust for the finale. Again basically conservative in approach, Szell's reading infuses the music with nervous energy that borders on maniacal at times. After racing toward the first hammer, it happens rather unnoticeably, and from there to the reprise the music seems to lose its spark. Szell recovers nicely as the opening *allegro* returns by driving the music forward with much spirit. Essentially, this is a straightforward reading by a conductor from whom we have all too few recorded Mahler performances.

TENNSTEDT, KLAUS/London Philharmonic - 2-Angel DS-3945; EAC 90180/81; CDC-47049 (1983); 10-EMI CMS7 64471-81 (1993) [87:07]*+   Unlike several of Tennstedt's effusive and self-indulgent readings, this performance shows that flexible tempi and mannered phrasing can be effective when applied idiomatically. A tendency to press forward into climaxes or drag through lyrical sections to elicit more emotion still characterizes this reading. But more often than not these aspects enhance the performance. The opening march is forceful and dynamic and the exposition material both energetic and exuberant. Although Tennstedt interposes some untoward affects (at #20 and 21) that disturb the musical flow, a few interesting interpretive nuances also appear (e.g., at m.205 a mysterious aura is created by an unusually slow tempo). A sense of urgency impresses itself upon the music through use of an agitated main tempo. Details are carefully rendered and playing is clear and precise. These characteristics also enhance the Scherzo movement. Tennstedt's reading of the trio is superb, bringing out Mahler's clever parody on the classical Viennese style through sharply accented sforzandi. Only some clipped playing is disturbing here. Few conductors (with the exception of Karajan) elicit as much expressivity in the slow movement as Tennstedt. While his manner is slightly affected it is far from overly sentimental. In fact, he creates a wistful mood tinged with just a hint of melancholy by letting the music breathe and treating each phrase with a tender gesture. At the climax, all the tragic passion of this exquisite movement comes through with bitter poignancy. The introduction to the finale is somewhat uneven (why speed up toward the cadence on the violin theme at the opening?). Tennstedt tends to rush through faster sections even if little intensity is achieved as a result. Much dynamic power is generated but not sufficient vitality. Strings sound generally weak while brass sometimes stand out too forcefully. The first hammer blow has a "slap-like" quality and what follows lacks sufficient impulse. As the music accelerates to a gallop, Tennstedt pulls in the reins too suddenly at m.394. After a shattering second hammer stroke, Tennstedt obeys the *pesante* marking too demonstratively and the stormy mood is too abruptly depleted. From here to the close, the music moves along with little energy as if a denouement had been reached. All considered, the many positive aspects of this performance outweigh its shortcomings and make it one of the best in Tennstedt's Mahler cycle.

WAKASUGI, HIROSHI/Tokyo Metropolitan Symphony - 2-Fontec FOCD 9022/23 (1989) [79:20]   When Wakasugi reads the score in his usually objective manner, sticking to the letter of its many markings, he shows himself to be an intelligent Mahler interpreter, if not a very engaging one. In this performance, however, he imposes too many mannerisms upon the score, causing thematic material to sag and the overall structure of movements to become sectionally segmented. While his main tempi are generally well-conceived, they often lose continuity, moving forward or holding back without justification in the score or the musical phraseology; it is most disconcerting when slight ritards are added before double bars. Another detraction is Fontec's weak, confined sonics, seriously diminish the effect of this powerful and moving score. The first movement has spirit and energy, even if it lacks full sonorities. Cowbells are virtually inaudible, as they are throughout the work. Wakasugi fails to render the trio of the Scherzo movement with any stylishness, playing it perfunctorily. Manufactured nuances appear in the *Andante Moderato* movement (e.g., a forced slow-up into the return of the main theme at 10:30), but pale timbres, uneven pacing and a reserved manner fail to impress. Many of the characteristics noted above pervade the finale. Too many hesitations, overly sluggish tempi, confined dynamic range, restrained temperament and frequent omission of Mahler's tempo adjustments (particularly where more motion is required) stultify the effect of this ode to human tragedy. Wakasugi does employ the third hammer stroke. Would that its inclusion were sufficient reason to recommend the performance.

WIT, ANTONI /Polish National Radio Symphony (Katowice) (perf. 15-19 Dec. 1992, Concert Hall of Polish Radio in Katowice) - 2-Naxos 8.550529/30 (1993) [84:04]*
Naxos engineers have juiced up the volume for this conservative, uninvolved, performance, in an attempt to make the ensemble sound full and strong. Their effort has both positive and negative consequences: enhanced inner voice audibility, on the positive side; undue stress on brass over woodwinds and strings, and a one-dimensional ambiance that lacks dimension and spatial breadth, on the negative side. An obvious example of the latter is the overbearing cowbells, too forward to give the intended pastoral impression. In a traditional reading, Wit handles the music respectfully, following the score carefully, and does not attempt to either interject unmarked affectations or overwhelm with enormous floods of sound or excessive speed. Some important elements tend to be underplayed, particularly the major-to-minor chords that overlay the outer movements with a tragic aspect and the Fate motto in the finale. The segments of repose in the first movement gently float on air (from 13'). Wit generates some spirit from his players in this movement; and they make a fine impression. He coordinates the Scherzo's main tempo with the first movement march; but the *altväterisch* music sounds drab, lacking graceful nuance and colorful characterization. Grotesqueries are mildly treated. Wit tries to pace the slow movement in long, spacious lines. He manages to keep things moving despite the difficulties in maintaining sonic fullness at such a broad tempo. Otherwise, his reading is traditional, yet not lackluster. Despite a rather meager opening string theme, the finale has much to recommend it. One senses that Wit has thought this music through and wants to make it unfold naturally and gradually, allowing climaxes to unfold without undue hast or impetuosity. Sometimes his intentions go awry (the second appearance of the fate motto should move forward more intently). Brass play their whoops and growls with panache, adding an eerie aspect to the tragic setting. Wit's moderate approach is successful on the whole: despite some balance problems, his reading hangs together, due to his consistency of approach and his ability to produce strong effects with relatively meager forces.

ZANDER, BENJAMIN /Boston Philharmonic (perf. 3/94) - 2-IMP Masters DMCD 93 (1995) [84:13]* Those who have attended any of Zander's performances of Mahler music know him to be a worthy advocate. His approach is usually straightforward and rarely does he either mishandle or toy with the score. In this Sixth, with a few exceptions this approach is maintained. But the severely diminished sonic levels so stifle the impact of this performance, and fail to compensate for orchestral weaknesses (particularly string sonority), that one wonders whether the live performance itself would have made more of an impression. What remains in memory here are the hammer blows: undoubtedly the most successful attempts at producing them ever recorded (n.b., Zander uses all three from the original version). However, it is extremely disappointing that the finale is so hampered by weak sonics and pale orchestral coloration that it fails to succeed. Zander's reading is undeniably intelligent and he elicits as much as could be expected from his orchestra; but some tempo choices and modifications are questionable: in the Scherzo, the fast main tempo lacks any *wuchtig* quality and does not coordinate well with the first movement, and tempo contrasts are played down so that the opening off-beat "march" in triple time is not distinguished enough from the *altväterisch* dance music. In the first movement, Zander smoothes over the "Alma" theme, tempering its dynamic thrust. He also glosses over the "N.B." pauses at 20:09, completely ignoring Mahler's instructions to hold up for a breath. Cowbells are hardly audible at all in the finale. After they appear following the second hammer stroke, Zander drags the tempo along mercilously, going both against the grain of the music's temperament here and the letter of Mahler's directions. What disappoints mostly is the restricted sound level that seriously mitigates against the success of this performance.

FOUR-HAND PIANO VERSION by Alexander von Zemlinksy:

SILVIA ZENKER and EVELINDE TRENKNER, duo pianists - Dabringhaus und Grimm MD + G L 3400 (1991) [74:25] This transcription for piano four-hands appeared in the same year as the symphony's premiere, 1906. Both Zemlinsky and Mahler performed it at Mahler's home with Arnold Schoenberg in attendance. Naturally, any reduction of this purely orchestral work severly restricts its impact. As a means for studying the symphony and clarifiying its many inner devices and designs, this transcription has merit. A pianistic rendition works best in the inner movements, capturing the romantic lyricism of the *Andante Moderato* and some of the special mimetic effects of the Scherzo without possibly matching an orchestral treatment of the grotesque and contrasting elements. Paced briskly, the first movement speeds along with more energy than character. The "Alma" theme appears more lyrical than passionate. The sweeping drama of the finale is reduced to a semblance of itself. Any insights into inner workings are outweighed but several inaccuracies in dynamic markings. The Fate motto is underplayed throughout, as is the soaring "string" theme of the introduction. While much excitement is generated, a quirkiness sometimes intrudes, out of sorts with the symphony's tragic sensibility. Overall, this recording is more of interest to a Mahler scholar than a casual listener.

SYMPHONY NO. 7 IN E MINOR ("SONG OF THE NIGHT")

Movements:

1. Langsam - Allegro con fuoco.
2. Nachtmusik I: Allegro moderato.
3. Scherzo: Schattenhaft. Fliessend, aber nicht schnell.
4. Nachtmusik II: Andante amoroso.
5. Rondo Finale. Allegro ordinario.

ABBADO, CLAUDIO/Chicago Symphony - 2-DG 413773-2 GH2 (1985); 10-DG 447 023 (1995) [78:27]*+   Abbado turns in one of the best performances in his entire cycle. Playing is strong and sharp, details carefully rendered and tempo settings and modulations well-conceived. The first movement makes a strong impression generally, although it sometimes lacks vigor and spontaneity and sounds too consciously artful (an awkward affectation at m.245 is evidence of the latter). *Nachtmusik* I seems slightly restrained and mellow, but Abbado's attentiveness to details brings out subtle nuances. Notice the marvelous echo effect made by placing the horns antiphonally in the opening measures. Muffled cowbells produce a choked rather than distant sound. The Scherzo movement is set at a brisk pace, breezing through the interweaving triplets too quickly to elicit a mysterious atmosphere. Otherwise, Abbado balances inner voices deftly. Also in quick tempo, *Nachtmusik* II is treated more like a bright, lively ditty than a moonlit serenade. Some more relaxed moments, such as at # 202-207, only highlight Abbado's animated reading. If much of the music up to this point seems to lack involvement, despite the spirited tempo, Abbado releases a torrent of energy and intensity in the boisterous finale. His conception of tempi (a very essential element in the overall design) is excellent, particularly in his treatment of the *grazioso* segments. He seems to lose control as the tempo presses forward too quickly, spoiling the parodistic *altväterisch* (old-fashioned) sections intended as a spoof on the classical style. Toward the close, Abbado maintains just the right attitude in his tongue-in-cheek treatment of repeated false cadences. One would wish for less noisy bells at #293 and a true *a tempo* at #296 (played for some reason very slowly). Mahler's unorthodox reversal of a typical final chord (a diminuendo instead of a crescendo leading to a final loud stroke) is timed perfectly. Sonics are clear but strings need more brilliance and bass could be better focussed.

ABRAVANEL, MAURICE/Utah Symphony - 2-Vanguard VSD 71141/2 (1966); 11-Vanguard 08.4013.79 (1995) [77:48]   This performance begins quite well but with each movement it gradually deteriorates until it reaches its nadir in the finale. The first movement is well-conceived, strong and demonstrative. Abravanel generates life here: playing is precise and involved, although the trumpet section is too restrained. Details are treated with care, though commas could be less awkwardly handled. While some energy and spirit spill over, in the second movement, Abravanel emphasizes the music's lyricism over its jocular aspect, imbuing the *grazioso* sections with more charm than parodistic character. Playing is not always secure, but is usually expressive, clear and well-balanced (notice the sauntering treatment of dotted rhythms). Cowbells sounds like clinking glasses. Abravanel rarely imposes himself upon the music, letting it flow freely and without unwanted affectation. But the Scherzo movement is too bland, overcautious and reserved; it fails to evoke a shadowy atmosphere and downplaying its grotesqueries are downplayed and weakly accentuation. In contrast, the trio is too agitated and misses the Viennese parody. Despite some lovely playing, the fourth movement is rather cool and detached for a moonlight serenade. A few interesting nuances appear: the gaily tripping rhythms of the opening and trills on all crotchets and minims in the guitar and mandolin. Carrying forward a lack of impetus and involvement from the preceding movement, the finale succumbs to stiffness and soon becomes deadly dull. Most of the satirical humor is glossed over. One senses that the performers are in a hurry to rid themselves of this music. This much-maligned and misunderstood symphony does not find a sympathetic advocate here, except in the first two movements.

BERNSTEIN, LEONARD/New York Philharmonic - 2-Columbia M2S 739 (1966); 3-CBS M3K 42200 (1986); 3-Sony SM3K 47585 (1992) [79:47]** No Mahler conductor on records has captured the spirit of this symphony to such captivating effect while eliciting from his orchestra such brilliant, precise and powerful playing as Bernstein. Each nuance is rendered in a completely characteristic manner; each transition is handled with perfect aplomb. Special plaudits must be given to the brass section which plays superbly throughout. Few conductors shape the lengthy and complex introduction as perfectly as Bernstein. When the allegro exposition is reached, he impels the music forward with vitality and imbues it with great strength. Bernstein holds up slightly before the effusive second theme and then swings into it with marvelously grand gesture. Details are clear, attacks sharp and tempi always ideal, with a natural swing that never hurries forward or lags behind. The return of the opening *allegro* is nothing short of overwhelming! It is difficult to imagine a better performance.

Clarity of inner voices, brilliant playing and excellent stylistic nuances also enhance the second movement. Bernstein makes the most of its devilishly parody. March rhythms are jaunty and strident, while lyrical passages are shaped with a loving touch (#89). Viennese waltz rhythms (before #79) are handled in perfectly idiomatic style. Bernstein may be the only conductor to master the subtleties of the Scherzo. His ability to create a spooky atmosphere from the sinewy interweaving triplet patterns in the strings during the opening section, decorated with offbeat sforzandi, is virtually unequalled. While the trio tempo is well-conceived, at the section marked *piu mosso*, Bernstein presses forward more than necessary. A delightfully jocular spirit reminds one of circus music in the waltz segment for tuba and trombone. Celli produce a shattering effect with their *fffff* pizzicato.

The lovely fourth movement is a shade on the slow side but evokes the atmosphere of a warm summer evening in the country. Bernstein's sensitivity and expressiveness result in an enchanting performance. As the movement proceeds to its conclusion, one feels it gradually tiring out with a final yawn as this "Night Music" ends the long day. Then the morning comes bursting forth with a rollicking timpani solo as the finale begins. Spectacular playing, perfect balances and marvelous sonics define this musical tour-de-force. Only Bernstein seems to understand the delightful Haydnesque joke that Mahler intended by the frequent shifts between contrasting sections. Each time we think we have arrived at a full cadence of the march theme, Mahler brings us back to the minuet with a devilish grin. Bernstein moves the final diminuendo/stroke rather quickly so that the close comes very abruptly. This magnificent performance is among the best of any Mahler symphony ever recorded!

BERNSTEIN, LEONARD/Vienna Philharmonic (perf. October, 1974, Vienna Musikverein Grosser Saal) - DG video 072 227-3 (1991) [84]**   Bernstein is the consummate master of this controversial symphony. In his first recording (see above), he captured its multifarious dimensions with an approach perfectly adapted to the music's unique style and structure. Few adjustments are made from that ground-breaking effort. But a live performance usually generates more intensity, as this one inevitably does. In the first movement, what impresses is Bernstein's perfectly natural pacing, especially when turning the many corners in the score that require gear-shifts. The first theme is slightly more agitated, the second more spirited, with much emphasis on the echo effects in solo horn. Again the romantic third theme, with its built-in rubato, is simply gorgeous. From beginning to end, Bernstein's reading thoroughly engages the listener. The opening of second movement is enhanced by the use of European horns. More temperate than his earlier reading, Bernstein still evokes a nocturnal atmosphere with subtlety and nuance. No other conductor creates such a ghostly aura in the Scherzo. In a whirlpool of swirling triplets, the strings wind their way around the main theme with bewitching gracefulness. Watching Bernstein's gyrations is like view a balletic treatment of this caricaturesque music. This time only the first *fffff* pizzicato in bass strings is played off the fingerboard. Notice how the woodwind eighths toward the close are treated in the same mode as the brief, interruptive figurational passages in the trio. No interpretive revisions are made in the slow movement either. One can literally breathe the enchanting scent of night air toward the close. Once again Bernstein's finale is both a *brilliante* spectacle and an education for those conductors puzzled by its juxtaposition of the demonstrative and the genteel. Bernstein seems best able to present these contrasting qualities perfectly. What makes his reading so interesting is its implicit recognition of the fascinating self-parody with which Mahler may have consciously or unconsciously infused the work. Possibly, it is also a self-parody of Bernstein. He even dances with the orchestra in the minuet-like grazioso segments. Having a visual as well as aural document of Bernstein's way with this symphony makes this video version all the more valuable.

BERNSTEIN, LEONARD/New York Philharmonic - 2-DG 419 211 (1986); 13-DG 435 162 (1992) [82:17]*+   To repeat the monumental success Bernstein had with his brilliant first recording of the Seventh with the NYP (see above) after so many years would be a remarkable achievement. Bernstein accomplishes it almost without exception. Rather than rethink his earlier reading, Bernstein tries to capture inner details with even more clarity than before. His approach is still dynamic and forceful, but the thrust and impulse that was generated by the excitement of tackling a relatively unknown and extremely difficult work has been tempered by familiarity, despite occasional experiments in nuanced phrasing. Toning down the volume of the opening to its *pp* marking, Bernstein sets the tone for what is to be a more balanced approach to dynamic levels than in his often brash, supersonic first recording. He also makes more of the second theme by slowing up measurably on its upbeat dotted rhythms. A tendency to press through segments paced more evenly before may be a result of the tension of a live performance. And the strings simply do not have their earlier brilliant sheen; brass, as strong as they still are, seem both less articulate and deeply committed.

Bernstein also tones down his treatment of the second movement, now in a slower, more deliberate tempo. Orchestral playing sometimes suffers from untidy entrances. A sense of spirited involvement which made this movement so captivating in the earlier version seems to have faded here. But Bernstein is still the master of the Scherzo movement. Like none other he reinforces the movement's spooky atmosphere by highlighting the swirling string triplets--

giving them an impish, darting quality--and emphasizing the sforzandi in winds that often pierce the musical fabric. Still, in the earlier recording the orchestra played with more urgency and character in this movement. Much the same can be said of the *Andante Amoroso* movement. Still ebulliently raucous and delicately prancing by turns, the finale is Bernstein's private showcase. No one understands and communicates this difficult movement, with its outrageous and virtually unremitting contrasts, as well as he does. Mahler's parody of his own use of march and dance music is delightfully wrought, yet without being played as strongly and securely as before. There was also a more fluid handling of the numerous tempo shifts and the *grazioso* second theme group is somewhat less mannered here. Even if both spontaneity and orchestral precision seem to have diminished, the performance still rises head and shoulders above most of its best rivals.

BERTINI, GARY/Cologne Radio Symphony - EMI CDC 7 54184 WDR (1991) [79:23]
*   While there is much to admire in the workmanlike precision with which Bertini renders the myriad complexities of this work, his detached manner sometimes chills the atmosphere. This is particularly evident in the *Andante Amoroso*, which should glow with the warmth of an enchanted summer evening. But Bertini's objectivity does not mitigate against his conveying the more eerie touches of "night music" which pervade much of the rest of the symphony. In the opening movement, a curiously foggy quality invests the tenor horn with a mysterious hue, like a beacon of light through thick mist. By contrast, the main material has much dynamic thrust, sometimes overly underscored, particularly in a demonstrative treatment of the dashing second theme. Yet frequently one senses a somewhat rigid hand at the helm which constricts what should seem unconfinedly ebullient (especially in brasses' square treatment of dotted rhythms). While generally well-conceived, the performance never gets below the surface of the music. After a fine introductory "call" and "answer," the second movement soon begins to flatten out, resulting in more mildness than urgency. The principal themes, while generally well presented, seems unconvincing, lacking stylishness in favor of over-emphasized clarity of line. Cowbells (5:55) are played in rapid trills but positioned so as to sound from afar. Bertini has a tendency to race to the top of a phrase and ease up at its cadence (12:45+), particularly in the common-time waltz sequences. But his reading of the Scherzo is simply superb! Only in Bernstein's recordings is this phantasmagorial music given as effective a turn. String triplets weave in and out of the musical fabric with a whispy quality that enhances the mystery of its nocturnal enchantment. Even bass string swells are audible and in perfect balance with the rest of the ensemble (2:02). Grotesqueries are excellently rendered and the entire movement is characterful and creatively endowed with effective nuances. Listen to the closing section, presented as a denouement in which the lower strings and winds struggle with each other for thematic fragments.

After a rather stark, cool and inflexive slow movement, lacking warmth and richness in the strings, the finale erupts with booming exuberance. Bertini does well with the contrasts between brash and delicate music: the march theme has panache while the *grazioso* material has a delightfully Haydnesque gentility. However one chooses to view this movement--as an exaggerated play on a romantic finale or a Mahlerian self-parody--Bertini's reading is generally well-conceived and full of spirit, even though his forces seem to de-energize before the final coda. Bertini stirs them up enough to give momentum to the final bars, the last measure (with its reversal of the usual procedure for a closing chord: diminishing from a *forte* to the final stroke rather than crescendoing into it) being perfectly timed.

CHAILLY, RICCARDO/Royal Concertgebouw Orchestra - 2-London 444 446 (1995) [83:54]*   Mahler's most "unbuttoned" humor, with its combination of societal caricature and self-parody, permeates this strange, often misunderstood symphony. Riccardo Chailly clearly understands the nature of its unrestrained mockery, emphasizing Mahler's many grotesqueries appear sometimes in sneering brass or contemptuous woodwind bleeps. Excellent sonic quality and balancing allow these numerous inner-voice fragments to come to the surface, adding greater dimension to Mahler's parodistic wit. Periodically, Chailly makes a conscious effort to keep the orchestra under control. The opening movement, while generally well-proportioned, sometimes seems slightly tempered, needing more *schwung* to drive home its point. Chailly's reading is thought-provoking, creating a special character for each theme group. The main allegro theme might seem slightly restrained, but the second theme (4:20) is enhanced by adding a nasty quality to the horn fragment of descending half-step notes which answers the jaunty string theme, while the romantic third theme is treated broadly and lithely, sounding more tender-hearted than passionate (N.B., how warm and sunny--even Mediterranean--this theme sounds in its final appearance). A tendency toward long ritards also keeps the forward motion in tow. Possibly Chailly sees the entire movement as Mahler's mockery of his many funereal first movements, causing Chailly to impress upon the movement a quasi-mournful quality. An unmarked full stop employed before the return of the opening section (at 15:33) seems out of place. The horn call-and-answer that opens the second movement is treated in march-like style in its many re-appearances throughout the movement. Chailly keeps the main theme at *pp* as written and tones down his treatment of grotesqueries for this *Nachtmusik*. Again inner voices come through provocatively. Only an unmarked long pause after the upbeat to the waltz-in-four at 3:50 (and later) is both awkward and inappropriate. Chailly seems to downplay the interweaving string triplets, favoring the more melodistic elements, which he imbues with sweet romanticism (3:45). He does have more fun with this movement than most conductors, letting its Mephistophelian spirit suffuse the music without restraint (listen to the wicked treatment of the woodwind skipping figures during the coda). A sloppy glissando on the opening note of the violin solo's cadential phrase that begins the *Andante Amoroso* movement bodes ill. In a later appearance of this cadence (8:50) for all the violins, Chailly forces the celli entrance in the next measure to sound like an echo of the opening octave leap of the cadence instead of the written grace-note octave leap. The main theme is briskly paced and perky woodwind rhythms are emphasized over the lyricism of the string line. One wonders if such a characterization is appropriately *amoroso*, or is this yet more Mahlerian mockery. Chailly finally comes in out of the sunlight in the closing coda, giving the main theme the character of a midnight serenade. The finale is a delightful romp, Chailly turning around the many corners of this complex movement more deftly than most of his colleagues. The key here is to have fun with Mahler's outrageous contrast of a boisterously vulgar march with a delicate, whimsical Viennese minuet, and Chailly does just that. Tempi set for both theme groups are well-conceived and frequent sudden shifts from one to the other brilliantly handled. One shudders at the timpanum's low D-flat *fff* roll at #286 (15:35)--the instrument created for Mengelberg just for this purpose. The closing measures provide a perfect ending to a marvelous performance.

DEWAART, EDO/Netherlands Radio Philharmonic - RCA 74321 276082 (1995) [79:13]

Given the rapidity with which the DeWaart/NRP complete cycle was produced, it is not surprising that this complex work was not given the attention it deserves. One senses that the performance was put together haphazardly, and the reading conceived either from pure intuition or without any overview of the work in mind. Edo DeWaart, throughout his cycle, has shown a preference for a traditional approach, uncluttered with affectation. But such an approach can devolve into routine if it also lacks personality and character, and the Seventh depends on the latter qualities for its success. They must, however, be drawn from the music authentically and naturally, and not forced from it artificially. In this performance, routine and the excess go hand in hand. A rocky, disjointed introduction features grossly loud woodwinds and a very close tenor horn that sounds more rude than morose. The main theme is played routinely, while the swashbuckling second theme is given an affectatious reading, weighing so heavily on the opening dotted rhythmic figures as to nearly cause it to collapse before it gets to the second beat. RCA has provided high-power sonics with a one-dimensional dynamic range (which is mostly on the high side) that distorts balances and buries or over-emphasizes inner voices. Long ritards, oozing lyricism and affectatious hesitations combine peculiarly with pale sonorities and heavy-laden brass. Sections are strung together in a motley array. For example, in the reprise, the second theme is played evenly, rather than dragged out as in its initial appearance.

DeWaart seems completely uninvolved in the second movement. It proceeds perfunctorily (after a strangely mournful first theme) with only an inauthentic attempt to stylize the waltz-in-four segment and an interesting effect on leaps in dotted rhythms that appear toward the close. Tempi are sometimes shaky and inconsistent (e.g., after 8'). The Scherzo lacks the very quality it requires: subtlety. After a dull, inarticulate opening that smoothes over sforzandi needed to created a shadowy, darting effect, and over-emphasizes glissandi, the trio section devolves into mere note-spinning. Too much tinkering here works against the flow of the music. Then the slow movement trips merrily along in bright sunlight, as if it had no idea that it was supposed to be a moonlight serenade. DeWaart's light, spirited approach seems to contradict his sugary treatment of the opening cadential phrase in violin solo. Tempo shifts push and pull the music too strongly. Dynamic levels could have been softened for what should have been a lilting, graceful *Nachtmusik*. The finale starts off well. Strong brass weigh in on the march theme, a sense of spirited resolve promising some relief from the confusion of the previous movements. But again dynamic levels remain at full blast (even the *ruthe* sounds unduly strong). The *grazioso* section (Tempo II) is hurried at first, requiring a tempo adjustment to fit its character (from c.6:45' to m.252). Thereafter, the march theme gives the impression of being merely dashed off and the *grazioso* counter-subject is extremely rushed, thereby losing its classical guise. Toward the close, DeWaart makes the frequent sudden shifts between these two theme groups work in tandem (even though he ignores the *pesante* marking at m.293). Unfortunately, the many problems with this performance are not remedied by its well-rendered close.

GIELEN, MICHAEL/SWF Symphony, Baden-Baden - Intercord INT 860.924 (1993) [77:19]* Gielen proves himself a masterful Mahlerian with this splendid performance. Only the last two movements are somewhat of a let-down. After superb readings of the first three movements, played with precision, clarity, and artful nuance, Gielen seems to distance himself from the lyrical romance of the slow movement and makes little of the petulently wicked caricature of the *grazioso* music in the finale. The first movement opens with a rhythmically-square treatment of the 32nd-note shakes in strings, tempering the underlying tension they should produce. The principal themes are strong, articulate and beautifully played at a spirited pace. Gielen rivals Bernstein here, and adds stronger inner voice clarity. Much the same may be said for the second movement: excellent playing, relaxed but never sluggish tempi, sharp instrumental pinpricks, and perfectly stylish nuances. Even the cowbells are superbly handled, playing in isolated jingles at a proper distance. Gielen gives a straight, idiomatic reading of the Scherzo as well. While no *danse macabre* ala Bernstein, it has many of the elements needed to be both captivating and atmospheric: fluid pacing, well-integrated inner lines and spirited dance music. In the *Andante Amoroso* movement, heightened volume levels and a detached approach stiffen musical flow. One feels more the briskness of a winter's eve than the warmth of a summer night. In the finale, Gielen pulls out all of the stops on the march theme, making it sound more raucous than majestic. But a straight, precision-oriented reading, with over-emphasis on inner voice clarity, sometimes causes a rigidity that hampers the music's spontaneity. More troublesome is a rather characterless rendering of the *grazioso* material, lacking in delicacy what the march exudes in pomposity and boisterousness. Any conductor who cannot see and project the sheer fun of this music will have difficulty engaging his audience. All of the hyped-up volume merely causes brass to sound screechy and does not produce an atmosphere of unabashed frivolity that should pervade this movement.

HAENCHEN, HARTMUT/Netherlands Philharmonic - 2-Laserlight 14 141; 3-Capriccio 10 643 (1994) [80:52] Haenchen might have considered waiting a while longer before tackling this complex and difficult symphony so early in his projected cycle, for he simply has no conception of what to do with the work. He either overplays or underplays so much of it that it often becomes a jumble of turgid blabbering or a distended bore. From the sluggish introduction, which seems to go on forever, Haenchen fails to elicit any of the movement's epic romance. Playing is stiff, stilted and matter-of-fact, unaided by high volume levels. The entire first movement drags along mercilously, threatening to collapse of its own weight. Even when Haenchen makes necessary (if unmarked) tempo adjustments for the galloping rhythms at m.88 or much later at 21'+, he cannot enliven this deadly dull performance. Brusquely rattling off the opening horns calls, the second movement is played too disinterestedly. The Scherzo lacks articulate playing and sharpness of focus, demonstrating only a meagre effort to highlight its many grotesque elements. Listen to how stiffly the lower strings play the dotted rhythms at 4:20 on the return of the main theme. When Haenchen ventures into creative nuance (e.g., slowing up slightly at #165 on violin theme or gradually working into Tempo I thereafter), the result is simply awkward. The sultry summer night air which should permeate the atmosphere of the second *Nachtmusik* is completely lost in Haenchen's dull, inexpressive reading. One-dimensional sonics also narrow depth of field and interfere with inner-voice balancing. While every marking is audibly rendered, the musical aesthetic seems anesthetized. So to in the finale. While the bustling march gets a strong, if overblown treatment, the *grazioso* material is just routinely played, lacking personality, delicacy and style. Brass become more raucous and vulgar as the movement approaches its close. What note is the trombone playing at m.446 (13:26)? It certainly is not the written D-natural! Even a microscopic analysis of this performance would not turn up much worthy of praise.

HAITINK, BERNARD/Concertgebouw Orchestra - 2-Philips 410 398 (1984); 10-Philips 434 053 (1992); 442 050 (1994)[75:49] Despite very clear sonics and good balances, Haitink fails to elicit enough energy to provide a fully satisfying performance. More intense and angular sections are smoothed over, playing is frequently stiff and unfocussed and dynamic level restrained. Starting at a trudgingly slow pace, the introduction has more of a mournful than intrepid character. Little energy is generated until the development section, itself on the mild side. Even though the reprise contains some interesting moments (e.g., a threatening trombone before #44 leading to a ebullient outbreak of passion), the final bars seem swallowed up. Haitink offers a routine, uninteresting reading of the second movement, seeming to wander aimlessly through this music. Playing here is too square and accents are smoothed over. The Scherzo movement, treated in much the same manner, lacks vibrancy, color and sufficient swing in the waltz sections. Also lackluster is the fourth movement, played in more of a jaunty than lilting manner as a result of a quick main tempo and a cool, objective approach. Haitink seems somewhat more involved in the finale, providing more energy and excitement there than anywhere else in this performance. But he paces the *grazioso* sections briskly, glossing over their wry humor. The final diminuendo chord seems to end with a slight crescendo anticipating the unexpected fortissimo stroke and ruining Mahler's clever, witty close.

HAITINK, BERNARD/Berlin Philharmonic (perf. 1992) - 2-Philips 434 997 (1995) [80:04] Once again Haitink's dour, severe manner weighs down this performance, making all the movements but Nachtmusik II appear as if they were haunted by the funereal opening. As is his wont, Haitink smoothes over the music's rough edges and sharp articulation, emphasizing tonal beauty over characterful playing. Consequently, the opening tenor horn sounds bright rather than forebodingly dark and the march-like rhythmic figure in strings that accompanies it is inarticulate. Tempi in the first movement sometimes drag, as if weighed down by the morose character of the opening. How cautiously the gorgeous BPO strings play the beautiful serenade-like theme at 12:20, and how gloomily they characterize the return of the opening *adagio* at 14:15. Restraint is also the order of the day in *Nachtmusik I*. But for a long unmarked hesitation into the 4/4 waltz at 3:35, most of the movement is tame, modest and unadventurous. The Scherzo completely lacks character: sforzandi are toned down; the swirling triplets of the opening are played like an exercise; the waltz music lacks spirit; and the sorrowful trio theme (3:24) sounds either sullen or dispassionate. For what conceivable reason does Haitink slow up at #165 for the string theme and weigh down the music at #167 when marked *subito Tempo I*? The closing coda sounds like a lumbering elephant trying to shake off a flea. Haitink paces *Nachtmusik II* briskly. Playing sounds too casual and the demeanor sometimes too serious (at 7:20). Such a combination of sternness and sprightliness downplays the romance of this nighttime serenade. Worst of all, the finale suffers from this same weightiness and severity. A tempered opening timpani flourish sets the tone for the entire movement. Haitink's reading lacks spontaneity and verve. Mahler's little joke in contrasting a Germanic march with a Viennese minuet simply doesn't come off in such a heavy-handed, controlled reading.

HALASZ, MICHAEL/Polish National Radio Symphony - Naxos 8.550531 (1995) [79:09]
This performance may have the dubious distinction of being possibly the least Mahlerian in the catalogue. From frequently misread directions, unidiomatic style, and an ill-conceived approach to certain tempi, one wonders how much time was given to preparation and rehearsal. Halasz tries too hard to make an impression, and fails at every turn. His schmaltzy approach to the third theme of the first movement simply oozes along vulgarly. From his uneven approach to the shifting tempi of the introduction to his lack of sufficient contrast between Tempos I and II in the finale (playing the latter so much faster than the former that he fails to create an appropriate contrast of styles between them), Halasz makes a mockery of both Mahler's clear directions and the symphony's musical aesthetic. He seems only capable of handling the main allegros, provided that no tempo variations are required. Miscues are both audible and telling: the first trumpet is caught napping in the first movement at 19:16, completely missing his important cue, and clarinets play concert E-natural instead of E-flat in the middle of bar 250 of the second movement. None of the middle movements evoke any sort of atmosphere. Playing is generally dull, smoothed over and pale. After a fine opening "call and answer" in horns, the rest of *Nachtmusik I* is one long bore, plodding along tiresomely. The Scherzo is too tame and mild. Halasz eases into Tempo I after the trio section, ignoring Mahler's direction to change the tempo suddenly (at 4'). He tends to smooth over such sudden tempo changes throughout the movement. Lack of variety in dynamic levels, colorless sonorities (e.g., the cello solo at 6:48 is supposed to be played "with full tone"), and a strange inconsistency in the main tempo (from long-lined at first to sprightly by 9:40) are serious detractions here as well. Halasz's ill-conceived tempi in the finale completely distort the movement. After having set Tempo II at such a quick pace, one wonders why he adjusts it to a more appropriate tempo at 12:10, and then later repeats his earlier rapid tempo. His reading is simply confused. Only the marvelous effect of *forte-diminuendo* into the final stroke works well.

HORENSTEIN, JASCHA/New Philharmonia Orchestra (perf. 29 Aug. 1969, Royal Festival Hall) - Descant 02 (1989); Intaglio INCD 753 (1993); Music & Arts CD 727 [73:57]* Horenstein generates much energy and excitement in this superbly recorded live performance. Though flawed in some detail, it emerges as an important statement on this controversial symphony by one of Mahler's greatest interpreters. The first movement opens with a deliberately tight rendering of the rhythmic pulse after a fudged tenor horn entrance. Horenstein establishes an energetic main tempo, and moves the movement along at a spirited pace. Some markings seem to elude him, however: he ignores the *molto pesante* at the change of key after #21, pressing to a poco ritard before #24 without hesitation despite the *nicht eilen* warning. From #45 to the reprise, Horenstein measures the build up with due deliberation, stretching out the closing ritard into the main theme. Another long ritard ushers in the final coda, but by then energy seems to wane. The same energy drain affects the opening of the second movement, but Horenstein's forces recover well enough to make a fine presentation. Most impressive is the Scherzo. Unlike many conductors, Horenstein refuses to make a tempo change for the trio section when none is marked. The Andante Amoroso seems brisk, Horenstein choosing to highlight the playful rhythmic elements (mostly in woodwinds) over the lilting romance of the serenade-like string theme. From #204 to before the return of the opening cadence, the NPO strings take the opportunity to display their beauty of tone and fullness. An awkward slow-up into #211 leaves a loose end. By the final return of the main theme, Horenstein's tempo hurries along too rapidly to capture the sweet perfumery of a summer eve's serenade. The finale, though less ebullient than Bernstein's boisterous frolic, has all of the energy and gaiety needed to generate the effect of a rollicking joy-ride. Horenstein presses forward throughout the *grazioso* section without sacrificing stylishness. Sometimes Tempo I also moves quicker than it did at first. As the juxtapositions of the caricaturesque march and minuet become more frequent, the tempo quickens and playing becomes more inflexible. The final moments aptly crown a fine performance.

INBAL, ELIAHU/Frankfurt Radio Symphony - 2-Denon 60CO-1553/54 (1987); 16-Denon CO 72589-604 (1989) [79:29]+ Inbal turns in a moderately successful performance. But he is no match for his major competitors (Bernstein, Levine, Abbado, Horenstein and Chailly). Tending toward brisk *allegros*, he often skims over what should have been given more breathing space. Conversely, a few indulgences exaggerate thematic material excessively, such as the morose treatment of the first movement's second theme. Brass often overpower and strings sometimes lack precision and tautness. Notwithstanding these problems, the first movement works well. Inbal makes little of the varied nuances in the second movement, brushing by them ineffectually. Sometimes he lets phrase-endings get swallowed up in the generally brisk musical flow. The Scherzo is well-played and also swiftly paced, brass emphasizing the mournful character of the *klagend* theme. But the *Andante Amoroso* movement feels too brisk and lacks warmth of expression. Inbal makes little of the "*grazioso*" parody in the finale, merely racing through this coquetish music without any stylistic inflexion.

KLEMPERER, OTTO/New Philharmonia - 2-Angel SB-3740 (1968); CDMB 64147 (1992) [99:01] An extremely wrong-headed approach to tempo throughout most of the work makes this version almost unlistenable at times and clearly unacceptable. Although greater clarity of line is achieved (with some perceptive moments), lagging tempi saps all the music's vitality. A lugubriously mournful quality pervades the introduction and the main *allegro* section seems hopelessly lifeless. The music just lumbers along throughout most of this movement. Awkwardly slow tempi also weigh down the second movement, resulting in a strangely mysterious atmosphere. The Scherzo has its moments (particularly in a fine treatment of the intermittent *piu mosso* interjections during the trio), even if it never sounds shadowy. A restful and mellow mood pervades the fourth movement. The finale also suffers from plodding tempi despite characterful treatment of the *grazioso* sections. What is missing is the *joie de vivre* that this music should convey, and a slight crescendo before the final stroke defuses its explosive quality.

KUBELIK, RAFAEL/Bavarian Radio Symphony - 2-DG 2707 061 (1971); 10-DG 429042 (1990) [72:36] Kubelik delivers a generally well-conceived if somewhat uneven performance. A fine introduction is laden with spotty brass playing and heavy vibrato on the tenor horn. From the exposition onward, the music is deftly handled (except after #30) but balances are not always well coordinated. More vitality and intensity enhance the reprise despite weak percussion and basses. A minor affectation stretches out the last measure. Kubelik holds on too tightly to the reins in the second movement, making its principal subject sound attentuated; yet, conversely, the waltz music is too brisk. Isolated, distant tones in cow bells evoke a pastoral atmosphere but timpani are too far removed. Generally, tempi are on the slowish side. Kubelik evokes an eerie quality in the Scherzo with an impishly quickish tempo. The trio section works well but for troublesome affects (from ##139-40). On returning to the scherzo section, a swift tempo blurs inner rhythms and the final moments contain some unwanted mannerisms. After a routine reading of *Nachtmusik* I, set at a brisk pace, the finale is more expressive and better played. Kubelik is not always attentive to dynamic markings and some moments seems either stiff (#255), hurried (before #260) or off the mark (##276-78). Notwithstanding these particularly problems, Kubelik shifts between Tempos I and II in an engagingly subtle manner.

LEVINE, JAMES/Chicago Symphony - 2-RCA ARC2-458; (1982); RCD2-4581 (1984) [80:01]*+ This splendid performance combines excellent orchestral playing with a well-conceived reading by Levine. Sound quality is full-bodied but suffers from fuzzy bass response. A well-coordinated introduction ushers in a strong allegro exposition. Levine slows up for the second theme, which is treated in a very expressive, mannered style. Some tempo changes are not deftly handled (such as around m.99 and between ##55 and 56), dynamics are restrained and the main tempo drags slightly. While the first movement is not as sharp and vital as it could be, it comes across effectively. A moderate approach to tempo in the second movement works well. Although Levine does not create as shadowy an atmosphere in the Scherzo as does Bernstein, the music flows smoothly if cautiously, and frequent brief and abrupt tempo shifts in the trio are well-coordinated. *Nachtmusik* II is very expressive without untoward mannerisms and the finale combines boisterous jocularity with graceful nuance in the *grazioso* segments. Levine handles the relentless alternation between this material and the march theme ably.

MAAZEL, LORIN/Vienna Philharmonic Orchestra - 2-CBS 12M 39860 (1986); 3-CBS M3K 42495 (1987); 14-Sony Classical SK14K 48198 (1992) [86:08] Little valuable space need be wasted on but another misguided rendering in the Maazel cycle. Even Klemperer's ponderous reading of the outer movements does not compare with Maazel's plodding rendition. Taking his cue from what he must presume to be the mournful character of the introduction, Maazel saps most of the first movement of its energy and spirit, as if to imbue it with a funereal quality. Such a conception may work in the opening movement of the Second Symphony but not here. At times, Maazel drags the tempo so mercilessly as to tear the music to shreds (e.g., before #61). More lyrical moments do have a warm, summery feeling. Best is the second movement, which is more characterful and spirited. But a stiff, disjointed Scherzo movement has little characater, sounding too mellow and rhythmically deliberate. None of Mahler's fascinating nuances are rendered with any special effect. Maazel makes an effort at capturing the wafting serenity of a moonlit night in the fourth movement, but with little success. The romance of this amorous music never becomes apparent in this cold reading. As for the finale, the one word that readily comes to mind is travesty. Lacking both spirit and humor, Maazel's reading brushes the movement aside as if it were utter nonsense, an unfortunately popular opinion among some unperceptive interpreters. The result is sheer boredom.

MADERNA, BRUNO/Vienna Symphony (perf. 27 May 1967) - Hunt CD 547 (1988) [74:34] Remarkably poor playing by the VSO leads one to wonder how much rehearsal time was given to this complex work. Not only is the playing imprecise and inarticulate, but the orchestra has difficulty following Maderna's extremely flexible approach to tempo. There are moments when some players are thoroughly lost (e.g., trumpets in the first movement from m.228). Much of the first movement's stronger sections are smothered in the thickness of their sonic morass, and an unpleasantly loud hiss underlies the entire recording. With virtually no pause, we are hustled abruptly into the second movement. Again messy playing predominates, starting with the third horn's blooper during the opening horn calls. At first the main tempo is sluggish, but Maderna sees the wisdom of moving it forward, unfortunately chosing to do so when Mahler directs otherwise (*nicht eilen*). The main tempo continues to increase throughout the movement. Quiet moments are distorted by high volume; cow bells sound like clinking glasses; and intonation problems abound. Maderna's penchant for affectation (from #95 to the return of the main theme) and extremely flexible tempi is taken to extremes. From the beginning of the Scherzo, one is uncertain as what is going on! Completely ignoring the direction *aber nicht eilen* (but not fast) for main tempo, Maderna races through the principal material, making the movement completely incomprehensible. While beginning well enough, the slow movement also suffers from an effusively mannered reading, overmiked mandolin, messy playing, and abrupt halts between sections (e.g., at m.252 before the return of the opening and at Tempo I before #216). A strong, strident march theme opens the finale. But soon tempi become either labored (the overdone *pesante* before #226 and into the return of Tempo I after #246) or extremely hurried (Tempo II seems to increase in speed throughout the movement). Such an unsteady, uneven, imprecise and generally unattractive performance may not be a fair example of Maderna's or the VSO's ability to handle this symphony.

MADERNA, BRUNO/ Milan RAI Symphony (perf. 24 Dec. 1971) - 4-Hunt/Arkadia CDMAD 028.4 (1993) [78:29]*+ For a conductor nothing beats working with an orchestra with which you have a long-standing relationship and complete rapport. With his own Milan orchestra, Maderna shows what he can do with the Seventh, having failed to do so in his VSO performance (see above). He demonstrates a total grasp of the symphony's idiom, infusing it with energy and spirit and eliciting better playing than he was able to obtain from the more renowned VSO. After a slightly flabby treatment of the opening rhythmic figure in strings, Maderna picks up the tempo slightly, building through the successive tempo up-grades that lead to the *allegro* main theme. Played demonstratively, with vibrancy and vitality, the first theme march has a majesterial quality that sets the mood for the entire movement. Refusing to conform to a mannerism that has become the custom in recent years, Maderna does not slow up for the second theme, but retains the main tempo for it, sometimes making it race like the wind. The romantic third theme reeks with emotion in an extremely mannered reading. Maderna handles much of the movement with character and subtlety, making the numerous tempo shifts deftly and generating much energy and excitement throughout. Sonics are close and strong but clear, revealing inner voices.

Maderna begins the first *Nachtmusik* movement somewhat on the mushy side, keeping the volume down as marked, after a marvelous chromatic slide into the main theme. Though mild at first, the mood becomes increasing agitated throughout the movement. Maderna eases up into the main theme at 10:52, its tempo now considerably faster than before, and increases to a spirited close. Also impressive is his brilliant handling of the spooky Scherzo. Holding the volume level to *p* as marked, Maderna imbues the music with a marvelously impish character, deftly weaving the triplet figuration, with its darting, jutting sforzandi on weak beats, in and out of the musical fabric. The trio is only slightly more relaxed, if still brisk, and the common-time waltz music played with *kitsch*. After a shaky start in supporting strings, the Andante Amoroso settles in to an expressive reading. Only high volume distorts the otherwise languid mood. Maderna exaggerates the ebb and flow of this music. Notice how he drags the augmented treatment of the main theme in bass strings at #193 (5:25), moving gradually into a lively cadence. While not as lilting as Bernstein's reading, it is still quite enchanting. How gently he eases up for the gorgeous final measures, which seem to waft sultry perfume over a calm summer eve.

Maderna's finale begins with a forceful, deliberate march. His treatment of the contrasting "classical" material (Tempo II) is aptly stylish. But high volume overplays the march's brashness and strips the Haydnesque dance music of its delicacy. Maderna soon presses forward, so that these contrasting themes become confusedly similar in tempo. By 9:25 the march theme is nearly in double-time. A much needed tempo adjustment finally occurs at 11:35. But Maderna overdoes it and the main material soon becomes overly weighty though marked *l'istesso tempo*, only to press forward yet again thereafter. Despite quick pacing, the minuet music is treated in pleasantly graceful style, especially at its highpoint (13:30). Frequent false cadences on the march theme that collapse into this stylized music are nicely handled. Maderna captures the music's playful spirit despite his deviations from the letter of the score.

MASUR, KURT/Leipzig Gewandhaus Orchestra - Eterna 827790 (1984); Tokuma 32TC33 (1985); Berlin Classics BER 2058 (1994) [73:34]   If Masur has any special interpretive vision to contribute to an understanding of this difficult and often misconstrued work, it is not evident here. Playing is not only stiff and uneasy, but sometimes untidy and disjointed. More disturbing is Masur's inconsistent manner in handling tempi: either his treatment is inordinately flexible, with little control or consistency, or rigidly measured and constricted. Consequently, the performance lacks a natural, comfortable fluidity which might have better held the attention. Examples abound: when the music threatens to sag during the lengthy first movement at #37 (9:40), Masur picks up the tempo for the trumpet tattoos despite the marking *etwas gemessener* (somewhat more measured). Later he slows up to emphasize the romantic violin phrase at 13:20, when Mahler directs him to return to the main tempo but more fleetingly. Then the tempo plods along dutifully into the reprise, now set more briskly than at first. Masur's attention to detail is so inconsistent as to evidence not only lack of spontaneity but also lack of a general overview. Most ineffectual in the first movement is the jaunty second theme (4:12). Here some creativity and subjectivity might have filled in for the lack of any tempo direction for this new theme, so much more effusive than its predecessor. Instead, Masur just maintains the same tempo faithfully, thereby producing an extraordinarily uninteresting theme. His treatment of the *Nachtmusik* movements is routine and flaccid, diffused by tempo inconsistencies and lack of natural musical flow. Had Masur sharpened his strings and been less rigid in the waltz material, he might have provided a more satisfying reading of the Scherzo. In the finale Masur tries to solve the problem of the movement's constant shifts from stalwart march to delicate Haydnesque minuet by virtually eliminating the difference in tempo between them. Making less of a contrast is just the reverse of what works best here. As a result the entire movement just runs by like a loud, disjointed *melange*, devoid of any parodistic humor.

NANUT, ANTON/Ljubljana Radio Symphony - 2-Digital Concerto CCT 743-4 (1990); 12-CCT 999701 (1992) [82:13] After a promising first movement whose only serious detraction is Nanut's overbroad and extremely vulgar treatment of the second theme, this performance becomes mired in the routine. After matter-of-fact manner opening horn solos in the second movement, the listener will soon succumb to boredom. The entire movement has a mellow, pale and bland flavor, replacing character with high volume. Typical of the current crop of budget CDs, every note is laid bare on a one-dimensional plane, eliminating the slightest degree of dynamic contrast. One is also struck by the lack of idiomatic playing: at 6:20 of Index #9, notice how the flute plays staccato because the marking reads *non legato*! Brass sometimes exceed proper balance, such as on their countertheme at Index 10/1:00 against the return of the main theme. The Scherzo is also given a mild, uninteresting reading. Lacking sharp articulation in strings, the lugubrious treatment of the main theme and self-indulgently oozing character of the trio work against any invocation of a ghostly atmosphere. Again high volume for inner voices is a serious problem: on the return of the opening at Index 2/1:45, the clarinet part is marked *ppp*, but sounds *ff*. Low brass are sometimes given a morose timbre and trumpets and horns sometimes sound nasty. For the most part, all we hear is habitual note-spinning. Many of these same qualities erode the slow movement: hyped volume levels, one-dimensional balances, insensitive playing and lack of personality. Exaggerated brass and underplayed strings subvert their importance in this movement (just listen to the dreadful "wah-wah" horn playing at Index 4/9:00). Nanut fails to evoke the atmosphere of a warm summer evening which the music clearly expresses. He seems more at home in the extroverted brashness of the finale. Ringing high brass blare out the march tune, sounding more crude than majestic. The *grazioso* caricature of the subsidiary subject is spun out routinely, underplaying Mahler's musical joke. What we hear is mainly loud and rattled off without any attempt at nuance or contrast, but for the extremely weighty treatment of the main theme before the closing coda.

NEUMANN, VÁCLAV/Leipzig Gewandhaus Orchestra - 2-Eterna 8 26 103-4 (1970); Berlin Classics 0090462 (1995) [76:02]+ After an energetic, vibrant and sharp-edged first movement that rivals Bernstein in its bravado, this performance gradually dissipates, concluding with a tiresome, reserved and lackluster rendition of the finale. Ironically, Neumann's tempi tend to be brisk, until his laggard treatment of the march theme in the closing movement. He brings out the heroic aspects of the first movement with panache enhanced by crisp, full-bodied and fiery playing from the LGO. Yet tempo and mood contrasts are moderated, so that the grayish opening measures sound nearly as bright and strong as the main material and some tempo markings are uneffectuated (e.g., the *molto pesante* on the return of the second theme). Sonic quality is excellent, with superb bass response and audible inner parts that add atmosphere, such as in the shimmering rhythms in second violins on the sudden return of the main theme at 9:20. The entire movement sparkles with brilliance and vibrates with dynamic urgency. But problems already become evident in the second movement. A fast pace (more *moderato* than *andante*) hastens the music along so hurriedly that opportunities to evoke stylish playing in the waltz trios are lost. Lacking a sense of mystery, possibly caused by not fine-tuning dynamic markings, such as *sforzandi*, and avoiding any nuance that might slacken the pace, the movement communicates little of its fascinating contrasts with its focus on the spirited march tempo that never lets up for the waltz. An unrelenting restlessness characterizes much of this movement. The waltz music in the Scherzo's trio section is also spirited, but the swirling triplets of the principal subject lack bite for smoothed over accentuation. Once again Neumann holds on unwaveringly to his main tempo when slight nuances would have added a touch of character. The fourth movement is much the same: he establishes a brisk pace that he maintains with little flexibility throughout. As a result this lovely moonlight serenade is rendered without as much charm and grace as, for instance, Bernstein elicits (see above). The finale, however, is the biggest disappointment. Without sufficient contrast between the march material and its *grazioso*, minuet-like counterpart, this movement simply does not work. Neumann's pacing of the march lags increasingly and fails to add any finesse to the *grazioso* music, allowing the movement to lose spirit and energy and become both tiresome and lackluster. Dynamic contrasts are also mitigated, becoming monotonously one-dimensional (except for horrendously over-balanced bells at 11:50). What began with a brilliant opening movement devolves into insignificance in the finale.

NEUMANN, VÁCLAV/Czech Philharmonic - 2-Pro Arte 2PAL-2003 (1979); 2-Supraphon 111 978 (1993); 11-Supraphon SUP 111860 [80:45]   Too many problems limit the effectiveness of this recording: sonics are weak and thin; dynamic contrasts are blurred; balances lack adequate proportion (brass overpower, especially trumpets); playing often misses the mark; and the overall effect is mostly dull and uninvolved until the finale. Cautious restraint in the opening movement has a debilitating effect upon the music's spirit, that is further impoverished by Neumann's tendency to smooth over interesting nuances and important inner voice detail. The second movement is too brisk, frequently too loud and generally lacks sensitivity. In the Scherzo movement, the swirling triplets are squared off too deliberately to produce a shadowy effect and in the trio section, a quick tempo fudges contrasts between it and the rapid interjections producing a disjointed performance. Neumann leads the fourth movement with a heavy hand; in combination with excessively high level dynamics, this results in a cold and insensitive reading. While transitions are not very smooth and the main tempo sometimes drags on lifelessly, the final moments are fairly effective. Strong dynamics and a more evident sense of involvement enliven the finale. But too many awkward passages, some constricted moments and frequently unidiomatic playing, particularly in the minuet parody, are serious distractions. Neumann manages to handle the frequent shifts between the *grazioso* parody and the march theme with a sense of wry humor.

OZAWA, SEIJI/Boston Symphony - 2-Philips 426 249 (1990); 14-Philips 438 874 (1995) [80:13]   As often occurs in the Ozawa cycle, the orchestra outshines the conductor, for while the BSO plays with refinement and tonal beauty, their conductor's reading tends toward the perfunctory, smoothing over abrupt interjections and grotesqueries while marking time in long-stretches. An impressionistic haze whitewashes too much of Mahler's demonic effects. For the dynamic first movement, Ozawa offers an extremely strident rendition of the principal theme, and an uneven, debilitated reading of the subsidiary theme. His reading lacks both impulse and urgency, favoring lyricism over dramatic power. For the most part, Ozawa lets the movement play itself, except for a curious slow up at #38 (10:30); the result is mild, uninvolved and often too rigid. Similarly, Ozawa takes a very legato approach to the second movement, smoothing over sforzandi that should interject a note of mystery here. Contrasts are also moderated. The jaunty march music at 13:25 is treated diminutively and sounds like a parade of little mice as a result. But the cowbells, played softly and in isolated tones, evoke the intended hint of nostalgia. Otherwise, Ozawa fails to captivate the imagination, even with such polished playing and vibrant sonics. The Scherzo is treated as a mere intermezzo, lacking any sense of mystery and covering up Mahler's impishly wicked grotesqueries. While the trio section is charming, the rest of the movement is a complete bore. Given Ozawa's propensity for the lyrical, one would expect the *Andante Amoroso* to be the one movement he does well. However, this lovely serenade falls flat under his direction, lacking both impulse in passionate sections and a proper blend of integral components. Big brass spew out the march theme of the finale with gusto and vibrancy, but the contrasting *grazioso* music is too inflexible to be charming or coquettish. Ozawa keeps the principal theme under wraps throughout. Sometimes too much background material comes to the surface (e.g., the bassoon after #274); elsewhere even important material loses pride of place (main theme in violins at 13:50). Why is the tempo so quick at 14:55 when marked *Feierlich* (solemnly)? This misunderstood symphony is given yet another unimpressive, unrevealing performance.

RATTLE, SIMON/City of Birmingham Symphony - EMI CDC 7 54344 (1992) [77:10]
* Rattle offers an energetic, vibrant and uncompromising reading, enhanced by superb work from the CBS and clear, brilliant sonics. Yet so many quick tempi follow in succession, that there is little time to catch one's breath. Moreover, sonic brilliance and extroverted playing- - often nervously impelled forward or rigidly measured--divert attention from the work's main focus: the *Nachtmusiken*. The opening section of the first movement is neither nocturnal nor funereal, but sounds strong and defiant. Rattle works out the many tempo shifts superbly, and establishes an excellent main tempo. He maintains this staunch pace in full vigor throughout the second theme group (4:23) which is usually stretched out with affectatious slow-ups by others. While his intense reading captures the music's vibrancy and romance, sometimes restraint and rigidity cause a lack of spontaneity. Climaxes are strong and given to extremes in isolation from their surroundings. Most disconcerting are the *Nachtmusik* movements. Each are briskly paced and strongly played, colored in bright tones that fail to capture the soft, pallid glow of a moonlit night. In *Nachtmusik* I, things that go bump in the night sound as if exposed to broad daylight. Again lack of stylish nuance and flexibility (unlike Rattle's usual approach) rigidifies much of this movement. Always on edge, he fails to evoke the music's nocturnal quality. So too in *Nachtmusik* II. Laced with a brisk tempo, Rattle's reading emphasizes the intermittent skipping rhythms in woodwinds rather than the lyric quality of the main theme in strings. Rattle pulls the movement along too hurriedly to create the sultry atmosphere of a summer evening. Only in the gorgeous final moments (after an almost neurotically impassioned climax) does the music radiate with the glow of moonlight. In the Scherzo, Rattle handles the undercurrent of swirling triplets with subtlety, eliciting a ghostly presentment. Few beside Bernstein have created such a marvelous contrast of mystery and jollity as Rattle has here. His finale rises to the occasion, surging with vitality and energy. All the raucous bravado of the march theme comes through without compromise. At times Rattle becomes over-zealous in his approach, pressing the march forward so intently as to lose sight of its pompousness (at 8:11). What can the marking *gemütlich* at #262 possibly be taken to mean if played at such a rapid pace? On a later return of Tempo I, Rattle pulls up abruptly, giving the principal subject a dirge-like quality, only to immediately race through the remainder of the section (to 11:30). Despite a boisterous reading of the march, the swift tempo applied to the contrasting *grazioso* music makes it sound even more boorish than the march. Rattle's approach is certainly uncompromising in his emphasis of the symphony's extroverted elements rather than its more charming *Nachtmusik* diversions, and he is in complete control throughout.

ROSBAUD, HANS/Berlin Radio Symphony - 2-Urania URLP 405 (1953); 2-Vox VUX 2008 (1963); 2-Vox Box CDX2 5520 (1995) [80:41] This outdated mono version has little redeeming value. The CD reissue compensates slightly for the poor sound quality of the original LP release. Orchestral precision is below par, with frequent sloppy attacks and improper balances. An extremely slow opening with a fatuous-sounding tenor horn projects a mournful tone. The gradual tempo increases go too far and require a slight ritard into the exposition. Rosbaud's dry, cerebral reading fails to evoke any kind of emotion from this music. The horn duet that opens the second movement is atrociously played, and the tempo set for the woodwind passage that follows is extremely fast. Eventually, the main allegro tempo becomes more comfortable, and then the music moves along nicely, only disturbed by sonic distortion at strong climaxes. In the Scherzo movement, weak accentuation on string triplets, frequently slow tempi and blurred inner voices are still apparent. Rosbaud sets a brisk tempo for

Nachtmusik II, breezing through what should be a relaxing serenade. Although the finale suffers from a sluggish and stiff reading, it manages to elicit some spirited moments. The witty *grazioso* segments work nicely, but bungling in the orchestra--particularly by the solo trumpet before the accelerando into #290--is most disturbing.

SCHERCHEN, HERMANN/Vienna Symphony (perf. 1960) - AS Disc AS 302 (1988); Notes PCP T1022 (1992) [73:45] This live performance suffers more from abundant sloppiness than from Scherchen's quirky mannerisms. Only glimpses of his superlative reading with the Vienna State Opera Orchestra come through the mess of inaccuracies here. Scherchen tends to extremes in tempi, sometimes stretching a lyrical section almost beyond endurance and then hurtling forward with nervous agitation. He belabors the funereal aspect of the opening section, heavily pacing the rhythmic tread and the tiered tempo increases, and causing much stiffness, but the main theme has spirit. Violins sound too piercing in the second theme and Scherchen overloads the third theme with much schmaltz. Some segments reveal his thorough understanding of the music (to #32), but again too many technical problems occur. What tempo is the harp in at m.317 marked *sehr breit* (very broad)? A sluggish treatment of the reprised introductory material contrasts with a slapdash approach to quicker sections (the Shostakovichian march in 6/4 before the final return of Tempo I is completely disjointed). Scherchen's elephantine tempo for the final coda (to be played in Tempo I) provides at least a consistent conclusion to his disjointed reading. Rough-hewn if natural horn calls open *Nachtmusik* I. Here playing is sharper, more angular and well-accented. Much *joie de vivre* comes through, particularly in the jaunty march sections, but wrong notes abound (e.g., in the flute before #87). Many sections move along too quickly to have much impact. In the Scherzo movement, Scherchen's treatment of the Viennese waltz music is extremely mannered and he plays up the darting grotesqueries that permeate the swirling opening section. Notice the curious off-beat accents on leaps at #158. Energy levels increase here noticeably. Untidiness mars an otherwise fine reading of the *Andante Amoroso*. Transitions could be cleaner and never disturb the serene atmosphere. A few affectations seem exaggerated (e.g., slowing up at the double bar before #201) but they blend in generally well. The finale is a jovial romp. Scherchen emphasizes the swaggering march over the parodistic minuet. Again imprecise playing distorts the performance, particularly during the minuet section (Tempo II) with its exposed inner voices. A huge luftpause holds back the flood of the final measures. Despite its many flaws, this performance improves with each succeeding movement.

SCHERCHEN, HERMANN/Toronto Symphony (perf. 1965) - King KICC 2077 (1990) [69:36]+ Except for a jumbled, erratic reading of the first movement, this performance is more in keeping with Scherchen's best work in the Seventh. While orchestral miscues and imprecision abound, his reading is characterful, spirited and often exciting. Given to eccentricities, especially in extreme tempo shifts, Scherchen emphasizes the juxtaposition of contrasting themes. The first movement is a maddening race. After driving the first theme home relentlessly, Scherchen comes to a halt for the second subject, giving it an uncharacteristically schmaltzy twist. The lyrical third theme is highly romanticized, in complete isolation from the surrounding material, played rapidly and impulsively. *Nachtmusik* I is also paced briskly, but works well enough to convey a sense of spirited gaiety. The Toronto Symphony (mislabelled "Tronto" on the jacket) seems uncomfortably harried, with their numerous miscues and straggly ensemble work, but they overcome their lack of familiarity with this complex work and Mahler's idiom admirably. Scherchen knows how to create a shadowy undercurrent in the Scherzo, which contrasts nicely with his lively treatment of the waltz tune. Strangely, the slap shot *fffff* pizzicatos do not seem to rebound off the fingerboard as they should.

The slow movement has a relaxed quality, a welcome diversion after what seems like three allegro movements. Mandolin and guitar have difficulty playing together. A few interesting nuances are added: a momentary slow-up into #201 (6:40) alternating with a lighter treatment of the plucking theme, and a long ritard on the return of the opening cadence before the impetuous climactic section preceding the coda. In the finale the orchestra responds more readily to Scherchen's eccentric conductorial style. Brass are more articulate in the energetic march. A brisk Tempo II works convincingly, if not optimally. But as the interpositions of the march and *grazioso* sections become more frequent, the orchestra begins to unravel, becoming confused and, consequently, less efficient. Scherchen has difficulty controlling the march tempo in its numerous unprepared reprises. He cops out in the final measure by adding a slight crescendo after the diminuendo on the closing chord into the final stroke.

SEGERSTAM, LEIF/Danish National Radio Symphony - 3-Chandos CHAN 9057-59 (1992) [88:22]+ Segerstam's penchant for over-emoting places inordinate demands upon an ensemble hardly at home with Mahler's idiom. While they give all they have, the players are uncomfortable with Segerstam's wayward approach. His direction either becomes so firm as to stifle flexibility or so loose that the orchestra has difficulty following him. Chandos tries to enhance orchestral sound by amplifing volume levels and brightening sonic quality, but the result, while positive for the most part, sometimes causes harsh brass sound in fortissimo passages. An extroverted character infuses the entire work. For instance, the opening sounds more dynamic and forceful than dirge-like. Contrasts in tempo are extreme, rapid-fire speed suddenly giving way to heavy-footed plodding. But some creative characterizations are impressive: the devilishly threatening tuba and deliciously quacky clarinet in the opening of the second movement (the latter also reappears in the Scherzo's trio section). Segerstam generates much momentum in the first movement. But frequent rubato inflections cause the musical flow to become disjointed and sound like overtly conscious efforts at showmanship. Huge slow-ups (into the second theme) are followed by intense agitation, that sometimes adds a measure of bravura to the first movement, but elsewhere seems overdone.

The three inner movements are also replete with affectations. While one could argue about the impropriety of each one, they do capture the attention. Martial rhythms in *Nachtmusik* I have a squarish bent; few conductors have treated them in the style of the Pan march of the Third Symphony as Segerstam does here. The waltz material is subjected to exaggerated luftpauses in an attempt to heighten the decorative aspects of its rhythmic sway. All the sweep and spookiness of the Scherzo comes through with much vitality, even if details are sometimes applied with a heavy hand (after #141). Cautious playing occasionally tempers these effects and flagrant quirkiness disjoints phrasing. The last bar, played twice as slow as before, misses the point of Mahler's little joke of cutting out the third beat of the waltz tune. In the *Andante Amoroso* movement, Segerstam again pours on his schmaltzy nuances like thick sauce. Any relationship to the term "*Nachtmusik*" has been lost both here and in the second movement. As expected, brass blare out the pompous march theme of the finale with undaunted arrogance, but the contrasting *grazioso* subject is languorously affected rather than parodistically graceful. As the movement proceeds, the march theme becomes more and more agitated, until 11:33 where Segerstam mercilessly drags it out in the huge *ff* brass chorale, holding on to his weighty tempo even into the return of Tempo II. Structurally, the performance lacks cohesiveness and fluency. In the final minutes, brass so overpower that the music becomes more sardonic than witty.

SINOPOLI, GIUSEPPE/Philharmonia Orchestra - 2-DG 437 851 (1994) [87:26]+
Sinopoli exposes the Seventh to the extremes of self-indulgence that make his reading possibly the most discombobulated ever recorded. He adds personal touches to the already voluminous markings whenever and wherever it strikes his fancy. Consequently, the push-pull

of the music is often stretched to the breaking point: slow-ups wrench phrases from their natural course, only to give way to fits of rapid propulsion that jar the nerves. Mahler requires many tempo divergencies and digressions throughout the score. Sinopoli's manipulations merely add confusion rather than enlightenment and fail to provide a cohesive viewpoint on this complex and expansive affair. Molto ritards become virtual fermatas; the occasional *nicht eilen* (do not rush) marking is read as if it meant *langsamer* (slower). These constant exaggerations are most disturbing in the first movement. What is one to make of all of these radical tempo shifts (beyond those that Mahler himself provides)? Examples of a hurry-up-and-wait manner are to numerous to mention here. Broad-lined themes become mercilously stretched out in Sinopoli's heavy-handed treatment. Just listen to how lugubriously the second theme plods along at 5:20, despite the *l'istesso a tempo* marking; or how suddenly Sinopoli rushes forward at 9:28 (before #30) without any direction in the score. Screaming trumpets pierce the air and, when they accompany the rest of the brass section, they overwhelm the rest of the orchestra in a flood of sound that exaggerates vulgarity to the hilt. Is this an attempt to trash the symphony? It certainly sounds like it. High sonic levels hype up climaxes to coincide with Sinopoli's other exaggerations. While the second movement opens with a well-wrought echo effect in horns, we are not free from Sinopoli's manipulations. The waltz that follows is vulgarized by a mid-stream slow-up. At least the cow bells are well rendered, played in isolated tones that blend well into the pastoral atmosphere of the choral-like bridge passages. But Sinopoli's emphatic approach to much of this music often makes it sound stilted and unnatural.

The Scherzo movement is more extroverted than spooky and needs a sharper edge for the string figuration. Sinopoli takes further liberties here: notice how he gradually goes into tempo before #139 (at c.4') so that the one measure *piu mosso* that interrupts it is not longer as abrupt as it was intended to be. Brass create too bright an atmosphere (at 6:59), getting in each other's way at times. The subito Tempo I at 8:30 is certainly not in Tempo I but much slower. An attempt to bring it up to speed fails, succumbing to sluggishness once again on the cello theme at #169. An effort at tender, caressing expression threatens to thicken the atmosphere during the beginning of the *Andante Amoroso* movement. The passage marked *gehalten* (halting) on a phrase from the first theme is treated charmingly. But Sinopoli's over-emoting often interrupts the natural musical flow, and his fussiness gets in the way of structural cohesion and inner-voice balance. During the passionate section at 13:40, Sinopoli even slows up into what should be a sudden return of Tempo I. One senses that nearly every measure has its own tempo. Sinopoli carries tempo inflection to such an extreme that his approach would not have been acceptable to even such a "flexible" conductor as Mahler. During the finale, Sinopoli tries to juxtapose a broadly-paced march theme with a sprightly minuet subject. But his unmarked slow-ups again infect the musical line too much variation in speed. Tempo I is sometimes disengaged incomprehensibly from its original pace. Sinopoli plays up molto ritards on false cadences during the frequent switches from march to minuet that should evoke humor, but does anything but. Despite excellent treatment of the final measures, Sinopoli fails to present a clear and convincing view of this music or have any fun with it. Possibly, acceptance of his tendency to exaggerate may be a matter of taste, and arguments have been made in its favor. But fluidity of line is one thing and distortion another.

SOLTI, GEORG/Chicago Symphony - 2-London CSA 2231 (1972); London 425041 (1992); 10-London 430 804 (1992) [77:20]*+ When first issued, this recording was rated in the class of those performances by Bernstein, Levine and Abbado, as one of the finest versions available. Sonics are excellent and Solti generally handles the music both idiomatically and with finesse. While the opening section seems on the deliberate side, the tenor horn has a marvelous tonal quality and tempo modulations are well handled up to the exposition. One minor annoyance is Solti's tendency to slow up affectedly for the second theme. Some brass problems occur, such as an awful third trombone at m. 346. Basically, the excitement Solti generates in the first movement would have been better served by eliminating unnecessary affectations and extreme ritards. The second movement is somewhat understated having less character and spirit than Bernstein's version, despite superb playing and marvelous cow bells. A very energetic and stylized Scherzo movement is every bit the equal of Bernstein's delightful reading. Yet Bernstein has a more attractive way of handling the lovely *Nachtmusik* II, even if Solti's version is beautifully played and meticulously detailed (listen to that clever *accelerando* trill in the flute at #219). Only minor annoyances crop up in the closing section: the flute is breathy, horn strange-sounding and an added comma before the last note is unnecessary. Solti's fast and furious treatment of the finale works extremely well. Sharply-honed articulation and fine balances enhance the overall effect. Tempo II is frolicking and jovial, if hard pressed at times. Since Tempo I also moves very quickly, adequate contrast between these two main tempi is sometimes lacking. A few passages could be better handled: brass lose power after #273 and the passage leading into #286 lacks cohesion, but Solti's whirlwind approach keeps one on the edge of one's seat to the end.

TENNSTEDT, KLAUS/London Philharmonic - 2-Angel DSB-3908; EAC 90058/59 (1981); 10-EMI CMS7 64471-81 (1993) [83:33]* This performance seems to lack both idiomatic playing and a sense of involvement throughout much of the first three movements but generates more beauty and intensity thereafter. Hampered by stiff and unsteady playing, Tennstedt has difficulty eliciting just the right effect in the opening movement. Dynamics seem muffled here. A bloated tenor horn and weak timpani are also detractions. Tennstedt slows up for lyrical passages and thereby sometimes loses vitality. The return to the main theme and the following *grandioso* climax are infused with a heightened sense of drama. Tennstedt elicits too much legato playing from the strings in the second movement, which also suffers from weak timpani and lack of cohesion. Squarish treatment of dotted rhythms and extremely quiet string triplets make Tennstedt's reading of the Scherzo rather uninteresting. While the trio section is generally fine, some awkward tempo shifts and distant timpani are detractions. A more lively tempo might have created a more flittering effect in the principal subject. A lovely reading of *Nachtmusik* II is enhanced by clearer if somewhat restrained playing. Tennstedt treats the music with more sensitivity toward the close than earlier. A brisk tempo is set for the opening of the finale but distant timpani again weaken what should be unabashed exuberance. In preparation for the march theme, Tennstedt brings the tempo back down to earth so that extroverted march is treated with all the majesty it richly deserves. He is better able than most to elicit the classical grace and charm called for in the second subject (Tempo II) but he seems to underplay the march tempo (Tempo I) as the movement proceeds. Alternating sections are well handled toward the final coda. Stronger timpani would have been preferable. More intensity is generated at the close than almost anywhere else in the entire performance.

WAKASUGI, HIROSHI/Tokyo Metropolitan Symphony - 2-Fontec FOCD 9024/25 (1989) [79:04] While principal tempi are generally well-considered, Wakasugi's reading alternates between the use of affectatious hesitations and slow-ups that heavily underline certain passages and a mechanical approach that lets the music play itself out without a trace of stylistic inflection while smoothing over what should be darting sforzandi and biting accents. Such a contrast of stylistic approaches appears unconvincing at both extremes. Notice how the jaunty second theme of the first movement (at 4', 9' and 17') becomes a gushing, lingering effusion of romantic emotion, and how leaden the march theme becomes during the finale's concluding section. So many conflicting emotions are highlighted in the first movement (from the morose tenor horn solo to the unnaturally fervid passion of the second theme) that it is unclear just what Mahler has in mind. Both *Nachtmusik* I and the Scherzo fail to conjure up anything nocturnal, lacking color, bite and dynamic flair. Occasional attempts to add character are noteworthy only for being uncharacteristic of the overall performance (e.g., the morose cello theme contrasting with mocking woodwinds toward the close of the Scherzo). In the fourth movement, Wakasugi holds back each time the opening cadential phrase reappears and eases in and out of virtually every paragraph or section in an overly sentimental manner. Yet the strings lacks sufficient sonority to beautify this romantic serenade. Much is made of the contrast between the string theme and light, frolicsome woodwind rhythms. After a jerky timpani volley, the opening of the finale begins in fine fettle, with an imperious march theme and fairly tasteful minuet counter-theme. But from the appearance of dreadfully loud, clangy low bells at 11:12 (are these church bells?), Wakasugi again indulges in exaggerated tempo contrasts, ignores many of Mahler's markings and tries too consciously to stretch out grandiose effects as much as possible in the finale moments, while underplaying the charm of the minuet (13'). Consequently, the remainder of the movement does not hang together.

TRANSCRIPTION FOR PIANO 4-HANDS by Alfredo Casella:

SILVIA ZENKER and EVELINDE TRENKNER, pianists - MD&G L3445 (1992) [77:27] As with his piano reduction of the Sixth (see above), Casella evidences his understanding of Mahler's idiom here while recognizing the virtual impossibility of reproducing every element of this orchestrally conceived work on one piano. Difficult choices are inevitable and Casella generally makes them intelligently. Yet, again as with Casella's Sixth transcription, one misses the special impact that only strings and winds can make with sharp edged embellishments that add color and character to the *Nachtmusik* movements. Of course, this version is not intended to replace Mahler's orchestration, but to shed light on inner workings for more intimate study. Smoothing over rough-edges hews down the many devilish grotesqueries to a mild distraction. This tendency may speak as much for the performance as the piano score itself. In the first movement, Zenker and Trenkner, after a mild-mannered opening, press energetically into the main allegro theme, which is rapidly paced. But the second theme's exaggerated dotted-rhythmic figure plods along in a squarish, flat-footed manner devoid of spirit, leading into a quiet but not very effusive reading of the romantic third theme. Tempo shifts seem angular and abrupt (even more than directions indicate they should be). Dissonances at #36-37 become more obvious. But the captivating romance of the third theme's variant that follows (c. 11:18+) requires the gorgeous string writing Mahler provided for it, sounding like music DeFalla might have written for his **Nights in the Gardens of Spain**. The awesome demonic section for brass that preceeds the final coda lacks intensity. But the middle movements work more effectively to capture the diverse aspects of Night so brilliantly evoked there. Casella omits the long chromatic slide into the first theme (though he keeps it into #92 at c.6:55), and, naturally, cow-bell and *col legno* effects are absent. Some touches work well, such as at Index #4 on an extention of the introductory triplets for woodwinds. But the pianists sometimes adversely affect the musical flow by slowing up into sections (at #108) or completely stopping before they proceed (10:20). The Scherzo is more evocative; played with only two pairs of hands the triplet rhythms flow more evenly than is often the case in the orchestral version. As musical textures are laid bare one becomes conscious of Adorno's interesting remark that Mahler's music often lacks any bass line. More accentuation would have added biting wit to the shadowy sections and more muscularity would have made their extroverted themes sound more dynamic.

Baroque ornamentations in the main theme seem more distracting than decorative in the fourth movement. But for the most part the reading as well as the piano reduction itself is light and charming. In the finale, after a heavy-laden opening leading into a mild march theme

SYMPHONY NO. 7

(perverted by a curious reverse swell), the pianists gradually catch the spirit of fun that should be evoked here. The importance of emphasizing the sardonic juxtaposition of boisterous pomposity and flirtacious charm is not lost in this piano version. From the march theme's rousing return at 11:02 to the close, the performance is a sheer delight.

SYMPHONY NO.8 IN E-FLAT MAJOR ("SYMPHONY OF A THOUSAND")

Movements:

Part I : Veni Creator Spiritus
Part II: Finale Scene from Goethe's *Faust, Part II*

ABBADO, CLAUDIO/Berlin Philharmonic; Cheryl Studer, Sylvia McNair, Andrea Rost, sopranos; Anne Sofie von Otter, Rosemarie Lang, altos; Peter Seifert, tenor; Bryn Terfel, baritone; Jan-Hendrik Rootering, bass; Berlin Radio Chorus; Prague Philharmonic Choir; Tölzer Knabenchor - 2-DG 445 843; 10-DG 447 023 (1995) [81:20]*+ At long last Abbado completes his symphony cycle for DG with this stunning performance accompanied by one of the best team of soloists ever to appear on a commercial recording of this massive choral symphony. With such notable vocalists as Cheryl Studer, Sylvia McNair and Bryn Terfel the recording promises much. True to their reputations they sing superbly. Choral forces are also excellent. DG's stunning sonics enhance the brilliant playing of the BPO, providing full dynamic range. The only surprise here is the lack of drive and intensity that characterized Abbado's early Mahler performances. Now a more temperate approach prevails, still generating enormous power but with a more majestic bearing. Without Abbado's earlier impetuosity, Part I seems mild and restrained. Legato playing is stressed over sharp articulation. In Part II, a warm glow pervades the opening and returns, after a moderately passionate *piu mosso* orchestral diversion, to the hushed *Wäldung* chorus colored in pastel shadings. Bryn Terfel as Pater Ecstaticus tries to sing passionately despite Abbado's mild mannered accompaniment. Too much restraint de-energizes the solo sections, causing intensity to abate. Studer, McNair and von Otter sing beautifully in their respective roles, and team up for a trio that blows by like a gentle breeze. Abbado maintains both a lyrical style and spacious tempo throughout most of what follows. After the Chorus Mysticus exudes a warm glow, he is able to move his forces forward ever so gradually to a conclusion well worth waiting for: overwhelming in its grandeur and magnificent in its proportions.

ABRAVANEL, MAURICE/Utah Symphony; Jeanine Crader, Lynn Owen, Blanche Christensen, sopranos; Nancy Williams, Marlena Kleinman, altos; Stanley Kolk, tenor; David Clatworthy, baritone; Malcolm Smith, bass; University of Utah Chorus; Children's Chorus, Salt Lake City Schools - 2-Vanguard VRS 1120/1 (1964); 11-

Vanguard 08.4013.79 (1995) [76:06] This mediocre performance suffers from constricted sonics, weak and often strained choral forces, an extremely uneven soloist ensemble and a routine, uninteresting reading. The best work here occurs in those sections that require the least flair or subtle nuance. Abravanel's reading seems uninvolved, producing a colorless performance which rambles on from section to section with little sense of shape or design. Choral forces smooth over accents and sometimes sound lifeless or unfocused. Soloists are generally either strained, heavyish or wobbly; the soprano duet in Part II is wretched and Mater Gloriosa is too closely miked to produce the desired "heavenly" effect. Playing is often imprecise, poorly tuned and weakened by watered-down dyanmics. The overall performance is simply too dull to be of any interest.

BERNSTEIN, LEONARD/London Symphony Festival Chorus & Orchestra; Erna Spoorenberg, Gwyneth Jones, Gwenyth Annear, sopranos; Anna Reynolds, Norma Proctor, altos; John Mitchinson, tenor; Vladimir Ruzdiak, baritone; Donald McIntyre, bass; The Leeds Festival Chorus; Orpington Junior Singers; Highgate School Boys' Choir; Finchley Children's Music Group - 2-Columbia M2S-751 (1967); 3-CBS M3K 42199 (1986); 3-Sony SM3K 47581 (1992) [79:07]** Although sonic technology has made it much easier to record this enormous choral symphony than it was when this recording was first produced, it still retains its popularity among Mahlerians. The primary reason is Bernstein's magic touch and knowing interpretive sense. He infuses the music with great vitality, bordering on nervous agitation. While some affectations appear (a tendency to slow up for more lyrical moments), they usually enhance the emotive quality without becoming unseemly. Phrases are shaped stylistically and sections molded with seamless contours. Orchestral and vocal forces produce every nuance clearly and stylishly. One extremely difficult aspect of this sprawling symphony is holding together the numerous sections (especially in Part II which contains a series of variations). Bernstein structures the work so that sections flow smoothly and naturely into one another. Some complex textures would have been better balanced with more advanced technology, yet choral climaxes are thrilling, especially in the closing section of Part I where the choral lines sound like planets hurling through space. A haunting yet soulful opening to Part II suddenly catches fire at #8 with an intense pathos reminiscent of the finale of the Sixth Symphony. Details are captured very effectively and stylishly. Tempi are flexible but never excessively pliant and structural balance is well-conceived. The vocal soloists are a fine lot: John Mitchinson sings engagingly, if sometimes lacking in subtlety; the female trio (after # 134) is gorgeous; the Penitent is very expressive and the Mater Gloriosa heavenly from her distant height. As wondrous and exciting as most of this performance is, nothing can compare to the sheer ecstacy of the Chorus Mysticus. Beginning as an almost inaudible hush giving off a warm glow, this mystical music builds to a magnificent climax, ending in a blaze of glory with trumpets roundly heralding redemption on the three-note "light" motif.

BERNSTEIN, LEONARD/Vienna Philharmonic; Edda Moser, Judith Blegen, Gerti Zeumer, sopranos; Ingrid Mayr, Agnes Baltsa, altos; Kenneth Riegel, tenor; Hermann Prey, baritone; Jose Van Dam, bass; Konzertvereinigung Wiener Staatsoperchor; Wiener Singverein; Wiener Knabenchor (perf. 1975, Salzburg) - DG video 072 216-3 NTSC (1989) [86]** It is a wonder that DG did not issue this version on CD, for most of this videotape is far superior to what was put together for the CD version. While most of the soloists are the same (Edda Moser and Ingrid Mayr replacing Margaret Price and Trudeliese Schmidt respectively), they sing more securely and with more self-assurance here. Of course, there are the usual imperfections of choral and orchestral ensemble work, but by and large Bernstein's sheer force of will, energy, and unrestrained enthusiasm makes this a performance worth treasuring. The manner in which he effects tempo shifts throughout Part I (e.g., speeding up into the return of the *"Veni"* chorus at 6:38, then holding up for its reprise at 18:37) is thoroughly captivating. The *"Hostem"* and *"Accende"* choruses are utterly thrilling. Unlike the CD version, the two sopranos sing beautifully in the final *"Gloria,"* bringing Part I to a magnificent, if slightly blurred conclusion. The beginning of Part II is especially impressive for its combination of subtle mystery in the opening and impetuousity in the impassioned orchestral segment that follows. Horns ring out in stentorian tones. Male vocalists sing impressively and with demonstrative assurance; even the stalwart Kenneth Riegel manages the high tessitura of Doctor Marianus with only a few flaws. The sopranos all sing admirably and mostly on pitch (Blegen is in much better voice here than in the CD version). Only Mayr has pitch problems and strains in her Samaritana role. Few can compete with Bernstein in providing energy and dramatic tension so necessary to the success of this work. He alone was responsible for bringing it to the attention of a new generation and offers a closing section that may be the best one ever recorded.

BERNSTEIN, LEONARD/Vienna Philharmonic; Margaret Price, Judith Blegen, Gerti Zeumer, sopranos; Trudeliese Schmidt, Agnes Baltsa, altos; Kenneth Riegel, tenor; Hermann Prey, baritone; Jose Van Dam, bass; Konzertvereinigung Wiener Staatsoperchor; Wiener Singverein; Wiener Sangerknaben (perf. 1975, Salzburg) - 2-DG 435 102 (1991); 13-DG 435 162 (1992) [83:05]* Issued hurriedly after Bernstein's untimely demise in order to complete his second symphony cycle, this Eighth has all of the virtues and flaws of a live performance: electricity and energy but also serious lapses in precision and ensemble co-ordination. From the opening, marred by an awful sounding organ on the second chord, Bernstein presses his huge forces to the limits of their capacity. The *"Accende"* (at #11) is a romp and *"Hostem"* is driven to the edge of madness. Bernstein hurls the billowing waves of sound from his orchestra into a shattering climax at #59 (Index 11 at 3:50). His frequent foot-stamping sometimes jump-starts strong entrances or climaxes (e.g., the *ff* string entrance at #8 in Part II, Index 1 at 4:15+). At the same time, balances are often distended and playing fudgy, clarity being far from a virtue here. The vocal ensemble rarely blends well, each soloist going his or her own way or trying to out shout the others (particularly the sopranos). Only Van Dam seems to rise above the satisfactory; while the indominitable Riegel and Prey do the best they can under the circumstances. Choral forces sound woolly, clearly strained by Bernstein's unremitting rapid-fire tempi. Yet with all of these imperfections, few can match Bernstein's electricity and intensity. He nearly stomps through the floorboard ushering the impassioned section at #56 in Part II (6') and pounds assertively on the augmented *"ewig"* motive before the Chorus Mysticus. One senses that more preparation might have spared us the many flaws that detract from this otherwise exciting performance.

BERTINI, GARY/Cologne Radio Symphony; Julia Varady, MariAnne Häggander, Maria Venuti, sopranos; Anne Howells, Florence Quivar, altos; Paul Frey, tenor; Alan Titus, baritone; Siegfried Vogel, bass; Cologne Radio Chorus; Prague Philharmonic Chorus; Stuttgart Radio Chorus; Little Singers of Tokyo - EMI CDC 7 54846 (1995) [79:03]* Gary Bertini and his supplemented Cologne-based forces provide an impressive performance that runs the gamut of emotions from an energetic Part I to an extremely broad, majestic closing section of Part II. The soloists work better individually than as a group, and choral forces make up in clarity for their deficiency in power. Close-miking has its usual positive and negative results: making audible important inner voices (particularly in the bass strings) while over-emphasizing instrumental parts better left as an integral part of the musical fabric, and heightening the volume of quiet sections. In Part I, Bertini's steady hand keeps the pace always fresh and enlivened. His handling of the entrance into the reprise without a ritard (such as Bernstein added), but without just crashing headlong into it, is superb. Part II opens with an engagingly mysterious atmosphere after a shaky *pp* cymbal on the first note. The intense drive of Part I has tapered off, and a feeling of restraint pervades the Anchorites chant, preceded by an impassioned orchestral section marked by visceral strength in strong accents (9'). Paters Ecstaticus and Profundis perform admirably, their weaknesses in resonance or projection overcome by close miking. The three female soloists who sing first individually and then as a trio are more comfortable in the former than the latter. Thereafter, Bertini picks up the energy level until the heavenly appearance of Mater Gloriosa, which is marred only by an unduly outspoken first horn accompaniment. Doctor Marianus' segment lacks urgency and vitality. From "Blikket auf," Bertini maintains a broad pace to the close, often ignoring Mahler's directions to pick up the tempo, but such a reading heightens the nobility and grandeur of the conclusion. How magnificently the horns call out their motif at the end of the choral section preceding the Chorus Mysticus; how thrillingly the chorus calls out *"ewig, ewig"* and the trombones intone their answer (Index 18 at 3:40). For some, Bertini's deliberate pace in the concluding section may seem plodding, but he clearly chose to use it to enhance the conclusion's majestic character.

BOULEZ, PIERRE/BBC Symphony; Edda Moser, Linda Esther Gray, Wendi Eathorne, sopranos; Elizabeth Connell, Bernadette Greevy, altos; Alberto Remedios, tenor; Siegmund Nimsgern, baritone; Marius Rintzler, bass; BBC Singers; BBC Choral Society; Scottish National Orchestra Chorus; Wandsworth School Boys Choir (perf. 1975, London) - 2-Artists FED 041.42 (1993) [86:33] Clarity is Boulez's principal concern in this performance and he achieves his goal for the most part, despite technical flaws. Extremely high recording levels and close miking virtually eliminate even a hint of softness, making more lyrical moments sound harsh. Boulez moves straight through the textural thicket of this music with consistency and spirit, if without much inflection or nuance. Stronger sections generate much power, which may be due more to the high volume level than dramatic strength. In Part II, the sound sometimes fades in and out of focus, distorting balances and continuity. Where Part I was brisk, Part II seems more weighty, even dogged at times, producing a milder, less intense effect. The vocal soloists generally sing well, with the exception of Remedios, who is overmatched in the high tessitura and succumbs sometimes to a whisper or falsetto. For the most part, Boulez keeps his huge forces together, but he evokes little magic in this objectified, sometimes rigid and sonically overblown performance. His best work comes at the closing moments of both Parts; but his forces are so exhausted by the very end that they barely make it through the final bars.

DEWAART, EDO/Netherlands Radio Philharmonic; Alessandra Marc, Gwynne Geyer, Regina Nathan, sopranos; Doris Soffel, Nancy Maultsby, altos; Vinson Cole, tenor; David Wilson-Johnson, baritone; Andrea Silvestrelli, bass; Netherlands Radio Choir; Leipzig Opera Chorus; City Boys Choir Elburg - 2-RCA 74321 276092 (1995) [83:18]
Hampered by an uneven vocal group, middling choral and orchestral forces and sonic overkill, this performance is too flawed to satisfy. Edo DeWaart gives a competent reading, but densely textured choral passages sometimes appear to ramble along aimlessly. He also lets his vocal soloists sing out to their collective hearts' content, whether their parts are marked *piano* or *forte*. In all the later symphonies in DeWaart's complete cycle, one senses inadequate preparation, causing rag-tag entrances that are most disturbing at the appearance of the final *"Alles vergänglische"* chorus. DeWaart starts Part I in fine style, with a strong, majestic main theme. But there is little relief from the high volume level of the opening, soft passages losing their delicate beauty from such overpowered sonics. Issue may be taken with a few of DeWaart's decisions: holding back into the *subito ff* outburst at #37 contrary to Mahler's

directions and speeding through the *"Hostem"* chorus more quickly than the preceding *"Accende"* passage. Part II begins ominously with a misfired cymbal entrance. DeWaart's opening *poco adagio* section seems on the brisk side, causing (with additional help from closely-miked woodwinds) the loss of the mysterioso quality that should make it shiver with anticipation. From here to the *Wäldung* chorus, one senses little personal involvement, particularly in the sluggish *allegro moderato* segment (Index 2). Volume levels are confined, ranging from *forte* to *mezzo-piano*. After an adequate, if not especially provocative Anchorite chant, the baritone and bass soloists sing adequately within the limits of their individual vocal abilities (the former sounding dry, the latter woolly). Only the tenor makes an interesting appearance during Index 9, when at least he tries to sing softly and tenderly despite his serious vocal limitations. As if captivated by the tenor's lovely *"Jung Frau"* passage, DeWaart matches the singer's gentle lyricism with a gorgeous rendition of the orchestral section that follows. Unfortunately, the female soloists have far too many vocal problems to pass muster. In the magnificent closing section, DeWaart sometimes stretches the pace considerably, as he does in the serene passage leafding into the Chorus Mysticus. What remains is too mediocre to save this performance from insignificance.

GIELEN, MICHAEL/Frankfurt Opera House-Museum Orch. & Chorus; Faye Robinson, Margaret Marshall, Hildegard Heichele, sopranos; Ortrun Wenkel, Hildegard Laurich, altos; Mallory Walker, tenor; Richard Stiwell, baritone; Simon Estes, bass; Figural Chordes Hessischen Radio; Frankfurter Kantorei and Singakadamie; Limburger Domsingknaben - 2-CBS 79238 (1981); Sony Classics SBK 48281 (1992) [79:05]
Recorded at a live concert given in Frankfurt on August 28, 1981, the most that can be said in favor of this cold, uninteresting and breezed-through performance is its conscious attempt to achieve clarity of line (especially in inner voices) often by close-miking. Tempi are consistently fast, playing is often clipped and square and choral forces sound raw or fuzzy. Gielen treats most of the music with little sensitivity and angular harshness. Despite careful balancing of inner voices, dynamic markings are sometimes ignored. Choral pronunciation has a curiously non-Latin affect (accende=assende; pacem=passem). Gielen's undramatic style communicates itself to the chorus which often sounds uninspired and lacks tightness of ensemble, especially during the difficult closing section of Part I. After a chilly opening to Part II, the more impassioned music that follows is strong and fiery if briskly paced. Clear pronunciation in the Gregorian chant section is helpful. Soloists are at best uneven: Ecstaticus is very dramatic, even operatic; Simon Estes as Profundis is too dry and woolly and the trio of female voices are dreadfully heavy-sounding and generally unpleasant. Gielen does generates some excitement in the bridge passage to the "scherzo" section of Part II and even adds subtle nuances to the passage before #77. As the music brightens, it begins to fly like the wind if only to be rudely hurled back to earth by a weak, shaky and strained tenor solo. Some untoward tempo changes interrupt the musical flow before #148. After the boys' choir enters, Gielen has difficulty keeping them together with the orchestra (## 157-161). Performances by the Penitent and Mater Gloriosa deserve praise. After a lovely Chorus Mysticus, an extremely jumbled choral entrance spoils the fortissimo climax and the final moments are run through with complete indifference.

HAITINK, BERNARD/Concertgebouw Orchestra; Ileana Cotrubas, Heather Harper, Hanneke van Bork, sopranos; Birgit Finnila, Marianne Dieleman, altos; William Cochran, tenor; Hermann Prey, baritone; Hans Sotin, bass; Collegium Musicum Amsteladamense; Toonkunstkoor, Amsterdam; De Stem des Volks, Amsterdam; Kinderkoor St. Willibrord and Pius X, Amsterdam - 2-Philips 6700 049 (1972); 420 543 (1988); 10-Philips 434 053 (1992); 442 050 (1994) [75:45]   Haitink's restrained approach works best in quieter, more lyrical sections, but stronger sections lack dramatic power. Choral forces are thin and distant until the very end, when Haitink lets them sing out. As for the soloists: Cochran is terribly strained throughout; Harper (Penitent) is somewhat shrill but sings stylishly; Prey (Ecstaticus) is very expressive; Sotin (Profundis) is strong but dry; Cotrubas (Peccatrix) is cautious and not very expressive; and Finnila (Samaritana) is rich and robust. Unless an understated approach is wanted, this version has little to offer. The major fault here is the lack of intensity, power and involvement. In short, a very controlled reading with little subtlety or nuance. A few bright spots are the buoyant scherzando of Part II (after #63); the lovely female trio at #136 (Part II) and the more engaging final section from the Chorus Mysticus to the close (though the trumpets could hold the "light motif" notes more fully).

INBAL, ELIAHU/Frankfurt Radio Symphony; Faye Robinson, Teresa Cahill, Hildegard Heichele, sopranos; Livia Budai, Jane Henschel, altos; Kenneth Riegel, tenor; Hermann Prey, baritone; Harald Stamm, bass; Chorus of Bavarian Radio; Chorus of North German Radio; Sudfunkchor Stuttgart; Chorus of West German Radio; Limberger Domsingknaben; Children's Chorus of Hessian Radio - 2-Denon 60CD 1564-65 (1987); 16-Denon 72589-604 (1989) [77:57]+ Inbal does an admirable job with the diverse forces provided him. His energy and intensity often enhance the more spirited passages of this work, but they sometimes unduly ennervate calmer sections. The clarity of linear material is impressive, even if brass sometimes overpower. What is missing is interpretive insight. Climaxes are powerful ("*Accende*" at #59 of Part I and much of the concluding section of Part II) but cannot sustain attention in their denouement. Soloists are adequate for the most part, even if integral ensemble work is sometimes faulty. In Part II, Robinson sings with force and security, which Budai lacks in high range. Henschel works well with her colleagues but has difficulty singing sweetly. As Mater Gloriosa, Heichele is not placed above or even distant from the rest of the array, but her lovely voice (even with scoops into high Bb) adds an enchanting quality to her heavenly urgings. As the Penitent, Cahill also makes a delightful impression, producing a marvelous superoctave slide after #116. Kenneth Riegel, the veteran tenor of many Eighths, sings his strenuous high tessitura with even more security here than for Bernstein (see above). Choral forces perform commendably, giving all they have in strong sections. Inbal cortrols his tendency to press forward with nervous impulsiveness in a spacious Chorus Mysticus. As he approaches the work's grandiose conclusion, instead of moving forward from #218 as written, he holds back, preparing for a climax at #220 that should have literally blown off the roof. Instead, he reserves some energy for the final build up to E-flat major, which seems almost anti-climactic in light of what preceded it. Overall, the performance is concise, and generally well-played with some memorable moments.

JÄRVI, NEEME/Gothenburg Symphony Orchestra, Gothenburg Opera Orchestra; Ulla Gustafsson, MariAnne Häggander, Carolina Sandgren, sopranos; Ulrika Tenstam, Anne Gjevang, altos; Seppo Ruohonen, tenor; Mats Persson, baritone; Johann Tilli, bass; Gothenburg Opera Chorus; Royal Stockholm Philharmonic Choir; Gothenburg Symphony Chorus Estonian Boys' Choir; Brunnsbo Children's Choir - BIS CD 700 (1994) [70:16]+ Recorded at a concert to raise funds for Estonian refugees, this version may be celebrated more for the event than the performance. The combination of diverse ensembles results in a mixed bag. Järvi conducts as if with one eye on the clock, concluding this performance in a record seventy minutes. His brisk, driven tempi work better in Part I, adding a sense of urgency and stirring up excitement. For the most part, Järvi coordinates the many divergences in this texturally-complex score effectively, while propelling the music forward intently. In Part II, however, where lack of breathing space can cause confusion in transitions between sections, Järvi's harried pace works against the natural musical flow and creation of an appropriate mood. Unremitting brisk tempi often become too inflexible (during the opening of Part II and the *Wäldung* chorus). When impulse and intensity are required, Järvi knows how to drive the point home. The *ff* entrance of celli at Index 9/3:29 has the quality of a sword thrust; the accentuation in strings at *Piu mosso* (Index 10) pierce the musical fabric to the core. In contrast, the Anchorites' chant (Index 11) seems pale, paced almost in march tempo. Most of the vocal soloists make a fair impression, with only the tenor straining noticeably. Much the same may be said for the diverse choral forces. Järvi winds his way through the vocal solos briskly, giving each performer little chance to catch his or her breath. Throughout many of the solo passages, one senses a fleeting quality which enhances underlying urgency without damaging the vocal line. By the *allegro* segment at Index 22, Järvi speeds along so swiftly that he should have to make a major adjustment for the *langsam* tempo change at 2:32. Instead, he plays through it in moderate tempo. Doctor Marianus has difficulty overcoming many vocal inadequacies (insecure pitch, wooble and frequent use of crutches). Järvi rushes through the build-up of the Marianus segment so quickly that he diminishes its impact after his spacious reading of the Mater Glorioso. He eases up for the chorus that follows, but the effect is counter-productive. While Järvi manages to hold things together for the most part, the sense of otherwordly mystery which should infuse the moments leading to the magnificent final chorus is missing, especially in the Chorus Mysticus, which is too uncoordinated with the rapid pacing that preceded it. A fast "*Alles vergängliche*" chorus concludes with an enormous (unmarked) ritard; and the final chord crescendos to a very strong bass drum cut off. The combination of rapid tempi and long ritards cause lack of cohesion and continuity

JOÓ, ÁRPÁD/Budapest Radio & TV Symphony; Éva Bártfai-Barta, Andrienne Csengery, Maria Tóth, sopranos; Júlia Hamari, Klára Takács, altos; András Molnar, tenor; Sándor Sólyom-Nagy, baritone; József Gregor, bass; Hungarian Radio & TV Chorus; Miskolc Children's Chorus; Nyregyhaza Children's Chorus - 2-Hungaroton SLPD 12543-4 (1984); 2-Sefel SEFD 5017-8 (LP) [77:13]*+   Why has this excellent recording been hiding these many years? Having never been re-issued on compact disc, its many merits are virtually lost to current audiences. Árpád Joó (whose recording of the First also deserved praise) handles this complex score in a superbly deft manner. He seems to know instinctively when to ease up into a new section or when to keep the forward motion unimpeded. The choral forces are also impressive. Perfectly balanced for both depth of field and clarity, they sing with conviction as well as precision. Such magnificent sections as the "*Accende*" and "*Hostem*" segments of Part I and the gorgeous Chorus Mysticus of Part II are thrilling. A full-bodied organ adds an extra dimension of power. Joó takes a brisk main tempo for much of Part I, but in doing so, he energizes the musical impulse without becoming overly hurried. While his forces sound overworked after #71 of Part I for a few moments, they come alive for the awesome closing section. Joó generates just as much excitement in Part II. Even if overall power levels could be stronger, an adjustment of amplifier volume serves adequately. For the most part the vocal soloists sing admirably, if the tenor and bass are somewhat weak. But the highest accolades go to the relatively unknown conductor, Árpád Joó, whose brilliant reading demands notice and praise.

KUBELIK, RAFAEL/Bavarian Radio Symphony Orchestra and Choruses; Martina Arroyo, Erna Spoorenberg, Edith Mathis, sopranos; Julia Hamari, Norma Procter, altos; Donald Grobe, tenor; Dietrich Fischer-Dieskau, baritone; Franz Crass, bass; NDR Radio and WDR Radio Choruses; Boys of the Regensburg Cathedral Choir; Women's Chorus of the Munich Motet Choir - 2-DG 2707 062 (1970); 413 232 (1988); 419 433 (1987); 10-429042 (1990); 447 529 (1995) [73:56]*+   One of the better recordings available, Kubelik's reading generates excitement throughout, even if his tempi are sometimes hard-driven. The

BRSO plays beautifully, choral forces sing clearly and the soloist group performs admirably, but for a weak tenor. Kubelik sets a quick, lively tempo from the opening of Part I, which sparkles with crisp playing and overflows with strength and excitement (listen to the dramatic outburst on "*Accende*" in Part I). Details are well-rendered; balances and sonics generally excellent. While most of Part I seems too brisk (the coda sounds almost jolly for its quick pace), Kubelik lets up enough to enable the swirling choral polyphony of the final bars come through clearly and to a stirring effect. Part II opens with a bearly audible bass pizzicato (which carries a basic motif). As the music proceeds, Kubelik elicits much energy and vitality from his players, particularly at ##18-20. Soloist passages are very expressive, especially Ecstaticus and Profundis. The "scherzo" section has a buoyant playful quality, highlighted by sharp, precise attacks and lovely female voices. All goes very well throughout much of the central section of Part II (except for a thin, dull tenor solo). Mater Gloriosa goes sour at times and the tenor's "*Blikket auf*" is weak and flabby. The choruses sing beautifully in a hushed if controlled Chorus Mysticus. Although the sopranos are on the shaky side thereafter, choral forces do themselves proud in the final moments. This is a performance still deserving of a high ranking, even among the many new versions enhanced by more modern sonics.

LENARD, ONDREJ/Shinsei Nihon Symphony; Konomi Nagoya, Fumiko Nishimatsu, Yoko Oshima, sopranos; Misato Iwamori, Yuko Ofuji, altos; Eiji Date, tenor; Hidenori Komatsu, baritone; Yasuo Yoshino, bass; Shinsei-Nikkyo Chorus; Tokyo Laien Chorus; The Little Spiritual Fantastic Singers in Arakawa, Japan - 2-Club la Boheme B-4505-6 (1990) [78:44]+   Lenard offers a respectable, generally conservative reading, enhanced by fine vocal and orchestral work. Choral forces are set in the foreground, yet can sing *pp* when called for. Clarity and proper balancing of ensembles are other pluses. Vocal soloists are generally up to par, with some weakness in the extreme ranges. Temperament is on the mild side throughout, with energy levels moderate. Lenard handles the many tempo changes expertly, only a few shifts (Part I/#54; Part II/#23) being too abrupt. His tempi are generally well-considered, both the orchestra and choruses responding to them well. One is occasionally reminded of Bernstein, minus his fire and impetuosity. In Part I more thrust is needed for the "*Accende*" chorus, while the following "*Hostem*" is sharp and intense. Like Bernstein, Lenard slows up slightly into the reprise, but without the same sense of arrival that Bernstein conveys. Some confusion in the final section of Part I is soon straightened out, and the Latin hymn concludes resoundingly. Stirring strings and brass enhance the more impassioned orchestral segments in the opening of Part II, but broader tempi (from the trumpet chorale to #23) cause momentary sagging. While the vocal soloists do not make a big impression, they cover their respective roles well enough here. Only the Penitent has a slight wobble and Soprano II cannot reach her high B-flat toward the final coda. Lenard stretches out the closing moments with majestic baring, which causes some sluggishness that detracts from the tension of the enormous build-up to the closing chorus. On the whole, however, Lenard's control, the intelligence of his conception, and the concentration and conviction of his players distinguish this performance.

MAAZEL, LORIN/Vienna Philharmonic; Sharon Sweet, Pamela Coburn, sopranos; Florence Quivar, Brigitte Fassbaender, altos; Richard Leech, tenor; Sigmund Nimsgern, baritone; Simon Estes, bass; Vienna State Opera Chorus; ORF Chorus; Arnold Schoenberg Chorus; Vienna Boys Choir - 2-Sony S2K 45754 (1990); 14-SK14K 48198 (1992) [89:39]   Given Maazel's tendency to be dispassionate and nonchalant, it is no wonder that even the splendid forces amassed for this recording fail to capture the spirit of Mahler's heaven-storming choral symphony. Lacking energy, intensity and impulse, Maazel's reading saps the music of its driving force and spiritual uplift. In addition, he tends to overplay the lyrical passages and smooth over the sharp-edged ones, e.g., the "*Accende*" section of Part

I at 6' nearly stands still for lack of motion. With few sparks generating from the podium, Part I borders on the routine, despite the more than adequate choral and orchestral ensembles. Part II comes alive periodically (for example, during the *ff* string outburst at #8); but more often the reading seems too fussy, sluggish and smoothed-over to attract attention. Even the *Wäldung* chorus treats the staccato markings on each note as detached legato signs, making their chant-like mysticism sound funereal rather than mysterious. Soloists are mostly up to their respective roles, without making any lasting impression. Maazel makes a few points: an interesting effect on minims in the chorus at Index 7/1:25, and a heavenly "*Jung Frau*" section from Index 12 to the entrance of Mater Peccatrix at Index 15. Lacking energy, Part II never gets off the ground. Even the strength of these choral forces are unable to make the final apotheosis memorable.

MITROPOULOS, DIMITRI/Vienna Philharmonic Orchestra and Choruses; M. Coertse, H. Zadek, sopranos; L. West, I. Malaniuk, contraltos; G. Zampieri, tenor; H. Prey, baritone; O. Edelmann, bass - 2-Everest SDBR 3189/2 (1960); 3359/12; 2-Enterprise LV 10001 (1995) [79:25] Although poor sonics distort a significant portion of this live performance, some parts are memorable and worth hearing, particularly in Part II. Most of Part I suffers from a severely plodding allegro tempo, played squarely and deliberately by orchestral forces that do not live up to the reputation they otherwise richly deserve. Soloists are closely-miked and generally over-balanced. Choral polyphony is often muddled but individual parts come through at times. Some affectations occur but they fail to make a positive contribution. Mitropoulos seems to lack sensitivity in his sluggish reading of much of Part I, despite a majestic close. In Part II, the opening section works fairly well at a slow tempo, adding weight to this mysteriously hushed music. The orchestra becomes more fired up for the impetuous second variation. In the Gregorian chant segment, Mitropoulos evokes a mystical, austere atmosphere. From there on the vocal solos are generally well sung to fine orchestral accompaniment, especially stirring at *sehr langsam* into #100. Some minor flaws in orchestral playing and balances detract, but the overall effect is satisfying. Tempi are unevenly treated: sometimes well controlled, at other times petulently modulated. The female vocal trio is lovely and a childlike Mater Gloriosa adds a touch of innocence to the heavenly chorus that follows. Mitropoulos imbues the Chorus Mysticus with a weighty dramatic presentment, assisted by strong bass strings. The closing section is most impressive for its majestic bearing. Even if sonics and orchestral playing could be cleaner, this performance has a few noteworthy moments.

MORRIS, WYN/Symphonia of London; Joyce Barker, Elizabeth Simon, Norma Burrows, sopranos; Joyce Blackham, Alfreda Hodgson, altos; John Mitchinson, tenor; Raymond Myers, baritone; Gwynne Howell, bass; New Philharmonia Chorus; The Bruckner-Mahler Choir of London; The Ambrosian Singers; The Orpington Junior Singers; The Highgate School Choir; Finchley Children's Music Group - 2-Independent SYM 1-2; 2-RCA CRL-2 0359 (1973); 2-IMP CPCD 1019 (1993) [91:46]+ Interpreted in the style of a traditional English oratorio, much of the work is rendered in a strong, yet stodgy manner. This interpretive approach works satisfactorily at times, particularly when a majestic character is needed, but elsewhere the music sounds ponderous, even pompous. Playing is often square and doggedly demonstrative. Morris' heavy hand renders lifeless the livelier or more impetuous passages by forcing them to mark time at a labored pace. Close miking has both its advantages and drawbacks: inner parts are audible but high volume sometimes ruins proper balances. Most impressive is the superlative performance of the choral forces, especially notable for clear pronunciation and well delineated polyphonic texture. While much of Part I is strongly assertive, a tendency toward restraint hinders what might have been a stirring performance. Part II opens very broadly, emphasizing legato phrasing, but fails to approach the more intense music that follows energetically. Morris produces some powerful moments with his weighty pacing but his tendency to smooth over sharp accents (as in the Gregorian chant section) is debilitating. His way of spinning out long, legato lines is marvelous though. The soloists are less than satisfying: the tenor is strained, Peccatrix and Aegyptiaca too heavy, Mater Gloriosa thin and colorless. Balance problems are often troublesome, some inner parts tending to protrude when they should fit more neatly within the musical context. Imbued with Elgarian pomp, the final section is only fairly effective. A few minor annoyances (a flat high C in the soprano and sloppy choral entrances) tarnish the lustrous beauty of the Mater Gloriosa and Chorus Mysticus sections.

NANUT, ANTON/Radio Symphony Orchestra of Ljubljana; Eva Kirchner, Elisabeth Kim, sopranos; Anne Schwanewilms, Etsuko Katagiri, mezzo-sopranos; Daniel Kim, tenor; Jochem Schmeckenbecher, baritone; Martin Krasnenko, bass; Hungarian Choir; Consortium Musicum and Chamber Choir RTV Ljubljana; Children's Choir RTV - 2-Digital Concerto CCT 745-6 (1993); 12-CCT 999701-9 (1994) [83:39]*   For an obscure budget label recording, this performance has much going for it. Choruses are well-balanced such that the complex inner voices come through with strength and clarity. Orchestral playing has a dimension of vitality and concentration unexpected from a regional ensemble. Undoubtedly, some of these positive qualities can be attributed to Anton Nanut, who has shown himself to be a fine Mahlerian interpreter. His perspective is essentially conservative -- he rarely ventures into interpretive by-ways contrary to Mahler's directions. He maintains steady control over his ensembles, while managing to engender a strong, vigorous response from them when needed. His tempi are generally well-conceived, rarely if sometimes succumbing to rigidity or flabbiness. Sonic levels are high and miking close, making the vocal soloists sound overbearing in ensemble passages. Male soloists range from a strong, passionate Ecstaticus (Schmeckenbecher) to a Marianus (Kim) and Profundis (Krasnenko) who sing clearly but whose respective upper ranges are limited, the former have some difficulty controlling a nervous edge that pushes the tempo. Female vocalists perform admirably, managing *pp* when called for, particularly important for the Mater Gloriosa, even if she has trouble with high B-flat. The *Wäldung* chorus has moderate bite and a mysterious atmosphere. Scherzandi elements are swift and fleeting. Nanut keeps tempi under control, maintaining a moderate pace that threatens to come apart momentarily in Part II during the "*Blikket auf*" segment. He closes it with a marvelous choral swell. From the Chorus Mysticus, Nanut takes a median tempo, neither too slow nor too brisk, gradually broadening the pace to produce a majestic close. While no match for the likes of Bernstein, Solti and Tennstedt, Nanut offers an admirable performance deserving of praise and wider distribution.

NEUMANN, VÁCLAV/Czech Philharmonic Orchestra; G. Beňačková-Čápová, D. Šounová, I. Nielsen, sopranos; V. Soukupová, L. Márová, altos; T. Moser, tenor; W. Schöne, baritone; R. Novák, bass; Prague Philharmonic Choir - 2-Pro Arte 2PAD 204; 2CDD-204 (1982); 2-Supraphon C37 7307-8 (1987); 3-111 972-2 (1993); 11-Supraphon SUP 111860 (1994) [78:54]   Neumann simply cannot muster up enough energy, dramatic intensity and sensitivity to do this massive work justice. His deliberate, restrained approach seems uncommitted and frequently becomes dull and lifeless. The orchestral performance is uneven, most seriously flawed by ragged brass playing. Choral forces are very distant and often muffled. Part I just plods along in disspirited fashion covered by hazy, constricted sonics. One would hope for more involvement in Part II, but to no avail. All seems pale and perfunctory from the opening *Adagio*. Most of the soloists are strained or rough-hewn, except for a fine Peccatrix, and the choruses lack cohesion, except for the marvelous children's group. Neumann maintains a plodding tempo throughout much of Part I, simply glossed over many sections with little effect. In Part II, a cold, harsh Mater Gloriosa and a very insensitive and brisk Adagio that follows are disappointing. The final choral climax is strong if slightly fatuous, Neumann adding crescendo to the final chord.

OZAWA, SEIJI/Boston Symphony; Faye Robinson, Judith Blegen, Deborah Sasson, sopranos; Florence Quivar, Lorna Myers, altos; Kenneth Riegel, tenor; Benjamin Luxon, baritone; Gwynne Howell, bass; Tanglewood Festival Chorus; Boston Boys' Choir - 2-Philips 6769 069; 7654069 (1981); 410 607 (1984); 14-Philips 438 874 (1995) [82:25]

This uneventful performance merits little note. Sonics are riddled with hiss and soloists are closely-miked. Ozawa sticks close to the score in a straightforward reading. Part I is rendered in a deliberate manner, sometimes squarely played and often lacking dramatic or stylistic insight. Too frequently, important voices are covered. Choral forces sound weak and unfocussed. Ozawa evokes a marvelously hushed atmosphere during the opening section of Part II. He has engaged a fine group of vocal soloists who sing well and with intelligence. Some passages come across tiresomely though (e.g., #106 and *"Blikket Auf"*). More well-defined sonics enhance the choral finale, but the brass do not play the 3-note "light" motif with which the work closes with sufficient sonic breadth.

SCHERCHEN, HERMANN/Berlin Staatskapelle; Rita Meinl-Weise and Sigrid Ekkehard, sopranos; Anneliese Müller, Gertraud Prenzlow, altos; Herbert Reinhold, tenor; Kurt Rehm, baritone; Willi Heyer-Krämer, bass; Choruses of Berlin State Opera (Perf. October 8, 1951, Berlin) {PART I ONLY} - 2-Tahra 110/111 (1994) [24:50]+

For the most part this performance of Part I is hardly distinguishable from Scherchen's recording of the entire work also made in 1951 (See Vol. I, pp. 114-115). Tempi are generally moderate but firm and well-conceived; balances favor singers over the orchestra; and vocal soloists sometimes push the tempo and rarely sing softly. Scherchen strikes a balance between weightiness and nervous energy, providing enough heft without losing impulse despite a few wavering moments into the reprise (to 17:56) and coda (#81). Choral sound is a bit raw at times but inner voice clarity is remarkable for such an early recording. How marvelous to hear the brightness of *"Lumen"* shine out from the boys' choir at 16:55, and the sharp-edged intensity of *"Hostem"* from full chorus. Moderate pacing succeeds in holding the thick-textured vocal counterpoint together. During the final bars, Scherchen holds back rather than pressing forward to enhance the conclusion's dramatic impact.

SEGERSTAM, LEIF/Danish National Radio Symphony; Inga Nielsen, Majken Bjerno, Henriette Bonde-Hansen, sopranos; Kirsten Dolberg, Anne Gjevang, altos; Raimo Sirkiä, tenor; Jorma Hynninen, baritone; Carsten Stabell, bass; Philharmonischer Chor, Berlin; Danish National Radio Choir; Copenhagen Boys' Choir - 2-Chandos CHAN 9305/6 (1994) [85:29]* Modern technology and Segerstam's juiced-up romanticism are responsible for much of the hype generated by this performance. It is remarkable how state-of-the-art sonics can boost what are actually rather mediocre forces to levels beyond their own capacities. Since it is clear from the flexive manner of Segerstam's reading that he intended pull out all the stops and give as overwhelming a performance as possible, it is no wonder that his tempi are sometimes either overbroad or set at break-neck speed. He weighs into the *"Spiritus"* and *"Accende"* choruses of Part I with a will, slows up into *"Tuorum vista,"* rushes at *etwas drängend* before calming down for *"Infirma"*, sails undauntedly into the reprise and races through the closing section. In Part II, we get much of the same tempo extremes: brisk, if vital *allegros*--all passionate and fertive--are juxtaposed with heavy underlining of particular phrases (e.g., a sudden unmarked slow up for the trumpet solo before #23 at 8:35). Whenever the direction *nicht eilen* (don't rush) appears, Segerstam takes it to mean slow down, sometimes abruptly. Sluggishness weighs down broadly paced passages (during Index 8). In fact, Segerstam maintains a broad pace for such a long stretch before the final moments that the music threatens to collapse (from #204). Given such an over-romanticized approach, an attempt to overwhelm with huge waves of percussion during the conclusion is not surprising. Yet Segerstam's overall handling of this massive score is sound, sometimes even revealing, despite his over-emphases. One particular improvement over many other recordings is the strong presence of the organ from the opening chord throughout the entire work. The soloist group is the weakest aspect of this performance, generally sounding thin and pallid and singing without complete assurance and vocal security. The orchestra, weak in string support, has a field day with strong sonic levels. Trumpets ring out blaringly at times and percussion are deafening at the close, where waves of crescendi are added to make the sonic onslaught simply overwhelming or unbearable, depending on one's taste.

SHAW, ROBERT/Atlanta Symphony; Deborah Voigt, Margaret Jane Wray, Heidi Grant, sopranos; Delores Ziegler, Marietta Simpson, mezzo-sopranos; Michael Sylvester, tenor; William Stone, baritone; Kenneth Cox, bass; Ohio State University Chorale; Ohio State University Symphonic Choir; Master Chorale of Tampa Bay; members of University of Southern Florida Chorus; Atlanta Boy Choir - Telarc CD-80267 (1991) [79:39]+ Renowned choral conductor Robert Shaw offers The Eighth as a 19th-century oratorio. But Mahler is not Verdi or romanticized Handel. Shaw's unfamiliarity with Mahler's idiom results in a dry, mild, and tenuous reading, that fails to soar to heavenly heights or generate much electricity or intensity. Orchestral playing, clearly subordinated to vocal forces, becomes a mere shadow of what it should be, rendered in a perfuctory manner and lacking Mahlerian flair. Strings barely rise above the foray when they carry principal material, taking a back seat to closely-miked soloists and carefully prepared, well-balanced choruses. Only during strong choral climaxes is any level of excitement apparent. Sobriety and civility are not Mahlerian characteristics; they sap his music of much of the wonderment it has to offer. Yet soloists sing well, especially in Part II. Of the male voices, tenor Michael Sylvester stands out as a welcome newcomer who could have a promising future in heldentenor repertory. Heidi Grant (Mater Gloriosa) sings with security of pitch and purity of tone, displaying a fine high B-flat. The female trio and Penitent also execute their parts admirably. But Shaw's reticence to let the music take wing stifles the entire performance, defusing the impact of these fine vocalists. For example, his studied, analytical approach mars what is possibly the most significant moment in the entire work, the thrilling "*Alles vergängliche*" chorus in the closing section. At the height of the huge choral crescendo ushering in this monumental pronouncement of Goethe's profound words, Mahler inserted a double bar that separates it from the chorus to follow. But Mahler carried the sopranos and altos of the second chorus over the double barline, making a sustained crescendo on the first syllable of "*Alles*" that follows. Bernstein, like most Mahlerians, ignores the tie-over and makes a clean break, while Tennstedt does the reverse but underplays it by way of compromise. Shaw, reading the markings strictly, makes the suspension of the sopranos and altos over the double barline so audible that it detracts from the dramatic impact the entrance of the full chorus should make. Such fussiness does not serve the music well but is characteristic of Shaw's entire reading.

SINOPOLI, GIUSEPPE/Philharmonia Orchestra; Cheryl Studer, Angela Maria Blasi, Sumi Jo, sopranos; Waltraud Meier, Kazuko Nagai, altos; Keith Lewis, tenor; Thomas Allen, baritone; Hans Sotin, bass; Philharmonia Chorus; Southend Boys' Choir - 2-DG 435 433 (1992) [84:13]* Sinopoli's symphonic conception of Part I is immediately engaging. His manner is strong and vital but neither spiritual nor reverential. Inflexibility and agitated *allegros* in powerful sections contrast with warm lyricism in softer passages. Gone is his penchant for rubato, although he impresses the music occasionally with his personal stamp, such as with a whispering Chorus II on "*Infirma,*" a shuddering bass tremolandi at Index 4, distant church bells, and a strong and weighty close to the reprise. Sinopoli always has a firm grip on tempo which enhances structural consistency. DG has provided spectacular sound quality, reverberant and spacious, presenting inner voices with brilliant clarity. Soloists sing better as a group than individually. Studer and Blasi grace this performance with superb vocality and thrilling high notes, but tenor Keith Lewis is miscast in this heldentenor role, often straining his white-sounding voice to the limit. Thomas Allen's top range has a ring to it that adds measurably to his impassioned reading of Pater Ecstaticus; but Hans Sotin distances himself from his Pater Profundis role, sounding woolly and colorless.

Sinopoli opens Part II rigidly, missing an opportunity to create a mysterious atmosphere by being overly concerned with proportion. But the assionate sections that follow are intensely engaging, strings digging in to each accented note forcefully. The *Wäldung* chorus is sung with too much legato to create an eerie atmosphere. But choruses of Angels and Young Angels have a captivating sprightliness which lets them breeze by untroubled. While making an effort to capture the particular character of each section of Goethe's complex text, Sinopoli consistently works them within the established framework of the whole. With some soloists (Allen) the orchestra takes priority, while with others (Blasi) the vocalist is in the foreground. The Mater Gloriosa's call heavenward does not come from afar as it should. Choral forces begin to tire before the Chorus Mysticus, yet Sinopoli maintains a very broad tempo for their final appearance, intending to build this enormous work to a grand conclusion. That he does so cannot be denied. Something is still missing: spiritual redemption is replaced by heaven-storming grandeur.

SOLTI, GEORG/Chicago Symphony; Heather Harper, Lucia Popp, Arleen Auger, sopranos; Helen Watts, Yvonne Minton, altos; Rene Kollo, tenor; John Shirley-Quirk, baritone; Martti Talvela, bass; Vienna State Opera Chorus; Vienna Singverein Chorus; Vienna Boys Choir - 2-London OSA 1295; 414 493 (1972); 10-London 430 804 (1992) [85:00]** This magnificent performance is still a favorite in spite of increasing competition. Recorded in sumptuous sound, excellently played and superbly sung (with one of the best soloist ensembles), it has so many assets that its dated sonics are no serious detraction While Solti is not as intense or as vital as Bernstein, he is both more faithful to the score and often at least as insightful. His approach is strong and dramatic but not sharp-edged or angular, except when appropriate, such as at the beginning of the development section of Part I. The "*Accende*" and "*Hostem*" sections of Part I are alive with excitement and passages leading up to the reprise are thrilling. Choral definition and balances could be more finely tuned at times, especially in the closing section which also seems too pressed. Soloists in Part II deserve special praise for both excellent vocal quality and very sensitive and passionate singing, particularly John Shirley-Quirk as a strong Ecstaticus, Martti Talvela as a dark and sinister Profundis and a superb female trio of Lucia Popp, Yvonne Minton and Helen Watts. Also praiseworthy is the self-assured singing of The Vienna Boys' Choir and the heavenly beauty of the Mater Gloriosa. Solti's interpretive sense is always on the mark. But one wonders at times whether the engineers had a hand in toning down some climaxes, particularly at the very end. Careful adjustments in stereo equipment settings will aptly compensate for any sonic shortfall.

STOKOWSKI, LEOPOLD/London Symphony; Frances Yeend, Uta Graf, Camilla Williams, sopranos; Martha Lipton, Louise Bernhardt, altos; Eugene Conley, tenor; Carlos Alexander, baritone; George London, bass; London Symphony Chorus - Penzance PR 19N (1950); 2-Music & Arts MUA 280; Arkadia CDGI 761 (1992) [77:57]

*   A rare and most interesting reading by the conductor who introduced this symphony to American audiences. Stokowski maintains a full head of steam until the soloist sections of Part II whereafter the performance loses energy to the very end. The opening *"Veni Creator Spiritus"* makes a strong impact. Soloists are marvelous (if overbalanced) and choral forces are clear and vibrant. From the development section, which begins briskly, Stokowski starts to hold back from around #29. Then suddenly a thrilling *"Accende"* (#38) bursts forth and the energy level picks up racing into the reprise. A momentary lapse (at #69) and the music again presses forward (at #76), almost falling over itself into the coda. Stokowski manages to hold back the flood for a very exciting close. Part II begins at a quick pace and proceeds through the Gregorian chant section hastily. At this point Stokowski's energy seems to fade. Ecstaticus is too slow if languidly romantic; London as Profundis sings dramatically but the tempo here begins to flag. Every time Stokowski tries to regain momentum, his efforts are short-lived, producing a sometimes labored reading. In fact, the Penitent section (from #148) drags along mercilessly, almost literally falling apart. Doctor Marianus sounds strained and Mater Gloriosa hesitates and loses pitch. What follows is ineffectual until a grand entrance at #213 where Stokowski makes a deliberate effort to infuse some life into the closing section. The result is a fast ending, devoid of percussion and only mildly exciting.

TENNSTEDT, KLAUS/London Philharmonic; Elizabeth Connell, Edith Wiens, Felicity Lott, sopranos; Trudeliese Schmidt, Nadine Denize, altos; Richard Versalle, tenor; Jorma Hynninen, baritone; Hans Sotin, bass; London Philharmonic Choir; Tiffin Boys' Choir - 2-Angel/EMI DSB/CDCB 47625 (1987); 10-CMST 64471-81 (1993) [82:34]**
Tennstedt's Eighth is among the best ever recorded. His reading is less intense than either Bernstein's or Solti's, but all the drama and spiritual uplift which this massive choral symphony should convey are brilliantly projected. Coming at the close of his complete cycle, this performance shows how Tennstedt's approach has developed over the years. His earlier affectatious tinkerings are replaced by a perfect sense of natural musical flow and an expert handling of tempo shifts and transition passages. He has also learned how to build into a strong climax without crashing into it abruptly. A few details could be criticized, but their importance is diminished in light of Tennstedt's overall extraordinary success. Choral forces are strong and well-handled if sometimes remote. Soloists vary from excellent sopranos and a strong baritone to a gutteral alto (Denize), a woolly, dry bass and a weak tenor. The Mater Gloriosa's pitch problems in high range are particularly disconcerting. EMI provides a spacious backdrop for this performance, sounding more natural than many recent issues and given a large concert hall ambience. Brass sometimes seem distant (particularly at the close of Part II) and strings lack a full measure of sonic breadth as well as sharp articulation. What impresses throughout is Tennstedt's intuitive sense of timing and natural sense of pacing. Significant inner parts are audible, yet they are presented in perspective to avoid fussiness or overbalancing. Some messiness occurs: from #92 to 96; an early cello entry at #98; an ineffective, confused female trio; and a few moments of tangled inner parts in the multiple choruses. But such defects are soon forgotten in the thrill of more magnificent moments, such as Tennstedt's brilliant reading of the deeply passionate orchestral prelude to the *Wäldung* chorus in Part II. An overwhelming feeling of release, empowered by Tennstedt's dramatic bearing, characterizes the final moments of this superlative performance.

TENNSTEDT, KLAUS/London Philharmonic Orchestra; Julia Varady, Jane Eaglen, Susan Bullock, sopranos; Trudeliese Schmidt, Jadwiga Rappé, altos; Kenneth Riegel, tenor; Eike Wilm Schulte, baritone; Hans Sotin, bass; London Philharmonic Choir; London Symphony Chorus; Eton College Boys' Choir (rec. Jan. 27/28, 1991, Royal Festival Hall, London) - EMI video 0777 7 40309/Laserdisc LDB 7 40308-1 (1993) [93]

** Despite the sonic limitations of a videotape, this version is one of the best ever recorded. Although Tennstedt's brilliant reading has not changed much from his 1986 recorded performance (see above), it is measurably enhanced by a better group of vocal soloists, more technical precision and polished playing by the LPO, and excellent balances. Without the electric shock of a Bernstein performance or the thrust and parry of Solti's, Tennstedt brings out the majesty and mystery of this glorious work as few have ever done. Most impressive is his captivating manner of rounding out sections in perfectly seamless style, shaping them naturally. One is especially grateful for the three sopranos, each of whom sings with complete vocal security throughout their respective ranges. How pleasing it is to hear a high C or Bb sung *p* as written, especially during the Mater Gloriosa's beckoning call heavenward. Even Hans Sotin sounds fuller and more impassioned here than in the earlier performance. One is not likely to forget how magically Tennstedt gradually draws his forces toward the symphony's final choral climax.

VANDERNOOT, ANDRE /Brabant Orchestra; Ruth Falcon, Roberta Alexander, Thea van der Putten, sopranos; Jard Van Nes, Elisabeth Cooymans, altos; Anton de Ridder, tenor; Siegfried Lorenz, baritone; Robert Holl, bass; Koninklijk Mannerkoor La Bonne Esperance; Philips Philharmonic Choir; De Eindhovense Christelijke Oratorium Vereniging; Eindhovens Chamber Choir; Eindhovens Madrigal Choir; Koninklijke Gemengde Zangvereniging De Volharding; Stedelijk Helmonds Concert Choir - 2-RCS 538/39 (1983) {LP} [73:07]   Despite the unexpected appearance of some notable soloists, this live performance, has few merits worth the effort it would take to obtain the recording. Vandernoot does not evidence an especially Mahlerian flair in his generally mild, smoothed over and frequently distended reading. Soloists vary from a fine pair of sopranos and a strong baritone and bass to heavyish sounding altos and an insecure, ineffective Mater Gloriosa, all of whom are too closely miked. The choruses sing clearly enough but are often confused. Orchestral playing is amateurish. In a few places the performers rise to the challenge. For example, the *piu mosso* orchestral passage in Part II, after the haunting mystery of the opening, is intensely passionate and extremely well handled. The Anchorite Chorus thereafter is suddenly twice as fast as the preceding section, despite the marking *wieder langsam* (slow again). Overall, too many elements are buried in sonic haze (such as the boys' chorus from #161 and the mandolin and celesta at #187). The lack of power adequate to meet the mighty demands of this huge work is a serious drawback. Into the final *"Alles vergänglische"* chorus, Vandernoot adds an unmarked crescendo in an attempt to compensate for this weakness, but neither such a gimmick nor his leaden tempo make the final moments as glorious as they should be.

WAKASUGI, HIROSHI /Tokyo Metropolitan Symphony; Shinobu Satoh, Misako Watanabe, Yukie Ohkura, sopranos; Naoko Ihara, Yuri Oh-Hashi, altos; Makoto Hayashi, tenor; Futoru Katsube, baritone; Keizoh Takahashi, bass; Shin-yukai Chorus; Tokyo Broadcasting Children's Chorus Group - 2-Fontec FOCD 9026/7 (1991) [77:41]
+   Despite severely restricted sonic levels and Fontec's failure to compensate for the placement of soloists behind the orchestra (Mahler so positioned them for the Munich premiere), Hiroshi Wakasugi again evidences his command of Mahler's idiom with a well-conceived reading. His temperament is reserved, placing more emphasis on lyricism than dramatic power and driving intensity, smoothing over strong contrasts and toning down biting accents. Within this context, Wakasugi handles the work intelligently and capably. He rarely strays from the score's many markings, except when he rushes through the close of the reprise of Part I (at 19:20)--giving little effect to the livelier tempo that suddenly appears after #80-- and abruptly slows down at 15:50 of Index 4 in Part II, anticipating the ritard before #164 by

6 measures. During the last 5 minutes of the symphony, Wakasugi broadens the tempo and ignores contrasting infusions of energy called for by *fliessend* (fleeting) markings to increase tension. Consequently, pacing slackens when it should move forward urgently.

DAS LIED VON DER ERDE

Movements:

1. Das Trinklied Von Jammer der Erde
   (The Drinking Song of the Earth's Sorrow)
2. Der Einsame Im Herbst (Autumn Loneliness)
3. Von Der Jugend (On Youth)
4. Von Der Schönheit (On Beauty)
5. Der Trunkene Im Frühling
   (The Drunkard in Spring)
6. Der Abschied (The Farewell)

ASAHINA, TAKASHI/Osaka Philharmonic; Naoko Ihara, alto; Makoto Hayashi, tenor - Firebird KICC 155 (1984) [63:42] Although Asahina's reading is intelligently conceived, it lacks personality and emotional involvement, sometimes sounding sterile and dispassionate. The Osaka Philharmonic perform admirably, but in a tight, constricted manner which lacks expressivity and stylistic nuance. Naoko Ihara has a strong, matronly voice with a wide vibrato. Closely miked, she buries the orchestral accompaniment at powerful climaxes in the finale, singing full-voiced throughout. The tenor also has a robust voice on top but he has trouble negotiating certain passages, coming in late on "*Du aber Mensch*" in the first song and sings too loudly throughout the *Trinklied*.

BARENBOIM, DANIEL/Chicago Symphony; Waltraud Meier, mezzo-soprano; Siegfried Jerusalem, tenor - Erato 2292-45624 (1992) [60:16]* Barenboim drives through the *Trinklied* fiercely, providing a high level of intensity in support of Jerusalem's strong, expressive reading. In fact, tenor and conductor seem more sympatico than do mezzo-soprano and conductor. The sprightly, light-hearted third and fifth songs are more characterful than the second, fourth and sixth. Barenboim appears to be more personally involved in the faster movements; but his detachment from the world-weary moody of the *Herbst* movement, the lilting charm of "On Beauty" and the profound mystery of *Der Abschied* make his rendition of these movements less than satisfying. His cool reserve is well matched with Meier's. While she has admirable vocal qualities, one senses lack of involvement, perhaps from an effort to maintain control, particularly in *Der Abschied*. That expansive final movement opens in an atmosphere of abysmal doom. As it progresses, Barenboim becomes too edgy, diving hurriedly into climaxes (before #13) or meandering dispassionately (at #17, c.7:40), despite the marking *zart leidenschaftlich* (gently passionate). Too frequently the tonal shading becomes mirky (c.9:10) or even washed out (c.12:15). Harshness sometimes pervades more rapid passages (c.16:40). Barenboim slows up into the climax at 4 measures after #46 (c.19') in a noticeably affected manner, but little that he does here or during much of the finale evokes a feeling of profound pathos. From "*Wohin ich geh?*," invoking the spirit of a Yiddish lullaby, all forces seem more in tune with the music's essence, even if the ultimate impact is still muted by a concentration on precision rather than characterization.

BERNSTEIN, LEONARD/Vienna Philharmonic; Dietrich Fischer-Dieskau, baritone; James King, tenor - London 36005; OSA 223 (1966); 417 783 (1989) [66:21]* Only a baritone of the calabre of Dietrich Fischer-Dieskau could put over the movements usually sung by a contralto with such stylish expressivity and sensitivity. Whether he is completely successful in supplanting his female alternate may be nothing more than a matter of taste (Mahler designated either voice acceptable). Personally, I prefer the contralto for greater vocal contrast with tenor and for more tenderness and warmth. Bernstein's approach waivers between nervous intensity, affectatious emotion and a moderately soulful quality akin to Walter's more sensitive treatment (see below). While many mannerisms appear, they are generally effective. James King sings admirably throughout. Fischer-Dieskau is best in "Autumn Loneliness," where his subtle manner of expression adds a touching sense of longing to these melancholy musings. Bernstein moves quickly through much of the first movement, building to a thrilling if hurried climax at the reprise. Some playing is squarish but always clean and polished. A light and airy treatment of the third song is quite charming, while exaggerated flexibility in the *Trunkene* song sounds artificial. Bernstein sets a comfortable if lingering pace for the fourth song ("On Beauty") but sometimes hesitates too long on especially evocative phrases. After a rapid middle section, Bernstein returns gradually to the original tempo which devolves into a weak and affected close. In the finale, however, the musical progress seems to border on the routine at first, despite some manneristic touches. Underlying agitation propels the music forward. What is missing is a consistently sensitive and soulful reading, notwithstanding Fischer-Dieskau's expressive vocalism. But Bernstein shows how moving he can be at ##13 and 32 and during the closing moments, which only lack the compassionate warmth of the female touch.

BERNSTEIN, LEONARD/Israel Philharmonic; Christa Ludwig, contralto; Rene Kollo, tenor - Columbia M-31919; 3-CBS M3X-37892 (1979); MK 42201 (1987); M3K 42200; Sony Classics SMK 47589 (1993) [62:20]* Taking a less mannered approach, Bernstein delivers a more temperate reading than with the VPO. Kollo is consistently more effective than King, and Ludwig (a great Mahler singer) imbues her beautiful voice with touching warmth and sensitive expression while showing outward signs of age. Although the IPO plays generally well, woodwinds sometimes treat dotted rhythms squarely. Affectations aside, Bernstein's interpretation has changed significantly only in "Autumn Loneliness," no longer treated lingeringly but more briskly paced. In *Der Abschied*, Bernstein's pacing is more hesitant, yet less affectatious. Intensity is diminished by smoothed-over accents and watered-down bass. Too often the finale seems forced and lacks sensitivity, unusual for a Bernstein reading of Mahler's music. But the overall effect is still satisfying.

BERNSTEIN, LEONARD/Israel Philharmonic; Christa Ludwig, mezzo-soprano; Rene Kollo, tenor (perf. 1972, Tel Aviv, Israel) - DG video 072 228 3 (1990) [67]* This videotape of a live performance made several years before the commercial recording with the same performers (see above) has much to offer. Both soloists are in fine form; and while the IPO appears to be slightly uncomfortable, Bernstein overcomes the players' insecurities by motivating them with the force of his deep commitment to the work. The result is sometimes quite moving. Strings sound pale in the outer movements, yet their less than rich and warm timbre produces a soft hue that suffuses the opening of the *Herbst* movement with a desert-like aura.Watching Ludwig at such close range, one is impressed by her complete control and poise, her sweet, affable smile adds a touching nuance in the finale. Kollo, while vibrant and dramatic, fails to produce a pianissimo on certain significant words in the *Trunkene* song (on "*Traum,*" "*Lenz*" and "*lacht*"). Notwithstanding a rather brisk treatment of the opening of *Der Abschied*, Bernstein makes up in intensity and depth of feeling for what the orchestra lacks in richness of sonority. During the closing of the orchestral interlude, Bernstein holds back the tempo measurably, producing a devastating denouement to this terrifying vision of Death's final victory. In the transcendental final moments, Bernstein conjures up the mystery of another world of unending bliss (although a softer upbeat entrance of the soloist on F beginning the last line of text before the final "*ewigs*" would have been preferred).

BERTINI, GARY/Cologne Radio Symphony; Marjana Lipovšek, mezzo-soprano; Ben Heppner, tenor (perf. 16/17 Nov. 1991, Suntory hall, Tokyo) - EMI CDC 7 54849 (1994) [61:55]* All participants are to be complimented on this fine performance. Bertini handles the score in a direct, unaffected manner that is neither forced nor detached from the work's dramatic and lyrical sensibilities. Both vocal soloists perform admirably, singing with expressivity and keep a watchful eye on dynamic markings. Each of the song movements is presented in a perfectly idiomatic manner, giving full expression to its particular dramatic character. In spite of some technical problems (e.g., woodwind timbre is sometimes quacky), Bertini clearly gets the most he can from this ensemble. Their years of experience with Mahler's music under Bertini have ripened them into a fine Mahlerian orchestra. While the oboe soloist's attempt at lip slurs at 22:35 of the finale, although somewhat awkward, is to be admired, one misses the impact that a more polished orchestra can make in this work. A tendency to stiffness and fussiness, and tight, clipped phrasing is a drawback; but more often than not the performance captures the spirit of the music in fine style.

DAVIS, COLIN/London Symphony; Jessye Norman, contralto; Jon Vickers, tenor - Philips 6514112; 7337112; 411 474 (1984) [68:41] Although the first appearance of these outstanding vocal soloists in a Mahler work is promising, Davis's misguided reading works against the contribution of his notable singers. This is also Davis's first effort at recording a Mahler work, and his unidiomatic reading makes that fact painfully clear. A furiously fast *Trinklied* rips roughshod over the music with little nuance or subtlety. Vickers attempts to gush out this dramatic music in fits and starts, as if he were back in Hunding's hut in *Die Walkure*. Although his heldentenor voice is strong and dynamic, Vickers is more effective as an opera singer. He has difficulty containing his stentorian tones in order to engender the lightness and delicacy required for "On Youth" and *Trunkene*. Even Norman's warm, tender voice seems veiled and her reading has a detached feeling. Such detachment works well in "Autumn Loneliness" but a lighter quality would have been more effective in "On Beauty." Davis soothes over the rougher, more accentuated details while concentrating on orchestral precision. He lacks a feeling for Viennese style, particularly in his brusque reading of "On Youth" and his stodgy, uninvolved rendition of "On Beauty." Norman's velvet-toned voice and warmth of expression are perfect for *Der Abschied*. Unfortunately, Davis's heavy-handed and stiff approach particularly in the orchestral interlude, and he has difficulty maintaining tempo control as well as eliciting an appropriately evocative atmosphere. All these problems seem like a distant memory at the close as Norman's luscious voice gradually melts into the shimmering orchestral texture.

GIULINI, CARLO MARIA/Berlin Philharmonic; Brigitte Fassbaender, contralto; Francisco Araiza, tenor - DG 413 459 (1984)*+ This superb performance might have outclassed much of the competition but for two serious detractions: a dry, wobbly contralto and an extremely fast and insensitive reading of the final moments. Giulini and the glorious BPO handle most of the work with precision, perfect balances, carefully rendered details, marvelous clarity, much dramatic strength and stylistic lyricism. Araiza (a virtual unknown to the Mahler *oeuvre*) sings with youthful spirit and in excellent voice. His vocal timbre has a whitish coloration but his voice has resonance and he sings clearly as well as intelligently. Giulini combines with him to produce one of the best readings of the *Trinklied* movement in recent memory. All the drama and pathos of this awesome music is evoked with power and depth of feeling as well as careful attention to detail. A *sotto voce* string accompaniment for the plaintive oboe solo provides a haunting yet soothing atmosphere at the opening of "Autumn Loneliness." But Fassbaender's lackluster vocal quality can only produce a dry, colorless reading. Giulini takes care in rendering details so that every accent and dynamic effect comes through the musical fabric in just the right manner. Araiza is light and carefree in "On Youth" and *Trunkene*. Throughout most of the finale Giulini's reading is so effective that it manages to compensate for Fassbaender's detachment. But a hint of what is to come occurs at the heavenly "*O Schönheit*" climax to the first part of the movement, where Giulini skips the upbeat fermata entirely and brushes this gorgeous phrase aside with shocking indifference. Yet the orchestral interlude is stunning in its dramatic intensity. Thereafter, Fassbaender makes every effort to sing with expression but her voice is too dry to evoke the spellbinding effect which a richer tone might produce. Worst of all, Giulini just takes off from #58 to the final chord despite a *langsam* marking, so that the closing pages are absolutely devoid of ethereal beauty, evoking rather a sense of earthy passion. This extremely surprising interpretive turnabout left this listener in no less than a state of shock!

HAITINK, BERNARD/Concertgebouw Orchrestra; Janet Baker, contralto; James King, tenor - Philips 6500 831; 7300362 (1975); 432 279 (1992) [64:50]*+ Haitink's version with these well-known Mahlerian singers, the superb playing of the Concertgebouw Orchestra, well-proportioned balances and excellent sound quality, remains one of his best Mahler recordings. Haitink's moderate approach is satisfying more often than not, especially in lyrical sections, where he is expressive within the confines of his objective approach. King still has enough vocal strength to drive home the drama of the *Trinklied*, although his voice does sound covered at times. Without resorting to high speed or excessive mannerisms, Haitink achieves a strong and profound reading. Baker's cool, detached manner works quite well in the "Autumn Loneliness" movement, even if some moments seem slightly overdone (e.g., at ##.9-10). A deathly cold atmosphere hovers over the music toward the close (#17). King could be lighter and more extroverted in the "On Youth" as he is to superb effect in the *Trunkene* movement. Baker's objective reading of "On Beauty" seems at odds with the lilting charm of its lyricism. After a fine middle section with its series of tempo gradations, Haitink addes a long caesura at #16, interrupting the musical flow. Although King is in fine voice for his last song, a slightly controlled, cautious orchestral treatment fails to elicit the feeling of carefree abandon that can give this song its special fascination. In *Der Abschied*, Baker could sing more warmly even when she is expressive. Haitink's tempered approach is only moderately effective but marvelous orchestral playing reproduced in very clear sonics enhance both the orchestral interlude and closing section.

HORENSTEIN, JASCHA/BBC Northern Symphony; Alfreda Hodgson, contralto; John Mitchinson, tenor - Discocorp T2; Baton 1004 (1984); Descant CD 01; Music & Arts CD 728 (1993) [67:56]** This is another highly sought-after performance by one of the all-time great Mahler interpreters. Not only are sonics quite passable, but the orchestral performance is as close to definitive as one could hope for. It is a tribute to Horenstein's mastery that he could have elicited such strength and precision from these forces, unfamiliar as they must have been with Mahler's idiom. Horenstein may be the only conductor to the term *"pesante"* in the opening tempo marking (*allegro pesante*) seriously by adding a measure of weightiness to the music's agitated intensity. Mitchinson's ability to color his voice to fit the mood is simply marvelous. Notice his dark, baritone-like quality at *"Das Firmament."* The movement's climax just before the reprise is utterly shattering. An evenly paced tempo for "Autumn Loneliness" sets an appropriately *ermüdet* (tired) mood without becoming lugubrious and enhances it with a soft, hazy glow. Hodgson has a strong voice but one senses that she keeps much in reserve while providing a warm and expressive reading. Listen to how poignantly she sings the line *"ich hab' Erquikkung not*!" The song "On Youth" has a delightful lilt and is set in a gently swaying tempo. Hodgson's pianissimos in "On Beauty" (at *"In dem Funklen"*) add a heavenly quality to the charming simplicity of Horenstein's accompaniment. He handles the tempo contrasts between movements with uncanny perfection. A restrained but comfortable approach to "On Beauty" gives way to an extroverted and energetic treatment of the *Trunkene* movement. Mitchinson's vocal gifts add colorful nuances: a dark foreboding character at *"Aus tiefstem Schauen"* and a light, devil-may-care spirit at *"und lacht."* The combination of Horenstein's unsurpassed reading and Hodgson's heavenly singing in *Der Abschied* put their performance on the level of the Ferrier/Walter version (see below). Although Horenstein gives the music its requisite weight and depth, Walter elicits more power here in his performances with The New York Philharmonic (having a much superior orchestra helps). Some special moments are worth mentioning: a broad, deeply felt reading of *"Du mein Freund"* and *"Wohin ich geh?"*; and the rare treat of a true *ppp* entrance of the soloist at #58 held to a slow tempo as marked. Hodgson sounds like an angel in the closing pages. This performance is a must for all Mahlerians as well as anyone who loves this moving masterpiece.

INBAL, ELIAHU/Frankfurt Radio Symphony; Jard Van Nes, contralto; Peter Schreier, tenor - Denon CO-72605 (1988); 16-Denon CO 72589/604 (1989) [61:20]*   This final entry in the Inbal cycle is among the best versions to appear in recent years. Inbal's generally objective approach that often produces a hard-edged, biting quality is less evident in this characterful, expressive and sometimes even thrilling performance. Schreier's voice may be too light to do the *Trinklied* justice, but he handles it servicably. Van Nes is also on the light side but she sings clearly and proficiently, if sometimes in an emotionally detached manner, particularly in *Der Abschied*. The *Trinklied* opening is thrilling in its awesomeness, Inbal setting the movement ablaze with intensity. Even Schreier seems to catch fire from Inbal's heat. The movement's fearsome climax, with its grotesque allusions, closes with a breathtaking slide on "*Lebens*." Van Nes does some of her best work in the autumn song, producing a melting lyricism that is especially captivating at #12 (*es gemahnt mich an den Schlaf*). Some distractions occur in the first two movements: after #39 in the *Trinklied* one can hear the sound of a door slamming; during the opening of the *Herbst* movement, someone seems to be humming. Van Nes' lower register is not as attractive as her middle and top ranges, darkening the otherwise lilting "On Beauty." Inbal sparks the orchestral interlude here with a sharp, quick-stepping treatment of the caricaturesque march tempo, but Van Nes seems unable to join in the fun. After an extroverted reading of the brief *Trunkene* song, Inbal makes an effort to evoke the dark, otherwordly atmosphere of *Der Abschied* by weighing heavily on accents, even in the opening oboe solo. Van Nes, while consistently proficient, sounds too detached, colorless and sometimes too loud to be fully satisfying. Even with Inbal's driving pace during the orchestral interlude, and his expressive reading of the closing section (marred by a brisk *langsam* at #58 and closely-miked final "*ewigs*"), the overall effect, while satisfying, is far from overwhelming.

KARAJAN, HERBERT VON/Berlin Philharmonic; Christa Ludwig, contralto; Ludowic Spiess and Horst Laubental, tenors (perf. 12/15/70, Berlin) - Hunt 739 CD (1990) [65:21]

*   Unique for its use of two tenors, this live performance, given several years before Karajan's commercial recording was released, evidences his strong commitment to the work. His reading is vigorous and expressive, and the BPO is in fine form, despite a few miscues (e.g., clarinet in the finale at the close of the "*Wohin ich geh*" verse). While no information is provided about which tenor sings what songs, Horst Laubental, being more of a heldentenor, is probably in service for the *Trinklied* (and possibly *Von der Jugend*), while Spiess appears in *Trunkene*. The former, despite his vocal limitations in the lower ranges, admirably puts across the fiery opening movement. In *Trunkene*, Spiess strains and wobbles on top but elicits soft and lovely pianissimi on "*Traum*" and "*und lacht.*" Of course, Christa Ludwig is one of the finest singers to grace this work since Kathleen Ferrier. Warmth and expressivity, together with security and beauty of tone, are her well known assets. Karajan often hurries through the music and jumps quickly from movement to movement without a hair's-breadth of hesitation, not allowing the close of each movement enough time to make a lasting impression. Some well-placed hesitations in the "*O Schönheit*" climax to the first poem add inflection to a rather stiff opening. Though recorded at high volume levels, *Der Abschied* is a marvel of beauty and depth of feeling. How poignant are the rising thirds after "*Die Welt schleff ein,*" calling to mind a similar use of this interval by English horn in the Nietzsche movement of the Third. Ludwig's questioning of the necessity of this farewell comes across as a cry from the depth's of her soul. Her final "*ewigs*" fade wistfully in the closing measures.

KARAJAN, HERBERT VON/Berlin Philharmonic; Christa Ludwig, mezzo-soprano; Rene Kollo, tenor (perf. 27 October, 1972, Salzburg) - Foyer 1CF 2056 (1991) [62:00]*
    Interpretively, little has changed here from Karajan's 1970 recorded performance in Berlin (see vol. 1, pp.124-125), but for Rene Kollo's appearance in the tenor parts. Once again the outer movements literally seethe with riveting intensity, while the four intervening songs are generally well characterized. The *Trinklied* requires a more stentorian vocal timbre than Kollo possesses. Yet he sings with expressive nuance and sufficient dramatic import. An underlying agitation seems a countervailing force to what should be a more "*ermüdet*" (weary) quality in the *Herbst* song. While Ludwig tries to convey that quintessential character in her reading, Karajan chills the atmosphere with her rigid approach to tempo. Some tempo problems also detract from what is an essentially cheery *Von der Jugend* movement. After a fine beginning, Karajan suddenly picks up the tempo at #1 and Kollo follows suit by doing the same elsewhere (while the solo trumpet at #5 tries to hold back the tempo sluggishly). Conversely, at around 2:35 into the "On Beauty" movement (into #8), Karajan makes an effort to weigh down the tempo slightly, causing some confusion. But Ludwig's marvelous combination of expressivity and control, and Karajan's restraint when accompanying her, combine nicely to provide a fine rendition. A spirited *Trunkene* finds Kollo ignoring most of the softer dynamic markings, thereby emphasizing the exuberant over the lyric elements of this brief but difficult lied. As in the earlier version, Karajan characterizes *Der Abschied* with more ferocity than austerity. Close-miking and high volume levels may give a false impression of actual performance balances. While the BPO sometimes sounds icy cold, Karajan makes its timbre sound even more chilling in an orchestral interlude of massive proportions, especially apparent in the gaping maw of the yowling three-note bass motif which frequently underlies or interrupts the section's musical progress. One is more dissapointed by the high volume levels and ragged sonic quality toward the close (especially disturbing from "*Die liebe Erde,*" where even Ludwig cools to Karajan's detachment). Otherwise, Ludwig is more responsible for the finer moments of the finale than any other performer here.

KEILBERTH, JOSEPH/Bamberg Symphony; Fritz Wunderlich, tenor; Dietrich Fischer-Dieskau, baritone (1963) - CinCin CCCD 1026 (1994) [59:58]*   Having probably the two best male singers available for this performance considerably increases its likelihood of success. Keilberth supports them with a generally well-conceived, traditional reading, the effect of which is diminished only by occasional orchestral lapses. Sonics are severely covered and distant. Each movement has character and is rendered with remarkable clarity. Keilberth's fierce, sharp-edged approach to the *Trinklied* provides a perfect setting for Wunderlich's brilliant performance. Notice how touchingly he accents the word *"leeren"* before #19 (at 2:50). His outburst on the vision of an ape crouching menacingly in the graveyard is truly shattering! (Curiously he replaces the word *"jetzt"* with *"so"* in the concluding section). Keilberth elicits an atmosphere of world-weariness by his fluid approach to tempo in the *Herbst* movement, that Fischer-Dieskau graces with tender lyricism (how lovely the sentiment before #10 on *"der Lotos bluten auf dem Wasser ziehn"* and how poignant at 4:30 on *"mein Herz ist müde"*). Each of the next three songs is treated in fine style by all concerned. Wunderlich's delightfully ebullient, head-in-the-clouds *Trunkene* is thoroughly captivating. As one might expect, Fischer-Dieskau captures the spirit of the *Der Abschied* as no other baritone in recent memory. Keilberth's reading is also impressive, particularly in the opening and closing moments. Listen to the deeply mournful horns wailing on the farewell motif in thirds during the opening section, and the softness and delicacy with which the closing measures fade into oblivion. While imprecision mars parts of the orchestral interlude, the section ends with frightening growls on low C in trombones. The English horn is sometimes over-exposed (after #53) and has difficulty with the theme thereafter. By and large this version succeeds due to the many merits of its two great vocalists.

KLEIBER, CARLOS/Vienna Symphony; Christa Ludwig, mezzo-soprano; Waldemar Kmentt, tenor (perf. 1967) - Nuova Era CD 2224 (1988); Memories 4189 (1992); Exclusive EXL 92553 (1993); Enterprise LV 905 [58:10]+   Kleiber offers an impulsive and riveting reading that is effective in the outer movements but is marred by orchestral flaws, a tendency to push tempi hastily, and an icy cold detachment in the finale. Close-miking ruins softer segments and is particularly disturbing in the finale moments of *Der Abschied* (at #58, where both a brisk tempo and high volume are contrary to Mahler's markings). Kleiber's almost savage ferocity drives the *Trinklied* to the height of dramatic intensity. Kmentt, in spite of his vocal limitations (straining in top range), makes it through this extremely difficult movement. He has similar problems in "On Youth," but his exuberant manner in *Trunkene* makes it the best number in this recording. Both high volume levels and a *mosso* tempo fail to engender an *ermüdet* (tired) feeling at the opening of the *Herbst* song. Thereafter, Kleiber handles the woodwinds nicely, and later (c. #9-10) creates an atmosphere of profound melancholy that poignantly accompanies Ludwig's world-weary musings. *Der Abschied* is somewhat of a disappointment. Although the first two measures are inaudible, loud volume subsequently takes its toll. Clipped rhythms and quick 32nd-notes create nervous anticipation rather than profound, eschatological contemplation. The main tempo (at #4) is brisk and what follows seems pressed and impulsive rather than meditative. While the principal subject is certainly a march, it is not a quick step. Given Kleiber's cold, detached presentment, the soulful spirit of this music turns into unnerving fearfulness. A glimmer of soulfulness appears occasionally, e.g., at #24 through #30, but the climax of the first poem (*"O Schöheit"*) vanishes too quickly. Nervous energy intensifies the orchestral interlude, spilling over beyond the soloist's return. The closing section is certainly passionate, and Ludwig sings beautifully; but is passion the emotion to be conveyed here or transcendental bliss?

KLEMPERER, OTTO/New Philharmonia Orchestra; Christa Ludwig, contralto; Fritz Wunderlich, tenor - Angel S-3704 (1967); CDC 47231 (1985) [63:07]*+   Considered by many to contain the ideal vocalist team, this version ranks securely among best. None of the tenors appearing on these numerous recordings surpasses Wunderlich in both his vocal quality and interpretive style. Ludwig is equally marvelous, capturing a broad range of emotions in her three songs in perfectly idiomatic style and conceptual understanding. Klemperer generates much intensity throughout the stronger sections of the first song, reaching a climax nothing short of immense. In the second song, he evokes a somber mood and Ludwig captures the feeling of desperate loneliness with assurance. While "On Youth" seems to be viewed from the distant vantage point of old age, a comfortable and easy manner elicits a dreamy effect enhanced by Wunderlich's thoroughly captivating expressivity. Klemperer takes a deliberate and restrained approach to "On Beauty," too moderate to be completely satisfying, particularly in the closing moments. *Trunkene* is too constricted to elicit much spirit, but Wunderlich evokes such a feeling of joyous abandon that Klemperer's more objective accompaniment fades into obscurity. Plumbing the depths with deep bass sound at the opening of *Der Abschied*, Klemperer sets the mood for a dramatic and sensitive reading of this profound movement. Ludwig sings as if in communion with another world. Her popularity among conductors of this work is a tribute to her brilliant interpretive sense and wondrous vocal quality.

KLETZKI, PAUL/Philharmonia Orchestra; Dietrich Fischer-Dieskau, baritone; Murray Dickie, tenor - Angel S-3607 (1960); Seraphim S-60260; EMI CDZB 62707 (1994) [60:22]
* The most attractive aspect of this recording is a more youthful Fischer-Dieskau than on Bernstein's version with the LSO (see above). Kletzki turns in a generally fine performance despite lack of orchestral precision and unfocussed sonics at high levels. He is usually on track stylistically even if tempi are frequently quick in all but the final movement. Murray Dickie has a light, constricted voice that he uses unevenly, yet he manages to sing characterfully throughout and is most effective in his spirited reading of the *Trunkene* song. Fischer-Dieskau adds a sense of stark melancholy to the meandering strains of "Autumn Loneliness." His lower register is richer here than with Bernstein and he uses it to engender much warmth in "On Beauty" and extremely profound sentiments in the finale, especially at the poignant "*Wohin ich geh?*" passage (#53). Kletzki presses intently through the development section in *Der Abschied* to reach the reprise and separates the booming trombone chords at the climax with long commas. While he elicits a disturbingly mournful effect from the horns after #49, he could be more evocative in the closing moments.

KRIPS, JOSEPH/Vienna Symphony; Anna Reynolds, alto; Jess Thomas, tenor (perf. 24 June 1972) - Orfeo 278 921 B (1992) [63:22]+ The bright, luscious voice of Anna Reynolds is one major attraction of this historical performance. Had Krips provided her with a more inspired reading, their collaboration might have been more satisfying. He seems too impersonal in his approach to either cajole emotion from his singers or encourage the orchestra to intensify the drama. In the outer movements where mildness or mere precision will not suffice, Krips's ministerial oversight weakens the overall impact. The high tessitura of the tenor part causes much strain on Jess Thomas's voice, made more noticeable by close miking. Krips is usually careful to follow Mahler's markings; however, a few lapses occur: a suddenly faster tempo at #25 and trumpet staccatos instead of accents at 6:28 in the *Trinklied*. Both singer and conductor make an effort to come up to the full measure of the gruesome climax in the first song. The four diverting songs that act like intermezzi between the more profound the outer movements are generally well rendered. A gentle lilting quality, tinged by bittersweet harmonies, provides a fitting accompaniment for Anna Reynolds' beautiful reading of the *Herbst* song (N.B., listen to the lovely expression of the cello at c.4:00). Even if Thomas shows signs of wear in "On Youth," he handles it deftly. "On Beauty" has a restive, if restrained quality, enhanced by Reynolds' captivating voice. In *Trunkene*, Thomas tries to capture its extroverted spirit; yet he could be more consistent in his treatment of dynamic markings: after a marvelous *ppp* on a high A-natural on "*Traum*" he sings "*Lenz*" after #8 loudly despite its *pp* marking. His only serious flaw is an early entrance on "*Ein Engel singt im Baum.*" Reynold's *Der Abschied* is aglow with warmth and character, but Krips restrains the orchestra so strongly that his reading falls flat. Although sound quality is clear and reverberant, strong background noises in soft passages at the end are distracting.

KUBELIK, RAFAEL/Bavarian Radio Symphony; Janet Baker, mezzo-soprano; Waldemar Kmentt, tenor (perf. 1975) - 2-Originals SH 806/7 (1994) [61:26]*
Unfortunately, no performance data is given for this important release. Baker is as deeply moving in her closing *Der Abschied* as she was under Szell (see below), nearly whispering her duets with the flute as if in confidence, and expressing each line and phrase beautifully. Waldemar Kmentt has a robust, darkly-toned voice, most impressive in the opening *Trinklied* and delightfully spry in "On Youth." Kubelik vitalizes his BRSO players, indulging rarely in affectations, if not always keeping to the letter of the score. In *Trinklied* he ignores the tempo markings after #2 and #16, choosing to return each time to the main tempo when the principal theme appears instead of earlier as marked. The *Herbst* song is slightly pressed and not always on target (violas lose control before #14), but Baker sings it with grace and style. Even with close-miking, Baker sings softly enough to delight in "On Beauty." Notice how Kubelik tries to get the flute/oboe figure before #21 to sound like the "*lebewohl*" (farewell) motif of a falling second. From some reason, he finds it necessary to make cuts in--of all songs --*Trunkene*. In fact, the characteristic line "*Ich trinke, bis ich nicht mehr kann*" is completely missing! Most of the first poem of *Der Abschied* goes generally well, enhanced by Baker's soft, lovely voice, which rises to the occasion for the climactic closing section. Some moments during the following orchestral interlude can make one shudder (e.g., the opening bass tremelandi and closing bass string sforzando on low C). In between Kubelik evokes a deep sense of world-weary sorrow. From Baker's return to the close, her deeply moving performance is simply out of this world.

LEPPARD, RAYMOND/ BBC Northern Symphony; Janet Baker, mezzo-soprano; John Mitchinson, tenor (perf. 22 Feb. 1977, Free Trade Hall, Manchester) - BBC Radio Classics BBCRD 9120 (1995) [64:19]+ This BBC radio transcription pairs two experienced Mahler singers against a conductor and orchestra having little experience with Mahler's music. The resulting contrast has a telling effect upon the performance. Raymond Leppard offers a neat and tidy reading, free of affectation but also uneven in mood of expression and depth of feeling. The first movement has plenty of dynamic thrust and intensity. Even though Mitchinson shows signs of vocal wear, his familiarity with the music and strong identification with its dramatic content sees him through its punishing vocalism in fine style. Leppard creates just the right atmosphere of forlorn moodiness to open the next movement, but he fixes his main tempo so inflexibly that the music sounds more vapid than bemused. Janet Baker, who is undoubtedly one of the greatest Mahler singers we have ever had the good fortune to hear in this work, sings nicely, despite close-miking and an obtrusively strong entrance. How poignant is her moving line "*Ich hab' Erquikkung Not!*"; and how contrastingly empty sound her last words, "*mild aufzutrocknen.*" Leppard gives her a wide berth, and she uses it expertly. In "On Beauty" Leppard deftly handles the sudden shift into the *andante* main theme after the tiered *allegro* segments. Mitchinson provides a characterful reading of the brief *Trunkene* movement. Listen to how he darkens his voice for "*aus tiefem Schauen lauscht' ich auf*" (2:50). The finale is most disappointing, however. Leppard and the BBC Northern seem to have no idea what moods are being expressed here. Lacking urgency and profundity, they take a back seat to Baker, providing her with an accompaniment wiped clean of emotion and played in a forced and rigid manner. But when Baker returns after an unimpressive orchestral interlude, she holds the listener spellbound with the purity of her voice, the gracefulness of her style and the expressivity of her reading. How movingly she touches the heartstrings when she tells us of an unhappy life (on *"das Glück nicht hold!"*), and how longingly she relates the tale of her search for meaning with the words *"ich wandre in die Berge."* Her final *"ewigs"* could melt the hardest heart. Had she had a more sensitive accompaniment, the result would have been even more unforgettable.

NANUT, ANTON/Radio Symphony Orchestra of Ljubljana; Glenys Linos, mezzo-soprano; Zeger Vandersteene, tenor - Pilz 160 124 (1990); 160 417 (1991); Onyx Classics 266 663 (1992); Digital Concerto CCT 689 (1990); 12-CCT 999701 (1992) [61:13]

Given the limitations of his orchestra but with the help of a fine heldentenor, Nanut manages a passable performance. The most serious drawback here is the mezzo-soprano. Her operatic treatment of each of her lieder is far off the mark. She sounds like a scolding schoolmarm in "On Beauty" and a Fata Morgana in *Der Abschied*. Nanut's approach is straight and invariable, sometimes lacking warmth and subtlety. He is at his best when letting the music speak for itself. When it requires a more refined, sensitive or poignant treatment, he only touches the surface, content to embellish strong orchestral sections with overplayed brass and percussion (N.B., are such loud tam-tam whacks at the close of the orchestral interlude in *Der Abschied* really necessary?). But Nanut can stir up passion when called for (the orchestral interlude is often quite dramatic); and he even adds a few touches of his own in the finale, slowing up for the clarinets into #48 before the soloist's recitation and before the voice enters at #50. Woodwinds and brass are played rigidly and not always securely (the first trumpet cannot manage a high C after #29 in the first movement). As in too many other recordings, close-miking detracts from appropriate atmospheres (particularly in the *Herbst* and *Der Abschied* movements). What one misses most here is a visionary atmosphere that transcends earthly woes in the closing moments.

NEUMANN, VÁCLAV/Czech Philharmonic; Christa Ludwig, mezzo-soprano; Thomas Moser, tenor (perf. 7 April 1983) - Praga PR 254 052 (1994) [58:40]* Christa Ludwig is the principal asset of this version. One has come to expect a high quality performance from her in this work, and she delivers, notwithstanding close miking and Neumann's detached, sometimes edgy approach. Tenor Thomas Moser strains and wobbles through the *Trinklied* but manages a competent performance with no surprises. His efforts in "On Youth" and *Trunkene* are more successful. In the *Herbst* song, Neumann begins to press forward from the outset, causing underlying agitation to detract from what should be a careworn feeling. His demonstrative treatment of the clarinets before #5 (and elsewhere) seems slightly out of character. Ludwig's subtlety of expression acts as a counterfoil to Neumann's rigidity. Uncharacteristically, he slows up into #19 (8') instead of pressing forward as marked. Ludwig's charming and graceful reading of "On Beauty" contrasts with Neumann's sprightly, vivacious approach. After an excellent opening that immediately establishes the proper mood, *Der Abschied* works well, except for unwanted high volume toward the close. Ludwig's pure, seamless tone, and her controlled but subtle manner combine to deliver a deeply poignant farewell. Neumann adds some effective touches, such as a haunting treatment of the horn call at 8:35 before the second vocal recitative. The mandolin starts mistakenly with a shake on dotted quarter notes at #23 (10:10), marring what should be a hushed opening of this section. Then unrelenting tension becomes unnerving and detracts from the solemnity of the drama. The opening of the orchestral interlude (13:44) has a cavernous quality, but raw orchestral timbre, intonation problems in woodwinds, a constant feeling of nervous agitation and emotional reserve make this important segment less convincing. A slow-up into the theme before #43 seems grotesque and out of place, but Neumann makes a strong impression as the section moves to a climax by hesitating slightly at its height (17:28+). Ludwig's rendition of *Der Abschied*'s second poem is simply gorgeous. Unfortunately, she is too strong on "*Die liebe Erde*" (#58), even making a crescendo on it; and she continues at too high a dynamic level into the final "*ewigs.*" She may well have been affected by Neumann icy treatment of these closing moments.

ORMANDY, EUGENE/Philadelphia Orchestra; Lili Chookasian, contralto; Richard Lewis, tenor - Columbia MS-6946 (1967); 3--CBS D3S 774 (1968); Sony SBK 53518 (1994) [58:07] Ormandy takes few chances in this reading done strictly by the book. Sonics are clear and bright and orchestral performance is excellent. Lewis tends to smooth over the rough spots in the *Trinklied*, singing with little verve in a square and rigid reading with questionable pronunciation. He is more satisfying in "On Youth" than in *Trunkene*; in the latter his constricted style is in opposition to the mood of gay abandon that should come through. Loud woodwinds throughout much of "Autumn Loneliness" hamper the quietly yearning sentiments of Chookasian's vocalism. Tempi are slightly on the pressed side. Chookasian sounds too hefty in "On Beauty," lacking the sense of personal intimacy that best serves this charming music. Worse still, Ormandy seems to lack inspiration in the finale, producing a generally uninvolved, cool and objective reading that downplays the dramatic aspects with brisk tempi.

REINER, FRITZ/Chicago Symphony; Maureen Forrester, contralto; Richard Lewis, tenor - RCA LSC 6087 (1959); VICS 1390; GL 43272; AGL 1-5248; 5248 (1987); 60178 (1989;1991) [62:26]* Reiner's approach is cool and detached, but he manages to provide some stirring moments, particularly during the climax ushering in the reprise in the *Trinklied*, from #10 in "Autumn Loneliness" and at the close of *Der Abschied*. As one might expect from Reiner, his reading is exceptionally detailed and precise. Richard Lewis produces a dry tone which is sometimes matched only by his own brand of objectivity, but he can be expressive when he gets caught up in the music. That seasoned Mahler singer Maureen Forrester sounds on the heavy side here even though she is expressive and perceptive, particularly in the closing pages. Rather strange, dullish brass usher in the opening movement which contains several unwarranted affectations in the form of brief ritardandi. Razor-sharp precision and underlying tension characterize the development section. Lewis adds a touchingly mournful quality to the end of the climactic section which precedes the reprise. Reiner captures the *ermüdet* feeling of "Autumn Loneliness" perfectly, maintaining a delicate balance between detached sensibility and deeply-felt melancholy. Though a very comfortable, yet playful setting is created for "On Youth," it takes several measures for Lewis to get into the mood. When he does, the spirits lighten measurably. Opening at almost the same tempo as its preceding movement, "On Beauty" deports itself with more manner of charm and grace, despite a cool orchestral accompaniment. Lewis is definitely not right for *Trunkene* even if he makes an effort to be expressive. While the opening of *Der Abschied* could be more poignant and the main tempo less emotive, Forrester sings beautifully with more tenderness and warmth in the closing pages than Reiner generates. He maintains such a distance from the aesthetic core of this music that he projects an iciness that which never melts sufficiently to warm the closing pages.

RODZINSKY, ARTUR/New York Philharmonic; Kirsten Thorborg, contralto; Charles Kullman, tenor (perf. 19 Nov. 1944) - Baton 1001 (1984); AS Disc AS 528 (1992) [58:35] * Performed with the identical soloists appearing in Walter's notable version with the VPO (see below), this performance sounds curiously similar to Walter's but for intermittent applause and Thorborg's difficulty in staying on pitch. Rodzinski provides a generally acceptable reading and the NYP sounds in relatively good shape despite troublesome surface and background noises. Kullman sings with enthusiasm and vigor. He only makes one miscue in the first movement, coming in late into #46. Thorborg has some pitch problems mostly in the lower register (more noticable in "Autumn Loneliness" and the finale *"ewigs"* of *Der Abschied*). While not very insightful, Rodzinski never brutalizes the music with disturbing affectations but sticks closely to the letter of the score. Kullman handles "On Youth" and *Trunkene* with youthful bravado. A lively approach to "On Beauty" lets the music flow along without uncomfortable restraint. Thorborg is in more control here. *Der Abschied* is generally fine, except for some hurried passages and sloppy playing at *"O Schönheit."* The orchestral interlude is forceful and dramatic but contains long caesuras before #40 that take too much of a slice out of the forward motion. The closing moments are not especially interesting, particularly marred by Thorborg's pitch problems.

ROSBAUD, HANS/Southwest German Radio Orchestra; Grace Hoffman, contralto; Helmut Melchert, tenor - Vox PL 10910; STPL 510912 (1959); STPL 510910 (1965); Turnabout 34220 (1968); Club National du Disque 804; Stradivarius STR 10011 (1989); 2-Vox Box CDX2 5518 (1995) [62:41] Rosbaud's reading is cool and controlled, yet there is some underlying tension which adds vigor to the opening movement. The performance is well played and sung, close miking adding linear clarity to what is lost in sectional balance. A very agitated but expressive first movement finds Melchert in heldentenor-like voice. A shattering climax caps a dynamic reading. While Hoffman is somewhat thin on top and gutteral in her bottom range, she sings stylishly if with too much spirit in "Autumn Loneliness." Despite a controlled pace, "On Youth" flows along nicely and is well sung, viewing its subject from the distance of age. Clarity of line enhances Rosbaud's perky if detached reading of "On Beauty." Although Melchert has a stentorian voice, he shows in the *Trunkene* lied that he can sing lightly and with youthful exuberance which adds spirit to Rosbaud's slightly cool approach. In *Der Abschied*, Rosbaud takes a quick tempo for the opening; his objective reading, while not lacking expression, seems on the harsh side at times, particularly at the aptly referenced *"O Schönheit"* climax of the first poem. Hoffman sings adequately but mirrors Rosbaud in her icy cold detachment. The orchestral interlude becomes so intense as to sound angry and the closing moments seem frozen in endless time and space.

ROSBAUD, HANS/Cologne Radio Symphony; Grace Hoffman, contralto; Ernst Haeflinger, tenor (perf., 18 April 1955) - Phoenix PX 701.1 (1995) [62:44]+ Rosbaud's generally objective approach differs little in this live concert performance from that presented in his commercial recording four years later, yet occasional moments of warmth and tenderness occur, as if out of context (e.g., at the beginning of the second poem in *Der Abschied*). Tempi and demeanor are generally on the brisk, cool side, except for a slackened pace and mild temperament in "On Youth," seeming to contradict the lightness and vigor one might expect from the title of this song. Unlike the later version, Rosbaud occasionally slackens the pace of the principal theme in the *Trinklied*, but manages to become more forceful and intense as this movement proceeds to its terrifying climax. Ernst Haeflinger sounds slightly raspier and more strained here than he does later under Bruno Walter (see below). Some balance problems intrude: an unduly loud trumpet into the developement section (4:25) becomes almost inaudible for its *ff* statement of the main theme at the close. Rosbaud sets a *mosso* pace for "Autumn Loneliness" that eases up nicely on the main theme's return at 6:40 (#15). Grace Hoffman sings softly and gently, despite exceedingly strong woodwind accompaniment. The climax of this song seems a bit mild (#18) for its textual import. In "On Beauty," Rosbaud plunges rapidly into the brisker middle section, rather than easing into it as directed, and imbues an almost angry presentment as he hurries through an orchestral segment marked *allegro*. Haeflinger is as characterful in the *Trunkene* movement as he will be later under Walter, deftly contrasting extroverted effusiveness with dream-like musing. Unaffected by Rosbaud's icy cold detachment, Hoffman projects warmth and touching sincerity into her reading of *Der Abschied*, which seems less apparent in her later recording with Rosbaud. She even tries to hold back Rosbaud's agitated opening tempo at her initial entrance. While she sometimes succeeds in defusing Rosbaud's objective manner, close miking of both her voice and some inner instrumental lines creates high volume that sometimes chills the atmosphere, particularly during the closing section. During the orchestral interlude, nearly two full measures after #41 are lost. Despite its many flaws and generally detached demeanor, this performance is preferable to Rosbaud's later commercial recording reviewed above.

SANDERLING, KURT/Berlin Symphony; Birgit Finnila, alto; Peter Schreier, tenor - Ars Vivendi 2100 207 (1991) [61:54] What the BSO lacks in orchestral color and fullness of string sound, Sanderling makes up for in his well-conceived, traditional reading. The one serious problem with this performance is the expressionless vocalism of Birgit Finnila. Her pale, bone-dry timbre anesthetizes Sanderling's aptly characterized *Herbst* movement; her gutteral leadenness weighs down "On Beauty;" and her inability to express the emotions of *Der Abschied* makes what should be profound music seem superficial. Although Peter Schreier starts the *Trinklied* by giving his usually liquid, if light vocal timbre a Beckmesserian character, he later sings full-voiced and clearly, rising to the occasion with the help of Sanderling's brilliant reading. In each of his other two contributions, Schreier's high-spirited approach is captivating. Given the spacious opening, *Der Abschied* might have succeeded with a more expressive vocalist. Sanderling seems to catch Finnila's detachment. Even the orchestral interlude seems underdone, with the closing moments failing to evoke Mahler's profound mystique.

SCHURICHT, CARL/Concertgebouw Orchestra; Kerstin Thorborg, mezzo-soprano; Carl Martin Ohmann, tenor (perf. 5 Oct. 1939, Amsterdam) - Archiphon ARCH 3.1 (1993) [62:40]+ This performance occurred on the eve of the Nazi invasion of Holland. Its historical significance is evident during the performance, when, at the close of the orchestral interlude in *Der Abschied*, a woman clearly calls out *"Deutschland über alles, Herr Schuricht!"* This attempt to provoke a disturbance seems to have little impact upon the performance. Thorborg is in fine voice, even if her approach is more operatic than songlike. She has difficulties in long-lined passages (in "On Beauty") and close-miking makes it difficult for her to contain her strong voice during the closing moments of *Der Abschied*. Carl Martin Ohmann's robust voice enhances both his forceful and dynamic mode of expression in *Trinklied* and his characterful reading of *Trunkene*. Schuricht's approach is generally well-conceived, overcoming scattered flaws in precision. The solo oboe in *Der Abschied* has a quacky, pinched intonation and hurtles over the grace-note turns during the opening too quickly; and the flute soloist skips two measures at the end of the duet with the vocalist, jumping headlong into #23 (10:46). A mournful note is struck by horns after #41 during the orchestral interlude that ends with terrifying jabs in the trombones. More delicacy, softness and spaciousness would have improved the atmosphere of the final moments.

SOLTI, GEORG/Royal Concertgebouw Orchestra; Marjana Lipovšek, mezzo-soprano; Thomas Moser, tenor - London 440 314 (1992) [62:58]+ Marjana Lipovšek's warm, pleasing voice is the main attraction in this otherwise only moderately appealing recording. Solti, from whom one expects much energy and intensity, shows less of these characteristics than usual. Fatuous horns at the very opening temper one's hope for a typical Soltian drive. Although the opening *Trinklied* is not free of Solti's urgent impulse, all but the climactic section before the final reprise give the impression of being on auto-pilot. Thomas Moser manages full-throated power when called for, despite wear on his voice from advancing years. He has less difficulty in "On Youth" and delivers a well-conceived characterization of a "Drunkard in Spring." The round tone and expressive quality of Lipovšek's rich sonosity provides the most pleasing vocalism here, especially in *Der Abschied*. Solti makes little effort to rethink his earlier reading, and while his overall approach is certainly appropriate, one senses an unaccustomed detachment. Consequently, orchestral playing becomes stiff when it should relax or faulty when precision would enhance the dramatic impact (at climaxes, such as at 6:35 of *Der Abschied*). Despite these problems, Lipovšek's warm lyricism carries the finale, especially with her enchanting *pianissimos* at the close.

SZELL, GEORGE/Cleveland Orchestra; Maureen Forrester, contralto; Richard Lewis, tenor (perf. 21 April 1967, Berlin) - Hunt/Arkadia CDGI 745 (1991) [62:44]* In this live performance, Szell's reading is basically the same as the one he gave for a Cleveland audience three years later (see below). He emphasizes the stark, fierce aspects of the outer movements while glossing over the simpler, more congenial moods of the inner movements. Even more than in his later performance, one senses an agitation that infects the lighter songs with hyper-tension (particularly noticeable in "On Beauty"). The horrific vision of the *Trinklied*'s "graveyard scene" is unreservedly laid bare, and Der *Abschied*'s orchestral interlude has rarely been so terrifying. From its opening shudder to the final knife-thrust (both in bass strings), Szell (and Mahler) depict a dark, barren underworld, with cavernous sounds and wailing cries that are reminiscent of the atmosphere Bartok created in **Bluebeard's Castle**. Elsewhere, Szell seems less involved. He rushes through passionate sections (such on "*O Schönheit*" at the height of the first part of *Der Abschied*), giving little time to elicit deeply felt emotions. Maureen Forrester, one of the best Mahler singers of her generation, makes an effort to keep her large, somes slightly shrill voice under control in order not to over-project during soft interludes. She sings with command but also with subtlety, conveying the loneliness expressed in the *Herbst* movement as well as the heart-felt pathos of *Der Abschied*. In the latter, Forrester sings just as softly as Janet Baker does in her later performance with Szell, but Forrester's darker timbre — especially evocative when she almost whispers her lines — is uncanny, as if coming from another world. An accompaniment rendered with more warmth of expression would have made the performance even more poignant.

SZELL, GEORGE/Cleveland Orchestra; Janet Baker, mezzo-soprano; Richard Lewis, tenor (perf. 1970) - Cleveland Orchestra 75th Anniversary Edition (1993) [62:56]*+
Szell's outstanding career was soon to come to a close when this performance was given. Within the context of a traditional approach akin to his earlier reading with the same orchestra (see above), Szell delivers a strong if not particularly spontaneous performance that is remarkable for its clarity and revelation of inner detail. The brilliant sheen and remarkable precision of his ensemble add measurably to the success of the performance. Janet Baker, who stands among the very few outstanding Mahler singers of our day, matches if not surpasses her best work in other versions. Her softness and delicacy in *Der Abschied* make it an unforgettable experience. While others, particularly Christa Ludwig and Dietrich Fischer-Dieskau take a more expressive approach, Dame Janet's soft, liquid style adds a touch of mystical detachment to the oriental transcendentalism of the text. Richard Lewis, also a veteran of many *Das Lied*s, does quite well in his advanced years, despite noticeable wear and tear on the voice. His evocation of awesome dread climaxing the *Trinklied*, with its devastating super-octave drop on "*Lebens*", is utterly shattering. As with Baker, Lewis's ability to sing softly when called for (in both of his other songs) helps him stay within Mahler's guidelines and makes his readings delightful. Notice how deftly Szell spins the sinuous line that opens the *Herbst* movement, leading wistfully to the gentle oboe melody that muses on the theme of loneliness or how poignantly he hangs ever so slightly on the last appoggiatura chord. In the finale, an unforgettable shutter in bass strings

starts the orchestral interlude, ending with a terrifying final *sf* for the same group. And then out of the abyss comes the hushed tones of the soloist seeking life's meaning as if from another world. The closing moments are among the best ever committed to disc.

TENNSTEDT, KLAUS/London Philharmonic; Agnes Baltsa, contralto; Klaus König, tenor - EMI CDC 7 54603 (1992) [66:53]+   After a moderately intense, sometimes even profound reading of the opening *Trinklied*, an increasing detachment objectifies and even chills the atmosphere of this performance. Despite a less than satisfactory tenor, who strains on top and abuses dynamic markings in an overbearing manner, Tennstedt manages to evoke the horrific vision of the climactic section. He also conveys an attentuated feeling of emotional exhaustion in earlier sections with frequent ritards on cadences (into #7). He sets a *mosso* tempo for the *Herbst* movement that chills the atmosphere, but the pace eventually settles down enough to enable the moodiness of this haunting music to come through, even if the LPO does not evoke the dreary grayness of autumn. Tennstedt often presses into the highpoint of phrases or climaxes, letting what preceded them wander aimlessly. Baltsa, while in fine voice, does not express the music's melancholy thoroughly. One is struck by several inconsistencies. For example, after a marvelous thrust to high C before #11, Tennstedt ignores the *zurückhalten* marking for the close of this section, forcing what should be unresolved closure to seem complete. Even with some fine legato string playing the music's melancholy musing hardly comes through. The tenor is in high spirits in "On Youth," belting out this movement with more force than bespeaks its light lyric. The performance of "On Beauty" seems only mildly befit its name, with the strings playing too loudly and sometimes coarsely. Despite well-conceived tempo progressions in the increasingly faster middle section, much of the movement seems merely manufactured rather than naturally expressive. A feeling of constriction also tempers the ebulliant mood of the *Trunkene* movement. Klaus König gives a characterful reading, more headstrong and ardent than carefree and suffering from pervasively high volume when softness is required. The finale is ultimately disappointing. Notwithstanding Tennstedt's conscious effort colorize certain instrumental effects, such as growling horns in low register in the opening and buzzy contrabassoons at 2:42, his reading is generally cold and detached, rather than tender, personal and profound. Baltsa's reading lacks warmth, color and variety of shading. Notice her abrupt and stiff entrance at 12:50+ and how uninvolved her singing appears during the climax before the orchestral interlude. Tennstedt often drives in and out of phrases willfully, important moments appearing and disappearing with little impact. Morbidity rather than human pathos pervades the orchestral interlude. The remoteness of Tennstedt's manner during the closing section is most disconcerting. The LPO hurries along nervously through transition and lead-in passages when more spaciousness would have better served them. Baltsa is too loud and moves too quickly from #58 (marked *pp* and *langsam*). At the work's end, rather than uplifted, we are left in the cold.

WAKASUGI, HIROSHI/Tokyo Metropolitan Symphony; Naoko Ihara, alto; Makoto Tashiro, tenor - Fontec FOCD 9030 (1991) [63:26]+   Fontec has given this performance wider dynamic range than others in Wagasuki's complete cycle and the Japanese Maestro uses it to full advantage. He delivers a forceful and commanding reading of the *Trinklied* and creates just the right undertone to evoke a feeling of loneliness at the beginning of the second song. Elsewhere, Wakasugi falls back into his usual reserve, letting the music play itself out with nothing more than strict attention to detail. Occasionally, he adds a nuance to a phrase he thinks should be emphasized, such as the morbid 3-note fragment which plays an important role in the orchestral interlude of *Der Abschied* (15:45). These infrequent affectations seem out of place in an otherwise objective, strict reading, however. The songs on "Beauty" and "Youth" fail to elicit much of either quality and *Trunkene* has little of the carefree exuberance that makes it so captivating. Naoko Ihara is a deep-throated, Erda-like alto. She has a strong voice that she has difficulty controlling, especially when Mahler asks for soft and delicate singing (e.g., in *Der Abschied* when the main theme returns after the orchestral interlude at 25:10 and during the entire closing section). Tenor Tashiro negotiates the difficulties of his songs well enough, notwithstanding some strain on top. Although he adds little character to *Trunkene*, singing in full voice when he should soften the tones, he is more impressive in the *Trinklied*; particularly noticeable is his marvelous long slide on the cadence that concludes the horrifying graveyard scene.

WALTER, BRUNO/Vienna Philharmonic; Kerstin Thorborg, contralto; Charles Kullman, tenor - Columbia 11307-13D (1937); Seraphim 60191 (1972); Perrenial 2004; Priceless D 19122 (1989); Pearl GEMM CD 9413 (1990); 5-Angel CDHE 64294 (1992); Music & Arts CD 749 (1992); 2-Palladio ENTPD 4172 (1994) [58:15]*+ Walter's earliest recorded performance (dating from May 24, 1936) has as its main attraction the nobility and grace of Kirsten Thorborg. Her vocal poise and regal bearing often seem above the music, but these special qualities also invoke a peculiar sense of distance completely appropriate in "Autumn Loneliness" and infuses *Der Abschied* with Erda-like profundity. Yet more warmth of tone and expression might be desired in the tenderer moments of the final song and more delicacy in "On Beauty." Walter seems to press forward too frequently, even if he evidences a knowing way with climactic sections. The VPO plays superbly and inner voices come through noticeably for such a vintage recording. Kullman sings idiomatically for the most part, but has some trouble interpolating the high notes in *Trunkene*. Interpretively, one would expect more sensitivity from Walter but he delivers a straight, brisk reading. His last version is much to be preferred in this regard, for it weaves a magic spell which is thoroughly ingratiating even with a less notable female vocalist.

WALTER, BRUNO/Vienna Philharmonic; Kathleen Ferrier, contralto; Julius Patzak, tenor - London LL 625-6; 4212 (1952); Richmond R 23182; London 414 194 (1986); 12-433 330 (1992) [59:40]** Long considered the standard against which later versions are compared and usually found wanting, the unanimous acclaim that this highly treasured performance has received is mainly due to the presence of Kathleen Ferrier, whom Walter described as the quintessential Mahler singer. Combining a unique delicacy of both tone and phrasing with a strong, yet not overbearing voice, she seems to have just the right vocal qualities for this music. Julius Patzak, on the other hand, seems strained in all but the *Trunkene* movement. In this song, he imbues his part with Wozzeckian character, which has an almost crazed sensibility. Yet his affected, Loge-like, treatment of "On Youth" seems somewhat jaded. Walter's reading is stronger and less hurried here than in his earlier version. Despite some minor instrumental quirks (a honky English horn, tired French horns in the finale, etc.), the VPO lives up to its splendid reputation, infusing the music with breadth and depth as well as immense power (witness the overwhelming climax to the first song which may well be the best ever recorded!). A feeling of aimless wandering rather than loneliness pervades the second song, Walter setting a *mosso* pace. Ferrier is superb here. Listen to her whisper the last words, "*mild aufzutroknen*" at #19. She is also very sensitive in "On Beauty," where her languid approach, particularly in the rapid central section, has a charming beauty all its own. Walter provides a few interesting touches toward the close. While I believe that overall Walter's treatment of *Der Abschied* still lacks that perfect balance of weighty profundity, dramatic intensity and languid serenity that he produces so convincingly in his last version, he still elicits a great performance enhanced by superb playing and the unequalled beauty of Miss Ferrier's voice. Her manner of expressive nuance is entrancing: listen to how dispairingly she utters "*Lebens truckne Welt*," how tenderly she asks "*Wohin ich geh?*" or how like a wandering spirit she sings the closing pages. Until Jessye Norman's ethereal reading, no one has captured the gradually fainter *"ewigs"* as softly or warmly as Ferrier.

WALTER, BRUNO/Vienna Philharmonic; Kathleen Ferrier, contralto; Julius Patzak, tenor (perf. May 17, 1952) - WSP WISPCD 25963 (1995) [62:41]*+ Willem Smith has unearthed a radio transcription made by the Ferrier/Patzak/Walter team during the taping of their London recording (see above). As one might expect, their reading here is virtually identical with that offered in the commercial issue. Sonics are patchy and sometimes muddled but such technical problems are of little consequence in light of the superior quality of the performance. While slightly tamer than the London version, Mahler's profound vision of the beauties and mysteries of life comes through thrillingly. A few special moments are worth noting: Walter's strong emphasis on the ascending 3-notes that begin the main theme into #14 of the *Trinklied* (2:10); Ferrier's touching close to the autumn reverie on *"mild aufzutrocknen"*; the lesson in coloration and characterization Walter gives us during the orchestral interlude of *Der Abschied*; and Ferrier's breathtaking *ewigs* that seem to float in infinite space.

WALTER, BRUNO/New York Philharmonic; Elena Nikolaide, contralto; Set Svanholm, tenor (perf. 22 Feb. 1953) - AS Disc 403 (1989); Seven Seas 2075 (1990); Notes PGP 11020 (1992) [57:14]*+ Once again Walter delivers a truly Mahlerian performance, with another pair of fine soloists. Although they are closely miked, both singers deliver splendid readings: Svanholm is full of enthusiasm and sings with great dramatic power, though he sometimes strains on top, ignores softer dynamic markings and swallows notes. Nikolaide, with a vocal bearing similar to Thorborg's if slightly more shrill, is vocally secure and expressive. Walter's reading is consistent with the weightier approach he took in his later years; however, he uses brisker tempi in a few of the middle movements (particularly before #17 in the *Herbst* song, during the energetic middle section of "On Beauty" and in *Trunkene*). The NYP is in excellent form (*pace* a momentary lapse in horns after #43).

WALTER, BRUNO/New York Philharmonic; Maureen Forrester, contralto; Richard Lewis, tenor (perf. 16 April 1960) - Curtain Call CD-206 (1985); Music & Arts CD 206 (1987) [64:40 including long applause]** Beyond another splendid reading by Walter (who, after all, premiered the work), the special attraction of this recording is the appearance of another great Mahler singer, Maureen Forrester. Her reading of *Der Abschied* is among the best ever recorded. Interpretively, Walter makes a few adjustments from his commercial recording issued shortly after this performance (see below): touches of added emphasis on accentuation and linear highlighting from #27 in the *Trinklied*, more *legato* string treatment in the finale's orchestral interlude, and deeply mournful horn "*Lebewohls*" in the opening of the finale. But Walter performs the entire work as he has always done, in a thoroughly convincing and captivating manner. Few conductors project the profound emotions conjured up in the outer movements as impressively as he does, while letting all the tenderness of the *Herbst* song and the charm and delicacy of the remaining movements pour forth in a completely natural manner. Richard Lewis may have a littler voice than is optimal for the *Trinklied*, but he knows the music thoroughly and performs it convincingly. He has more difficulty with *Trunkene*, coming in incorrectly at first and straining thereafter. But one forgets his limitations completely when Maureen Forrester finishes her deeply moving performance of *Der Abschied*. Each line lingers after the words are sung; each nuance imbues the phrase in which it appears with an added dimension of meaning. The closing moments are perfection, each "*ewig*" floating farther and farther into eternity.

WALTER, BRUNO/New York Philharmonic; Mildred Miller, contralto; Ernst Haeflinger, tenor - 2-Columbia M2S-617; MS-6424 (1961); D3S-744; Odyssey 430043; CBS 61981; MP-39027; MK 42034 (1987) [63:03]** Walter's orchestral performance is too thrilling to be affected by the weaknesses of the soloists, who overcome their own limitations under the influence of Walter's brilliant reading. It is a great tribute to the genius of Bruno Walter that he can evoke such deeply expressive and sensitive singing from these vocalists while eliciting magnificent and perfectly idiomatic playing from the NYP. No version to my knowledge has been re-recorded as many times on domestic and foreign labels. The sheer vibrancy and power that Walter and the NYP generate are nothing short of stupendous! While Haeflinger does not have the strength or security of the younger Kollo, his inspired reading of the *Trinklied* is completely captivating. Notice how maddeningly he sings "*Jetzt nehmt den Wein!*" at the end of the climactic section ushering in the reprise. Walter wrenches every ounce of emotion from this frighteningly intense music while capturing the profound meaning of "*Dunkel ist das Lebens*" with an eerie sense of mysticism (listen to the main theme of Schumann's Symphonic Etude). Never does his vision or inspiration fade. While slightly more "*ermüdet*" than in earlier performances, Walter takes the same basic approach to "Autumn Loneliness" (see above). Miller's voice is on the thin side compared to her predecessors (which may be unfair) but she sings warmly and with tender expression. A lovely oboe adds a touch of plaintive melancholy to her beautifully shaped phrasing. "On Youth" is treated in a light, easy-going yet somewhat restrained Viennese style. How like a lullaby Miller tenderly sings "On Beauty." Notice how perfectly Walter handles the rapid middle section, sliding so deftly into *subito a tempo*. Haeflinger is better in this recording than in either of his previous efforts. His light, delicate lieder style is delightfully idiomatic in *Trunkene* (what a joyous "*und lacht!*"). No conductor has given us a reading of *Der Abschied* that is more profound, sensitive and dramatic than Walter. While Miller is sometimes too thin-sounding, her singing is so ingratiatingly expressive and lovely that it is never less than entrancing. In her recitative accompanied by solo flute ("*Es wehet kuhl*"), she really seems to be saying farewell to life (the word "*Lebewohl*" ends the passage). Walter eases into phrases smoothly and shapes sections with the understanding of a life-long Mahler advocate. His treatment of the orchestral interlude is stupendous in its awesome profundity. Each motivic element is given just the right attention and the climax with its bitter *fff* knife-thrusts in trombones is utterly shattering. Some particularly beautiful passages are worth mentioning: the tender sentiment of "*Du, mein Freund*"; the loving Yiddishkeit feeling of "*Wohin ich geh?*"; Miller's heavenly entrance on "*Die liebe Erde*" (#58) and the dream-like quality of "*blauen licht die Fernen*" which floats on air in the outer reaches of infinite time and space. Walter evokes such a soothing sense of repose in the final pages that it never fails to bring tears to my eyes.

PIANO VERSION (by Mahler):

BRIGITTE FASSBAENDER, mezzo-soprano; **THOMAS MOSER**, tenor; **CYPRIEN KATSARIS**, piano - Teldec 2292-46276 (1990) [60:35]+ Mahler's piano version is interesting because of how it differs, both in text and music, from the orchestral version. For example, the third, fourth and fifth lieder are entitled "*Der Pavillon aus Porzellan,*" "*Am Ufer*" (By the Brook) and "*Der Trinker im Frühling*" ("The Drinker in Spring") respectively, and several words of the poems vary from the later orchestral version. Mahler also changed a few musical phrases and altered some tonalities (e.g., on the final line of the *Trinklied* movement). Otherwise, comparisons with the orchestral version are pointless. A few disconcerting nuances seem at odds with the aesthetic quality in certain songs (e.g., numerous trills during the *Trinklied* have a decorative effect which overrides the music's dramatic import). Mr. Katsaris, a devotee of piano versions of Mahler scores, treats the work more as a song cycle than as a symphony, often dashing off important solo passages hastely. As a result it is difficult for him to elicit the full emotional impact of the outer movements even with his energetic and expressive playing. Thomas Moser's voice is light and heady; he appears to strain on top and sounds moderately cautious where he should sing with abandon (in the *Trunkene* lied). Ms. Fassbaender has a fine voice but sings without a trace of expression or sentiment. Her treatment of the *Herbst* song is simply too strong and forthright to capture the music's introspective mood. More problemmatic is her reading of the finale: cold, sterile and loud throughout. Sometimes her unattractive wobble becomes disconcerting. Katsaris sets a brisk main tempo for her in this huge closing movement, juxtaposing moments of profound sensitivity with displays of mere virtuosity. While he plays expressively in the solo interlude section, his manner of playing grace notes in the closing bars is offensive and disturbs the ethereal atmosphere. Overall, this version may have more interest as an musicological curio than an engaging performance.

FUMIKO NISHIMATSU, soprano; EIJI DATE, tenor, YASUKO FURUKAWA, piano - OCD 0504 (1992) [66:28] This Japanese release provides a less satisfactory rendition of Mahler's piano version than the Teldec recording (see above). The pianist plays in an extremely stylized manner, often indulging in exaggerated hesitations with excessive emphasis on fragments of thematic material. At other times he merely offers a rigid, confused reading of texturally complex passages. Both vocal soloists have fine voices but do not always succeed in communicating the dramatic import of the text. This failing is most evident in the *Herbst* movement. Neither of these soloists sings softly enough when the score directs, especially the tenor on key words in the *Trunkene* song, such as on "*Traum*" and "*Lenz*"). The alto's wide vibrato, pitch problems and consistent scooping up into notes are serious difficulties in *Der Abschied*.

CHAMBER ORCHESTRA VERSION (by Arnold Schoenberg):

HERREWEGHE, PHILIPPE/Ensemble Musique Oblique; Birgit Remmert, alto; Hans Peter Blochwitz, tenor - Harmonia Mundi (France) 901477 (1994) [62:40]+
Schoenberg's transcription for chamber orchestra brings out with stunning clarity the intimacy of much of this music. One is struck by how well the work lends itself to a pared down orchestration. Yet one misses the haunting atmosphere, warm lyricism and depth of emotion at climaxes that are achieved more effectively in Mahler's orchestration. The result is reminiscent of the linear style of Schoenberg's **Chamber Symphony No.1**. While all of the essential musical elements of Mahler's orchestral version are reproduced here, some of Schoenberg's instrumental choices sound ineffectual (e.g., piano replacing trumpet). One would think that a smaller group would enhance flexibility, but Herreweghe keeps a tight rein on his players, sometimes becoming too rigid and intractable. Pacing seems too measured at times during the *Herbst* movement and too sluggish and constricted in "On Youth." For the most part, the score is given an adequate reading. Occasionally, one misses a full string compliment (e.g., at 7:50 in the second movement). Both soloists have fine voices and sing well, despite close miking. The alto keeps her strong voice under control, singing softly when called for and with warmth and charm. While this leaner version makes for greater transparency, it is naturally but a shadow of the orchestral version, and therefore much less able to evoke the breadth and depth of emotions that make this extraordinary masterpiece so moving.

VANSKA, OSMO/Sinfonia Lahti Chamber Ensemble; Monica Groop, mezzo-soprano; Jorma Silvasti, tenor - Bis CD 681 (1994) [60:31] +   Again the Schoenberg transcription makes the same general impression: effective in its linear clarity but not in its dramatic or emotive impact compared to the full-orchestra version. Angularity and tonal ambivalence are more emphasized here. Vanska's reading is quite adequate; sharp-edged in the opening movement; straightforward yet appealing in its calm, relaxed pacing in the *Herbst* song; and light and sprightly for the next three movements. *Der Abschied* is treated more lightly than its dramatic nature calls for, but its intimate moments, such as the recitatives for singer and flute, work well. The mezzo-soprano has a lovely lyrical voice, although her reading of the finale seems too extroverted at times. The tenor has a somewhat lightweight voice that he uses characterfully, sometimes giving it a sharp edge. Tempi move quickly, sometimes hastily, but with much intensity, particularly in the finale. Again the reduced forces seem to sap much of the depth of feeling from this work, while giving us a clearer view of its inner workings.

WIGGLESWORTH, FRANK/The Premiere Ensemble; Jean Rigby, mezzo-soprano; Robert Tear, tenor - RCA BMG 09026-68043-2 (1995) [68:42]   Both soloists in this version of Schoenberg's chamber-music arrangement have significant vocal limitations. Their voices would probably be smothered by a full orchestra. Here they can be heard, but they sing with such reserved expression that powerful sections lose their impact. Robert Tear sings well enough, but strains on top and sometimes clips phrases to avoid breathlessness. His vocal weaknesses are most severely limiting in the *Trinklied* and *Trunkene* movements. Jean Rigby sings softly throughout, but her reading, particularly of *Der Abschied*, is devoid of expression. Mark Wigglesworth sets well-conceived tempi for the first five songs. But the opening movement lacks ferocity, sounding more impish than horrifying in the graveyard section. A legato treatment of the *Herbst* movement might have evoked that "*ermüdet*" (tired) feeling which makes this song so beguiling, but neither soloist nor ensemble manages to convey that feeling. Only the last line is sung with sensitivity. Tear does not have the vocal heft or ebullient temperament needed for a characterful reading of the *Trunkene* song. In "On Beauty," Wigglesworth tries to create a lazy, summery atmosphere but this approach falls flat and soon becomes tiresome. Notice how he wades flatulently into the tiered allegro segments at 2:40. In a complete reversal of his objectified manner in the earlier movement, Wigglesworth handles the finale in an extremely affected manner, making it seem like one long dirge. From the lugubrious opening section, he creates a mournful mood that becomes increasing overladen with tragedy. The oozing portamenti with which the solo violin embellishes his part is particularly unattractive, if not ludicrous. Rigby sings softly, even when the emotions should heighten, particularly at "*O Schönheit*" (15:30). Long pauses and stretched-out cadences further lengthen this already extensive movement. The result is mostly sterile and tiring.

SYMPHONY NO.9 IN D MAJOR

Movements:

1. Andante comodo.
2. Im Tempo eines gemächlichen Ländlers.
   Etwas täppisch und sehr darb.
3. Rondo. Burleske. Allegro assai.
   Sehr trotzig.
4. Adagio. Sehr langsam und noch zurückhaltend.

ABBADO, CLAUDIO/Vienna Philharmonic - 2-DG 423 564 (1988); 10-DG 447 023 (1995) [80:17]* Abbado's reading has a harsh, acrid and often edgy quality that sometimes gives the impression of anger rather than suffering. Strong dynamic contrasts and emphases on grotesque elements abound in the first movement and affected caricatures in the second. Sharper definition in string sonics would have presented the VPO in a better light. Muddy bass strings sometimes blur lower-voiced counterpoint, especially in strong sections for full orchestra. Nevertheless, Abbado elicits a spirited performance, most vibrant and alive in the Scherzo movement and impassioned in the finale. While one might characterize Abbado's approach as objective, it does not want for dramatic impact in the outer movements or rough-and-tumble vigor in the middle movements. In the more forceful moments, during both the opening and final movements, an almost accusatory tone pervades, as if demanding an explanation for life's unremitting tragedy. By way of contrast, Abbado underlines the *derb* (rough) marking over the second movement by a labored treatment of the 16th-note upbeat to the opening ländler. His tendency to infuse *allegro* movements with urgency works well in the third movement, where the mad whirl of everyday life is most tellingly mocked in burlesque fashion.

ABRAVANEL, MAURICE/Utah Symphony - 2-Vanguard C-10075/76 (1970); 11-Vanguard 08.7013.79 (1995) [81:58] As with most of Abravanel's cycle, a strong tendency toward restraint results in a lifeless, uninteresting and unperceptive reading, further numbed by stiff, imprecise playing, colorless sonics and constricted dynamics. After a slow and awkward opening, Abravanel inserts strange swells on the first beat of each measure in the celli. In the first movement's exposition, a plodding main tempo, weakened accents and watered-down volume produce a tiresome, even morose effect. Shifting tempi are not handled with deftness but abruptly, fast tempi are rushed while slower ones linger ineffectually. Abravanel's reading lacks both personality and subtlety of nuance. Although the second movement begins in a slightly spirited manner (Tempo I), the waltz tempo (Tempo II) is too restrained (Abravanel simply misses Mahler's pun here) and the minuet (Tempo III) seems on the mournful side, being strangely affected. Playing is consistently weak, stiff and awkward. The closing section just wanders aimlessly. Worst of all is the Burleske, which is a complete wash-out. Lacking spirit, intensity, proper instrumental balances and dynamic levels, the movement just lumbers along routinely. Abravanel seems more involved during the hymn-like strains of the finale as he renders this music with more commitment and conviction, but at *stets sehr gehalten* (still very held back) in the development section his interest wanes and he never really evokes a feeling of serene calm in the final moments.

ALBRECHT, GERD/Hamburg Philharmonic State Orchestra - 2-Insider OS 114 (1992) [81:01]+ Gerd Albrecht offers an expressionistic reading that combines vigorous tempi, sharp-edged articulation and strong emphasis on brass dissonances with a direct, unaffected interpretive manner and transparency of polyphonic textures. His approach works best in the Scherzo. Here greater agitation and biting intensity enhance the movement's virulence. Horns scream out in anger at times (e.g., at #38). Harsh brass grotesqueries often evoke a demonic image, giving the development section of the first movement a ghostly character and the ländler of the second movement a certain brusque quality. In the latter movement, the ländler has good heft and the waltz theme moderate spirit. Although Albrecht's reading is generally well-conceived, a few tempo modulations are awkwardly handled: the return to the waltz music after #23 and the imposition of a ritard into what should be a sudden reappearance of the ländler. A weighty, dark d-minor chord ushers in the second subject of the first movement, suddenly dispelling the calm, relaxed mood of the opening theme. The finale is briskly paced and has a stark, hard-edged temperament that adds a cutting edge to the spiritual nature of the movement's main theme. Because it lacks full sonorities and consistently true intonation, the HPSO is not fully equipped to bring out the full measure of this work's sonic dimensions; however, they do an admirable job with the difficult contrapuntal interweaving of voices and generally play without serious precision problems.

ANCERL, KAREL/Czech Philharmonic - 2-Supraphon SUAST 51813-4 (1967); 2-Crossroads 22260005-6 (1969); 2-Quintessence 2700 (1979); Supraphon SUP CD 11954 (1995)* Essentially a fine performance if slightly on the cool and objective side, this early Supraphon recording has finally been reissued on compact disc. Although some precision problems occur and playing style seems stiff at times (particularly in the first movement), Ancerl offers a powerful and generally well-conceived reading. His approach in the first movement is straightforward and temperate. Given his reserved manner of expression, little emotive depth comes across. But at more dramatic moments, Ancerl provides some measure of intensity, even if he rarely gets to the heart of the music. The coda is captivating despite a rather harsh flute solo. Most of the second movement is well-rendered except for a rapidly paced Tempo I. Against this brisk ländler tempo, the waltz (Tempo II) seems too restrained at first but gradually accelerates to whirlwind speed. Best is Ancerl's spirited approach to the Burleske movement, enhanced by sharp, articulate playing and well-proportioned balances. The finale is passionate without being overbearing. The main theme is strong and broadly stated in radiantly sonorous strings. While some moments seem to be glossed over (c. #90 and the beginning of the coda), the final *Adagissimo* is simply sublime.

ASAHINA, TAKASHI/Osaka Philharmonic - 2-Firebird KICC 158/9 (1984) [86:18]*
The opening movement of this performance leaves you feeling defeated even before the

battle for life has begun. Within his strict, objective approach, Asahina's tempi are laggard when more urgency is needed, especially into the high point of the development; rigid when inflection would be more ingratiating, particularly on the main theme; and dispassionate when the reverse is called for, such as on the angular second theme. These problems attenuate the drama and dissipate its impact. It is as if the hero were either too exhausted to fight or did not have the will to go on living. The second movement, notwithstanding a generally straight reading (but for a few anticipated ritards) and inflexive manner, comes to life with an energetic waltz theme. Asahina creates the impression of intensity in the third movement with forceful and full-bodied playing rather than propulsive speed. He usually lets the music speak for itself, in an intelligent, if depersonalized, reading. Given his reserved style, he fails to charge the increasingly animated closing section with much energy. Heavy accents and very strong playing intensify Asahina's otherwise objective reading of the finale. Despite some confusion in contrapuntal inner voices, the build-up to the climax of the development is monumental, and the *sforzandi* on high C-flats in violins that conclude it are riveting. The Osaka Philharmonic deserves praise for its accomplishments: high-level precision, forceful playing and rich, full-bodied sonorities.

BARBIROLLI, JOHN/Berlin Philharmonic - 2-Angel S-3652 (1963); EAC 50057/58; CDM 63115 (1989) [78:23]*+ Barbirolli's interpretive approach works very effectively here. His penchant for stretching slow tempi to the limit of endurance (witness the funeral march of the Fifth Symphony) creates an exceptional effect when applied to the opening section. Lumbering along hesitantly, Barbirolli is able to evoke a sympathetic response to the feeling of weariness with life's struggles that this music should convey. Clearly, Mahler's hero has sustained mortal injuries in fighting off his antagonist and has little strength left for the final conflict. The second theme maintains this approach notwithstanding its more hard-edged, intense material. From the return of the main theme in the exposition, Barbirolli begins to gather momentum, moving along more quickly and with less hesitation. He paces the remainder of this section as if it were a chronicle of the hero's regeneration. Tempi become increasingly pressed, ending the exposition in a state of uncontrolled fury. Into the development, excessive speed sometimes takes over, interrupted by minor affectations. Approaching the reprise with extreme haste and harshness, the sudden *fff* outburst on the "Fate" motif in trombones is shattering. Brisk tempi enliven the second movement, further enhanced by strong accents, powerful brass and excellent sound quality. While some tempi seem uncomfortably hurried, the general approach is not unduly energetic. The mocking irony of life's inane bustle emerges from the breathless whirl of the Scherzo. Strong playing is definitely a plus here. More impressive is Barbirolli's deft handling of the extremely complex and diverse material; the sole detraction is a minor affectation at the beginning of the second theme (not repeated on its later return). By the time we reach the finale, our hero has undoubtedly overcome his adversaries and faces his final moments with courage and noble deportment. For Barbirolli this was his hero's finest hour. Strongly accented, markedly demonstrative, dramatically weighty and extremely sensitive, this deeply personal statement is among Barbirolli's finest moments as well. After #73 (before the *Das Lied* quote), he begins to press forward, treating this entrancing passage with surprisingly little sensitivity and rushing toward the climax as if driven with passion. In the closing pages, gorgeous string portamenti and sobbing violins imbue life's final stirrings with heart-rending emotion.

BARBIROLLI, JOHN/Torino RAI Symphony (perf. 25 Nov. 1960) - 2-Fonit Cetra LAR 8 (1981); Hunt/Arkadia CDMP 403 (1988) [74:13] This Barbirolli reading is dwarfed by his superb rendition with the BPO (see above). Seriously hampered by an underrehearsed orchestra, the performance is too poorly played to have much of an impact. Even from a Mahler collector's viewpoint, it is difficult to determine whether Barbirolli's conception of the work has actually undergone any revision during the years between these performances. The opening drags along mournfully and in a rough-hewn manner. Often incongruous and imprecise playing mars the exposition. An effort to highlight the dramatic aspect of the monumental development section and sensitize the coda of the first movement goes awry because of serious performance problems, including a veritable barrage of miscues. In the second movement, Barbirolli sets slightly better tempi, but the overall reading lacks cohesion and polished playing (with wide oboe vibrato and distorted violin sound). Most disappointing is the Burleske, performed sloppily, disjoinedtly and with little vitality or direction. By the opening of the finale (played horrendously by the strings), Barbirolli seems to have had it! The music moves quickly and without sentiment, very different from his later recording. But he comes to the fore with imposing strength at the close of the exposition, even if he returns to his earlier debilitated manner as the development begins. The movement is replete with shoddy playing (e.g., a late entrance by the flute at m.99 and anticipated bass string entrances). Although the reprise moves forward too quickly, Barbirolli makes an effort to render the closing pages with sensitivity.

BARSHAI, RUDOLF/Moscow Radio Symphony (perf. 13 April 1993, Great Hall of Moscow Tchaikowsky Conservatory) - BIS CD 632 (1993) [75:58] Barshai's straight-and-narrow reading combined with the MRSO's uneven, raw-toned playing provide little satisfaction. Tempi are brisk and sometimes hasty (this is particularly counter-productive in the finale). Balances are uneven: brass overwhelm already weak strings with harsh blaring tone; inner voices are either over-emphasized or disappear in a welter of brass sound; and woodwinds overplay their hand in segments that demand a hushed atmosphere, such as at the close of the first movement. Particularly in the outer movements, Barshai handles the music without nuance or inflection, touching only the surface of the symphony's profound emotions. The orchestra's lack of experience with Mahler's idiom exacerbates the problem. Their sonorities range from harsh to pale and want for Mahlerian shadings. While tight, marcato playing enhances the second movement's main material, the Viennese parody is missing. The Scherzo seems washed out, lacking sufficient spirit because of controlled pacing. The result is simply uneventful. Barshai sets more of an *andante* than an *adagio molto* pace for the finale. Strings play out strongly here but without any conception of Mahlerian style, sounding stiff and harsh (e.g., at 6:35). For some inconceivable reason, Barshai adds a crescendo to the bass strings at m.51 (c.5:50). Woodwinds are often too loud, further robbing the symphony of its spiritual quality.

BERNSTEIN, LEONARD/New York Philharmonic - 3-Columbia MS 7024-6; D3S-776 (1968); 3-CBS M3K 42200 (1986); 3-Sony SM3K 47585 (1992) [79:34]* In comparison with several live performances of this work by Bernstein with both the NYP and VPO, this version seems pressed, lacks the degree of sensitivity and depth which we have come to expect from Bernstein and seems either ill-prepared or recorded on an off-day for the NYP. Of course, there is still much to praise here, but overall the performance leaves one cold. A lingering and expressive, if mannered, opening leads to a very smooth and tranquil first theme, well contrasted with a hard-edged and intense second theme. As the movement develops one is painfully aware of the absence of warmth and tenderness that Walter and Horenstein bring to this music. Moreover, the orchestra does not respond to Bernstein as well as in other Mahler symphonies. Some affectations creep in but are not as troublesome as the muddled effect produced in complex contrapuntal sections (e.g., before #13) and the hard-driving intensity that spills over into several sections where it becomes a hindrance. At moments when such intensity is called for, Bernstein is at his best. A restless feeling permeates the second movement, sometimes blurring tempo contrasts. The ländler frequently appears in gross caricature, while the waltz theme seems rough and bristly. Even if tense moments build to virtual pandaemonium, too much of this movement seems to lack involvement. But for sheer shock value Bernstein cannot be matched. His agitated approach would have worked well in the Burleske as it does in many of his live performances, but strangely enough he is more restrained than impulsive here. A whimsical attitude sometimes comes through if less so than in Haitink's version. Moving rapidly in and out of the myriad byways of this complex movement with little nuance, Bernstein again seems in a hurry to close. Playing and balances are not what they should be here. While we do have marvelous theatrical effects (grotesque dives and a breathtaking closing section), the religious quality of the finale is treated with more fervent passion than tender emotion. There is much impulse but little sensitivity. The best moments occur from the climactic section before the reprise. After being brought to a fever pitch at this climax, the underlying agitation subsides and Bernstein proceeds to the close with greater sensitivity, eliciting a more beautiful tone from the orchestral in the final pages than he does elsewhere in this performance.

BERNSTEIN, LEONARD/Vienna Philharmonic (perf. March 1971, Berlin Philharmonie) - DG video 072 229-3 (1991) [83]*+ What a world of difference there is between this thrilling performance and Bernstein's first NYP version (see above)! Even with the limitations of video sonics and the occasional imperfections that a live performance inevitably includes, the VPO are in excellent form. Few modern conductors have generated such intensity from an orchestra in the outer movements. Bernstein handles every nuance of this complex score splendidly, proving his complete mastery of the work. How furiously he pounces upon the angry second theme of the first movement, building it to magnificent heights! He then holds up slightly into the *a tempo* at m.47 and eases, at first imperceptibly then intently, into the return of the first theme, as if to enhance the emotive polarity between these themes. A ghostly aura permeates the opening of the development section, leading to a curious counterpoise of hesitent gurgling in lower strings and hasty grace-note embellishment of the violin lead-in to the main theme's return, sounding much like a paraphrase from Johann Strauss Jr.'s waltz *Freut euch des Lebens* ("Enjoy Life"). At the vigorous section marked *Mit Wut* (with fury) during the development, Bernstein drives forward willfully, leaving one breathless when he holds back to underline the quote from the opening *Trinklied* of *Das Lied* on "*Du aber Mensch*," recurring a few times during the movement. The climactic section here hurtles defiantly to its doom, evoked by an horrific outburst of the opening rhythmic motto *fff* in brass and intensified by tam-tam. Calming down into the first theme of the reprise as if to catch his breath, Bernstein proceeds apace into the coda. Here somewhat measured pacing detracts from the sense of suspension that should pervade the final measures. The second movement, a battle among waltz, ländler and minuet, is treated to a robust fun-filled reading. In the succeeding Scherzo, Bernstein lets lose all his nervous energy. With furious, nearly frantic intensity, he hurls out the vehement opening theme. The VPO brass show what can be done to make this music come alive. One is constantly at the edge of one's seat through the fiery closing moments. After such ferocity, the finale is deeply moving in every respect, from its intensely reverential main material to the hushed repose of its transitional passages and final coda. The result is nothing less than overwhelming. Has there ever before been such a leave-taking?

BERNSTEIN, LEONARD/Berlin Philharmonic (perf. 1979, Berlin Philharmonie) - 2-DG 435 378 (1992) [81:52]*+ Given the cool relationship between the BPO and Bernstein over the years, it is remarkable how much he gets from this great orchestra. For he drives them to heights of intensity and dramatic power beyond what they were accustomed to under Karajan. Bernstein even exceeds his usual self-indulgence, turning up all burners to produce a performance at white heat. His tempi are agitated and impulsive and give way to huge ritardandi at climaxes, that conclude only to renew their previously high tension. It is remarkable how well the BPO stays with Bernstein as he frequently follows instinctive impulses to underline a point or drive home a climactic section. He digs into the angry second theme of the first movement forcefully and races through the enraged *mit Wut* section in a veritable witches' sabbath of wild ferocity (Index 3). Then he holds back on the horns' entrance at 4:30 as if having glimpsed the immensity of the unknown. Torrid, even harsh string sonics and eerie, sometimes weird brass timbres give added dimension to the ghostly atmosphere pervading this movement. Rarely has this music been rendered so frenetically as to border on the maniacal. At the end, we are both exhausted and devastated. Brisk tempi also heat up the two middle movements, both driven by the same impulse as the first. Bernstein heightens the parodistic aspects of the second movement with impressively detailed characterizations. Any felicitous feeling generated by the ländler music is shattered by the mad whirl of the Scherzo that follows. Again tempi are hard-driven with little relief, even during the calmer middle section with its counterpoise of serenity and mockery. And the finale itself keeps up the heat: from its opening bars, Bernstein gives an impassioned, seethingly intense reading. No reverential, cathedral-like prayer this, but a deeply moving indictment against the tragedy of life and, possibly, even its Creator. Strings are ablaze with burning passion (Index 14), yet the main tempo is not as long-lined as it will become in Bernstein's later recording with the Concertgebouw Orchestra. An anguished climax gives way finally to the close, strings weeping with grief through the dissolution of the remaining strands of life at the end of this extraordinary performance.

BERNSTEIN, LEONARD/Concertgebouw Orchestra - 2-DG 419 208 (1987); 13-DG 435162 (1992) [88:39]* Bernstein's tortuous, almost tragic reading of the outer movements may not appeal to some. As is Bernstein's wont, extremes in tempi, especially during climactic ritards that are stretched to their limits, create an atmosphere of dread that is often overwhelming. His self-indulgence sometimes leads to confusion, principally in the orchestral playing itself. Horns need to warm up until the first theme's initial appearance. But thereafter brass playing is unevenly balanced: it sometimes overpowers weak-sounding strings, elsewhere seems too reserved, and darker sections of the first movement sound too bright and extroverted. Bass sonics are lacking in depth, color and definition; and in percussion, timpani can be obtrusive, such as in the first appearance of the vitriolic second theme of the first movement, while the bells are bearly audible at the opening movement's reprise. Strong sections sometimes become cluttered, while softer moments can bring tears to one's eyes. Bernstein's mannerisms work well in the second movement, underlining its parody. One could easy call to mind the picture of a Dickensian character trotting along on his loping nag. As for the Scherzo, there are no new insights. After the speedy tempo set for the main material, the calmer middle section also seems to hurry along, lessening the effect of its role as a portent of the finale. In that final movement, Bernstein is more tender and devotional than ever before, adding a good three minutes to his earlier timings. The pulseless closing moments seem unfettered by time, gradually dissipating into the infinite.

BERTINI, GARY/Cologne Radio Symphony - 2-EMI CDS 7 45387 (1992) [86:38]*
Bertini's reading combines two diverse aesthetic approaches, objective and subjective, in as near perfect a balance as Haitink achieved in his 1986 recording with the Concertgebouw Orchestra (see below). In a straight, unaffected manner, Bertini evokes the symphony's diverse moods with just the right emotive qualities--from deeply tragic to light-hearted, from tender and sensitive to vehement and willful. In the first movement, after a warm and gentle principal theme, the more angular and distraught second theme comes in more like a tragic sigh than an angry accusation. Climaxes are shattering during the development section, particularly into the great plunge at 11:50 and the demolitional outburst of the opening motto in brass at 18:10. Bertini's intelligent sense of balance, both aesthetic and musical, measurably enhances the

overall result. His manner of juxtaposing contrasts in the following dance movement is well-conceived. Intense agitation is balanced with calm serenity in the following burlesque. Bertini deftly handles the valedictory finale. His pacing is further evidence of his balanced approach, neither extremely broad nor overly aggressive. The creepy cello/double bassoon ascending phrase that follows the first theme sends shivers up the spine. Bertini's sensitive manner of expression shows his deep commitment to the work. Had the CRSO played with more precision, fuller sonority, more secure pitch levels, Mahlerian flavor and greater thrust and panache, this performance would compete with the best available.

BOULEZ, PIERRE/BBC Symphony (perf. 6 June 1971, London) - 2-Arkadia CDGI 754 (1991) [84:12]* Boulez may have the distinction of having provided the most unusual performance of this symphony ever recorded! His approach flies in the face of tradition with undaunted directness and self-assurance. Main tempi for all but the finale are completely out of line with most versions. Yet there is much dramatic weight and characterization here, even if rendered in an extraordinarily esoteric manner. He takes more time for the first movement than any of his colleagues, lingering measurably through what may be the longest, most lugubrious opening on record. Primal gurglings seem steeped in mud at first, but Boulez moves forward gradually to establish a suitable tempo for the first theme. Rather than irate or vehement, the second theme seems more heartbroken and disparing. One imagines the melancholy musings of a dying man in deep anguish, yet not really in severe pain. Sonics are weak and not well balanced, however; horns sounding particularly distant. After a shudderingly fearful beginning, the development begins to take on a dream-like quality. Grotesqueries are given their due, and Boulez handles most of them with finesse as well as sensitivity. He may be accused of over-dramatizing stronger sections (e.g., by literally sitting on certain notes to heighten the tension), but each wave of the struggle has immense dramatic impact. Listen to how he holds back on the horns into *etwas fliessender* (somewhat more fleeting) during the development, as if preparing to hurl himself yet again into the battle. The climax of the development, with its awesome outburst in mid-measure of the opening arhythmic heartbeat motto, is followed by terrifying timpani whacks on the normal heartbeat motto also appearing during the introduction, only to succumb to a ghostly apparition hovering zombie-like over the orchestra in violin figuration. Boulez draws out the main theme for all it is worth during the reprise, yet moves briskly into the closing coda. Here, with little hesitation, he brings this life-drama to a measured close.

After such a melodramatic first movement, the rapid tempo Boulez sets for the ländler movement that follows seems out of character. Even more uncharacteristic is Boulez's plodding treatment of the waltz music. In comparison to it, Tempo III (the easy-going minuet theme based upon the "farewell" motif) seems in an untoward hurry. Given such disjunctive tempi, it is difficult to determine just what sort of parody the music is meant to evoke. Again turning the tables on generally accepted tempi, Boulez sets a heavy-footed pace for the Burlesque movement. Mild, squarish, restrained and characterless, the opening Scherzo material virtually falls apart under its own weight. Yet Boulez presses through the middle section, which Mahler directs to be paced more comfortably. Only in the closing moments does Boulez try to inject any vitality into the Scherzo, with little success.

In the finale, interrupted before the end of the exposition by a disc change, Boulez does establishes a reverential, if detached, atmosphere. His approach is more traditional here than elsewhere in this performance, but the combination of thin-sounding strings and lack of emotive depth (except in the carefully rendered final moments) makes little impression. Boulez presses in and out of tempo at times, as if to make up in inflection for what his ensemble lacks in sonic resonance.

BOULEZ, PIERRE/BBC Symphony (perf. 22 Oct. 1972, London) - 2-Memories HR 4493/94 (1993); 2-Enterprise 901 (1993) [74:44]+ A mere sixteen months after his earlier performance, Boulez has shed his radical approach and adopted a more traditional one. Cutting a full six-and-one-half minutes off the timing of the opening movement, Boulez no longer drags out the opening bars sluggishly. In fact his pacing seems even more appropriate as a vehicle for achieving an objective interpretation. He manages to capture some of the first movement's profound sense of human pathos, appearing to be thoroughly engaged in the deep emotions of its life-and-death struggle. Playing is not particularly Mahlerian. Strings need more heft and fullness, brass play matter-of-factly and sometimes imprecisely, and woodwinds are often too loud. But the timpani are heard when important mottos sound out. Sonics are muddy despite good bass definition and volume levels too high due to close miking. Boulez tempers the speed of the opening ländler in the second movement, so that there is a better balance among the three main tempi presented here than in his earlier reading. Yet the ländler and the minuet still seem hurried in comparison with the heavy-footed tread of the waltz. Such tempo contrasts fit the characterization of an old man caught in a reverie of youthful pleasures. Boulez tries to energize the waltz on its return at 10:57 by noticeably increasing the volume of the two-measure vamp that ushers it in, but in the Scherzo he does his best and most revisionary work. Gone is the tiresome plodding pace of the earlier performance. Now the main tempo is more vital and urgent, and the middle section more serene. Having retrenched this far, Boulez seems unwilling to revise his thinking about the finale. The main tempo moves along at a moderate pace, neither broad nor spacious, and stronger sections are briskly handled. While some sense of spiritual reverence comes through, it has little chance to make a significant impression until the quiet chamber-like moments at the symphony's close. Although inner voices are distinct and well-balanced, abrupt, angular playing chills the atmosphere. Yet Boulez has come a long way from the radical approach he took in his earlier effort.

DEWAART, EDO/Netherlands Radio Philharmonic - 2-RCA 74321 276102 (1995) [84:12]+ After a relatively half-hearted reading of the first movement and an artificial, often lumbering second movement, Edo DeWaart and his Dutch ensemble seem to come alive, giving a strong and intense performance of the Scherzo and finale. Some interesting stylistic effects do appear in the first movement, such as a shuddering timpani roll that ushers in the second theme (2:11) and a nasty aspect to brass grotesqueries (c.14:45). The NRPO simply do not have the requisite sonic brilliance in strings, and woodwinds are over-balanced and brass covered at times. Sonics are confined in climactic passages. As in the other recordings in his Mahler cycle, DeWaart's approach is direct, unaffected and often objective, sometimes to the point of lacking personality. Given these characateristics, it is no surprise that the first movement fails to convey what should be a devastating experience. In the following movement, DeWaart weighs down the ländler theme and tempers the spirit of the waltz music to a mild-mannered spin. The entire movement bogs down in routine and colorless playing. DeWaart imposes a ritard into what is intended to be a sudden return of the ländler toward the close (13:20).

In contrast, the Scherzo has vitality and is articulately played. A chaotic quality adds character to the main theme group, while a tender sentiment warms the softer middle-section. Yet more subtlety and urgency could have made hints of the opening theme's impending return more interesting. When the principal subject suddenly jumps in, it seems even more agitated than earlier. In the finale, DeWaart elicits as much full-bodied, well-accented string playing as his ensemble can muster. Although his approach is objective, keeping strong emotions in tow, he provides a steady, well-conceived reading here. Most impressive are how forceful and detached the violins play the high C-flats that pierce through the climax of the development section, producing a version of the opening "heartbeat" motto in augmentation. A broadly paced, gentle and touching treatment of the closing coda is only marred momentarily by a loud piccolo at m.147.

GIELEN, MICHAEL/SWF Symphony, Baden-Baden - Intercord INT 860.913 (1990/1)
[79:05]   Although he takes his usual detached and cerebral approach, Gielen evokes much emotion without losing sight of structural design, even linear flow and proper ensemble balances. Gielen sometimes seems overly studious, particularly when underlining specific points, climaxes or phrases. During the first movement tempi seem either pressed (such as at the return of the main theme at 2:55) or overly inflexive, while linear material sometimes sounds stiff, agitated or sodden. Climaxes make only a mild impact, often because of excessive speed. The SWF Symphony lacks sufficient string sound to soar to Mahlerian heights. Horns give a sinister quality to *gestopfs*, but trombones hold back from giving the movement's important mottos their due. Sonics are compressed and sometimes unfocussed. Playing is generally angular, agitated and taut, lacking warmth and tenderness in the first theme and dramatic impact in the important climaxes. But Gielen's heady approach works well in the middle movements. His rough-shod manner with the opening ländler of the second movement brings out the earthiness of this peasant dance. The waltz theme seems too moderate by contrast. When it returns later (at 11:50) it has a menacingly aggressive aspect. The Tempo III minuet is merely pleasant rather than charming. The sudden return of the opening ländler at 13:30 retains too much of the motion of the preceding waltz to feel like a completely unprepared intrusion as it should be. Hard driven from the outset, the Scherzo movement combines vigorous tempi with sharp angularity to evoke its demonic spirit. But beginning at a fast pace, it leaves little room to speed up to the close. The middle section, with its glimpse of heavenly serenity foreshadowing the finale--while sometimes mocking it--contrasts aptly with the constant tension that surrounds it. Unfortunately, amplified volume works against the feeling of peace evoked here. In the finale, Gielen opts for an objective, cool approach. After setting a properly religious mood at the outset, continuously pressed tempi seem to rebel against too much emotion, resulting in a performance devoid of soulful expression. Only in calm, sustained passages does Gielen apply more tender expression; but when the music swells or becomes more forceful, it freezes solid.

GIULINI, CARLO MARIA/Chicago Symphony - 2-DG 2707097 (1977); 423 910 (1989)
[87:55]*+   This superb performance is further evidence of Giulini's intelligent and impressive Mahlerian interpretive style. While the CSO sounds somewhat craggy and stiff at times, Giulini elicits crisp and precise playing. Sound quality is sharp and clear. The mood of the first movement's opening is appropriately subdued and the tempo hesitant. The first theme sounds of bittersweet melancholy, while the second theme is treated with restrained passion. Giulini de-emphasizes the more painful aspects of this movement in a broad and lyrical approach that lacks expressiveness during the development section. His restrained tempo never seems unduly sluggish. From the horrific climax ushering in the reprise, all goes extremely well, especially in the serene coda. Giulini's conception of the second movement has some interesting aspects. The ländler theme (Tempo I) is appropriately hefty, but the waltz theme (Tempo II) is very emphatic and somewhat plodding. At this slow tempo, the parodistic clowning that Mahler boldly interjects here has a pleasant rather than rollickingly humorous quality. A curious conceptual problem arises as Tempo I changes character and gradually increases with little regard for its initial deportment; especially when Tempo II remains temperate and constricted. The Burleske, on the other hand, has a good measure of vitality, juxtaposing vibrancy, delicacy and power. Playing while precise seems uncomfortable, balances are uneven and momentum begins to wane toward the close. Giulini offers one of the best versions of the finale ever committed to disk. His hymnal approach to the principal theme lets the music evolve

naturally without losing impulse or becoming tiresome. Clear and vibrant playing are further assets. Giulini works magic at the close of the exposition by taking his time and building to the ultimate climax with an underlying sense of purpose without increasing tempo (he actually holds back). The closing pages are simply exquisite.

HAITINK, BERNARD/Concertgebouw Orchestra - 2-Philips 6700021 (1971); 416 466 (1986); 10-434 053; 442 050 (1994) [80:05]** This performance is one of Haitink's greatest achievement on disk as a Mahler conductor. Not only does the orchestra play with immaculate precision, imposing strength and vitality, but Haitink provides a reading that captures the dramatic import of this work with sensitivity and searing intensity without succumbing to extremes or extraneous mannerisms. Balances are superb in thickly contrapuntal sections and sound quality is clear and clean. In the first movement, a slowish tempo for the introduction evokes a tired, almost melancholy feeling. As the main theme appears, the tempo picks up ever so slightly, its legato treatment in perfect contrast with the almost angry intensity of the second theme. After reaching a thrilling climax, the return of the principal theme is handled with unerring deftness. While some moments seem hurried, Haitink's quicker pace simply adds fuel to the fire as the movement builds to its overwhelming climax. At times, the tension is almost unbearable. Haitink is equally capable of eliciting just the right effect in quieter sections (e.g., at *schattenhaft* in the development and in the coda). His interpretive approach is just as satisfying in the second movement. Perfect tempi, smoothly handled transitions, sharp playing and audible details combine to produce a marvelous performance. Haitink even adds some interesting effects: slowing up at the change of key before *subito Tempo I* toward the final section and setting a husky tempo before #26. One could easily run out of adjectives to describe the Burleske: it is vibrant, exciting, fierce, thrilling, crisply played, perfectly balanced, incredibly detailed and sonically spectacular! Each nuance, from the mocking E-flat clarinet theme to the marvelously sinister transition to the return of the scherzo theme has just the right character. The closing generates all the excitement of Bernstein's whirlwind rendition without its break-neck speed. Haitink takes a conservative approach to the finale. The main tempo is broad but not in the extreme and accents are not over-emphasized. Yet again Haitink proves that a reading that does not exaggerate the music's emotional content can be just as sensitive and full of expression as a more self-indulgent one. While his interpretation does not create a restful atmosphere in the more subdued sections (seeming somewhat measured and often too loud), Haitink generates an underlying intensity that works propels the music to a seething climax that concludes the development section. The closing pages are beautifully handled, without being stretched to the breaking point.

HAITINK, BERNARD/European Community Youth Orchestra - 2-Philips 438 943 (1993) [84:57]* Haitink's objective approach has become more weighty and wearisome since his earlier recording with the Concertgebouw. While this young orchestra, formed by Claudio Abbado, performs admirably for its tender years of experience, it lacks sufficient string sonority to be fully satisfying in this work. Haitink's controlled, cautious manner often causes rigidity to set in, weakening the level of intensity in more dramatic moments and smoothing over sharp edges. Although playing is strong, it sounds more blatant than dynamic and sometimes exhibits a nervous edge. The first movement suffers from these problems within a generally well-handled reading. A few moments capture the intended effect, especially with the chilling atmosphere established in the section marked *schattenhaft* (shadowy). Some unmarked tempo shifts (at m.47 and thereafter) and an awkward slow-up on the "*Du aber Mensch*" quote from the *Trinklied* movement of *Das Lied von der Erde* either distort the musical flow or backfire as an effort at strong emphasis. The second movement suffers most from tempo lag. Both the ländler (Tempo I) and the minuet (Tempo III) drag along sluggishly, and the waltz theme (Tempo II) lacks spirit. Somehow the world-weary feeling that pervades the first movement also hovers over the second. Yet the performance awakens from its doldrums for the Scherzo movement. Here Haitink drives his forces more intently than anywhere else in this performance. In the finale, Haitink's weighty approach works splendidly. The level of concentration increases tension measurably as he forces the strings to dig into accents and shapes their long-lined phrases masterfully. Haitink tries to hold back into the climax of the movement (at 16:30) but some players anticipate the highpoint and spoil its impact. A few audible noises from the hall distract both listener and players. Haitink delivers a fine performance of the finale, matched only by some splendid work in the Scherzo.

HALASZ, MICHAEL/Polish National Radio Symphony (Katowice) - 2-Naxos 8.550535-6 (1993) [83:59] After a mild reading of the first two movements, Halasz offers a vital and vigorous Scherzo and intense finale. While he elicits some depth of feeling in the first movement, one senses a world-weariness which defuses the energy needed to convey the import of this heroic life-struggle. Part of the problem may lie with the orchestra, less than ideal because of its weak strings, blaring brass and tendency to play stiffly and unstylishly, often clipping dotted rhythms. Sonics could also be improved; they sound boxy and lack vibrancy. The first movement fails to capture the drama that should be presented here, given Halasz's straight, uninvolved reading. Although the second movement has character, it borders on the routine too often to be convincing. The waltz theme lacks impulse; the minuet theme (Tempo III) is lumpy, wanting warmth and grace. From its inception, the Scherzo makes up in vitality for what the preceding movements lacked. Even playing improves. Notice how Halasz builds gradually into the return of the opening material from around 10:50, thus undercutting the intended suddenness of its return moments later. Halasz takes a moderate approach to tempo in the finale, neither dragging out the main material nor moving it along with haste. Antiphonal violins add dimension here, as they do throughout the performance. But the main tempo sags into the development, causing the players to slump along routinely until the music becomes more agitated. The ultimate climax works well enough, even if Halasz tries too hard to separate the high C-flats in violins that ring out the opening "heartbeat" motto in augmentation. Yet he draws out from his ensemble as much as they can give in the reprise. Now the main theme catches fire, its burning quality made all the more searing by the orchestra's rough-edged timbre at high volume. An atmosphere of quiet, accepting serenity permeates the closing measures.

HORENSTEIN, JASCHA/Vienna Symphony - Vox PL 7600 (1952); VBX 116; 2-Turnabout TVS 34332/33 (1970); 2-Vox Box CDX 5509 (1993) [89:12]*+ Although hampered by severe technical problems (poor sonics and imprecise playing), Horenstein provides a masterful reading that captures the pathos and intensity of this complex score with profound insight. His special interpretive style gets to the core of this very personal work without either extreme theatrics or gushing sentimentality. Each phrase is rendered knowingly, producing just the right effect whether by a soft, lyrical touch, a demonic twist or a powerful outburst. Horenstein rarely lingers, moving apace in measured but not constricted motion. The first movement has all of the above characteristics. However, serious sonic problems spoil climaxes and blur complex ensembles. A hefty approach to the ländler that opens the second movement is in perfect character; however, orchestral problems soon intercede (e.g., awful oboe tone). Horenstein is one of the few conductors who returns to Tempo I at *piu mosso subito* (m. 230) as indicated (most other conductors apply Tempo II). Usually a Horenstein reading avoids affectation, but a strange mannerism stands out noticeably when he slows up at m. 243. Otherwise, tempo shifts are deftly handled and the devilish grotesqueries of the last section come through with mocking irony. In the Burleske, lack of adequate orchestral forces is a serious problem. Notwithstanding, Horenstein delivers a strong and vital performance in a basically straight reading (but notice that curious affect at #64 where he slows up for no apparent reason). At the close, after stirring up the momentum to the point of frenzy, Horenstein pulls hard on the reigns for the last few measures. The finale is a study in depth of expression, without being overladen with emotion. Certain small details add intensity: strong accents, subtle gradations of dynamic levels and audible grace-note entrances (such as at the return of the main theme in the exposition). Quieter moments seem appropriately thoughtful (e.g., at m.28) and more passionate sections are simply thrilling (e.g., at m.70). No conductor in memory has made more of an effort to tie in the strongly accented C-flats in strings at the ultimate climax before the reprise with the syncopated motto of the symphony's opening as emphatically as Horenstein does. The closing section is heavenly, embellished with lovely string portamenti. Much can be learned from this insightful reading, which would have been even more effective with a better orchestra and improved sonics.

HORENSTEIN, JASCHA/London Symphony (perf. 1966) - 2-Music & Arts CD-235 (1986) [89:13]*+ Few interpretive adjustments to his earlier recording (see above) are made in this fine performance. And sonic problems and spotty orchestral playing are the most serious drawbacks here as well. After very deliberate pacing at the outset, the first movement settles in to a comfortable main tempo. Yet faster tempi seem on edge (e.g., an unduly fast pace from m.47 on the main theme). Minor technical problems aside, one can have little doubt about Horenstein's mastery of Mahler's idiom, particularly from the deft manner in which he handles the diverse twists and turns engaged here. From the depths of tragic pathos that the development evokes to the eerie shudder of primal stirrings in transition passages, this reading captures the pure essence of Mahler's last complete symphony. At the height of the development, the thunderous "heartbeat" motto in timpani seems to pound the very stuff of life to a pulp. In perfect contrast, Horenstein plays up the parodistic aspect of the next movement, even indulging in a few affectatious hesitations for good measure (at m.74, 76-7). When the ländler theme loses its way, interjecting itself into the waltz section, we sympathize with its many attempts to find a way out. The waltz itself has all the swing and carefree gaiety of Vienna's golden age which Mahler caricatures here. Only a break before the sudden return of Tempo I after the 16th-note upbeat to the ländler theme (in Tempo II) is disconcerting. While Horenstein does not race through the Scherzo as rapidly as others do (e.g., Bernstein), he stirs up enough energy to make the often dizzying excursion through this movement exciting. In fact, he seems to impose a threatening aspect upon the main material, reinforcing it in a demonstrative, deliberate manner. Where Horenstein weighs more heavily into the main tempo on its final appearance, he does so forcefully, leaving enough room for increases in tempo to the close while trying thereby to avoid the many pitfalls that an unduly fast pace before these tempo increases can cause. The finale is soulful and sensitively played, set in a broad, but not overly lingering tempo. More accentuation in inner strings would be welcome. Playing remains steady until a sloppy entrance at m.45 shakes things up. From the return of the second theme (m.49, marked *molto adagio subito*), Horenstein begins very slowly but works into a more bearable *adagio* as he proceeds. Then at m.57 he suddenly moves more rapidly, causing a slight muddle. His reading of climax that closes the development section is deeply moving. Only sonic flaws, uneven playing and intrusive audience noise are serious detractions here.

HORENSTEIN, JASCHA/Orchestre National de France (perf. 6 June 1967) - 2-Disques Montaigne WM 362 (1988) [82:37] Given the deficiencies of the ONF and its apparent lack of experience with this work, little of Horenstein's otherwise proven ability meets with satisfactory results. All but the finale is severely beset by the orchestra's shortcomings, ranging from pitch problems in winds, balance problems amongst various ensembles and generally unidiomatic playing style. Horenstein's reading of the first movement seems unusually detached. Only more intense moments are treated with passion and demonstrative force; the rest borders on the routine. Tempi relationships seem somewhat discombobulated in the second movement. A brisk opening ländler works well enough (despite an untoward affectation around m.74), but is followed by a sagging waltz replete with flawed brass playing. The Tempo III minuet simply does not hang together, being paced differently in its various appearances. The entire movement seems to have been forced unwillingly from the orchestra. A temperate Scherzo movement lacks impulse and is played with restraint and caution. Sounding more exhausted than wildly frantic, even the closing stretto breaks down from imprecision. The best movement by far is the finale. Here Horenstein seems better able to engender more precise, sensitive and well-accented playing, at least from the strings. Consequently, the music's emotions survive interference from technical distractions. Horenstein's approach to the central climax is deeply moving. He emphasizes the high C-flats in violins--a variant of the opening arhythmic "heartbeat" motto in augmentation--by having the players take their bows off the string between these notes. Close miking unduly amplifies some of the quieter moments; fortunately, it does not impair the quiet that should pervade the restful, submissive conclusion.

HORENSTEIN, JASCHA/American Symphony (perf. 10 Nov. 1969, Carnegie Hall, New York)- 4-Music & Arts CD-785 (1994) [89:30] In what was to be his final appearance in New York, Horenstein gave a memorable performance of the Ninth despite flawed orchestral precision. One wonders how much rehearsal time he had. Suffering from weak strings, overbearing brass and percussion, imprecise ensemble work and numerous miscues, it is a wonder that the performance makes any impression. Interpretively, Horenstein stays with his well-documented basic approach. In the first movement, a moderately brisk first theme is contrasted with a deeply impassioned second. Tempi are flexible but not too loose. The ASO has difficulty at times turning tricky corners. Gradual tempo changes seem more abrupt than they should, possibly because of the nervous tension of a live performance, but they are more troublesome given the ASO's probable lack of familiarity with this work. Horenstein does try to make a few points (e.g., underlining the *"Du aber Mensch"* quote from the *Trinklied* movement of *Das Lied Von Der Erde* at 10:22), but missed entrances (e.g., the horn's first *"lebewohl"* motto at 4:25; and an early entrance of trombones at 18:32 on the same motto) balderdize the performance. Playing in the second movement suffers from lack of character and sonic imbalance. Even the three contrasting dance tempi seem a bit stiff, and the ritards are abrupt, sounding more like full-fledged tempo changes. A cautious rendering of the Scherzo suffers from fussiness probably caused by concentration on getting the notes right, though without much success. Even the more restful moments of the middle-section seem uncomfortably pressed and perfunctory. In the finale playing again causes problems, especially lack of sufficient accentuation in strings, which sound fuller here given the relative absence of brass. The climbing string phrase that ends the exposition is thrilling. While this great Mahlerian conductor manages to capture the profound spirit of this soulful movement--particularly in the more attenuated closing moments--muddled playing is simply too much of a distraction. Many of those who attended thought this might very well be Horenstein's own "farewell." He died 4 years later.

INBAL, ELIAHU/Frankfurt Radio Symphony - 2-Denon 60CD-1566/7 (1987); 16-Denon CO 72589/604 (1989) [80:59]+ Inbal's cool, objective approach does little to summon up the emotions that make each of the outer movements an unforgettable experience or stylishly invoke the caricatures of country and cosmopolitan dances paraded wantonly in the second. As with many of the performances in the Inbal/FRSO cycle, playing seems taut, angular and sometimes reserved. Tempi tend to press forward hurriedly and with little inflection. Trumpets (especially the soloist) are sometimes overbearing or sound fatuous in isolated appearances, particularly when they clip dotted rhythms. Inbal's generally brisk and tight manner works better in the Scherzo, but frequent distancing from the music's aesthetic core produces little to hold the attention. In the rush to complete this cycle in chronological order, one wonders if less than full attention was payed to this late symphony. One minor example of lack of preparation: notice how brass must increase in volume in the first measure of the scherzo theme's return at m.522. The treatment accorded the finale by these performers might be most aptly described as mere note spinning, imbued with passion only by an increase in volume. The final moments are soft and tender, despite an emotionally detached reading of the main material.

JUDD, JAMES/Gustav Mahler Youth Orchestra - 2-Nuova Era 6906/7 (1990) [81:33]
*+   The conception of the Ninth as a dichotomy between youth and old age is given an ironic twist in this performance. Can a youth orchestra and young conductor succeed in bringing to light the more mature aspects of such musical dualism while capturing both its profound and paradoxical nature? If this performance is any indication, the answer is a resounding yes. The young James Judd reveals himself to be a superb Mahlerian, able to engender not only youthful energy and intensity but also a depth of vision that evidences maturity of both a musical and intellectual variety. His orchestra responds well, for the most part, and appears to be thoroughly committed to the work. Antiphonal placement of violins adds a dimension to inner voice balancing, enhancing the contrapuntal interweaving of diverse lines. Sometimes Judd lets his energetic spirit and enthusiasm go unrestrained, witness the climax of the first movement's development section on the outburst of the "heartbeat" motto and the beginning of the layered tempo increases which cap the Scherzo. He generates so much excitement that considerations of speed seem secondary. Contrasts are exaggerated in the second movement, playing up Mahler's grotesqueries to the hilt. The bucolic roughness of the ländler is emphasized in heavy-laden foot-stamping; the whirlwind waltz whizzes by without a care; and the mellow minuet of Tempo III has just the right lilt and charm. One might question a few affectations here and there (e.g., why take a breath before Tempo III's first appearance), but the end result is so captivating that Beckmesserian nit-picking would be out of place here. Much the same can be said for the Scherzo. Contrasts are highlighted, as they should be, and the main material is as energetic as the calmer middle section is warm and restful. Although strings could be better accented in the finale, Judd handles this fervant prayer with such deftness and ardency, that his ensemble plays beyond its limitations.

KARAJAN, HERBERT VON/Berlin Philharmonic - 2-DG 410 726-2(1985)   This second Karajan effort was recently issued on compact disk only. If it were possible to improve upon his earlier performance (see vol. 1, pp.140-141) in any respect, Karajan has done it here at every turn. His overview remains basically the same, but a conscious effort was clearly made to highlight certain aspects which may not have come through with equal force in the earlier release. The clarity and larger-than-life sonics of the compact disk format serves this purpose quite well. String highs have a disturbingly piercing tone quality which may have put more of a rough edge on their brilliant sheen than Karajan may have intended. Slightly less languid than before, the first theme of the opening movement has a subtle yet lyrical quality which is in perfect contrast with the dynamic thrust of the second theme. Karajan holds on ever so carefully to the appoggiatura of the *ewig* motto without producing too awkward an affect. All the power and drama comes through here with even more force than in the earlier version. Karajan builds to the great orchestral dive into #11 with fierce intensity. After a magnificient closing section at #13, a dark, almost eerie atmosphere imbues what follows. The stormy climax to the development is shattered by a terrifying return of the "Fate" motif of the opening (the tam-tam is given some whack here!). Only the second-beat sforzandi need more emphasis in the reprise. Again the parodistic effects in the second movement are hard-edged in a *danse* *macabre* treatment, but the three main tempi are better balanced and more characteristic than before. The ländler has just the right snap, while the waltz is slightly on the heavy side. Karajan elicits all the maddening whirl of this movement with gusto, especially in the racy return of the waltz theme (listen to the brass at m.405!). The closing section sounds like a distant memory of what went on before. No disturbing mannerisms mar the surging *wildheit* of the Burleske this time. Alive with energy and gusto, this movement keeps you on the edge of your seat from beginning to end. In the more lyrical middle section, Karajan elicits some lovely moments without over-emoting, reaching a climax that sounds like a premonition of doom. More gradual pacing into the return of the scherzo section would have been preferable, but the final presto is simply thrilling. Most improved is the finale. Karajan imbues this music with even more profound expressivity than previously, plumbing the deepest regions of the soul with awesome power (especially toward the close of the exposition). As the climax of the development section is reached, those searing C-flats now come forth with unmatched accentuation. After a very strong reprise, Karajan interweaves the isolated tones of the coda into a seamless texture of sustained sound, evoking a spellbinding sense of eternal calm during the final moments.

KLEMPERER, OTTO/Vienna Philharmonic (perf. Aug. 1968) - 2-Hunt CD 578 (1990) [85:10]+ At the end of his long and productive life, Otto Klemperer conducted Mahler's "Farewell" Symphony as if it were his own. His tempi in slower sections wound down measurably in his final years, but he could still energize an *allegro* with fiery impulse. His entreme age caused not only an overall slowing down, but more serious problems in producing a definitive, communicable beat. The VPO clearly has difficulty following him, as is evidenced by numerous miscues, wrong entrances and untidiness in contrapuntally dense passages. To add to these difficulties, sonics are muddled and unbalanced due to uneven use of close-miking. All that having been said, Klemperer manages to produce a strong reading, both deeply felt and, for the most part, well-conceived. While he claimed to distain emotionalism, his reading of the first movement, from its tired, care-worn opening through its fiercely chilling highpoints, could not have been wrought in the abstract. While one does sense that he catches himself short of over-involvement at times and becomes more detached (at mm.58-77), when he gets into the thick of the musical argument he is thoroughly committed and intrenched. How else could such remarkable intensity be stirred up at *mit Wut* (#9), with its chilling horn calls. Some moments seem somewhat slapdash; for example, the *allegro moderato* statement of the main theme during the exposition. A few curious divergencies from the score might be mentioned: holding up into the *allegro* at the close of the exposition and for the trumpet into *bewegter* (m.285). Such quirks are unnecessary in the second movement. Here Klemperer plays up the raucousness of the ländler with almost wicked tenacity. How heavily he stomps through the opening peasant dance, much like he might if he were to have joined in it at his advanced age. Then he whisks through the waltz as a younger man might. All of Mahler's grotesque stabs and jolts in brass are given due emphasis to highlight their caricaturesque aspect, but numerous wrong entrances and a strange slow up at the close are distracting.

Klemperer still finds the energy to generate a forceful and vital Scherzo. His approach to the light second theme is almost chipper; then he takes his time getting into the mood of the calmer middle section. When Mahlerian *angst* is called for, there is no want of it, as when Klemperer builds to a gigantic climax that ends with an enormous octave plunge in violins. The finale is also deeply felt. From the tearful opening measures, Klemperer maintains a moderate pace, encouraging the strings to cut emphatically into each accented note. Despite his reserve, this reading is undoubtedly very personal. Again wrong entrances intrude, interrupting the serenity of the development's opening section. At the height of the movement's main climax, a curious crescendo in the trumpets buries the high C-flats, which mirror the opening "heartbeat" motto of the symphony. The final page is heartbreakingly slow, virtually dripping with the last vestiges of lifeblood. What a pity that so many miscues mar this otherwise moving performance.

KLEMPERER, OTTO/Vienna Philharmonic (perf. 9 June 1968) - 2-Hunt/Arkadia 563 (1989) [82:38]* This performance was given during the Edinburgh Festival in 1968, in the same year as the Klemperer/VPO performance reviewed above. As one might expect, Klemperer's reading is essentially the same in both versions. False entrances and other slippages still occur, but are less significant given the fact that the VPO seems in better form here. Brass and strings make a strong impression, the former especially in the Scherzo, the latter most notably in the finale. Klemperer starts off with less deadening weightiness than in the other 1968 performance. His tempi for the three dance themes of the second movement are slightly less exaggerated. In fact, tempi throughout seem more comfortable and better coordinated; balances are better defined and inner voices more focussed. As before Klemperer presents a dramatic and forceful reading, thrilling in its power in the outer movements and well-turned in evoking the parodistic and demonic aspects of the middle movements.

KUBELIK, RAFAEL/Bavarian Radio Symphony - 2-DG 139345/6 (1967); 415 634 (1986); 10- 429 042 (1990) [76:51] The basic approach, typical of Kubelik, is objective yet characterized by flexible tempi and numerous mannerisms. The outer movements lack the spaciousness that would have allowed the music to breathe more naturally and fully. One particularly valuable asset is the antiphonal placement of violins, highlighting the contrapuntal intricacies often developed between firsts and seconds. After an appropriately hesitant opening, Kubelik paces the first movement briskly setting the music on edge. Affectations in the form of slight ritards at the height of a phrase seem somewhat overdone within the context of a generally *mosso* tempo (e.g., notice the grandiose affect at m.196, after which the music gallops toward a long plunge). One might conclude that Kubelik becomes involved in the music only at its big moments. While the second movement is essentially well-conceived, setting and coordinating the three principal tempi in fine proportion, many sections seem slightly forced or stiff (clipped dotted rhythms can produce this result). Antiphonal violins are used to good effect in the Burleske, where they seem sharper than elsewhere, but brass sometimes lag behind and horns are out of phase in the opening. Tempi are again flexible: Kubelik slows up for the second theme, speeds up before the final return of the scherzo, and then eases up after having reached it. Ironically, the one movement in which he might have put his flexible approach to good use is the finale, yet Kubelik's reading is measured and almost completely devoid of feeling until the ultimate climax before the reprise. From here he moves along smartly, gracing the music with gorgeous string portamenti. A touching sense of repose diffuses the intensity of the finale in its last moments.

KUBELIK, RAFAEL/Bavarian Radio Symphony (perf. 1975) - 2-Originals SH 806/7 (1994) [79:26]+ Unfortunately, little detailed information about this performance is provided in this release. The essential elements of Kubelik's interpretation remain unchanged from that of his commercial recording. Had sonic quality been even tolerable (loud tape hiss, high and close volume levels and muddy, raspy tone quality) and the BRSO in better form, this recording might have been more satisfying. Kubelik tends to highlight the more powerful and agitated sections of the first movement over the easy-going principal theme, which sometimes has a stiff and hurried character. As a result strong climaxes, such as at the close of the development (18'+), stand out disproportionately. Elsewhere a tendency toward hastiness often affects the lyrical flow. While Kubelik sets each of the three dance tempi in the second movement at an appropriate pace, he often treats some of these tempi (particularly for the Tempo III minuet) with such elasticity that one is not certain what the tempo is. He sometimes interjects hesitations or slow-ups that work both against Mahler's directions and a steady linear course (e.g., at 12:50 before the sudden return of Tempo I in the second movement and at 10' in the third). The Scherzo exudes much energy, even if Kubelik tries to mellow the character of the second theme. In the finale, Kubelik is uncharacteristically spacious in his treatment of the principal theme. Soft segments have a tender, pliant quality, given more breathing room than Kubelik provides anywhere else in the performance. The BRSO strings certainly have enough breadth of tone and dynamic thrust to fulfill the imposing requirements of the main theme, with its sustained *forte/fortissimo* dimensions and textural complexity. Brass, on the other hand, sound too rigid in strong passages. The final page is beautifully and sensitively played and is well worth waiting for.

LEVINE, JAMES/Philadelphia Orchestra - 2-RCA ARL2-3461 (1979); RCD2-3461 (1986)** Again Levine shows his deep commitment to Mahler's music by providing one of the most sensitive, expressive and thoughtful performances of The Ninth ever recorded. Each nuance is handled with care in a very personal, emotive approach. Rarely have the demonic intensity of the Scherzo and the heavenly rapture and prayerful ardor of the finale been captured with such interpretive understanding. One would only wish that RCA sonics were less constricted and jagged in bass tones. A *sotto voce* opening (which smothers a statement of the "Fate" motif on harp) gives way to a lingering but genuinely expressive main theme. In perfect contrast is Levine's harsh treatment of the antithetical second subject. Tempi are sometimes flexible but generally well-conceived. Levine adds furious intensity to more passionate moments (e.g., at *mit Wut*) and drives home the dramatic effect of powerful passages with a will. Some efforts at expressivity seem forced, such as the awkward treatment of the second theme in the development section. Strangely enough, the trombone outburst on "Fate" that ushers in the reprise seems unduly subdued for such an overpowering moment. In the second movement, sharp, angular playing by antiphonal violins is very effective in a restrained treatment of the opening ländler section. The waltz theme (Tempo II) has a snappy quality and the slower Tempo III (on the "*ewig*" motif) is very languid, if not tired. Although string portamenti are well done and percussion strong (as is typical of Levine), the orchestral playing style seems slightly uncomfortable at times. But the Burleske is absolutely thrilling! Levine captures the driving intensity and devilishness of this music in perfectly idiomatic style. He elicits very strong and precise playing from the Philadelphians. As vibrant and exciting as is the Scherzo, so deeply moving are the more lyrical sections of the Burleske. The finale may be the most emotive ever recorded. Without resorting to untoward affects, Levine's reading is so moving that it must evidence a deeply personal commitment to this music. Details are rendered with the utmost care, especially strong accents and subtle nuances of phrasing. Levine achieves moments of overwhelming power as well as heavenly serenity in a performance that takes one's breath away.

MAAZEL, LORIN/Vienna Philharmonic - 2-CBS 12M 39721 (1986); 14-Sony SK14K48198 (1992) [84:06] It is ironic that the conductor given the honor of recording a complete Mahler symphony cycle with the modern successor of Mahler's orchestra would turn in such a completely unimpressive performance of Mahler's last complete work (premiered by this orchestra in 1912). Judging from the lack of sensitivity, involvement and dramatic impact of his reading, Maazel clearly has no feeling for the work. Only in his lingering approach to the final page is there evidence of what this sprawling masterpiece might be all about. As for the remainder of the symphony, it seems devoid of feeling, intensity, and any sense of conception. The dramatic conflict of the opening movement is completely absent; the music is merely dashed off with little attention given to the dramatic aspects of its moments of crisis or repose. Even the orchestral playing seems uninvolved. Transitions are roughly handled and polyphonic texture frequently blurred. Undoubtedly, all the notes are there somewhere but they are not put together to make the music say anything profound. The second movement lacks any particularly Viennese style. In its place is left a dull, flatulence, lacking color and nuance. Maazel takes the opening ländler tempo on the hurried side (certainly not *sehr gemächlicher*), yet the waltz theme seems heavy-footed and the tender *Lebewohl* minuet (Tempo III) merely a brief "tah-tah." If this movement should portray the maddening whirl of daily life, it could do so only after a post mortem. Much the same could be said of the Rondo-Burleske. Lacking any intensity or drive, this movement simply moves along lifelessly (even the final coda is simply dull). Equally cold and insensitive is Maazel's reading of the finale. Accents are underdone and underlying tension completely absent. Only in the quieter sections and the closing coda do moments approaching blissful serenity appear. Even Maazel's usual interest in clarity of line is not evident, especially in high powered and thickly-textured passages.

MADERNA, BRUNO/BBC Symphony (perf. 31 March 1971, London) - Hunt/Arkadia CDMAD 016 (1991) [78:02]*+   Composer/conductor Bruno Maderna makes a singularly personal statement here. He stretches out slow tempi and ritards to the breaking point and then presses forward with exasperating willfullness in faster sections. Such a flexive approach, although sometimes taken to extremes, makes for a vital, often riveting performance, provided that one makes allowances for Maderna's many diversions from Mahler's directions. Loping sluggishly through the opening measures, lingering on appoggiaturas, Maderna still manages to convey warmth and tenderness in the first movement's principal theme, emotions completely dispelled by the hard thump of timpani that ushers in the harsh, agitated second theme. As the music builds to an early climax before return of the principal theme, Maderna draws out the climbing string phrase with such long lines--virtually placing a fermata over the high F# with which it closes--that the effect is nothing less than breathtaking. Then the principal theme appears more assertive and agitated. Extremes in tempi are the order of the day; but they do not cut deep. The profound struggle between the forces of Life and Death implicit here takes on more urgency than in many competing versions. While Maderna's free manner with tempi may not be to everyone's taste, it is difficult to turn a deaf ear to the outpouring of emotion that he achieves. How forcefully the development builds to a climax (c.10+), prefigured with a wrenching statement of "*Du aber Mensch*" from the *Trinklied* movement of *Das Lied von der Erde*, then hurtling to its own doom. Thereafter, horn "farewells" become ghostly apparitions of horrific presentment, underlined in long strokes. Before the reprise offers hoped for relief, trumpets blare out their tattoos demonstratively, as if in defiance of Fate.

In the second movement, Maderna sets a brisk pace for the ländler. During a marvelously extroverted waltz section, notice how shyly the 16th-note upbeat to the ländler wanders in and out of place. Maderna's decision to stop in his tracks at the end of a long, drawn out ritard into the Tempo III minuet (at 11:45) is questionable, however. The Scherzo is full of vigor, brass playing emphatically throughout. Naturally, Maderna makes much of the wilder moments, particularly at the close. But the mediating glimpse of heaven which forms the inner core of the movement is mercifully not stretched out too far, but played *legato* without over-indulgence. How poignantly the horns blare out after 7', as if recalling life's deep woes. When scherzo elements begin to stir in the undercurrent, Maderna treats them weightily at first (at 9:15) until they become more assertive. The closing moments are a devil's dance of victory. In the final movement, Maderna sets a moderately brisk main tempo, establishing a mood more intense and agitated than ardently spiritual. One senses that the struggle is far from over. A feeling of cool detachment sets in, underlying tension rarely giving way to repose. After a long pause into the subordinate theme (4:45), Maderna pursues the exposition's climax fiercely, climbing fervently to its highpoint only to resolve into nothingness (7:27+). The development moves along with little hesitency or spaciousness, losing the sense of suspension that makes its loftly sentiments all the more spellbinding. Just before the reprise (at 11:52), Maderna calls a halt to let the music catch its breath. Now unmarked hesitancies occur, infusing the main theme's return with an acute feeling of worldly suffering. Approaching the final moments, intensity and agitation subside. Maderna takes nearly five minutes for the last two pages. Each note is treated as a strand of life-tissue, holding onto existence with every fibre of its being. However controvertial Maderna's exaggerations might be, the entire performance is an event that is difficult to forget.

MADERNA, BRUNO/Orchestra Sinfonica di Torino della RAI (perf. 22 Dec. 1972, Torino) - 4-Hunt/Arkadia CDMAD 028.4 (1993) [77:48]*+ Maderna offers essentially the same perspective that flaunted all convention in his earlier BBC performance (see above). As in the latter, his extremely pliant pacing and the orchestra's inexperience with this complex work cause many technical problems, yet under these trying circumstances, the Turin ensemble plays admirably, if not flawlessly. Sonics are cleaner and better balanced than in the BBC recording. But a few new problems crop up. For instance, the timpani comes in with the "heartbeat" motto two bars late at the enraged *mit Mut* section of the first movement. While brass still play up the grotequeries that haunt the second movement, the opening ländler seems less sprightly and gay than in the BBC version. Maderna's long, drawn out ritard into Tempo III leaves the horn strangely exposed. While the Scherzo is as agitated and uneven as before, the finale opens in a broader tempo, that becomes brisker at *Straffer im Tempo* (in stricter tempo) and becomes restless and passionate, rather than spiritual and reverent, until the closing coda. Here, as before, Maderna slows up substantially in order to draw out as much as possible this simple but moving depiction of life's final moments.

MASUR, KURT/New York Philharmonic - Teldec 4509-90882 (1995) [78:35]*
Throughout the opening movement Masur's competent and steady hand is applied consistently. Tempi are well-conceived, mood swings aptly juxtaposed from the relaxed opening theme to the ardent counter-subject. Masur does not try to overwhelm at strong climaxes, but places them conceptually within the context of the whole. He also eschews mannerisms, tending to stiffen the line at times rather than succumb to flabbiness or undue haste. We find no interesting revelations here; just well-wrought, professional music-making, yet Mahler's idiom may require much more than merely skillful management. Compromising the impression made by extreme contrasts weakens their impact, and thereby tempers the shock of sudden, sometimes violence vicissitudes. Inner voices are audible and properly balanced; but brass cover strings during strong tutti sections. Many of the same characteristics are found in the ländler movement. Masur makes no attempt to endow the opening dance theme with an especially countrified character, diminishing the effect of Mahler's parody of *fin de siecle* Viennese cosmopolitan life vs. Provincial rusticity. The waltz theme gradually becomes very brisk, hastily sped through on its return, thereby causing the reprise of the ländler thereafter to hurry forward. One strange nuance is applied at 11:35, when without benefit of any suggestion to this effect in the score, Masur morosely grinds down nearly to a halt the closing segment of the mild-mannered minuet (Tempo III) before what Mahler intended to be an unanticipated return of the opening ländler. The result is startlingly grotesque and detracts from what should be a sudden tempo change for the unexpected return of the opening ländler theme.

What makes this performance admirable is the brilliant treatment afforded the last two movements. Masur sweeps one away with his vital and energetic pacing of the Scherzo's principal subject. He also handles the calmer middle section quite effectively. It is in the urgent impulse applied to the Scherzo that enables Masur to capture the mad whirl of modern life so engagingly. Masur seems more involved in the finale than in the first two movements, getting more deeply into the emotive essence of this increasingly intense prayer. Pacing is brilliantly conceived, flowing evenly yet with suppleness and nuance. Without over-emphasis, Masur adds weight and accentuation to the opening theme. Quieter transition passages are hauntingly beautiful. Climaxes build steadily and with the application of just enough pressure to impel the music forward without undue haste. Each of the isolated tones on the final page is rendered lovingly, with such warmth and tenderness as would betoken a touching last farewell.

MITROPOULOS, DIMITRI/New York Philharmonic - 2-Replica RPL 1460/1 (1980); Hunt/Arkadia 521 (1988) [73:09] The performance recorded here was given at Carnegie Hall on January 23, 1960. As to be expected, Mitropoulos provides a cold and generally pressed reading, far removed from the emotive core of the music. His tendency to move along with little effect or sensitivity seems bare and harsh. When the music calls for a more hard-edged or intense approach, Mitropoulos is right on target (as in the second theme of the first movement). Quickly paced and icy cold, the first movement lacks depth of emotion and lyric expressivity. Powerful moments seem subdued. Tempi are frequently pressed and too flexible, Mitropoulos often having to overcompensate in transitions to reach the appropriate tempo or simply ignoring tempo markings altogether. The second movement is completely ruined by very fast tempi for both the ländler and the minuet. At these tempi, what results is a second scherzo! Strangely enough, in the very last measure the tempo suddenly drops to a crawl! Mitropoulos does capture the spirit of the Burleske after a mild opening. Although objective in approach, some touching moments occur in the lyrical middle section. The transition back to the opening scherzo theme is handled ever so cautiously. Of the finale, one could simply say that it certainly would not melt butter. Tempi are fast and the overall effect is cold and detached. Only in the coda's fragmented lyricism does a glimmer of warmth come through.

MORRIS, WYN/Symphonia of London - 2-Peters PLE-116/7 (1978); 2-IMP DPCD 1025 (1993) [91:23]* Possibly Morris' most satisfying performance of a Mahler symphony on disk, this splendid version seems more characteristically Mahlerian than Morris's Anglicized readings of the Second and the Fifth Symphonies. The uncomfortably stiff playing and plodding tempi that happened the musical flow in these earlier symphonies are generally absent here. In the Ninth, Morris is more securely on the mark: his reading is idiomatic, sensitive and powerful. After an evenly paced if objectified opening, the first movement settles in comfortably with a plaintive first theme, countered by a darkly foreboding second subject. While the development section contains some clumsy (before #9) and disspirited moments (at *mit Wut*), a few very interesting aspects should be mentioned: controlled tempi never drag and terrifying intensity is achieved without excessive speed. Playing is not always comfortable and could be sharper and more robust. Antiphonal strings enhance clarity of line. Tempi in the second movement are basically fine: the ländler is sprightly if controlled and the waltz theme is effervescent, but Tempo III is set so close to the ländler tempo, that it seems too brisk. Morris frequently overdoes ritards, making them sound awkward to the point of caricature.

The orchestra comes alive in the Burleske. Exuding strength and excitement, this movement displays excellent playing, except for a pressed and rough treatment of the second subject. The main tempo is controlled but not constricted. Following upon a fine middle section, Morris seems to run out of gas with the return of the scherzo material. But his energies are regenerated in the finale, where his reading is both intense and sensitive. One could only wish for more consistently strong and less insecure playing. Notwithstanding, Morris delivers a quality performance to match the reputation he had rightfully earned in England by reason of his several concert offerings of the Ninth.

SYMPHONY NO. 9

NANUT, ANTON/Radio Symphony Orchestra of Ljubljana - 12-Digital Concerto CCT 999701 (1992) [81:54] This performance, included in a budget series from Yugoslavia, has little to offer. Conductor Nanut misses the many opportunities for expression that this work affords. Control and restraint take the place of nuance and dramatic impetus. The Ljubljana orchestra sounds stiff, unexpressive and uninvolved. Strings have little substance and brass are either constricted when they should play out strongly or overpowering when they should blend better into the orchestral texture. Sonic quality is yet another detraction, volume levels having been severely dampered.

NEUMANN, VÁCLAV/Czech Philharmonic - 2-Pro Arte 2PAD 207; 2CDD-207 (1982); Supraphon C37-7340 (1987); SUP 111980 (1993); 11-Supraphon 111860 (1994) [76:59] As with most of Neumann's cycle, this performance lacks sufficient dramatic punch and sensitivity to be completely satisfying. A cool detachment pervades much of the music. Neumann rarely gets to the heart of the matter, seeking instead to moderate both dynamic levels and depth of feeling. Tempi are brisk when they should be more tempered or lingering and weighty when a quicker pace would be more appropriate. While Neumann moves along without hesitation in the first movement in a rather impersonal manner, some fairly impassioned moments break through, but no cataclysms occur, even at the thunderous return of the "Fate" motif in trombones at the height of the storm in the development that ushers in the reprise. The CPO plays generally well but has a tendency in brass to clip dotted rhythms. Neumann's tempi in the second movement are too fast, and the ländler bounds along aimlessly. Even if the principal tempi are consistent, tempo changes are often abrupt when they should be smoother. An abominably untoward affect appears toward the end (at the double bar at m.516) that ruins the suddenness with which Tempo I should reappear. In the coda Neumann also sets a speedy pace, ignoring all markings to the contrary (*gehalten*; *nicht eilen*). On the other hand, the Burleske is ponderously dull and sluggish. Lacking intensity in the scherzo section and warmth in the lyrical middle section, the reading seems completely out of touch with the music. The finale opens more idiomatically, promising at least a satisfying close to this otherwise disappointing performance. In a basically conservative approach, Neumann elicits more passion here than elsewhere in the symphony. Yet warning signs of a change in direction begin to appear during the development section, where Neumann presses the tempo forward despite contrary signals. Playing becomes routine and lackluster, a blaring trumpet spoiling the climax. Just as it would seem that he has come out of this momentary lapse, Neumann takes the final Adagissimo extremely fast in complete disregard of both Mahler's intentions and the aesthetic content of these very sensitive and tender closing measures.

NEUMANN, VÁCLAV/Leipzig Gewandhaus Orchestra - 2-Eterna 825946 (1969); Berlin Classics 0021872BC (1994) [76:03]*+ Finally resurfacing after many years of limited availability, Neumann's Leipzig Gewandhaus performance is a revelation. Unlike in his later version with the Czech Philharmonic (see above), Neumann now demonstrates his complete grasp of the score's conceptual and emotive essence as well as his deep commitment to the work. No sense of detachment is apparent. Throughout the opening movement, heightened impulse and urgency sweep the music forward with gusto. The second theme has more thrust, angularity and textural richness and climaxes have more dynamic thrust (e.g., the *mit Wut* section is a shocker, horns hurling out their virulent pronouncements forcefully). More typical of Neumann's approach is the tendency to press forward briskly, here in the service of greater vitality. Sometimes Neumann overdoes it, for instance when approaching the reprise. Each of the three dance themes in the second movement is aptly paced and handled stylishly, with emphasis on their respective caricaturesque qualities. An unwarranted slow-up on the trumpet fragment of the Tempo III minuet at 12:20 disengages the effect of a sudden shift back to the rustic Tempo I ländler that follows. Neumann gives plenty of impetus to the Burlesque movement without shifting into overdrive. Playing is as articulate here as it is throughout the performance. The return of the second theme at 4:49 has a delightful march-like character. Neumann sets a brisk pace for the calmer middle-section, giving the impression of being unaccustomed to its serenity, having undergone the maniacal turbulence of the preceding section. How wickedly brass infiltrate this otherwise heavenly vision with their nasty premonition of the frenzied opening theme's return. For the final movement, Neumann sets a perfectly appropriate pace, broad and flexible but not exceedingly loose. Inner strings are both clear and well-accented. In a passionate reading, the second theme literally reeks with emotion. Unlike many conductors, Neumann choses to ease up to the highpoint of the exposition (10+) rather than press forward. While sonic quality is excellent, softer sections come out too strongly to create a serene atmosphere when the music requires it, particularly during the opening of the development. Here Neumann moves forward hastily at the outset, passing over without attention Mahler's tempo markings into the climax of the section calling for gradually brisker motion. When Neumann eases up for the return of the main theme during the reprise, the oboe solo at 18:58 suddenly rushes, breaking the mood and possibly causing the tempo to press hurriedly into the final coda. As later with the CPO, Neumann sets more of an *adagio* than *adagissimo* tempo for the last page. A sense of remoteness from the moving emotions of this touching farewell pervades the final moments.

OZAWA, SEIJI/Boston Symphony - 2-Philips 426 302 (1989/1991); 14-Philips 438 874 (1995) [82:25]+ As with most of Ozawa's Mahler recordings, what is missing here is the dramatic conflict, the life-and-death struggle that finally ends in calm resignation. While the latter comes through beautifully, the former does not. Even with much energy and vigor applied to the quicker sections of the opening movement, Ozawa tempers their effect either by defanging the biting grotesqueries in brass and woodwinds or pressing forward so ardently that the dramatic impact of climaxes becomes a mere momentary flash. Emphasizing warmth of tone and smoothness of expression, he downplays the intense emotions that pervade this movement. This interpretive style is no less apparent in the second movement. Here all is brightness, jollity and good spirits; but where is the biting parody and the sarcastic witticisms which expose the demonic side of this music? Ozawa handles the many tempo changes in this movement well enough, but the parody of its contrasting dance themes never comes to the surface. The opening ländler has a snappy quality, while both waltz and minuet seem restrained or pale by comparison. Ozawa generates much vitality in the succeeding Scherzo movement, but it never draws one to the brink of disaster. In the calmer middle section, Ozawa tries for effusive effects by interjecting several luftpausen (e.g., at 5:55), but when the piccolo clarinet comes in with its mockery of the finale's main theme, it sounds merely tame, its wicked, demonic aspect being entirely absent. The brilliant sheen of the BSO strings pervades the finale. While generally well-paced, little depth of feeling comes to the surface during the impassioned build-up to the huge climax of the development. From there complex textures become jumbled. The closing coda is treated broadly and sensitively, but without engendering the feeling that this ending came out of a long, arduous struggle with negative forces constantly threatening catastrophe.

PESEK, LIBOR/Royal Liverpool Philharmonic - 2-Virgin VCDS 791219 (1991) [85:16]
* Pesek's account of the Ninth is impressive for an initial entry into the field of Mahler recordings. His reading of the finale is especially notable for its depth of emotion and sensitivity. Despite brilliant characterizations of Mahler's frequently wicked treatment of brass and woodwinds intrusions, what seems lacking at times is his willingness to let loose. The dark, doleful aspects of the first movement are presented in the bright light of day. Pesek employs driving tempi to heighten the intensity of dramatic sections, such as at the enraged *mit Wut*

segment (10:30). Playing sometimes becomes rigid and constricted, although the RLPO makes a strong general impression throughout. At times, one senses that Pesek, with all of his concentration on the threatening aspect of this life-death struggle, seems one degree removed from the music's passions. Yet his harsh, malevolent treatment of brass and woodwind motifs is uncompromising. Without a moment's hesitation, Pesek dives into the second movement, setting a pesky pace for the opening ländler without emphasizing its rustic character. By contrast, his waltz tempo is more laid back, if not particularly *schwungvoll*. Low brass crudely mock the waltz music as if denigrating its cosmopolitanism (3:30+). No intellectual subtleties here, just good raucous fun. Rather than calming down at the close, Pesek lets the movement unwind naturally until a slight ritard on the last phrase adds poignancy to the undaunted ribaldry of the proceedings.

In the succeeding Scherzo, Pesek sets a brisk pace in an effort to set fire to this angry music, while highlighting its brash character. Again grotesqueries are unmitigatingly vulgar (horns at c.5'). Pesek's treatment of the calmer middle-section is impressive, with its portentious, if bizarre rendition of a fragment from the finale's hymn-tune. Notice how nastily the E-flat clarinet hesitates on this mocking version of that theme, before the return of the opening scherzo material. When the principal subject again bursts on the scene, Pesek drives it furiously to a sensational close. In the finale, the RLPO strings sound full and resplendent. Accentuation and inner voice balancing are superb. Horns bray out over the throng, adding a brilliant tonal overlay to climactic moments (9:25 to 10:20). Pesek sometimes presses forward in calmer sections (e.g., into the development). He and his orchestra are deeply committed to this music, and their high level of concentration is most apparent in the closing moments, when the musical elements dissipate in a representation of life's gradual demise.

ROSBAUD, HANS/Southwest German Radio Symphony, Baden-Baden (perf. 1960s) - Arkadia CDGI 757 (1991) [74:06]*+ On occasion those who rummage through performance tapes from the past come up with an important discovery. Such is this superlative issue of a noted Mahlerian conductor, Hans Rosbaud. Despite his orchestra's lack of tonal brilliance and precision, he turns in a marvelous performance. The opening movement virtually seethes with intensity through heightened agitation, which increases to ferocity at 8:30. Here heroic horn calls evoke a terrifying vision of intense rage which ends by plunging to the depths of despair. Suddenly Rosbaud pulls up the tempo at the close of this section (10:50) to usher in a ghostly atmosphere, overladen with distant horns in a apparitional presentment. From there the music drives forward urgently until an awesome outburst of the opening Fate motto shatters all that preceded it, striking such a terrible blow that its previous vigor is completely decimated. In the second movement, Rosbaud shows his natural kinship with the stylistic elements of both rustic and cosmopolitan dance music in a witty, yet sarcastic rendition. His opening ländler has heft as well as bite yet enough weight to appear as a distant memory in old age of the joyous delights of youth. A vigorous waltz contrasts well with a charming minuet. Like dancing marionettes the players prance along merrily without a care in the world. Rosbaud dives into the Scherzo-Burlesque movement with a will, heightening the tension it creates with vital energy. Again his reading of the calmer middle section provides a perfect contrast to the Scherzo's dark demonic character. Rosbaud's sense of timing is superb; notice how he hesitates just enough to make the climax at around 8:00 in this movement simply devastating. In the finale, Rosbaud offers a devoutly reverent reading, full of pathos and recalling the fervent spirituality of Bruckner (to whom both the title "*Adagio*" given by Mahler for this movement and its opening measures refer).

SANDERLING, KURT/Berlin Symphony - 2-Eterna 827433 (1981); 2-Tokuma 32TC-108/109 (1986); 2-Ars Vivendi 2200 224 (1991) [80:04] + An inveterate harshness permeates this entire performance, sometimes giving it a rough-hewn quality, at other times heightening intensity to the level of polemic. This austerity appears not only at the interpretive level and in playing style, but also seems to infect the sonic quality, and is often painfully oppressive at strong climaxes. Sanderling rarely relaxes his forces between the sluggish opening and the spacious close. He energizes the more passionate sections of the first movement with feverish urgency: witness how he relentlessly he presses to the enormous outburst of the fate motto at the end of the development, or propels forward hurriedly to the great plunge into the abyss at #11. In his hands the angular second theme sounds both darkly foreboding and intensely fertive, yet moments of stark coldness run through the veins of this movement as well (e.g., around #16). Unfortunately, inner voices sound fudged and brass distant. In the second movement, Sanderling's raucous treatment of the opening ländler and his rough-and-ready manner with the waltz lessens the contrast between them, while highlighting their difference from the more languid strains of the minuet. A chilly aura hovers over the movement. Again in the Scherzo, brusqueness, bordering on acrimoniousness, marks the main material, even placing its stamp upon the lighter second theme. A hard-driven undercurrent, continuously subject to unremitting high volume, gives the scherzo subject a frigid aspect. Tensions rarely subside, even in the quieter middle section. The closing stretto really begins from the return of the scherzo theme, already paced so briskly that the marked tempo increases up to the presto close are given little effect. In the final movement, coarse sonics at high volume levels heighten the music's fiery passion but diminish its devotional spirituality. Sanderling keeps the tension going by pressing forward without let-up, until some relief is provided in the quieter moments, where he merely lets the music play itself, causing a rigidly measured pace. In an otherwise straight and unadventurous reading, Sanderling suddenly speeds up at mm.136-140. The closing moments are handled with sensitivity, that might have been enhanced by more legato in the strings.

SANDERLING, KURT/Philharmonia Orchestra - 2-Erato 2292 45816-2 (1992) [82:16]

Those who may be tempted to acquire this version in hopes that it may be more representative of Sanderling's interpretive approach than his BSO reading of some years earlier (see above) should be forewarned. In this recording, Sanderling fails to generate much energy or intensity, moving through his paces in such a superficial, if not sometimes awkward, manner that the entire performance is unimpressive. He generates little life in the first movement, failing to project the profound conflict between heroic and demonic forces. Playing is mild, pale and smoothed over; sonics weak and unfocussed. After a taut, rigid and severely clipped first theme, the angular second subject seems rather bland by comparison. Plodding along with little inflection, the movement remains tightly controlled, the intensity of its passions falling flat. The same mild manner pervades the second movement, where the ländler appears like a mere apparition of itself. Such an unimaginative, antiseptic and, but for some mercilously long ritards, inflexible reading provides little to attract attention. Brass weigh down the music further with grossly exaggerated vulgarities at 14'. The Scherzo's fierce temperament is also abated, lacking force and robust playing. Cautious, stiff or routine playing take the place of spontaneity and involvement. Even the lyrical middle section sounds cool and the closing stretto matter-of-fact. Sanderling tempers the emotion-charged finale so severely that all of its impulse and tension is drained dry. Contrapuntal strings are indistinct, weak and colorless. This seriously flawed performance has even less to offer than Sanderling's earlier BSO version.

SCHERCHEN, HERMANN/Vienna Symphony (perf. 19 June 1950, Grosser Saal, Vienna) - Orfeo C228901A (1990) [69:04]; Melodram CDM 18038 (1991) [70:01]

Scherchen's frenetic approach to tempo in the first movement combines with any icy cold demeanor to make for an extremely harsh, insensitive and often slap-dash performance.

The VSO has great difficulty keeping up with his mad dashes (e.g., at the close of the exposition and into the huge dive which plunders the first climax of the development), which cause confusion and insecurity. As impulsive as Scherchen is here, he can also be extremely inflexible, especially with the principal subject. When intensity increases, the music behaves like a wild beast. What we have here is either careless lack of involvement or unrestrained madness. The closing coda provides welcome relief. More in character, the ländler movement has the virtue of stylish dance tempi: a hefty, bumpkinesque opening ländler, energetic waltz and somewhat languidly mannered minuet. Scherchen's tempo adjustments conflict with Mahler's directions: for example, applying a gradual instead of sudden return to the opening ländler at 12:40. Ritards are stretched out to the limit (c. 8:40). An early miscue in celli (2:46) causes an entire measure to be omitted (m.87). One wonders how much rehearsal time was given to this performance.

Scherchen's impulsive manner works better in the Scherzo, even if it causes the strings some difficulty in handling their fugetto figuration. Anticipating the return of the scherzo section after the calmer middle section by pressing the tempo forward early, Scherchen has difficulty coordinating the brisk tempo he finally sets for.the scherzo subject with the tiered tempo increases of the closing stretto. But what a wild devil's dance it is! For the finale, Scherchen removes himself from this moving music, setting brisk tempi that result in more technical problems (e.g., for the second violin at m.73). Skimming over the surface of this deeply impassioned music causes playing to straddle between being perfunctory and imprecise. Only at the close does Scherchen try to be more sensitive. But atrocious string sound and loud, harsh sonics (with audible street noise in the Melodram edition) make what should be moments of blissful serenity unbearably noisy.

SEGERSTAM, LEIF/Danish National Radio Symphony - 3-Chandos CHAN 9057-59 (1992) [90:57]* Segerstam's tendency to underline and highlight particular effects reminds one of similar efforts by Bernstein in his early recordings. While lack of audience familiarity with Mahler's idiom may have justified such an approach in the past, it cannot be said to do so now. What results from so many hesitations, long ritards, stretched swells and overly pronounced inner voices is either an extremely fussy or over-indulgent reading. While Segerstam makes every effort to create a dramatic effect, too much of a good thing may have its negative consequences. His view of the first movement is deeply tragic, and he uses every means at his disposal to enhance this conception. How sorrowful, rather than turbulent, sounds the angular second theme, yet how furiously he drives through the *mit Wut* section (12:10), even adding curious hesitencies that momentarily interrupt the oppressively fast tempo. After #13, the "*lebwohl*" motif becomes frighteningly stark where it might have been consoling. A mournful quality infuses the shadowy atmosphere at 17:10 with tragic presentment. At 20:45 the "*Du aber Mensch*" quote from *Das Lied von der Erde* is momentarily held at the edge of a vast precipice, threatening to hurl one down into the abysmal depths only to be blown away from the precipice by an enormous outburst of the "heartbeat" motto in low brass. Even the calmer chamber-like section that precedes the final moments is treated expressively.

In the ländler movement, Segerstam plays up the grotesque elements, but strings do not have enough heft to make the ländler theme sound sufficiently rustic. His penchant for stretching out ritards and jutting forward abruptly characterize also this movement. The waltz is gay and the minuet lilting. When the opening ländler suddenly reappears before the close, woodwinds cry out in vain to stop the unremitting madness. Most impressive is the wildly furious Scherzo movement, and especially interesting are Segerstam's emotive exaggerations in the middle section. Notice how hesitently the solo oboe plays the turn theme before brass intrude threatening the scherzo's return (10:40). A no-holes-barred stretto closes the movement with as much wild ferocity and raw power as these forces can muster. After a broadly paced, heartfelt opening theme, the finale becomes more emotively antiseptic as it increases in volume. Little touches try to enhance the music's compassionate quality, such as a weepy solo violin, but the main tempo seems choppy and the principal subject segmented, so that the overall impression is more one of studied concentration than convincing expressivity. Minor details stand out obtrusively (e.g., the low horn swell at 8:30). In quieter moments a sense of bittersweet contemplation comes through; but stiff playing, especially on dotted rhythms, makes the main theme material sound squarish. After a nearly unending pause, Segerstam manages to elicit tender and sensitive playing during the closing coda. His is an interesting and thoughtful reading, but more so for his treatment of details than an insightful overview.

SINOPOLI, GIUSEPPE/Philharmonia Orchestra - 2-DG 445 817 (1995) [82:39]**
In his Norton lectures, Bernstein interpreted the Ninth as a prophetic warning against the dehumanization of mankind that Mahler presumably envisioned would become increasingly apparent in the twentieth century. If such a view--whether meritorious or not--is taken as a focal point, Sinopoli's reading of the symphony seems to concentrate upon the negative characateristics inherent in that prophecy, as if implicitly fulfilled. For here we have a Ninth for the 90s: cold, aggressive, harsh, impersonal, insensitive, embattled and ultimately nihilistic. Only in the finale does the reality of man's inhumanity cause moments of painful guilt to rise to the surface, although they are sometimes presented in an accusatory tone. The depersonalized level to which we have fallen in this century is characterized relentlessly in the first three movements. Sinopoli takes a staunchly objective approach to the opening movement. His view of the life-and-death struggle it represents is so impersonal that it lacks any of the human qualities--warms, tenderness, sensitivity--that should provide a counterbalance to the negative forces with which they struggle for the conquest of humankind. One suspects from this performance that the battle is long over and the anti-human forces have had the victory.

The entire first movement has a hard-edged, rigid, angular character, tinged with harshness and devoid of the "comodo" quality that should characterize at least the first theme group (as Mahler indicated). Tempi are generally aggressive, making much of the stronger sections fly in the face of the listener rather than gnaw at his innards. Even the lilting string theme in the development section (Index 3 at 2:28), with its kinship to Strauss's *Freut euch des Lebens* waltz, has no Viennese charm, sounding unnaturally tight and hurried. At times, the music seethes with intensity, sometimes gushing over with overbearing anguish but without inflective nuance. Yet the climax of the struggle (when the "heartbeat" motto blasts out of wildly racing string figuration) seems less shocking than what might be expected from the unremitting aggressiveness of the preceding music. Even the return of the main theme at the reprise (Index 7) is exceedingly demonstrative, overly confident and hard-edged, producing a chilling sense that little remains of humanity's caring, loving sensibilities. Mahler's frightening vision has been realized without reservation.

The second movement has many of the same characteristics. A brisk, rough and acrid demeanor infects the ländler theme, with none of its light-hearted rusticity or easy, free-swinging gaiety in evidence. Thus it offers little contrast with the waltz theme, here treated in a curt and brusque manner. Even the minuet exudes little warmth and charm. Curiously, the final return of the ländler (Index 15) is measurably slower than at the beginning of the movement. A pervasive sense of power, harshness and aggression overpowers any humane sentiments. Such qualities are appropriate for the Scherzo movement, and they are certainly present in Sinopoli's rendition of it. His driving force intensifies the principal subject; but the middle section--that should anticipate the soulful nature of the finale--sounds cold, slightly rigidified and certainly not sympathetic. Once again we are confronted with evidence of the fulfillment of Mahler's dreadful prophetic vision.

Having had to endure nearly one hour of unrelenting aggressiveness, intensity and impersonal disposition, the finale provides little relief. This increasingly ardent prayer for redemption from worldly suffering begins with an edgy, constricted temperament that could only be a reaction to the icy detachment of the preceding movements. Again the atmosphere is cold, harsh and barren. No sentiment here; but as the music becomes more fervent, one senses more heart-felt expression. How profoundly the brass intone the "turn" theme, transfigured from its mocking premonition in the Scherzo's middle section on an E-flat clarinet. Toward the end of the exposition, as the music builds to what is to be aborted closure, a rare glimpse of humaneness manages to break through in a pathetic prayer for relief from the harshness of the modern world. As the development approaches its climax, what was a fervent prayer now becomes an accusation. But if humankind has bled itself dry of its own humanity, it has no one to blame but itself. There is implicit in the strong, sharp-edged brass at the height of the reprise a recognition of this unbearable truth. During the denouement that follows Sinopoli has soft strings play long, sinewy glissandi that sound like the faint cry of an unborn child.

Technically, both the recording and the performance are outstanding. Sound quality is pure, dynamic and transparent. The Philharmonia Orchestra plays brilliantly, with full, rich sonorities. Such is to be expected from the better performers in our technologically proficient age, for which this performance stands as both a brilliant representative and perceptive indictor.

SOLTI, GEORG/Chicago Symphony - 2-London LDR 72012; 410012 (1983); 10-London 430 804 (1992) [85:00]*+ A vast improvement over his prior version (see vol.1, pp.147-148), much of Solti's earlier underlying agitation in the outer movements has disappeared, replaced by a more tempered approach that lets the music flow smoothly and evenly. Also impressive is a perfectly coordinated second movement, where the three main tempi are interrelated in just the right perspective. High-powered sonics make powerful sections larger-than-life (especially in brass) while inner voices are more distinctly audible. A comfortable tempo in the first movement (even the second theme has a legato quality) does not impede Solti's capacity to generate tension and dramatic impact. While he does keep tempi under control, there are no boundaries to the level of excitement or vitality he generates. Timpani and brass are sometimes unduly suppressed. In the second movement, Solti's extreme care in structuring tempi might have been the cause of slightly forced playing, but no such problem exists in the Burleske. Hard-driven and wickedly demonic, Solti pushes the scherzo material to the breaking point in a rendition that smacks of Bernstein's *furioso* readings (see above). Although the main theme of the finale is paced slightly slower and played more softly than in his previous version, the overall effect is cool if expressive. Solti dives into phrases somewhat abruptly but achieves a thrilling climax and a gorgeous closing section.

SZELL, GEORGE/Cleveland Orchestra (perf. 9 May 1968) - Stradivarius STR 10012 (1988); 2-Memories HR 4180/81 (1990); Documents (Enterprise) LV 963 (1994) [74:54] * At the end of his glorious years with the Cleveland Orchestra, George Szell offered a Ninth which in many ways summarizes his general interpetive approach. His ability to bring out with remarkable clarity and equipose Mahler's diffuse details is still unsurpassed. While his temperament is objectively detached, he can build up to and release a climax as overpowering as can the best of the more self-indulgent conductors. How magnetic is his power to draw the listener into the maze of this human drama during the development section of the first movement, bringing each wave of passionate effusion to a devastating climax. Yet he paces the main theme briskly, sometimes driving it forward with unremitting urgency. Steeped in the European traditions from which Mahler drew much of his music, Szell handles the diverse dance themes of the second movement in a delightfully parodical style, pitting a foot-stomping ländler against an unabashedly gay waltz. Mahler's terrain of frequent, unprepared tempo shifts is deftly traversed. Yet Szell interposes an abrupt slow-up at the double bar at m.516, anticipating what should be a sudden return of the opening ländler tempo soon thereafter. Despite some instrumental flubs, the brass and woodwinds give due significance to Mahler's many grotesqueries. The succeeding Scherzo movement literally vibrates with energy. Even a few miscues do not diminish the pleasing effect of generally articulate playing here. Szell pulls up only slightly during the calmer middle section, only to drive his musicians all the harder during the stretto coda. In the finale, Szell sets a moderately slow tempo that does not detract from the emotive impact of his impassioned reading; in fact, his pacing gives off such heat as to energize and intensify the music. The exposition closes calmly, if without much hesitation. Szell drives his team ardently to the climax of the development, with an impulse that carries over into the reprise. In the final pages, as emotional intensity subsides, Szell holds both his players and his audience suspended in long stretches of pure sound, warmed by the gorgeous Cleveland strings.

TENNSTEDT, KLAUS/London Philharmonic - 2-Angel SZ-38991; EAC 80586/7; CDC-47112 (1980); 10-EMI CMS7 64471-81 (1993) [84:25]* One must accept Tennstedt's rather self-indulgent approach to appreciate this performance. His penchant for over-emoting lyrical passages and pressing intently forward to climaxes which are then elongated may not be to everyone's taste. While the opening of the first movement has a lingering quality which adds tender sentiment to the first theme, the harsher, almost angry second theme is treated too tamely to contrast effectively. Undoubtedly, Tennstedt feels the movement's deeply emotional essence, but frequent attempts to create a certain impression or emotion by slowing up or pressing forward (contrary to Mahler's directions) seem forced and sometimes fail to evoke the intended reaction. The LPO plays well but for momentary lapses in precision and stylistic treatment. Curiously, Tennstedt pulls in the reins at the huge climax on the "Fate" motif that appears before the reprise, while rendering other minor climaxes more strongly if with little profundity. The coda rambles on in an uninteresting manner. Although the ländler tempo in the second movement is brisk, the other two dance tempi are well paced. What becomes disturbing here are several overly long or added ritards and a tendency to push tempi forward upon return of the main thematical material. Moments of chipper frolicking add comic relief to Tennstedt's otherwise mannered reading. A rapid scherzo tempo in the Burleske movement (particularly apparent in the second theme) causes imprecise attacks and blurs polyphonic texture, yet also fails to elicit a whimsical spirit. Otherwise, the movement is generally well handled but for an occasional unmarked tempo shift or fudged detail. In the opening section of the finale, Tennstedt takes a mild if sentimental approach. Intensity increases as the movement proceeds, reaching a strong climax at the height of the exposition which desolves into a restful transition to the development. From here things move along routinely through the height of the development, marred only by unfocussed sound. Tennstedt elicits some gorgeous playing in a soft and serene coda.

WAKASUGI, HIROSHI/Tokyo Metropolitan Symphony - 2-Fontec FOCD 9028/9 (1991) [81:55]* In the context of an objective approach, sprinkled with occasional emphasis on material not often so highlighted, Hiroshi Wakasugi presents an intelligent, generally well-conceived reading. As is his wont, he never attempts to overwhelm and usually lets the music speak directly without cluttering it with awkward affectations. What results is usually stylish and well-wrought, if lacking personality. The TMSO has had much experience with Mahler's music during the completion of its symphony cycle with Wakasugi, and its progress can be measured by comparing earlier recordings to this one. Much of the tightness and rigidity in figuration that was apparent in earlier Mahler releases has gone and the orchestra plays in fine Mahlerian style. In the first movement, a straightforward reading makes only a moderate impression. Only Wakasugi's decision to hold up on a thematic fragment for horns (m. 184) during the *mit Wut* section, after pressing into it, seems out of place and detracts from the more important *Das Lied* quote ("*Du aber Mensch*") that soon follows (11:15). After a spiritless ländler movement (despite the quickening of Tempo I when its theme recurs toward the close), the Scherzo has much drive and urgency. In the middle section, the horns sound weary, as if exhausted from the fury of the opening section. Wakasugi's finale makes the most consistently satisfactory impression of any of the movements. While his interpretive style is objective, he still elicits strong feelings and a profound sense of peace at the close. Had Wakasugi been more compelling in the opening movement and more spirited throughout the second, this performance would have been a complete success.

WALTER, BRUNO/Vienna Philharmonic - Victor 13522-31; LCT 6015 (1954); 2-Electrola 1C 14701402/1; 2-Turnabout THS 65008/9; Angel CDH 63029 (1989); 2-Palladio PD 4172 (1994) [69:39]*+ While this early issue (of a concert given on January 16, 1938) has undeniable importance for the Mahlerphiles and has received many well deserved plaudits as the premiere recording of this work by the conductor who give its first performance, I still find Walter's reading here to be extremely pressed, even rushed, sometimes lacking in that tender warmth that was to characterize his later recording. Playing is sometimes unsteady and imprecise. There is no doubt that Walter captures much of the music's pathos without emotional excesses but his later reading is much more sensitive and less frenetic. While Walter's tempi are more flexible here than later, he knows just when to make the appropriate effect by use of a stylistic nuance (although at least one attempt seems awkward: at m.148 on the return of Tempo I). Aggressive intensity causes Walter to hurry through the *mit Wut* and *shattenhaft* sections), but he does evoke movement's dramatic sweep. Extreme tempo contrasts characterize the second movement, particularly by reason of a fast waltz (Tempo II) which accelerates at times to a furious clip. Walter captures the Viennese style caricatured here in a thoroughly delightful manner. He begins the ländler with heavy strides that gradually quicken into the main tempo. The Burleske is hard-driven and nervously agitated, especially unnerving in the more subdued middle section even if the climax to this section is given a weighty and dramatic reading. Walter sets a brisk pace for the finale, sometimes seeming overly aggressive. Even if he evokes much passion here, tenderness and serenity are sacrificed to this *mosso* pacing.

WALTER, BRUNO/Columbia Symphony Orchestra - 2-Columbia M2S-676; D3S 744; Odyssey Y2-30308 (1962); CBS-S77275; CBS/SONY 40AC 1834-5; 2-CBS M2K 42033 (1986) [81:10]*+ Compared to Walter's earlier version (see above), this reading is clearly that of an older and more mature conductor. Weightier and more sensitive, the performance succeeds more by its evocation of tragic pathos than by the passionate intensity engendered by brisker pacing in his earlier recording. Although passages occur that seem somewhat laggard, few performances achieve such dramatic power and emotive depth. In fact, tempo control sometimes elicits an underlying tension that builds to shattering climaxes in the first movement. At times, Walter has a problem maintaining a consistent tempo. But his warm and tender treatment of lyrical passages and subtle approach to atmospheric nuances add to the immense pleasure this performance can give. Listen to the mantra-like suspension of tone in the coda, seeming to come from the farthest reaches of space, and the mysterious quality of the transition to the development which languishes indeterminately as if unsure of its fate. Few conductors treat the parodistic elements of the second movement with more aplomb than Walter. Stomping heavily on the first beat of the ländler, he creates an almost caricaturish effect akin to the Austrian equivalent of a Western hoedown. So as not to overplay the waltz, its tempo is set only slightly faster than the ländler (as marked), while the lilting minuet (Tempo III) has a charming Viennese quality without resorting to unnecessary mannerisms. More vitality could have improved particular moments, but the overall effect is very satisfying. Much the same could be said of the Burleske. Never overly fast, the scherzo subject is strong and lively, its intensity derived from underlying impulse rather than excessive speed. The middle section is not treated as a slow movement within a faster one but *etwas gehalten* (slightly held) as written. Walter's genius here is his ability to engender excitement and intensity without extreme tempi or awkward nuances. As one who conducted the premiere performance of this work, he understood the importance Mahler placed upon linear clarity and, consequently, pays careful attention to inner voice placement and proper balances. Walter still moves quickly in the finale, although not so much so as in his earlier version. Some special moments are memorable, such as the end of the climbing phrase to m.73 and the closing page, but elsewhere remnants of the *mosso* approach Walter applied in the previous recording produces a cool effect, particularly in the exposition. Walter may have conceived this approach to avoid unduly self-indulgent emotionalism.

SYMPHONY NO. 10 IN F-SHARP MAJOR (UNFINISHED)

Movements:

1. Adagio.
2. Scherzo I: Schnelle viertel.
3. Purgatorio: Allegretto moderato.
4. Scherzo II: Allegro pesante.
    Nicht zu schnell.
5. Finale

ADAGIO ONLY:

ABBADO, CLAUDIO/Vienna Philharmonic - 2-DG 423 564 (1988); 10-DG 447 023 (1995) [27:19]* Abbado offers a strong, passionate reading that showcases the VPO's glorious brass and brings out inner voice detail and pin-point sforzandi, yet the mood evoked sometimes has a hard edge and seems more aggressive than soul-searching. An emptiness of feeling diminishes the effectiveness of quieter moments (e.g., from m. 91 to m. 99) and more subtle shadings might have enhanced orchestral color. The low brass exude a deathly sound in the piled-on thirds segment linked by deafening trumpet A-naturals.

ABRAVANEL, MAURICE/Utah Symphony - 2-Vanguard SRV 321/2 SD (1975); 11-Vanguard 08.4013.79 (1995) [23:11] Abravanel takes a languid but sensitive approach that is too lyrical to elicit much intensity in the more dramatic moments. The sting of stronger segments is lost in legato playing and smoothed-over accentuation. Rhythmic subsidiary material that should sound devilish only seem innocently lighthearted. Sometimes Abravanel's broad-lined, subtly-phrased style can be effective (at #6), but he underplays climactic passages to a fault.

BERNSTEIN, LEONARD/New York Philharmonic - Columbia M33532 (1970); 3-CBS 42200 (1986); 3-Sony SM3K 47585 (1992) [26:29]* While essentially a well-wrought performance, the general effect seems somewhat edgy and over-anxious. After an expansive and soulful treatment of both the *andante* and *adagio* themes, reaching a climax of profound human pathos at #8, one might expect a more dramatic treatment of the piled-on-thirds climax. Bernstein hurries through this crucial section, as if embarrassed by its extreme dissonance (his remarks on Mahler's alleged flirtation with modernisms are well-known), but the "scherzando" rhythmic material has an appropriately devilish character and the coda is warm and tender. Sonics are clear but strings seem thin and slightly rough in the upper register, putting a jagged edge on soaring string passages.

BERNSTEIN, LEONARD/Vienna Philharmonic (perf. October 1974, Vienna Musikverein, Grosser Saal) - 2-DG 435 102 (1991); DG video 072 515-3 (1991); 13-DG 435 162 (1992) [27:48]* While essentially the same interpretative stance Bernstein took with the NYP a few years earlier, this film version makes visible Bernstein's uncharacteristicly detached manner. His unwillingness to accept Mahler's flirtation with modernistic dissonances may be the reason for his distancing himself from the entire piece, leaving its more powerful moments underdone. Calmer sections are beautifully rendered, enhanced by the VPO strings in full bloom, and scherzando segments have a lusty frivolity and gypsy-like character.

BERNSTEIN, LEONARD/Vienna Philharmonic (perf. 1986) - 2-DG 435 102 (1991); 13-DG 435 162 (1992) [25:57]* Bernstein seems more involved in this performance than he did in his performance with the VPO more than ten years earlier. Now he captures the depths of this symphonic drama with all of the profundity that we have come to expect from his Mahler readings. The opening *andante* breathes with lingering expressivity, and its *adagio* counterpart is just as engaging. Unlike others, Bernstein does not disturb the flow of tempo on the appearance of the contrasting scherzando material at m 28 by quickening the pace, but he does move along more briskly here. The glorious VPO horns are resplendent in their full-blown brilliance at climaxes (e.g., at Index 3/2:50), sometimes stifling strings. By Index 4, the *adagio* theme seems more hurried, and at #30 the *andante* theme has slowed to an *adagio* tempo. Even if Bernstein does not give full vent to the horrifically dissonant chords that mark the dramatic apex of this movement, he still penetrates to its inner soul with profound insight.

BERTINI, GARY/Cologne Radio Symphony - 2-EMI CDS 7 45387-2 (1992) [26:04]+
Heavy accents, occasional slow-ups, long ritards and strong tempo contrasts characterize this uneven performance. One senses a conscious effort to underline details, but with mixed results. The *adagio* theme is broadly paced, while the *andante* opening is steady and unyielding at first, then later more aggressive. Scherzando elements have an easy, lilting quality. Of the several idiosyncrasies Bertini imposes upon the movement, the most egregious occurs on the last two beats into #21 (at 15:23), where Bertini makes a big ritard at the end of a lively scherzando segment. Thereafter, mere note spinning takes the place of interpretation until the *adagio* theme returns, sounding more languid than earlier. Horns crowd out the rest of the orchestra at climaxes, jumping in a hair too soon on the enormous dissonant chords that climax the movement. Sometimes lyrical material seems stiff, volume levels excessive in softer passages and playing uncomfortably edgy.

GIELEN, MICHAEL/Southwest German Symphony, Baden-Baden - Saphir INT 830.875 (1990) [22:13]+ Gielen takes an objective approach, characterized by slightly pressed tempi and cool detachment. He deviates from this with a few affectatious slow-ups that seem counter to his otherwise reserved manner. The Southwest German orchestra often seems tense, yet Gielen rarely urges them to dig into heavily accented passages or hone their articulation on the impish scherzando elements. The result is mostly tame, despite occasional mannered touches.

HAITINK, BERNARD/Concertgebouw Orchestra - Philips 6700 048 (1971); 2-Philips 420 543 (1988); 10-Philips 434 053 (1992); 442 050 (1994) [24:33]** Haitink's reading is still one of the best ever recorded. Superbly played and brilliantly interpreted, little happens here with which to take issue. An expansive treatment of the main themes is enthralling. The introduction has an ominous quality, as if foreshadowing the drama to come. Accents are strong and woodwinds are crisp and well-balanced. The "scherzando" rhythmic material is given a spooky aspect rarely encountered in performances by others who usually gallop through these passages with little subtlety. At #26, the huge A-flat minor outburst is chilling as is the climatic piled-on-thirds segment. Clarity and balances are excellent. Haitink imbues the closing moments with a captivating dream-like quality.

HAITINK, BERNARD/Berlin Philharmonic - 2-Philips 434 997-2 (1995) [26:43]*
A broad *adagio* theme provides an fitting contrast to the opening *andante*. Haitink tempers most of the harshness of this music severely, thereby diminishing its fervent passions and the shock-value of its powerful climaxes. Extremely dissonant tones that should jab through to the heart are merely whispered, especially the violin's high D-flat at #8 (8') and their high D-natural after the massive dissonant chords from 19:44. Haitink falls lumpishly into the terrifying A-flat minor orchestral outburst at 18:55. After favoring the middle tones of the huge dissonant chords that follow, he goes right into the *andante* theme as if totally unaffected by the horrific vision that just occurred. Beautiful playing by BPO strings (*pace* some raggedness) tempers rather than enhances the dramatic impact of this performance.

INBAL, ELIAHU/Frankfurt Radio Symphony - 2-Denon 60CD-1566/7 (1987); 16-Denon CO 72589-604 (1989) [22:56]*   Inbal treats both the *andante* and *adagio* subjects with emotive depth of feeling and sensitivity. The faster sections have a darting angularity that adds a sprightly quality to the impish scherzando elements. Although his tempo choices generally work well, at m.100 on an important rhythmic phrase in celli, Inbal is forced to ease up in order not to lose the significance of this passage in the generally brisk pace leading to it. His reading is mostly free of mannerisms; a single exception occurs into m.128, where he holds back on the upbeat. After a fairly successful presentation of the huge dissonant chords before the reprise, he might have eased up for the return of the second theme and quieted down his strings for their entrances in this passage. The final pizzicato is played so loosely that it sounds almost like a short glissando.

JUDD, JAMES/European Community Youth Orchestra (perf. 31 Aug. 1987) - 2-Nuova Era 6906/7 (1990) [26:30]*   Judd's instinctive sensitivity to Mahler's idiom counter-balances the young players' cautious reserve, encouraging them to be both expressive and forceful when appropriate. Given the broad pacing of both principal themes, the ECYO's degree of concentration and control is a tribute to Judd's remarkable talents. Judd does not hesitate to use his creative talents either, filling in a few "gaps" in tempo markings during transitions by slowing up or holding back deftly into thematic reprises (e.g., at 11:50, to 14:45 and 16:40). One is again conscious of the performers' youth in the energetic treatment of the scherzando elements. The terrifying orchestral explosion of A-flat minor and its consequent accumulated dissonant chords that climax the movement do not overwhelm but are treated as a transition to the final statement of the main themes. A lively coda closes the movement in hushed stillness.

KUBELIK, RAFAEL/Bavarian Radio Symphony - 2-DG 139341/2 (1969); 10-DG 429 042 (1990) [23:55]   After a calm but foreboding introduction, Kubelik sets a very slow tempo for the main *adagio* in a richly expansive reading. As the drama unfolds, he presses forward slightly, giving the rhythmic material that follows a devilish aspect. A few moments seem on the harsh side (#21), but a suspenseful hush settles over the orchestra before the great A-flat minor outburst, slightly anticipated by brass while enhanced by audible harp swirls. One might have wished for more weight in the piled-on-thirds segment, however. The high A in the trumpet covers the soaring super-octave high D in violins at this point, tempering the chilling dissonance of the latter which should pierce disturbingly through the massive orchestral sound. For some reason, Kubelik takes the return of the second theme more slowly at #30 than earlier and some affectations creep in. Gorgeous string playing in the coda is marred by excess speed and harsh second violin attacks at #35.

MAAZEL, LORIN/Vienna Philharmonic - 2-CBS I2M 39721 (1986); 14-Sony SK14K 48198 (1992) [26:19]* Maazel provides a long-lined and often quite profound reading of this movement. He is particularly effective with a lingering approach to the *andante* opening theme and a spacious treatment of the other principal material. Tempi are generally well-conceived if controlled, although Maazel adds a few rallentandi at cadences. The VPO's usual dynamic forcefullness seems absent in stronger sections, particularly the segment containing the piled-up dissonant chords. In the closing moments, Maazel maintains a sustained tempo, eliciting more sensitivity that he does in similar passages elsewhere in his Mahler performances.

MEHTA, ZUBIN/Israel Philharmonic (perf. March 1992, Tel Aviv) - 2-Sony S2K 52579 (1993) [23:32]+ Apparently content to display the finely polished sheen of the vastly improved IPO strings, Mehta makes virtually no attempt to uncover the movement's dramatic power or depth. Smoothing over extremes and dynamic contrasts produces an homogenized quality, short on temperament, thrust and drama. A few affectations (e.g., at c. 13:53 and after #30) seem out of place in such a tame, straightforward reading.

NANUT, ANTON/Radio Symphony Orchestra of Ljubljana - 2-Digital Concerto CCT 748-9 (1991); 12-CCT 999701 (1992) [27:04] This routine performance has little to offer. Nanut reads straight through the movement without any emotive depth, urgency or linear flexibility. He lets the music move along without stylistic nuance and at consistently high dynamic levels. Such a one dimensional approach makes little impact, Nanut makes no effort to balance ensembles or apply any variety of shadings and contrasts. The Ljubljana orchestra has neither the stylistic manner nor the richness of sonority that this music requires.

NEUMANN, VÁCLAV/Czech Philharmonic - 2-Pro Arte 2PAL 2019 (1982); Supraphon 11 0721-2; 11 1970 (1994) [22:40]+ Neumann offers an essentially adequate but not very impressive performance. Many sections seem hurried, even hard-driven, but his reading is both expressive and soulful. A few harsher passages are smoothed over (e.g., #8), yet rhythmic material has a delightful flitting quality. Climaxes are fairly strong; the only drawback is the trumpets' high A covering the high D in violins at the conclusion of the piled-up-thirds section. In a quick-moving coda, a few measures might have been better coordinated (after #37).

OZAWA, SEIJI/Boston Symphony - 2-Philips 426 302 (1991); 14-Philips 438 874 (1995); [29:02]+ As is true of most of the Ozawa/BSO cycle, excellent playing and sonic quality are the principal merits of this recording. Ozawa's mild temperament never gets to the heart of this deeply profound music. After establishing a suspensful atmosphere for the opening *andante* theme (contrarily laden with heavy accents), the *adagio* theme has a sweet, languorous quality that is not in keeping with its passionate, yearning character. Scherzando material is read through without any attempt at characterization (such as Mephistophelian cynicism). A few slow-ups beg the question (at 16:40, 18:25), offering little insight into the pathos expressed here. Brass outplay strings in the climactic conclusion to the development section. A curious C-natural replaces a written C-sharp in the second violins at m.189. (What version is used here?) The closing coda has a warm and restful quality; the feeling of repose it generates is less effective when it follows such a tame reading of the life-death struggle that preceded it.

PESEK, LIBOR/Czech Philharmonic - 2-Virgin Classics VCDS 791219 (1991) [23:33]
After the splendid Ninth which accompanies this version, the icy cold atmosphere created here comes as something of a surprise. Brisk pacing, especially for the scherzando elements, combined with straight, inflexible musical flow, devoid of breathing space, create a sense of urgency that replaces the overwhelming feeling of dread that this movement expresses. Deviations from this approach occur: a long ritard into the return of the scherzando material at c.14:30; more hesitancy during the hushed prelude to the huge A-flat minor orchestral outburst (15:02); and a bloated mid-theme luftpause at 18. The infamous dissonant chords sound like dull thuds over which the solo trumpets' A-natural shrieks defiantly. The quiet coda brings little relief from the shock of the nightmarish visions that it tries but fails to completely dissolve.

RICKENBACHER, KARL ANTON/Bamberg Symphony - Virgin Classics VC 7 90771-2 (1989) [32:04] Long-lined pacing, a somber atmosphere and legato phrasing serve here to extended this already lengthy movement to epic proportions. Rickenbacher seems to view this music as a euology for a fallen hero, much like Wagner composed for Siegfried in the Funeral March from *Götterdämmerung*. The principal themes are pulled along in a gloomy dirge-like procession. Such a lumbering pace sometimes produces enough dramatic weight to sound heroic; however, in the crucial moments, where abysmal fears of humanity's ultimate annihilation should come terrifyingly to the fore, a heavy tread is not enough to generate the desired effect. Scherzando material set at this ponderous pace sounds more pixyish than satanic. One wonders whether such an expansive approach would have been taken had this movement been presented not in isolation but as the opening movement of the completed symphony.

SCHERCHEN, HERMANN/Leipzig Radio Symphony (perf. 4 Oct. 1960) - 2-Tahra TAH-101 (1992) [20:40] With his typical contrariness, Scherchen tries to refashion this movement into a standardized first movement of a traditional nineteenth-century romantic symphony. To accomplish this he merely reverses the tempo for the opening long-lined theme (marked *andante*) and the succeeding theme (marked *adagio*), so that the former is paced as the latter and vice-versa. In making this tempo switch, Scherchen creates a sense of urgency in the main thematic material and agitation in the scherzandi segments. But his quirk of moving arbitrarily in and out of tempo works against the natural flow of the musical line. Tempo shifts and ritards are severely stretched (12:18) in a most unwieldly fashion when they preceed a return to the sluggish *andante* theme. As is often the case with Scherchen, his wayward manner causes confusion in the orchestra, already suffering from ragged sonorities. An audible grace note into the huge A-flat minor outburst diffuses the impact of its sudden appearance. Thereafter, Scherchen slows up into the piled-on dissonant chords only to rush through them unstintingly. Only in the closing coda does he let the music speak for itself.

SEGERSTAM, LEIF/Danish National Radio Symphony - 2-Chandos CHAN 9305/6 (1994) [29:26]+ Long, lingering lines and heavy brass chords give the *adagio* theme a spacious and languid aura, while the opening *andante* subject is aptly paced and phrased with dutiful solemnity. As this half-hour movement proceeds, time becomes suspended as strings climb to the heights with seething emotion. The countervailing scherzando material has a perky character. With only minor exceptions, Segerstam's reading is free of inter-linear hesitations and affectations; he only adds a few ritards into and out of thematic segments. Brass generally cover strings in fortissimo climaxes. Antiphonal placement of violins would have enhanced the frequent interplay between firsts and seconds. Most of the movement works well, if presented more blatantly than with nuance or subtlety. Segerstam lets the music go its own way for the most part, and as a result the performance is never much more than either restful languidity or overbearingly loud. A sense of urgency and impending doom are wanting here.

SINOPOLI, GIUSEPPE/Philharmonia Orchestra - 2-DG 423 082 (1987) [32:40]+
Sinopoli approaches this movement as one long *adagio* with little variety in tempo but with an underlying restlessness that sometimes grows wearisome. It may be that Sinopoli views the piece as a continuation of the finale of the Ninth, which concluded in a state of virtual lifelessness suspended in time. While Mahler's long-lined themes sound warm and restful, more powerful moments have an attentuated impact, glossed over as fleeting, peripheral disturbances in an otherwise calm and untroubled scenario.

TENNSTEDT, KLAUS/London Philharmonic - Angel SZB-3883; CDC-47103 (1979); 10-EMI CMS7 64471-81 (1993) [27:58]+   Tennstedt's effusively romantic style is put to good use here. Tempi are treated broadly and the main themes are vital and sensitive in expression. Unwanted affectations frequent in Tennstedt readings are absent here and the linear flow is extremely fluid and seemless. He captures the music's pathos without over-indulgence and with profound emotive effect. Orchestral performance is superb and details are quite audible. Notice how deftly Tennstedt eases in and out of certain sections (e.g., before #12 and into #24). In such an expansive treatment, it is surprising to find him moving quickly through the piled-up-thirds climax (the trumpet is overbalanced here). A dream-like quality hovers over the opening of the coda, but the closing moments seem slightly intense, even harsh.

WAKASUGI, HIROSHI/Tokyo Metropolitan Symphony - 2-Fontec FOCD 9028/9 (1991) [26:56]*   Wakasugi delivers an intelligent, well-considered reading in his usual objective manner. He eschews sensationalism and affectation in favor of letting the music make its own points, and makes those points compellingly and in a thoroughly Mahlerian style. An excellent performance by the TMSO makes this performance a fitting conclusion to their complete cycle, indicative of their deep commitment to Mahler and evidencing the remarkable progress they have made in developing a Mahlerian sound.

ADAGIO & PURGATORIO:

SZELL, GEORGE/Cleveland Orchestra - Epic LC 3568; BC 1024 (1959); Columbia M2 31313 (1972); Sony SBK 53259 (1993) [22:10/3:55]**   This is the only recording that conjoins these two movements. Although tempi are slightly brisk, gorgeous and passionate playing from strings and a perfectly idiomatic reading from Szell make this performance of the *Adagio* movement one of the best versions ever recorded. Szell makes a strong argument for avoiding an extremely heavy tempo in the first movement, but the forward motion sometimes goes beyond the opening *andante*. The lighter rhythmic music is brisk as well. Yet Szell's deft handling lets the music breathe, even at this slightly *mosso* pace. The great A-flat minor explosion bursts forth with awesome power and the piled-up thirds have sufficient dramatic weight to produce a shattering climax. The coda is simply beautiful. Szell gives the brief *Purgatorio* movement a straightforward but strong reading. The opening section is sprightly and in perfect contrast with the more dramatic middle section. At the close, an orchestral outburst like a sudden gust of wind sweeps away all that preceded it.

SYMPHONY NO. 10

DERYCK COOKE VERSIONS:

ORIGINAL VERSION:

INBAL, ELIAHU/Frankfurt Radio Symphony - Denon CO-75129 (1992) [70:49]+
Using the Cooke version of 1964 rather than his final version of 1972, Inbal makes some wise choices and some questionable ones. His inclusion of the xylophone in the second Scherzo has merit, for it enhances the spectral atmosphere; and his omission of the interlinking muffled drum stroke that both concludes the fourth movement and begins the finale is also defensible. Most disconcerting is his mercilessly long glissando on the heart-wrenching sigh that ends the symphony. Such an affectation evokes a feeling foreign to the one Mahler conjures up here, a last welling up of emotion at the loss of his beloved. Overall, Inbal's approach is detached and reserved. He favors brisk tempi that have an underlying nervous edge, particularly in the opening movement where such pacing combined with an inflexible manner produces a shallow reading that never reaches to the heights or depths of emotion explored here. Even the tender closing moments lack warmth and sensitivity. Inbal is at his best in the first Scherzo, where he is more lively and brasher than Ormandy. Perky woodwinds, natural propulsion and a languid waltz theme add character to the movement's maddening whirl. The *Purgatorio* needs more atmosphere; one could take a hint from Mahler's Wunderhorn song *Das Erdische Leben* that contains a similar rhythmic undercurrent. Instead of sounding phantasmagorical, it appears too good-natured. In the second Scherzo, faulty balances cause important rhythmic motives to fade into insignificance; horns clip dotted rhythms; and mannerisms (in the waltz at 2:05 and elsewhere) impede a natural musical flow. An egregious hold on the upbeat to the *schwungvoll* segment exemplifies Inbal's inner contradiction: between general detachment and occasional over-emoting. A marvelously eerie atmosphere opens the finale, properly much softer than in Ormandy's version. Despite boosting of volume levels (to reinforce thin-sounding strings), this movement lacks the sense of urgency and the rich string sonorities that the Philadelphians provided for Ormandy. Rattle is more intense here and Ormandy more dramatic. The *allegro moderato* moves along hurriedly, taking on a scherzando quality that matches similar elements in the first movement. Inbal's liberties with the lyrical line sometimes sound like mere caricature (e.g., after the huge *fff* chord at m.179). He rarely lets the music breathe enough in its long-lined melodism to engender a feeling of coming to the end of life's long struggle.

ORMANDY, EUGENE/Philadelphia Orchestra - 2-Columbia M2S 335/D3S 774 (1965); CBS MPK 45882 (1990) [70:10]** The CD transfer of this first recording of Cooke's original version does not capture the full-bodied sheen of the Philadelphia strings that made this performance so engaging. Some critics felt that Ormandy's tempi in the outer movements were too brisk; nevertheless, the overall performance remains thoroughly captivating. Ormandy's performance is undeniably thrilling and deeply moving. The Philadelphians outclass the other orchestras that have recorded the revised version by leaps and bounds, including its own later rendition under Levine. While not over-indulgent stylistically when compared with later recordings by Morris (see vol.1, p.159) and Levine (see below), Ormandy shows clearly that in a master's hands music of such soulful expression need not be wrenched from the orchestra to be highly effective. The opening *andante* and succeeding *adagio* themes are perfect examples. Although phrases could be produced more lingeringly, they still are rendered expressively as well as with sonorous beauty. When more hesitancy is needed to infuse the shatteringly dissonant climax of the first movement with sufficient dramatic weight, Ormandy adds just the right heft to each chordal entrance to produce an unforgettable climax. The closing coda is restful and sensitively played. Superb ensemble balancing enhances the rhythmic vitality of the middle movements. Ormandy handles the difficult meter shifts of the second movement with agility and seamless cohesion. His treatment of the ländler of the second movement and waltz sections of the fourth movement is lively and perfectly idiomatic. The first Scherzo is a whirlwind of complex offbeat rhythms and the second Scherzo has the force and determination of a dynamo. Underlying tension pervades the strange *Purgatorio* movement, so akin in spirit to *Das Irdische Leben*. Details are always audible and inner-voice placement is excellent. While Ormandy sets a brisker pace in the finale than his colleagues, the overall effect is deeply moving. Neither langourous nor over-emotive, Ormandy's reading captures the heart-rending emotion of the main theme with unexcelled beauty and profound expressivity. The foreboding opening with its shattering drum strokes ushers in an unsurpassably beautiful main theme in solo flute that lingers in memory long after the work concludes. While the return of the overpoweringly dissonant chords of the opening movement seems somewhat fast-paced, some of the music that follows is agonizingly intense. The final "sigh" at life's leave-taking on the closing page is simply unbearable! Even if some may criticize Ormandy's tempi, one would have to be a stone wall not to be moved by the gorgeous string sound and stirring emotions evoked when in the main theme is restated in strings *fortissimo* before the final coda.

REVISED VERSION:

CHAILLY, RICCARDO/Berlin Radio Symphony - 2-London 421 182 (1988) [73:29]*+
 Chailly's first venture into Mahler territory on disc deserves high praise. His marvelous rendition of the metrically tricky and structurally convoluted first Scherzo is particularly noteworthy. Chailly handles the wealth of intricate detail with the ease and fluency of a seasoned Mahlerian and captures every mood in fine Mahlerian style. Notice how naturally the ländler section emerges at m.165 and how deftly Chailly shifts gears suddenly at m.416. While avoiding mannerism his reading demonstrates a certain creative intelligence. For example, after the hullabaloo of the jerky principal section unexpectedly exhausts itself (at m.416), Chailly evokes a reverie of bygone happiness rather than letting the music succumb to *ennui*. The other inner movements are equally interesting and convincing. Chailly conjures up an atmosphere of mystical fantasy in the *Purgatorio* movement, closing with a booming plunge that leaves an uneasy feeling, as if anticipating what follows. Such discomfort is well-founded as the raucous sounds of the second Scherzo wreck their savage fury upon the ear. Sharp articulation and strong dynamic levels enhance the intensity of this blatantly cynical music. Passages that devilishly taunt the senses have just the right rhythmic bite (e.g., m.123+), while contrastingly quieter sections seem completely untroubled (e.g., before *schwungvoll* at m.312). Only in the important outer movements do serious problems occur. Chailly's reading is not as much at fault for his rendering of details as for the overall effect he produces. Dramatic and deeply emotive, both of these movements demand an adequate display of power and expressivity. But here Chailly seems too restrained. In the opening movement, after a well-conceived principal subject, Chailly backs away from any characterization of the wickedly satanic scherzando material. *Fliessend* (fleeting), a marking that Mahler used when he wanted more motion, is virtually written out of the score by Chailly, and as a result he again levels out contrasts. When the climactic section is introduced by an enormous A-flat minor outburst, Chailly seems reluctant to let it erupt volcanically as it should. Consequently, this terrifying moment and the dreadful vision created by a series of extraordinarily dissonant chords that follow lack sufficient impact, brass being kept in reserve. Again in the finale Chailly keeps dynamic levels in check. The shocking muffled drum stokes that open the movement are toned down to puny thuds.

When they appear later in the movement (marked *fff*), they are even quieter than before. But volume alone does not produce a feeling of power. The absence of a foreboding presentment during calmer interludes detracts from the impact of the more powerful sections that follow. Only upon the *ff* return of the principal theme in violins toward the close does one feel a deeper level of intensity. Notwithstanding these detractions, Chailly's version should take its place among the best recordings of this important reconstruction of Mahler's unfinished final statement.

LEVINE, JAMES/Philadelphia Orchestra - 2-RCA ARC2-4553 (1981); CTC2-3726; RCD2-4553 (1985)*   Although Levine's reading makes a sincere effort at plumbing the depths of this moving work, overall, it makes only a moderate impression. As with Rattle's version (see below), the main emphasis is on the finale. Rattle is satisfied to let the music speak for itself, while Levine tends to indulge in over-sentimentality. Another serious problem is with the sound quality. RCA's digital sonics have a raw and constricted quality with little reverberance. The Philadelphians sound embarrassingly tarnished in comparison with their performance under Ormandy. Levine's soulful reading of the first movement is generally effective, but his lyrical, heavily-accented and demonstrative approach does not engender as much chilling intensity as does Ormandy. Soft and serene moments have a lofty aspect but stronger passages seem underplayed. Taken at a pace similar to Ormandy's, Scherzo I is less articulate and jagged edges are smoothed over harmlessly. On the other hand, Levine's treatment of the ländler sections are wonderfully warm and lilting. In a fine *Purgatorio* movement, he exaggerates the *gehalten* sections that return in the finale. Scherzo II seems to lack sufficient dramatic punch, yet calmer moments, especially the lovely waltz music, are delightful. In the finale, the opening drum strokes have a dark, thuddy quality, less overpowering than in either the Ormandy or Rattle versions. A serene calm pervades the beautiful main theme but the *allegro moderato* section is uncharacteristically jocular. Dotted rhythms are clipped sharply, even more so than with Rattle (see below) or Morris (see vol.1, p.159). Levine's reading is deeply searching; sometimes he lingers over a phrase, even in a very broad tempo. He captures the feeling of yearning with profound insight but without any sense of urgency. The stirring *fortissimo* statement of the main theme in strings before the quiet coda is almost as gripping as in Ormandy's version and the overwhelming "sigh" on the last page is given such weight as to carry the burden of the entire symphony on its shoulders.

MARTINON, JEAN/Resident Orchestra of the Hague - 2-Residentie 6812 102-3 (1975) [65:35]   This recording of a live performance given on June 13, 1975, is a noble effort but too flawed to be of importance. The Hague orchestra, otherwise a competent ensemble, is simply not up to the task. Wrong notes, sloppy entrances and insecure playing are major detractions. Martinon makes a laudable effort to evoke Mahler's profound, sometimes terrifying vision dramatically, but the first movement comes across on the mild side, needing more punch and poignancy. Martinon races through the first Scherzo raucously, calming down for the subsidiary waltz theme that seems uncomfortably rigid. After a fairly well-rendered *Purgatorio*, the first theme of the second Scherzo hurries along in a slapdash manner, giving way to an affectatious treatment of the waltz counter-subject. Martinon goes right into the finale without a moment's hesitation and provides a straightforward reading that is again subjected to the inadequacies of his ensemble.

RATTLE, SIMON/Bournemouth Symphony - 2-Angel DS 3909 (1980); 2-EMI 47301 (1985); Angel CDC 54406 [75:32]**   With much conviction and intelligence, Rattle provides one of the best recordings of Cooke's revised version. He produces a much better paced, more convincing and deeply emotive reading than Morris (see vol.1, p.159). Although

Levine's version is competitive, Rattle does him one better at almost every turn. Tempi are more appropriate, broader than Ormandy's but less extreme than Morris' or Levine's. Discounting the unmatched tonal quality and polish of the Philadelphians, Rattle's ensemble plays with strength and vigor enhanced by excellent sonics. While Ormandy is more intense in the first movement, Rattle's legato approach is just as valid and undeniably beautiful. One may prefer Ormandy's weigher treatment of the dissonant thirds at the climax, however. Again in Scherzo I, Rattle's tempo strikes a middle ground between Ormandy and Morris, thus perfectly capturing the music's spirit. He handles the injected *drängend* measures in a manner similar to their use in the scherzi of the Sixth and Seventh Symphonies, making a perfectly logical connection. In the transition to the final return of the scherzo material, Rattle adds a lovely Straussian quality which makes this brief respite most enchanting. The *Purgatorio* movement flows nicely and tempo changes in the middle section are well-coordinated. While Rattle handles the difficult Scherzo II with spirit, some inner parts are buried and crisp, and clear playing is wanting. Rattle merges the two drum strokes, one of which ends the fourth movement and the other of which opens the finale, into one. These strokes sound awesome, stronger and more reverberent than in most other recordings. The finale's introduction evokes an ingratiatingly mysterious atmosphere and the heavenly principal theme is played with equal beauty on solo flute and strings. A spirited *allegro moderato* contains some unwanted clipping but moves along nicely. From the return of the dissonant thirds of the first movement to the coda, Ormandy is stronger and more brilliant. In the coda, Rattle evokes an aura of everlasting peace, interrupted only by that deeply moving final "sigh."

SANDERLING, KURT/Berlin Symphony - 2-Eterna 8 27 435-6 (1981); Tokuma 32TC 72 (1987); Ars Vivendi 2100 225 (1991) [73:17]**   Kurt Sanderling and the BSO may have given the most satisfying performance of Cooke's revised version to date. Adding his own small touches to Cooke's score, Sanderling reads the work in a straightforward yet expressive manner, never either over-indulging in swoons of passion or merely beating time. His essentially conservative approach works well throughout. Tempi are consistently well-conceived, playing strong and articulate, and mood swings and characterizations impressively wrought. Weeping violins in high register add to the first movement's pathetic character. Perfect timing adds to the shock of the A-flat minor orchestral outburst that precedes the dissonant chordal pile-up --perhaps the most horrific moment in all tonal music. In the first Scherzo, Sanderling brings in cymbals to highlight punctuation and characterization. The BSO perform admirably, with acute articulation, clear lines and full sonorities enhancing the mood of joyful abandon. A mysterious air pervades the brief *Purgatorio* movement, to which Sanderling again makes slight adjustments in scoring. Percussive retouchings add to the contrasting moods evoked in the second Scherzo. An appropriately boisterous opening subject is deftly juxtaposed to a stylish waltz section.

Without a strong and heart-rending finale, this symphony would not have the impact it should. Sanderling and the BSO come to the fore splendidly. The muffled drum strokes are awesome, shattering the silence with a deafening thud. The heavenly principal theme, first enunciated by the solo flute, is allowed to breathe naturally. By way of contrast, the *allegro moderato* subject, scherzo-like in character, has a sharp, brash and angular quality and is enlivened by much underlying agitation. One might take issue with Sanderling's use of drum rolls to accompany the long-held A-natural in trumpets that separates the awesome dissonant chords at the movement's horrific climax. The effect seems to bring down to earth the otherworldly aspect of this overpowering passage. Other touches, such as the use of xylophone for the important 3-note motto from earlier movements, are well-conceived. Heavy doublings in strings provide rich sonority for the heart-rending *fortissimo* statement of the principal theme toward the close. A deeply-moving final "sigh" closes this brilliant performance.

WIGGLESWORTH, MARK/BBC National Orchestra (perf. 26 Nov. 1993, Royal Concert Hall, Nottingham) - BBC Music Magazine BBCMM 124 (1994) [74:05]

After a promising first movement in which this young conductor lets the music speak for itself and its long-lined themes breathe properly, the weaknesses of the BBC ensemble become increasingly evident and the rest of the performance pales into insignificance. Strings are often smothered by heavy-laden brass in strong tutti sections, despite the antiphonal placement for violins. Given this orchestra's apparent unfamiliarity with the score, Wigglesworth concentrates on getting the notes and markings right, giving the performance a studied quality. Yet over-emphasis on precision can also go awry: witness the all-too-audible grace-note in bass strings into the massive A-flat minor orchestral outburst at 16:20 that weakens the shock of its unexpected eruption. The dissonant chords that follow have enough strength to make an impression.

In the first Scherzo sharper articulation, more vitality and better drawn characterization are needed. Either the music is hurled at the listener (c.7:20) or mildly read through (c.6'). The *Purgatorio* movement also lacks character, shading and nuance. Brass overplay their hand in orchestral *fortes*, burying the strings, a characteristic especially troublesome at 2:28 on a significant motivic statement. One wonders if the young maestro has any idea of what to make of the second Scherzo. After a very morose 4-bar introduction, clarity is soon lost, awkward mannerisms interjected and stylistic treatment of the waltz subject lacking. Important reference material (e.g., the quote from *Das Lied von der Erde* at 3:20) is smothered in a welter of sound. The entire movement seems a mere jumble of disjointed fits and starts.

In the finale, the BBC Welsh strings make their best impression in softer, more relaxed passages, lacking sufficient sonic dimension to fulfill stronger thematic sections. They make a noble effort at playing beyond their own limitations, and succeed, if not completely, at least measurably. But the *allegro moderato* subject is a complete wash-out, played weakly and in mild temperament. Balances are uneven (winds are too close and strings too covered), dynamic markings not always applied (e.g., the horns after the piled-on dissonant chords should play *forte*) and playing is generally stiff and unstylish. Strong accents in the huge crescendo to 19:13 only try to impress. An excruciatingly long glissando on the upward thrust of the closing "sigh" seems out of sorts with the emotions stirred into consciousness at the symphony's close, one final breath of life giving way to the complete acceptance of life's finality.

EDITION BY REMO MAZZETTI, JR.:

SLATKIN, LEONARD/Saint Louis Symphony - RCA 09026-68190 (1995) [75:28]*

Remo Mazzetti's edition of a completed Tenth was premiered in 1989 and receives its first recording here. A comparative analysis of this edition with other completed versions by Maestro Slatkin is contained on an accompanying disc. Mazzetti takes a middle ground here between the leaner, more respectful "performing version" by Deryck Cooke (as revised by him) and Clinton Carpenter's attempt at a more fully realized completion that clutters Mahler's sketches with numerous fragmentary inner parts that thicken the texture and create instrumental coloration (particularly in brass and percussion) that sometimes sound foreign to Mahler's idiom. In Mazzetti's version, more counterpoint is filled in than in the Cooke Revised Version but less than in Carpenter's edition. The result is often quite convincing, even if one could argue about instrumental choices, imposition of sometimes excessive, not always idiomatic contrapuntal elements and a marked change in the character of passages and entire movements, particularly the finale.

Slatkin is a proficient, intelligent conductor, who handles this score ably, letting the music speak for itself without imposing upon it a personal perspective. Such would be an appropriately deferential stance in most instances under similar circumstances. However, for the Tenth, more is required if the performance is to be truly inspiring. Slatkin's reading of this powerful, deeply emotional score is too moderate in expression, detached in temperament and artful in style. Much the same can be said of the SLS: it plays very competently but its string sonorities are not luxurious and brass too often sound disconcertingly harsh.

In the first movement, the main theme is played more dispassionately than in many competing versions, while the scherzando material is perky and bright. Even the climax before the final coda seems a shade underdone. One gets the feeling that Slatkin merely reports on the profound emotions expressed here rather than taking part in them. Scherzo I has an acrid, angular temperament, in keeping with its modernistic ametrical content. Mazzetti chooses to reinforce the arhythmic quasi-ländler more than the parodical waltz tune. His added counterpoint here goes to the limits of acceptability, threatening at times to match Carpenter in excessive littering of thematic material with motivic fragments. At times, the orchestral pallette he uses creates coloristic effects that seem foreign to Mahler's orchestrational style. Would he have succumbed to the expressionistic instrumentation of the young Viennese radicals whom he befriended in his last years? We will never know.

Mazzetti's edition is most effective in the brief middle movement (he eliminates the title "Purgatory" that appeared on the first page of one sketch), where a whispy, impish main theme is succeeded by grotesque interplay of brass and woodwinds tinged with biting wit, and in Scherzo II, where harsh, steely brass fit the music's antithetical juxtaposition of acrid, brash sarcasm and lilting caricature. Such a contrast is typical of Mahler's mocking irony, here taken to the ultimate extreme. Quotes from the *Trinklied* of **Das Lied von der Erde** (3:21) and the Scherzo of the Fifth Symphony (4:49) are more audible here than in the Cooke version. Mazzetti fills in background in Scherzo II more completely than Cooke but does not create the jumbled confusion that permeated Carpenter's edition. What is still missing is a Mahlerian flavor that seems to have been buried in a profusion of harsh brass. Harshness also pervades the finale. Heavy-laden with soaring brass that brutalize this deeply personal expression of lost love, this rendition retains little of the beautiful lyricism that made the Cooke version a revelation. Rather than profound anguish, the music seems to convey over-wrought anger. Even the huge "sigh" that comes before the final measures ends with a timpani thud that sounds like the pounding of a fist. Little warmth and tenderness is generated here, or anywhere in this performance. Part of the reason is Mazzetti's creative woodwind and brass sonorities and the way he mixes timbres, sometimes having different instruments carry parts of a line in sequence, characteristic of Webern's compositional style. It is interesting to speculate how far Mahler would have gone beyond what we know of his style in deference to the new ideas of the second Vienna group. Even if Mazzetti could make a strong argument for the contention that Mahler would have developed an expressionistic style had he lived longer, we still miss the warmth of his bittersweet lyricism and the depth of his profound vision in the welter of harsh sonorities that tinge too much of this music with an acrimonious taint.

EDITED BY CLINTON A. CARPENTER:

FARBERMAN, HAROLD/Philharmonia Hungarica - Golden String GSCD 024 (1995) [65:42]+ With the first recording of Clinton Carpenter's realization, we now have all but Joe Wheeler's version represented on disc. Carpenter takes a very different approach in completing the symphony than did Deryck Cooke. While the latter only attempted to provide what he called a "performing version" of Mahler's sketches, completing empty measures and providing mostly what Mahler noted as instrumentation with a few necessary exceptions, Carpenter attempts to complete the symphony as a fully realized work. In order to do so, he made an extensive study of Mahler's music and his compositional procedures. After several of his own versions, Carpenter has settled upon this one. When I heard one of his versions in a performance several years ago in New York City, I was concerned about the extent to which he flooded his version with so many contrapuntal lines and fragmentary motivic references. As a result, textures became cluttered, sometimes even incomprehensible, especially in the scherzo movements. Such thick textures, overladen with numerous musical devices, seem out of joint with Mahler's almost maniacal concern in his last years with clarity of line. While there still exist some passages burdened in this manner with possibly too many cross-currents, this version seems to work more consistently than did the earlier performance.

What is more significant is the vast difference in the aesthetic nature of Carpenter's version compared with Cooke's. The latter thought the Tenth significant because he felt that it indicated that Mahler's final state of mind was not riddled with the despair evident in the Ninth. A feeling of hope emerged here that was absent in the earlier symphony. Apparently, Carpenter disagrees, for his version is harsh, dark, pervasively cold and bitter and devoid of the soulful quality that made Cooke's less "filled-in" edition so moving. If the Ninth was a prophetic vision of the horrors of de-humanization that Mahler envisioned would characaterize this century, Carpenter's Tenth is the realization of that prophecy. Even the beautiful theme of the finale takes on a stark, icy cold image in this version, forced to play over harsh brass chords and jutting motivic fragments. Gone also is the powerful impact of the muffled drum strokes in the finale, reduced in Carpenter's version to soft pings that hardly even provide punctuation much less dramatic strokes that shatter the otherwise calm, if foreboding atmosphere. Carpenter believes that Mahler could not have heard much more than this from the eleventh floor of his New York apartment when he happened to witness a funeral procession that stopped momentarily in the street below. Apparently, Carpenter thinks little of Mahler's sense of imagination, not to mention his dramatic proclivities!

These criticisms are not meant to denigrate the many interesting touches intelligently applied by Carpenter through the score. His refusal to repeat the opening section of the brief third movement verbatim on its return is conceptually sound. In the Scherzo movements, his use of motivic elements in woodwinds scattered around the main material provides appropriately demonic filigree. The choice of double basses to intone the rising stepwise motif in the finale instead of Cooke's morose tuba is sensible; although the correlation of this phrase with the quiet interlude between themes in the finale of the Ninth may suggest the use of the contrabassoon here. More intricate scoring in the closing moments of Scherzo II than Cooke applies (who reduces the instrumentation to percussion alone) has merit. Yet a cymbal crash on the second piled-on-thirds chords in the first movement is an untoward distraction, and the middle movement's modest close seems miles away from the portent of dread to which it plunges in Mazzetti's more interesting version.

Minutia aside, the most serious consideration here is the basic aesthetic presentment of stark, cold and bleak existence devoid of any feeling other than pain and piteous inanity. Mahler may well have been in such a state of mind at the end; but I believe he would not have so denigrated life as to call down a malediction up it, as might be implicit in this version.

Harold Farberman's reading enhances the desolate, acrid temperament of Carpenter's scoring by consistently applying fast tempi, creating intensity that impels the music forward sometimes in spite of its temperament. Thus, the opening *andante* theme is in a *moderato* tempo and the *adagio* theme that follows is set at an *andante* pace. A similarly hurried impulse is generated in the finale. In fact, there seems to be no slow movement in this version at all! Farberman adroitly handles the many twists and turns of the middle movements. The Philharmonica Hungarica is to be complimented on consistently articulate and precise playing.

****

BIBLIOGRAPHY

BIELEFELDER KATALOG: 1986-1995.

DIASPASON CATALOGUES: 1986-1995.

DISQUES CATALOGUE: 1989.

ETERNA KATALOG: 1984-1989

GRAMOPHONE CLASSICAL RECORD CATALOGUE: 1985-1995

IN TUNE (San Francisco, Calif.): 1993-1995

JAPAN CLASSICAL RECORDS: 1984-1995

MAHLER DISCOGRAPHY (Ed. Peter Fülöp): New York (1995)

SCHWANN/OPUS CATALOGUE (Santa Fe, New Mexico): 1986-1995.

INDEX TO CONDUCTORS

(N.B., "DL" refers to *Das Lied von der Erde*)

Conductor	Symphony	Page
ABBADO, CLAUDIO		
	No.1	1-2
	No.2	33-34
	No.3	59
	No.4	81
	No.5	107-108
	No.6	141-142
	No.7	167
	No.8	189
	No.9	225
	No.10 (Adagio)	255
ABRAVANEL, MAURICE		
	No.1	2
	No.2	35
	No.3	59-60
	No.4	81
	No.5	108
	No.6	142
	No.7	167-168
	No.8	189-190
	No.9	225-226
	No.10 (Adagio)	255
ADLER, F. CHARLES		
	No.3	60
ALBRECHT, GERD		
	No.9	226

INDEX TO CONDUCTORS

ANCERL, KAREL
No.1   2
No.9   226

ANDREESCU, HORIA
No.1   2

ASAHINA, TAKASHI
No.2   35
DL   205
No.9   226

ASHKENAZY, VLADIMIR
No.3   60

BARBIROLLI, JOHN
No.2   35
No.3   61
No.4   82
No.5   108
No.6   142-143
No.9   227-228

BARENBOIM, DANIEL
DL   205

BARSHAI, RUDOLF
No.9   228

BERNSTEIN, LEONARD
No.1   3-5
No.2   36-37
No.3   61-63
No.4   82-84
No.5   109-111
No.6   143-145
No.7   168-170
No.8   190-191
DL   206-207
No.9   228-230
No.10 (Adagio)   255-256

BERTINI, GARY
No.1   5
No.2   37
No.3   63
No.4   84
No.5   111

INDEX TO CONDUCTORS

BERTINI, GARY (cont.)
	No.6	145
	No.7	170
	No.8	191
	DL	207
	No.9	230
	No.10 (Adagio)	256

BLOMSTEDT, HERBERT
	No.2	38

BOULEZ, PIERRE
	No.2	38
	No.3	64
	No.5	111-113
	No.6	146-148
	No.8	192
	No.9	231-232

BOULT, ADRIAN
	No.1	5

BUTT, YONDANI
	No.1	5

CASADESUS, JEAN-CLAUDE
	No.1	6
	No.2	39
	No.4	85
	No.5	113

CHAILLY, RICCARDO
	No.6	148
	No.7	170
	No.10 (Revised Cooke Version)	262

CONLON, JAMES
	No.4	85
	No.5	113

DANIEL, JOSIP
	No.3	64

DAVIS, COLIN
	No.1	6
	DL	207

DEWAART, EDO

No.1	7-8
No.2	40
No.3	65
No.4	85
No.5	113
No.6	148
No.7	171
No.8	192
No.9	232

DOHNANYI, CHRISTOPH VON

No.1	8
No.4	86
No.5	114
No.6	149

EDELMANN, HANS

No.1	8

FARBERMAN, HAROLD

No.1	9
No.4	86
No.10 (Carpenter version)	266

FEDOSEYEV, VLADIMIR

No.1	9

FISCHER, IVAN

No.1	9

FRIED, OSKAR

No.2	40

FROMENT, LOUIS DE

No.5	114

GIELEN, MICHAEL

No.4	87
No.7	172
No.8	193
No.9	233
No.10 (Adagio)	256

GIULINI, CARLO MARIA

DL	207
No.9	233

INDEX TO CONDUCTORS

HAENCHEN, HARTMUT
- No.4 — 87
- No.6 — 149-150
- No.7 — 173

HAITINK, BERNARD
- No.1 — 10
- No.2 — 40-41
- No.3 — 65-66
- No.4 — 88
- No.5 — 114-115
- No.6 — 150-151
- No.7 — 173-174
- No.8 — 193
- DL — 208
- No.9 — 234-235
- No.10 (Adagio) — 256-257

HALASZ, MICHAEL
- No.7 — 174
- No.9 — 235

HAYASHI, CHIHIRO
- No.1 — 11

HERBIG, GÜNTHER
- No.5 — 115

HERREWEGHE, PHILIPPE
- DL (chamber version) — 223

HORENSTEIN, JASCHA
- No.1 — 11
- No.3 — 66
- No.4 — 89
- No.6 — 151
- No.7 — 175
- DL — 208
- No.9 — 235-237

HORVATH, MILAN
- No.2 — 41
- No.4 — 89

INBAL, ELIAHU
- No.1 — 11
- No.2 — 42
- No.3 — 67

INBAL, ELIAHU (cont.)
No.4	89
No.5	115
No.6	152
No.7	175
No.8	194
DL	209
No.9	237
No.10 (Adagio)	257
No.10 (Original Cooke Version)	261

INOUE, MICHIYOSHI
No.4	90
No.5	116
No.6	152

JANSONS, MARISS
No.2	42

JÄRVI, NEEME
No.1	12
No.3	67
No.4	90
No.5	116
No.6	152
No.8	194

JOÓ, ÁRPÁD
No.1	13
No.8	195

JORDAN, ARMIN
No.1	14
No.3	68
No.4	90

JUDD, JAMES
No.1	14
No.9	238
No.10 (Adagio)	257

KAPLAN, GILBERT
No.2	43

KARAJAN, HERBERT VON
No.6	153
DL	209-210
No.9	238

INDEX TO CONDUCTORS

KASPRZYK, JACEK
　　　　　　　　No.1　　　　　　　　15

KEGEL, HERBERT
　　　　　　　　No.1　　　　　　　　15
　　　　　　　　No.4　　　　　　　　91

KEILBERTH, JOSEPH
　　　　　　　　DL　　　　　　　　　210

KLEIBER, CARLOS
　　　　　　　　DL　　　　　　　　　211

KLEMPERER, OTTO
　　　　　　　　No.2　　　　　　　　44-46
　　　　　　　　No.4　　　　　　　　91-93
　　　　　　　　No.7　　　　　　　　175-176
　　　　　　　　DL　　　　　　　　　211
　　　　　　　　No.9　　　　　　　　239-240

KLETZKI, PAUL
　　　　　　　　DL　　　　　　　　　212

KNESS, WALTER
　　　　　　　　No.3　　　　　　　　68

KOBAYASHI, KEN-ICHIRO
　　　　　　　　No.1　　　　　　　　16
　　　　　　　　No.5　　　　　　　　117

KONDRASHIN, KIRIL
　　　　　　　　No.5　　　　　　　　118

KONOYE, VISCOUNT HILDEMARO
　　　　　　　　No.4　　　　　　　　93

KOSLER, ZDENEK
　　　　　　　　No.1　　　　　　　　16

KRIPS, JOSEPH
　　　　　　　　DL　　　　　　　　　212

KUBELIK, RAFAEL
　　　　　　　　No.1　　　　　　　　17
　　　　　　　　No.2　　　　　　　　46
　　　　　　　　No.3　　　　　　　　69
　　　　　　　　No.4　　　　　　　　93
　　　　　　　　No.5　　　　　　　　118-119

KUBELIK, RAFAEL (cont.)

No.6	153
No.7	176
No.8	195
DL	213
No.9	240-241
No.10 (Adagio)	257

LEINSDORF, ERICH

No.1	17
No.5	119

LENARD, ONDREJ

No.1	17
No.5	119
No.8	196

LEPPARD, RAYMOND

DL	213

LEVI, YOEL

No.5	120

LEVINE, JAMES

No.1	17
No.4	93
No.5	121
No.6	153
No.7	176
No.9	241
No.10 (Revised Cooke Version)	263

LITTON, ANDREW

No.1	18
No.5	121

LOMBARD, ALAIN

No.5	122
No.6	154

LUDWIG, LEOPOLD

No.4	93

MAAZEL, LORIN

No.1	18
No.2	47
No.3	69
No.4	94

INDEX TO CONDUCTORS

MAAZEL, LORIN (cont.)
	No.5	122
	No.6	154
	No.7	176
	No.8	196
	No.9	241
	No.10 (Adagio)	258

MACKERRAS, CHARLES
	No.1	19
	No.4	94
	No.5	122

MADERNA, BRUNO
	No.3	69-70
	No.5	123
	No.7	177-178
	No.9	242-243

MARKEVITCH, IGOR
	No.1	19-20

MARRINER, NEVILLE
	No.4	95

MARTINON, JEAN
	No.10 (Revised Cooke Version)	263

MASUR, KURT
	No.1	21
	No.7	178
	No.9	243

MATA, EDUARDO
	No.2	47

MEHTA, ZUBIN
	No.1	21-22
	No.2	47-48
	No.3	70
	No.5	124-126
	No.10 (Adagio)	258

MENGELBERG, WILHELM
	No.4	95

MITROPOULOS, DIMITRI
	No.1	22

MITROPOULOS, DIMITRI (cont.)
	No.3	70-71
	No.5	126
	No.6	155
	No.8	197
	No.9	244

MORRIS, WYN
	No.4	95
	No.5	126
	No.8	197
	No.9	244

MUTI, RICCARDO
	No.1	23

NANUT, ANTON
	No.1	23
	No.5	126
	No.6	155
	No.7	179
	No.8	198
	DL	214
	No.9	245
	No.10 (Adagio)	258

NEUMANN, VÁCLAV
	No.1	24
	No.2	48-49
	No.3	71
	No.4	96
	No.5	127-128
	No.6	156
	No.7	179-180
	No.8	198
	DL	214
	No.9	245-246
	No.10 (Adagio)	258

ORMANDY, EUGENE
	DL	215
	No.10 (Original Cooke Version)	261

OTAKA, TADAAKI
	No.5	128-129

OZAWA, SEIJI
	No.1	24

INDEX TO CONDUCTORS

OZAWA, SEIJI (cont.)
	No.2	49
	No.3	72
	No.4	96
	No.5	129
	No.6	157
	No.7	180
	No.8	199
	No.9	246
	No.10 (Adagio)	258

PESEK, LIBOR
| | No.9 | 246 |
| | No.10 (Adagio) | 259 |

PREVIN, ANDRÉ
| | No.4 | 97 |

RATH, GYÖRGY GYÖRIVANYI
| | No.5 | 130 |

RATTLE, SIMON
	No.1	25
	No.2	49
	No.6	157
	No.7	181
	No.10 (Revised Cooke Version)	263

REINER, FRITZ
| | No.4 | 97 |
| | DL | 215 |

RICKENBACHER, KARL ANTON
| | No.10 (Adagio) | 259 |

RODZINSKY, ARTUR
| | DL | 215 |

RÖGNER, HEINZ
| | No.3 | 72 |
| | No.6 | 158 |

ROSBAUD, HANS
	No.1	26
	No.6	159
	No.7	181
	DL	216-217
	No.9	247

SANDERLING, KURT
	DL	217
	No.9	247-248
	No.10 (Revised Cooke Version)	264

SALONEN, ESA-PEKKA
	No.4	97

SARASTE, YUKKA-PEKKA
	No.5	130

SCHERCHEN, HERMANN
	No.1	26
	No.2	50
	No.3	73
	No.5	131-132
	No.6	159
	No.7	182-183
	No.8 (Part I)	199
	No.9	248
	No.10 (Adagio)	259

SCHURICHT, CARL
	No.2	51
	No.3	73
	DL	217

SCHWARZ, GERARD
	No.5	132

SCHWARZ, RUDOLF
	No.5	132

SEGERSTAM, LEIF
	No.1	27
	No.2	52
	No.3	74
	No.5	133
	No.6	160
	No.7	183
	No.8	199
	No.9	249
	No.10 (Adagio)	259

SHAW, ROBERT
	No.8	200

INDEX TO CONDUCTORS

SINOPOLI, GIUSEPPE
No.1	27
No.2	52
No.3	75
No.4	98
No.5	134
No.6	161
No.7	183
No.8	200
No.9	250
No.10 (Adagio)	260

SKROWACZEWSKI, STANISLAW
No.4	99

SLATKIN, LEONARD
No.1	29
No.2	53
No.10 (Mazzetti Version)	265

SOLTI, GEORG
No.1	29
No.2	53
No.3	75
No.4	100
No.5	134-136
No.6	162
No.7	184
No.8	201
DL	217
No.9	251

STOKOWSKI, LEOPOLD
No.2	54
No.8	201

SUITNER, OTMAR
No.2	54
No.5	136

SVETLANOV, YEVGENY
No.3	76
No.6	163

SWAROWSKY, HANS
No.4	100

SZELL, GEORGE

No.4	101
No.6	163
DL	218-219
No.9	251
No.10 (Adagio and Purgatorio)	260

TEMIRKANOV, YURI

No.2	55

TENNSTEDT, KLAUS

No.1	29-31
No.2	56
No.3	76
No.4	101
No.5	136-137
No.6	164
No.7	185
No.8	202-203
DL	219
No.9	252
No.10 (Adagio)	260

THOMAS, MICHAEL TILSON

No.3	77

TSUTSUMI, SHUNSAKU

No.4	101

VANDERNOOT, ANDRE

No.8	203

VANSKA, OSMO

DL (chamber version)	224

VIS, LUCAS

No.5	137

VONK, HANS

No.2	56
No.3	77

WAKASUGI, HIROSHI

No.1	31
No.2	57
No.3	78
No.4	102
No.5	137

INDEX TO CONDUCTORS

WAKASUGI, HIROSHI (cont.)
	No.6	164
	No.7	185
	No.8	203
	DL	219
	No.9	252
	No.10 (Adagio)	260

WALTER, BRUNO
	No.1	31-32
	No.2	57
	No.4	102-104
	No.5	138
	DL	220-222
	No.9	253-254

WESLER-MÖST, FRANZ
	No.4	104

WIGGLESWORTH, MARK
	DL (Chamber Version)	224
	No.10 (Revised Cooke Version)	265

WIT, ANTONI
	No.2	58
	No.3	78
	No.4	105
	No.5	138
	No.6	165

ZANDER, BENJAMIN
	No.6	165

INDEX TO ORCHESTRAS

(N.B., "DL" refers to *Das Lied von der Erde*)

Orchestra	Symphony	Page
AMERICAN SYMPHONY		
	No.9	237
AMSTERDAM PHILHARMONIC		
	No.1	13
ATLANTA SYMPHONY		
	No.5	120
	No.8	200
BAMBERG SYMPHONY		
	DL	210
	No.10 (Adagio)	259
BAVARIAN RADIO SYMPHONY		
	No.1	6, 17
	No.2	45, 46
	No.3	69
	No.4	92, 93
	No.5	118-119
	No.6	153
	No.7	176
	No.8	195
	DL	213
	No.9	240-241
	No.10 (Adagio)	257
BBC NATIONAL ORCHESTRA		
	No.10 (Revised Cooke Version)	265

INDEX TO ORCHESTRAS

BBC NORTHERN SYMPHONY
	DL	208, 213

BBC SYMPHONY
	No.2	38
	No.3	64
	No.4	82, 94
	No.5	111-113
	No.6	146
	No.8	192
	No.9	231-232, 242

BBC WELSH SYMPHONY
	No.5	128

BERLIN PHILHARMONIC
	No.1	1, 10
	No.2	41
	No.3	61, 66
	No.4	88
	No.5	107, 115
	No.6	142, 150, 153
	No.7	174
	No.8	189
	DL	207, 209-210
	No.9	227, 229, 238
	No.10 (Adagio)	257

BERLIN RADIO SYMPHONY
	No.3	72
	No.4	94
	No.6	158
	No.7	181
	No.10 (Revised Cooke Version)	262

BERLIN STATE OPERA ORCHESTRA
	No.2	40

BERLIN STAATSKAPELLE
	No.2	54
	No.5	136
	No.8 (Part I)	199

BERLIN SYMPHONY
	No.5	115
	DL	217
	No.9	247
	No.10 (Revised Cooke Version)	264

BOSTON PHILHARMONIC
No.6	165

BOSTON SYMPHONY
No.1	17, 24
No.2	49
No.3	72
No.4	96
No.5	119, 129
No.6	157
No.7	180
No.8	199
No.9	246
No.10 (Adagio)	258

BOURNEMOUTH SYMPHONY
No.10 (Revised Cooke Version)	263

BRABANT ORCHESTRA
No.8	203

BUDAPEST RADIO & TV SYMPHONY
No.8	195

CHICAGO SYMPHONY
No.1	29-31
No.2	33, 53
No.3	73
No.4	93, 97, 100
No.5	107, 134-136
No.6	141, 162
No.7	167, 176, 184
No.8	201
DL	205, 215
No.9	233, 251

CITY OF BIRMINGHAM SYMPHONY
No.1	25
No.2	49
No.6	157
No.7	181

CLEVELAND ORCHESTRA
No.1	8
No.4	86, 101
No.5	114
No.6	149, 163
DL	218-219

INDEX TO ORCHESTRAS

CLEVELAND ORCHESTRA (cont.)
    No.9   251
    No.10 (Adagio & Purgatorio)   260

COLOGNE PHILHARMONIC
    No.4   85
    No.5   113

COLOGNE WDR (RADIO) SYMPHONY
    No.1   5
    No.2   37
    No.3   63, 71
    No.4   84, 91
    No.5   111
    No.6   145, 155
    No.7   170
    No.8   191
    DL   207, 216
    No.9   230
    No.10 (Adagio)   256

COLUMBIA SYMPHONY
    No.1   31
    No.9   253

CONCERTGEBOUW ORCHESTRA OF AMSTERDAM
    No.1   4, 10
    No.2   40, 44
    No.3   65
    No.4   83, 88, 95, 100
    No.5   114
    No.6   148, 150
    No.7   170, 173
    No.8   193
    DL   208, 217
    No.9   230, 234
    No.10 (Adagio)   256

CZECH PHILHARMONIC
    No.1   2, 24
    No.2   48
    No.3   71
    No.4   96, 100
    No.5   127
    No.6   156
    No.7   180
    No.8   198
    DL   214

CZECH PHILHARMONIC (cont.)
No.9	226, 245
No.10 (Adagio)	258-259

DALLAS SYMPHONY
No.2	47
No.5	121

DANISH NATIONAL RADIO SYMPHONY
No.1	27
No.2	52
No.3	74
No.5	133
No.6	160
No.7	183
No.8	199
No.9	249
No.10 (Adagio)	259

DRESDEN PHILHARMONIC
No.1	15

DRESDEN STAATSKAPELLE
No.1	31

ENSEMBLE MUSIQUE OBLIQUE
DL (chamber version)	223

EUROPEAN COMMUNITY YOUTH ORCHESTRA
No.3	60
No.9	234
No.10 (Adagio)	257

FESTIVAL PHILHARMONIC
No.3	68

FINNISH RADIO SYMPHONY
No.5	130

FLORIDA PHILHARMONIC
No.1	14

FRANKFURT OPERA HOUSE-MUSEUM ORCHESTRA
No.8	193

FRANKFURT RADIO SYMPHONY
No.1	11
No.2	42

INDEX TO ORCHESTRAS

FRANKFURT RADIO SYMPHONY (cont.)
No.3	67
No.4	89
No.5	115
No.6	152
No.7	175
No.8	194
DL	209
No.9	237
No.10 (Adagio)	257
No.10 (Original Cooke Version)	261

GIOVANILE ITALIANA ORCHESTRA
No.5	130

GOTHENBERG OPERA ORCHESTRA
No.8	194

GOTHENBERG SYMPHONY
No.8	194

GURZENICH ORCHESTRA
No.4	85
No.5	113

GUSTAV MAHLER YOUTH ORCHESTRA
No.9	238

THE HAGUE PHILHARMONIC
No.2	56
No.3	77
No.6	154

THE HAGUE RESIDENT ORCHESTRA
No.10 (Revised Cooke Version)	263

HALLE ORCHESTRA
No.4	99

HAMBURG PHILHARMONIC STATE ORCHESTRA
No.9	226

HESSIAN RADIO SYMPHONY
No.2	51

HUNGARIAN STATE SYMPHONY
No.1	16

ISRAEL PHILHARMONIC

No.1	21
No.2	47-48
No.3	70
DL	206
No.10 (Adagio)	258

JAPAN PHILHARMONIC

No.5	117

KIROV OPERA & BALLET THEATER ORCHESTRA

No.2	55

LEIPZIG GEWANDHAUS ORCHESTRA

No.5	127
No.6	156
No.7	178-180
No.9	245

LEIPZIG RADIO SYMPHONY

No.3	73
No.4	91
No.6	159
No.10 (Adagio)	259

LJUBLJANA RADIO SYMPHONY

No.1	23
No.5	126
No.6	155
No.7	179
No.8	198
DL	214
No.9	245
No.10 (Adagio)	258

LONDON PHILHARMONIC

No.1	5, 26
No.2	56
No.3	76
No.4	89, 101, 104
No.5	136
No.6	164
No.7	185
No.8	202
DL	219
No.9	252
No.10 (Adagio)	260

INDEX TO ORCHESTRAS

LONDON, SYMPHONIA OF
    No.5   126
    No.8   197
    No.9   244

LONDON SYMPHONY
    No.1   5, 9, 15, 17, 29
    No.2   36, 37, 43, 53
    No.3   66, 77
    No.4   86, 95
    No.5   132
    No.6   153
    No.8   190, 201
    DL   207
    No.9   236

LOS ANGELES PHILHARMONIC
    No.4   97
    No.5   124

MILAN RAI ORCHESTRA
    No.3   69
    No.5   123, 131
    No.7   177

MINNEAPOLIS SYMPHONY
    No.1   22

MINNESOTA ORCHESTRA
    No.1   7

MOLDAVIA PHILHARMONIC
    No.1   2

MOSCOW RADIO LARGE SYMPHONY
    No.9   228

NETHERLANDS PHILHARMONIC
    No.4   87
    No.6   150
    No.7   173

NETHERLANDS RADIO PHILHARMONIC
    No.1   7
    No.2   40
    No.3   65
    No.4   85
    No.5   113

NETHERLANDS RADIO PHILHARMONIC (cont.)
  No.6   148
  No.7   171
  No.8   192
  No.9   232

NETHERLANDS YOUTH ORCHESTRA
  No.5   137

NEW PHILHARMONIA ORCHESTRA
  No.2   45
  No.5   108
  No.6   143
  No.7   175
  DL   211

NEW TOKYO SYMPHONY
  No.4   93

NEW YORK PHILHARMONIC
  No.1   3, 21, 31
  No.2   36, 57
  No.3   61-63, 70
  No.4   82, 102, 103
  No.5   109, 125-126, 138
  No.6   143
  No.7   168, 169
  No.8   213, 221-222
  No.9   228, 243-244
  No.10 (Adagio)   255

ORCHESTRE NATIONAL BORDEAUX AQUITAINE
  No.5   122

ORCHESTRE NATIONAL DE FRANCE
  No.1   20
  No.4   104
  No.9   236

ORCHESTRE NATIONAL DE LILLE
  No.1   6
  No.2   39
  No.4   85
  No.5   113

ORCHESTRE NATIONAL DE PARIS
  No.2   51

INDEX TO ORCHESTRAS

L'O.R.T.F. NATIONAL ORCHESTRA
    No.5   132

L'ORCHESTRE DE LA SUISSE ROMANDE
    No.1   14
    No.3   68
    No.4   90

OSAKA PHILHARMONIC
    No.2   35
    DL   205
    No.9   226

OSLO PHILHARMONIC
    No.2   42

PHILADELPHIA ORCHESTRA
    No.1   23
    No.2   54
    No.5   121
    DL   215
    No.9   241
    No.10 (Original Cooke Version)   261
    No.10 (Revised Cooke Version)   263

PHILHARMONIA ORCHESTRA
    No.1   27
    No.2   44, 52
    No.3   75
    No.4   92, 98
    No.5   134
    No.6   161
    No.7   183
    No.8   200
    DL   212
    No.9   248, 250
    No.10 (Adagio)   260

PHILHARMONIA SLAVONICA
    No.6   149

PHILHARMONICA HUNGARICA
    No.10 (Carpenter version)   266

POLISH NATIONAL SYMPHONY (KATOWICE)
    No.1   11
    No.2   58
    No.3   78

POLISH NATIONAL SYMPHONY (KATOWICE) (cont.)
No.4	105
No.5	138
No.6	165
No.7	174
No.9	235

PREMIERE ENSEMBLE
DL (chamber version)	224

RADIO LUXEMBOURG SYMPHONY
No.5	114

RAI TORINO ORCHESTRA
No.1	19

ROYAL LIVERPOOL PHILHARMONIC
No.1	19
No.5	122
No.9	246

ROYAL PHILHARMONIC
No.1	18
No.4	90
No.5	116
No.6	152

ROYAL SCOTTISH NATIONAL ORCHESTRA
No.1	12
No.3	67
No.4	90
No.5	116
No.6	152

RUSSIAN STATE SYMPHONY
No.3	76

SAN FRANCISCO SYMPHONY
No.2	38

SAINT LOUIS SYMPHONY
No.1	29
No.2	53
No.10 (Mazzetti Version)	265

SAXON STATE ORCHESTRA
No.4	93

INDEX TO ORCHESTRAS

SHINSEI JAPAN (NIHON) SYMPHONY
No.1   17
No.5   119
No.8   196

SINFONIA LAHTI CHAMBER ENSEMBLE
DL (chamber version)   224

SLOVAK PHILHARMONIC
No.1   16

SLOVENE PHILHARMONIC
No.2   41

SOUTHWEST GERMAN RADIO SYMPHONY
No.1   26
No.2   35
No.4   87
No.6   159
DL   216
No.9   233, 247

STOCKHOLM PHILHARMONIC
No.6   151

STUTTGART CONSERVATORY ORCHESTRA
No.1   8

STUTTGART RADIO SYMPHONY
No.3   73
No.4   95

SWF SYMPHONY, BADEN-BADEN
No.7   172
No.9   233
No.10 (Adagio)   256

TOKYO CITY PHILHARMONIC
No.4   101
No.5   128, 132

TOKYO METROPOLITAN SYMPHONY
No.1   31
No.2   57
No.3   78
No.4   102
No.5   137
No.6   164

TOKYO METROPOLITAN SYMPHONY (cont.)

No.7	185
No.8	203
DL	219
No.9	252
No.10 (Adagio)	260

TORINO RAI SYMPHONY

No.9	227, 243

TORONTO SYMPHONY

No.7	182

USSR ACADEMIC SYMPHONY

No.6	163

USSR RADIO & TV LARGE SYMPHONY

No.1	9
No.5	118

UTAH SYMPHONY

No.1	2
No.2	35
No.3	59
No.4	81
No.5	108
No.6	142
No.7	167
No.8	189
No.9	225
No.10 (Adagio)	255

VIENNA PHILHARMONIC

No.1	3, 18
No.2	33-34, 44, 47
No.3	59, 63, 69
No.4	81-82, 94, 102-104
No.5	109-111, 122
No.6	144, 147, 154
No.7	169, 176
No.8	190-191, 196-197
DL	206, 220-221
No.9	225, 229, 239-241, 253
No.10 (Adagio)	255-256, 258

INDEX TO ORCHESTRAS

VIENNA STATE OPERA ORCHESTRA
| | No.2 | 50 |
| | No.5 | 131 |

VIENNA SYMPHONY
	No.1	11
	No.3	60
	No.6	141
	No.7	177, 182
	DL	211-212
	No.9	235, 248

ZAGREB RADIO & TV SYMPHONY
| | No.3 | 64 |
| | No.4 | 89 |

INDEX TO SOLOISTS

(N.B., "DL" refers to *Das Lied von der Erde*)

Soloist	Symphony	Page
AGHOVÁ, LIVIA (soprano)		
	No.2	48
ALEXANDER, CARLOS (baritone)		
	No.8	201
ALEXANDER, ROBERTA (soprano)		
	No.4	88
	No.8	203
ALEXANDROVA, OLGA (mezzo-soprano)		
	No.3	76
ALLEN, THOMAS (baritone)		
	No.8	200
AMELING, ELLY (contralto)		
	No.2	40
	No.4	97
ANDOR, EVA (soprano)		
	No.4	89
ANNEAR, GWENYTH (soprano)		
	No.8	190
ARAIZA, FRANCISCO (tenor)		
	DL	207

INDEX TO SOLOISTS

ARMSTRONG, SHEILA (soprano)
            No.2   36
            No.4   94

ARROYO, MARTINA (soprano)
            No.8   195

AUGER, ARLEEN (soprano)
            No.2   49
            No.8   201

BAKER, JANET (contralto)
            No.2   36-37, 45, 49
            No.3   77
            DL   208, 213, 218

BALTSA, AGNES (mezzo-soprano)
            No.3   69
            No.8   190-191
            DL   219

BARKER, JOYCE (soprano)
            No.8   197

BÁTFAI-BARTA, ÉVA (soprano)
            No.8   195

BATTLE, KATHLEEN (soprano)
            No.2   53
            No.4   94

BENACKOVÁ, MARTA (contralto)
            No.2   48

BEŇAČKOVÁ-ČÁPOVÁ, GABRIELA (soprano)
            No.2   48
            No.8   198

BERNHARDT, LOUISE (contralto)
            No.8   201

BINDENAGEL, GERTRUD (soprano)
            No.2   40

BJERNO, MAJKEN (soprano)
            No.8   199

BLACKHAM, JOYCE (contralto)
    No.8   197

BLASI, ANGELA MARIA (soprano)
    No.8   200

BLEGEN, JUDITH (soprano)
    No.4   93
    No.8   190-191, 199

BLOCHWITZ, HANS PETER (tenor)
    DL (chamber version)   223

BOESE, URSALA (contralto)
    No.3   69

BONDE-HANSEN, HENRIETTE (soprano)
    No.8   199

BORK, HANNEKE VAN (soprano)
    No.8   193

BUCHANAN, ISOBEL (soprano)
    No.2   53

BUDAI, LIVIA (contralto)
    No.8   194

BULLOCK, SUSAN (soprano)
    No.8   202

BURROWS, NORMA (soprano)
    No.8   197

CAHILL, TERESA (soprano)
    No.8   194

CAIRNS, CHRISTINE (mezzo-soprano)
    No.3   60

CERVENA, SONA (contralto)
    No.3   73

CHOOKASIAN, LILI (contralto)
    DL   215

CHRISTENSEN, BLANCHE (soprano)
    No.8   189

INDEX TO SOLOISTS

CLATWORTHY, DAVID (baritone)
No.8 — 189

COBURN, PAMELA (soprano)
No.8 — 196

COCHRAN, WILLIAM (tenor)
No.8 — 193

COERTSE, MIMI (soprano)
No.2 — 50
No.8 — 197

COKU, ALEXANDRA (soprano)
No.4 — 87

COLE, VINSON (tenor)
No.8 — 192

CONLEY, EUGENE (tenor)
No.8 — 201

CONNELL, ELIZABETH (soprano/mezzo-soprano)
No.8 — 192, 202

COOYMANS, ELISABETH (contralto)
No.8 — 203

COTRUBAS, ILEANA (soprano)
No.8 — 193

COX, KENNETH (bass)
No.8 — 200

CRADER, JEANINE (soprano)
No.8 — 189

CRASS, FRANZ (bass)
No.8 — 195

CSENGERY, ANDRIENNE (soprano)
No.8 — 195

CUNDARI, EMILIA (soprano)
No.2 — 57

CURRY, CORINNE (soprano)
No.4 — 86

INDEX TO SOLOISTS

DATE, EIJI (tenor)
    No.8   196
    DL (piano version)   223

DAVRATH, NETANIA
    No.4   81

DELLA CASA, LISA (soprano)
    No.4   97

DENIZE, NADINE (contralto)
    No.8   202

DERNESCH, HELGA (mezzo-soprano)
    No.3   75

DIADKOVA, LARISSA (contralto)
    No.3   65

DICKIE, MURRAY (tenor)
    DL   212

DIELEMAN, MARIANNE (contralto)
    No.8   193

DOLBERG, KIRSTEN (contralto)
    No.2   52
    No.8   199

DONATH, HELEN (soprano)
    No.2   35, 42
    No.4   89

EAGLEN, JANE (soprano)
    No.8   202

EATHORNE, WENDI (soprano)
    No.8   192

EDELMANN, OTTO (bass)
    No.8   197

EKKEHARD, SIGRID (soprano)
    No.8   199

ESTES, SIMON (bass)
    No.8   193, 196

INDEX TO SOLOISTS

FALCON, RUTH (soprano)
    No.8   203

FASSBAENDER, BRIGITTE (mezzo-soprano)
    No.2   52
    No.8   196
    DL   207
    DL (piano version)   222

FERRIER, KATHLEEN (contralto)
    No.2   44
    DL   220-221

FINLEY, ANNE (soprano)
    No.2   45

FINNIE, LINDA (contralto)
    No.3   67
    No.4   90

FINNILA, BIRGIT (mezzo-soprano)
    No.2   35
    No.8   193
    DL   217

FISCHER-DIESKAU, DIETRICH (baritone)
    No.8   195
    DL   206, 210, 212

FORRESTER, MAUREEN (contralto)
    No.2   43, 53, 57
    No.3   65
    DL   215, 218, 221

FREY, PAUL (tenor)
    No.8   191

FURUKAWA, YASUKO (piano)
    DL (piano version)   223

GEYER, GWYNNE (soprano)
    No.8   192

GJEVANG, ANNE (contralto)
    No.3   74
    No.8   194, 199

GODOY, MARIA LUCIA (mezzo-soprano)
No.2   54

GOROHOVSKAYA, YEVGENIA (mezzo-soprano)
No.2   55

GRACELJ, OLGA (soprano)
No.2   41

GRAF, UTA (soprano)
No.8   201

GRANT, HEIDI (soprano)
No.8   200

GRAY, LINDA ESTHER (soprano)
No.8   192

GREENBERG, SYLVIA (soprano)
No.2   47

GREEVY, BERNADETTE (contralto)
No.8   192

GREGOR, JÓZSEF (bass)
No.8   195

GRIST, RERI (soprano)
No.4   82

GROBE, DONALD (tenor)
No.8   195

GROOP, MONICA (mezzo-soprano)
DL (chamber version)   224

GRUBEROVA, EDITA (soprano)
No.4   98

GUEDEN, HILDE (soprano)
No.4   103

GUSTAFSON, NANCY (soprano)
No.2   48

GUSTAFSSON, ULLA (soprano)
No.8   194

INDEX TO SOLOISTS

HAEFLINGER, ERNST (tenor)
    DL   216, 222

HÄGGANDER, MARIANNE (soprano)
    No.8   191, 194

HAJOSSYOVA, MAGDALENA (soprano)
    No.2   54
    No.4   96

HALBAN, DESI (soprano)
    No.4   102

HAMARI, JULIA (contralto)
    No.2   42
    No.8   195

HARGAN, ALISON (soprano)
    No.4   99

HARPER, HEATHER (soprano)
    No.2   45, 53
    No.4   82, 94
    No.8   193, 201

HAYASHI, MAKOTO (tenor)
    No.8   203
    DL   205

HEICHELE, HILDEGARD (soprano)
    No.8   193

HELLEKANT, CHARLOTTE (mezzo-soprano)
    No.2   38

HENDRICKS, BARBARA (soprano)
    No.2   36
    No.4   97

HENSCHEL, JANE (contralto)
    No.8   194

HEPPNER, BEN (tenor)
    DL   207

HEYER-KRÄMER, WILLI (bass)
    No.8   199

HEYNES, AAFJE (soprano)
- No.2 — 40

HODGSON, ALFREDA (contralto)
- No.2 — 45
- No.8 — 197
- DL — 208

HOFFGEN, MARGA (contralto)
- No.2 — 51

HOFFMAN, GRACE (contralto)
- DL — 216

HOLL, ROBERT (bass)
- No.8 — 203

HORNE, MARILYN (mezzo-soprano)
- No.2 — 33, 49

HOWELL, GWYNNE (bass)
- No.8 — 197, 199

HOWELLS, ANNE (contralto)
- No.8 — 191

HYNNINEN, JORMA (baritone)
- No.8 — 199, 202

IHARA, NAOKO (mezzo-soprano)
- No.2 — 35, 57
- No.3 — 78
- No.8 — 203
- DL — 205, 219

ISOLOSKI, SOILE (soprano)
- No.4 — 85

IWAMORI, MISATO (contralto)
- No.8 — 196

JERUSALEM, SIEGFRIED (tenor)
- DL — 205

JO, SUMI (soprano)
- No.8 — 200

INDEX TO SOLOISTS

JONES, GWYNETH (soprano)
    No.8   190

KASAPIETORA, SERESTYNA (soprano)
    No.4   91

KATAGIRI, ETSUKO (mezzo-soprano)
    No.8   198

KATSARIS, CYPRIEN (piano)
    DL (piano version)   222

KATSUBE, FUTORU (baritone)
    No.8   203

KENNY, YVONNE (soprano)
    No.4   90

KIBERG, TINA (soprano)
    No.2   52

KILLEBREW, GWENDOLYN (contralto)
    No.3   63

KIM, DANIEL (tenor)
    No.8   198

KIM, ELISABETH (soprano)
    No.8   198

KING, JAMES (tenor)
    DL   206, 208

KIRCHNER, EVA (soprano)
    No.8   198

KITASAYA, SAKAYE (soprano)
    No.4   93

KLEINMAN, MARLENA (contralto)
    No.8   189

KMENTT, WALDEMAR (tenor)
    DL   211, 213

KOLK, STANLEY (tenor)
    No.8   189

KOLLO, RENE (tenor)
    No.8   201
    DL   206, 210

KOMATSU, HIDENORI (baritone)
    No.8   196

KÖNIG, KLAUS (tenor)
    DL   219

KOPLEFF, FLORENCE (contralto)
    No.2   35

KOVALEVA, GALINA (soprano)
    No.2   55

KRASNENKO, MARTIN (bass)
    No.8   198

KREBS, BEATRICE (contralto)
    No.3   70

KROOSKOS, CHRISTINA (contralto)
    No.3   59

KULLMAN, CHARLES (tenor)
    DL   215, 220

LAKI, KRISZTINA (soprano)
    No.2   37

LANG, ROSEMARIE (contralto)
    No.8   189

LAUBENTAL, HORST (tenor)
    DL   209

LAURICH, HILDEGARD (contralto)
    No.8   193

LEECH, RICHARD (tenor)
    No.8   196

LEISNER, EMMI (contralto)
    No.2   40

LEWIS, KEITH (tenor)
    No.8   200

INDEX TO SOLOISTS

LEWIS, RICHARD (tenor)
DL	215, 218, 221

LINDERMEIR, ELISABETH (soprano)
No.4	92

LINOS, GLENYS (mezzo-soprano)
DL	214

LIPOVŠEK, MARJANA (mezzo-soprano)
DL	207, 217

LIPTON, MARTHA (mezzo-soprano/alto)
No.3	61
No.8	201

LISOWSKA, HANNA (soprano)
No.2	58

LONDON, GEORGE (bass)
No.8	201

LORENZ, GERLINDE (soprano)
No.4	100

LORENZ, SIEGFRIED (baritone)
No.8	203

LOTT, FELICITY (soprano)
No.2	42
No.4	104
No.8	202

LUDWIG, CHRISTA (contralto)
No.2	36
No.3	62-63, 71
DL	206, 209-210, 211, 214

LUXON, BENJAMIN (baritone)
No.8	199

MALANIUK, IRA (mezzo-soprano)
No.8	197

MARC, ALESSANDRA (soprano)
No.8	192

MARGIONO, CHARLOTTE (soprano)
    No.2   40
    No.4   85

MÁROVÁ, LIBUSE (contralto)
    No.8   198

MARSHALL, MARGARET (soprano)
    No.4   85
    No.8   193

MARTON, EVA (soprano)
    No.2   47

MATHIS, EDITH (soprano)
    No.2   46, 56
    No.4   82
    No.8   195

MAULTSBY, NANCY (contralto)
    No.8   192

MAYR, INGRID (contralto)
    No.8   190

MCINTYRE, DONALD (bass)
    No.8   190

MCNAIR, SYLVIA (soprano)
    No.2   41, 47
    No.4   88
    No.8   189

MEIER, WALTRAUD (contralto)
    No.2   34
    No.8   200
    DL   205

MEINL-WEISE, RITA (soprano)
    No.8   199

MELCHERT, HELMUT (tenor)
    DL   216

MILLER, MILDRED (contralto)
    DL   222

INDEX TO SOLOISTS

MINTON, YVONNE (mezzo-soprano/alto)
    No.3   64
    No.8   201

MITCHINSON, JOHN (tenor)
    No.8   190, 197
    DL   208, 213

MOLNAR, ANDRÁS (tenor)
    No.8   195

MORISON, ELSIE (soprano)
    No.4   93

MOSER, EDDA (soprano)
    No.8   190, 192

MOSER, THOMAS (tenor)
    No.8   198
    DL   214, 217
    DL (piano version)   222

MÜLLER, ANNELIESE (contralto)
    No.8   199

MYERS, LORNA (contralto)
    No.8   199

MYERS, RAYMOND (baritone)
    No.8   197

NAGAI, KAZUKO (contralto)
    No.8   200

NAGOYA, KONOMI (soprano)
    No.8   196

NATHAN, REGINA (soprano)
    No.8   192

NEBLETT, CAROL (soprano)
    No.2   33

NIELSEN, INGA. (soprano)
    No.8   198-199

NIKOLAIDE, ELENA (contralto)
    DL   221

NIMSGERN, SIGMUND (baritone)
No.8   192, 196

NISHIMATSU, FUMIKO (soprano)
No.8   196
DL (piano version)   223

NORMAN, JESSYE (contralto)
No.2   47
No.3   59, 72
DL   207

NOVÁK, RICHARD (bass)
No.8   198

NOVZAK-HOUZKA, EVA (contralto)
No.2   41
No.3   64

OFUJI, YUKO (contralto)
No.8   196

OH-HASHI, YURI (contralto)
No.8   203

OHKURA, YUKIE (soprano)
No.8   203

OHMANN, CARL MARTIN (tenor)
DL   217

ORAN, MARIA (soprano)
No.2   56

OSHIMA, YOKO (soprano)
No.8   196

OTTER, ANNE SOFIE VON (contralto)
No.8   189

OWEN, LYNN (soprano)
No.8   189

PALMER, FELICITY (soprano)
No.2   38

PATZAK, JULIUS (tenor)
DL   220-221

INDEX TO SOLOISTS

PERSSON, MATS (baritone)
    No.8   194

PLOWRIGHT, ROSALIND (soprano)
    No.2   52

PODLES, EWA (contralto)
    No.2   39
    No.3   78

POPP, LUCIA (soprano)
    No.4   84, 101
    No.8   201

PRENZLOW, GERTRAUD (contralto)
    No.8   199

PREY, HERMANN (baritone)
    No.8   190-191, 193-194, 197

PRICE, MARGARET (soprano)
    No.4   89
    No.8   191

PRIEW, UTA (contralto)
    No.2   54

PROCTER, NORMA (contralto)
    No.2   46
    No.3   66
    No.8   190, 195

PUETZ, RUTH MARGRET (soprano)
    No.2   51

PUTTEN, THEA VAN DER (soprano)
    No.8   203

QUIVAR, FLORENCE (mezzo-soprano/alto)
    No.2   37, 47
    No.3   70
    No.8   191, 196, 199

RANDOVA, EVÁ (contralto)
    No.2   48

RAPPÉ, JADWIGA (contralto)
    No.2   58

RAPPÉ, JADWIGA (contralto) (cont.)
    No.3   68, 72
    No.8   202

RASKIN, JUDITH (soprano)
    No.4   101

REHM, KURT (tenor)
    No.8   199

REINHOLD, HERBERT (tenor)
    No.8   199

REMEDIOS, ALBERTO (tenor)
    No.8   192

REMMERT, BIRGIT (contralto)
    No.2   40
    DL (chamber version)   223

REYNOLDS, ANNA (contralto)
    No.8   190
    DL   212

RIDDER, ANTON DE (tenor)
    No.8   203

RIEGEL, KENNETH (tenor)
    No.8   190-191, 194, 199, 202

RIGBY, JEAN (mezzo-soprano)
    DL (chamber version)   224

RINTZLER, MARIUS (bass)
    No.8   192

ROBINSON, FAYE (soprano)
    No.8   194, 199

ROOTERING, JAN-HENDRIK (bass)
    No.8   189

ROSSL-MAJDEN, HILDE (contralto)
    No.2   44
    No.3   60

ROST, ANDREA (soprano)
    No.8   189

INDEX TO SOLOISTS

ROZARIO, PATRICIA (soprano)
No.4 — 95

RUOHONEN, SEPPO (tenor)
No.8 — 194

RUSSELL, LYNDA (soprano)
No.4 — 105

RUZDIAK, VLADIMIR (baritone)
No.8 — 190

SANDGREN, CAROLINA (sorpano)
No.8 — 194

SASSON, DEBORAH (soprano)
No.8 — 199

SATOH, SHINOBU (soprano)
No.2 — 57
No.8 — 203

SCHLEMM, ANNY (soprano)
No.4 — 93

SCHMECKENBECHER, JOCHEM (baritone)
No.8 — 198

SCHMIDT, TRUDELIESE (contralto)
No.8 — 191, 202

SCHÖNE, WOLFGANG (baritone)
No.8 — 198

SCHREIER, PETER (tenor)
DL — 209, 217

SCHULTE, EIKE WILM (baritone)
No.8 — 202

SCHWANEWILMS, ANNE (mezzo-soprano)
No.8 — 198

SCHWARZ, HANNA (contralto)
No.3 — 75

SCHWARZKOPF, ELIZABETH (soprano)
No.2 — 44

SCHWARZKOPF, ELIZABETH (soprano) (cont.)
    No.4   92, 104

SEEFRIED, IRMGARD (soprano)
    No.4   102-103

SEIFERT, PETER (tenor)
    No.8   189

SELIG, EDITH (soprano)
    No.2   51

SHIRAI, MITSUKO (soprano)
    No.4   95

SHIRLEY-QUIRK, JOHN (baritone)
    No.8   201

SIEWERT, RUTH (contralto)
    No.3   73

SILLS, BEVERLY (soprano)
    No.2   35

SIMON, ELIZABETH (soprano)
    No.8   197

SIMPSON, MARIETTA (mezzo-soprano)
    No.8   200

SILVASTI, JORMA (tenor)
    DL (chamber version)   224

SILVESTRELLI, ANDREA (bass)
    No.8   192

SIRKIÄ, RAIMO (tenor)
    No.8   199

SMITH, MALCOLM (bass)
    No.8   189

SOFFEL, DORIS (soprano)
    No.2   42, 56
    No.3   67
    No.8   192

INDEX TO SOLOISTS

SÓLYOM-NAGY, SÁNDOR (baritone)
No.8 — 195

SOTIN, HANS (bass)
No.8 — 193, 200, 202

SOUKUPOVÁ-MULIER, VERA (contralto)
No.8 — 198

ŠOUNOVÁ, DANIELA (soprano)
No.8 — 198

SPIESS, LUDOVIC (tenor)
DL — 209

SPOORENBERG, ERNA (soprano)
No.8 — 190, 195

STABELL, CARSTEN (bass)
No.8 — 199

STADE, FREDERICA VON (soprano)
No.4 — 81

STADER, MARIA (soprano)
No.4 — 104

STAHLMAN, SYLVIA (soprano)
No.4 — 100

STAMM, HARALD (bass)
No.8 — 194

STIWELL, RICHARD (baritone)
No.8 — 193

STONE, WILLIAM (baritone)
No.8 — 200

STUDER, CHERYL (soprano)
No.2 — 34
No.8 — 189, 200

SVANHOLM, SET (tenor)
DL — 221

SWEET, SHARON (soprano)
No.8 — 196

SYLVESTER, MICHAEL (tenor)
No.8 — 200

TAKÁCS, KLÁRA (contralto)
No.8 — 195

TAKAHASHI, KEIZOH (bass)
No.8 — 203

TALVELA, MARTTI (bass)
No.8 — 201

TASHIRO, MAKOTO (tenor)
DL — 219

TEAR, ROBERT (tenor)
DL (chamber version) — 224

TE KANAWA, KIRI (soprano)
No.2 — 49
No.4 — 96, 100

TENSTAM, ULRIKA (contralto)
No.8 — 194

TERFEL, BRYN (baritone)
No.8 — 189

THOMAS, JESS (tenor)
DL — 212

THOMAS, MARJORIE (contralto)
No.3 — 69

THORBORG, KERSTIN (contralto)
DL — 215, 217, 220

TILLI, JOHANN (bass)
No.8 — 194

TITUS, ALAN (baritone)
No.8 — 191

TÓTH, MARIA (soprano)
No.8 — 195

TOYODA, KIYOMI (soprano)
No.2 — 35

INDEX TO SOLOISTS

TOYODA, KIYOMI (soprano) (cont.)
    No.4   102

TRENKNER, EVELINDE (piano)
    No.6 (trans, Zemlinsky)   166
    No.7 (trans, Casella)   186

TROETSCHEL, ELFRIEDE (soprano)
    No.4   91

TROYANOS, TATIANA (contralto)
    No.2   38

TYLER, VERONICA (soprano)
    No.2   54

UPSHAW, DAWN (soprano)
    No.4   86

USAMI, RURI (soprano)
    No.4   101

VALENTE, BENITA (soprano)
    No.2   43

VAN DAM, JOSE (bass)
    No.8   190-191

VANDERSTEENE, ZEGER (tenor)
    DL   214

VAN NES, JARD (contralto)
    No.2   41, 47, 56
    No.3   66, 77
    No.8   203
    DL   209

VARADY, JULIA (soprano)
    No.8   191, 202

VENUTI, MARIA (soprano)
    No.8   191

VERSALLE, RICHARD (tenor)
    No.8   202

VICKERS, JON (tenor)
    DL   207

INDEX TO SOLOISTS

VINCENT, JO (soprano)
- No.2 — 44
- No.4 — 95

VISHNEVSKAYA, GALINA (soprano)
- No.2 — 44

VOGEL, SIEGFRIED (bass)
- No.8 — 191

VOIGT, DEBORAH (soprano)
- No.8 — 200

WALKER, MALLORY (tenor)
- No.8 — 193

WATANABE, MISAKO (soprano)
- No.8 — 203

WATTS, HELEN (contralto)
- No.2 — 53
- No.8 — 201

WENKEL, ORTRUN (contralto)
- No.3 — 76
- No.8 — 193

WEST, LUCRETIA (contralto)
- No.2 — 33, 50
- No.3 — 61, 71
- No.8 — 197

WHITTLESEY, CHRISTINE (soprano)
- No.4 — 87

WIENS, EDITH (soprano)
- No.4 — 90
- No.8 — 202

WILLIAMS, CAMILLA (soprano)
- No.8 — 201

WILLIAMS, NANCY (contralto)
- No.8 — 189

WILSON-JOHNSON, DAVID (baritone)
- No.8 — 192

INDEX TO SOLOISTS 321

WITTEK, HELMUT (boy soprano)
    No.4   83

WOYTOWICZ, STEFAN (soprano)
    No.2   33

WRAY, MARGARET JANE (soprano)
    No.8   200

WUNDERLICH, FRITZ (tenor)
    DL   210-211

YEEND, FRANCES (soprano)
    No.8   201

YOSHINO, YASUO (bass)
    No.8   196

ZADEK, HILDE (soprano)
    No.8   197

ZAKAI, MIRI (contralto)
    No.2   53

ZAMPIERI, GIUSEPPE (tenor)
    No.8   197

ZARESKA, EUGENIA (contralto)
    No.2   51

ZENKER, SILVIA (piano)
    No.6 (trans., Zemlinsky)   166
    No.7 (trans., Casella)   186

ZEUMER, GERTI (soprano)
    No.8   190-191

ZIEGLER, DELORES (mezzo-soprano)
    No.8   200

ZIESAK, RUTH (soprano)
    No.2   38

ZYLIS-GARA, TERESA (soprano)
    No.2   39

INDEX TO CHORUSES

(N.B., "DL" refers to *Das Lied von der Erde*)

Chorus	Symphony	Page
AMBROSIAN SINGERS		
	No.3	66
	No.8	197
AMERICAN BOYCHOIR		
	No.3	72
AMSTELADAMENSE COLLEGIUM MUSICUM		
	No.8	193
AMSTERDAM DE STEM DES VOLKS		
	No.8	193
AMSTERDAM TOONKUNSTKOOR		
	No.8	193
AMSTERDAM WOMEN'S CHORUS		
	No.3	65
"ANKOR" CHILDREN'S CHOIR, THE		
	No.3	70
ARDWYN SINGERS, THE		
	No.2	43
ARNOLD SCHOENBERG CHOIR (CHORUS)		
	No.2	34
	No.8	196

INDEX TO CHORUSES

ATLANTA BOY CHOIR
    No.8   200

BAVARIAN RADIO SYMPHONY CHORUS
    No.2   45, 46
    No.3   63, 69
    No.8   194, 195

BBC CHORUS AND CHORAL SOCIETY
    No.2   38
    No.3   64
    No.8   192

BBC SINGERS
    No.3   64
    No.8   192

BBC WELSH CHORUS
    No.2   43

BERLIN PHILHARMONIC CHORUS
    No.8   199

BERLIN RADIO CHORUS (WOMEN & CHILDREN)
    No.3   72
    No.8   189

BERLIN STATE OPERA CHORUSES
    No.8   199

BOSTON BOYS' CHOIR
    No.8   199

BROOKLYN BOYS' CHOIR
    No.3   62

BRUCKNER-MAHLER CHOIR OF LONDON
    No.8   197

BRUNNSBO CHILDREN'S CHOIR
    No.8   194

CARDIFF POLYPHONIC CHOIR
    No.2   43

CATHEDRAL CHOIR, BERLIN
    No.2   40

CHICAGO SYMPHONY CHORUS
No.2   33, 53
No.3   75

CHURCH OF THE TRANSFIGURATION, BOYS' CHOIR
No.3   61

CITY OF BIRMINGHAM SYMPHONY CHORUS
No.2   49

COLLEGIUM JOSEPHINUM, BOYS' CHOIR, BONN
No.3   63

COLOGNE RADIO (WDR) SYMPHONY CHORUS
No.2   37
No.3   71
No.8   191

COPENHAGEN BOYS' CHOIR
No.3   74
No.8   199

CRACOW BOYS' CHOIR
No.3   78

CRACOW PHILHARMONIC CHOIR
No.3   78

CRACOW RADIO & TV CHOIR
No.2   58

CZECH PHILHARMONIC CHORUS
No.3   71

DALE WARLAND SINGERS
No.2   42

DALLAS SYMPHONY CHORUS
No.2   47

DANISH NATIONAL RADIO SYMPHONY CHOIR
No.2   52
No.3   74
No.8   199

DUTCH THEATER CHOIR
No.2   56

INDEX TO CHORUSES 325

EBERHARD LUDWIG GYMNASIUM KNABENCHOR
No.3   73

EDINBURGH FESTIVAL CHORUS
No.2   36, 37

EINDHOVENS CHAMBER CHOIR
No.8   203

EINDHOVENSE CHRISTELIJKE ORATORIUM VERENIGING
No.8   203

EINDHOVENS MADRIGAL CHOIR
No.8   203

ELBURG CITY BOYS' CHOIR
No.3   65
No.8   192

ERNST-SENFF CHOR
No.2   41
No.3   66

ESTONIAN BOYS' CHOIR
No.8   194-195

ETON COLLEGE BOYS' CHOIR
No.8   202

FESTIVAL CHORUS
No.3   68

FINCHLEY CHILDREN'S MUSIC GROUP
No.8   190, 197

FRANKFURTER KANTOREI AND SINGAKADAMIE
No.3   67
No.8   193

FRANKFURT OPERA HOUSE-MUSEUM CHORUS
No.8   193

FRANKFURT SINGAKADAMIE CHORUS
No.2   51

GLEN ELLYN CHILDREN'S CHORUS
No.3   75

GERMAN STATE OPERA CHORUS, BERLIN
No.2   54

GOTHENBURG OPERA CHORUS
No.8   194

GOTHENBURG SYMPHONY CHORUS
No.8   194

HAARLEM KOORSCHOOL ST. BAVO BOYS' CHOIR
No.3   77

HARTFORDSHIRE COUNTY YOUTH CHOIR
No.3   64

HESSIAN RADIO CHILDREN'S CHORUS
No.8   194

HESSIAN RADIO FIGURAL CHORUS
No.8   193

HESSIAN RADIO SYMPHONY CHORUS
No.2   51

HIGHGATE SCHOOL BOYS' CHOIR
No.8   190, 197

HOLLAND FESTIVAL CHORUS (1951)
No.2   44

HUNGARIAN CHOIR
No.8   198

HUNGARIAN RADIO & TV CHORUS
No.8   195

"IHUD" CHOIR, THE
No.2   47

ISRAEL KIBBUTZ CHOIR
No.3   70

ISRAEL NATIONAL CHOIR "RINAT"
No.2   47
No.3   70

KANSEI GAKUIN GLEE CLUB
No.2   35

INDEX TO CHORUSES

KIROV OPERA & BALLET THEATER CHORUS
No.2   55

KONINKLIJKE GEMENGDE ZANGVERENIGING DE VOLHARDING
No.8   203

KONINKLIJK MANNERKOOR LA BONNE ESPERANCE
No.8   203

KONZERTVEREINIGUNG, VIENNA
No.2   47

KUHN BOYS' CHOIR
No.3   71

LATVIAN STATE ACADEMIC CHOIR
No.2   42

LEEDS FESTIVAL CHORUS
No.8   190

LEIPZIG OPERA CHORUS
No.8   192

LEIPZIG RADIO CHORUS (WOMEN & CHILDREN)
No.3   73

LIMBURGER DOMSINGKNABEN
No.3   67
No.8   193

LITTLE SINGERS OF TOKYO
No.8   191

LITTLE SPIRITUAL FANTASTIC SINGERS IN ARAKAWA, JAPAN
No.8   196

LJUBLJANA ACADEMIC CHOIR, "IWAN GORGAN KOVACIC"
No.2   41

LJUBLJANA RTV CHAMBER CHOIR, CHILDREN'S CHOIR & CONSORTIUM MUSICUM
No.8   198

LONDON PHILHARMONIC CHOIR
No.2   38, 56

LONDON PHILHARMONIC CHOIR (cont.)
    No.3   76
    No.8   202

LONDON SYMPHONY CHORUS
    No.2   53
    No.3   77
    No.8   190, 201, 202

MAITRISE DU CONSERVATOIRE POPULAIRE DE MUSIQUE DE GENEVE
    No.3   68

MILAN RAI CHORUS
    No.3   69

MISKOLC CHILDREN'S CHORUS
    No.8   195

MOSCOW BOYS' CAPELLA
    No.3   76

MUKOGAWA WOMEN'S UNIVERSITY CHORUS
    No.2   35

MUNICH MOTET CHOIR, WOMEN'S CHORUS
    No.8   195

MUSIQUE VOCALE DE LAUSANNE
    No.3   68

NATIONAL DE PARIS CHORUS
    No.2   51

NDR RADIO CHORUS
    No.8   195

NETHERLAND RADIO CHORUS (CHOIR)
    No.2   40
    No.3   65
    No.8   192

NEW LONDON CHILDREN'S CHOIR
    No.3   75

NEW PHILHARMONIA CHORUS
    No.2   45
    No.8   197

INDEX TO CHORUSES

NEW YORK CHORAL ARTISTS
    No.3   62

NORTH GERMAN RADIO (NDR) CHORUS
    No.2   42
    No.8   194

NYREGYHAZA CHILDREN'S CHORUS
    No.8   195

OHIO STATE UNIVERSITY CHORALE
    No.8   200

OHIO STATE UNIVERSITY SYMPHONIC CHOIR
    No.8   200

ORF CHORUS
    No.8   196

ORPINGTON JUNIOR SINGERS
    No.8   190, 197

OSLO PHILHARMONIC CHORUS
    No.2   42

PHILHARMONIA CHORUS
    No.2   44, 52
    No.8   200

PHILIPS PHILHARMONIC CHOIR
    No.8   203

PIUS X KINDERKOOR
    No.8   193

PRAGUE PHILHARMONIC CHORUS (CHOIR)
    No.2   48
    No.8   189, 191, 198

RADE KONCAR, CHILDREN'S CHOIR
    No.3   64

REGENSBURG CATHEDRAL CHOIR BOYS
    No.8   195

RESIDENT KAMERKOOR, THE HAGUE
    No.3   77

ROTTERDAM KAMERKOOR
  No.3   77

ROYAL ACADEMY OF MUSIC CHOIR, SWEDEN
  No.3   60

ROYAL SCOTTISH ORCHESTRA CHORUS
  No.3   67

ROYAL STOCKHOLM PHILHARMONIC CHOIR
  No.8   194

RUSSIAN ACADEMIC CHOIR OF TV "OSTANKINO"
  No.3   76

**ST. HEDWIG'S CATHEDRAL CHORUS,
  WOMEN & CHILDRENS**
  No.3   61

SAINT LOUIS SYMPHONY CHORUS
  No.2   53

ST. WILLIBRORD CHURCH, BOYS' CHORUS
  No.3   65
  No.8   193

SALT LAKE CITY SCHOOLS CHILDREN'S CHORUS
  No.8   189

SAN FRANCISCO SYMPHONY CHORUS
  No.2   38

SCHOLA CANTORUM, WOMEN'S CHORUS
  No.3   61

SCHOLA DI COLOGNE BOYS' CHORUS
  No.3   71

SCOTTISH NATIONAL ORCHESTRA CHORUS
  No.8   192

SHINSEI-NIKKYO CHORUS
  No.8   196

SHIN-YUKAI CHORUS
  No.2   57
  No.8   203

INDEX TO CHORUSES

SINGING CITY CHORUS (CHOIR)
　　No.2　　　　　　　　　　　　　　54

SOUTHEND BOYS' CHOIR
　　No.3　　　　　　　　　　　　　　76, 77
　　No.8　　　　　　　　　　　　　　200

SOUTHERN FLORIDA UNIVERSITY CHORUS
　　No.8　　　　　　　　　　　　　　200

STAATL HOCHSCHULE FUR MUSIK, CHOR DER
STEDELIJK HELMONDS CONCERT CHOIR
　　No.8　　　　　　　　　　　　　　203

STOCKHOLM'S BOY'S CHOIR
　　No.3　　　　　　　　　　　　　　60

STUTTGART DARSTALLENDE KUNST CHOIR
　　No.2　　　　　　　　　　　　　　35

STUTTGART ORATORIO CHORUS
　　No.2　　　　　　　　　　　　　　39

STUTTGART STATE SCHOOL CHOIR
　　No.2　　　　　　　　　　　　　　35

SUDFUNKCHOR, STUTTGART
　　No.2　　　　　　　　　　　　　　35, 37
　　No.3　　　　　　　　　　　　　　73
　　No.8　　　　　　　　　　　　　　191, 194

TAMPA BAY MASTER CHORALE
　　No.8　　　　　　　　　　　　　　200

TANGLEWOOD FESTIVAL CHORUS (CHOIR)
　　No.2　　　　　　　　　　　　　　49
　　No.3　　　　　　　　　　　　　　72
　　No.8　　　　　　　　　　　　　　199

TEL AVIV PHILHARMONIC CHOIR
　　No.2　　　　　　　　　　　　　　47

TIFFIN SCHOOL BOYS' CHOIR
　　No.8　　　　　　　　　　　　　　202

TÖLZER KNABENCHOR
　　No.3　　　　　　　　　　　　　　66
　　No.8　　　　　　　　　　　　　　189

TOKYO BROADCASTING CHILDREN'S CHORUS GROUP
    No.3   78
    No.8   203

TOKYO COLLEGE OF MUSIC, FEMALE CHORUS
    No.3   78

TOKYO LAIEN CHORUS
    No.8   196

UTAH UNIVERSITY CHORUS
    No.8   189

UTAH UNIVERSITY CIVIC CHORALE
    No.2   35
    No.3   59

VIENNA AKADEMIE KAMMERCHOR
    No.2   50

VIENNA BOYS' CHOIR
    No.3   59, 63, 69
    No.8   190-191, 196, 201

VIENNA PHILHARMONIC CHORUS
    No.8   197

VIENNA SINGVEREIN DER MUSIKFREUNDE
    No.2   44
    No.8   190-191, 201

VIENNA STATE OPERA CHORUS
    No.2   33, 47
    No.3   59, 63, 69
    No.8   190-191, 196, 201

WANDSWORTH SCHOOL BOYS' CHOIR
    No.3   66
    No.8   192

WDR RADIO CHORUS (WEST GERMANY)
    No.3   63
    No.8   194-195

WEST LONDON YOUTH CHOIR
    No.3   64

INDEX TO CHORUSES

WESTMINSTER CHOIR
    No.2   36, 57
    No.3   70

ZAGREB RADIO & TV WOMEN'S CHOIR
    No.3   64

INDEX TO RECORD LABELS

(N.B., "DL" refers to *Das Lied von der Erde*)

Record Label	Symphony	Page
ANDROMEDA		
	No.5	131
ANGEL		
	No.1	23
	No.2	44
	No.4	89, 92, 97
	No.5	108, 136
	No.6	164
	No.7	175, 185
	No.8	202
	DL	211, 212, 220
	No.9	227, 252, 253
	No.10 (Adagio)	260
	No.10 (Revised Cooke Version)	263
ARCHIPHON		
	No.3	73
	DL	217
ARKADIA		
	No.2	33, 35
	No.3	61, 69, 70
	No.4	92, 104
	No.5	111, 123, 126
	No.6	141, 142, 143, 155
	No.7	177
	No.8	201
	DL	218
	No.9	227, 231, 240, 242

INDEX TO RECORD LABELS

ARKADIA (cont.)
    No.9   243, 244, 247

ARS VIVENDI
    DL   217
    No.9   247
    No.10 (Revised Cooke Version)   264

ARTISTS
    No.3   64
    No.6   146
    No.8   192

ARTS
    No.1   13

AS DISC
    No.1   31
    No.7   182
    DL   215, 221

ASV
    No.4   90

AUDIOPHILE
    No.5   118

AUDIO PLUS
    No.2   47

AUROPHON
    No.1   13

BATON
    DL   208, 215

BBC MUSIC MAGAZINE
    No.5   128
    No.10 (Revised Cooke Version)   265

BBC RADIO CLASSICS
    No.4   94
    DL   213

BERLIN CLASSICS
    No.1   15
    No.4   93
    No.5   127

INDEX TO RECORD LABELS

BERLIN CLASSICS (cont.)
    No.6   156
    No.7   178
    No.9   245

BIS
    No.8   194
    DL   224
    No.9   228

BLACKPEARL
    No.5   114

BRUNO WALTER SOCIETY
    No.2   40
    No.4   104

CAMERATA
    No.5   128

CANYON CLASSICS
    No.1   16, 24
    No.2   48
    No.5   117, 127

CAPRICCIO
    No.4   95
    No.6   150
    No.7   173

CAROMAN
    No.5   130

CDI
    No.2   47

CETRA
    No.3   70

CHANDOS
    No.1   12, 27
    No.2   42, 52
    No.3   67, 74
    No.4   90
    No.5   116, 133
    No.6   152, 160
    No.7   183
    No.8   199

INDEX TO RECORD LABELS

CHANDOS (cont.)
	No.9	249
	No.10 (Adagio)	259

CINCIN
	DL	210

CLASSIC
	No.1	2

CLASSICS FOR PLEASURE
	No.4	89

CLEVELAND ORCHESTRA (75TH ANNIVERSARY)
	DL	218

CLUB LA BOHEME
	No.5	119
	No.8	196

CLUB NATIONAL DU DISQUE
	DL	216

COLLINS CLASSICS
	No.1	15
	No.4	95
	No.5	126

COLLINS QUEST
	No.1	15

COLUMBIA/CBS
	No.1	3, 18, 21, 22, 31
	No.2	36, 57
	No.3	61, 77
	No.4	82, 94, 101, 102
	No.5	109, 122, 138
	No.6	143, 154, 163
	No.7	168, 176
	No.8	190, 193
	DL	206, 215, 220, 222
	No.9	228, 241, 253
	No.10 (Adagio)	255, 258
	No.10 (Adagio & Purgatorio)	260
	No.10 (Original Cooke Version)	261

CBS\SONY
	No.1	3, 18

INDEX TO RECORD LABELS

CBS\SONY (cont.)
	No.2	47
	No.4	102
	No.9	253

COLUMBIA: ODYSSEY
	No.1	31
	No.2	57
	No.4	102
	No.5	138
	DL	222
	No.9	253

CROSSROADS
	No.1	2
	No.9	226

CURB CLASSICS
	No.5	115

CURTAIN CALL
	DL	221

DABRINGHAUS UND GRIMM (MD + G)
	No.6	166
	No.7	186

DATUM
	No.6	159

DECCA
	No.2	44
	No.4	93

DENON
	No.1	11
	No.2	42
	No.3	67
	No.4	89, 93
	No.5	115
	No.6	152
	No.7	175
	No.8	194
	DL	209
	No.9	237
	No.10 (Adagio)	257
	No.10 (Original Cooke Version)	261

INDEX TO RECORD LABELS

DESCANT
| | No.7 | 175 |
| | DL | 208 |

DEUTSCHE GRAMMOPHON (DG)
	No.1	4, 17, 27
	No.2	33, 34, 36, 46, 52
	No.3	59, 62, 69, 75
	No.4	81, 83, 93, 98, 103
	No.5	107, 110, 119, 134
	No.6	141, 144, 147, 153, 161
	No.7	167, 169, 176, 183
	No.8	189, 191, 195, 200
	DL	207
	No.9	225, 229, 230, 233, 238, 240, 250
	No.10 (Adagio)	255, 256, 257, 260

DG PRIVILEGE
| | No.5 | 119 |

DG RESONANCE
| | No.1 | 17 |

DG VIDEO CONCERTO
	No.1	1, 3
	No.2	37
	No.3	63
	No.4	82
	No.5	109
	No.6	144
	No.7	169
	No.8	190
	DL	206
	No.9	229
	No.10 (Adagio)	256

DIGITAL CLASSICS
| | No.3 | 60 |

DIGITAL CONCERTO
	No.1	22
	No.2	41
	No.3	64
	No.4	89
	No.5	126
	No.6	149, 155

DIGITAL CONCERTO (cont.)
	No.7	179
	No.8	198
	DL	214
	No.9	245
	No.10 (Adagio)	258

DISCOCORP
	DL	208

DISQUES MONTAIGNE
	No.1	20
	No.9	236

DISQUES REFRAIN
	No.2	44

DOCUMENTS (ENTERPRISE)
	No.2	38, 45
	No.9	251

DORIAN
	No.5	121

ELECTRECORD
	No.1	2

ELECTROLA
	No.9	253

EMERGO
	No.5	127

EMI
	No.1	5, 19, 21, 23
		25, 29
	No.2	37, 49, 56
	No.3	63, 76
	No.4	84, 85, 101
	No.5	108, 111, 113, 136
	No.6	145, 157, 164
	No.7	170, 181, 185
	No.8	191
	DL	207, 212, 219
	No.9	230, 252
	No.10 (Adagio)	256, 260
	No.10 (Revised Cooke Version)	263

INDEX TO RECORD LABELS

EMI/ANGEL
- No.2 — 56
- No.3 — 76
- No.4 — 101
- No.5 — 136
- No.8 — 202

EMI CLASSICS
- No.1 — 23
- No.4 — 92, 97

EMI EMINENCE
- No.4 — 104
- No.5 — 122

EMI VIDEO
- No.1 — 30
- No.8 — 202

ENIGMA CLASSICS
- No.1 — 16

ENTERPRISE (PALLADIO)
- No.2 — 45
- No.3 — 71
- No.5 — 111
- No.6 — 146
- No.8 — 197
- DL — 211
- No.9 — 232

EPIC
- No.10 (Adagio & Purgatorio) — 260

ERATO
- No.1 — 14
- No.4 — 90
- DL — 205
- No.9 — 248

ETERNA
- No.1 — 15, 31
- No.2 — 54
- No.3 — 72
- No.5 — 115, 136
- No.6 — 158
- No.7 — 178, 179
- No.9 — 245, 247

ETERNA (cont.)

No.10 (Revised Cooke Version)	264

EURODISC

No.5	118

EVEREST

No.1	5
No.5	132
No.8	197

EXCLUSIVE

DL	211

FIDELIO

No.5	126

FIREBIRD

No.2	35
DL	205
No.9	226

FNAC

No.3	60

FONIT CETRA

No.3	70, 71
No.6	155
No.9	227

FONTEC

No.1	11, 31
No.2	57
No.3	78
No.4	102
No.5	137
No.6	164
No.7	185
No.8	203
DL	219
No.9	252
No.10 (Adagio)	260

FORLANE

No.1	6
No.2	39
No.4	85
No.5	122

INDEX TO RECORD LABELS   343

FOYER
              DL   210

FUN HOUSE
              No.5   132

GOLDEN STRING
              No.10 (Carpenter version)   266

HAGUE PHILHARMONIC ORCHESTRA (HPO/RESIDENTIE)
              No.2   56
              No.3   77
              No.6   154
              No.10 (Revised Cooke Version)   263

HARMONIA MUNDI (FRANCE)
              No.5   132
              DL   223

HARMONIA MUNDI (GERMANY)
              No.3   60
              No.6   115

HARMONIA MUNDI (U.S.)
              No.1   14
              No.3   60

HELIDOR
              No.1   26

HUNGAROTON
              No.1   9
              No.8   195

HUNT
              No.2   33, 35, 45
              No.3   61, 70
              No.5   112, 126
              No.6   141-143, 155
              No.7   177
              DL   209, 218
              No.9   227, 239, 240,
                                              242-244

IGI
              No.2   44

IMP CLASSICS (MASTERS)
No.1	5
No.4	99
No.5	126
No.6	165
No.8	197
No.9	244

INDEPENDENT
No.8	197

INSIDER
No.9	226

INTAGLIO
No.4	82
No.7	175

INTERCORD
No.7	172
No.9	233

JOD
No.1	17

KING
No.7	182

KULTURA (VIDEO)
No.2	47

LASERLIGHT
No.1	23
No.4	87
No.6	150
No.7	173

LEGEND
No.1	31

LEOPOLD STOKOWSKI SOCIETY OF AMERICA
No.2	54

LONDON
No.1	8, 21, 29
No.2	38, 53
No.3	75
No.4	86, 100

INDEX TO RECORD LABELS

LONDON (cont.)
	No.5	114, 124, 134-135
	No.6	148-149, 162
	No.7	170, 184
	No.8	201
	DL	206, 217, 220
	No.9	251
	No.10 (Revised Cooke Version)	262

LONDON RICHMOND
	DL	220

MCA CLASSICS
	No.1	26
	No.2	43, 50

MC CLASSICS: ARTS & ELECTRONICS
	No.6	163

MELODRAM
	No.2	51
	No.9	248

MELODIYA
	No.1	9
	No.2	55

MEMORIA
	No.4	91

MEMORIES
	No.1	19
	DL	211
	No.9	232, 251

METEOR
	No.5	118

MMG
	No.1	9
	No.4	86

MONITOR
	No.4	89

MURRAY HILL
	No.5	132

MUSIC & ARTS
No.2	44
No.4	103-104
No.6	151
No.7	175
No.8	201
DL	208, 220-221
No.9	236-237

MUSICAL HERITAGE SOCIETY
No.5	118

NAXOS
No.1	16
No.2	58
No.3	78
No.4	105
No.5	138
No.6	165
No.7	174
No.9	235

NONESUCH
No.3	66
No.4	94
No.6	151

NOTES
No.1	31
No.7	182
DL	221

NOVALIS
No.1	6

NSO
No.5	137

NUOVA ERA
No.2	45
No.4	104
No.5	111
DL	211
No.9	238
No.10 (Adagio)	257

ONYX CLASSICS
DL	214

INDEX TO RECORD LABELS

OPAL
No.2 — 40

ORFEO
DL — 212
No.9 — 248

ORIGINALS
No.1 — 20
No.2 — 51
No.4 — 102
DL — 213
No.9 — 240

PALLADIO
No.1 — 26
No.2 — 50
No.5 — 131
DL — 220
No.9 — 253

PARLOPHONE (JAPANESE)
No.4 — 93

PEARL
No.2 — 40
No.4 — 94
DL — 220

PENZANCE
No.8 — 201

PERRENIAL
DL — 220

PETERS
No.5 — 126
No.9 — 244

PHILIPS
No.1 — 10, 24
No.2 — 40-41, 49
No.3 — 65-66, 72
No.4 — 88, 95-96
No.5 — 114-115, 127, 129
No.6 — 150, 156-157
No.7 — 173-174, 180
No.8 — 193, 199

INDEX TO RECORD LABELS

PHILIPS (cont.)
	DL	207-208
	No.9	234, 246
	No.10 (Adagio)	256-258

PICKWICK (PWK CLASSICS)
	No.2	47

POLYDOR
	No.2	40

PILZ
	No.1	23
	No.5	126
	DL	214

PRAGA
	DL	214

PRELUDIO
	No.1	11

PRICELESS
	DL	220

PRO ARTE
	No.2	47
	No.3	71
	No.7	180
	No.9	245
	No.10 (Adagio)	258

QUADRIFOGLIO
	No.3	68

QUINTESSENCE
	No.9	226

RAY
	No.4	101

RCA VICTOR
	No.1	7, 17
	No.2	40
	No.3	65
	No.4	85, 93, 97
	No.5	113, 119, 121
	No.6	148, 153

INDEX TO RECORD LABELS

RCA VICTOR (cont.)
No.7	171, 176
No.8	192, 197
DL	215
DL (chamber version)	224
No.9	232, 241, 253
No.10 (Revised Cooke Version)	263
No.10 (Mazzetti Version)	265

RCS
No.8	203

REPLICA
No.5	126
No.9	244

REVOLUTION
No.3	60

ROYAL PHILHARMONIC ORCHESTRA (RPO)
No.5	116
No.6	152

SAISON RUSSE
No.3	76

SAPHIR
No.4	87
No.10 (Adagio)	256

SEFEL
No.1	13
No.8	195

SERAPHIM
No.4	92
DL	212

SEVEN SEAS
DL	221

SONY
No.1	3, 18, 21
No.2	36, 47
No.3	61, 69-70
No.4	82, 94, 97, 101-102
No.5	109, 122, 138
No.6	143, 154, 163

SONY (cont.)
	No.7	168, 176
	No.8	190, 193, 196
	DL	206, 215
	No.9	228, 241, 253
	No.10 (Adagio)	255, 258
	No.10 (Adagio & Purgatorio)	260

SONY VIDEO
	No.5	135

SPA
	No.3	60

STRADIVARI CLASSICS
	No.1	16, 23

STRADIVARIUS
	No.1	19, 26
	No.3	73
	No.5	131
	DL	216
	No.9	251

SUPRAPHON
	No.1	2, 24
	No.2	48
	No.3	71
	No.4	96, 100
	No.5	127
	No.6	156
	No.7	180
	No.8	198
	No.9	226, 245
	No.10 (Adagio)	258

TAHRA
	No.3	73
	No.6	159
	No.8 (Part I)	199
	No.10 (Adagio)	259

TELARC
	No.1	29
	No.2	53
	No.5	120
	No.8	200

INDEX TO RECORD LABELS

TELDEC
No.1	21
No.2	48
No.5	125
DL (piano version)	222
No.9	243

THEOREMA
No.1	22
No.2	50

TOKUMA
No.2	54
No.3	72
No.4	91
No.5	136
No.6	158
No.7	178
No.9	247
No.10 (Revised Cooke Version)	264

TURNABOUT
No.1	11
No.4	95
DL	216
No.9	235, 253

TUXEDO MUSIC
No.1	11

UNICORN
No.3	66

UNICORN-KANCHANA
No.3	66
No.6	151

URANIA
No.7	181

VANGUARD
No.1	2
No.2	35
No.3	59-60
No.4	81
No.5	108
No.6	142
No.7	167

VANGUARD (cont.)

	No.8	189
	No.9	225
	No.10 (Adagio)	255

VANGUARD CARDINAL

	No.5	127

VANGUARD CLASSICS

	No.2	35

VARESE SARABANDE

	No.4	102

VERONA

	No.2	44

VIA CLASSICS

	No.4	94

VICTOR INDEPENDENT

	No.5	126

VIRGIN CLASSICS

	No.1	7, 18
	No.5	130
	No.9	246
	No.10 (Adagio)	259

VIVACE

	No.1	23
	No.2	56
	No.5	126

VOX

	No.1	11
	No.7	181
	DL	216
	No.9	235

VOX BOX

	No.1	9, 11
	No.4	86
	No.7	181
	DL	216
	No.9	235

INDEX TO RECORD LABELS

WESTMINSTER
	No.1	26
	No.2	50
	No.5	131

WSP
	DL	221

XENOPHONE
	No.1	8

ZYX CLASSICS
	No.2	41
	No.5	126
	No.6	155

About the Author

LEWIS M. SMOLEY is the author of *The Symphonies of Gustav Mahler: A Critical Discography* (Greenwood, 1986), a companion volume to this work. Smoley has written and lectured extensively on Mahler's music and has performed and conducted with The Town Hall Orchestra of New York and The Suffolk Chamber Orchestra. He received his musical training at Queens College and the Juilliard School. He currently serves as vice president of the Gustav Mahler Society of New York.